Jonathan Swift

Jonathan Swift

HIS LIFE AND HIS WORLD

Leo Damrosch

Yale UNIVERSITY PRESS

New Haven and London

Published with assistance from the Annie Burr Lewis Fund and from the foundation established in memory of Philip Hamilton McMillan of the Class of 1894, Yale College.

Yale University Press books may be purchased in quantity for educational, business, or promotional use. For information, please e-mail sales.press@yale .edu (US office) or sales@yaleup.co.uk (UK office).

Designed by Nancy Ovedovitz and set in Adobe Garamond type by Newgen North America. Printed in the United States of America.

Library of Congress Cataloging-in-Publication Data
Damrosch, Leopold.
Jonathan Swift : his life and his world / Leo Damrosch.
pages   cm.
Includes bibliographical references and index.
ISBN 978-0-300-16499-2 (clothbound : alk. paper)
 1. Swift, Jonathan, 1667–1745.   2. Authors, Irish—18th century—
Biography.   I. Title
√PR3726.D27 2013   C ,2
828'.509—dc23
[B]

A catalogue record for this book is available from the British Library.

This paper meets the requirements of ANSI/NISO Z39.48–1992 (Permanence of Paper).

10 9 8 7 6 5 4 3 2 1

Contents

Gift
4-19-22

Illustrations

Acknowledgments

I want to express my gratitude to Robin Dublanc, expert copyeditor; to Jennifer Banks, whose editorial insight was invaluable in shaping this story; and to Joyce Van Dyke, whose imagination and advice improved every page of the book. My research and the acquisition of illustrations were generously supported by a grant from the Andrew W. Mellon Foundation.

Prologue

In the 1720s a brilliant and beautiful young woman was entangled in a troubled affair with a man twenty years older. She had fallen passionately in love with him in London, and when he moved home to Dublin she followed him there. He was strongly attracted to her but reluctant to commit himself, and he insisted they keep their relationship secret. They were apart much of the time and communicated by letter, and she was sometimes near despair when he seemed to be rejecting her: "I am sure I could have bore the rack much better than those killing, killing words of yours." At other times, though, he did reply in the way she wanted. "Be assured," he declared, "that no one on earth has ever been loved, honored, esteemed, adored by your friend but yourself." Whenever he wrote like that, she would be joyful—"You are good beyond expression, and I will never quarrel again if I can help it."[1] For a time they met covertly once a week at someone else's house in Dublin.

In the letters they had a private code. The man suggested that "a stroke thus ——— ——— ——— ——— signifies everything that may be said." In her letters from then on, the dashes flew thick and fast: "I have worn out my days in sighing and my nights with watching and thinking of ———, ———, ———, ———."[2] Only they knew what words were meant.

Evidently, the word *coffee* was part of the same code. In a number of letters from the man over several years, "coffee" has a suggestive aura: "I wish I were to walk with you fifty times about your garden, and then—drink your coffee";

"I drank no coffee since I left you, nor intend till I see you again, there is none worth drinking but yours"; "Without health, you will lose all desire of drinking your coffee." At one point the absence of her coffee is so disturbing that it interferes with his work as a writer: "I am not cheerful enough to write, for I believe coffee once a week is necessary to do that."[3]

The man in this strange romantic story was Jonathan Swift, and the book he was trying to write was *Gulliver's Travels*. He liked to be mysterious toward everyone, not just toward the young woman, and even those who knew him best were baffled by his contradictions. One friend said that his character was "exceedingly strange, various, and perplexed," and another called him "my hieroglyphic friend."[4] He became a public figure of great distinction, dean of St. Patrick's Cathedral, and a champion of Irish rights, yet he was profoundly skeptical and he claimed to despise Ireland. He was a great writer, yet he almost never signed his name to his work.

Even the basic facts concerning Swift's origins are open to question. He inherited the name of a Jonathan Swift who died before he was born, but it is not entirely certain that that was his real father. His wet nurse abducted him from Dublin when he was an infant and took him to England with her; amazingly, his family let him stay there with her for several years. Why? When he was finally brought back to Dublin, why did his mother then leave for England herself, and why did he not see her again until he was an adult? After his mother left, an uncle in Dublin become his guardian and paid for an expensive education. So why did Swift despise his uncle and declare that he had been given "the education of a dog"?[5]

It wasn't just Swift's childhood that was mysterious; his most intimate and enduring adult relationships were mysterious too. After college he spent ten years as confidential secretary to a distinguished retired diplomat in England in whose household there was a bright nine-year-old girl, the housekeeper's daughter. The diplomat arranged to have his servant's child tutored by Swift, and at his death she received an extraordinarily large bequest. As an adult she became Swift's closest friend for the rest of her life, and she too moved to Dublin when he returned there. Even though they were apparently never together without a third party present, many who knew them were convinced that they were secretly married. But if they were married, why did it have to be secret? And how much did the close friend (or wife) know about her young rival with the coffee? Was it an actual love triangle, or only a virtual one?

This man of mystery produced a book that became world-famous. Everybody recognizes the image of Gulliver tied down on the ground by a host of tiny people, even if they have not read the masterpiece from which it comes. A stunningly original fantasy, it is uncanny in Freud's sense of that term: strange and yet familiar, absurd and yet believable. Many children, and many adults too, have loved *Gulliver's Travels*. George Orwell, though he was critical of Swift's politics, confessed that he read it over and over, and would put it on any list of "six books which were to be preserved when all others were destroyed."[6] To this day, at least two dozen publishers are keeping it in print, and it is a universal classic, its fame extending beyond the English-speaking world.

But few know much about the man who wrote *Gulliver's Travels*, or about the long-ago world that for him was the present moment. This book is an invitation to time travel, in quest of what a historian has called "the sensations of being alive in a different time." Swift was alive during a time of revolutionary

1. Gulliver on Dollymount Strand. A seventy-foot fiberglass model of Gulliver in Lilliput, constructed to correct scale, just east of Dublin. Swift would have loved this picture, not to mention the effigy, since he often rode his horse on this beach.

change, when a king was deposed in a sensational revolution, the modern political system came into being, and Britain became a world power. It was at that time that an Irish national consciousness was born, in opposition to control by England, and Swift's was a crucial voice in forging it. "We should see certain men and women," Yeats said, with Swift in mind, "as if at the edge of a cliff, time broken away from their feet."[7]

Swift was known as a great talker. Unlike Samuel Johnson, described by Boswell as "talking for victory, and determined to be master of the field," Swift was open and relaxed in conversation. And although his flow of humor was noted by everyone who knew him, it seldom took the form, as Johnson's did, of quotable bon mots. "He was by no means in the class with those," his relative Deane Swift said, "who pour down their eloquence like a torrent, driving all before it. Far from any desires of that sort, he equally loved to speak, and loved to hearken."[8]

Something of Swift's style of talking comes through in his letters, often playful, at times angry. He complained to a former patron that he was wasting away in Ireland, and expected to die there "in a rage, like a poisoned rat in a hole." Especially revealing is the daily journal he kept during one extended period, sent in installments to the woman who was his closest friend, and whom he may have secretly married. He had a wonderful ear for the way people talk, and he loved to act out and impersonate: "I dined today with Patty Rolt at my cousin Leach's, with a pox, in the city. He is a printer, and prints the *Postman*, oh ho, and is my cousin, God knows how, and he married Mrs. Baby Aires of Leicester. . . . I wish you could hear me repeating all I have said of this in its proper tone, just as I am writing it. 'Tis all with the same cadence with 'oh hoo,' or as when little girls say, 'I have got an apple, miss, and I won't give you some.'"[9]

Numerous writers have pondered Swift's life, but one biography in particular needs to be considered here: Irvin Ehrenpreis's monumental *Swift: The Man, His Works, and the Age*, which filled two thousand pages by the time the third volume came out in 1983, two decades after the first. I was Ehrenpreis's colleague for fifteen years at the University of Virginia, at a time when I had no notion of ever writing a life of Swift. Since then an outpouring of scholarship has thrown new light on many aspects of Swift's career and writings, and has reopened serious questions that Ehrenpreis chose not to notice. Strangely, though a man of subtle irony himself, he insisted that literature always means exactly what it says, and that Swift's thinking and life were massively conventional—his views on religion, politics, and love were all tepidly middle of the road.[10]

Since for nonspecialists the Ehrenpreis biography may still seem authoritative, something must be said about its very real limitations. His grasp of details is encyclopedic, and he traces the week-by-week course of Swift's career with complete assurance. It might seem, then, that his opinions about personalities and motives are equally authoritative, but in fact he indulges constantly in invention without saying so. He tells us, for instance, that "Swift's relatives trained him in an austere religion and a harsh morality," that he was "harshly disciplined as a child," and that he was "brought up to consider his essential character as naturally corrupt and to consider the corruption as rooted in his flesh."[11] Yet there is not the slightest scrap of evidence for a single one of these assertions. We know nothing whatever about Swift's upbringing, or for that matter about the moral convictions of his relatives, except that as moderate Anglicans they were very unlikely to have held the beliefs Ehrenpreis attributes to them. This is pure projection on his part, laying the groundwork for a now very dated Freudian interpretation of personality, in which every relationship is translated into a single reductive pattern. An older man—even if just a few years older—must be a father figure, or else resented for not being one. A woman Swift's age or older is a mother figure. And, inevitably, a younger woman is a daughter figure. These interpretations lead to startling distortions of Swift's most important relationships, and they permit Ehrenpreis to ignore a mass of thought-provoking evidence, ambiguous though it may be, that raises important questions about Swift's parentage and his sexual life.

For Ehrenpreis not only presents his highly subjective interpretations as simple fact, he also omits a great deal of well-attested evidence. The puzzles surrounding Swift's personal life were a subject of fascination to his contemporaries, including his closest friends, and many of them left striking anecdotes that Ehrenpreis ignores. He doesn't discuss them in order to dismiss them; he doesn't even mention them in passing; he simply ignores them. On the first page of his first volume he declares, "Those readers who look for my views on a long train of legendary Swiftiana will search in vain. Here, neither Swift nor Stella is made a bastard; Swift does not say, 'My uncle gave me the education of a dog;' Dryden does not say, 'Cousin Swift, you will never be a poet;' and Temple does not seat Swift and Stella at the servants' table."[12] Every one of these "legendary" stories deserves consideration, and to categorize them as "Swiftiana" is to marginalize them unjustly. It is very possible that all of them are true, and at least two—Stella's probable illegitimacy, and Swift's relationship with the uncle who acted as his guardian—are of great importance in understanding his story. Together with many other pieces of evidence that Ehrenpreis ignores, they suggest a far more complex, enigmatic, and challenging Swift than the conventional character presented in Ehrenpreis's biography.

There have been several biographies since Ehrenpreis's, of which the most ambitious is David Nokes's *Jonathan Swift, a Hypocrite Reversed* (1985). The title comes from a comment by Swift's friend Bolingbroke that he was a *hypocrite renversé:* with a horror of seeming to pretend to be better than he was, he let it appear that he was worse.[13] Nokes's book is subtitled *A Critical Biography*. Like Ehrenpreis, he is confident that he knows Swift's real motives at every turn, but for him they are nearly always discreditable. A reviewer recently called his book "a story of Swift's life told by an enemy."[14] What has apparently not been noticed is how heavily dependent Nokes is on Ehrenpreis, often deploying the same quotations in the same order, and for long stretches virtually paraphrasing his book. Victoria Glendinning's brief *Jonathan Swift* (1998) is much more generous, but breezy and impressionistic, and makes little use of recent scholarship; she rightly calls it a selective "portrait" that focuses on personal relationships and only glances at Swift's public career.[15]

This book draws on discoveries that scores of researchers have made during the past thirty years about the details of Swift's life. It also takes seriously some daring speculations about his family and his relationships that differ radically from the official story. Unlike a fictional mystery, Swift's can't have a pat ending, but some of the possible scenarios are at least as plausible as the official story—more plausible, in fact. And some very suggestive bits of evidence, recorded in out-of-the-way places and presented here, have never been fully assembled until now.

Some of these ideas have been available for many years, but with the exception of Glendinning, biographers have dismissed or ignored them completely. They did so because they refused to consider anything that couldn't be conclusively proved, and also because they saw them as marginal to Swift's public life in politics and the Church. But to Swift himself, they were anything but marginal. A man of powerful emotions, he loved secrecy and disguise. Keeping his intimate relationships mysterious was an essential strategy of self-protection.

It is no accident, too, that much of Swift's writing was issued under assumed names: Isaac Bickerstaff; M.B., Drapier; Lemuel Gulliver. As with his gift for mimicry, he relished the game of becoming someone very different from himself as he appropriated a voice—people from the lower classes, politicians he despised, household servants, patrician ladies. And much more than playfulness was involved. Impersonating a different voice liberated the subversive side of Swift's imagination, and that could be very subversive indeed.

This book differs too from previous biographies in seeking not just to recount the events of Swift's career, but also to bring him to life as a complex, compelling human being. Hidden though he wanted his inner life to be, he was anything but a recluse. "He always appeared to the world in a mask," his godson Thomas Sheridan said, "which he never took off but in the company of his most intimate friends."[16] But with them he did take it off, and they all testified to his magnetic personality and infectious playfulness. Listening to Swift's own words, together with those of his wide circle of friends, we can form an intimate acquaintance with him.

In addition, rich contemporary descriptions of life in Ireland and England are available, and they bring back the sights, sounds, and smells of Swift's world—he was acutely sensitive to them all. This book also has many more illustrations than is usual, often drawn from little-known sources, for as Alice said, "What is the use of a book without pictures or conversations?" Pictures sometimes do more than words to give reality to the people and places Swift knew. Because small black-and-white reproductions of oil paintings look indistinct, contemporary engravings have generally been chosen. Instead of being segregated in a glossy section by themselves, they appear wherever the narrative will benefit from them.

Swift still matters, three and a half centuries after his birth, because he was a great writer and a great man. If his political views were sternly conservative, it was because he feared anarchy in a turbulent era, and also because he was tempted by anarchic impulses within himself. His was a restless personality, embattled in what Sir Walter Scott called "the war of his spirit with the world."[17] When he felt mistreated he fought back fiercely, and because he could empathize profoundly with the mistreatment of others, he became the hero of an oppressed nation. What made him great was a resolute character and a probing, lucid intelligence. Looking back fifty years after Swift's death, a philosopher and novelist convincingly called him "perhaps the man of the most powerful mind of the time in which he lived."[18]

Rather than narrating Swift's life in a strict year-by-year sequence, this book at times takes up important issues and relationships in separate narratives. Since Swift's views of human behavior, though not of English and Irish politics, changed very little throughout his life, his comments are not always quoted in connection with the occasions when he made them. *Gulliver's Travels*, in particular, gathers up a wide range of his long-standing preoccupations. A chronology at the end of the book sets out the important dates.

Spelling is modernized, and punctuation sometimes altered slightly for clarity.

CHAPTER I

Beginnings

VANISHED TRACES

The story that Jonathan Swift told is that he came into the world on November 30, 1667, in the house of his uncle Godwin Swift, in a little Dublin alley known as Hoey's Court. He was born there because his father had recently died at the age of twenty-seven, and his mother, Abigail, had moved in with her Swift relatives. The baby was named Jonathan, after his father. Abigail also had an eighteen-month-old daughter, Jane, and hardly any money.

These, at least, were the facts as Swift understood them. But strangely, nothing is certain about his early years, including the date of his birth. The year may not even have been 1667. He was presumably baptized in the nearby parish church, St. Werburgh's (which he pronounced "Warbrow's"). But when he had the church register searched years later, there was no record of the baptism. This may or may not be significant; a colleague of his thought the omission must have been "due to the carelessness of the vestry clerk at that time."[1] On the other hand, it's conceivable that he was baptized someplace else, and not necessarily in a church at all. Swift was told that his father had died seven months before his birth, "just time enough to save his mother's reputation," as he often remarked.[2] But there is no official record of his father's death either. We know only that his parents were married in 1664. It may even be that the baby's real father was someone else, a startling possibility that Swift

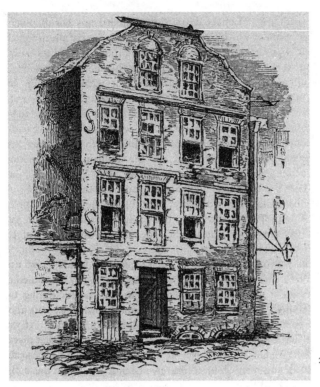

2. Godwin Swift's house,
Hoey's Court.

himself may eventually have suspected. There is no solid evidence for that, but if those concerned wanted to keep it secret, they could have made sure that there would be no evidence. And in fact many aspects of Swift's early life are puzzling, to say the least.

Hoey's Court has vanished, too. If you go in search of Swift sites in Ireland, you will usually search in vain, and all that remains today of Godwin Swift's house is a plaque on a wall that was put there in 1912: "In No. 7 Hoey's Court (now demolished) about 100 feet NW of this spot, it is reputed that JONATHAN SWIFT, Dean of St. Patrick's Cathedral, was born on the 30th day of November 1667." Whoever composed this was sufficiently well informed to use the word "reputed."

HOW THE SWIFTS CAME TO IRELAND

Swift liked to say that he had been unluckily "dropped" in Ireland—a term from animal husbandry. He claimed that his birth happened in Dublin

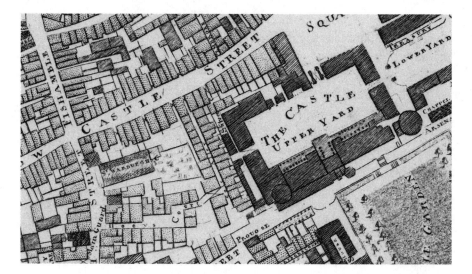

3. Swift's first neighborhood. To the left of the massive castle from which Ireland was governed, Hoey's Court (which no longer exists) appears as a narrow passageway. Just above it is St. Werburgh's, where Swift was presumably baptized.

only because his widowed mother was too far along in her pregnancy to risk a sea voyage to her English home in Leicester. "As to my native country (as you call it), I happened indeed by a perfect accident to be born here, my mother being left here from returning to her house at Leicester, and I was a year old before I was sent to England; and thus I am a Teague, or an Irishman, or what people please, although the best part of my life was in England."[3] Abigail did have relatives in Leicestershire, and evidence has fairly recently been found to suggest that she may have been born in a village just outside the town of Leicester. Ehrenpreis guessed that her father was a clergyman named James Ericke who emigrated to Ireland in 1634, but another possibility is a butcher named Thomas Ericke (also spelled Herrick). If so, she was not the same age as her husband, as Ehrenpreis assumed, but ten years older.[4]

The Swifts were recent arrivals, four brothers in all, beginning in 1658 (two others remained in England). After the Restoration of 1660 brought an end to the Puritan rule that had succeeded the civil wars of the 1640s and '50s, large numbers of Protestant English and Scots were encouraged to settle in Ireland, where they were awarded land that used to belong to Catholics. An English governor at the time compared the process to "flinging the reward upon the death of a deer among a pack of hounds, where everyone pulls and tears what he can for himself." The brothers Swift, sons of a clergyman and seeking employment in Dublin as lawyers, arrived to pull and tear. It has been well said that they were Irishmen in the sense that Camus was an Algerian. Jonathan Swift would often observe that colonists in North America were regarded as still English, and that the Anglo-Irish ought to be as well.[5]

Jonathan Swift the elder, our Jonathan's father, was the youngest but the first to arrive. The oldest brother, Godwin, was thirty-nine when his nephew was born in 1667; William was thirty and Adam twenty-five. We know that in later years William sometimes gave his nephew financial help, more in fact than Godwin did. (Two other brothers had stayed in England and died young.) It used to be thought that Godwin was unusually generous toward his young nephew; Ehrenpreis says that Jonathan's "early years were sheltered by an uncle's hospitality," and that his assistance "must have been an act of disinterested kindness."[6] But as we will see, there are good reasons to doubt this comfortable picture.

KIDNAPPED?

When Swift was about a year old, a remarkable event apparently happened. His wet nurse took him across the Irish Sea to Whitehaven, a small town on the northwest coast of England, and he remained there for several years with no contact with his family. Ehrenpreis calls this a kidnapping and says that the Swift family's failure to get him back seems most peculiar.[7] But was it?

It was common for middle-class families to send their children out to wet nurses. Almost always the infant would live with the nurse, sometimes nearby, sometimes in a village far away. Not many parents visited the children regularly, and the infant's first bonds would be formed with the nurse rather than the mother.

Given the importance of the role, wet nursing was a well-paid occupation. Nurses were usually artisans' wives with several children of their own. Weaning to "pap" (flour or breadcrumbs cooked in water) happened toward the end of the first year, but the stay with the nurse was normally much longer. For this reason, the nurse's speech and education were considered important; it was she who would teach the child to talk, and even to read and write. She might remain a valued friend for years. When Alexander Pope's nurse died, he erected a memorial in the local church:

> To the memory of Mary Beach
> who died Nov. 25, 1725, aged 78.
> Alex. Pope, whom she nursed in his infancy,
> and constantly attended for twenty-eight years,
> in gratitude to a faithful old servant erected this stone.[8]

Thus it may have seemed perfectly normal for Swift to remain with his nurse. Here is the story as he relates it in the third person, in a brief autobiographical sketch:

> When he was a year old, an event happened to him that seems very unusual, for his nurse, who was a woman of Whitehaven, being under an absolute necessity of seeing one of her relations who was then extremely sick, and from whom she expected a legacy; and being at the same time extremely fond of the infant, she stole him on shipboard unknown to his mother and uncle, and carried him with her to Whitehaven, where he continued for almost three years. For when the matter was discovered, his mother sent orders by all means not to hazard a second voyage till he could be better able to bear it. The nurse was so careful of him that before he returned he had learned to spell, and by the time that he was three years old he could read any chapter in the Bible.[9]

Whether or not Swift was exaggerating his precociousness, this shows that his nurse was literate. And since she was looking forward to a legacy, she was probably not poor. Most important, she was affectionate. What was unusual may not have been that she took the baby away, but that she gave no advance warning.

Long afterward a friend of Swift's, Laetitia Pilkington, reported the story with even greater emphasis on the affection:

> He was given to an Irish woman to nurse, whose husband being in England, and writing to her to come to him, as she could not bear the thoughts of parting with the child, she very fairly took him with her, unknown to his mother or any of his relations, who could learn no tidings either of him or her for three years, at the end of which time she returned to Ireland and restored the child to his mother, from whom she easily obtained a pardon, both on account of the joy she conceived at seeing her only son again, when she had in a manner

lost all hope of it, as also that it was plain the nurse had no other motive for stealing him but pure affection, which the women of Ireland
generally have in as eminent degree for the children they nurse as for
their own offspring.[10]

Still, the only evidence for what happened is what Swift himself was told,
or said he was told. It has even been conjectured that the story was "one more
elaborate fiction of Swift's old age to extenuate the fact of his Irish birth." A
relative recalled that he enjoyed spinning yarns about this mysterious episode:
"It gave occasion to many ludicrous whims and extravagancies in the gaiety of
his conversation. Sometimes he would declare that he was not born in Ireland
at all, and seem to lament his condition, that he should be looked upon as
a native of that country; and would insist that he was stolen from England
when a child, and brought over to Ireland in a bandbox."[11]

And then there is the letter written toward the end of his life, already
quoted, in which Swift said, "I was a year old before I was sent to England."
So he might have been "sent," not abducted. And we know nothing for certain about how he returned to Dublin—whether someone was sent to get
him, or the nurse brought him back herself.

And what about Uncle Godwin? By the time Jonathan was born, Godwin
had been married four times, each wife bringing a generous dowry, and he
was relatively well off. However, he had eight children of his own to support,
and when those grew up, he acquired at least fifteen grandchildren. In addition, his financial affairs were starting to go downhill. Why would he have
wanted to take on his late brother's widow and two small children? Might he
not have been glad to see the baby go to England? Perhaps he hoped it would
be an inducement for Abigail to follow.

At any rate, by the time Jonathan was in college, Godwin unquestionably
disliked being responsible for his nephew, who in turn was bitter about the
way his uncle treated him. "Sure it is," Godwin's grandson admitted with
regret, "that Dr. Swift never loved his uncle, nor the remembrance of his
uncle, to the hour of his death." He didn't care for lawyers as a class, either,
though some of his good friends were lawyers. In Houyhnhnmland, Gulliver has to explain to the rational horses what it is that lawyers do. "I said
there was a society of men among us, bred up from their youth in the art of
proving by words multiplied for the purpose that white is black and black
is white, according as they are paid. To this society all the rest of the people
are slaves."[12]

ABANDONED

When Swift was finally brought back to Dublin, what happened is surprising. His mother, Abigail, left for England, taking Jane with her and settling permanently in Leicester. In all likelihood she made the move because she was desperately broke. But why would she leave little Jonathan behind? Ehrenpreis suggests that she probably came back to Dublin to see him from time to time, but there's no evidence whatsoever for that, or indeed that Jonathan saw her at all before he moved to England himself at the age of twenty-one.[13] He may not have minded much. Surely what hurt most at the time was not separation from the mother whom he would not even have recognized when he returned from Whitehaven, but from the nurse who loved and cared for him during his first few years.

We don't know the nurse's name, or anything about the child's life with her in Whitehaven, which was a fishing village with a dock from which Cumberland coal was shipped over to Ireland. But there must have been relatives and probably playmates. He may have felt more secure there than he ever did again, and it would have seemed like normal life to him until it abruptly ended. There would be more abrupt endings to come.

Jonathan Swift was now effectively an orphan. We know that in later life he regarded family affection with suspicion, if not contempt. Gulliver clearly speaks for him when he reports that the Lilliputians "will never allow that a child is under any obligation to his father for begetting him, or to his mother for bringing him into the world; which, considering the miseries of human life, was neither a benefit in itself, nor intended so by his parents, whose thoughts in their love encounters were otherwise employed."[14] When Swift was living in London in his forties he had a close friend named Abigail Masham, who was the confidante of Queen Anne. Because her two-year-old son was dying, she was absent from court at a critical time, and Swift commented angrily, "She stays at Kensington to nurse him, which vexes us all. She is so excessively fond it makes me mad; she should never leave the Queen, but leave everything to stick to what is so much the interest of the public as well as her own. This I tell her, but talk to the winds." It is remarkable, in fact, how seldom Swift mentioned mothers during the whole course of his life.[15]

Perhaps Swift would have agreed with Kafka that "the selfishness of parents—the authentic parental emotion—knows no bounds."[16] Kafka's problem was an overwhelmingly dominant father. Swift never knew his father, was abandoned by his mother, and felt humiliated by the uncle who grudgingly raised him. There is no recorded comment of any kind about the aunt he must have known, Godwin's fourth wife. A social historian remarks, "'Walk me through your childhood home,' we say, 'for opening the creaky front door unlocks the library of memory.'"[17] Swift slammed that door shut and locked it.

A MYTHIC ANCESTOR

Swift's paternal grandfather, who had died nine years before he was born, became something of a hero to him. Swift always liked to personalize history, and he made the most of the Reverend Thomas Swift's role in the English civil wars. Thomas Swift was vicar of Goodrich in Herefordshire, and although not wealthy, he was able to mortgage his estate for "three hundred broad pieces of gold." Concealing the money in the lining of his waistcoat, he presented it to the beleaguered King Charles I. The result was martyrlike persecution. "He was plundered by the Roundheads six and thirty times (some say above fifty)." Jonathan may also have felt vicarious resentment of maternal mistreatment, since he had heard that Thomas's mother was "a capricious, ill-natured and passionate woman" with "a good deal of the shrew in her countenance," and that she disinherited her son "for no greater crime than that of robbing an orchard when he was a boy."[18] Swift loved fruit.

His grandfather's military exploits take up the longest single account in the brief autobiographical sketch that Swift wrote down when he was sixty. He reports with evident relish, "Mr. Swift having a head mathematically turned, he contrived certain pieces of iron with three spikes, whereof one must always be with the point upwards. He placed them overnight in the ford where he received notice that the rebels would pass early the next morning, which they accordingly did, and lost two hundred of their men, who were drowned or trod to death by the falling of their horses, or torn by the spikes." Actually the spiked device, known as a caltrop, had been in use since the Middle Ages, and it wouldn't have worked unless there were four spikes, not three. As a younger relative of Swift's later commented, this story puts Thomas's saintly sufferings in a rather different light: "It was undoubtedly for actions of this kind that he was considered by the fanatics in the character of a soldier, and deprived of his church livings, together with the profits of his estate, so very early."[19]

Late in life Swift told his friend Alexander Pope, "I am utterly void of what the world calls natural affection, and with good reason, because they [that is, his family] are a numerous race, degenerating from their ancestors, who were of good esteem for their loyalty and sufferings in the rebellion against King Charles the First."[20] Recalling the name of Goodrich, Pope once sent him some playful verses:

> Jonathan Swift
> Had the gift,
> By fatheridge, motheridge,
> And by brotheridge,
> To come from Gutheridge,
> But now is spoiled clean
> And an Irish Dean.[21]

BOARDING SCHOOL BOY

Born into the Anglican minority in Ireland that later became known as the Ascendancy, from a political point of view Swift had a relatively auspicious start in the world. Although Anglicans made up at most 10 percent of the Irish population, they were the only citizens allowed to vote, attend the university, or hold government office. They also owned most of the land, which had been confiscated from Catholics over the years. Another 15 percent were Presbyterian Dissenters. The remaining 75 percent were Catholics, regularly referred to by the Irish Parliament—whose members were all Anglicans, of course—as "the common enemy."[22]

Jonathan was sent to Kilkenny College, the best school in Ireland. He remembered having started there when he was six, but he was often muddled about dates; Ehrenpreis notes that the usual age of entrance was nine.[23] Perhaps Swift just remembered it as distressingly early. This was an expensive education. It has been generally assumed that his uncle Godwin paid for the schooling at Kilkenny, but only one of his own sons went there. Why would Godwin choose to educate Jonathan at the expense of his own sons? Was there a patron in the shadows who wanted the boy to receive the best possible schooling? And if so, why? A possible answer to this puzzle will emerge later on.

Seventy miles southwest of Dublin on the river Nore, Kilkenny had been a cathedral city and a center of Anglo-Irish power since the thirteenth century, though the cathedral had recently been trashed by the Puritans and wouldn't be restored until the nineteenth century.

After the Restoration, the Duke of Ormonde, newly raised to that high rank by a grateful King Charles II, worked to promote peace among the various factions. A visitor in 1680 called Kilkenny the pleasantest and most delightful town in the whole of Ireland. The surrounding region was heavily Catholic, as indeed most of Ireland was. Roughly 70 percent of Dubliners were Protestant, but only 20 percent were Protestant within the Pale, a British-dominated zone that extended from Dublin about forty miles to the west. Beyond that—literally beyond the pale—up to 90 percent of the people were Catholic. Kilkenny was unusual, however, for religious tranquility, and there were thriving tradesmen of three different faiths: Catholics (who lived in a section known as Irishtown), Huguenot refugees from France, and members of the established Church of Ireland.[24]

The great Ormonde family (also spelled Ormond) presided over the town and County Kilkenny from its imposing castle. Replacing an earlier grammar school, the first Duke of Ormonde founded Kilkenny College to meet the needs of Protestant families that were otherwise "fain to send their children to Popish schoolmasters."[25] Catholics and Presbyterians were not admitted.

The actual school Swift attended no longer exists. It occupied an Elizabethan building near the cathedral that was torn down when a replacement was erected in 1784 across the river.[26] (Two centuries later, in 1985, the school migrated to its present quarters outside of town.) Kilkenny College was not a large institution; in 1686, four years after Swift left, there were just fifty-one students. The routine was rigorous. The boys had to get up at six and attend morning prayer, after which they had classes until eleven and again from one to five, ending the day with evening prayer. They did get the afternoon off on Thursday and Saturday, but catechism study was mandatory on Sunday, followed, of course, by church.[27]

Education was essentially restricted to Latin and Greek, with few of the subjects we would now expect—no science, no mathematics, no history. The diarist Samuel Pepys went to St. Paul's, one of the best schools in England, and afterward to Cambridge, but when he became a civil servant he had to hire a tutor to teach him the multiplication table.[28] A centerpiece in the Kilkenny curriculum was double translation, in which the student would translate a passage from Latin into English or from Greek into Latin, set it aside for a while, and then try to put it back into the original as accurately as possible. This exercise gave insight into the differences between languages, since word-for-word literal translations are always clumsy and frequently ridiculous.[29]

In later life Swift read Latin with ease and was grateful for this rigorous training, but not for the way it was enforced. When he was forty he remarked that it was common to sentimentalize one's youth—"our memories lead us only to the pleasant side"—but that his experience of school had actually been pretty grim. "I formerly used to envy my own happiness when I was a schoolboy—the delicious holidays, the Saturday afternoon, and the charming custards [prohibited treats, perhaps?] in a blind alley; I never considered the confinement ten hours a day to nouns and verbs, the terror of the rod, the bloody noses and broken shins."[30] Beatings were indeed considered the best incentive to learn. Fielding gave Tom Jones a tutor called Thwackum, and Gibbon said that a school was "the cavern of fear and sorrow: the mobility of the captive youths is chained to a book and a desk. . . . They labour, like the soldiers of Persia, under the scourge." Samuel Johnson did remark, though, "There is now less flogging in our great schools than formerly, but then less is learned there; so that what the boys get at one end, they lose at the other."[31]

Swift made a number of friends at Kilkenny, notably William Congreve, who would become a famous playwright while still in his twenties. Long after Congreve's death Swift said that he loved him "from my youth" and that he was always "a very agreeable companion."[32] Another friend, though they eventually parted ways, was a cousin about his own age named Thomas Swift, a year or two older. Thomas had been sent to Ireland at the age of five after his clergyman father died in England. This, in fact, was another fatherless nephew that the Dublin Swifts had on their hands. Still another Swift cousin, Godwin's son Deane, was three years older than Jonathan and was also at Kilkenny.

It was at Kilkenny that Swift formed a lifelong fondness, amounting virtually to addiction, for a verbal game in which the words look like Latin but make sense in English when spoken. One example he later recalled was "Mi dux et amasti cum."[33] This turns out to mean "My ducks ate a masticum." "Ate" was (and still is) commonly pronounced "et"; a masticum was medicine intended to be chewed.

Hardly anything else is known about Swift's years at Kilkenny, not even whether he spent the holidays at Uncle Godwin's house or someplace else. Two anecdotes have survived. When he was past sixty he recalled gloomily, "When I was a little boy, I felt a great fish at the end of my line which I drew up almost on the ground, but it dropped in, and the disappointment vexes me to this very day, and I believe it was the type of all my future disappointments."[34] "Type" was a religious term: "that by which something is prefigured," as Johnson defined it in his *Dictionary*.

The other anecdote is more dubious. As told a century later by George Faulkner, Swift's Dublin publisher, when he was dean of St. Patrick's he offered advice to a young clergyman who had made an imprudent marriage

4. Kilkenny Castle. The castle rises above the river Nore, which was then navigable
(if just barely) down to the sea at Waterford thirty miles to the south.
It was here that Swift lost his fish.

and been cut off by his family. Faulkner's account isn't very clear, but the gist is that as a schoolboy Swift gave a man all the money he had, 1 shilling and sixpence, for a mangy horse that was about to be killed for its hide. He rode it around town for a while, envied by some of the boys and mocked by others, and only then realized that he had no way to feed it. "But the horse died immediately," Faulkner concludes, "which gave the owner great relief." After hearing this the young clergyman exclaimed, "Sir, your story is very good, and very applicable to me. I own I deserve it."[35] Of course, Swift might have just made the story up to put a point across—an unattractive one, if he was comparing an unwise marriage to buying a mangy horse.

One Swift relic survived for a while in Kilkenny. Until the school was torn down in 1784, visitors were shown a desk on which he had carved his name in full, JONATHAN SWIFT. The school desks were then bought by a local shopkeeper who used the boards as flooring for his shop.[36] Nobody knows where they are today, if they exist at all.

"THE EDUCATION OF A DOG"

After leaving Kilkenny Swift was enrolled as a paying "pensioner," together with his cousin Thomas, at Trinity College, Dublin. This happened on April 24, 1682, when he was fourteen, a quite usual age to enter college in those days, and it is the earliest documented date in his life. Like Kilkenny College, Trinity as he knew it no longer exists, though the modern Trinity College still occupies the same site. For that matter, the entire city of Swift's youth has mostly vanished. St. Stephen's Green was being developed, the large and elegant park around which handsome Georgian mansions would eventually rise, as Dublin grew to take on the aspect of a modern European capital. But during Swift's youth it was still much like the congested, ramshackle medieval town it had once been.[37]

Trinity College had been founded ninety years previously by Queen Elizabeth as a Protestant seminary. (There were no divinity schools as such, and a university degree was the prerequisite for ordination.) Not every graduate

5. The Dublin Custom House. Not many images survive of the Dublin Swift knew, even in later life. The custom house shown here, built in 1707 at the Essex Quay, was replaced by a grander structure in 1791.

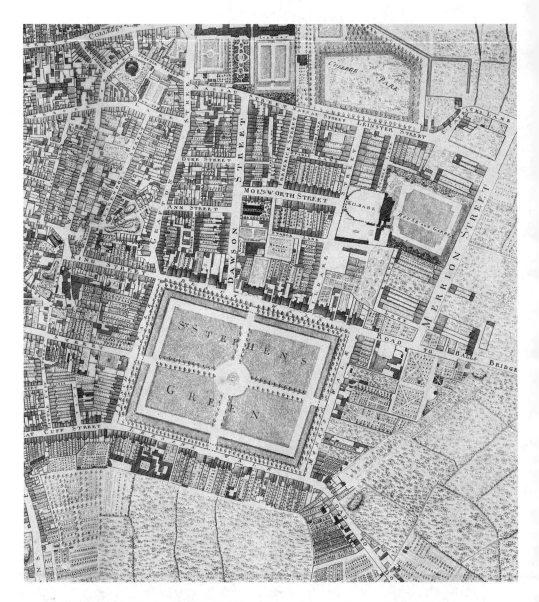

6. Map of Dublin showing Trinity College. The college, a mile east of Swift's birthplace, occupies the area at the top, bounded by Grafton Street to the west and Nassau Street to the south. When this map was made in 1756, houses were in place around most of St. Stephen's Green, but there were still open fields to the south and east.

went into the ministry, but all students had to be members of the Church of Ireland; no Presbyterians need apply, and of course no Catholics either. Swift had been baptized and would make his career in the Church of Ireland, the officially established state Church, separate only bureaucratically from the Church of England; its bishops were appointed by the English Crown.

The subjects Swift loved best were history and poetry. But history wasn't in the curriculum at all, and at Trinity, just as at Kilkenny, the emphasis in Latin and Greek was on grammar and composition. His godson Thomas Sheridan recalled that when he himself was at Trinity, "he asked me, 'Do they teach you English?' No. 'Do they teach you how to speak?' No. 'Then,' said he, 'they teach you *nothing*.'"[38] Sheridan said that on another occasion, "he told me that he had made many efforts, upon his entering the College, to read some of the old treatises on logic writ by Smeglesius, Keckermannus, Burgersdicius, etc., and that he never had patience to go through three pages of any of them, he was so disgusted at the stupidity of the work. . . . Swift asked [his tutor] what it was he was to learn from those books? His tutor told him, the art of reasoning. Swift said that he found no want of any such art, that he could reason very well without it."[39] (Burgersdicius, author of a logic textbook, would come in for derision in Sterne's *Tristram Shandy*.)

In later years Swift often mocked this aridly formal style of education, which he described as "the art of being deep-learned and shallow-read." Reasoning by syllogism seemed to him like arguing in circles: "Words are but wind; and learning is nothing but words; ergo, learning is nothing but wind." In a joint satire written with friends he quoted actual examples of mind-numbing abstraction: "*An praeter esse reale actualis essentiae sit aliud esse necessarium quo res actualiter existat?* In English thus: whether besides the real being of actual being, there be any other being necessary to cause a thing to be?"[40]

The provost of the college when Swift entered was Narcissus Marsh, a distinguished scholar, though not in disciplines that appealed to Swift. "I untied a difficult knot in algebra," Marsh wrote in his diary, "for which I praise the Almighty"; and again, "After great study I had a good invention in conical sections, for which God's Holy name be praised." Before long Marsh became a bishop and resigned the provostship with relief. "I was quickly weary of 340 young men and boys in this lewd and debauched town, and the more so because I had no time to follow my always dearly beloved studies." He rose eventually to be Primate of All Ireland, the archbishop at the head of the national Church, but Swift never thought much of him. Marsh did leave a bequest for a fine library, which was in place in the grounds of St. Patrick's Cathedral by the time Swift became its dean.[41]

At some point Swift wrote a devastating character sketch of Marsh as a person with "neither friend nor enemy, without joy or grief," whose sole passion was pedantry. "It has been affirmed that originally he was not altogether devoid of wit, till it was extruded from his head to make room for other men's thoughts. . . . No man will be either glad or sorry at his death, except his successor." Swift found Marsh personally repellent, too. Apparently he seldom bathed, "so that the most honourable place at his table is much the worst, especially in summer."[42]

Someone Swift did admire was his tutor, St. George Ashe, just ten years older than he, who became a lifelong friend. Swift didn't share all of Ashe's interests, though. Like Marsh, Ashe was an enthusiastic member of the Dublin Philosophical Society, which conducted amateurish scientific experiments, some of which seem today like a complete waste of time. In *Gulliver's Travels* Swift would describe researchers who kill a dog by pumping air into its anus, encourage pigs to root around in fields in order to save the cost of plowing ("they had little or no crop"), and breed sheep that grow no wool ("to propagate the breed of naked sheep all over the kingdom").[43] But some of the work of the Philosophical Society was genuinely valuable. Like many of his friends in later life, Swift failed to appreciate the potential promise of modern science.

Swift's academic performance was uneven. College records show that he got *bene* in Greek and Latin, *male* ("bad") in philosophy, and *negligenter* in theology. In later years he showed no interest in theological dogma, regarded abstract philosophizing with contempt, and loved the classics. But *male* is not the worst mark he could have received; some of his classmates received *pessime*, or "worst," and nearly half were *mediocriter in omnibus*, right across the board. Dickens's friend John Forster, who wrote a biography of Swift, studied these results with scrupulous care and noted that only one student, a certain Thewles, got *bene in omnibus*, and he "has not been heard of since." Swift liked to make the same point himself: "What becomes of all the fine boys one hears of in the world? Can anyone show me one of them grown up into a fine man?"[44]

What Swift did indulge at Trinity was a love of socializing. A classmate recalled that "when he was a young man in the University of Dublin, he never understood one word of Stierius or Smiglesius. But—for cards and poetry!" Someone else remembered him as "remarkable for nothing else in College except for making a good fire."[45] In fact he was something of a rebel. There was compulsory chapel attendance three times every day (at six and ten in the morning, and four in the afternoon), with additional services on special occasions. It was necessary to get a pass to leave the college precincts, and even then one was permitted to leave for no more than two hours at a time. The records show, without giving details, that Swift was disciplined often for cutting chapel and for staying out in the town too long. But there is no evidence of the behavior that got two classmates expelled, "indecent conversation with women in Stephen's Green, and of unseasonable walking in the night." That sounds more like Joyce than Swift. Still, on one occasion he did take part in some sort of disturbance for which he was required to beg the dean's pardon on bended knees.[46]

Trinity students were constantly involved in troublemaking, rising at times to full-scale rioting. Their lives centered more on partying than on books, though Swift himself was a moderate drinker, and claimed he was never drunk in his life. A poet catalogued the contents of a typical student room at Trinity:

> Imprimis, there's a table blotted,
> A tattered hanging all besnotted. . . .
> A penny pot and basin, this
> Designed for water, that for piss.
> A trencher and a College bottle
> Riding on Locke and Aristotle,
> A smutty ballad, musty libel,
> A Burgersdicius and a Bible,
> A prayer book he seldom handles,
> Item, a pound of farthing candles.[47]

There are no portraits of Swift before the age of forty, which is roughly when the one reproduced here was painted (figure 7). It shows him in a clerical gown and an expensive periwig (this one cost £2 1/2). George Faulkner, Swift's friend and Dublin publisher, gave the most extended description of his appearance: "The Dean was of middle stature, well made and comely, with very good regular features, an high forehead, handsome nose, large sparkling blue eyes very piercing (which had their luster to the last, although he read very much, but never made use of spectacles or glasses), an exceeding agreeable mouth, a fine regular set of teeth, and round double chin with a small dimple. His complexion a light olive, or pale brown." The poet Alexander Pope was similarly struck by the eyes: "Though his face has a look of dullness

7. Jonathan Swift, by Charles Jervas, 1710.

in it, he has very particular eyes: they are quite azure as the heavens, and
there's a very uncommon archness in them."[48]

Thanks to a joking comment by Swift, we also know his height. When Julius Caesar was mentioned in conversation, a friend named Ambrose Philips
suggested that he must have been "of a lean make, pale complexion, extremely

neat in his dress, and five feet seven inches high," all of which described Philips himself. Swift commented pleasantly, "And I, Mr. Philips, should take him to have been a plump man, just five feet five inches high, not very neatly dressed, in a black gown with pudding-sleeves." That was the name of the puffy sleeves of a clergyman's gown.[49]

In that era of poor nutrition, average heights were much lower than today. On one occasion a description was posted of four soldiers who had deserted from the army, and the tallest of them was five feet six. The imperious Louis XIV was five feet five inches tall, William III only an inch taller than that, and Charles I barely five feet.[50]

We know from Swift's rhymes, incidentally, that he pronounced many words in the Irish way: *meals* rhymes with *fails*, *weavers* with *savers*, and so on. He was aware that the English looked down on Irishness, and he sometimes joked about it, punning for instance on the name of William Wood:

> Teague made a good pun by a brogue in his speech,
> And said, "By my shoul he's the son of a BEECH.[51]

In 1686, when he was nineteen, Swift was awarded his B.A. degree *speciali gratia*, "by special grace," which seems to mean that he barely squeaked by. Patrick Delany, a close friend, said the shock of taking a humiliating degree was what spurred him to study eight hours a day for the next several years. Another friend, John Lyon, confirmed that *speciali gratia* indicated "some degree of dishonor," and Patrick Delany flatly called it a "disgrace."[52] Swift may well have been the brightest student at Trinity for many years, and that was his problem.

During the graduation ceremonies it was customary for a student known as the *terrae filius*, "son of the earth," to interrupt with a derisive speech in barbarous Latin and indecent English. This would be produced as a collaborative effort by a group of students, and Swift almost certainly took part. The fragmentary scripts that have survived from that period are far from brilliant, but one passage suggests his later verse style, in which the vice provost appears as a "waddling doctor":

> A wight inferior to none
> For ponderosity of bum.[53]

It was probably at Trinity too that Swift sketched some notes for a project he never developed, a Kingdom of Absurdities that had glass bells with iron clappers, houses made of gunpowder with candles alight inside them, and exceptionally alarming privies: "There is a sort of flying insect in their jakes [privies], which has cruel teeth, and is fond of human testicles; so that when a man goes there upon his occasions, it is forty to one but he comes away without them. Nothing is so easy as to destroy those animals, and yet ask the reason why they do it not, they say it was their ancestors' custom of old."[54]

Speaking of his Trinity years, Swift once declared that his uncle Godwin gave him "the education of a dog." Ehrenpreis dismisses the story as incredible, but Sir Walter Scott heard the story from one of Godwin's grandsons, who would have been likely enough to remember such a shocking statement, especially in view of the public occasion at which it was delivered: "Whittingham, the Archdeacon of Dublin, demanded insultingly at a banquet whether Swift owed his education to his uncle Godwin. Swift at first ignored the question, but when it was repeated, answered 'Yes! He gave me the education of a dog.' Grinning maliciously, Whittingham retorted, 'Then you have not the gratitude of a dog,' at which point the Bishop had to intervene to prevent them from coming to blows."[55]

Several commentators suggest that what Swift probably meant was that he was kept on a very meager allowance, which he doubtless was.[56] His detestation of financial dependence encouraged a tendency to keep track of even the smallest expenses, and for the rest of his life everyone who knew him would notice this concern, which amounted really to an obsession. Yet he was far from being a miser, since he would give away much of his disposable income.

One relative did come through, handsomely and unexpectedly. That was a cousin seven years older than Jonathan, Godwin's son Willoughby, who by now was a successful merchant in Lisbon. Godwin's grandson Deane Swift got the story from Willoughby's daughter, and it deserves to be heard at length:

> It happened when [Jonathan] was at the University of Dublin that one day he was looking out of his window pensive and melancholy, his pockets being then at the lowest ebb, having spied a master of a ship gazing about in the college courts. "Lord," thought he, "if that person should now be inquiring and staring about for my chamber, in order to bring me some present from cousin Willoughby Swift, what a happy creature should I be!" He had scarce amused himself with this pleasing imagination when the master of the ship, having come into his chamber, asked him if his name was Jonathan Swift. He told him it was. "Why then," said the master, "I have something for you that was

sent to you by Mr. Willoughby Swift;" whereupon he drew out of his pocket a large greasy leather bag, and poured him out all the money that it contained on the table. As the sum which he had now received was much greater than ever in his life he had been master of before at any one time, he pushed over without reckoning them a good number of silver cobs (for it was all in that specie) to the honest sailor, and desired he would accept of them for his trouble. But the sailor would not touch a farthing. "No, no, master," said he, "I'ze take nothing for my trouble; I would do more than that comes to for Mr. Willoughby Swift."[57]

Ehrenpreis never mentions this story, though it seems well enough attested. Perhaps he felt that it highlights Godwin's lack of generosity, which it certainly does.

Willoughby's kindness continued. Several years later Swift asked his cousin Deane (father of the biographer of the same name), who had been at Kilkenny with him and had gone to Lisbon too, to tell Willoughby "how extreme sensible of his goodness and generosity I am."[58] Quite possibly Godwin's sons were embarrassed by the way their father treated their cousin. None of Swift's biographers has pointed out that they must have grown up together in Hoey's Court, more like siblings than cousins. Years later, when Willoughby's daughter married a clergyman, Swift took him on as a curate and offered to lend him the huge sum of £800 to settle an onerous debt. He told the lawyer who was involved in the affair, "He married the daughter of my near relation, for whom I had great kindness, and to whom I owe some obligations."[59]

REVOLUTION

Charles II had been welcomed back to the throne in the Restoration of 1660, with an appetite for pleasure that gained him the nickname of the Merry Monarch. Swift was eighteen when the king died in 1685, as he wryly recalled late in life, when most of his friends were much younger than himself:

> He's older than he would be reckoned,
> And well remembers Charles the Second.[60]

Unluckily, Charles left no legitimate heir, though plenty of the other kind— fourteen children by seven mothers. As the poet Dryden wittily put it, he "scattered his maker's image through the land." When the king lay dying, his latest mistress, the Duchess of Portsmouth, insisted that a Catholic priest hear his confession and administer the last rites. Macaulay describes the strange group that gathered to say farewell: "His natural children were brought to his bedside, the Dukes of Grafton, Southampton, and Northumberland, sons of the Duchess of Cleveland; the Duke of Saint Albans, son of Eleanor Gwynn; and the Duke of Richmond, son of the Duchess of Portsmouth. Charles blessed them all."[61]

What had long been suspected was now certain: that ever since returning from exile in France, Charles had been a secret Catholic. His brother succeeded him as King James II, and James was not only openly Catholic but determined to re-Catholicize England. He set out to replace bishops, academics, and judges on a massive scale. Equally alarming to his Protestant subjects— who in England and Scotland made up 98 percent of the population—was that James wanted to create an authoritarian central government on the pattern of Louis XIV's in France. Still, since he and his queen were childless, most people were willing to await the time when he would be succeeded by his daughter Mary, who had remained a Protestant and was married to the Protestant William of Orange, *stadholder*, or leader, of the United Provinces of the Netherlands.

In June of 1688, however, the queen bore a male heir who took precedence over Mary, and events unraveled quickly. A group of highly placed nobles invited William and Mary to eject James by force, and public opinion was clearly in agreement. William actually had a claim of his own, since he was a grandson of Charles I as well as husband of James's daughter. He was thus both second cousin and son-in-law to James.

For a brief time the clergy of the established Church, whose appointments were conditional upon an oath of loyalty to the Crown, attempted to follow a policy of passive "nonresistance," but as a noblewoman commented to a group of bishops, "You have made a turd pie, seasoned it with passive obedience, and now you must eat it yourselves."[62]

On November 5—Guy Fawkes Day—William of Orange landed with his army in Devonshire and prepared for battle. James was intimidated and irresolute, and gave up the fight after a couple of minor engagements in which little blood was shed. His support was rapidly melting away. The defection of John Churchill, the future Duke of Marlborough, was an especially wounding blow. And then James's other daughter, Anne, also went over to the rebels. "God help me!" the king cried, "my own children have forsaken me."[63] In December he left England forever, and would live and die in France.

There was now intense debate about how to proceed. One faction wanted William to be named regent rather than king, but he refused to consider that solution and threatened to go home to Holland. In the end it was decided that James had effectively abdicated, leaving the throne vacant, and that it would be occupied jointly by William III and Mary II. After their deaths Mary's sister Anne was to succeed as queen.

In England the fighting was over. But in Ireland, where the Catholic majority still hoped to recover lands that had been confiscated over the years and given to Protestants, it was just beginning. Irish soldiers rallied to James's cause, and he landed near Belfast with an army of continental mercenaries in March of 1689. It was the first time in three hundred years that a British king had set foot in Ireland, and he was serenaded in Dublin by pipers playing "The king enjoys his own again."[64]

Thus began what was known as the War of the Two Kings, William III and the deposed James II, who led their troops into battle at the Boyne River northwest of Dublin. William's victory there has been celebrated ever since by the Orangemen of Northern Ireland. Despairing of success, James left his army in the lurch and went back to France for good. His sudden desertion of his Irish troops caused lasting bitterness, and they referred to him thereafter as Séamus an Chaca, "James the Shithead." But the fighting dragged on for another whole year, ending only after the bloodiest battle in modern Irish history at Aughrim in July of 1691. The Treaty of Limerick finally brought peace, but throughout the island it had been a period of protracted violence, with brutality and pillage on both sides. When it was finally over, twenty-five thousand soldiers and countless civilians had died.[65]

Swift thus came of age at a historical turning point of far-reaching significance. The stakes were frighteningly high: a person's choices could ruin him forever, or make him rich and powerful. He was a keen observer of these events, but he didn't watch them unfold in Ireland. In February 1689, just before James II landed, the fellows of Trinity College decided that "all those who thought fit to withdraw themselves from the College for their better security might have free liberty to do so." Ten of the fifteen fellows did so, along with most of the students. James's troops requisitioned the college as a garrison and prison, and according to its register, "the scholars were all turned out by soldiers, and ordered to carry nothing with 'em but their books."[66] At some point early in that year Swift had already followed the advice of the college and departed for Leicester, where his mother still lived. As far as we know, he had not seen her since he was a young boy.

Meanwhile, immense changes were under way. It had been established at last that in times of crisis Parliament was supreme over the monarch, who could neither levy taxes nor dismiss a parliament without its own consent. These and other limitations of royal power were laid out in the Bill of Rights of 1689. In the Whig tradition, which saw British history as a progressive achievement of popular liberty, it was truly a Glorious Revolution. "This revolution, of all revolutions the least violent," Macaulay wrote in 1849, "has been, of all revolutions, the most beneficent."[67]

Beneficent or not, the Revolution of 1688 was a decisive stage in the evolution of a modern society. Steve Pincus has argued in a comprehensive study that it even deserves to be called "the first modern revolution," since James II and his opponents were all radical modernizers.[68] Like Louis XIV, James wanted to develop a powerful centralized bureaucracy, and like Louis, he wanted to enrich his nation by extending its worldwide empire. The middle-class opponents who evicted him wanted the same things, but with authority based in Parliament rather than the throne, and with a focus on commercial growth instead of landed possessions. "The Revolution is looked upon by all sides as a new era," Swift's ally Bolingbroke wrote; "from thence we must date both king and people."[69]

Swift was now living in Leicester with the mother he scarcely knew. As his godson Sheridan pointed out, his prospects were far from bright. He had no money. He had emerged from the university with an undistinguished degree, and he had none of the powerful patrons who could help a young man to rise. However, he was fiercely ambitious, and a sense of great abilities kept down was a powerful motivator. "It is to those very circumstances, probably," Sheridan commented, "that the world owes a Swift: to the want of money, want of learning, want of friends."[70] He would soon find a patron and he would acquire more learning. As for money, that would be a source of anxiety for the rest of his life.

CHAPTER 2

————◆◆◀◁▩⬥▷▶◆◆————

ᴄᴀ *Patron and Two Mysteries*

REUNION WITH ABIGAIL

For the first time since he was a child, Swift sailed to England, setting out from Ringsend near Dublin, where the river Liffey enters the sea. He probably took a small packet boat, so called because it carried packets of mail as well as passengers, and he would have landed either at Holyhead in Wales or Chester in England. Holyhead was the port nearest to Dublin, at the western tip of the island of Anglesea; Chester, on the river Dee, was seventy miles further inland. In later years he made the crossing many times and used both destinations.

It is not easy today to appreciate how difficult crossing the Irish Sea could be. It might take as few as fifteen hours to cross, but it might also be necessary to wait a week for a favorable wind. Terrifying storms could blow up without warning in what a 1691 guidebook called "a violent and unruly sea."[1] Milton's college classmate Edward King drowned there, as immortalized in *Lycidas*, and so did Wordsworth's brother John, who was a professional sea captain. Today the trip can be made comfortably on a high-speed ferry named the *Jonathan Swift* ("travelling at a speed of 39 knots, your arrival time is as quick as 1 hour 49 minutes").[2]

Swift then traveled by road, quite possibly on foot, to the town of Leicester in the Midlands, ninety miles from Holyhead or seventy from Chester.

33

8. Holyhead in 1742. At anchor below the church are two of the packet boats that plied
between Wales and Ireland, with a third setting out to sea.

There he settled down for several months with his mother. Whatever their relationship had been previously, they quickly became fond of each other, and in the coming years he would always stop off to see her when he made the trip from London back to Ireland. No doubt they wrote to each other as well, but no letters have survived, except for one draft that begins "Dear Mother" and then breaks off, used thereafter for miscellaneous notes on Swift's reading.[3] His sister, Jane, was living with their mother too, but his relations with Jane were always distant.

Swift liked Leicester, and in later years he kept a map of it in his bedroom.[4] It was a market town of modest size on the river Soar, nothing like the manufacturing center it would become after the Industrial Revolution, and its history went back to Roman times. The legendary King Lear was supposedly buried by the river, and Richard III's remains were flung into it after his defeat nearby at the battle of Bosworth Field.

When Abigail was growing up, Leicester had been rather backward, overshadowed by Nottingham twenty miles away. A visitor in the 1670s called it "an old stinking town situated upon a dull river," and a historian says that even in the eighteenth century "our main impression of the streets of the town would probably have been smell and dirt." That would have been true almost anywhere, though, and a 1741 map of Leicester shows spacious gardens all through the town and open countryside close by. By the time Swift arrived it had a thriving industry of knitted wool stockings, and was relatively prosperous.[5]

For the first time we hear of romance, or flirtation at least. As Swift recalled forty years later, he got so interested in a clergyman's daughter, Betty Jones, that "my prudent mother was afraid I should be in love with her." What prompted that memory was a letter from a young woman who turned up in Dublin in 1729 when he was out of town, claiming to be Betty's daughter and asking for a loan. He thought her story sounded dubious, but he asked his

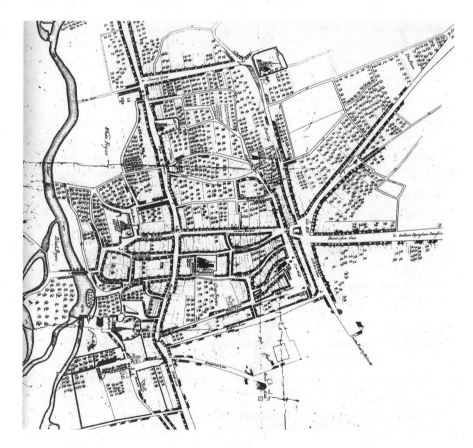

9. Leicester in 1741. There were about seven thousand inhabitants. Leicester still has the street pattern shown here, but almost none of the buildings from Abigail's time.

vicar to interview her, and if she seemed honest to give her £5 "on account of her mother and grandmother, whom my mother used to call cousin."[6]

A trace of this amour, if that's what it was, may survive in a letter Swift wrote in 1699 to a friend who was packing up some papers for him: "I remember those letters to Elisa; they were writ in my youth. You might have sealed them up, and nobody of my friends would have opened them. Pray burn them."[7] If Swift gave Elizabeth Jones the poetical name Elisa, as he gave names to other women later, this could be the same person.

One other letter—the first by Swift that we have—may refer to this Betty, or else to another Leicester acquaintance. A clergyman who had married a cousin of his wrote to inquire what his intentions were toward an unnamed young woman. Swift replied that he had no thought of getting married until he was better established in the world, and that anyway the relationship with what he called "the woman in hand" wasn't serious. "I could remember twenty women in my life," he said, "to whom I have behaved myself just the same way, and I profess without any other design than that of entertaining myself when I am very idle, or when something goes amiss in my affairs."[8] It's not clear why flirtation would be provoked by something going amiss—as a distraction, perhaps. We do know that all his life Swift loved to tease and flirt. Perhaps it had already begun when he was at Trinity.

In his autobiographical sketch Swift says that he stayed in Leicester "for some months." Then he acquired a patron, and an exceptionally distinguished one: Sir William Temple, a retired diplomat who lived near London. The connection was made by Abigail Swift, though we know nothing about the terms under which Temple agreed to take Jonathan on. What we do know is that Temple's father, Sir John, had been an important figure in the Dublin legal establishment and was close to the Swifts. Jonathan later called him "a great friend to the family," and as we shall see, there is reason to suspect that Sir John Temple may have been much more than a friend to Abigail herself.[9] At any rate, it was a great stroke of luck for Swift to receive this appointment. He was interested in a career in politics or government, and Sir William was well known to be a close friend of King William III.

It was a journey of 220 miles from Leicester to London, on truly terrible roads. They were unpaved, of course, and deep in mud when it rained. Roads throughout the country were maintained only by the farmers whose land happened to adjoin them, and deep jolting ruts were the norm. Not only were the roads bad, they were anything but direct. "Straight lines were not prominent in the landscape," Trevelyan remarks. Chesterton made a John Bull virtue out of it:

> Before the Roman came to Rye or out to Severn strode,
> The rolling English drunkard made the rolling English road.[10]

Difficult the journey may have been, but Swift probably enjoyed it all the same. In later life he liked to recall that as a young man he possessed boundless energy. Deane Swift the younger, one of the few relatives he liked, heard that "he was prodigiously fond of rambling," and that his stamina, which remained impressive right into old age, had been extraordinary then. "He ran like a buck from one place to another. Gates, stiles, and quicksets [hedges] he no more valued than if they had been so many straws."[11]

Swift's friend and biographer Lord Orrery, a snob if ever there was one, said that "he often went in a wagon, but more frequently walked from Holyhead to Leicester, London, or any other part of England. He generally chose to dine with wagoners, hostlers, and persons of that rank, and he used to lie at night in houses where he found written over the door 'Lodgings for a Penny.' He delighted in scenes of low life. The vulgar dialect was not only a fund of humour for him, but I verily believe was acceptable to his nature." The point about wagons was that he ought to have traveled in respectable stagecoaches. A French visitor called the wagons "great carts, covered in, that lumber along but very heavily; only a few poor old women make use of this vehicle." Samuel Johnson suggested that the real reason Swift traveled that way was "a passion which seems to have been deep fixed in his heart, the love of a shilling." But one of his friends remembered being told that he liked to disguise himself as an ostler, waiter, or shoemaker "to get into the knowledge of their professions."[12]

SIR WILLIAM AND HIS DEVOTED ENTOURAGE

Swift's destination was Sir William Temple's pleasant country house, known as Moor Park, near Farnham in Surrey, forty miles southwest of London. Temple was the first employer he had ever had, and although he was paid a very modest £20 per year, there was reason to hope that this opportunity would be the start of a brilliant career. In the days before competitive exams and interviewing committees, positions of all kinds were in the gift of the patrons who bestowed them. More than half of the seats in the House of

Commons were controlled by private individuals or by government ministers; parish priests were appointed to their "livings" by local landowners; and
bishoprics, for the few clergymen who rose that high, were in the gift of the
Crown.[13]

The word *patronize* didn't yet have the negative connotations that it would
later acquire. Joseph Addison, for example, wrote in the *Spectator* that a good
man "patronizes the orphan and widow, assists the friendless, and guides the
ignorant."[14] Likewise, *condescend* was positive in meaning; Johnson defines it
as "To depart from the privileges of superiority by a voluntary submission;
to sink willingly to equal terms with inferiors." Temple himself didn't have
positions to bestow, but he had very highly placed friends who did, above all
the king. Swift was counting on Temple to condescend and patronize, and his
failure to do so would provoke enduring resentment.

Sir William represented a type that Swift had probably never encountered
before. He was urbane, cosmopolitan, fluent in French, well read in the clas-

10. Sir William Temple in
his youth.

sics, and a gentleman of leisure who had retired after a distinguished diplomatic career. He was exceptionally good-looking as well.

Temple's career had begun back in the 1660s, when Charles II entrusted him with important negotiations in Holland. Two important treaties were the result, but after a while Temple realized that although he was supposed to be promoting England's alliance with Holland against France, the king was actually colluding secretly with Louis XIV in return for secret subsidies. It was a betrayal. "My wings are cut," Temple lamented in a letter, "and that frankness of my heart which made me think everybody meant as well as I did is much allayed."[15]

Deeply disillusioned, Temple nevertheless continued with diplomacy for a few more years, during which he developed a close friendship with the Dutch prince William of Orange and negotiated his marriage with King Charles's niece, Princess Mary. But in 1681, at the age of fifty-three, he renounced his career and settled with his wife in the village of Sheen (now part of Richmond), close to London. There they were joined by William's younger sister Martha. She had married Thomas Giffard in 1662 when she was twenty-three, but lost her husband to a sudden illness just two weeks later. Lady Giffard never remarried, and remained her brother's close companion for the rest of his life.

When the Revolution of 1688 ejected James II, Temple's friends William and Mary ascended the British throne. The new king invited him to become secretary of state, one of the highest positions in the governing ministry, but he declined, holding to his resolution to live as a simple country gentleman. In memoirs that he left for Swift to publish after his death he declared, "I take leave of all those airy visions which have so long busied my head about mending the world, and at the same time, of all those shining toys or follies that employ the thoughts of busy men; and shall turn mine wholly to mend myself."[16]

The Temples' marriage had been a love match. They fell for each other in 1648, when William was twenty and Dorothy Osborne nineteen. Though they were both highly independent spirits, their engagement dragged on for six years because they weren't rich, and both families wanted them to marry other people who had more money. The lively, intelligent letters Dorothy wrote during their separation were published in 1888 and became famous (Virginia Woolf admired them).[17] It should be noted, however, that Sir William was a notorious ladies' man, and he probably saw marriage as no obstacle to sexual liaisons. One that may well have occurred will shed light on some of the mysteries at Moor Park.

Infant mortality was dreadful, since there was no real protection against infectious disease. Seven Temple children died in infancy, and a beloved daughter was fourteen when she succumbed to smallpox. But a son named John grew to adulthood. When John was thirty-two, King William came to the throne and gave him a government post. There, John immediately gave some advice that backfired disastrously. He persuaded the king to release an Irish officer, Richard Hamilton, from the Tower of London so that he could go to Ireland and negotiate the surrender of the rebels. As soon as Hamilton got to Ireland, however, he went over to the rebels himself, and commanded James II's troops at the infamous siege of Derry.

Disgraced, young Temple filled his pockets with stones and jumped from a boat into the Thames. On the seat he left a heartbreaking note: "'Tis not out of any dissatisfaction with my friends [the term could imply "family" in those days], from whom I have received infinitely more kindness and friendship than I deserve, I say it is not from any such reason that I do myself this violence, but having been long tired with the burden of this life, 'tis now become insupportable. From my father and mother I have had especially of late all the marks of tenderness in the world." On this scrap of paper his mother wrote: "Child's paper he writ before he killed himself." In a memoir after Sir William's death, his sister Lady Giffard said, "This cruel blow brought a cloud upon the remainder of his life, and a damp upon the good humor so natural to him that nothing could ever recover."[18]

THE GARDENS OF EPICURUS

When the Temples acquired their new home in 1686, the brick Elizabethan house was known as Compton Hall. They renamed it Moor Park after a house in Hertfordshire where they had spent their honeymoon. The name was appropriate since it stood at the edge of a great expanse of heath land, full of gorse and bracken and scraggly pines. Less than two miles from the bustling town of Farnham, it remains isolated to this day, surrounded by woods and reachable only by a narrow lane. A Swiss visitor when Swift lived there called it "a pleasant retreat, far enough from town to be protected from visits, the air wholesome, the soil good, the view limited but pretty, a little stream which runs near making the only sound to be heard; the house small, convenient, and appropriately furnished. . . . I saw Monsieur Temple healthy and gay, and though he is gouty and getting on in years, he tired me in walking."[19]

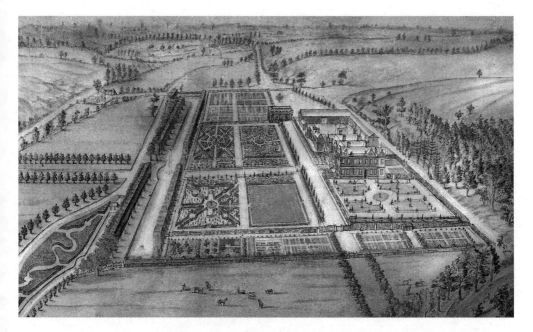

11. Moor Park in Temple's time.

Temple laid out his garden in the rectangular style that he had gotten to know in Holland. In front of the house he arranged to have a placid little river—"chalky Wey, that rolls a milky wave," Pope called it—channeled into a long, straight canal. Temple's great passion was raising fruit, in which he became expert. He also enjoyed writing relaxed, conversational essays, and in one of them, called "Upon the Gardens of Epicurus," he specified that "the only good nectarines are the Murry and the French; of these there are two sorts, one very round, and the other something long; but the round is the best."[20]

Indeed, Epicureanism was Temple's chosen philosophy of life. Its critics thought the term was synonymous with insatiable pleasure seeking; one of them said that synonyms for *Epicurean* were "godless, voluptuous, sensual, bestial, beastly, dissolute, vicious, wallowing, swinish, self-pampering, self-pleasing."[21] Some seventeenth-century Epicureans were indeed like that, the rake-poet Rochester, for instance, but Temple was not. He was what the French would call a libertine in the sense of being liberated from cares, living according to nature and enjoying tranquil pleasures. Temple ended his

12. Moor Park today. The house, now divided into private apartments, stands where it always did, but with a façade completely altered since Swift lived there. The immense cedar tree was planted after his time, a reminder of just how long ago that was. In the foreground is a surviving vestige of Sir William's canal.

memoirs with a vow to pursue "that old and excellent counsel of Pythagoras, that we are, with all the cares and endeavours of our lives, to avoid diseases in the body, perturbations in the mind, luxury in diet, factions in the house, and seditions in the state." He also said that the things of the world were mere baubles in comparison with "old wood to burn, old wine to drink, old friends to converse with, and old books to read."[22]

Sir William enjoyed an attentive female support system at Moor Park. It included Lady Temple; Lady Giffard, Sir William's widowed sister; John Temple's widow, together with her mother and two daughters; the housekeeper, Bridget Johnson, and her young daughter, Hester; and Lady Giffard's waiting woman, Rebecca Dingley. We know little about Swift's relations with any of these, with two exceptions. Hester Johnson, now best known as Stella, was nine years old when he arrived and would become his lifelong closest friend. Rebecca Dingley would be Stella's inseparable companion.

AN EXACTING MASTER

Temple had hired Swift as a secretary, one of several he engaged over the years.[23] Among other duties, he was asked to read aloud to Temple, a task for which his excellent command of Latin was an advantage. He may have helped to keep the household accounts, though there was a steward whose job that probably was. But the chief duty was to work with Temple on preparing his essays and correspondence for eventual publication. Swift read aloud from earlier drafts, took down changes as directed, and wrote out the revised texts in fair copies suitable for sending to a printer.

Figure 13 shows an example of Swift's labors. In his careful secretarial hand he has written out a preliminary draft of Temple's *Some Thoughts upon Reviewing the Essay on Ancient and Modern Learning.* Considering it, Temple toned down the self-praise in "perhaps more distinguisht by his Writings than by the great Employments he has had or refused" by crossing out "distinguisht" and replacing it with "knowne."

13. A page of Swift's work as secretary to Sir William Temple.

What was the relationship between Swift and Temple? Ehrenpreis takes it for granted that Swift had been yearning for a father and found one in Temple, to whom he surely listened "with eager attentiveness." Under "Temple" in Ehrenpreis's index there are three separate entries for "father-son relation." Yet it's quite clear that Temple was, to quote a recent writer, "a self-important old pontificator," and Swift detested pontificators.[24] There is no evidence at all that Temple became a father figure for Swift, and even less that Swift was like a son to Temple. How could a newly arrived stranger replace the son who had so recently killed himself?

Our information about the whole decade of the 1690s is sparse, but what there is of it suggests a very different picture. Thirty years ago A. C. Elias published a scrupulously researched investigation, *Swift at Moor Park*. This book was ignored at first because although Elias was a gifted scholar, he was not an academic Swiftian. But gradually his findings have found acceptance, and they confirm Thackeray's judgment that Swift's Moor Park years were full of bitterness, "as that of a great genius bound down by ignoble ties, and powerless in a mean dependence." The indelible image of a helpless Gulliver, tied to the ground by tiny ropes, reflects an all too frequent experience in Swift's life. Macaulay put it still more robustly: "Little did Temple imagine that the coarse exterior of his dependent concealed a genius equally suited to politics and to letters, a genius destined to shake great kingdoms, to stir the laughter and the rage of millions, and to leave to posterity memorials which can perish only with the English language."[25]

Of course, Swift's humble status made it easy for Temple to take him lightly. Half a century later Jean-Jacques Rousseau also worked as a secretary, doing laborious research for wealthy patrons who were would-be writers. When he afterward burst on the literary scene as a major thinker, one of them cheerfully acknowledged that she was amazed: "But tell me, Monsieur Rousseau, who would have suspected it of you?"[26] Temple apparently saw Swift as nothing more than an intelligent secretary, and Swift would spend the rest of his life proving how wrong Temple had been.

A close friend of Swift's, Patrick Delany, commented long afterward, "His spirit was formed with a strong reluctance to submission of any kind." But submission was what Sir William demanded. As he said himself in writing, subordinates needed to be handled with severity as well as kindness: "Whoever will be well served must compass it by the continual employment of those two general and natural governors of mankind, hope and fear."[27]

In addition to imperiousness, Temple had a short temper. His adoring sister acknowledged that he was troubled "by cruel fits of spleen and melancholy, often upon great damps in the weather." The south of England is subject to damps. He was also tormented by gout, which deposits sharp crystals in the joints that cause exquisite pain. Diet was thought to be at the bottom of the disease, and in an essay on its management Temple recommended temperance, "that gives indolence of body, and tranquility of mind."[28] That was the Epicurean ideal, but he often failed to achieve tranquility.

Even in good health, Temple could be difficult. He was notoriously vain, and Swift detested vanity. Years later, reading a historian's account of these years, Swift filled the margins with abusive comments, but made no remark at all when he read the characterization of Temple, which suggests that he agreed with it: "Temple was a vain man, much blown up in his own conceit, which he showed too indecently on all occasions."[29]

Dr. Arbuthnot, Swift's close friend in later years, told a story that must have come from Swift himself. Temple was once visiting a nobleman who showed him his pictures and other collections, and as they came to each of them, it would turn out that Temple had ones that were better. "Lord Brouncker at length very gravely replied, 'Sir William, say no more of the matter. You must at length yield to me, I having lately got something which it is impossible for you to obtain, for my Welsh steward has sent to me a flock of geese; and these are what you can never have, since all your geese are swans.'" One can imagine that Temple required regular doses of flattery from his entourage. Joyce alluded to Swift in *Finnegans Wake* as Temple's "private privysuckatary."[30]

A few documents survive from the Moor Park years that have been taken to prove that Swift worshiped Temple unreservedly, but all of them are open to other interpretations. In a letter in 1692, for instance, he made this remarkable assertion about Temple: "I never read his writings but I prefer him to all others at present in England, which I suppose is all but a piece of self-love, and the likeness of humors makes one fond of them as if they were one's own." The recipient of this letter was Swift's cousin Thomas, who also spent some time at Moor Park. Thomas was eager to curry favor with Sir William, and Jonathan doubtless expected that this tasty morsel would be passed on to their employer. Actually, it was preposterous to claim "likeness of humors" since, as Elias says, he and Temple were temperamental opposites.[31]

There is no way to know to what extent Swift was treated as an equal rather than as a member of the domestic staff, but one startling story was told later on by a member of the Temple family. According to Temple's nephew Jack, who visited Moor Park and would eventually inherit it, "Sir William hired Swift, at his first entrance into the world, to read to him and sometimes to be his amanuensis at the rate of £20 a year and his board, which was then high preferment to him; but Sir William never favoured him with his conversation because of his ill qualities, nor allowed him to sit down at table with him."[32] The "ill qualities" presumably refers to a lack of social graces, with the implication that Swift had to eat with the servants.

This was secondhand hearsay, since it came from the novelist Samuel Richardson, who remembered hearing it from Jack Temple. Richardson had a streak of malice and may have exaggerated the story for effect. It is also possible that Swift's status in the household began like that and improved as time went on. Still, the social distance was very real. One of Temple's Victorian biographers commented approvingly, "It was quite natural that, at first, the young clerk should not be admitted to any intimacy with his patron, or sit at his table." As for the wages of £20, Elias studied Moor Park records and found that this was probably the correct figure. It would have left Swift with the same sense of financial pressure that he had endured back in Dublin, and we know that at Moor Park he was grateful for continued remittances from his uncle William and his cousin Willoughby.[33]

There are a number of other clues to this difficult relationship. In his forties Swift remarked to Stella, "Don't you remember how I used to be in pain when Sir William Temple would look cold and out of humour for three or four days, and I used to suspect a hundred reasons?" At that time Swift was becoming close to the brilliant young Henry St. John, soon to be named Viscount Bolingbroke, and he told Stella, "One thing I warned him of, never to appear cold to me, for I would not be treated like a schoolboy—that I had felt too much of that in my life already (meaning from Sir William Temple)."[34] So Temple provoked unhappy memories of Kilkenny College, and perhaps also of Godwin Swift.

Another reference may also evoke this period. When he had servants of his own, Swift was himself a demanding master, though also a fair-minded and generous one. For many years he amused himself by writing up a set of witheringly ironic "directions to servants," urging them to cheat and thwart their employers in all sorts of ways. Among these, the instructions to the butler seem highly suggestive of Moor Park: "If an humble companion, a chaplain, a tutor, or a dependent cousin happen to be at table, whom you find to be little regarded by the master and the company, which nobody is readier to discover and observe than we servants, it must be the business of you and the footman to follow the example of your betters by treating him many degrees worse than any of the rest; and you cannot please your master better, or at least your lady."[35]

When Swift had been at Moor Park for less than a year, Temple tried to send him away. May of 1690 was the month when King William, feeling secure on his British throne, was setting out to fight James II in the battle of the Boyne. One of Temple's friends, Sir Robert Southwell, was accompanying him and would stay on as the representative of the Crown in Ireland. As soon as he heard of this mission, Temple dispatched Swift to London with a letter to Southwell. We don't know whether Swift saw its actual wording, but most likely not, since it was remarkably lukewarm:

> I venture to make you the offer of a servant, in case you may have occasion for such a one as this bearer. He was born and bred there (though of a good family in Herefordshire), was near seven years in the College of Dublin, and ready to take his degree of Master of Arts, when he was forced away by the desertion of that college upon the ca-lamities of the country. Since that time he has lived in my house, read to me, writ for me, and kept all accounts as far as my small occasions required. He has Latin and Greek and some French, writes a very good and current [cursive] hand, is very honest and diligent, and has good friends though they have for the present lost their fortunes in Ireland, and his whole family having been long known to me obliged me thus far to take care of him.[36]

"Obliged me thus far to take care of him" seems unenthusiastic. "Thus far" implies that one year was more than enough, and to call Swift a servant was hardly flattering, though Forster thought it might simply mean "someone you may wish to employ."[37]

Swift did indeed go back to Ireland at this point, but apparently South-well wasn't interested in employing him, and soon (there are few definite dates in these years) he returned to Moor Park. In his only mention of this trip, almost fifty years later, he said that he made it "by advice of physicians, who weakly imagined that his native air might be of some use to recover his health." He said nothing about Southwell.[38]

A final piece of evidence for Swift's view of Sir William is a remarkable page of resolutions, headed "When I come to be old," that he jotted down at the end of his Moor Park stay. They make fascinating reading:

14. "When I come to be old." Scratching with a quill wasn't easy, and in casual writing Swift could be rather slapdash.

Not to marry a young Woman.

Not to keep young Company unless they reely desire it.

Not to be peevish or morose, or suspicious.

Not to scorn present Ways, or Wits, or Fashions, or Men, or War, &c.

Not to be fond of Children, ~~or let them come near me hardly~~.

Not to tell the same Story over and over again to the same People.

Not to be covetous.

Not to neglect decency, or cleenlyness, for fear of falling into Nastyness.

Not to be over severe with young People, but give Allowances for their youthfull follyes, and Weeknesses.

Not to be influenced by, or give ear to knavish tatling Servants, or others.

Not to be too free of advise nor trouble any but those that desire it.

To desire some good Friends to inform me wch of these Resolutions I break, or neglect, & wherein; and reform accordingly.

Not to talk much, nor of my self.

Not to boast of my former beauty, or strength, or favor with Ladyes, &c.

Not to hearken to Flatteryes, nor conceive I can be beloved by a young woman, et eos qui hereditatem captant odisse ac vitare [and detest and avoid those who try to catch an inheritance].

Not to be positive or opinionative.

Not to sett up for observing all these Rules, for fear I should observe none.^39

A few of these resolutions reflect lifelong concerns of Swift's, for example, the emphasis on cleanliness. But for the most part they suggest close and unsparing observation of his employer. Temple was peevish and morose, and very likely suspicious. He probably encouraged tattling servants to tell tales. He may well have been covetous, since he was unquestionably stingy. He scorned modern ways, talked about himself, boasted about his good looks and his exploits with women, welcomed flattery, and loved to impart opinions and advice. (Swift's modern editor reads the word in the next-to-last entry as "opiniative," but the correct reading may be *opiniâtre*, "stubborn." In that case, Swift might be ironically invoking Temple's vanity in speaking French.) As for expecting to be "beloved by a young woman," is that a hint that his philandering wasn't finished?

Perhaps the oddest resolution is "Not to be fond of Children, or let them come near me hardly." Forster's explanation is that "we do not fortify ourselves with resolutions against what we dislike, but against what in our weakness we have reason to believe we are only too much inclined to."^40 Yet nothing in Swift's life suggests any such inclination. In *Gulliver's Travels*, the Lilliputians have a system that Swift clearly approved of. Infants are consigned to public nurseries, where "their parents are suffered to see them only twice a year; the visit is not to last above an hour; they are allowed to kiss the child at meeting and parting, but a professor, who always standeth by on those occasions, will not suffer them to whisper, or use any fondling expressions, or bring any presents of toys, sweetmeats, and the like."^41

Sir William, however, was indeed drawn to children, as his sister recalled: "He had a very agreeable way of conversing with all sorts of people, from the greatest princes to the meanest servants, and even children, whose imperfect language and natural and innocent talk he was fond of."[42] There was probably something complacent about this easy geniality, which would have made it all the more galling that Temple didn't treat Swift himself like that. Servants and children were no threat; the ferociously intelligent Swift was.

Temple's own children were all deceased by now. But there was one child at Moor Park of whom he was remarkably fond: the housekeeper's daughter, little Hester Johnson.

SWIFT'S STELLA

In addition to his other duties at Moor Park, Swift acted as Hester's tutor in reading and writing. Why was the daughter of the housekeeper, who was being trained as a maidservant, given a tutor at all? We don't know why this arrangement was made, or how their relationship developed at first. What we do know is that as an adult she became his lifelong companion until her death in 1728, and that seventeen years after that Swift was buried by her side in St. Patrick's Cathedral.

Nowadays Hester is usually referred to as Stella, the name Swift gave her much later in some affectionate poems. She signed her name Esther, though she had been christened Hester, and no doubt those were considered versions of the same name. Lady Giffard, whom she served as a servant when she was old enough, called her Hetty.[43]

Swift was twenty-two when he met Stella, and she was nine. He was no Lewis Carroll (it's been said of Carroll that his only two interests were formal logic and little girls, and he put them both into a single book). But he was unquestionably taken with Stella, and enjoyed tutoring her. Years later he reminded her that he had been her "writing master," and among letters by Temple that he copied out for publication, there is one in a hand very like his but with variations that show it to be Stella's. She made a few minor errors in transcription, all of which he corrected. In later years she remained grateful for Swift's instruction, and in a poem for his fifty-fourth birthday she called him "my early and my only guide."[44]

On the day of Stella's death, a heartbroken Swift sat down to record his memories from those first years: "She was sickly from her childhood until about the age of fifteen, but then grew into perfect health, and was looked upon as one of the most beautiful, graceful, and agreeable young women in London, only a little too fat. Her hair was blacker than a raven, and every feature of her face in perfection." No authentic portrait survives, which has not deterred biographers from including various dubious portraits and calling them "Stella." Since these clearly show a number of different women, it would be an arbitrary choice to pick any one of them.[45]

When Stella was sixteen and visiting London with the Temples—whether as Lady Giffard's servant or as a companion isn't clear—Swift wrote to her from Moor Park in a way that shows they shared a playful wit. It also shows that he enjoyed life when the Temples were away:

> Loory [a parrot] is well, and presents his humble duty to my Lady [Temple], and love to his fellow-servant, but he is the miserablest creature in the world, eternally in his melancholy note, whatever I can do; and if his finger does but ache, I am in such a fright you would wonder at it. . . . Aeolus has made a strange revolution in the rooks' nests; but I say no more, for it is dangerous to meddle with things above us. I desire your absence heartily; for now I live in great state, and the cook comes in to know what I please to have for dinner. I ask very gravely what is in the house, and accordingly give orders for a dish of pigeons, or etc. . . . We all keep home like so many cats.[46]

Parrots do sulk when the person they've bonded with is away, and their claws do look like fingers, but it was a deft touch to imply that the bird and Stella were "fellow-servants." She was clearly supposed to know also what Aeolus was the god of, and to appreciate the humor in literalizing "things above us."

In the note he wrote after Stella died, Swift recalled, "Some presents of gold pieces being often made to her while she was a girl, by her mother and other friends, on promise to keep them, she grew into such a spirit of thrift that in about three years they amounted to above two hundred pounds." Perhaps this inspired the episode in which Gulliver gives a present to the nine-year-old Brobdingnagian girl who looks after him, which she puts in her pocket "to keep among other trinkets, of which the girl was very fond, as children at her age usually are."[47]

What exactly was Stella's status at Moor Park? Her mother, the housekeeper Bridget Johnson, was paid the modest wage of £10 per year. She was hardly in a position to give her daughter £200 in gold pieces. Swift mentions "other friends" who also gave her presents, and it's easy to suspect that the most important was Sir William Temple. In his will he left Stella property worth at least £1,000, an enormous sum for a servant's daughter. Bridget got £20 plus half a year's wages, and most of the staff got the latter only.[48]

Why such extraordinary largesse to young Hester Johnson? Like Edgar Allan Poe's purloined letter, overlooked because in plain view, an essential clue has been available ever since 1757. However, it was published anonymously in a magazine, and under the bizarre initials C.M.P.G.N.S.T.N.S., so biographers naturally dismissed it. The one exception was Victoria Glendinning in 1998, who rightly took it seriously, but without realizing that the identity of the writer had already been convincingly established. In 1967, in a fine piece of detective work that unfortunately appeared only in an obscure University of Tulsa publication, a researcher was able to show that the author was the Reverend John Geree, a friend of Swift's at whose Berkshire rectory he made a ten-week visit in 1714. At that time Swift referred to him in a letter as "an old friend and acquaintance whom I love very well."[49]

When the Reverend Geree was in his twenties, he actually lived with the Temple family at Moor Park (his father was rector of the church in neighboring Farnham), and he had personal memories of everyone there. Once this is known, his testimony becomes immensely valuable. Geree's letter to the magazine begins by describing Stella's mother. She was the widow of a merchant who imported goods from Holland, and came to Moor Park "in the character of a housekeeper." This account—the only description we have of Bridget Johnson—has never been quoted before in any biography of Swift:

> She was a person of a surprising genius; few women ever exceeded her in the extent of her reading, none in the charms of conversation. She had seen the world; her address and behavior were truly polite; and whoever had the pleasure of conversing with her for a quarter of an hour were convinced that she had known a more genteel walk in life than her present situation confined her to. She was not so happy in her person as in her mind, for she was low of stature, and rather fat and thick than well-shaped; yet the imperfection of her shape was fully compensated by a set of fine features and an excellent complexion, animated by eyes that perfectly described the brightness of her genius.[50]

Bridget's other two children, like herself, weren't especially attractive, but Stella was beautiful. The other siblings were fair-haired whereas Stella was dark. Here is Geree's description of the young Stella, with whom he was obviously smitten:

> Esther's, or, as she was usually called in the family, Miss Hetty's eyes and hair were of a most beautiful black, and all the rest of her fea-

tures bore so strong a resemblance to those of Sir Wm T—— that no one could be at a loss to determine what relation she had to that gentleman. And could the striking likeness have been overlooked, Sir William's uncommon regard for her, and his attention to her education, must have convinced every unprejudiced person that Miss Hetty Johnson was the daughter of one who moved in a higher sphere than a Dutch trader. . . . Her shape was perfectly easy and elegant; her complexion exquisitely fine; her features were regular, with the addition of that nameless something that so often exceeds the most exact beauty, and which never fails to add to it when they meet together. Her teeth were beyond comparison; her eyebrows and hair, of the most glossy black; and her eyes—but those I pretend not to describe; her mien and air were equal to the rest of the piece. Such was her exterior appearance. Her mind was yet more beautiful than her person, and her accomplishments were such as to do honour to the man who was so happy as to call her daughter.

Temple had black hair and was famously handsome.

In 1757, at the age of eighty-five, Geree was addressing the widely read *Gentleman's Magazine* to correct what he saw as errors in recently published biographies by Orrery and Delany. As for C.M.P.G.N.S.T.N.S, a cryptanalyst has surmised that the letters stand for *cum paganis satanas*, implying truth telling, whereas "the devil is with the pagans."[51]

Ehrenpreis was aware of the *Gentleman's Magazine* letter, but its author had not been identified when the first volume of his Swift biography came out, and he understandably dismissed it. But he made no serious attempt to explain why Stella should have received such an enormous bequest. And, most unusually, he made a factual error as well: he asserted that Edward Johnson, Bridget's deceased husband, "had been Temple's steward in his time."[52] That is incorrect. Bridget did marry a steward of Temple's, but not until after Temple's death, and that husband's name was Ralph Mose.

So who was Edward Johnson? Here the detective work has been done by two Dublin writers, Denis Johnston and Sybil Le Brocquy. Like Elias, they were long ignored by Swift specialists because they weren't Swiftian scholars, but they were able researchers and they came up with an arresting hypothesis. Their suggestion is that the intelligent, well-read, and charming Bridget Johnson was Temple's mistress, and that Temple was Stella's father. When Bridget got pregnant he would have arranged a suitable marriage for her (we don't know the date), and the husband he found was Captain Edward Johnson, who traded regularly with Holland. Having lived for a long time in Holland himself, Temple could well have known Johnson there.

We do know when Stella and her siblings were born, since baptisms for all three are recorded in the parish register at Richmond, close to the house at Sheen where the Temples were then living. Hester was born in 1681, Anne in 1683, and Edward in 1688. So here is the conjecture: Stella, the oldest of the three, was indeed Sir William Temple's daughter. Anne and Edward, however, were the children of Edward Johnson, which is why Temple took no interest in them. Anne remained in London, where she married in 1700; Edward was put into a school in Farnham, close to his mother at Moor Park, and died young.[53]

It was quite usual for an affluent gentleman to provide for his illegitimate children. James Boswell, when still in his early twenties, fathered two of them and provided honorably for their mother. And Temple, like Boswell, was known to be not only sexually adventurous but proud of it. A young diplomat reported in 1677, "He held me in discourse a great long hour, of things most relating to himself, which are never without vanity, but this most especially full of it; and some stories of his amours, and extraordinary abilities that way, which had once upon a time very nearly killed him."[54]

An anonymous reviewer of Orrery's biography of Swift commented, "It is well known that Sir William Temple was a very amorous man, and much addicted to intrigue with various women; and it is not improbable that such a man as Sir William should take uncommon precautions to provide well for his natural children, without letting the public, or even themselves, know that they were such." Ehrenpreis, though he dismisses without explanation the possibility that Temple was Stella's father, does remark, "A man who enjoys such an indulgence at fifty does not sacrifice it at sixty-five."[55] Temple was in his mid-fifties when Stella was born.

Another clue to Temple's extramarital life comes in a criticism of him that a foreign diplomat published in 1693. He would refrain, he said, from mentioning discreditable information that he evidently had: "I shall enlarge no further, that I may not engage myself to publish the misfortune of Sir William's family, which I suppose would not be like a gentleman. I have no reason that I know of to complain, neither of his lady, nor of his son, nor of his daughters."[56] This is a fine example of the rhetorical device of *occupatio*, in which you say you won't draw attention to something and then proceed to do so. The hint in the plural "daughters" seems strong. Temple had only one legitimate daughter, Diana, and she had died in 1684.

Until her death in 1694, Lady Temple spent most of her time in London, while her husband's sister, Lady Giffard, presided at Moor Park. We don't know exactly when Bridget and Stella arrived at Moor Park, but if Lady Temple was aware that Stella was Sir William's illegitimate daughter, the girl's presence after the suicide of their only son might well have provoked her to leave. And it was Lady Giffard, whom Denis Johnston accurately describes as Temple's "managing, loyal sister, his standby throughout his life," who took Bridget and then Stella into her service.[57]

One piece of testimony may seem to undermine this theory, though it does confirm that gossip about Stella's parentage was widespread. According to Orrery, "the general voice of fame" made Stella and Swift relatives by blood, but Swift's sister, Jane, who spent some time as a Moor Park servant, always denied it. Jane assured Orrery that "Stella was the daughter of Sir William Temple's steward. She was allowed by the Dean's sister (a bitter enemy of hers) to be the very picture of her mother's husband; and this, Mrs. Fenton [Jane's married name] would insist on whenever she heard the aspersion of her being Sir William Temple's daughter mentioned, because, as she expressed herself, 'she ought to give the devil his due.'"[58]

Jane probably did hate Stella, to whom her brother was obviously attached. But whomever Stella looked like—and Geree's testimony carries more weight than what Orrery heard much later—it could not have been the steward Mose. And since Captain Johnson was dead before Bridget and Stella moved to Moor Park, there is no way Jane could have seen him. What is notable is that she felt obliged to repudiate the gossip "whenever" it came up, which was evidently often. It even reached friends of Swift's in England who had never met Stella.[59]

In short, the belief that Stella's father was the steward might be yet another cover story of Swift's, repeated over the years until it came to seem authoritative but with no real basis at all. And that could be the motive behind a curious comment he made in his memorial description of Stella: "She had little to boast of her birth." That seems a strange sort of put-down, coming from a man heartbroken with grief—unless it was intended to forestall the suspicion that she had, in fact, very much to boast of.[60]

Orrery, accepting the story that Stella was the steward's daughter, said that Temple "bequeathed her in his will one thousand pounds, as an acknowledgement of her father's faithful services." Orrery can only have gotten this impression from Swift, who clearly wanted people to believe it. This too had to be a cover-up. The bequest wasn't cash, it was property that was worth at least that much, and not just any property, but property in Ireland. This is what Temple's will states: "I leave a lease of some lands I have in Monistown, in the county of Wicklow in Ireland, to Esther Johnson, servant to my sister Giffard."[61] Was giving Stella land in Ireland, where she had never been, a way of inducing her to move there? And could there have been an understanding that Swift would accompany her there and take over Temple's role as guardian?

There is one further stunning piece of evidence that Stella was very likely Temple's daughter. It has been ignored until now, so far as I know, because it was mentioned in a casual aside by someone studying the Temple family papers who didn't make the connection with the question of paternity. This is a letter from Stella to a member of the Temple family, dated May 21, 1723. She was forty-two at the time and had been living in Dublin for over twenty years. This letter gratefully acknowledges receipt of the very large sum of £432.[62] It looks very much as if the Temple family continued to provide her with financial assistance indefinitely, as though that had indeed been the wish of Sir William. Since the letter begins simply with the word "Sir," we can't be sure which Temple it was addressed to, but Sir William's nephew Jack would be a good guess.

And what about Ralph Mose, the steward whom Bridget did eventually marry? We don't know how long he had been at Moor Park, since few records survive, but he was there no later than 1697. A year or two after that, his first wife died (she had been the cook) and he began importuning Bridget with proposals of marriage, which she repeatedly turned down. But then she accepted. Geree was told by a friend of Bridget's "that she had heard Mrs. Mose, in her freer hours, declare that she was obliged by indispensable necessity to marry the man whose servile manners her soul despised." What necessity could have been so decisive? Geree offered a plausible guess: "Mose might be privy to certain secrets that she was unwilling to have divulged, and therefore she might not dare to reject his proposals, for fear of drawing his resentment upon her."[63] Whether or not this guess is correct, there were clearly plenty of secrets, and a determination to keep them that way.

ANOTHER MYSTERY

During Swift's lifetime and immediately afterward, there were persistent rumors in Dublin not only that Stella was Sir William Temple's daughter, but that Swift was his son. "A torrent of scandal," Deane Swift said, kept this notion alive.[64] This was easily disproved by Swift's first biographers, since they could verify that Temple was in Holland at the time when Swift was conceived in Dublin. But there is another possible paternity for Swift— far-fetched, unquestionably, but worth considering.

It needs to be emphasized that, as a recent biographer says, "There is no evidence whatsoever to suggest that Swift was the son of anyone other than Jonathan Swift senior."[65] Still, there is little evidence about anything in Swift's early years, and the official story is pretty far-fetched in its own right. If we accept that story, we must believe the following: a baby is abducted by his nurse from Ireland to England, with no reaction from the mother or her family for several years. Just when the child is brought back to Dublin, the mother herself departs for England. One of the child's uncles thereupon gives him the best possible education, even though he can't afford to do so for most of his own children. Despite this exceptional generosity, the child develops a lifelong resentment of the uncle. And finally, when he grows up, a distinguished Englishman willingly takes him on as a private secretary although he has never met him before.

In his 1959 book *In Search of Swift*, Denis Johnston advanced a thought-provoking hypothesis, building upon suggestions he had first offered in 1941. Johnston was a Dublin playwright and broadcast producer who rose to a high position in the BBC, and he had a passion for painstaking research, especially in the records of the law courts where the Swift brothers were employed. His standards were high, as he scrupulously weighed evidence and commented on the suspicious absence of certain kinds of it. But as he acknowledged with ironic understatement, his argument would "possibly be unwelcome in some circles," presuming as he did to enter a "heavily mined area."[66] He was right about that. The few professional Swift scholars who noticed his book at all denounced it as amateurish nonsense, and Ehrenpreis never once mentions it in the two thousand pages of his biography.

Here is the scenario that Johnston puts forward. It is far more speculative than the hypothesis that Stella was Temple's daughter. But Johnston's theory would make sense of some of the mysteries that surround Swift's early years, and at the very least it establishes that there are far more questions than answers.

First, there is a matter of dates. We know that Jonathan Swift the elder died before the younger Jonathan was born. The son believed that his mother was two months' pregnant when she became a widow. But there is no record of the father's death, and Johnston suggests that it might have been a good deal earlier. He notes that the elder Jonathan Swift stopped making entries in a legal ledger known as the Black Book of King's Inns in November 1666, a full year before the birth of young Jonathan. Might he have fallen ill at that time and died soon after? None of Swift's biographers has addressed this gap in the record. We do know that on April 15, 1667, Abigail Swift submitted a petition to her late husband's employers for financial assistance as a widow. What we don't know is how long she waited after her husband's death to do so.

It is also remarkable that there is no baptismal record to confirm the younger Jonathan Swift's date of birth. We have seen that he had a search made of the St. Werburgh's church register (which no longer exists) and that no trace of his baptism was found. Swift's friend Lyon ascribed the omission to "the carelessness of the then vestry clerk."[67] But what if the baptism did not take place at St. Werburgh's at all? It could have been performed privately, in which case no parish record would have been made. For that matter, the birth too could have taken place elsewhere, if secrecy was important. Swift often told friends that he was born in Godwin's house in Hoey's Court, but even if he believed that, it might not have been true.

It is possible, in fact, that Swift had serious doubts about the story he had been told. When he had the church register searched, he could have been hoping to establish the date when his father died as well as his own birth date. A reviewer of Orrery's biography in 1751 made a telling point that later biographers ignored: Swift could have silenced rumors about his origins "by producing the necessary proofs and circumstances of his birth, yet we do not find that ever this was done, either by the Dean or his relations."[68]

Pondering these puzzles, Denis Johnston reviews what little we know about the elder Jonathan Swift. With no formal legal training, he spent several years doing odd jobs for the law offices that were known in Dublin, like those in London, as the Inns of Court. In his autobiographical sketch, the younger Jonathan says vaguely that his father "had some employments and agencies." Finally, in late 1665 or early 1666, the elder Jonathan was appointed steward of the Inns. This was not a distinguished position. The duties were to keep routine records of billing for meals and to supervise the laundress, cook, and other servants. Wale, Swift's predecessor, had been a butler before being promoted to steward. Yet the very day after Swift's appointment, he was made an attorney, suddenly achieving a status that had eluded him for years, and that carried the likelihood of increased income in the future. This notation was entered into the Black Book: "The petitioner [the elder Jonathan Swift] for these six or seven years last past hath been much conversant about the said

Inns, and is very well acquainted with the duty and employment belonging unto the steward thereof, he having assisted the said Thomas Wale in entering up the orders of your Honors, and in the settling and ordering other things belonging to the said employment."[69]

The story of Swift's mother is likewise unclear. Ehrenpreis says, "I assume she was born in Dublin," but he admits that there is no evidence. He also says she was twenty-four when she got married, the same age as her husband, but the alleged source for this "fact" is an obscure article by himself that actually says nothing at all about her age. And although he states that no record of her baptism has been found in Leicestershire, that may not be true. As Johnston points out, a Leicestershire antiquarian did a search of parish registers and found that an Abigail Ericke was baptized on May 16, 1630, in the village of Wigston Magna, five miles south of the town of Leicester.[70]

Ehrenpreis guesses that Abigail's father was the Reverend James Ericke, who was expelled from an English church in 1634 for Puritanical leanings and then emigrated to Ireland. He acknowledges that Swift never mentioned the Reverend Ericke, which seems strange, since he would surely have told people if he knew that both grandfathers had been clergymen. Ehrenpreis surmises that he was so appalled by James Ericke's religious attitude that he made a point of ignoring his existence. But perhaps Swift never mentioned him because there was no reason to. If his mother was the Abigail recorded in the Wigston Magna register, her father, Thomas Ericke (sometimes spelled Herrick), was a butcher there.

Whoever Abigail was, we don't know why she married an impecunious young clerk at the law courts, who may even have been ten years younger than herself. Nor we do we know why she made no effort to recover her son when his nurse spirited him off to England. But that whole story may be a fiction. There is no evidence whatsoever that after the alleged kidnapping she remained in the household of Godwin Swift, who already had more than enough people to support. She may well have gone home to Leicester at that point, not three or four years later at the very moment when her son was brought back to Dublin.

What follows is only Denis Johnston's conjecture, and perhaps a wild conjecture at that. Still, it bears thinking about. Swift's father could not have been Sir William Temple. But the persistent rumors to that effect might have sprung from a confused recollection of a different Temple. Sir William's father was Sir John Temple, born in Ireland and educated at Trinity. When the Swift brothers arrived in Dublin in the late 1650s and early 1660s, Sir John was highly placed in their profession. He was a widower, for his wife had died in 1638 after giving birth to Sir William's sister, whom we know as Lady Giffard.

The position Sir John Temple held was master of the rolls, an important appointment in charge of the "rolls," or scrolled-up records in the Chancery court. He was also treasurer of King's Inns, which is where Jonathan Swift the elder began to pick up odd jobs around 1658, and where he was eventually appointed steward. Jonathan the younger knew that Sir John "had been a great friend to the family." In his letter of recommendation to Sir Robert Southwell, Sir William Temple himself said that the whole family of Swifts "were long known to me." Deane Swift grew up hearing that his grandfather Godwin Swift and Sir John Temple "spent much of their time together, and as they frequently dined and passed the remainder of the day at each other's houses, the whole family of the Swifts became intimately acquainted with that open, generous, disinterested man. . . . This friendship continued for many years without interruption, even to the last hour of Sir John's life."[71]

Sir John Temple had close connections with Leicester in England, for his friend and patron was the Earl of Leicester, whom he is known to have visited at his Leicestershire estate.[72] Now, here is Denis Johnston's hypothesis. Sir John met Abigail in Leicester, and at some point brought her to Dublin to act as his housekeeper, and probably as something more than that. Johnston suggests that Sir John, in his early sixties and concerned for Abigail's future security, provided her with a husband in a young man to whom he could give a start in the legal profession.

Jonathan Swift the elder could have been the actual father of Jane, and of Jonathan the younger too. But if there was a sexual relationship between Sir John and Abigail, it might conceivably have continued after she was married. Another possibility is that the elder Jonathan was already ill with the disease that would kill him, and was no longer sexually active. In that case Sir John would know that the child was his own.

We will never know if these guesses are close to the truth. But if they are, then Sir John might well have provided for the education of his son, funneling the money through Godwin Swift. And it could make sense of another mystery, the story of the abduction by the nurse. If the child was born inconveniently late after the death of the legal father, the nurse might have been paid to take little Jonathan away, and Abigail too might have been advised to go back to England. Jonathan would have been brought back to Godwin's house as a way station for Kilkenny College, which could explain why he entered the school at an unusually early age. As was only recently pointed out by an Irish Swift specialist, Sir John Temple spent a great deal of time at his country estate in Carlow. Carlow is twenty miles from Kilkenny.[73]

When young Jonathan was ten, in 1677, Sir John died, leaving a will that unfortunately no researcher examined before it was destroyed during the 1922 insurrection, when a massive explosion shattered the Irish Public Records Office. Johnston suggests that the will may have provided funds for Jonathan's continuing education, which would then have been administered by Godwin Swift as a duty rather than as an expression of affection. Once Jonathan graduated from Trinity, Godwin would have felt that his obligations were at an end, and that it was high time for the Temples to do their part. After the young graduate rejoined his mother in Leicester in 1689, she sent him on to Sir William Temple, Sir John's son and—just possibly—Jonathan's half brother.[74]

Deane Swift had heard that the reason Abigail suggested that her son apply to Sir William Temple was that her family was distantly related to his. That may possibly be true, but again, one suspects an invention. If members of the Swift family were concerned to clear their famous relative from the suspicion that a Temple was Jonathan's father, it might have been expedient to imagine some other kind of family obligation. Jonathan Swift himself, always proud of distinguished family connections, would probably have mentioned that he was related to the Temples if he had heard of it, but he did not.[75]

Unless further evidence should somehow come to light, this is where we must leave the question of Swift's parentage. Denis Johnston never claimed to offer more than a hypothesis, and it may well seem improbable. Still, it's not impossible, and something like it would certainly make more sense than the story Swift himself told.

CHAPTER 3

"Long Choosing, and Beginning Late"

STROLLING WITH THE KING

The profession for which Swift was most qualified was the ministry. He was in no hurry, though, to climb into the pulpit. Sir William was well placed to get him launched instead in politics or government service, and that track appealed to him strongly. He detested being financially strapped, and he was well aware that the clergy were deplorably underpaid. At the end of the eighteenth century the clergyman Sydney Smith lamented that a minister "is thrown into life with his hands tied, and bid to swim; he does well if he keeps his head above water." If Swift did choose that route, his goal would be a bishopric, which would ensure prestige and a fine income for life. But for now, he awaited developments. As Milton said of himself in *Paradise Lost*, he was "long choosing, and beginning late."[1]

It was a heady experience at first to meet friends of the Temples, whether at their London town house or at Moor Park. Their most eminent friends were none other than the newly crowned king and queen. William III had been close to the Temples in Holland, and he was a frequent visitor at Moor Park. As Macaulay says, he found there, "among the heath and furze of Surrey, a spot which seemed to be part of Holland, a straight canal, a terrace, rows of clipped trees, and rectangular beds of flowers and pot-herbs."[2]

Remarkably, the unworldly young Dubliner found himself strolling in the garden with the king of England, since Temple was often laid up with the gout and His Majesty wanted someone to chat with. It was a very rare privilege for an obscure commoner to be on conversational terms with the monarch. Samuel Johnson, after he became famous and George III asked to meet him, experienced the privilege with awe.

There is no record, unfortunately, of what they said during these chats, or even what language they spoke. Swift was fairly good at French and the king preferred it to English; he almost certainly spoke French with Temple. In later life Swift did like to recall that the king showed him "how to cut asparagus (a vegetable which his Majesty was extremely fond of) in the Dutch manner."[3] This would have been in the garden, not at the table, and one can visualize the king taking out his penknife and bending over the plants. Asparagus is a perennial, and if too much of the stalk is cut off at one time, it will be weakened for the following year.

15. King William III. The artist has caught the stern demeanor of this able bureaucrat, diplomat, and warrior.

Personally, the king was somewhat off-putting. As Macaulay describes him, he had "a slender and feeble frame, a lofty and ample forehead, a nose curved like the beak of an eagle, an eye rivaling that of an eagle in brightness and keenness, a thoughtful and somewhat sullen brow, a firm and somewhat peevish mouth, a cheek pale, thin, and deeply furrowed by sickness and by care." His discomfort speaking English may excuse the ponderousness of his attempts at wit; he told a clergyman named William King, "You and I have almost the same name—you are William King and I am King William."[4]

Naturally, Swift was hopeful that this acquaintance would lead to an attractive appointment in public office or the Church, but Temple was reluctant to encourage it. Swift told his uncle William at the time, "I am not to take [holy] orders till the King gives me a prebendary; and Sir William Temple, though he promises me the certainty of it, yet is less forward than I could wish, because I suppose he believes I shall leave him, and upon some accounts he thinks me a little necessary to him." Swift's expectation was that after putting in his time at Moor Park, he would be rewarded with the prestige and comfortable income of a prebend at Canterbury or Westminster. He might not even have to reside there, for a prebend was simply the income from a cathedral appointment, and its recipient, the prebendary, had no actual duties at the cathedral. (Confusingly, Swift and others used the terms *prebendary* and *prebend* interchangeably.) A historian says, "The attractiveness of the royal prebends lay primarily in their revenue," typically about £300 per year, or fifteen times as much as the salary Sir William was paying Swift. A Canterbury prebend was worth £350, Oxford £400, and St. Paul's Cathedral a spectacular £800.[5]

No prebend ever materialized, but King William did make Swift a surprising offer: to become a "captain of horse" in the army. Actually, this was not as bizarre as it must seem. Commissions in the army were often awarded through patronage, and the recipients might have no relevant experience at all. When Swift's journalist friend Richard Steele left Oxford and became a cavalry officer, his first task was to learn to ride a horse.[6]

Johnson accurately remarked, "King William's notions were all military."[7] The reason he took the huge risk of deposing James II was to strengthen the Dutch position against France. Louis XIV was determined to make himself master of the Continent, and the Low Countries were in grave peril. With Britain on their side, everything would change. It was only because William had married Princess Mary—a calculated move, of course—that this now became possible. Dynastic arrangements among royal houses could determine the course of history.

16. Queen Mary II. Given her rather
stodgy later image, this portrait of
Mary in her youth may seem surprising.
She is depicted with the sultry expression
and encouraging breasts of a
Restoration court lady.

From 1689 onward, Britain would be at war for all but four years of the next twenty-four. The War of the League of Augsburg began in that year and continued for most of the time Swift was at Moor Park; from 1697 to 1702 there would be an interlude of peace; and then the tremendous War of the Spanish Succession would drag on until 1713. Endless fighting would play a key role in the political affairs that would engross Swift in the years to come.

Though the royal marriage had been politically expedient, it was much deeper than that. When the queen was dying of smallpox in 1694, William told a bishop who was attending her, "I was the happiest man on earth, and I am the most miserable. She had no fault, none; you knew her well, but you could not know, nobody but myself could know, her goodness."[8]

Still, in that era it was not considered inappropriate for a monarch to have mistresses. On one occasion at the court of George I, the Countess of Dorchester, who had been a mistress of James II, happened to meet the Duchess of Portsmouth and the Countess of Orkney, who had been mistresses respectively of Charles II and William III. "Who would have thought," she asked pleasantly, "that we three whores should have met here?"[9]

In fact King William's sexual life was quite indiscriminate, and Swift found it distasteful. When he read much later in a history book that William "had no vice, but of one sort, in which he was very cautious and secret," he commented in the margin, "It was of two sorts—*male* and *female*—in the *former* he was neither cautious nor secret." And when another author referred to the Earl of Albemarle as "King William's constant companion in all his diversions and pleasures," Swift wrote, "Very infamous pleasures."[10]

Spending time with the monarch gave Swift lasting immunity to hero worship, not that he was ever very susceptible to it. He once said in a sermon, "Princes are born with no more advantages of strength or wisdom than other men, and by an unhappy education are usually more defective in both than thousands of their subjects." According to Orrery, "his aversion to kings was invincible," and he was often heard to say that "he should be glad to see half a dozen kings dissected, that he might know what it was that stamped a greater value upon one prince than upon eleven millions of people."[11]

Sir William did entrust Swift with one important mission. In 1693, fearing that King William was beginning to govern high-handedly, Parliament tried to pass a Triennial Act that would require him to call a new election no later than three years after the previous one, instead of only when he felt like it. The fear was that he might pack the House of Commons with paid dependents and then prolong its life indefinitely, avoiding fresh elections that might work to his disadvantage.

Temple understood that intransigence on this point could jeopardize the king, and he dispatched Swift to convey his arguments to King William. As Swift described it long afterward, with his usual fuzziness about dates, "Mr. Swift, who was well versed in English history although he were then under three and twenty years old [he was twenty-five], gave the King a short account of the matter, but a more large one to the Earl of Portland; but all in vain, for the King by ill advisers was prevailed upon to refuse passing the bill. This was the first time that Mr. Swift had ever any converse with courts, and he told his friends it was the first incident that helped to cure him of vanity."[12]

The next year, however, the king relented and allowed the Triennial Act to pass. As with much else, it was a concession forced by his war policy. A guarantee that parliaments would meet regularly was the House of Commons' price for voting the funds he needed to keep fighting the French.[13] As it turned out, what ensued were the most frequent elections in British history, no fewer than ten in the next twenty years.

"THAT OLD VERTIGO IN HIS HEAD"

Even before Swift's first arrival at Moor Park, when the Temples were at Sheen near London, Swift experienced some alarming physical symptoms. They turned out not to be dangerous, but they could be incapacitating, and he would suffer increasingly severe recurrences for the rest of his life. As he described it in his autobiographical sketch, "He happened before twenty years old, by a surfeit of fruit, to contract a giddiness and coldness of stomach that almost brought him to his grave, and this disorder pursued him with intermissions of two or three years to the end of his life." At another time he said that he contracted the illness "by eating a hundred golden pippins at a time, at Richmond," adding that the first attack of deafness came on several years later after he fell asleep outdoors. For a while the nausea and vertigo seemed to come on independently, but eventually they tended to coincide, and Swift was often tormented by "a hundred oceans roaring in my ears."[14] He became progressively deaf as well, first in one ear and later in both. The dizziness affected his balance, and he referred to it variously as "tottering" and "vertigo."

Blaming too much fruit sounds absurd today, but it didn't then. John Locke, who was a physician as well as a philosopher, wrote grimly, "Fruit makes one of the most difficult chapters in the government of health, especially that of children. Our first parents ventured Paradise for it, and 'tis no wonder our children cannot stand the temptation, though it cost them their health." In the next century Sir Walter Scott could still say that professors of medicine thought an excess of fruit "in every respect adequate to produce such consequences." It needed the common sense of Johnson to point out, "The original of diseases is commonly obscure. Almost every boy eats as much fruit as he can get, without any great inconvenience." We know that Johnson thought well of Temple's essays, and this may have been a recollection of what Temple himself had written: "All men will eat fruit that can get it."[15]

So although Swift loved fruit, and would later emulate Sir William in planting fruit trees of his own, he forced himself to consume it sparingly. At the age of forty-four he lamented, "The peaches are pretty good, and there are some figs; I sometimes venture to eat one, but always repent it." And again, "I envy people maunching and maunching peaches and grapes, and I not daring to eat a bit." At sixty there was a recurrence of "my old disease of giddiness, a little tottering" and he was sure that "cider and champagne and fruit have been the cause." Six weeks after that he had a more severe bout, so nauseated that he threw up, and he resolved to be even more abstemious: "In the midst of peaches, figs, nectarines, and mulberries, I touch not a bit."[16]

We tend to forget how primitive was what passed for medical knowledge until recent times. As a martyr to gout, Temple gave much thought to possible remedies for that affliction, and was sure he had found the answer:

> The next specific I esteem to be that little insect called millipedes: the powder whereof, made up into little balls with fresh butter, I never knew fail of curing any sore throat. It must lie at the root of the tongue, and melt down at leisure upon going to bed. I have been assured that Doctor Mayerne used it as a certain cure for all cancers in the breast; and should be very tedious if I should tell here, how much the use of it has been extolled by several within my knowledge, upon the admirable effects for the eyes, the scurvy, and the gout; but there needs no more to value it, than what the ancient physicians affirm of it in those three words: *Digerit, Aperit, Abstergit:* It digests. It opens. It cleanses.[17]

The millipedes would certainly purge the digestive system, but they wouldn't do much for gout, ailments of the eye, or breast cancer.

It is often hard to tell, from symptoms reported by eighteenth-century sufferers, just what were the diseases that afflicted them. In Swift's case there can be no doubt, but no one then had the faintest idea of the truth. He recognized that his vertigo and nausea were symptoms of a single disease, but he was convinced that the deafness was entirely different. Actually, his Dublin physicians had the impressive intuition that all three apparently separate symptoms were interconnected. "The doctors here," he told a friend in 1733, "think that both these ailments in me are united in their causes." But since the disease is progressive and there is no deafness at first, he understandably disagreed with them.[18]

Not until 1861 did a French specialist named Prosper Ménière finally identify the disease that now bears his name. Due to a disturbance of the labyrinthine canals in the inner ear, Ménière's syndrome produces four classic symptoms, and Swift had them all: irregular attacks of "rotational vertigo" that can last for weeks; progressive hearing loss, especially in the lower frequencies; tinnitus (the roaring noise); and a feeling of fullness or pressure in the ears. It is common for sufferers to feel deep depression, and as the years went by and the symptoms worsened, that is indeed what Swift felt, lively and energetic though he had been in his prime. Referring to himself in a late poem, he lamented,

> That old vertigo in his head
> Will never leave him till he's dead.[19]

Johnson's *Dictionary*, giving these lines as an illustration, shows that "vertigo" was then accented on the second syllable, "ver-TYE-go."

Swift's malady did have one positive consequence, for he became convinced that exercise was beneficial, in an era when medical theory discouraged it and most people avoided it. At Moor Park, as he told Deane Swift long afterward, he would work for two hours and then take a break by running up to the top of a nearby hill and down again. "This exercise he performed in about six minutes; backwards and forwards it was about half a mile." As he got older he stopped running but walked long distances and rode horseback frequently. When he was walking with Laetitia Pilkington in his sixties, a rainstorm drove them indoors. "The Dean then ran up the great stairs, down one pair of back stairs, up another, in so violent a manner that I could not help expressing my uneasiness to the good gentlewoman [his housekeeper] lest he should fall and be hurted; she said it was a customary exercise with him when the weather did not permit him to walk abroad." For the rest of his life Swift's doctors kept trying to persuade him to stop.[20]

Swift had one trait that may deserve to be called neurotic, reflected in his resolving "not to neglect decency, or cleenlyness, for fear of falling into Nastyness." His friend Patrick Delany gave the fullest description of how this manifested itself: "His hands were not only washed, as those of other men, with the utmost care, but his nails were kept pared to the quick, to guard against the least appearance of a speck upon them. And as he walked much, he rarely dressed himself without a basin of water by his side, in which he dipped a towel and cleansed his feet with the utmost exactness." With this passage in mind Johnson said unsympathetically, "He had a kind of muddy complexion, which, though he washed himself with oriental scrupulosity, did not look clear."[21]

It is hard to know how extreme Swift's behavior was. As Glendinning says, few people in those days had the standards of hygiene that are usual today, and "to be clean was an idiosyncratic luxury." Ehrenpreis makes a persuasive point, though: "Swift had in fact the classic traits of a compulsive personality. He made lists, he collected books, he saved money, he kept himself unusually clean; he was often obsessional."[22] Now that obsessive-compulsive disorder is well known, however, it is Johnson, whose friends all noticed his bizarre repetitive rituals, and not Swift who seems likeliest to have suffered from it.

Only the cleanliness seems really suggestive in Swift's case, and curiously, that was one trait Johnson definitely did not share, with his slovenly dress and disgraceful wig.

More interesting psychologically is something Swift told a Leicester relative not long after settling at Moor Park: "A person of great honour in Ireland, who was pleased to stoop so low as to look into my mind, used to tell me that my mind was like a conjured spirit, that would do mischief if I would not give it employment." The implication is that Swift's mind was volatile and constantly humming, and needed to focus on specific tasks to keep it in balance. In a poem written at about the same time, he lamented his "fatal bent of mind, / Still to unhappy restless thoughts inclined."[23]

Yet motion was better than stasis, absolutely necessary in fact. When Swift's cousin Thomas complained that he was feeling anxious about his prospects for employment, he replied, "I protest I cannot much pity your present circumstances, which keep your mind and your body in motion, and myself was never very miserable while my thoughts were in a ferment, for I imagine a dead calm to be the troublesomest part of our voyage through the world."[24]

A CAREER IN IRELAND

It has been said that an eighteenth-century Englishman got his sense of identity from four sources: his family, his social rank, his property, and his occupation.[25] In Swift's case the first two were unimpressive and the third nonexistent. It would have to be in a career that he would achieve social standing. Apart from the law, the family profession of which he took a dim view, the obvious choice was the Church. He seems always to have thought of it as a career, not as a spiritual vocation. His friend and fellow clergyman Delany said that "he found in himself uncommon talents for writing and speaking in public," and therefore chose the profession that would best reward them.[26]

We don't know at what point Swift made his decision, but in 1692 he took the preliminary step of acquiring an M.A., a prerequisite for ordination. In later life he liked to give the impression that he had actually studied at Oxford, rather than just stopping by to pick up a degree. "I had the honor to be for some years a student at Oxford," he claimed forty years later. But in those days no extra work was required to earn the degree, just payment of a fee after an interview to confirm that the candidate's work for the B.A. had been satisfactory.[27] Accordingly, Swift spent a few weeks at Hart Hall (later Hertford College), collected the M.A., and returned to Moor Park.

Two years had passed and Temple had still done nothing to help Swift find employment, even though he was helping his cousin Thomas, who showed up at Moor Park and was promised the "living" of Puttenham near Moor Park once its elderly rector died. That person was Simon Geree, brother of John Geree at Farnham, whose son John would long afterward publish his reminiscences under the initials C.M.P.G.N.S.T.N.S. In the meantime Thomas was serving as curate at another town further away.

The Puttenham living was a royal appointment, so in this, at least, Sir William made use of his friendship with the king. It's conceivable that Puttenham was offered first to Jonathan Swift and that he turned it down, since it had only a modest income of £70 a year.[28] If he did so in the expectation of getting something better, he soon grasped that it was never going to happen. He would have to take his chances back home in Ireland.

So in the summer of 1694 Swift stopped off in Leicester to see his mother and then sailed for Dublin. He expected to be ordained in September, but there was an embarrassing complication. Eight years had gone by since he took his B.A., and he was now twenty-seven, an unusually advanced age for ordination. Church rules required a testimonial confirming the "good life and behavior" of a candidate, and the Irish bishops he approached insisted on getting it. But Swift had evidently left Moor Park against his employer's wishes, so that asking him for a recommendation was awkward in the extreme. Writing from Leicester to his cousin Deane, Swift said, "He was extreme angry I left him, and yet would not oblige himself any further than upon my good behavior, nor would promise anything firmly to me at all; so that everybody judged I did best to leave him."[29] But it was to Temple that he must now appeal.

There was no help for it. "I shall stand in need of all your goodness," Swift wrote abjectly, "to excuse my many weaknesses and follies and oversights" and to confirm that his departure was not "occasioned by any ill actions of mine." Nokes calls Swift's language here "strictly conventional," but it may not have been. Swift could often be prickly, and he was surely aware that he sometimes gave offense. On the other hand, Elias thinks the groveling pose is overdone: "How low I am fallen in your Honor's thoughts . . . all entirely left to your Honor's mercy . . . all I dare beg at present from your Honor." In Elias's opinion, "a disgraced butler might have written in such terms and meant them. With Swift it is hard to avoid a sense of something angrier and more complicated going on."[30]

At any rate, Temple behaved generously and sent the testimonial without delay. In October Swift was ordained deacon, the preliminary step to the priesthood, in Christ Church Cathedral. It is extremely rare for a city to have more than one cathedral, but Dublin did, as a result of a quirk of history. Christ Church is the older, founded in the eleventh century. In the sixteenth century Henry VIII, owing to some sort of quarrel with Christ Church, converted a priory to St. Patrick's Cathedral, and it was there that Swift would be named dean in 1713.

Christ Church was the seat of the archbishop of Dublin, and that was Narcissus Marsh, the former provost of Trinity whom Swift had greatly disliked when he was a student there. The feeling was no doubt mutual. So the ordination was performed instead by Bishop William Moreton of Kildare, who subsequently ordained Swift to the priesthood in January of the next year.[31]

In his autobiographical fragment long afterward, Swift told an odd story about what happened right before he decided to be ordained. Sir William now had his father's former title as master of the rolls in Ireland, which had become a sinecure that did not require him ever to go there. "Though his fortune was very small," Swift said of himself in his third-person account, "he had a scruple of entering into the Church merely for support, and Sir William Temple, then being Master of the Rolls in Ireland, offered him an employ of about £120 a year in that office; whereupon Mr. Swift told him that since he had now an opportunity of living without being driven into the Church for a maintenance, he was resolved to go to Ireland and take holy orders."[32]

What this apparently means is that Swift thought he would be suspected of getting ordained merely to secure an income, rather than from any sense of vocation. Even so, it's hard to make sense of the story. Sheridan believed that Sir William really made the offer but intended it as an insult. Craik agreed: "As Temple no doubt expected, Swift refused. To have held a petty and subordinate post in the very law courts where some of his kinsmen had been, and where others still were, leading counselors, would have wounded his pride to the quick." Ehrenpreis's interpretation is that Temple was trying to keep Swift from leaving Moor Park, since "the memory of his son's fate would have made protective measures appear kinder than efforts to give Swift independence." That seems unlikely. Once again, Elias's interpretation is the most persuasive:

since Swift never once mentioned this alleged offer in the 1690s, in letters where it would normally have come up, it looks like a post facto attempt to describe his career choice as an expression of principle instead of as a fallback position when nothing else was working out.[33]

The appointment Swift now received was disappointing in the extreme. He might have expected a parish in Dublin, or at least in the Anglo-Irish Pale close by. Instead, he got what he referred to in his autobiographical sketch as "a prebend in the north, worth about £100 a year."[34] In the north it certainly was.

BURIED ALIVE IN KILROOT

In March of 1695 Swift arrived at his first parish, Kilroot in County Antrim, ten miles east of Belfast and a hundred miles north of Dublin. The appointment was probably negotiated by his old tutor St. George Ashe, by now provost of Trinity College and soon to be promoted to bishop of Cloyne.

17. The Irish Sea. This 1695 map shows Carrickfergus, the town adjacent to Kilroot, lying within sight of Scotland. (At the inland tip of the bay, further west, Belfast was still just a small town.) To the southeast across the sea, Holyhead in Wales is the nearest port to Dublin.

It wasn't much, but it was the best Ashe could manage.[35] Close by was the town of Carrickfergus, the very spot where William III had landed five years previously, on his way to victory over James II.

It was no accident that the king had chosen to go ashore in the north, for that part of Ireland was dominated by Protestants. Ever since the early seventeenth century a massive "plantation" campaign had populated the province of Ulster with Scottish Presbyterians, and during the 1690s forty thousand more of them arrived.[36] They didn't have far to travel: in clear weather the coast of Scotland, just twenty-seven miles away, could be seen from Kilroot.

Kilroot formed part of a "union" of three parishes, as was common when Church of Ireland congregations were small, many churches in disrepair, and the income from a single parish not enough to support a priest. Technically, Swift was rector of Ballynure, ten miles away over the hills, and vicar of Kilroot and Templecorran. The only difference was in income, not duties.

At Kilroot, although it gave its name to his position, the church had been in ruins for a century or more, and Swift may never have gone there except to bury people. The graveyard continued to be used right into the nineteenth century, but by then nothing remained of the church except a fragment of wall and a font, standing in the open air, in which rainwater collected that was reputed to cure warts. The other two villages did have churches, and he may have lived in Templecorran, but nobody knows. He may equally well have lived in Carrickfergus.[37]

Swift's first clerical appointment was thus to a place that barely existed and that had no church at all. And there were few parishioners in his other two villages, since Anglicans in County Antrim were a small minority. A bishop wrote at the time, "Some parishes have not ten, some not six, that come to church, while the Presbyterian meetings are crowded with thousands covering all the fields." There wasn't much incentive for an Anglican clergyman to labor diligently. Swift's predecessor had been ejected for drunkenness and "incontinency of life."[38]

Presbyterians were Protestants, of course, but Swift regarded that as irrelevant—only the officially established Church had any rights. So far as he was concerned, people could believe whatever they liked, but they were obligated to support the Church of Ireland with their tithes, officially 10 percent of income, though no one ever paid that much. Needless to say, this regulation infuriated Presbyterians and Catholics, but Swift and his colleagues didn't care. In an era when local government was minimal, it was the parish that was responsible for everything from road maintenance to poor relief, which is why Catholics and Dissenters were expected to contribute tithes to a Church they didn't belong to.[39]

Swift's position was not very different from that of the tutor in *Tom Jones*, who declares belligerently, "When I mention religion, I mean the Christian religion; and not only the Christian religion, but the Protestant religion; and not only the Protestant religion, but the Church of England." In addition, Swift detested the Scots. Even before he got to Ulster he had described them in verse as "that discontented brood / Who always loudest for religion bawl," and who "pine us like a chronical disease." What especially enraged him was the memory of the rebels who killed Charles I and turned the nation upside down. When in later years he read a history of that period, he filled the margins with exclamations: "a Scotch dog," "cursed Scottish hellhounds forever," "a rogue, half as bad as a Scot," "cursed, abominable, hellish Scottish villains everlasting traitors." The only good he ever said of the Presbyterians was to acknowledge their work ethic, which he described in terms that foreshadow Max Weber's *The Protestant Ethic and the Rise of Capitalism*: "These people, by their extreme parsimony, wonderful dexterity in dealing [that is, business], and firm adherence to one another, soon grow into wealth from the smallest beginnings."[40]

The Kilroot position did carry with it the prebend that Swift wanted, entitling him to a small income from the cathedral of the diocese of Connor. But even this was ludicrously minimal. The actual cathedral had originally been in Down, but after it was demolished in the sixteenth century, a parish church at Lisburn had to substitute for it. The bishop of Down and Connor seldom showed up in Ireland, and was known jokingly as the bishop of Hammersmith because he preferred to reside in that London suburb.[41]

FIRST LOVE?

At the outset, Swift's prospects were bleak. As Sheridan put it, "He found himself situated in an obscure corner of an obscure country, ill accommodated with the conveniencies of life, without a friend, a companion, or any conversation that he could relish." But his sociable disposition soon generated friendships with local clergy and landowners. An especially good friend was the Reverend John Winder, who would become his successor at Kilroot. Another valuable acquaintance was Richard Dobbs, a former mayor of

Carrickfergus, who gave him free use of his excellent library. Swift no doubt encountered Dobbs's seven-year-old son, Arthur, who would grow up to be governor of North Carolina.[42]

During Swift's brief time at Kilroot he fell in love. Twenty-year-old Jane Waring, seven years younger than Swift, was the daughter of a deceased Church of Ireland clergyman named Roger Waring. Other members of her family still lived in Waringstown, the village their forebears had established, thirty miles west of Carrickfergus in County Down, and were prominent members of the local squirearchy. Swift's contact with this family may have been due to his friendship at Trinity with two of Jane's cousins. (His early biographers believed he had roomed with her brother, but that was erroneous.) But Jane was not as far away as Waringstown, for at this time she was living with her widowed mother in Belfast.[43]

Swift liked to bestow romantic names on women, sometimes constructed anagrammatically from their actual names, and in the two letters to Jane that survive he calls her Varina. He even proposed marriage, or at least talked about it seriously. Previously, he had been contemptuous of anyone who got married without financial security, remembering his own parents, of course. When a Leicester relative was questioning him about his flirtations in that town, he wrote back indignantly, "Among all the young gentlemen that I have known to have ruined themselves by marrying (which I assure you is a great number) I have made this general rule, that they are either young, raw and ignorant scholars, who for want of knowing company believe every silk petticoat includes an angel, or else they have been a sort of honest young men who perhaps are too literal in rather marrying than burning, and so entail miseries on themselves and posterity by an overarching modesty." This is the very first letter of Swift's that has been preserved. The allusion is to St. Paul's "It is better to marry than to burn," a grudging concession that someone who can't control his sexual desires would do better to marry than burn in hell.[44]

Swift apparently controlled his desires successfully. Nokes oversimplifies when he comments, "Throughout his career Swift was fascinated with exposing what exactly was contained within a silk petticoat."[45] We don't know that. He almost never mentions the most interesting thing under the petticoat, unlike that other witty clergyman, Laurence Sterne, whose *Tristram Shandy* is full of muffs and clefts and fingers in the pie.

Jane Waring played hard to get; she probably thought that a young clergyman with little money was an unpromising prospect. And it turned out that Swift was only briefly in her neighborhood. By April of 1696 he had decided to return to Moor Park, eighteen months after leaving there. In a long letter he reproached Jane for her behavior in elevated romantic language:

> Would to Heaven you were but a while sensible of the thoughts into which my present distractions plunge me—they hale me a thousand ways, and I am not able to bear them. 'Tis so, by Heaven: the love of Varina is of more tragical consequence than her cruelty. Would to God you had hated and scorned me from the beginning. It was [your] pity opened the first way to my misfortunes, and now your love is finishing my ruin. . . . By Heaven, Varina, you are more experienced and have less virgin innocence than I. Would not your conduct make one think you were highly skilled in all the little polite methods of intrigue? . . . Oh Varina! how imagination leads me beyond my self and all my sorrows—'Tis sunk, and a thousand graves lie open—No Madam—I will give you no more of my unhappy temper, though I derive it all from you.[46]

It was evidently Jane's power over him that Swift feared.

The other surviving letter is a strange one. It dates from 1700, four years later. Swift and Jane Waring must have continued to correspond, for he speaks of "your letters," but he now complains that her "great sweetness of nature and humour" had given way to "a severe indifference." Perhaps there was a physical obstacle as well. "You told me the doctors advised you against marriage, as what would certainly hazard your life." Jane's health was poor, and the implication was that childbirth would be too risky. At any rate, Swift says that if the doctors have changed their mind, he is prepared to offer marriage, but only with clear provisos:

> Have you so much good nature as to endeavour by soft words to smooth any rugged humour, occasioned by the cross accidents of life? Shall the place wherever your husband is thrown be more welcome than courts or cities without him? In short, these are some of the necessary methods to please men who, like me, are deep read in the world. . . . These are the questions I have always resolved to propose to her with whom I meant to pass my life; and whenever you can heartily answer them in the affirmative, I shall be blessed to have you in my arms, without regarding whether your person be beautiful or your fortune large. Cleanliness in the first, and competency in the other, is all I look for.[47]

Is he saying that he would love her even if she weren't beautiful, or that she actually isn't? Her fortune is a sore point too, since she might suspect he is after her for her money.

It is quite possible, as Ehrenpreis suggests, that Swift didn't really want this marriage anymore, and was offering it in the coolest possible terms so that Jane would be sure to refuse. But it may also be that she had continued to tease, and that he was simply asking whether she could consent wholeheartedly to be his wife. "To this not unreasonable query," Denis Johnston says, "he seems to have got no reply. So there the matter ended."[48]

What did Swift carry away from his year at Kilroot? Nothing but disappointment. There was the romantic interest that turned sour, professional ambitions that seemed hopelessly stalled, and a renewed consciousness of being an outsider—a southerner in the north, a Church of Ireland priest in a sea of Presbyterians.

All that survives from Swift's time at Kilroot is the abandoned churchyard, in which the oldest gravestone dates from 1743. That stone commemorates a resident who was old enough to have heard Swift preach in her youth: "Here lyeth the body of Margrat Stevenson who died May the 16th 1743 aged 99 years."[49] If Swift could see the place today it might fulfill his grimmest expectations. The site is dominated by a gigantic power plant, a cement works, and the entrance to an underground network of salt mines. The salt is inferior in quality and is used on icy roads.

CHAPTER 4

Moor Park Once More

THE WAITING GAME

In 1695 Swift had been eager to escape from Moor Park; a year later he was ready to return. His chances for advancement could hardly be worse there than they were in Kilroot. His cousin Thomas had taken his place as Temple's secretary, but Thomas now went off to his curacy, and Jonathan resumed his old position. He retained the Kilroot living for a couple of years, probably for the income, while someone else handled the minimal duties. Then he resigned it in favor of his friend John Winder.

Temple had advised Swift to hold on to Kilroot indefinitely. "I would not consent to it," Swift told Winder. Temple was still making no effort to get Swift an appointment in England, and Swift was apparently burning his Irish bridges in an effort to force Temple's hand. It was impossible to force. For a while Swift hoped that an appointment might be arranged by one of Temple's friends, the Earl of Sunderland, who held the high position of lord chamberlain. But in December of 1697 Sunderland resigned, and Swift wrote to Winder, "My Lord Sunderland fell and I with him. Since that, there have been other courses, which if they succeed I shall be proud to own the methods, or if otherwise, very much ashamed." Craik interprets this as meaning "that though he is sure of the honesty of his means, he will still be ashamed of having tried at all, if these means do not end successfully."[1]

Temple may not have been as much at fault as Swift believed. Louis Landa, in his account of Swift's career in the Church, makes a notable point. He had set his sights on the royal prebends at Canterbury and Westminster, but they were valuable and prestigious, and he was an obscure young man with hardly any experience. Why should the commission of six bishops in charge of appointments have considered him qualified?[2] But Swift was always sure of his own merits, and a grudge collector too.

For an entire three-year period, from 1696 through 1698, we have almost no information about Swift's doings. The only surviving letters are the three that have already been quoted, to Jane Waring, to Winder, and to Stella (the one about the parrot and the rooks). A single incident happened to get recorded, and it gives a glimpse of Swift's characteristic fearlessness. The story comes from William Flower, who was related to the Temple family, and who wrote to Swift many years later: "As several little accidents make indelible impressions upon the minds of schoolboys, near thirty years ago, when I was one, I remember I was committed to your care from Sheen to London. We took water at Mortlake; the commander of the little skiff was very drunk and insolent, put us ashore at Hammersmith, yet insisted with very abusive language on his fare, which you courageously refused. The mob gathered; I expected to see your gown stripped off, and for want of a blanket to take a flight with you in it. But by your powerful eloquence you saved your bacon and money, and we happily proceeded on our journey." We don't have Swift's reply, but when Flower was raised to the peerage later on, Swift wrote to congratulate him.[3]

SELF-EDUCATION AT MOOR PARK

If Swift couldn't gain employment at court or in the Church of England, he could at least improve his education, which had been very narrow at Trinity College. Temple was a voracious reader with a superb library, and Swift took advantage of it. During the single year of 1697, for which a list still exists, he read the *Iliad*, the *Odyssey*, and the *Aeneid* twice each, and the poems of Horace as well. (Incidentally, he read Latin with ease, but probably not Greek, unless it was printed with a facing Latin translation.)[4] He also read numerous books in French, and histories in both French and English.

History was a favorite genre for the rest of Swift's life. What mainly interested him was the interplay of personalities, with their complicated motives, covert betrayals, and heavily masked truth. He would undoubtedly have

agreed with Voltaire's conclusion to his massive *Essai sur les moeurs:* "Since nature has placed self-interest, pride, and all the passions in the human heart, it
is not surprising that we have viewed, over a span of ten centuries, an almost
continuous succession of crimes and disasters." Long after Moor Park, Swift
made Gulliver tell the story of English history to the king of Brobdingnag,
who then summarizes it as "an heap of conspiracies, rebellions, murders, mas-
sacres, revolutions, banishments; the very worst effects that avarice, faction,
hypocrisy, perfidiousness, cruelty, rage, madness, hatred, envy, lust, malice,
and ambition could produce." After hearing Gulliver praise England and its
ways, the king declares, "By what I have gathered from your own relation,
and the answers I have with much pains wringed and extorted from you, I
cannot but conclude the bulk of your natives to be the most pernicious race
of little odious vermin that Nature ever suffered to crawl upon the surface of
the earth."[5] Statements like this earned Swift a reputation for misanthropy
and, as we will see, he didn't altogether disagree.

In later days Swift was deeply proud of the way he had educated himself.
"If anyone was cried up to him as a great scholar," Delany remembered, "his
first question was, How old is he? and the next, How many years he had
passed in a close application to his studies? And if the space fell short of his
period, he answered with contempt, 'He a scholar? 'Tis impossible! No man
can be a scholar that has not passed many years in hard study, and an application to good books.'"[6]

"When I am reading a book, whether wise or silly," Swift once wrote, "it
seemeth to me to be alive and talking to me." The books he owned that have
survived show that he constantly talked back, filling the margins with comments and objections, as he did when he referred to King William's morals.
Describing this period ten years later, he said of himself, "The author was
then young, his invention at the height, and his reading fresh in his head. By
the assistance of some thinking, and much conversation, he had endeavoured
to strip himself of as many real prejudices as he could."[7] That was his lifelong
goal: to be faithful to firm principles, but only after thinking them through.

In one important way, Sir William was a model. In an era when prose was
often wordy and pretentious, Temple's was notable for colloquial directness.
Patterned after Montaigne's essays, though without Montaigne's complexity and depth, Temple's offered genial, relaxed good sense. He was especially
good at pithy analogies: "The abilities of man must fall short on one side or
other, like too scanty a blanket when you are abed: if you pull it upon your
shoulders, you leave your feet bare; if you thrust it down upon your feet, your

shoulders are uncovered."[8] That sentence could easily be mistaken for one by Swift.

The persona Temple projected was attractive, too. Years later David Hume, a gifted stylist himself, praised the relaxed, familiar quality of Temple's writing: "We enter into acquaintance with the character of the author, full of honour and humanity, and fancy that we are engaged not in the perusal of a book, but in conversation with a companion." Samuel Johnson made a less obvious point: "Sir William Temple was the first writer who gave cadence to English prose. Before his time they were careless of arrangement, and did not mind whether a sentence ended with an important word or an insignificant word, or with what part of speech it was concluded." Despite the magniloquence of Johnson's own style, he said he modeled it originally on Temple's.[9]

Thirty years after Swift left Moor Park, when young Sheridan was entering Trinity College, Swift urged him to spend some time every day studying English—which was not included, of course, in the curriculum. "When I asked him what authors he would advise me to read, he immediately replied, Sir William Temple."[10]

"COUSIN SWIFT, YOU WILL NEVER BE A POET"

Sir William was a fan of the poet Abraham Cowley, who had died in the year of Swift's birth. Swift now claimed to love Cowley too. But the handful of poems Swift wrote at Moor Park in Cowley's style are truly awful.

Cowley was an imitator of the Greek poet Pindar, and his Pindarics became a fad. "All the boys and girls," Johnson said in his *Life of Cowley*, "caught the pleasing fashion, and they that could do nothing else could write like Pindar." Pindar wrote irregular, rhapsodic, obscure verse that was meant to express emotional excitement. Dryden called Pindar "wild and ungovernable," and Cowley himself praised Pindar's "impetuous dithyrambic tide . . . which neither banks nor dikes control." Possibly Swift did find that kind of verse exciting, since he wrote to his cousin Thomas, "I am Cowley to myself." More likely, he was trying to impress Temple, and counted on Thomas to pass this hyperbole along.[11]

One of Swift's early poems is *Ode to the King*, exalting the greatness of Sir William's friend, and another is *Ode to the Honorable Sir William Temple*. The very first word of that one is "Virtue," the subject of one of Temple's own essays. A. C. Elias, debunking the myth that Swift worshiped Temple, notes drily that this poem dwells on a subject "close to Temple's heart: Temple's own greatness and goodness." Sure enough, Virtue is embodied in Sir William, and it is to be found at Moor Park:

> Sing (belov'd Muse) the pleasures of retreat. . . .
> Sing of thy vales, sing of thy woods, sing of thy fields.

The river Wey shares this feeling, "loath to see the hated court and town."[12]

Far from hating court and town, that was where Swift wanted to be. Perhaps flattering Sir William would help him to get there.

> Those mighty epithets, learn'd, good, and great,
> Which we ne'er joined before, but in romances meet,
> We find in you at last united grown. . . .
> Shall I believe a spirit so divine
> Was cast in the same mold with mine?

Flattery was a diet that Temple never tired of, but it didn't pay off in tangible rewards for Swift. Did Temple pay attention to what comes next?

> Why then does Nature so unjustly share
> Among her elder sons the whole estate?

In a society based on primogeniture, only the eldest son could inherit an estate. It was in this context that Swift called himself, years later, "a younger son of younger sons." Since he had no brother, he must have been using the term metaphorically—he was *like* a younger son, lacking inherited advantages.[13]

Similarly calculated to please Temple was *Ode to the Athenian Society*, in praise of a periodical called the *Athenian Gazette* (later renamed the *Athenian Mercury*) that supplied answers to supposedly fascinating questions. Temple thought highly of the society and no doubt encouraged Swift to write this poem. It duly appeared in the periodical—his first publication, and for nine years his only one. Ehrenpreis thinks it endows the Athenians with "incandescent perfections," but it's hard to believe Swift was such a fool as to believe that.[14]

Some of the Athenian questions were pretty silly, and those are the ones that occasionally get quoted: "How does a horse produce a square turd when its fundament is round?" But mostly the *Athenian Mercury*, which filled two huge folio volumes when collected, is sensible and often generous:

> QUEST. Whether there be two men in the world with an
> equal number of hairs on their head?

ANSW. The question is unanswerable, for it admits of
neither experiment nor argument.
QUEST. Whether it be proper for women to be learned?
ANSW. On the whole, since they have as noble souls as we,
a finer genius, and generally quicker apprehensions, we see
no reason why women should not be learned.
QUEST. Is not kissing an insipid thing? Is there any real
pleasure in it?
ANSW. We must leave that to your own experience, though
'tis much as the person is.[15]

There is surely a hint of irony in a reference in this poem to Swift's "young
and (almost) virgin muse."[16] Almost virgin! Perhaps he already suspected what
soon turned out to be true, that there was no Athenian Society at all, just a
hack journalist named John Dunton and a couple of his friends.

In the *Ode to Temple* Swift describes himself as "to the Muse's galley tied."
Bondage to the Muse might be worth it if it led to a well-paying position, as
did happen to a number of young writers. But it didn't for Swift. To make
the disappointment more bitter, William Congreve, his Kilkenny schoolmate
and two years younger, had already scored a triumph as a London playwright.
An ode to Congreve, which Swift wrote at this time, was ostensibly meant as
praise, but jealousy and rivalry keep breaking through:

> This could I do, and proudly o'er him tower,
> Were my desires but heightened to my power.[17]

Swift hoped his poem would appear in a published version of one of Congreve's plays, giving his own reputation a boost. He had to feel chagrined
that when the play did appear, it was accompanied instead by a masterly
tribute by John Dryden, a prominent playwright and the greatest poet of the
time. Dryden opens with effortless authority, passing the torch to the younger
generation:

> Well then; the promised hour is come at last,
> The present age of wit obscures the past.

Dryden's colloquial ease makes Swift's Pindarics look laboriously old-
fashioned. Dryden ends on a movingly personal note:

> Already I am worn with cares and age,
> And just abandoning th' ungrateful stage . . .

And take for tribute what these lines express;
You merit more; nor could my love do less.[18]

For Swift, Dryden was to become a bête noire. In a story that comes down from several sources, Swift introduced himself to Dryden in London, showed him his poems, and received the humiliating verdict, "Cousin Swift, you will never be a poet." They were cousins only in a remote sense, since Dryden's grandfather and Swift's maternal great-grandfather were brothers, making them second cousins once removed. In another version what Dryden said was "Young man, you will never be a poet."[19]

If the exchange took place at all, it's possible to put a different spin on it. In a version that may have originated with Swift himself, what Dryden really said was "Nature has never formed you for a Pindaric poet." Years afterward, Swift might have had to agree. In any event, he always had it in for Dryden. Long afterward he bitterly recalled the scene at Will's coffeehouse in London, where "Battus"—clearly Dryden—"reclining on his elbow-chair / Gives

18. John Dryden late in life. The great poet has the air of cool superiority that infuriated Swift.

judgment with decisive air" while disciples lap up his opinions. Swift especially disliked Dryden's talent for self-promotion. "The world would never have suspected him to be so great a poet," he later wrote, "if he had not assured them so frequently in his prefaces, that it was impossible they could either doubt or forget it."[20]

Long afterward, Swift observed, "Although men are accused for not knowing their own weakness, yet perhaps as few know their own strength." By then he had become a celebrated writer, and in public affairs the most admired man in Ireland. He had come to understand that his strength was best exerted in satire, and there is an anticipation of that in the Congreve poem:

> My hate, whose lash just heaven has long decreed
> Shall on a day make sin and folly bleed.

In another early poem the aggressiveness is even more startling: "Each line shall stab, shall blast, like daggers and like fire."[21]

In the *Ode to Temple* Swift lamented that writing lyric poetry was for him "an incurable disease." He was soon cured of pretentious odes, at any rate, and a poem about Temple's recovery from illness bids farewell to a nonexistent Muse:

> There thy enchantment broke, and from this hour
> I here renounce thy visionary power;
> And since thy essence on my breath depends,
> Thus with a puff the whole delusion ends.[22]

BATTLING BOOKS

Some poets, Dryden and Pope, for instance, excelled in verse satire, but Swift was learning that his best medium was prose. At Moor Park, he began to experiment with it. A mock epic called *The Battle of the Books* embodied some of Swift's deep convictions, but was mainly intended as a gift for Sir William Temple.

The occasion of this piece was an unseemly public quarrel over the authorship of an obscure Greek text, which became the pretext for a culture war with important implications. The reason Swift weighed in was that Sir William Temple had already done so, and was rightly regarded as having made a complete fool of himself. In itself the affair was trivial, but it is worth describing because Temple was defending a privileged way of life.

In France, where science was struggling to free itself from the ancient Greeks and Romans, its spokesmen had recently attracted notice by championing the "moderns" over the "ancients." Charles Perrault, best known today for his collection of fairy tales, claimed provocatively that the French poet Boileau was greater than Horace, and the French playwright Corneille greater than Sophocles.[23] British traditionalists rose to the bait, and Temple saw his chance. Like others of his class, and indeed like Swift himself, he had been brought up to believe that the classics were the foundation of civilized life, an indispensable preparation for politics, the Church, and the law. So in 1690 he published *An Essay upon the Ancient and Modern Learning*, which attracted a good deal of attention.

In a way Temple was wasting his time, since he had to admit that the champions of the moderns conceded "the preeminence of the ancients in poetry, oratory, painting, statuary, and architecture." But that wasn't enough for Temple. He insisted that the moderns were no good at science, either. "There is nothing new in astronomy to vie with the ancients," he declared, "unless it be the Copernican system; nor in physic, unless Harvey's circulation of the blood." He thought that neither theory had been proved, and that even if they could be proved it would make no difference, since they "have been of little use to the world."[24]

What Temple really cared about was literature, and there he was certain that the moderns were pigmies. The only English writers of any note, he said, were Sir Philip Sidney, Francis Bacon, and John Selden—no mention of Milton or Shakespeare. It was impossible to rival the great geniuses of old, and Temple incautiously gave an example: "I think the *Epistles* of Phalaris to have more race, more spirit, more force of wit and genius, than any others I have ever seen, either ancient of modern."[25] Phalaris was a ruler in Sicily in the fifth century B.C. Some pedants, Temple acknowledged, had doubted the authenticity of those letters, but that only showed their inability to appreciate great writing.

What happened next was that a new edition of the Phalaris letters appeared at Oxford, inspired perhaps by Temple's praise. The choice of text and editor were both rather casual. The head of Christ Church College at Oxford was in the habit of asking his brightest undergraduates to produce new editions of minor works, and Phalaris fell to seventeen-year-old Charles Boyle, a favorite because he was the younger brother of the Earl of Orrery. Boyle accordingly sent word to the King's Library in London that he would like someone to collate the manuscript copies there (it did not occur to him to do the work himself), and he claimed afterward that the head of the library had insultingly refused access to his assistant.

That librarian was the formidable Richard Bentley, one of the greatest classicists England has ever produced, who would soon play a decisive role in the debate. A learned friend of Bentley's, William Wotton, had already published a critique of Temple's views on Phalaris, and in a second edition he included a *Dissertation* in which Bentley totally demolished young Boyle, proving that the so-called Phalaris mentioned events that occurred long after he lived, referred to cities that didn't yet exist, and used a dialect not yet current. Temple had cut off his own retreat. It might have been possible to argue that even if the *Epistles* were not by Phalaris, they were still excellent, but since his claim was that the human mind was at its best in earliest antiquity and degenerated thereafter, he was trapped with no way out.[26]

What was at stake, really, was not the merits of the obscure Phalaris, but a privileged culture that preferred urbane wit to what it regarded as dreary pedantry. Christ Church was not just an educational institution, it was a feeder for worldly success, and its members were extremely well connected. Macaulay says that they were "dominant at Oxford, powerful in the Inns of Court and the College of Physicians, conspicuous in Parliament and in the literary and fashionable circles of London." In a collective rejoinder called *Dr. Bentley's Dissertations Examined*, the Christ Church gang rested their case on Temple's cultural superiority, "mixing wit with reason, sound knowledge with good manners, and making the one recommend and set off the others." Never mind Bentley's arguments from history and philology. Phalaris was a king. Temple "had written to kings and they to him, and this has qualified him to judge how kings should write, much better than all Dr. Bentley's correspondence with foreign professors."[27]

Swift's contribution, written but not published in 1697, was a mock epic called *The Battle of the Books*. Its theme is not just ancients versus moderns, but the larger opposition between two different ways of reading and living. To Swift, as to Temple, the classics were living voices; to scholars like Bentley, they were apparently just documents to be analyzed. So in Swift's satire, the books in the King's Library divide into armies and join battle, with the ancients of course victorious. Fighting on their side is Sir William Temple, and when Wotton hurls a lance at him, "Temple neither felt the weapon touch him, nor heard it fall." Before long Wotton and Bentley, represented insultingly as homosexual lovers, are skewered by a single javelin from Boyle. Dryden gets another kick, too. When he has to face off against Virgil, whom he had translated brilliantly into English, he rides a "gelding of a monstrous size"—big but castrated—and his helmet is "nine times too large for the head."[28]

The Battle of the Books is clever and energetic, but for most readers today, too deeply invested in a long-forgotten controversy to have much appeal. The most interesting thing in it is the very first sentence: "Satire is a sort of glass, wherein beholders do generally discover everybody's face but their own." For the rest of his life Swift would continue to experience that truth. The second most interesting thing is a fable about a spider and a bee, adapted from various earlier sources. The spider is the modern artist with his cult of originality, proud of creating out of his own vitals. His weapons are poison and a flimsy web. The bee, on the other hand, ranges freely from flower to flower, injuring nothing while gathering nectar, and his product is honey and wax, "sweetness and light" (wax as used in candles).[29] So Bentley is a spider sucking the juices from books that he has stung to death, while Temple is a lover of literature gathering sweet sustenance as he roves.

The affair soon blew over, for as Gibbon said eighty years later, "The *Epistles* of Phalaris have been pronounced spurious after a much fuller hearing than they deserved."[30] It is not known why Swift didn't publish *The Battle of the Books* right away, when the controversy was still going on. Temple disliked satire, and may have advised against publication. It is definitely an odd piece of work, and like much else that Swift would go on to write, paradoxical. On the one hand, it displays a probing, ironic, skeptical intelligence; on the other hand, it asserts a reactionary commitment to an idealized past. All his life Swift would declare that Homer had more genius than any writer who ever lived, more even "than all the rest of the world put together."[31]

GOOD-BYE TO ALL THAT

In January 1699, Sir William Temple died at the age of seventy-one. During the last few months of his life Swift kept a detailed record of Temple's health, but his Dublin friend Dr. Lyon, who had seen it, quoted only the final sentence: "He died at one o'clock in the morning, and with him all that was great and good among men." Lacking the rest of the entries, we have no way of knowing what their tone was, or even why Swift made them. Elias suggests persuasively that it was Lady Giffard, who monitored her brother's condition attentively, who asked him to do it. In that case the eulogistic conclusion would have been intended for Lady Giffard.[32]

Shortly after Temple's death Swift wrote on the flyleaf of a Bible, no longer extant, this eulogy: "He was a person of the greatest wisdom, justice, liberality, politeness, eloquence, of his age and nation; the truest lover of his country, and one that deserved more from it by his eminent public services than any man before or since; besides his great deserving of the commonwealth of learning, having been universally esteemed the most accomplished writer of his time." Ehrenpreis calls this "extravagant," which it certainly is, and "reverently admiring," which is less certain. Swift doesn't say that it's his own opinion that Temple was the greatest writer of the age, but claims improbably that everybody thought so. And it's hard to believe that no one could have been as wise and liberal as the self-important and tight-fisted Temple. Elias makes the suggestion that a Bible at Moor Park could have been available for anyone to see, and that these words too were for Lady Giffard's benefit.[33]

The years at Moor Park were now ended, and it was surely discouraging to reflect on how many those years had been. When Swift arrived he was a hopeful twenty-one. He was leaving just shy of thirty-one, totally unknown. His one attempt to strike out on his own, at Kilroot, had been a disaster. He was now a clergyman without a church. And no one could possibly have thought of him as a writer, since his sole publication was the unimpressive and anonymous *Ode to the Athenian Society* back in 1692.

The first thing to do was to wind up Sir William's affairs. Swift helped with arrangements for the funeral in London, and together with the rest of the Moor Park staff he was measured for mourning clothes, the cost of which was charged to the household account. His own share was 8 shillings for breeches and a waistcoat. On the same bill Ralph Mose, the steward by now, received 13 shillings.[34]

Sir William was laid to rest in Westminster Abbey. His heart, however, remained at Moor Park, as specified in his will: "I desire and appoint that my heart may be interred six feet underground, on the southeast side of the sundial in my little garden at Moor Park." The will also gave detailed instructions for bequests, including the amazingly generous one to Stella, and it had a curious codicil that reflected Temple's experience as a diplomat: his granddaughters would forfeit their inheritance if they married Frenchmen.[35]

"To Mr. Jonathan Swift, now dwelling with me," went a legacy of £100, along with an obligation that would prove onerous. Swift was to finish collating and editing Temple's papers and to oversee their publication, with any profits to go to himself. Due to his high opinion of his own writing, Temple may have thought that this would make Swift rich, but it did nothing of the kind, and required much labor over a period of years. There were seven volumes in all: one of *Letters*, three of *Miscellanies*, and three of *Memoirs*, published from 1705 to 1709. So for ten years after Temple's death, Swift was still working for him. His total income from all of the books was somewhere between £200 and £250, spaced out over a decade.[36]

. What happened after that, in 1709, brings out Swift's bitterness at the haughty way Sir William had treated him. Lady Giffard complained that he had published her brother's *Memoirs* from an "unfaithful copy." His reply was wounded and indignant. As Temple's secretary, he explained, it had been his job to write down every word that Temple intended to print, under the author's direct supervision. Beyond that stenographic function, "I pretend not to have had the least share in Sir William Temple's confidence above his relations or his commonest friends. (I have but too good reasons to think otherwise.)"[37]

Two years later, Swift told Stella, "I thought I saw Jack Temple and his wife pass by me today in their coach, but I took no notice of them. I am glad I have wholly shaken off that family." Jack was the nephew who would inherit Moor Park after Lady Giffard's death, and who told the story about Swift not eating at the Temples' table. Three months later Swift ran into Jack Temple at court, where it wasn't possible to avoid him, "so we talked two or three careless words, and parted."[38]

Swift nursed this resentment of the Temples for a long time. As late as 1726 he got into a name-calling exchange with Sir William's nephew, Viscount Palmerston. Swift was writing to complain that someone he had recommended was mistreated and another person dismissed solely because it was Swift who recommended them—"but these are some of the refinements among you great men, which are above my low understanding." Palmerston defended his conduct in a spirited reply, adding insultingly, "I fear you hugged the false report to cancel all feelings of gratitude that must ever glow in a generous breast and to justify what you had declared, that no regard to the family was any restraint to you. These refinements are past my low understanding, and can only be comprehended by you great wits." The charge of ingratitude infuriated Swift: "I own myself indebted to Sir William Temple," he retorted, "for recommending me to the late King, although without success, and for his choice of me to take care of his posthumous writings. But I hope you will not charge my living in his family as an obligation, for I was educated to little purpose if I retired to his house on any other motives than the benefit of his conversation and advice, and the opportunity of pursuing my studies. For, being born to no fortune, I was at his death as far to seek as ever, and perhaps you will allow that I was of some use to him."[39]

This was not just disappointment at lack of career advancement; it reflects a deep sense of injury in being treated as a mere stenographer. Certain that he himself was a great writer, Temple never considered that Swift might be one.

When Swift was leaving Moor Park, his sister Jane told their cousin Deane, "My poor brother has lost his best friend, Sir William Temple, who was so fond of him whilst he lived that he made him give up his living in this country [Kilroot in Ireland] to stay with him at Moor Park, and promised to get him one in England; but death came in between, and has left him unprovided both of friend and living."[40] It had probably been several years since Jane was at Moor Park, and there is no way of knowing how much genuine fondness she perceived there. As for "friend," the word had a wider range of meanings than it does today, and is used here in the sense defined in Johnson's *Dictionary:* "favourer, one propitious."

Perhaps, though, bygones were finally bygones. In 1737 Jack Temple wrote to Swift to ask whether he could buy a portrait of Lady Giffard that Rebecca Dingley possessed. Swift wrote back courteously to say that he was welcome to it, and that it would be generous to make some gift as well to the aged and impoverished Dingley. Jack was living by then at Moor Park, and Swift added a pleasant reminiscence: "The tree on which I carved those words, *factura nepotibus umbram* [may it give shade to the nephews], is one of those elms that stand in the hollow ground just before the house; but I suppose the letters are widened and grown shapeless by time."[41]

For six months or so in 1699, Swift hung about London, hoping that a couple of noblemen with Temple connections would help him to the long-desired prebend at Canterbury or Westminster. They didn't, and probably couldn't. The young clergyman with little experience was setting his sights too high. The best thing he was able to secure was a chance to be chaplain to Lord Berkeley, on his way to Ireland to govern the country as the representative of the Crown.

A new century was at hand, and it struck many people as a turning point. In 1700 Dryden captured the transition in a theatrical piece called *The Secular Masque* ("secular" means "of the century"). The god Janus embodies the end of one era and the start of the next. Diana represents the court's love of hunting in the early 1600s, Mars the civil wars of midcentury, and Venus the amorous intrigues of the Restoration. At the end Momus, god of laughter, puts them all in their places:

Momus.	All, all of a piece throughout:
[pointing to Diana]	Thy chase had a beast in view;
[to Mars]	Thy wars brought nothing about;
[to Venus]	Thy lovers were all untrue.
Janus.	'Tis well an old age is out,
	And time to begin a new.[42]

A month later, just as Dryden's masque was receiving its first performances, he died at the age of sixty-nine.

CHAPTER 5

The Village and the Castle

A MODEST HOME

In addition to his duties with Lord Berkeley, Swift expected an appointment or "preferment" in the Church, and one was duly found, though not nearly as distinguished as he had hoped. In September of 1700 he became vicar of Laracor, a tiny hamlet close to the town of Trim, twenty-three miles from Dublin and an easy day's journey on horseback. Laracor lay in County Meath, in a landscape far less dramatic than the one at Kilroot. Northerners had a saying, "Ulster sits in the middle of five thousand hills, but the county of Meath lies level as a board."[1]

After a century of privation, the towns in the area were unprepossessing. "They were generally small and almost invariably shabby," a historian says, "their approaches lined with poor hovels, their streets interspersed with ruins." Trim, however, was described in a 1691 guidebook as "a borough and market town of good trade, reckoned the chief in the county." Then as now, it was dominated by Trim Castle on the river Boyne, the biggest Anglo-Norman castle in all of Ireland. It is an emblem both of English domination and of the wrenching vicissitudes of history. What had been impregnable in the days of bows and arrows was helpless against cannons, and like a neighboring abbey of which only a gutted bell tower remains, it was nothing more than a majestic ruin.[2]

19. Trim Castle.

Beyond Dublin, the situation of the Irish Church was bad. In the relatively affluent diocese of Meath, only a fifth of the parishes had churches fit for use. Laracor did have one, but no usable vicarage, so Swift had to live elsewhere, probably in Trim. When a new bishop arrived in the diocese he found not a "bishop's palace" awaiting him, as would have been the case in England, but a single-story house with floorboards so rotten that a stick would go right through to the dirt beneath.[3]

Still, Swift grew deeply fond of Laracor, a valued rural retreat even after he moved permanently to Dublin. He had the vicarage rebuilt, "a neat cabin," as a church document later described it, and he began to plant. A stone's throw from the church was a little river, hardly more than a stream (the name Laracor comes from the Gaelic Lathrach Cora, meaning "the site of the weir"). He had the banks altered to make a miniature ornamental canal, in imitation of the one at Moor Park, and he planted rows of willows. In later years there were apple and cherry trees as well. He remarked in a letter, "My river walk is extremely pretty, and my canal in great beauty, and I see trouts playing in it."[4] He seems to have taken no interest in a prehistoric tumulus

20. Laracor Church. This drawing was made in 1852, shortly before the building Swift knew was torn down and replaced.

21. Laracor Communion table.

next to the church; in those days the romance of ancient Ireland had yet to be born.

Swift's duties at Laracor were far from exacting, since Protestants were a small minority. On one occasion Swift wrote, "I am this minute very busy, being to preach today before an audience of at least 15 people, most of them gentle [that is, "gentlefolk," the well born] and all simple." All of the neighboring peasants were Catholic. The Communion table from Laracor has been preserved, and can be seen in a side aisle of St. Patrick's Cathedral in Dublin. Its extreme simplicity suggests how modest the services must have been. Sometimes no one at all showed up. Swift's Dublin friends enjoyed a story relating how he arrived at church one Sunday and found no one there except the parish clerk, whose first name was Roger. As Orrery told it, instead of saying, "Dearly beloved brethren, the Scripture moveth you and me in sundry places," Swift began, "with great composure and gravity, but with a turn peculiar to himself, 'Dearly beloved Roger.'" The younger Sheridan, however, was sure that Swift would never have made a mockery of the service in that way, suggesting that he merely thought of doing it. "They who heard this, as is frequently the case on such occasions, thought it would improve the story much by making him carry it into execution, and related it accordingly."[5]

MONEY

Clergymen had to pay close attention to finances, because their "livings," as their appointments were known, came not from salaries but from tithes and rents. In most cases what they could collect was discouragingly low. Tithes were paid by the landowners in the parish, but they always tried to pay less than they were supposed to, and had often acquired a legal right to the tithes themselves. Getting even partial payment was a struggle that exasperated Swift for the rest of his life. "Although tithes be of divine institution," he remarked, "they are of diabolical execution."[6]

Rents, on the other hand, came from property owned directly by the local church, including farmland known as the glebe. Laracor had barely an acre of glebe, though Swift augmented it later by purchases out of his own pocket. Johnson, who defines *glebe* as "the land possessed as part of the revenue of an ecclesiastical benefice," illustrates it with a quotation from Swift: "Many parishes have not an inch of glebe." As late as 1728 an Irish archbishop reported that the majority of parishes had no glebe, and no parsonage either.[7]

In these circumstances, the only way to make ends meet was to join two or more parishes under a single minister, as had been the case at Kilroot. So together with Laracor, Swift took on Rathbeggan, halfway between Laracor and Dublin, and Agher, a few miles south of Laracor. Agher provided a modest income, but a recent writer says that it had "no church in repair, no curate, and possibly no Protestants." At Rathbeggan there were definitely no Protestants. Three parishes held by one priest was very common; there were instances in which eight or even ten would be joined for a meager total income of £40 per year.[8]

In Victorian times this practice of holding multiple livings would be denounced as corrupt "pluralism," and there were certainly eighteenth-century examples of that. Richard Watson, bishop of Llandaff in Wales later in the century, had a princely income of £2,200 a year, cobbled together from seven churches in Llandaff, two churches in Shropshire, two in Leicestershire, two in Cambridgeshire, and three in Huntingtonshire. Watson employed low-paid curates in all of those far-flung dependencies, the majority of which weren't even in Wales. But for the humbler clergy there was no possibility of affluence. Macaulay paints a vivid picture of their status in England at just the time when Swift was going to Laracor:

> Hardly one living in fifty enabled the incumbent to bring up a family comfortably. As children multiplied and grew, the household of the priest became more and more beggarly. Holes appeared more and more plainly in the thatch of his parsonage and in his single cassock. Often it was only by toiling on his glebe, by feeding swine, and by loading dung carts that he could obtain daily bread; nor did his utmost exertions always prevent the bailiffs from taking his concordance and his inkstand in execution. . . . His children were brought up like the children of the neighbouring peasantry. His boys followed the plough, and his girls went out to service. . . . Even a keen and strong intellect might be expected to rust in so unfavourable a situation.[9]

Since pluralism was an economic necessity, it infuriated Swift to hear it criticized. "The clergy having been stripped," he said, "of the greatest part of their revenues, the glebes being generally lost, the tithes in the hands of laymen, the churches demolished, and the country depopulated; in order to preserve a face of Christianity, it was necessary to unite small vicarages, sufficient to make a tolerable maintenance for a minister."[10]

With their own and their parishioners' income dependent on farming, rural clergymen had a strong personal interest in agriculture. When Swift turned Kilroot over to John Winder he described its income in detail, which "at eighteen pence per acre, oats, amounts to better than £100 a year—with cows, sheep, cats, and dogs etc.," and he called himself proudly "an understanding man in that affair." Laracor and the other two parishes were worth £200 in years of good harvests, but numerous expenses had to be paid. There was taxation on church property, which came out of the vicar's pocket, and generous pay (more than £50) for the curate who took charge whenever Swift was away. There were personal outlays, of course: in addition to food, wine,

22. Swift's account book. Swift recorded expenses by the month and totaled his income at the end of each year. Here tithes and rents for 1703 at Laracor and Agher are listed in pounds, shillings, and pence. Swift's agent Isaiah Parvisol collected £132, 8 shillings (at the top, just before £6 from "Mr. Bumford").

and clothing, there was also £15 for a personal servant, £10 for feeding and stabling two horses, £10 for clothing, and so on.[11]

This attention to finances made Swift more interested in economic issues than a modern clergyman might be. Throughout his life he would publish pamphlets on economic subjects. In the 1720s his intervention in an especially controversial issue would make him an Irish national hero.

As is true of nearly all Irish sites associated with Swift, hardly anything remains today of the Laracor he knew. Though the name still appears on maps, there is not even a hamlet there, and as a current resident has written, "Laracor exists today only in the concerns of Swiftian aficionados and local historians." Swift's church was torn down in 1856 in favor of a Victorian replacement, which has since been converted to a private residence. The old graveyard is still there, choked with weeds, and it contains gravestones of some parishioners Swift must have known. The most interesting is the gravestone of a gentleman mentioned by Swift as "Goodman Bumford" and his wife: "They lived together in wedlock 50 years in this parish and were descended from good ancient English families. They had many children to whom they gave virtuous example and education being tender parents, loving neighbours, devoted frequenters of the church and constant benefactors of the poor. . . . He departed life the 25th of March 1720 aged 103 years and she the 25th of January 1722 aged 89 years."[12]

As for the rectory that Swift repaired and used, no trace at all remains, except for a fragment of medieval masonry that was once thought to be part of it. In actuality it was never incorporated in the house, and was never mentioned by Swift. Down by the little river, his plantings are long gone and his canal filled in.

A LONG-SOUGHT APPOINTMENT

Seven months after being appointed to Laracor, Swift got a second position, the prebend of Dunlavin in St. Patrick's Cathedral. Even now he felt resentment, because Archbishop Marsh, who had been provost of Trinity when Swift was a student there, seems to have delayed the appointment due to dislike of Swift. "He hath found out the secret," Swift later said bitterly, "of preferring men without deserving their thanks; and where he dispenses his favours to persons of merit, they are less obliged to him than to fortune."[13]

The cathedral had eighteen prebendaries whose duties were minimal: they only had to take turns preaching there and to show up for an annual meeting.

There was a modest income, but out of it Swift had to pay a curate to look after the parish of Dunlavin thirty miles to the south. In no way was this a distinguished appointment, as Laurence Sterne wryly acknowledged in his own case, when he had Pride tell him that he would never be anything more in the Church than "a lousy prebendary."[14] Yet this turned out to be a crucial stage in Swift's career, for it gave him a foothold in the cathedral, and that would lead to an ever more impressive career.

In 1702 Swift achieved another goal when he received the degree of doctor of divinity from Trinity College. Like the Oxford M.A., this one required no extra work, just payment of a hefty sum of money—£44 in "fees and treats," presumably for the college officials. He was referred to thereafter as "Dr. Swift," a title he clearly enjoyed.

AT HOME IN THE CASTLE

The appointment that mattered most to Swift was his chaplaincy to Lord Berkeley, the king's representative in Ireland. Whenever the Irish Parliament was in session, for six to eight months every other year, this dignitary was required to be present. He was known by several titles. Usually he was referred to as the lord lieutenant, but sometimes as the viceroy or the lord deputy. During the extended periods when no lord lieutenant was present, three lords justices would act as a governing committee. When Berkeley took up his position, there was no Parliament sitting, so that technically he governed as one of the lords justices.

The royal representative enjoyed a certain amount of power, but the position was largely ceremonial. Each new incumbent—there were thirteen between 1703 and 1745, the year of Swift's death—would progress to the castle in an ornate coach drawn by eight horses, with foot guards and battle axes marching in front, in a procession that took four hours to cover a distance that normally needed only half an hour. "The joy of the people was such," claimed a 1732 account, "as besides huzzas, bells ringing, great and small guns firing, bonfires and other illuminations, wine and ale was given away in plenty to the populace."[15] That helps to account for the joy.

Swift's new employer was Charles Berkeley, second Earl Berkeley, a former diplomat who had recently succeeded his father to the earldom. Berkeley was a cultivated, intelligent man, though Swift later described him as "intolerably lazy and indolent, and somewhat covetous," and his appointment would be withdrawn after less than a year.[16]

23. Lord Berkeley.

Swift's job as domestic chaplain was essentially a sinecure, reading family prayers and preaching now and then to dignitaries at the castle. But he liked to manage his own time, and disliked being constantly available for minor duties, rather as he had been at Moor Park. Years later he said, "I will be no man's chaplain alive."[17] To look after Laracor when he wasn't there, he employed a reliable curate.

A notable perk for the chaplain was that he got to live in the handsome family apartments in the castle, close to Hoey's Court where Swift's uncle Godwin had lived until his death in 1695. He became something of a favorite in the Berkeley family, especially with a pretty fifteen-year-old daughter named Elizabeth. In London in the coming years he often visited them, and he kept up a warm lifelong correspondence with Elizabeth, known after her marriage in 1706 as Lady Betty Germaine.

Deane Swift heard about one near disaster:

In the year 1699 Swift had like to have burnt the Castle of Dublin, and the Lord Berkeley in the midst of it. For the Doctor [he wasn't in fact a doctor yet], whose bedchamber was the next room to his Excellency's, having grown drowsy over his book while he was reading in bed, dropped asleep without extinguishing his candle; which happening to fall upon his quilt set it on fire, and burnt its passage quite through the bedclothes until it reached his thigh. Swift, roused by the pain, leaped out of bed and extinguished the fire, which by this time had burnt part of the curtains. He took care to have the damages repaired, and by throwing away some guineas in hush money, the accident was never made known in the Castle.[18]

Swift's appointment began awkwardly, and thanks to Louis Landa's patient research, it illustrates the way he often harbored unjustified resentment. His autobiographical sketch breaks off at exactly this point after describing a double offense. At first, it had been his understanding that he was going to be Berkeley's secretary as well as chaplain, with more pay and status. But a rival candidate "had so far insinuated himself into the Earl's favor, by telling him that the post of secretary was not proper for a clergyman, nor would be of any advantage to one who aimed only at Church preferments, that his Lordship after a poor apology gave that office to the other."[19]

The new secretary, Arthur Bushe, was indeed something of a schemer, but what Swift narrates next makes him sound downright diabolical. "In some months the deanery of Derry fell vacant, and it was the Earl of Berkeley's turn to dispose of it. Yet things were so ordered that the secretary having received a bribe, the deanery was disposed of to another, and Mr. Swift was put off with some other Church livings [that is, Laracor] not worth above a third part of that rich deanery, and at this present time not a sixth. The excuse pretended was his being too young, although he were then 30 years old."[20]

Reading through the correspondence of everyone involved, Landa shows that Swift once again overestimated his own qualifications, and wrongly suspected treachery. The person with the right to bestow the deanery was the Earl of Galway, not Berkeley. Galway was responding to a bishop's plea that this especially difficult post in the Presbyterian north should go to an experienced man of prudence and piety. John Bolton, who did get the deanery, had been an able clergyman for twenty-three years, whereas Swift had left the only parish he ever served after a single year. Moreover, far from angling for Derry, Bolton was so unenthusiastic about going there that it had to be sweetened by letting him keep the income from a parish near Dublin. It's not even clear that Berkeley ever pushed for Swift's appointment, or that he should have. Bolton had been his chaplain too.[21]

Swift's behavior in incidents like this is not very attractive, nor is his habit of spinning a circumstantial but groundless story to explain it. Yet there were positive consequences too. Such experiences fueled his indignation against injustice, and later on he would focus that indignation on issues of public concern, with spectacular results.

THE PLAYFUL SWIFT

Swift was now spending a lot of time with sophisticated people from high society. It amused him to mimic the vacuous entries that a lady's guests would write in her table book, which he imagined as interspersed with her own jottings.

> Here you may read (*dear charming saint*)
> Beneath (a new receipt for paint);
> Here in beau spelling (tru tel deth)
> There in her own (far an el breth);
> Here (lovely nymph pronounce my doom),
> There (a safe way to use perfume);
> Here, a page filled with billets-doux,
> On t' other side (laid out for shoes);
> (Madam, I die without your Grace),
> (Item, for half a yard of lace).[22]

The fourth line must refer to a sweetener "for an ill breath."

It was probably at this time, too, that Swift began making entries in a collection of "polite conversation" whose triteness fascinated and exasperated him; he went on adding to it for the rest of his life. Its purported author is one Simon Wagstaff, who boasts "that there is not one single witty phrase in this whole collection which hath not received the stamp and approbation of at least one hundred years." In other words, these are stalest of clichés, prefabricated phrases that might have been clever once but no longer are. A few are still around today:

> LADY SMART. Madam, do you love bohea tea?
> LADY ANSWERALL. Why really, madam, I must confess I
> do love it, but it does not love me.
>
> LADY ANSWERALL. Pray, how old do you take her to be?
> COLONEL ATWIT. Why, about five or six and twenty.

LADY ANSWERALL. I swear she's no chicken; she's on the
wrong side of thirty if she be a day.

The complacent exchanges plod on for sixty pages.[23]

Swift's friends testified that he was a brilliant mimic, and he loved to ventriloquize voices from different social strata. Lady Berkeley had a garrulous
servant named Frances Harris, who was horrified one day to realize that she
had lost her purse, containing the large sum of £7, 4 shillings, and sixpence.
Swift impersonated her in an inspired piece of verse, *The Humble Petition of
Frances Harris, Who Must Starve, and Die a Maid, if It Miscarries*:

> So next morning we told Whittle, and he fell a-swearing;
> Then my dame Wadgar came, and she, you know, is thick of hearing.
> "Dame," said I, as loud as I could bawl, "do you know what a loss I
>   have had?"
> "Nay," said she, "my Lord Collway's folks are all very sad,
> For my Lord Dromedary comes a-Tuesday without fail."
> "Pugh!" said I, "but that's not the business that I ail."
> Says Cary, says he, "I have been a servant this five and twenty years,
>   come spring,
> And in all the places I lived I never heard of such a thing."
> "Yes," says the steward, "I remember when I was at my Lady
>   Shrewsbury's,
> Such a thing as this happened, just about the time of gooseberries."[24]

"Lord Collway" was Galway, and "Lord Dromedary" was Drogheda. The implication is that Frances Harris hopes to present her petition to the lords
justices of Ireland, but is too obtuse to realize that two of the three justices
are these very guests.

There is another twist in the poem as well. It seems that Frances has aspirations to marry the castle chaplain, which is to say, Jonathan Swift. She
offends him, however, by asking him to cast an astrological "nativity," and he
stalks off, since a priest would have no business dabbling in astrology.

> Well, I thought I should have swooned. "Lord," said I, "what shall I do?
> I have lost my money, and shall lose my true love too."

What Swift thought of servants who fantasized about marrying chaplains is
apparent in his instructions to the waiting maid in his collection of ironic
advice called *Directions to Servants*. She is advised to yield sexual favors to

her master, but only sparingly, in order to squeeze money out of him—"five guineas for handling your breast is a cheap pennyworth, although you seem to resist with all your might." In the unlucky event that she gets pregnant, however, "you must take up with the chaplain," who might perhaps be lured into marriage.[25]

This ability to ventriloquize would provide the basis for some of Swift's greatest satires. "Swift seems," Scott said admiringly, "like the Persian dervish, to have possessed the faculty of transfusing his own soul into the body of anyone whom he selected—of seeing with his eyes, employing every organ of his sense, and even becoming master of the powers of his judgment."[26]

In London a couple of years later, Swift used this ability to play a practical joke on Lady Berkeley. She often asked him to read aloud from Robert Boyle's *Occasional Reflections upon Several Subjects*, a compendium of trite moralizing. Craik calls the *Occasional Reflections* a "pious sedative" for Lady Berkeley, and Swift quickly got sick of them. Boyle is known today as the great chemist for whom Boyle's Law is named, but in this work his theme was that ordinary sights could inspire "pious reflections, devout soliloquies, ardent ejaculations, and other mental entertainments of a religious soul." A typical homily is based on "killing a crow (out of a window) in a hog's trough, and immediately tracing the ensuing reflection with a pen made of one of his quills." Boyle solemnly explains, "This method is not unusual to divine justice towards brawny and incorrigible sinners, whose souls, no less black than this inauspicious bird's feathers, do wear already the livery of the Prince of Darkness, and with greediness do the works of it, whose delights are furnished (as the feasts of crows are by carrion) by their own filthy lusts."[27]

When Lady Berkeley called for the *Occasional Reflections* one day, Swift was ready. He solemnly announced that the next piece was called *A Meditation on a Broomstick*. "Bless me!" Lady Berkeley exclaimed, "what a strange subject! But there is no knowing what useful lessons of instruction this wonderful man may draw from things apparently the most trivial. Pray let us hear what he says upon it." Swift then read a parody he had hidden in the volume, in which human beings are compared to brooms in absurdly inventive ways. The prank was exposed only when Lady Berkeley mentioned to some visitors that it was an especially fine piece, and when they opened the book the paper in Swift's handwriting fell out. "A general burst of laughter ensued," Sheridan says, "and my Lady, when the first surprise was over, enjoyed the joke as much as any of them, saying, 'What a vile trick has that rogue played me! But it is his way, he never balks his humor in anything.'"[28]

Swift's parody is doubly interesting, because characteristically he could be mocking and serious at the same time. "Surely mortal man is a broomstick," his fake meditation proposes. The once-clean twigs of a tree are "handled by every dirty wench, condemned to do her drudgery, and by a capricious kind of fate, destined to make other things clean and be nasty itself." But as the comparison proceeds, Swift virtually describes the kind of satirist he would soon become: "A broomstick, perhaps you will say, is an emblem of a tree standing on its head; and pray what is a man but a topsy-turvy creature? his animal faculties perpetually mounted on his rational, his head where his heels should be, groveling on the earth. And yet, with all his faults, he sets up to be a universal reformer and corrector of abuses; a remover of grievances; rakes into every slut's corner of Nature, bringing hidden corruptions to the light, and raiseth a mighty dust where there was none before; sharing deeply all the while in the very same pollutions he pretends to sweep away."[29] There is much self-knowledge, and even wisdom, in that practical joke.

THE RETURN OF STELLA

After less than a year King William became disenchanted with Lord Berkeley, who may indeed have been as lazy as Swift said he was, and recalled him to England in April 1701. Swift traveled there in the Berkeley party, stopped off at Leicester to visit his mother, and then proceeded to London. And now something of great personal significance happened: he was reunited with Stella. She may have been living at the Temples' house in Sheen, since her mother continued to work there for Lady Giffard, or she may have been with Rebecca Dingley in Farnham.[30] At any rate, she and Swift evidently reached an understanding. In September he returned to Dublin, working now for a new lord lieutenant, the Earl of Rochester. By then, Stella and Rebecca were already living there.

The sole information we have about this remarkable development is in the account that Swift wrote down on the evening of Stella's death:

She lived generally in the country, with a family, where she contracted an intimate friendship with another lady of more advanced years [Rebecca]. I was then (to my mortification) settled in Ireland; and about a year after, going to visit my friends in England, I found she was a little uneasy upon the death of a person on whom she had some dependence. Her fortune, at that time, was in all not above fifteen hundred pounds, the interest of which was but a scanty maintenance, in so dear a country, for one of her spirit. Upon this consideration, and indeed very much for my own satisfaction, who had few friends or acquaintance in Ireland, I prevailed with her and her dear friend and companion, the other lady, to draw what money they had into Ireland, a great part of their fortune being in annuities upon funds. Money was then at ten per cent in Ireland, besides the advantage of turning it and all necessaries of life at half the price. They complied with my advice, and soon after came over.[31]

Why is Sir William Temple mentioned only vaguely as "a person on whom she had some dependence"? Why was she still uneasy about his death after two years had gone by? Why is the "intimate friendship" with Rebecca Dingley given such emphasis? Perplexingly, Rebecca remains an altogether shadowy figure, even though she and Stella were together from this moment on.

Most significant of all, why does Swift place such stress on finances, and mention only casually that Stella's presence in Dublin was "very much for my own satisfaction"? She had just turned twenty that March, and he was thirty-three. He goes on to say that in Dublin "her person was soon distinguished," which must refer to her good looks. And then he acknowledges, though only to dismiss them, the obvious suspicions that arose: "The adventure looked so like a frolic, the censure held for some time as if there were a secret history in such a removal; which, however, soon blew off by her excellent conduct."[32]

It was indeed true that the cost of living was higher in England than in Ireland, where, as Swift told English friends much later, you could still get a sedan chair for sixpence instead of 12, and a chicken for 7 pence instead of 18.[33] But Stella had never seen Ireland in her life; was this really sufficient inducement to go and settle there? Whatever Swift might say, suspicions about a romantic relationship by no means "soon blew off." But it remains true, as a leading specialist says, that we know "next to nothing" about Hester Johnson—her parentage, her move to Ireland, and above all, the hidden aspects of her relationship with Swift.[34]

One thing we do know. During the next few years, many people took it for granted that Swift and Stella were planning to marry. In 1707 his cousin Thomas Swift asked their uncle Deane "whether Jonathan be married? or whether he has been able to resist the charms of both those gentlewomen that marched quite from Moor Park to Dublin (as they would have marched to the north or anywhere else) with full resolution to engage him?"[35]

And what of the shadowy Rebecca, joined with Stella in Thomas Swift's jocular remark about "the charms of both those gentlewomen"? She was related to the Temple family, her grandmother having been a sister of Temple's mother, and no doubt that is why she was taken in at Moor Park. The only descriptions we have of her come from people who knew her much later, and they say nothing about charm; the younger Deane Swift heard that she was "by all accounts a very insipid companion." Some later poems by Swift suggest a fussy scatterbrain, but if he showed them to Rebecca herself, he may have been only teasing her. At the time of the move she was at least thirty-five, perhaps forty, and thus roughly twice Stella's age. Supposedly, but unprovably, Stella and Swift were never alone together, and Rebecca served as a convenient chaperone.[36]

We know also that Swift gave Stella and Rebecca an annual allowance of £50 each as well as advising them on investing their modest holdings. Tactfully, he pretended that Rebecca's allowance likewise came from investments that he was managing on her behalf. For Rebecca the move to Ireland must have been a welcome solution to her predicament. She didn't have enough money to live on by herself, and in that world, as a historian notes, "independence was a pipe dream for most spinsters."[37]

One incident from these first Dublin years left a paper trail, though its implications are ambiguous. In 1703, when Swift was in London and Stella was still in Dublin, he had been corresponding with a clergyman friend of theirs, William Tisdall. Perhaps Tisdall was sometimes a victim of Stella's sharp tongue, for Swift offered this suggestion: "I'll teach you a new way to outwit Mrs. Johnson. It is a new-fashioned way of being witty, and they call it a bite. You must ask a bantering question, or tell some damned lie in a serious manner, and then she will answer or speak as if you were in earnest; then cry you, 'Madam, there's a bite.' I would not have you undervalue this, for it is the constant amusement in Court, and everywhere else among the great people."[38]

In his next letter Swift acknowledged Tisdall's intimacy with Stella and Rebecca, hinted that he might be jealous, and made an uncharacteristic obscene innuendo: "You seem to be mighty proud (as you have reason, if it be true) of the part you have in the ladies' good graces, especially of her you call the *Party*. I am very much concerned to know it; but since it is an evil I cannot remedy, I will tell you a story. A cast [cast-off] mistress went to her rival, and expostulated with her for robbing her of her lover. After a long quarrel, finding no good to be done, 'Well,' says the abdicated lady, 'keep him, and

stop him in your ar[se].' 'No,' says t'other, 'that won't be altogether so convenient; however, to oblige you, I'll do something that's very near it.'" There was
also some condescending advice concerning Tisdall's thoughts of becoming a
writer: "I look upon you as under a terrible mistake, if you imagine you cannot be enough distinguished without writing for the public. Preach, preach,
preach, preach, preach, preach—that is certainly your talent."[39]

A month or so after receiving this last advice, Tisdall made a remarkable
request. His letter has not been preserved, but Swift's reply makes clear what
it said. Tisdall demanded to know what Swift's own intentions were toward
Stella. If he did not plan to marry her himself, then Tisdall hoped that he
would act as a go-between in asking her mother for her hand on Tisdall's behalf. What we do have is Swift's reply, which seems both reasonable and generous. As with Varina, he lays emphasis on having enough money for marriage,
which Tisdall does have. But he also indicates that his "humour," defined by
Johnson as "general turn or temper of mind," does not incline him to marry.

> I think I have said to you before that if my fortunes and humour
> served me to think of that state, I should certainly, among all persons
> on earth, make your choice, because I never saw that person whose
> conversation I entirely valued but hers. This was the utmost I ever gave
> way to. And secondly, I must assure you sincerely that this regard of
> mine never once entered into my head to be an impediment to you;
> but I judged it would, perhaps, be a clog to your rising in the world,
> and I did not conceive you were then rich enough to make yourself
> and her happy and easy. . . . I told the mother immediately, and spoke
> with all the advantages you deserve. But the objection of your fortune
> being removed, I declare I have no other; nor shall any consideration
> of my own misfortune in losing so good a friend and companion as
> her prevail on me against her interest and settlement in the world. . . .
> I have always described her to you in a manner different from those
> who would be discouraging; and must add that though it hath come
> in my way to converse with persons of the first rank, and of that sex,
> more than is usual to men of my level and of our function [that is,
> clergymen], yet I have nowhere met with a humour, a wit, or conversa-
> tion so agreeable, a better portion of good sense, or a truer judgment
> of men and things."[40]

Stella turned Tisdall down, and there is no way to know why. Deane Swift
and Sheridan suspected that she had encouraged him only as a way of provok-

ing a commitment from Swift. But they were writing fifty and eighty years later, respectively, and that can only be guesswork. Maybe she just wasn't attracted to Tisdall. As for Swift's position, it is hard to agree with Ehrenpreis that he felt "elementary panic" at the thought of losing "a dependent, compliant confidant, part daughter, part pupil, part mistress." The most we can say for certain is that Swift acknowledged it would be painful for him to see less of Stella. It is sometimes claimed that from then on he nursed cold contempt for Tisdall, but that is based on a single offhand remark he made nine years later: "Do his feet stink still?"[41] Swift was always hypersensitive to smells.

Some biographers have imagined Stella as a fragile, dependent creature, but a story Swift told about these early Dublin years suggests a very different character. In the memoir written immediately after her death, he described her remarkable behavior in a crisis:

> With all the softness of temper that became a lady, she had the personal courage of a hero. She and her friend having removed their lodgings to a new house which stood solitary, a parcel of rogues, armed, attempted the house, where there was only one boy. She was then about four and twenty. And having been warned to apprehend some such attempt, she learned the management of a pistol; and the other women and servants being half dead with fear, she stole softly to her dining room window, put on a black hood to avoid being seen, primed the pistol fresh, gently lifted up the sash, and taking aim with the utmost presence of mind, discharged the pistol loaden with the bullets into the body of one villain, who stood the fairest mark. The fellow, mortally wounded, was carried off by the rest and died the next morning, but his companions could not be found. The Duke of Ormonde hath often drank her health to me upon that account, and had always an high esteem of her.[42]

John Geree, the English clergyman friend who had known Stella at Moor Park, added a few details that he must have heard from Swift himself. The gang's interest had been aroused by Stella's elegant lifestyle, which gave rise to rumors that she must have a lot of money and jewels. She stayed up unusually late that night reading, and therefore wasn't asleep as the thieves expected. And the thief she shot was on a ladder at the time, from which he fell to the ground.[43]

Swift was always critical of conventional female timorousness. In *A Letter to a Young Lady, on Her Marriage* he commented, exactly as the feminist

Mary Wollstonecraft later would, "There should seem to be something very capricious, that when women profess their admiration for a colonel or a captain on account of his valour, they should fancy it a very graceful, becoming quality in themselves to be afraid of their own shadows; to scream in a barge when the weather is calmest, or in a coach at the ring; to run from a cow at an hundred yards distance; to fall into fits at the sight of a spider, an earwig, or a frog." Stella was admirable for being altogether different:

> For Stella never learned the art
> At proper times to scream and start,
> Nor calls up all the house at night,
> And swears she saw a thing in white.[44]

It's notable that no mention is made in these accounts of trauma or remorse at having killed a man. And indeed in shooting him Stella was entirely within her rights, for as a legal manual stated, "Man's home or habitation is so far protected by the law that if any person attempts to break open a house in the nighttime, and shall be killed in such attempt, the slayer shall be acquitted and discharged."[45]

CHAPTER 6

London

BUILDING BOOM

Swift adored London, with its endless variety and turbulent energy. In 1700 it was the largest city in Europe, with a population of six hundred thousand. That was three times as many people as in Shakespeare's day, and one-tenth of all the inhabitants of England. The London Shakespeare had known, less than a century earlier, was gone. In the Great Fire of 1666, four-fifths of the city center had been demolished, including the medieval St. Paul's Cathedral. Its stones, the diarist John Evelyn said, "flew like grenados, the melting lead running down the streets in a stream, and the very pavements glowing with fiery redness."[1]

A year later, a poet captured the sense of astounding loss:

> The city now is the once-city's tomb,
> A skeleton of fleshless bones become.
> Its venerable ruins have the name
> Of what it *was*, but little else the same.[2]

An immense rebuilding campaign was soon under way, and continued for decades. Sir Christopher Wren's new St. Paul's wasn't finished until 1710, thirty-five years after construction began. Wren and others proposed razing the tortuous old streets and alleys, replacing them with broad avenues on the

24. St. Paul's Cathedral in 1695. The upper sections, including
the great dome, are yet to be constructed.

continental model, but those plans were defeated by legal wrangling over
property boundaries. In the end, new houses occupied pretty much the same
spaces as the old. To the west of the burned zone, however, there were still
empty fields, and development went forward energetically. All the time that
Swift was in London, new buildings were going up and elegant squares taking shape.

London was divided into three regions. To the west, Westminster was the
site of the court, once dominant but now yielding to the financial "City" to
the east. In between was the sophisticated "polite" world, commonly referred
to as "the Town."[3] Swift lived in various lodgings in that zone.

The 1695 map shown here (figure 25) is full of interest. Some familiar land-
marks were already in existence (though not identified on this map), such as
the Tower of London and St. Paul's. Westminster, with its abbey and Houses
of Parliament, was separated from the rest of the city by open fields. Names
that today identify stations on the Underground—Earls Court, Kensington,
Knightsbridge, Paddington, Marylebone, Tottenham Court—appear on the
map as isolated villages. Shepherds still tended sheep at Shepherds Bush,
and people still gathered nuts on Notting Hill ("Noding Hill" on the map).
Hampstead, with its hill and heath, lay far off to the north, and Chelsea, from

25. Part of Middlesex County, 1695.

which Swift would later walk through the fields into London, was a hamlet to the west.

The spaces between the outlying towns were being rapidly filled in. "We see several villages," Defoe wrote in 1724, "formerly standing as it were in the country and at a great distance, now joined to the streets by continued buildings, and more making haste to meet in the like manner." But the countryside was still close by, and as Macaulay says, "He who then rambled to what is now the gayest and most crowded part of Regent Street found himself in a solitude, and was sometimes so fortunate as to have a shot at a woodcock."[4]

London Bridge, lined on both sides with houses and shops, was the only bridge over the Thames. To cross the river elsewhere, people hired watermen with rowboats. Sailing ships came right up to the city, docking below the bridge because the spaces between its piers were low and narrow. Small boats

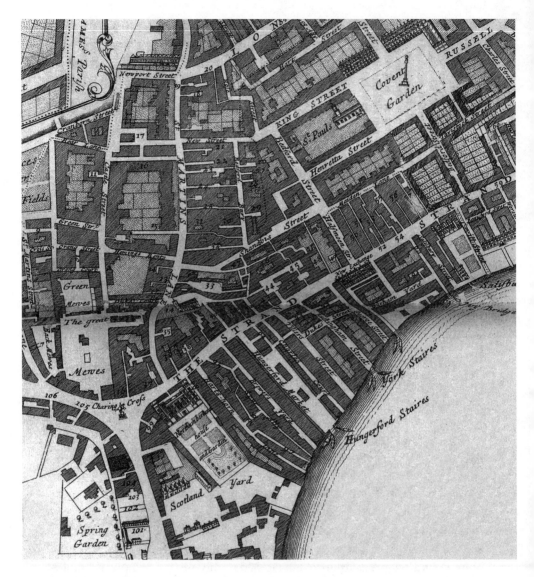

26. Part of central London, 1720.

could get through, but that was perilous, since the current narrowed and speeded up. You could drown there. Swift had learned to swim at Kilkenny, but at the time few people knew how.

Detailed city maps began to be produced, but were often unreliable, and even with a map it was hard to find your way, since houses weren't numbered and there were no street signs. Even if there had been signs, you would still need local knowledge—there were no fewer than fourteen King Streets scattered all over the city, and you would have to explain that you meant King Street near St. Anne's Church, or King Street in Covent Garden, or King Street by Bloomsbury Square, or one of the eleven other King Streets. Only hackney coachmen, like taxi drivers today, really knew their way around.[5]

A 1720 map of St. James's parish shows a section of London that Swift knew well, and would recognize immediately if he could see it today (figure 26). Covent Garden, Charing Cross, and Scotland Yard are all shown. But there have been plenty of changes as well. There was a market then at Covent Garden, but not the neoclassical arcades that went up in 1830; there was a Piccadilly, but no Piccadilly Circus. And facing St. Martin's in the Fields were stables called "the Great Mews," on the site now occupied by the National Gallery and Trafalgar Square.

Street names often embody associations that are now forgotten. Piccadilly was named for Elizabethan ruffs called pickadillies that were once sold there. Rotten Row alongside Hyde Park was more recent, created during Swift's time by King William III. It was originally known as the Route du Roi, the king's road. Naturally enough, street names often denoted trades practiced there. Another section of the 1720 map shows a Love Lane, which was a euphemistic revision of the original Gropecunt Lane.[6]

STREET LIFE

London was alive with bustle and noise. "The full tide of human existence," Johnson later said, "is at Charing Cross." On another occasion he could have been speaking for Swift: "You find no man, at all intellectual, who is willing to leave London. No, Sir, when a man is tired of London, he is tired of life; for there is in London all that life can afford." In 1729 a writer tried to reduce the teeming goings-on to alphabetical order and came up with thirty-seven entries for just the letter A, including Accidents, Accusations, Adulteries, Affidavits, Affronts, Aggravations, Agonies, Alarms, Allurements, Amours, Animosities, and Assignations.[7]

If London was exciting, it was also intimidating. Anyone who may feel nostalgic about town houses filled with Queen Anne furniture should note a historian's description: "There was an edge to life in the eighteenth-century which is hard for us to recapture. In every class there is the same taut neurotic quality—the fantastic gambling and drinking, the riots, brutality and violence, and everywhere and always a constant sense of death." A recent book provides a needed breath of bad air: *Hubbub: Filth, Noise and Stench in England, 1600–1770*.[8]

Street life was aggressive. Carts and wagons were dangerous, herds of livestock pushed past pedestrians, and since there were no sidewalks, it was impossible to avoid the traffic and the dirt. That was why bullies went close to the walls of buildings while everyone else had to give way. Johnson recalled his mother's account of London back in Swift's day: "There were two sets of people, those who gave the wall and those who took it, the peaceable and the quarrelsome. When I returned to Lichfield after having been in London, my mother asked me whether I was one of those who gave the wall, or those who took it."[9]

These aspects of experience are captured by the artist Swift called "humorous Hogart" ("Thou, I hear, a pleasant rogue art").[10] Among other things, Hogarth's engraving *The Second Stage of Cruelty* is a reminder that the streets were crowded with animals. A horse has stumbled, overturning the coach it was pulling, and a group of lawyers is trying to emerge. Even though the

27. William Hogarth,
*The Second Stage of
Cruelty* (1751).

horse's foreleg is broken, the coachman is flogging it. In the foreground a flock of sheep is being driven to market, and the owner is brutally beating one that has collapsed. Just beyond him, a small boy is being crushed by a heavy wagon whose driver has dozed off, oblivious to the beer gushing from an open barrel. In the middle distance, a donkey is struggling to carry a huge load and two men as well. Further away, a dog is baiting a bull, abetted by an excited crowd, and the bull has just tossed a boy into the air. The only sympathetic figure is the man by the horse's head, taking down the number of the coach so he can report the abusive coachman.

There was a good deal of crime; the city offered anonymity and many places to hide. Forty years after Swift was there, Henry Fielding, writing in his capacity as a magistrate, called London "a vast wood or forest, in which a thief may harbor with as great security as wild beasts do in the deserts of Africa or Arabia." But it is easy to exaggerate the element of threat. So far as we know Swift was never robbed, and he always went about on foot. He loved walking, and it saved money, since coaches and sedan chairs were expensive (a shilling an hour for an enclosed chair carried by two men).[11]

Swift was captivated by the human comedy in the streets; he said that a display at Charing Cross "where painted monsters are hung out" held him "fastened by the eyes." He also had a fine ear for the way people talked. "A mountebank in Leicester Fields had drawn a huge assembly about him. Among the rest, a fat unwieldy fellow, half stifled in the press, would be every fit [repeatedly] crying out, 'Lord! what a filthy crowd is here! Pray, good people, give way a little. Bless me! what a devil has raked this rabble together? Zounds, what squeezing is this! Honest friend, remove your elbow.'"[12]

On one occasion Swift was impressed by a diorama on rollers that scrolled through a wide landscape, though he claimed to be ashamed of bothering with it: "I went to see a famous moving picture, and I never saw anything so pretty. You see a sea ten miles wide, a town on t'other end, and ships sailing in the sea and discharging their cannon. You see a great sky with moon and stars etc. I'm a fool." Buried in Swift's account books is an entry showing that he paid 1 shilling, 4 pence to view "dwarfs." Some of these sights perhaps suggested elements of *Gulliver's Travels:* in addition to dwarves, there were giants, performing animals, miniature buildings, and clockwork automata. When the giant king of Brobdingnag "saw me walk erect, before I began to speak, [he] conceived I might be a piece of clockwork."[13]

All his life Swift had a low threshold of disgust, and despite his fascination with city life, there was plenty to be disgusted by. London stank. A poem by

his friend John Gay, *Trivia; or, The Art of Walking the Streets of London*, is full
of revolting smells. Walking the streets, one might manage to keep one's feet
out of the mud mixed with excrement, but there was no escaping the smell of
fat and "train oil" (from whale blubber) being rendered for candles, or rotting
meat and fish on open stalls.

> Here steams ascend
> That, in mixed fumes, the wrinkled nose offend.
> Where chandlers cauldrons boil, where fishy prey
> Hide the wet stall, long absent from the sea;
> And where the cleaver chops the heifer's spoil,
> And where huge hogsheads sweat with trainy oil,
> Thy breathing nostril hold.[14]

Chamber pots were supposed to be emptied into the carts of "night soil
men," but often they were just dumped in the street. A privy was known as
the "house of office," or sometimes the "house of ease," after the French *lieu
d'aisance*—hence the modern British "loo." Pepys mentions an unpleasant
surprise when he went down to his cellar and "put my foot into a great heap
of turds, by which I find that Mr. Turner's house of office is full and comes
into my cellar, which doth trouble me." Worst of all was the appalling effluent
known as Fleet Ditch, an urban river that was effectively an open sewer that
flowed into the Thames. Defoe described it as "a nauseous and abominable
sink of public nastiness."[15]

URBAN ANTI-PASTORAL

During his London years Swift wrote two splendid anti-pastorals. In 1709
he published a little poem called *A Description of the Morning*, and his friend
Richard Steele commented accurately that "he has run into a way perfectly
new, and described things exactly as they happen." The poem is a succession
of snapshots of a city waking up:

> Now hardly here and there an hackney coach
> Appearing, showed the ruddy morn's approach.
> Now Betty from her master's bed had flown,
> And softly stole to discompose her own.
> The slipshod prentice from his master's door

Had pared the dirt, and sprinkled round the floor.
Now Moll had whirled her mop with dext'rous airs,
Prepared to scrub the entry and the stairs.

There's tongue-in-cheek irony as the housemaid Betty rumples her bed to make it look slept in, an allusion to Aurora, goddess of dawn, who blushes emerging from the sea where she's been with her lover. Swift is remembering Dryden's translation of Virgil: "Now rose the ruddy morn from Tithon's bed."[16]

The hackneys were ubiquitous, the equivalent of modern taxis; eight hundred of them plied the narrow streets. Paving stones were bumpy and the coaches had stiff suspensions; a German visitor complained that they "jolt most terribly." Pepys, forty years earlier, was more explicit, coming home in pain "from my riding a little uneasily tonight (for my testicles) in the coach."[17]

There was no provision for street cleaning, so each householder had to clear the area directly in front of his door, moving the dirt out into the traffic. Sprinkling helped to keep the dust down. As daylight broadens, noise increases:

The small-coal man was heard with cadence deep,
Till drowned in shriller notes of "Chimney sweep;"
Duns at his Lordship's gate began to meet,
And brickdust Moll had screamed through half the street.

Chimney sweeps were shrill because they were young boys, the only people small enough to clamber through narrow, winding chimneys. Hawkers needed to be loud, to be heard over the racket of wheels on cobblestones and pigs grunting and squealing. Pigs were welcome since they devoured street garbage, but they inspired a saying, "He that loves noise must buy a pig."[18]

In Swift's mock pastoral, the hawkers' cries are an equivalent to rural birdsong. A foreign visitor commented, "The curious tones that they call or sing can be freakishly imitated on the violin." Joseph Addison wrote a playful essay about their musical qualities—"Nor can I forbear being inspired with a most agreeable melancholy, when I hear that sad and solemn air with which the public is often asked if they have any chairs to mend."[19]

Swift didn't always appreciate the cries. A couple of years after this poem, he wrote to Stella, "Here is a restless dog crying 'Cabbages' and 'Savoys' plagues me every morning about this time, he is now at it, I wish his largest cabbage was sticking in his throat." (The Savoy, still eaten today, was a

Four for Six pence Mackrell
Maquereux quatre pour SixSols
Quatre Sgombri ß sei Soldi
Mauron delin: F.Tempest exc:
                                  Cum Privilegij:

28. Mackerel seller. She is slightly better off than the desperately poor, but still living hand to mouth, with shabby clothes that have been mended repeatedly.

particularly good kind of cabbage.) At other times it amused him to put the cries into verse, extolling, for instance, the aphrodisiac property of oysters:

> Charming oysters I cry,
> My masters, come buy;
> So plump and so fresh,
> So sweet is their flesh,
> No Colchester oyster
> Is sweeter and moister;
> Your stomach they settle,
> And rouse up your mettle,
> They'll make you a dad
> Of a lass or a lad.[20]

The "small coal" that Swift mentions in *A Description of the Morning*, cheap because it came in little scraps, had become the principal fuel in London. A foreign visitor admired St. Paul's but regretted that only thirteen years after it was inaugurated "it is already so black with coal smoke that it has lost half its elegance." Decades earlier, John Evelyn was already complaining of "pernicious smoke, superinducing a sooty crust or fur upon all that it lights, and corroding the very iron bars and hardest stone with those piercing and acrimonious spirits which accompany its sulfur."[21] The duns in Swift's poem are hanging about in hopes of getting a nobleman to pay his debts, notoriously difficult to do. As for what "brickdust Moll" had for sale, no one has been able to figure out what that was for.

The poem ends with three more urban types, described with similar clarity:

> The turnkey now his flock returning sees,
> Duly let out a-nights to steal for fees.
> The watchful bailiffs take their silent stands,
> And schoolboys lag with satchels in their hands.[22]

In the world of pastoral, a shepherd would be sending out his flock to graze; the jailer's flock is just coming home from a different kind of grazing. The prisoners would pay him for privileges in jail, and he would let them out at night to get hold of the money. The bailiffs know this, of course, and are waiting to intercept them and get a piece of the action. Meanwhile, living in a different time frame, the schoolboys are as reluctant as at any other period in history.

Swift's London was boisterous and noisy, but he never described the seamier regions, as an irrepressible journalist named Ned Ward did in *The London Spy*: "By this time we were come to Billingsgate, and in a narrow lane, as dark as a burying-vault, which stunk of stale sprats, piss and sirreverence [excrement], we groped about like a couple of thieves in a coal-hole. . . . At last we stumbled upon the threshold of a gloomy cavern where, at a distance, we saw lights burning like candles in a haunted cave where ghosts and goblins keep their midnight revels." An inebriated woman asks him to join her for a drink, and when he cheerfully agrees, she exclaims, "Why, then, here's a health to mine arse, and a fart for those that owe no money!" Ward relished the argot of the streets: a "bumsitter" was a prostitute, a "deadmonger" an undertaker, a "fuddle-cup" a drunk, and a "Posture Moll" a prostitute specializing in flagellation.[23]

Swift did comment on the dirt and garbage. His other London poem is called *A Description of a City Shower*, a takeoff on Virgil's *Georgics* in which farmers read nature's warning signs to know when a storm is brewing. In Swift's version,

> Careful observers may foretell the hour
> (By sure prognostics) when to dread a shower:
> While rain depends, the pensive cat gives o'er
> Her frolics, and pursues her tail no more.
> Returning home at night, you'll find the sink
> Strike your offended sense with double stink.

Citing Swift's line as an illustration, Johnson defines "sink" as "a drain; a jakes." Swift wrote to Stella when he was working on this poem, "I'll give ten shillings a week for my lodging, for I am almost stunk out of this [one] with the sink, and it helps me to verses in my *Shower*."[24]

The poem ends with a revolting glimpse of Fleet Ditch:

> Filth of all hues and odours seem to tell
> What street they sailed from, by their sight and smell. . . .
> Sweepings from butcher's stalls, dung, guts, and blood,
> Drowned puppies, stinking sprats, all drenched in mud,
> Dead cats and turnip-tops come tumbling down the flood.

Swift wasn't making this up: there were prosecutions for creating a "nuisance" by throwing animal viscera, blood, and excrement into the street.[25] The sights and smells are horrible, but the poem is fresh. Readers were bored with rural idealization, and Swift's two *Descriptions* were hugely popular.

Over the years from 1702 to 1714, Swift would spend about a third of his time in London, with repeated trips back and forth to Ireland.[26] He longed to live in London permanently, and for a time, as he became an important player in public affairs, he had good reason to believe that this dream would be realized. But it was not to be, and it isn't Swift the Londoner that posterity remembers, but Swift the Dubliner.

CHAPTER 7

"A Very Positive Young Man"

In 1701 Swift was thirty-four years old, stalled in his career, and utterly unknown to the public. That was about to change.

Working for the new lord lieutenant, the Earl of Rochester, Swift repeatedly accompanied his employer from Ireland to England and back again. He also spent time with the Berkeley family in London and with other friends. But we know next to nothing about his life at this time; no letters have survived from the middle of 1700 to the end of 1703. What we do know is that he became deeply interested in English politics. This was by no means unusual for a churchman, since the established Church was intimately bound up with the political system, and since all bishops sat in the House of Lords.

The details of political infighting in these years are bewilderingly complex, but the basic issues are clear. One was the problem of royal succession, for in 1700 the only child of Princess Anne died at the age of eleven, which meant a possible opening for the exiled Stuarts to reclaim the throne. To forestall that possibility, an Act of Settlement was passed in 1701, affirming that no Catholic could ever reign. Anne duly became queen in 1702, when King William died at the age of fifty-one after falling from his horse. The Act of Settlement specified that next in line after Anne would be the aged Electress Sophia of Hanover, a granddaughter of James I, "and the heirs of her body being Protestants."[1] As it happened, the electress would die in 1714, two months before Anne, and the lucky heir of her body would become King George I.

His descendants later adopted the name Windsor and are still on the British throne.

The succession was thus settled, but controversy was not. The exiled James II died in 1701, and there were still a large number of Jacobites (from Jacobus, the Latin form of James) who insisted that his son, known as the Pretender, was rightfully James III. In addition to drinking enthusiastic toasts to "the king over the water," they added a toast to "the little gentleman in the velvet coat," the mole whose hole had tripped up King William's horse.[2] Not until 1745 would attempts at a Jacobite rebellion come to an end. Theirs was a lost cause, but in 1702 no one could be sure of that. Flirtation with the Pretender would one day wreck the careers of some of Swift's closest associates, and he himself would fall under grave suspicion.

Beyond the dynastic question, the political system itself was far from stable. The Revolution of 1688 was a recent memory, and with the Pretender hoping to return, a new civil war seemed all too possible. Meanwhile the modern party system was coming into being, together with the names Whig and Tory. Like so many terms that describe groups—Quaker and Methodist, for example—they were originally derogatory. The Whig name came from Scottish Presbyterian rebels in 1648 (a "whiggamore" was a Scottish horse driver), and the Tory name from Irish Catholics whose rebellion was put down in 1641.

In many ways the two parties did have their roots back in the civil wars. Whigs were heirs of the roundheads who deposed Charles I. They didn't want a Puritan theocracy ever again, but they did want Parliament to be clearly superior to the monarchy. They drew their strength from the Dissenters— non-Anglican Protestants—and from London merchants and financiers, many of whom were Dissenters themselves.

Tories were heirs of the cavaliers who fought for Charles I, and who welcomed his son joyously at the Restoration. Most of them no longer believed that kings had a divine right to do anything they pleased, but they did fervently support the monarchy. Their strength came from the country gentry who dominated provincial society, and from the clergy whose status and incomes were dependent on the established Church.

Many thoughtful individuals had opinions that overlapped with both parties. As a firm supporter of the "revolution principles" that had ejected James II, Swift agreed with the Whigs. As a firm supporter of the Church of England, he agreed with the Tories.

It would be a mistake to imagine that Whigs were progressive and Tories conservative. In important ways they were all conservative, although the term *conservatism* didn't yet exist. It was born in the reaction against the French Revolution at the end of the eighteenth century, as was the distinction between left wing and right wing. That was the seating arrangement of the French Chamber of Deputies, with the more radical members on the left.

Swift entered the political debate in 1701 with a sixty-page pamphlet written in excitement and haste. It was called *A Discourse of the Contests and Dissensions between the Nobles and the Commons in Athens and Rome, with the Consequences They Had upon Both Those States.* Today, it would strike any casual reader as a dry and detailed historical survey. What made it brilliant was that although England was barely mentioned in it, every ancient personality and controversy had a direct parallel in modern English history. Decoding the analogies was an enjoyable game, and more than that. For people brought up to admire the Greeks and Romans, it was like seeing ancient history come alive.[3]

The device of pretending to talk about the distant past had another advantage: it was an effective way to avoid prosecution. You could describe an outrageous tyrant in ancient Rome and count on readers to figure out which modern politician you had in mind; conversely, you could praise a noble figure from antiquity as a contrast to some despised contemporary. In 1695 the Licensing Act that required censorship before publication had been abolished, but that only meant that the authorities could no longer block a work from being published at all. Once it did come out, they could still prosecute the author and printer for blasphemy, libel, or sedition. This they frequently did, and throughout Swift's life he had to take great care to steer a course beyond the reach of the law.

The profound implications of the 1688 revolution were still being worked out. What kind of government was England going to have, and where did ultimate authority lie? Whigs and Tories were beginning to close ranks, and the Tories, who were currently in the minority in Parliament, saw their chance to exploit tectonic shifts taking place at the time in the geopolitics of Europe.

The all but insoluble problem was Spain. When the sickly and practically imbecilic Carlos II, with no son of his own, finally got around to dying, who would succeed him? That person would rule not only Spain and its empire, but far-flung regions of Europe as well. Large parts of Italy were under Spanish rule, as was a section of the Low Countries known as the Spanish Netherlands. At this critical moment, due to interlocking dynastic marriages, the apparent heir to the Spanish throne had a plausible claim to both the king-dom of France and the Habsburg Empire. It was to block Louis XIV's plan to rule the world that William III negotiated, behind the scenes, a Partition Treaty that would make sure the Bourbons of France would never occupy the throne of Spain.

In 1700 Carlos finally did die, after thirty-five hapless years on the throne, and a full-blown crisis was at hand. Louis XIV prepared to make his bid to control Spain. The result would be the War of the Spanish Succession, which would dominate English politics for the next decade, and ultimately make England a world power. But at this moment no one had any idea what the future would hold.

A governing alliance of five Whig peers, known as the Junto from the Spanish *junta*, had negotiated the Partition Treaty in secret. That was per-fectly legal, but the Tories argued that it was against the best interests of a nation that was sick of fighting on the Continent. In 1701 they managed to impeach the Whig peers, and they asked the king to dismiss them from his cabinet. Thus the crucial question of 1688 came to the foreground: was the House of Commons now the supreme power in the land?

In the long run Swift would be more Tory than Whig, but in this crisis he was on the Whig side. Many Tories were Jacobite sympathizers, and no Irish Protestant, in a land with a huge Catholic majority, was likely to risk the re-turn of the Stuart monarchy. Swift even had a chance to explain this to King William himself: "I told the King that the highest Tories we had with us [in Ireland] would make tolerable Whigs there."[4] It was Swift's firm belief that a nation should preserve an equal balance among the three forces of monarch, nobles, and commons, and it appeared that the House of Commons was de-termined to upset the balance.

The theme in Swift's *Contests and Dissensions*, therefore, was the disasters that ensued in ancient times when political leaders were imprisoned or os-tracized—an obvious parallel to the current impeachment of the king's min-isters. A tyranny by the people, he thought, was even worse than a tyranny by oligarchy or monarchy, because someone would be sure to seize executive power and become a dictator. It happened with Julius Caesar, it happened with Oliver Cromwell, and it could well happen again.

In those days hardly anyone argued for total democracy, and Swift be-lieved as others did that the people were all too easily led. They were like sheep, he said in the *Contests and Dissensions*, so that "whoever is so bold [as] to give the first great leap over the heads of those about him (although he be the worst of the flock) shall be quickly followed by the rest." In an even more contemptuous analogy, they were mindless silkworms, exploited by "some single tyrant, whose state and power they advance to their own ruin, with as blind an instinct as those worms that die with weaving magnificent habits for beings of a superior nature to their own."[5]

Like most of what Swift would go on to write, this pamphlet was a direct response to current events, and was intended to influence them. After the *Contests and Dissensions* came out, he boasted that it was "greedily bought and read," and he believed that it was partly due to his arguments that the House of Lords threw out the impeachment. And he had the satisfaction of hearing it praised by people who had no idea who wrote it. According to Johnson, a bishop declared in Swift's presence that the author could only be Gilbert Burnet, the distinguished bishop of Salisbury. "When he seemed to doubt Burnet's right to the work," Johnson says, "he was told by the bishop that he was 'a young man,' and still persisting to doubt, that he was 'a very positive young man.'"[6]

Deane Swift had a different and more elaborate version of the story, in which Swift had to listen to a pompous old man tell him that he knew nothing about style. Bishop William Sheridan (not related to Swift's friend of that name) encountered Swift at the Dublin house of his favorite uncle, William Swift. This version is plausible, since Swift never forgot insults and put-downs:

> "I can assure your Lordship," replied the Doctor [Swift], "Bishop Burnet was not the author of it." "Not the author of it?" said the bishop. "Pray, sir, give me your reason for thinking so." "Because, my Lord, that discourse is not written in the bishop's style." "Not in the bishop's style!" replied old Sheridan, with some degree of contempt. "No, my Lord, the style of that pamphlet is, I think, wholly different from the style of the bishop." "Oh, Mr. Swift," replied Sheridan, "I have had a long acquaintance with your uncles, and an old friendship for all your family, and really I have a great regard for you in particular. However, let me assure you notwithstanding that you are still a great deal too young to pronounce your judgment on the style of authors. If Bishop Burnet was not the author if it, pray, sir, let me know who it was that did write it." "Why, really, my Lord, I writ it myself."[7]

In Swift's later account, "the vanity of a young man prevailed with me to let myself be known for the author." It was more than vanity. This was his bid for recognition by the magnates who ruled England, and the gamble succeeded. "My Lords Somers and Halifax, as well as the bishop above mentioned [Bishop Burnet himself], desired my acquaintance, with great marks of esteem and professions of kindness; not to mention the Earl of Sunderland, who had been of my old acquaintance."[8]

Bishop Sheridan would have been even more surprised if he could have known this positive young man would be remembered as one of the greatest writers in the English language. Swift himself would probably have been surprised. His few attempts at poetry had fallen flat, and his energies now were dedicated to making a career in public life, with writing a useful tool to that end. But he did have one major work in preparation for the press, and it would change his life in more ways than one. Its brilliance was immediately recognized, but so was its potential subversion of the very religion he claimed to defend. In the long run it would prove to be an insuperable obstacle to the advancement he longed for.

CHAPTER 8

The Scandalous Tub

In May of 1704 a peculiar book was offered for sale. It was called *A Tale of a Tub*, a proverbial expression for a pointless cock-and-bull story, and it was a hodgepodge of religious allegory, learned parodies, and rambling digressions explicitly labeled "Digressions." The whole thing was a wild medley of sources and allusions, piled on with irreverent glee. The title page carried no author's name, and it wouldn't have meant much if it had. The only thing of any note that Swift had yet published was the *Discourse of the Contests and Dissensions in Athens and Greece*, and that was anonymous too.

Swift had been working on this book for years. The idea may have originated during his undergraduate days. A good deal of it was probably written at Kilroot, which would explain why it treats Dissenting Protestants with great rancor, and it was more or less finished at Moor Park in 1696. Why he waited so long to publish is unknown. It would undoubtedly have offended Sir William Temple, but he had been dead for five years when it finally appeared.

Actually, *A Tale of a Tub* is two different books scrambled together. One is a story about three brothers quarreling over their father's will, which represents the New Testament, with the brothers as three rival branches of Christendom. But the narrative is interrupted repeatedly by anarchic digressions that finally take over completely.

29. Frontispiece of *A Tale of a Tub*.

The frontispiece is a visual image of the metaphor that inspired the book's title. Thomas Hobbes's *Leviathan*, the grim might-makes-right treatise from the civil war period, was anathema in Swift's day, and he begins by recalling it.

Seamen have a custom, when they meet a whale, to fling him out an empty tub by way of amusement, to divert him from laying violent hands upon the ship. This parable was immediately mythologized: the whale was interpreted to be Hobbes's *Leviathan*, which tosses and plays with all other schemes of religion and government, whereof a great many are hollow, and dry, and empty, and noisy, and wooden, and given to rotation. . . . It was decreed that in order to prevent these Leviathans from tossing and sporting with the Commonwealth (which of itself is too apt to fluctuate), they should be diverted from that game by a *Tale of a Tub*.[1]

Swift loved to spin out analogies like these: schemes of religion and government are hollow, and wooden, and given to rotation. And he liked to make familiar clichés absurd. People lay violent hands, whales don't.

No one knew what to make of the *Tale of a Tub*, but everyone read it, and three more editions came out within a year. Seventy years later Samuel Johnson, whose opinion of Swift was unfavorable on the whole, said that the book was so good, someone else must have written it—"There is in it such a vigour of mind, such a swarm of thoughts, so much of nature, and art, and life." The political journalist William Cobbett, born in Farnham half a century after Swift left nearby Moor Park, related how as an eleven-year-old, the son of a gardener, he found his curiosity aroused by seeing the odd title *A Tale of a Tub* in a shop window. He gave his last 3 pence for a copy and sat down by a haystack to read it. "Though I could not understand some parts of it, it delighted me beyond description, and produced what I have always considered a sort of birth of intellect. I read on until it was dark, without any thought of supper or bed." Recently Harold Bloom, even though admitting that "I dislike this great book as much as I admire it," has called it "the most powerful prose work in the language."[2]

Swift was intensely proud of his achievement. During his declining years, when a relative read aloud from it, he exclaimed, "Good God! what a flow of imagination had I, when I wrote this!"[3] Anyone who dips into it will see the truth of that, but unlike *Gulliver's Travels*, published two decades later, it is heavy going for a modern reader. Two main points concern us here. One is the way the *Tale* revealed Swift's great gifts, hidden until then. The other is the way it seriously damaged his career.

In a defense later on, Swift emphasized that "there generally runs an irony through the thread of the whole book."[4] Irony can be simple when a speaker obviously means the opposite of what he's saying, but in this book it's seldom obvious. A Swiss reviewer commented perceptively, "An odd game goes on through the book, where we often do not know whether the author is making fun or not, nor of whom, nor what his intention is." Swift's ironies are maddeningly hard to pin down. Dr. Lyon remembered a wit calling him "the first left-handed genius in the world; this metaphor is taken from fencing, where a left-handed adversary makes the wickedest pass, and the most difficult to be parried."[5] Or as we might say today, the ball comes at you with an unfamiliar spin. The trickiness is all the more disconcerting because Swift often speaks ingratiatingly—"Hark in your ear"—and at the same time abuses the reader. Claude Rawson remarks "the note of quarrelsome intimacy that is the hallmark of Swift's satire."[6]

MODERNISM AND GRUB STREET

A Tale of a Tub, like *The Battle of the Books*, which was published in the same volume, jeers at modernism of every kind. (The first citation for the word *modernism* in the *Oxford English Dictionary* is from a letter by Swift, though he meant by that only faddish expressions, not a worldview.) "I claim an absolute authority in right," declares the mock author of the *Tale*, "as the freshest modern, which gives me a despotic power over all authors before me." Homer, he says, is grossly overrated, because we know so much that Homer didn't. "What can be more defective and unsatisfactory than his long dissertation upon tea?"[7] Obviously, Homer had never heard of tea.

Swift's models were Erasmus's *Praise of Folly*, Rabelais' *Gargantua and Pantagruel*, and the Greek satires of Lucian. Fielding saw the affinity: "To translate Lucian well into English is to give us another Swift in our own language." But Lucian is relaxed and genial, whereas Swift is challenging and intense. Rabelais isn't a close model either, though Pope said Swift was "a great reader and admirer of Rabelais," and imagined seeing him "laugh and shake in Rabelais' easy chair." Coleridge got it right, quoting Rabelais himself: "Swift was *anima Rabelaisii habitans in sicco*—the soul of Rabelais dwelling in a dry place."[8]

Among other things the *Tale* is a mock book, parodying the cut-and-paste quality of many productions of the day. It takes forever to get started. First there's a dedication to a politician, next a message from "the Bookseller," then a dedication to "Prince Posterity," then a "Preface," and at long last "Section I: The Introduction." In some ways the *Tale* anticipates postmodernism.[9]

One of Swift's targets is Grub Street, defined by Johnson as "originally the name of a street in Moorfields in London, much inhabited by writers of small histories, dictionaries, and temporary poems; whence any mean production is called *grubstreet*." Johnson's mention of dictionaries was no accident. When desperately poor, he had labored there himself.

These writers were a new type, dependent not on wealthy patrons but on publishers who were feeding the demand of a middle-class reading public. What kept them in poverty was not just the ephemeral nature of what they churned out—one of them compared his job to slaving in a coal mine, except that he got to work in daylight—but the nonexistence of royalties.[10] That concept did not exist. In 1710 a Copyright Act would finally protect publishers from having their books pirated, but it was still the publisher who owned a book outright. Only a really famous author could negotiate a good price, and no matter how well the book sold he would never get another penny.

Pope derided Grub Street "hacks" for their poverty, but Swift never did. Throughout his career he made constant use of this new publishing industry. He was a prolific writer of political pamphlets, and many of his poems also appeared first as single-page broadside sheets. What Swift did despise was mindless, formulaic writing with nothing to say. At the end of the *Tale* he imagines being reduced "to write upon nothing; when the subject is utterly exhausted, to let the pen still move on, by some called the ghost of wit, delighting to walk after the death of its body."[11]

Off and on, *Tale* mimics the ramblings of a bad writer, who introduces himself as a Grub Street regular: "The shrewdest pieces of this treatise were conceived in bed, in a garret; at other times (for a reason best known to myself) I thought fit to sharpen my invention with hunger; and in general, the whole work was begun, continued, and ended under a long course of physic, and a great want of money."[12] But the voice is always Swift's own, even when it's ironic and parodic. And the left-handed ironies allow him to suggest things that he would never dare to say straight out.

DEFENDING RELIGION OR SUBVERTING IT?

Swift disliked the whole tendency of modern thought, centering in the scientific program of the Royal Society that threatened to reduce all of life to a materialist explanation. But that wasn't what made the *Tale of a Tub* notorious—it was the allegorical story of the brothers and their father's will.

Since the brothers are triplets they ought to be equals, but competition soon breaks out. Peter, representing Roman Catholicism, brazenly claims that he is the eldest and has a right to be obeyed. Jack, named for John Calvin, fights back ferociously. Martin, recalling Martin Luther, is more temperate, and represents something like the Anglican middle way.

The allegory begins like a fairy tale. "Once upon a time, there was a man who had three sons by one wife, and all at a birth; neither could the midwife tell certainly which was the eldest. Their father died while they were young; and upon his deathbed, calling the lads to him, spoke thus: 'Sons, because I have purchased no estate, nor was born to any, I have long considered of some good legacies to bequeath you; and at last, with much care as well as expense, have provided each of you (here they are) a new coat.'"[13]

Peter smothers his coat in fancy decorations, symbolizing the worldly ostentation and doctrinal inventiveness of Catholicism, and then has to concoct far-fetched reinterpretations of the will, which stipulated that the coat must never be altered. He locks up the will so that his brothers can't see it, but they break open his strongbox and make copies for themselves (Protestant translations of the Bible, which the Catholic Church restricted to the Latin Vulgate). Jack, a Puritan determined to be as different from the Catholics as possible, rips the decorations off his own coat and leaves it in shreds. "Ah, good brother Martin," he pleads, "do as I do, for the love of God! Strip, tear, pull, rent, flay off all, that we may appear as unlike the rogue Peter as it is possible." The moderate Martin removes only such frills as he safely can, and refuses to damage his coat any further.[14]

What ignited criticism was not so much the story as the way Swift told it. "Everything spiritual and valuable," William Empson says with Swift in mind, "has a gross and revolting parody, very similar to it, with the same name. Only unremitting judgment can distinguish between them."[15] In his later satires Swift usually planted clues to guide that judgment, but in the *Tale of a Tub* the ironies keep turning inside out. Many readers felt that it wasn't just abuses in religion that were under attack, but religion itself. And when the author's identity became known, it was scandalous that such a subversive satire had been written by a clergyman.

Swift's fondness for making abstractions concrete led to serious problems. Why isn't it blasphemous to make the three brothers pleasure-seekers in modern London? "They writ, and raillied [exchanged witty repartee], and rhymed, and sung, and said, and said nothing; they drank, and fought, and whored, and slept, and swore, and took snuff; they went to new plays on the first night, haunted the chocolate-houses, beat the watch, lay on bulks, and got claps [beat night watchmen, slept on shop stalls, and caught venereal disease]; they bilked hackney coachmen, ran in debt with shopkeepers, and lay with their wives; they killed bailiffs, kicked fiddlers downstairs, ate at Locket's, loitered at Will's."[16] Locket's was a fashionable eating house at Charing Cross; Will's was the coffeehouse, favored by writers, where Dryden used to hold forth.

It was likewise outrageous to suggest that divine inspiration was really the result of disgusting vapors with a physiological cause. Swift invents a sect of Aeolists who hold that air is the principle of all things, and that belching is "the noblest act of a rational creature." Puritans liked to use the biblical term *vessel* to refer to the body ("he shall be a vessel unto honour, sanctified"), and Swift made it literal: "At other times were to be seen several hundreds linked together in a circular chain, with every man a pair of bellows applied to his neighbour's breech, by which they blew up each other to the shape and size of a tun; and for that reason, with great propriety of speech, did usually call their bodies their *vessels*." Like Greek oracles, these people are inspired by vapors that penetrate their bodily orifices, women being especially gifted because their organs are "better disposed for the admission of those oracular gusts."[17] Freud would have been impressed. Here are both anal and genital sources for religious emotion.

In a slighter work published together with the *Tale*, *The Mechanical Operation of the Spirit*, Swift made that point explicitly. "Persons of a visionary devotion, either men or women, are in their complexion of all others the most amorous; for zeal is frequently kindled from the same spark with other fires. . . . I have been informed by certain sanguine brethren of the first class that in the height and *orgasmus* of their spiritual exercise, it has been frequent with them * * * * *, immediately after which they found the spirit to relax and flag of a sudden with the nerves."[18] Swift was fond of using asterisks as if parts of the manuscript had been lost, as editors of classical texts often did. Needless to say, many readers took offense at the implication that religious emotion was a symptom of repressed or displaced sexuality.

One of the original illustrations to the *Tale* shows three ways in which men gratify their egos by rising above their fellows. It is dominated by a lugubrious Puritan preacher, high above his glum congregation (they were encouraged to brood on their unworthiness). Puritans favored simplicity in their pulpits, which were popularly derided as tubs, here made literal. In the distance, climbing a ladder to the gallows, a condemned man mirrors the preacher's gesture in his farewell statement, achieving a final celebrity. And just below, a mountebank on a stage prepares to amaze the crowd with some sort of magic trick. All three are phonies, and by implication, all in the same way.

A fundamental doctrine of Calvinism was predestination, the inability of human beings to alter the fate foreordained by God. Swift translates that theology into everyday terms:

> [Jack] would shut his eyes as he walked along the streets, and if he
> happened to bounce his head against a post or fall into the kennel (as
> he seldom missed either to do one or both), he would tell the gibing

30. The preacher in his tub.

prentices who looked on that he submitted with entire resignation, as to a trip or a blow of fate, with whom he found by long experience how vain it was either to wrestle or to cuff, and whoever durst undertake to do either would be sure to come off with a swingeing fall or a bloody nose. "It was ordained," said he, "some few days before the Creation, that my nose and this very post should have a rencounter, and therefore Providence thought fit to send us both into the world in the same age, and to make us countrymen and fellow citizens. . . . 'Tis true, I have broke my nose against this post, because Providence either forgot or did not think it convenient to twitch me by the elbow and give me notice to avoid it."

This was very risky on Swift's part. Anglicans might not believe in predestination, but they did believe in Providence, and it was easy to suspect that Providence itself was under attack. Swift had second thoughts, and when he brought out a new edition both mentions of "Providence" had disappeared, replaced by the innocuous words "Nature" and "Fortune."[19]

A sect that worships tailors holds that the universe is "a large suit of clothes," and each person "a micro-coat, or rather a complete suit of clothes with all its trimmings." Values and ideals are thus external and easily shed.

> Is not religion a cloak, honesty a pair of shoes worn out in the dirt, self-love a surtout, vanity a shirt, and conscience a pair of breeches, which, though a cover for lewdness as well as nastiness, is easily slipped down for the service of both? . . . 'Tis true, indeed, that these animals, which are vulgarly called suits of clothes or dresses, do according to certain compositions receive different appellations. If one of them be trimmed up with a gold chain, and a red gown, and a white rod, and a great horse, it is called a Lord Mayor; if certain ermines and furs be placed in a certain position, we style them a judge; and so an apt conjunction of lawn and black satin we entitle a bishop.[20]

It wasn't news that religion could be used as a hypocritical mask, or that a bishop could have high status but no inner worth (Johnson defines "lawn" as "fine linen, remarkable for being used in the sleeves of bishops"). But Swift's description sounds all too much like what someone who actually did despise religion would say. Voltaire commented, "He claims to have respected the father while giving a hundred strokes of the birch to the three children. People of a difficult turn of mind believed that the stick was so long it reached to the father as well."[21]

As for Catholicism, there are a lot of knockabout jabs at relics, holy water, miracles, and so on, but the critical issue is transubstantiation, the doctrine that the consecrated bread and wine in the Eucharist are literally the body and blood of Christ. When Peter invites his brothers to a dinner of roast mutton, he serves up instead a loaf of bread. Jack protests:

> "By God, my Lord," said he, "I can only say that to my eyes, and fingers, and teeth, and nose, it seems to be nothing but a crust of bread." Upon which the second [brother] put in his word: "I never saw a piece of mutton in my life so nearly resembling a slice from a twelve-penny loaf." "Look ye, gentlemen," cries Peter in a rage, "to convince you

what a couple of blind, positive, ignorant, willful puppies you are, I will use but this plain argument: by God, it is true, good, natural mutton as any in Leadenhall Market, and God confound you both eternally if you offer to believe otherwise." Such a thundering proof as this left no further room for objection.[22]

This captures the aggressive anger that true believers can give way to, but that's not all it does. Protestants held that Communion bread was only a sign or symbol, not literally Christ's body, but still, what it symbolized was Christ. And since Christ was regularly referred to as the Good Shepherd and the Lamb of God, it was outrageous to see him represented as mutton.[23]

THE HAPPINESS OF BEING WELL DECEIVED

These religious issues have cooled with time, but one section of the *Tale*, "A Digression concerning Madness," still speaks with unsettling power. Like Erasmus's *Praise of Folly*, but far more bitterly, it bundles together every kind of human craziness. Whether in religion, science, or politics, people are all too frequently insane. War, for example, is the acting out of irrational aggression, and like emotional religion, it may reflect displaced sexuality. "Having to no purpose used all peaceable endeavours, the collected part of the semen . . . ascended to the brain. The very same principle that influences a bully to break the windows of a whore who has jilted him naturally stirs up a great prince to raise mighty armies, and dream of nothing but sieges, battles, and victories. *Teterrima belli causa*." In Swift's Latin quotation the crucial word, *cunnus*, is discreetly omitted. Horace is referring to Helen of Troy and saying that "a cunt was the most dreadful cause of war."[24]

In all of these versions of madness, the focus of Swift's satire is obvious. But then the digression veers in a new direction, and exposes the human impulse to be in denial more generally. Or is it not just an impulse, but a psychological necessity?

Whatever philosopher or projector can find out an art to solder and patch up the flaws and imperfections of Nature, will deserve much better of mankind, and teach us a more useful science, than that so much in present esteem of widening and exposing them (like him who held anatomy [that is, dissection] to be the ultimate end of physic). And he whose fortunes and dispositions have placed him in a convenient station to enjoy the fruits of this noble art; he that can with Epicurus content his ideas with the films and images that fly off upon his senses from the superficies of things; such a man, truly wise, creams off Nature, leaving the sour and the dregs for philosophy and reason to lap up. This is the sublime and refined point of felicity, called *the possession of being well deceived*, the serene peaceful state of being a fool among knaves.[25]

No one wants to be a fool, Swift least of all. But is the alternative to be a knave? We know that Swift was deeply suspicious of Epicurus's materialism, according to which all we can perceive is the superficial "films" that objects give off. We also know that he had a disillusioned view of human nature, and no sympathy with attempts to patch and solder it. "He is fond of probing wounds to their depth," Orrery said, "and of enlarging them to open view. He prefers caustics, which erode proud flesh, to softer balsamics, which give more immediate ease."[26]

Here is another question. Sir William Temple was a disciple of Epicurus. Was Temple, then, one of those people whose "fortunes and dispositions" gave him the luxury of being well deceived? But if being like that makes you happy, what's the catch? Erasmus has Folly say, "People say it's sad to be deceived. Not at all—it's far sadder *not* to be deceived." More cynically, a woman in one of Rochester's poems says that lovers shouldn't pry into their mistresses' secrets:

> They little guess, who at our arts are grieved,
> The perfect joy of being well deceived.[27]

So here is the dilemma: what if deception can be life giving and healthy? "In the proportion that credulity is a more peaceful possession of the mind than curiosity, so far preferable is that wisdom which converses about the surface to that pretended philosophy which enters into the depths of things, and then comes gravely back with informations and discoveries that in the inside they are good for nothing. . . . Last week I saw a woman flayed, and you will hardly believe how much it altered her person for the worse."[28]

Women weren't actually flayed, of course, but prostitutes were regularly flogged in public, and continued to be until the nineteenth century. In the library at Trinity College, Swift would have seen the actual flayed and stuffed skin of an executed rebel, with an especially grotesque aspect that a visitor to Dublin noted: "In this passive state he was assaulted by some mice and rats, not sneakingly behind his back, but boldly before his face, which they so much further mortified, even after death, as to eat it up; which loss has since been supplied by tanning the face of one Geoghagan, a Popish priest, executed about six years ago for stealing; which said face is put in the place of Ripley's."[29]

What makes Swift's comment about the flayed woman shocking is the off-hand expression "you will hardly believe." Of course it would be horrifying to see someone flayed. But can we really understand *how* horrible if we've never actually witnessed it? And who would witness it if they could avoid it? Maybe outsides aren't so bad after all. "It is better, by and large," Denis Donoghue says, pondering this passage, "to take things as they come and leave them as they are."[30]

The argument in favor of being well deceived has always struck readers as a high point of the *Tale of a Tub*, yet it has provoked endless argument. The whole point of a paradox is to entertain incompatible views without choosing between them. "Wisdom" that demands a definite conclusion—either it's very good to be deceived, or else it's very bad—is just as reductive as the kinds of wisdom that Swift mocks with a cascade of analogies: "Wisdom is a fox, who after long hunting will at last cost you the pains to dig out. . . . Wisdom is a hen, whose cackling we must value and consider, because it is attended with an egg. But then, lastly, 'tis a nut, which unless you choose with judgment, may cost you a tooth, and pay you with nothing but a worm."[31]

A passage in the "Digression concerning Madness" may have special implications for Swift. "When a man's fancy gets astride on his reason, when imagination is at cuffs with the senses, and common understanding as well as common sense is kicked out of doors, the first proselyte he makes is himself."[32] In the empiricist psychology that was then standard, imagination was a threat, since wish-fulfilling fantasy can overwhelm rational judgment and even lead to insanity. Is Swift appealing to reason as a defense against his own anarchic impulses? The *Tale of a Tub* is one long feat of imagination, and its ambiguities suggest that the imagination is not always under control. "Perhaps the ideological substance was orthodox," Rawson suggests, "because beneath it lay a temperament (reflected in the style!) that knew itself to be subversive."[33]

This line of thinking could explain why middle-of-the-road Martin, the second of the three brothers and Swift's exemplar of true religion, doesn't do or say much, and is described as "extremely phlegmatic and sedate." That must be meant to suggest the stability of the Church of England, but "phlegmatic" and "sedate" are words that no one would ever associate with Jonathan Swift. It's Jack and Peter, not Martin, who interest him, because they represent the psychopathology of religious experience.[34]

31. Bedlam.

Swift's fascination while he was in London with Bedlam, the popular name for Bethlehem Hospital, is especially interesting. Mental illness was thought to be the result of a physiological imbalance that could be corrected by forcing invisible "animal spirits" back into their proper channels. A wide range of tortures was prescribed. There were purging and bleeding, of course, as was done for every kind of illness. But in addition patients were suspended from the ceiling in a chair and whirled round until they lost consciousness, or blistered with hot irons, or dropped into icy water, and they were routinely chained up and beaten.

Bedlam was a tourist attraction, where "keepers" charged a penny to show their charges like animals in a zoo. In a *Tale of a Tub* illustration, visitors are shown peering through the gratings. The chained inmate in the foreground is acting out Swift's description, in which he is ironically referred to as a student, with his keepers as the professors: "Is any student tearing his straw in piecemeal, swearing and blaspheming, biting his grate, foaming at the mouth, and emptying his piss pot in the spectators' faces?" Swift recommends that depending on their particular obsessions, the inmates be sent into the army, the law courts, or the royal court, where they will feel right at home.[35]

On at least one occasion Swift saw Bedlam up close.[36] It must have made a strong impression, since he was later elected one of the hospital's governors. Presumably he asked to be. At the end of his life he made plans to found a mental hospital in Dublin, and left his entire fortune for that purpose. In that city the majority of the mentally ill simply wandered the streets helplessly, badly needing an institution to take care of them. Swift felt deep sympathy for their plight, especially after he began to experience symptoms of dementia, and he wanted to ensure that they would be treated more humanely than the inmates of Bedlam were.

HOSTILE REACTIONS

In the *Tale* Swift pretends to believe that it would be impossible to misinterpret his meaning. If seven scholars were locked up for seven years to write commentaries, "whatever difference may be found in their several conjectures, they will be all, without the least distortion, manifestly deducible from the text."[37] But isn't that a tongue-in-cheek way of saying that the text can be made to mean almost anything? Plenty of readers were certain they knew what it meant, and they were outraged.

One broad and disparate group was especially indignant, and that was the Dissenters. Jack, in the *Tale*, represents the radical extreme of Protestantism, but Swift habitually lumped together, as he said elsewhere, every sect that stayed outside of the Anglican Church—"the whole herd of Presbyterians, Independents, Atheists, Anabaptists, Deists, Quakers, and Socinians." In actuality there were drastically different versions of Dissent, ranging from sober Presbyterians to wild inner-light visionaries, and the visionaries were by now a tiny minority. Swift was being outrageous in tarring them all with the same brush to make the whole lot look like a menace to society.[38]

Daniel Defoe, who once hoped to enter the Presbyterian ministry, soon guessed that Swift was the author of the *Tale*, and turned his "Aeolist" metaphor against him. "All his notion dissolved in its native vapour called *wind*, and flew upward in blue strakes of a livid flame called blasphemy, which burnt up all the wit and fancy of the author, and left a strange stench behind it that has this unhappy quality in it, that everybody that reads the book smells the author, though he be never so far off—nay, though he took shipping to Dublin, to secure his friends from the least danger of a conjecture."[39]

Dissenters weren't the only ones who found the *Tale* objectionable. Martin gambles and whores just as much as his brothers do, and that seems a strange way to defend the Church of England. It was also easy to detect irreverence in passages like this one: "The fumes issuing from a jakes [privy] will furnish as comely and useful a vapor as incense from an altar." An Anglican critic named William Wotton, Temple's old opponent in the ancients versus moderns controversy, complained that Swift was playing "a game at leapfrog between the flesh and spirit," reducing spiritual experience to disgusting physicality. St. Paul, mysteriously but memorably, testified that he was afflicted with "a thorn in the flesh." In Swift's account of fanaticism, Wotton observes, "he tells us 'that the thorn in the flesh serves for a spur to the spirit,' and it seemed to Wotton that this was meant as ridicule of St. Paul.[40]

Even Swift's admirers foresaw trouble ahead. Francis Atterbury, dean of Carlisle and later a bishop, told a friend, "Bating the profaneness of it in some places, it is a book to be valued, being an original in its kind, full of wit, humour, good sense, and learning. . . . The town is wonderfully pleased with it." But then Atterbury added, "The author of *A Tale of a Tub* will not as yet be known; and if it be the man I guess, he hath reason to conceal himself, because of the profane strokes in that piece, which would do his reputation and interest in the world more harm than the wit can do him good."[41] Atterbury was right about that.

Six years later, smarting from criticisms, Swift brought out a new edition of the *Tale* with an "Apology" at the beginning, declaring that he would "forfeit his life, if any one opinion can be fairly deduced from that book which is contrary to religion or morality." He also had the clever idea of co-opting the critical comments that Wotton had published, inserting them as footnotes of his own. And he continued ever after to insist that his satire supported true religion:

> Humour and mirth had place in all he writ:
> He reconciled divinity and wit.[42]

There was one last minor irritant. To Swift's disgust, his "little parson cousin" Thomas went around hinting that he was the real author of the *Tale of a Tub*. Swift figured out what had happened. "Having lent him a [manuscript] copy of some part of, etc., and he showing it after I was gone for Ireland, and the thing abroad, he affected to talk suspiciously, as if he had some share in it." (The "etc." was to avoid naming the *Tale of a Tub* in writing.) It's possible that at Moor Park the cousins had shared some ideas for a satire, and that when the *Tale* finally appeared Thomas recognized bits and pieces from those days.[43] After Swift challenged his cousin to prove his authorship publicly, Thomas shut up, but whatever their relationship had once been, it was now over for good.

When it came time for the English bishopric that Swift believed he deserved, it would be the *Tale of a Tub* that would ruin his career hopes, for it would convince the pious Queen Anne that he must never be made a bishop. And although he was willing to have his authorship suspected, he never acknowledged it explicitly. Anonymity was a protection from prosecution, of course, but it was also a strategy for disguising his voice and disavowing his own words. He wanted to taunt readers with impunity, and he was always unwilling to give away much of himself, even from behind a mask. In a startling analogy he remarked, "A copy of verses kept in the cabinet, and only shown to a few friends, is like a virgin much sought after and admired; but when printed and published, is like a common whore, whom anybody may purchase for half a crown."[44]

CHAPTER 9

Swift and God

THE HIDDEN GOD

Throughout Swift's life he was hounded by accusations that he was too irreverent for a clergyman, and maybe not even a believer at all. When he was installed as dean of St. Patrick's Cathedral, some mocking verses were allegedly tacked to the door:

> Look down, St. Patrick, look we pray,
>   On thine own church and steeple;
> Convert thy Dean on this great day,
>   Or else God help the people.

A hostile writer later commented that Swift's "affection to the Church was never doubted, though his Christianity was ever questioned."[1]

Swift's inverted hypocrisy was partly to blame, since he avoided any conventional display of piety. Did it flatter his pride to know that he was better than people thought he was? At any rate, those who knew him best never doubted his sincerity. Patrick Delany, a fellow clergyman, once lived with him for a period of months without suspecting that the servants reported to him every evening for prayers, "without any notice from a bell, or audible call of any kind, except the striking of the clock." Delany was impressed also by the way Swift said grace at meals, "with an emphasis and fervor which everyone around him saw and felt; and with his hands clasped into one another, and lifted up to his breast, but never higher." Swift's secretiveness seemed quixotic to Delany, though. "How happy had it been, both for himself and the world, had he carefully governed his life by that apostolic and truly divine precept, *abstain from all appearance of evil*."[2]

And there is no reason to doubt the genuineness of Swift's faith. In this regard, a striking anecdote from his final years has not been noticed by biographers. According to a servant who attended him when his dementia was getting worse, "Whilst the power of speech remained, he continued constant in his private devotions; as his memory failed they were gradually shortened, till at last he could only repeat the Lord's Prayer. That, however, he continued to do till the power of utterance forever ceased." Swift's friend Dr. Lyon preserved his personal prayer book, "which, being fouled with the snuff from his fingers, shows the parts of it which he most approved."[3]

There is an important difference, however, between sincerity and authenticity. However earnestly Swift performed his devotions, in private as well as in public, he may still have harbored doubts. And if he did, it's inconceivable that he would have allowed anyone to know it.

With his probing, corrosive intelligence, Swift surely experienced a temptation to skepticism. Johnson, a fierce defender of orthodoxy, acknowledged that "everything which Hume has advanced against Christianity had passed through my mind long before he wrote." In his *Dictionary* Johnson defines "belief" as "credit given to something which we know not of ourselves, or on account of the authority by which it is delivered." In some unpublished remarks, Swift took the same position. "The Scripture system of man's creation is what Christians are bound to believe, and seems most agreeable of all others to probability and reason. Adam was formed from a piece of clay, and Eve from one of his ribs." C. S. Lewis comments, "Is it possible that this should not be irony?"[4] But if Christians are "bound to believe" the Bible story, that only means that they should try to believe it and keep quiet if they can't.

Swift says in another note, "To say a man is bound to believe is neither truth nor sense. You may force men, by interest or punishment, to say or swear they believe, and to act as if they believed. You can go no further." Lip service is preferable to denial. "The want of belief," he adds, "is a defect that ought to be concealed when it cannot be overcome." And again: "I am not answerable to God for the doubts that arise in my own breast, since they are the consequence of that reason which he hath planted in me, if I take care to conceal those doubts from others, if I use my best endeavours to subdue them, and if they have no influence on the conduct of my life."[5]

What evidence there is suggests that Swift's God was distant and impersonal. He despised "fanatics" who claimed to enjoy direct communication with the Almighty, and he would have appreciated the comment by the psychiatrist Thomas Szasz, "If you talk to God, you are praying; if God talks to you, you have schizophrenia." We know that he owned a copy of Pascal's *Pensées*, and he probably agreed with Pascal that "men are in darkness and remote from God, who is hidden from their knowledge; this is the very name which he gives himself in the Scriptures, *deus absconditus*." The biblical text is Isaiah 45:15: "Verily thou art a God that hidest thyself, O God of Israel."[6] The hidden God is a deity in Swift's own image.

The historian Lecky put it well: "That Swift would have been a skeptic if he had not been a clergyman is very probable; but this is no disparagement to his sincerity." In *The Mechanical Operation of the Spirit* Swift wrote, "It is a sketch of human vanity for every individual to imagine the whole universe is interested in his meanest concern. . . . Who, that sees a little paltry mortal, droning, and dreaming, and driveling to a multitude, can think it agreeable to common good sense that either Heaven or Hell should be put to the trouble of influence or inspection upon what he is about?" This is not far from Voltaire, who makes a Turkish dervish say to Candide, "When his Highness sends a ship to Egypt, do you suppose he worries whether the ship's mice are comfortable or not?"[7]

Swift's religion was a practical one, and he had little interest in theology. A clergyman's job, he said, was "to tell the people what is their duty, and then to convince them that it is so." As for the thorny questions that theologians liked to debate, "I defy the greatest divine to produce any law, either of God or man, which obliges me to comprehend the meaning of *omniscience, omnipresence, ubiquity, attribute, beatific vision*, with a thousand others so frequent in pulpits."[8]

One of the thorniest theological questions was the nature of the Trinity, three persons yet a single God. Increasing numbers of writers were finding that doctrine untenable, and liberal thinkers were branded with the dread titles of Socinians, Sabellians, and Arians. We know what Swift said in public about the Trinity because he devoted a sermon to it: it was a mystery, and mysteries are by definition impossible to understand. "If you explain them," he said, "they are mysteries no longer; if you fail, you have labored to no purpose." Johnson similarly told Boswell, "If you take three and one in the same sense, to be sure you cannot believe it; but the three persons in the Godhead are Three in one sense, and One in another. We cannot tell how; and that is the mystery!"[9] Swift would surely have appreciated the story of the Oxford dons who saw an open car go by with three men seated in a row. One of them commented, "There goes an allegory of the Holy Trinity," and the other replied, "No, for that, you must show me one man in three cars."

RELIGION AND SOCIAL ORDER

During the first decade of the eighteenth century Swift wrote often about religion, confirming that doctrine mattered to him only in institutional terms. Remembering the chaos of the civil wars, he thought that an established state church was the essential bedrock of a stable society. To keep it secure, a legal sanction was required, and such a sanction existed. Hated by Dissenters but energetically defended by Swift, it was the Test Act of 1673, still very much in force.

When Swift makes Peter insist that a loaf of bread is really mutton, he is parodying the Catholic doctrine of transubstantiation, according to which sacramental bread and wine retain their outward appearance but are literally the body and blood of Christ. It's doubtful that Swift cared much about transubstantiation as such. In *Gulliver's Travels* he deplores the fact that "difference in opinions hath cost many millions of lives; for instance, whether flesh be bread or bread be flesh; whether the juice of a certain berry be blood or wine."[10] What he did care about was the usefulness of transubstantiation as a litmus test for political loyalty.

Under the title "An act for preventing dangers which may happen from popish recusants," the Test Act required every holder of civil or military office to receive Communion in the Church of England at least once a year, and to take this oath: "I do solemnly and sincerely, in the presence of God, profess, testify and declare that I do believe that in the sacrament of the Lord's Supper there is not any transubstantiation of the elements of bread and wine into the body and blood of Christ, at or after the consecration thereof by any person whatsoever; and that the invocation or adoration of the Virgin Mary, or any other saint, and the sacrifice of the Mass, as they are now used in the Church of Rome, are superstitious and idolatrous."[11]

Swift regularly used the term "popish," not "Catholic," because the Anglican Church regarded itself as embodying the authentic Catholicism from which Rome had strayed. But Swift had utter contempt for the founder of his

Church, Henry VIII. Mad for power, Henry "cut off the head of Sir Thomas More, a person of the greatest virtue this kingdom ever produced, for not directly owning him to be head of the Church." In addition, by confiscating the vast wealth of the Church, Henry gravely weakened it. The margins of Swift's copy of a biography of Henry VIII are filled with imprecations: "Bloody inhuman hell-hound of a king"; "Dog, villain, king, viper, devil monster"; "Nero was emperor of Rome, and was a saint in comparison of this dying dog Henry"; "I wish he had been flayed, his skin stuffed and hanged on a gibbet, his bulky guts and flesh left to be devoured by birds and beasts for a warning to his successors forever. Amen."[12]

"We have just religion enough," Swift once wrote, "to make us *hate*, but not enough to make us *love* one another." For that very reason he thought it essential to enforce conformity. It wasn't really Catholics that he was worried about, since their rights had been severely curtailed after 1688. It was dissenting Protestants, especially since the Whigs were eager to extend toleration by repealing the Test Act. Swift did claim once that he was in favor of "a proper indulgence to all Dissenters," but that only meant that they would be left alone so long as they shut up. In one of his unpublished *Thoughts on Religion*, he said that although we have a right to "our own thoughts and opinions," they must not provoke political unrest. "Liberty of conscience, under the present acceptation, produces revolutions, or at least convulsions and disturbances in a state."[13]

What it came down to was that you were free to believe what you liked but not to say so. The king of Brobdingnag tells Gulliver, "He knew no reason why those who entertain opinions prejudicial to the public should be obliged to change, or should not be obliged to conceal them . . . for a man may be allowed to keep poisons in his closet, but not to vend them about for cordials." And in the religion of Lilliput there is bitter doctrinal fighting over which end of an egg is proper to break. The Lilliputian Bible, however, directs only "that all true believers shall break their eggs at the convenient end; and which is the convenient end seems, in my humble opinion, to be left to every man's conscience, or at least in the power of the chief magistrate to determine." (Swift himself, as it happens, broke neither end. He had his eggs hard-boiled, and cracked the shells on his plate.)[14]

Swift's polemical energy was focused on rival Christian sects, but there was also another threat to his position—"freethinking," also known as deism or natural religion. This was the claim that human reason was capable of figuring out everything worth knowing about religion. An intelligent and

well-meaning creator—the *deus* of deism—must have been responsible for
the orderly structure of the universe, but there was no evidence that he loves
us, or punishes us for sin, or will reward good behavior with eternal life.

Swift thought deism so obviously wrong that his attempts to confront it
are often weak. He succeeds best with offhand jabs, like this one at a freethinking clergyman:

> He shows, as sure as God's in Gloucester,
> That Jesus was a grand imposter;
> That all his miracles were cheats,
> Performed as jugglers do their feats.

God was proverbially at home in Gloucester in the Middle Ages, when that
county was supposedly swarming with monks.[15]

"LAUGH US INTO RELIGION"

Irony served Swift better than polemics, and the controversy over the Test
Act inspired one of his most brilliant satires, a short piece entitled *An Argument to Prove that the Abolishing of Christianity in England May, as Things Now
Stand, Be Attended with Some Inconveniencies, and Perhaps Not Produce Those
Many Good Effects Proposed Thereby*. What Swift was discovering was that he
could make his points most forcefully, and at the same time delight his readers, through a deadpan impersonation of somebody else.

An Argument against Abolishing Christianity, as it's commonly known, cri-
tiques a totally imaginary bill in Parliament. Swift's targets include freethink-
ers who did want to get rid of Christianity, and also Socinians—later to be
called Unitarians—who rejected the Trinity. But the immediate occasion was
the Whig agenda to abolish the Test Act, so that Dissenters could be eligible
for public office.[16]

Swift adopts the voice of a man of the world who despises "daggle-tail
parsons" like Jonathan Swift, and it becomes apparent that he is a member of
Parliament as well. With modest tact, he urges, "I do not yet see the absolute
necessity of extirpating the Christian religion from among us." What makes
the *Argument* great is that it rises above specific issues to make the point that
"nominal Christianity" is all that really exists any more.

> I hope no reader imagines me so weak [as] to stand up in the defense
> of *real* Christianity, such as used in primitive times (if we may believe

the authors of those ages) to have an influence upon men's belief and actions. To offer at the restoring of that would indeed be a wild project; it would be to dig up foundations; to destroy at one blow all the wit and half the learning of the kingdom; to break the entire frame and constitution of things; to ruin trade, extinguish arts and sciences with the professors of them; in short, to turn our courts, exchanges, and shops into deserts.

Swift the moralist wasn't always identical to Swift the politician. From the point of view of the moralist, even if the Church was invaluable as a bulwark of social order, it had forgotten its true mission, to recover the Christianity that once influenced people's lives. "If, notwithstanding all I have said, it shall still be thought necessary to have a bill brought in for repealing Christianity, I would humbly offer an amendment: that instead of the word *Christianity*, may be put *religion* in general . . . which, by laying restraints on human nature, is supposed the great enemy to the freedom of thought and action."[17]

In the years to come Swift would return often to this mode of impersonation, which evidently satisfied a psychological need. It was a way of standing outside himself, inhabiting someone else's mind and then subverting it from within. And getting the joke was pleasurable to readers in a way that preaching couldn't be. "He judged rightly," Orrery said, "in imagining that a small treatise, written with a spirit of mirth and freedom, must be more efficacious than long sermons or laborious lessons of morality. He endeavours to laugh us into religion, well knowing that we are often laughed out of it." Scott, in the next century, called the *Argument* "one of the most felicitous efforts in our language to engage wit and humour on the side of religion."[18]

CHAPTER 10

First Fruits

SWIFT AS A POLITICAL PLAYER

In 1704 Swift's story starts to gather momentum again, and in fact this was the turning point of his career. It hinged on a financial issue that was of marginal significance even at the time. This was an ancient law, a tax on the income of the clergy, established in the Middle Ages, with the arcane name of the First Fruits and Twentieth Parts. When a minister took up a new position, he had to pay the state the equivalent of a year's income. That was the First Fruits, so called from a biblical text, "Honour the Lord with thy substance, and with the first fruits of all thine increase."[1] Each year thereafter the tax was 5 percent of income, hence the Twentieth Parts.

In England, where most clergymen were very badly paid, the law was obviously unjust. Queen Anne recognized that, and in 1704 she diverted its proceeds to assist the neediest of the clergy. Yet the British government continued to collect the tax in Ireland, where the clergy were even worse off than in England. As vicar of Laracor, Swift felt the financial pinch personally. Beyond that, he and his colleagues saw the issue as fundamentally important: was the impoverished Church of Ireland just an emaciated cash cow, or did it have a right to its own resources?[2]

The newly appointed archbishop of Dublin was William King, a valiant defender of his Church and a worthy collaborator (if sometimes antagonist) for Swift. King realized that Swift was well suited to argue the Irish case in London, since he was a persuasive speaker and had made useful contacts there. When the clergy assembled in their annual meeting, they accordingly authorized Swift to negotiate on their behalf.

Unfortunately, there was a catch. The Whig ministry in London did indicate a willingness to remit the First Fruits, but only on a condition that was utterly unacceptable to the Irish. The quid pro quo they demanded was abolition of the Test Act in Ireland, where it had only recently become law. The Test Act excluded Dissenters from a wide range of public employment, and the Church of Ireland leaders regarded it as an essential bulwark against both Presbyterianism and Catholicism. For them, the Test Act was nonnegotiable. So negotiations on the First Fruits would drag on for years, and Swift would be exasperated by a series of politicians who promised support and then reneged. King flatly called one hopeful prediction "a mouthful of moonshine."[3] But in a larger sense Swift was in his element at last, a significant player in the public world, and he was paving the way for deeper involvement in the future.

THE STATE OF PLAY IN POLITICS

Since the queen had the power to appoint and dismiss members of the cabinet, and since she attended its meetings every week, her concerns mattered greatly.[4] Though Swift never had an opportunity to meet her personally, it must have seemed auspicious to him that she was devoted to the Church and took seriously her title of Defender of the Faith. She was the last British monarch to "touch for the King's Evil," a laying on of hands that could supposedly cure the lymphatic disorder known as scrofula. When Samuel Johnson was a little boy he contracted a tubercular condition from infected milk, and his mother took him on a long journey to London to be touched by Queen Anne.

Unlike her brother-in-law, the masterful William, Anne was ill at ease and temperamentally depressive. Her longtime friend, the Duchess of Marlborough, said that "there was something of majesty in her look, but mixed with a sullen and constant frown, that plainly betrayed a gloomy soul and a cloudiness of disposition within." The duchess added that although the queen had an extraordinary memory, "she could, whenever she pleased, forget what others would have thought themselves obliged by truth and honour to remember, and remember all such things as others would think it an happiness to forget."[5]

ANNA D. G. ANGLIÆ. SCOTIÆ.
FRANCIÆ ⊕ HIBERNIÆ REGINA.

32. Queen Anne. The inscription is the text of the Great Seal of England, identifying her as queen of England, Scotland, France, and Ireland. By her time, of course, the French part was wishful thinking.

Relatively young though she was—thirty-seven when she ascended the throne in 1702—the queen was in poor health. By 1707 a Scottish diplomat described her as "under a very severe fit of the gout, ill dressed, blotted in her countenance, and surrounded with plasters, cataplasms, and dirty rags."[6] Her depression would deepen after her royal consort died in 1708. He was Prince George of Denmark and Duke of Cumberland, a mild and ineffectual figure who had been selected as a spouse when England needed Scandinavian support against the Dutch. Notwithstanding this arrangement, Anne was devoted to Prince George and distraught at his death.

At this stage in history, the two houses of Parliament were in theory equal, though since the Commons controlled finances it often had the upper hand. But the House of Lords could reject legislation passed by the Commons, which meant that peers continued to hold great power. Their number was held down by the rule of primogeniture, which allowed only the eldest son to inherit a title. In 1688 there were just 160 lords temporal, the peers with he-

reditary titles, and in addition 26 lords spiritual, Church of England bishops
who likewise sat in the House of Lords.[7]

Swift knew and admired many peers, but like Edmund Burke after him,
he had no illusions about the intellectual and moral qualities of the peerage
as a whole. In Gulliver's description, "A weak diseased body, a meager countenance, and sallow complexion, are the true marks of noble blood; and a
healthy robust appearance is so disgraceful in a man of quality that the world
concludes his real father to have been a groom or a coachman. The imperfections of his mind run parallel with those of his body, being a composition of
spleen, dullness, ignorance, caprice, sensuality, and pride. Without the consent of this illustrious body, no law can be enacted, repealed, or altered; and
these nobles have likewise the decision of all our possessions, without appeal."[8]

Orwell thought it an obvious defect in Swift that "he does not seem to
think better of the common people than of their rulers." That is true, but he
didn't think worse of them, either. And it's important to recognize that there
was nothing democratic about the House of Commons. The electorate was
small, since only one man in seven (no women, of course) owned enough
property to vote. It was usual to bribe electors, and since there was no secret
ballot, it was easy to verify the results. Many "pocket boroughs" were personally controlled by big landowners, and some were so unrepresentative that
they became known as "rotten boroughs." The worst was Old Sarum, near
Salisbury, which had two members of Parliament but no inhabitants at all. Its
handful of voters would show up from other places and solemnly conduct an
election in the empty fields where there had once been a town.[9]

The governing ministry was the coalition of Whig noblemen known as
the Junto. Its members had sonorous titles: the Earl of Halifax, Baron Somers, the Earl of Wharton, Earl Cowper, the Earl of Orford, and the Earl of
Sunderland. A seventh peer, holding the influential office of lord treasurer,
gradually acquired more power than the rest. This was Sidney, Earl Godolphin, who had the good fortune to be related by marriage to the Duke of
Marlborough, currently winning battles abroad, and his duchess, Queen
Anne's intimate friend. (Godolphin's son had married the Marlboroughs' eldest daughter in 1698.)

To many people the Junto looked like a secretive and manipulative cabal,
but in historical hindsight it was a necessary response to the evolving needs
of party government. The queen might think of the cabinet as simply a group
of her personal advisers, but since ultimate power lay with Parliament, that

was no longer a practical way to govern. For the first time, it became usual to draw the cabinet from the majority party rather than from able men of both parties. There was, as yet, no formal office of prime minister, but the lord treasurer increasingly assumed that role.

The Junto ministers had reason to be well disposed to Swift, since Orford, Halifax, and Somers were among the peers whose impeachment Swift had condemned in *The Contests and Dissensions in Athens and Rome*. Eventually he would break with them all, and Wharton, in particular, would excite his withering scorn. But at this point they represented his best chance of getting a distinguished appointment in the Church of England, and he placed his highest hopes in Somers.

John, Lord Somers, fifty-three years old, fully deserved Swift's admiration. He was acknowledged to have the most brilliant legal mind in England, and he had been the principal author of the Declaration of Rights that limited William III's powers. Somers fascinated Swift by combining intense emotion with severe self-control. "No man is more apt to take fire," Swift later wrote,

33. Lord Somers.

"upon the least appearance of provocation; which temper he strives to subdue with the utmost violence upon himself, so that his breast hath been seen to heave, and his eyes to sparkle with rage, in those very moments when his words and the cadence of his voice were in the humblest and softest manner." Swift probably identified personally with Somers's achievement in rising to "the greatest employments of the state, without the least support from birth or fortune."[10]

Since Somers was literate and witty, Swift had a bright idea. In 1704 *A Tale of a Tub* was about to be published, and he would dedicate it to Somers. Dedications in those days were overt bids for patronage, and Macaulay comments, "Books were frequently printed merely that they might be dedicated." The great Dryden wrote dedications, Johnson said, "in a strain of flattery which disgraces genius, and which it was wonderful that any man that knew the meaning of his own words could use without self-detestation. . . . When he has once undertaken the task of praise he no longer retains shame in himself, nor supposes it in his patron."[11]

Swift had to find a way to avoid fulsome flattery, and his characteristic solution was praise by ironic understatement. "To ply the world with an old beaten story of your wit, and eloquence, and learning, and wisdom, and justice, and politeness, and candor, and evenness of temper in all scenes of life; of that great discernment in discovering and readiness in favouring deserving men; with forty other common topics; I confess I have neither conscience nor countenance to do it."[12] Swift regarded himself, of course, as one of those "deserving men."

No doubt Swift believed that the entire *Tale* would appeal to Somers and his colleagues, since it embodied a cynical wit very congenial to the style of the rakish grandees. In the lengthy "Apology" that Swift published six years later, he explained with evident embarrassment, "The author . . . was then a young gentleman much in the world, and wrote to the taste of those who were like himself; therefore, in order to allure them, he gave a liberty to his pen which might not suit with mature years or graver characters." "Liberty," with a positive spin, was a Whig slogan, and in hindsight Swift must have realized that it was a political faux pas to dedicate to Somers.[13]

Right from the start, there were obvious ways in which Somers's principles differed from Swift's. He had close ties with City financiers, whom Swift deeply distrusted, and he strongly supported toleration for Dissenters. That didn't stop Swift from seeking his help in getting a cushy Church position, though his own worldly demeanor was becoming an obstacle. He later recalled what happened when Somers recommended him to the archbishop of Canterbury: "His Grace said he had heard that the clergyman used to play at *whisk* and *swobbers;* that as to playing now and then a sober game at *whisk* for pastime, it might be pardoned, but he could not digest those wicked *swobbers.*"[14] "Whisk" was whist; as for "swobbers," Johnson, citing this passage from Swift, defines them as "four privileged cards that are only incidentally used in betting at the game of whist." His Grace clearly thought that a clergyman shouldn't gamble. Swift went right on playing for small sums for the rest of his life.

IRELAND ONCE MORE

It soon became obvious that the First Fruits campaign was going nowhere, so by the end of 1704 Swift returned to Ireland, and there he would remain for the next three and a half years. The expenses of London had forced him to live beyond his means, so that he badly needed to retrench. And Archbishop King took a dim view of absentee clergymen. If the First Fruits mission wasn't succeeding, he expected Swift to come home.[15]

The period from 1704 to 1707 is a biographical blank. All we know is that Swift divided his time between Laracor and Dublin, and got increasingly involved in the affairs of St. Patrick's Cathedral. He played a role, for example, in complicated maneuvering that went into getting his friend John Stearne appointed its dean.[16] He remained on good terms with Dublin Castle, too, becoming close to the Duke of Ormonde, the last Irish-born lord lieutenant in the eighteenth century, and after that to Ormonde's successor, the Earl of Pembroke.

The *Complete Peerage* says of Pembroke that his reputation for "humour and oddness" was "remarkable and indeed most extraordinary."[17] He was just the kind of person, in fact, whom Swift liked. Pembroke enjoyed punning and wordplay, as did a young aide of his named Sir Andrew Fountaine, who would later be a favorite companion of Swift's in London. Also in the social circle were the three Ashe brothers, Thomas, Dillon ("Dilly"), and St. George, Swift's former tutor who was now bishop of Clogher.

On one occasion Swift came up with a brilliant multilingual pun. A lady who was swirling her gown unluckily swept a fine violin off a table and smashed it. Swift exclaimed, "Mantua ve miserae nimium vicina Cremonae!" Virgil's line means "Mantua, alas! too close to unfortunate Cremona"—

Mantua was Virgil's birthplace, and land in Cremona had been confiscated for settlement by army veterans. The pun depends on knowing that Stradivarius made his great violins in Cremona, and that a mantua was a loose gown worn over other clothing.[18]

Swift's most important relationship during these years was with Stella, but it left no paper trail. We have seen that his cousin Thomas Swift wondered in 1707 "whether Jonathan be married," but whatever people expected, there was no marriage at this point, or perhaps ever.

At some point Swift's mother came over from Leicester for a visit. She evidently shared her son's love of playful imposture, for when she checked in at her Dublin boardinghouse, she pretended she was there for an assignation with a lover. Only after Swift appeared did she explain to the landlady that he was her son.[19] This little anecdote was recorded after Swift's death by one of his friends, who must have heard it from him. But like many of the stories about Swift, it raises curiosity without satisfying it. Did mother and son treat each other flirtatiously, or was Abigail just having fun with a credulous landlady?

Swift was in the habit of jotting down aphorisms, somewhat in the style of the great Rochefoucauld, whom he admired, and he wrote the collection *Thoughts on Various Subjects* in the year 1706. A number of aphorisms speak directly to his own experience, particularly this one: "It is a miserable thing to live in suspense; it is the life of a spider. *Vive quidem, pende tamen, improba, dixit.*"[20] The allusion is to Ovid's *Metamorphoses*: "Live then, but hang, presumptuous one." Having woven a tapestry superior to one made by Minerva (whom the Greeks called Athena), the country girl Arachne rashly exults in her victory. Her punishment is to grow a tiny head, big belly, and slender legs, and to hang forever after in her web. Stuck in Ireland and once again seemingly going nowhere, Swift apparently saw himself bleakly as the spider of the *Battle of the Books* instead of as the productive bee.

THE UNION WITH SCOTLAND

In 1707 a momentous event carried profound implications for Ireland. This was the union of England and Scotland, symbolized by combining the crosses of St. George and St. Andrew in the Union Jack. But although Scotland was now fully integrated, Ireland continued to be ruled as a dependent colony, and it would be nearly a century before Ireland too would join the Union, with the cross of St. Patrick added to the flag.

Swift wrote bitterly at this time,

> The Queen has lately lost a part
> Of her entirely-English heart,
> For want of which, by way of botch,
> She pieced it up again with Scotch.

This was an allusion to the queen's well-known declaration that she had "a heart entirely English."[21] The part she lost was the Irish part. Swift never published this little poem; to do so would have jeopardized his hopes for advancement.

Another comment that Swift didn't publish was a prose allegory called *The Story of the Injured Lady, Written by Herself.* It's a slight piece of work, but valuable for the insight it gives into his ambiguous position as an Anglo-Irishman. The lady is grieving because a neighboring landowner who had seduced her, "half by force and half by consent, after solemn vows," has deserted her and is now about to marry another neighbor instead. When *The Injured Lady* was eventually published after Swift's death, the publisher added a subtitle: *Being a True Picture of Scotch Perfidy, Irish Poverty, and English Partiality.*

Scotland, the neighbor who has gained the landowner's hand, is represented as "tall and lean, and very ill-shaped; she hath bad features and a worse complexion; she hath a stinking breath, and twenty ill smells about her besides, which are yet more insufferable by her natural sluttishness, for she is always lousy, and never without the itch." As for Ireland, she is still beautiful, although "pale and thin with grief and ill-usage." She is compelled to employ servants who belong to her faithless lover, and to sell her produce to no one but him.[22] Yet her heart is true and she loves him still.

The reason Swift's position was ambiguous is that he was speaking both for Ireland as a whole and for the ruling Anglo-Irish Ascendancy to which he belonged. Future Irish patriots would characterize their history as a rape, rather than as an engagement to be married. But Swift couldn't do that, because his own class had committed the rape.[23] This fundamental ambiguity— a spokesman for Ireland who didn't necessarily speak for the people as a whole—would haunt his writings even after he became a national hero.

As a member of the Church of Ireland, Swift had another reason for alarm. In Scotland the Presbyterian Church now enjoyed the status of the official establishment (to this day, when the monarch visits there, he or she worships as a Presbyterian). Swift was convinced that if the Test Act, requiring all officeholders to take Communion in an Anglican church, was ever repealed, the Church of Ireland would be shoved aside in the same way by the energetic, militant Presbyterians. "We are verily persuaded," he wrote in 1709, "the consequence will be an entire alteration of religion among us, in no great compass of years."[24] Defending the Test Act would remain an idée fixe of Swift's.

Archbishop King, willing to try once more to tackle the First Fruits issue, agreed at this point to send Swift back to London on the old quest. No doubt Swift implored him to do it. When Lord Pembroke sailed for England in November of 1707, Swift went with him.

CHAPTER II

The War and the Whigs

The overwhelming concern of British public life for over a decade, from 1701 to 1713, was the War of the Spanish Succession. The Whigs were an enthusiastic war party, and their hero was the charismatic general-in-chief of the allied armies, the Duke of Marlborough.

Marlborough wasn't always a duke, or even a peer. He was born John Churchill in 1650, son of Sir Winston Churchill, ancestor of the twentieth-century Sir Winston. This Sir Winston had fought for Charles I in the civil wars, and was well placed for rewards when Charles II recovered his throne. John Churchill was handsome, charming, and a dashing ladies' man. When he was twenty he began a protracted affair with Lady Castlemaine, ten years older than himself, even though she was the mistress of King Charles II. On one occasion the king turned up and Churchill escaped detection by leaping from her second-story bedroom window. But in 1675, when he was twenty-five, he fell passionately in love with a fifteen-year-old maid of honor named Sarah Jennings. In 1677 they married, and he remained in her thrall for the rest of his life. His sister Arabella, incidentally, who has been described as a person of "considerable intelligence and rampant sexuality," was a mistress of James II.[1]

Churchill was a canny political survivor, always landing on his feet through the vicissitudes of five reigns. Queen Anne's biographer comments dryly,

"Churchill's family motto was 'Faithful but Unfortunate,' but his whole career was to belie it. He intrigued against every English monarch from James II to George I, while managing to amass the largest private fortune in Europe."[2] Over the years he kept accumulating titles, usually as rewards for choosing the winning side. In 1682 he became Lord Churchill of Eyemouth, and was raised to Baron Churchill three years later when he helped to put down a rebellion against the newly crowned James II. In 1689 it was James's turn to go, and for deserting him at a crucial moment Churchill became the Earl of Marlborough. In 1702, after his first victories on the Continent, Queen Anne made him a duke, the highest rank in the peerage, and his military glory also brought him the titles of prince of the Holy Roman Empire and prince of Mindelheim, a tiny Bavarian principality that he visited only once, but of which he was very proud.

Marlborough's career was sustained not only by his personal abilities, but by his relationship with the queen. When Sarah Churchill was nineteen, she and then Princess Anne became fast friends. Sarah was a maid of honor to

34. The Duke of Marlborough.

Anne's stepmother, and was beautiful, brilliant, and a controlling personality. The shy and awkward princess developed a powerful crush, and it is sometimes suggested that they were in love. In the long run, however, their temperamental difference would prove fatal to the relationship. In the beginning, Princess Anne was "a willing slave," in Macaulay's words, "to a nature far more vivacious and imperious than her own."[3] When Anne became queen she delighted in pretending to be an ordinary citizen, and insisted that her friends use private names: Queen Anne was "Mrs. Morley" and the Marlboroughs were "Mr. and Mrs. Freeman." Lord Godolphin, whose son was married to the Marlboroughs' daughter, also had a pet name, "Mr. Montgomery."

As her reign continued, however, Anne began to resist being pushed around by the imperious Sarah. Sarah, in turn, grew more dictatorial than ever and refused to back off, even though her husband begged her to. Swift's assessment of the duchess's character is severe but accurate: "Three furies reigned in her breast, the most mortal enemies of all softer passions, which were sordid avarice, disdainful pride, and ungovernable rage."[4] He didn't know either the

35. The Duchess
of Marlborough.

duke or duchess personally, however; it was their inordinate influence over national affairs that he despised.

THE PROGRESS OF THE WAR

The stakes were very high in the War of the Spanish Succession, which had begun in 1702. If Louis XIV could control Spain, together with its territory in the Spanish Netherlands, every other nation in Europe would be in grave danger. Accordingly, England joined a "Grand Alliance" whose other members were the United Provinces of Holland and the Habsburg Empire, which comprised most of Germany, Austria, and Hungary. The Duke of Marlborough was named commander in chief of the combined forces.

Marlborough proved to be a tactician of genius, able to grasp intuitively the progress of a battle, carry out deceptive feints, and strike decisively at the critical place and time. His courage was exceptional. During one victory he was swinging his leg across his horse's saddle when a cannonball passed under his leg and decapitated the officer assisting him. Another officer wrote afterward that he had "fulfilled that day all the parts of a great captain, except that he exposed his person as the meanest soldier," and the incident was celebrated in a pack of playing cards whose ten of diamonds showed Marlborough in the saddle and the dead officer standing beside him with blood spouting from his headless trunk.[5]

That was far from all. Marlborough was also a superb planner, able to organize and deploy huge forces under several different allied commanders (only nine thousand of the fifty-six thousand men in the army were British). He was a gifted diplomat too, and needed to be. The alliance was unwieldy in the extreme, and given to exasperating delays, because the Dutch had the most to lose in defeat and were predisposed to caution. There were no fewer than seven separate governments in the United Provinces of Holland (Holland itself was just one of them), and even when they could agree on a policy, it didn't always suit the emperor in Vienna. In addition, Marlborough had to coordinate his campaigns with a partner, the gifted Prince Eugene of Savoy, with whom he fortunately formed a warm friendship.

After a couple of years of inconclusive fighting, the great turning point was the battle of Blenheim in 1704, which stopped the French in their tracks and ranks with Agincourt and Waterloo as a pinnacle of British military achievement. Blenheim (properly Blindheim) was a Bavarian village on the Danube, around which the engagement was desperately close fought. The carnage was appalling. In Trevelyan's words, "With the darkness, sheets of rain descended in pitiless brutality on the maimed and dying men, gathered from all the four quarters of Europe to perish together on that tragic hill."[6] Blenheim ended Louis' dreams of conquest, and from then on, a negotiated peace was inevitable, though it would take nearly a decade to bring it about.

On the back of a tavern bill Marlborough scribbled a note to his wife: "I have not time to say more, but to beg you will give my duty to the Queen, and to let her know her army has had a glorious victory. M. Tallard and the two other generals are in my coach."[7] That last line was arresting: Tallard was the French commander in chief.

It was more than a week before anyone in England knew what had happened. For four days a Colonel Parkes galloped day and night across the face of Europe, and then adverse winds kept him from sailing for another three days. At last, on August 10, he reached London, gave the Duchess of Marlborough her husband's note, and hastened on to Windsor to inform the queen. The duchess spread the news, and within minutes the cannons in the Tower of London were booming salutes, bells were ringing in all the churches, and people were pouring into the streets. Not long afterward the queen, overjoyed at her dear friend's triumph, got Parliament's consent to grant him the royal manor of Woodstock in Oxfordshire, with sixteen thousand acres and funding to build a grandiose palace.[8]

Joseph Addison, a former Oxford fellow and minor poet who was hoping to make a career in government service, saw a wonderful opportunity. He hastened to bring out a poem called *The Campaign*, which has been called "a sensational propaganda success."[9] Marlborough was now an epic hero:

> Rivers of blood I see, and hills of slain,
> An Iliad rising out of one campaign. . . .
> In vengeance roused, the soldier fills his hand
> With sword and fire, and ravages the land:
> A thousand villages to ashes turns,
> In crackling flames a thousand harvests burns.

That was an elegant way of saying that at Blenheim the French lost thirty-four thousand men and the allies fourteen thousand (only twenty-two hundred of whom were British). In an analogy that became famous, Marlborough was nothing less than an agent of divine wrath:

> And, pleased th' Almighty's orders to perform,
> Rides in the whirlwind, and directs the storm.[10]

The poem made Addison's career, and before long he was an undersecretary of state.

Further allied victories followed, mostly in the Low Countries now—Ramillies in 1706, Oudenarde in 1708. The French were ready to reach an accommodation, but the Whig ministry was not. It had become clear that it would be impossible to eject the Bourbons from Spain, but Marlborough and the Junto felt obliged to honor their commitment to the Austrian emperor to keep trying. They also feared that if they abandoned their campaign in Spain, it would expose the incredible wastefulness of the war. So their slogan became "No Peace without Spain."

Hoping to force an unconditional surrender, the allies decided to make a drive for Paris. The drive ended in horrifying bloodshed in the battle of Malplaquet in Belgium. The allied army lost twenty-one thousand killed and wounded, and the French army eleven thousand. "In many places," a British general wrote, "they lie as thick as ever you saw a flock of sheep. . . . I hope in God it may be the last battle I may ever see." A corporal recalled later, "All the hedges and ditches were lined with disabled men, the horrible cries and groans of the wounded terrified my soul."[11] Even if doctors had been available, the primitive state of medicine meant that there was little they could have done for these men, who were left to die slowly.

France claimed victory, but it was a Pyrrhic one; a French general said that a few more victories like that one would destroy his army. Perhaps the most lasting consequence of the battle was the derisive folk song "Malbrouk s'en va-t-en guerre"—"Marlborough Went Off to War."[12] The war dragged on, more dispiritingly than ever.

BLOOD AND TREASURE

Tories loathed the Whig war policy not just because it destroyed human lives, but because of the way it was financed. Wars had formerly been paid for with temporary, ad hoc taxation, but that meant that Parliament could effectively end them by cutting off the money supply. To secure a dependable way of supporting a protracted campaign, William III's ministers created the first national debt in 1693, and once in existence it inevitably grew. People gladly bought government-backed securities and annuities, which were known as "the funds." Before long everyone with money to invest had some of it in the funds, Swift included.

This was a financial revolution, creating a modern system of credit and public debt in order to sustain what John Brewer has called a "fiscal-military state." Public expenditure rose during the war from £3 million a year to £13 million, and the national debt from £10 million to £50 million. At least 75 percent of government expenditure in eighteenth-century Britain went to war, and at times it would reach 85 percent.[13] There were profound civilian consequences. In order to manage these new obligations, a centralized bureaucracy was created, as had already happened in France.

These changes were much to the taste of the Whigs and their supporters in the financial City. Winning the war would bring Britain a world empire, and empire would bring unprecedented wealth. Addison, who soon became a leading Whig spokesman, paid unctuous tribute to the Royal Exchange: "As I am a great lover of mankind, my heart naturally overflows with pleasure at the sight of a happy and prosperous multitude, insomuch that at many public solemnities I cannot forbear expressing my joy with tears that have stolen down my cheeks. For this reason I am delighted to see such a body of men thriving in their own private fortunes, and at the same time promoting the public stock."[14]

The Tories hated the fiscal-military state, and Swift would soon join them. In the years to come he repeatedly used the expression "blood and treasure," which he may have coined. There was a very practical reason why most country squires were passionately Tory. Individual incomes were largely secret, so it was impossible to tax income or even investments. The swelling national debt, along with subsidies to foreign allies and maintenance of the army, were largely funded by a tax on landowners. And this meant that the country squires, who deeply opposed the debt and the war, found themselves obliged to pay for them.[15]

Meanwhile, investors in the debt, who drew regular interest and got richer and richer, appeared to have a selfish stake in a war that must never end. Fashionable London carriages, Swift wrote, were filled with profiteers and army officers cashing in the spoils of battle, "a species of men quite different from any that were ever known before the Revolution, consisting either of generals and colonels, or of such whose fortunes lie in funds and stocks; so that power, which according to the old maxim was used to follow land, is now gone over to money."[16]

Years later, when a speculative scheme known as the South Sea Bubble imploded, Swift felt vindicated. "I ever abominated that scheme of politics (now about thirty years old) of setting up a moneyed interest in opposition to the landed. For I conceived there could not be a truer maxim in our government than this: that the possessors of the soil are the best judges of what is for the advantage of the kingdom. If others had thought the same way, funds of credit and South Sea projects would neither have been felt nor heard of." Swift also declared, "I have often wished that a law were enacted to hang up half a dozen bankers every year."[17]

The War of the Spanish Succession did make Britain a world power. The modern Churchill said of his ancestor: "By his invincible genius in war, and his scarcely less admirable qualities of wisdom and management, he completed that glorious process that carried England from her dependency upon France under Charles II to ten years' leadership of Europe."[18] But after the fiasco of Malplaquet, the war was increasingly unpopular, and Swift would play a leading role in the campaign to end it. Beyond that, he would always fiercely condemn the entire policy of British imperialism.

COURTING THE GREAT WHIGS

During 1707–8, Swift kept pushing his First Fruits agenda and working to ingratiate himself with the ministry. He sent regular reports to Archbishop King, and although it's sometimes said that there was bad feeling between them at this stage, the evidence doesn't support it. King did find Swift headstrong at times, and Swift did think that King could have tried harder to advance his career. But they always treated each other with respect, and appreciated a mutual disinterestedness that was rare in the Church hierarchy. "I never was a favourite of any government," King wrote to Swift, "nor have I a prospect of being so, though I believe I have seen forty changes, nor would I advise any friend to sell himself to any so as to be their slave." Swift in turn told King that his letters were "full of everything that can inspire the meanest pen with generous and public thoughts." And although Swift didn't always disclose everything he knew—there was much that was confidential—he sent full accounts of the political ebb and flow. King, in return, offered sensible advice, for example, that to argue that a given measure would benefit Ireland was a sure way to get it blocked.[19]

When we read accounts of the Whig grandees, they may seem interchangeable as well as remote—Whigs in wigs. The two words do overlap; Swift once teased Stella: "Who are those *Wiggs* that think I am turned Tory? Do you mean Whigs? Which *Wiggs* and *wat* do you mean?" He also made the connection in his *City Shower:*

Here various kinds, by various fortunes led,
Commence acquaintance underneath a shed;
Triumphant Tories and desponding Whigs
Forget their feuds, and join to save their wigs.[20]

Among these powerful men, Swift found the witty, brilliant Somers the most attractive, and the formidable Godolphin the most off-putting. Immensely privileged patricians, all of them moved in a far different world from the vicar of Laracor. Of Godolphin, for example, Trevelyan said approvingly, "Newmarket [racetrack] was his spiritual home, and not the least of his services to England was done in the capacity of breeder of race horses."[21]

In after years Swift liked to claim that he never flattered the great, but that was far from true. He did flatter them, until it became obvious that they were never going to help him. For a while his hopes were placed in the Earl of Halifax, whose portrait captures his ironic worldliness.

Sometimes Swift would even suggest that he was the perfect candidate for a specific vacancy. After declaring that Halifax had "fifty times more wit than

36. Lord Godolphin. On his shoulder is the emblem of the Order of the Garter, with the cross of St. George and the legend *Honi soit qui mal y pense;* at the left is the white staff that denoted the office of lord treasurer.

37. Lord Halifax.

all of us together," he suggested, "Pray, my Lord, desire Dr. South to die about the fall of the leaf, for he has a prebend of Westminster which will make me your neighbor, and a sinecure in the country, both in the Queen's gift; which my friends have often told me would fit me extremely." The sinecure was the parish of Islip, just four miles from Oxford. Halifax replied politely that Dr. South was not immortal, "and upon all occasions that shall offer, I will be your constant solicitor, your sincere admirer, and your unalterable friend." He never did anything, however, and Swift noted later, "I kept this letter as a true original of courtiers and court promises." And when he came upon a writer's claim that Halifax was "a great encourager of learning and learned men" and "patron of the Muses," Swift wrote in the margin, "His encouragements were only good words and dinners—I never heard him say one good thing, or seem to taste what was said by another."[22]

In the long run, the politician who would matter most to Swift was Robert Harley, though they were not close at this time. Harley was the leader of a group known as the Country Whigs, because they promoted the "country interest" of landed gentlemen as opposed to the "city interest" of merchants and financiers. From 1704 to 1708 Harley held office as secretary of state, but he was distrusted by his colleagues, who saw him as a closet Tory, and in due course he would indeed become the Tory leader.

Harley had a stable of journalists who were also information gatherers, and might even be described as spies. Their access was literally through the back door, as he indicated in a note to one of them: "I will be ready, upon your giving three knocks at the back door, to let you in."[23] The most effective of these agents was Daniel Defoe, not yet a novelist. His relationship with Harley furnishes an interesting glimpse into a political underworld that Swift kept clear of.

Defoe fell into Harley's lap because he got into trouble with the law. Brought up a Dissenter—he once mentioned that he had thoughts of becoming a Presbyterian minister—he was outraged by the Test Act and published a satiric attack called *The Shortest Way with the Dissenters*. Unfortunately, *The Shortest Way* mimicked bigoted Tories all too well, and many people thought

38. Daniel Defoe.

at first that one of them had written it. Shrewder readers understood the ironic intention, and after a relentless search Defoe was identified. He was put on trial, convicted of "seditious libel" threatening the stability of the nation, forced to stand in a pillory, and consigned to Newgate Prison.

Desperate to be released, Defoe got in touch with Harley, who responded by persuading the queen that the prisoner was harmless and by paying his fine out of the "Queen's bounty." Thereafter Defoe toured England and Scotland under assumed names, gossiping in coffeehouses and taverns in order to pick up information and plant useful rumors. For this work he received £400 a year from the government. In addition he turned out a stream of political pamphlets, as well as a periodical called *A Review of the State of the British Nation*—the *Review* for short—that presented the Whig party line.[24]

It isn't clear how often Swift and Defoe met, but they were definitely aware of each other. When Harley went over from the Whigs to the Tories, Defoe did not, and from then on he and Swift were opponents. But since they published anonymously, they were opponents in the dark, with readers only guessing at the authorship of pamphlets, and often guessing wrongly. It was altogether a strange moment in political history, with modern party alignments just beginning to take shape, and a new breed of propagandists getting out their message and defaming the other side's.

In a pamphlet of his own on the Test Act, Swift dismissed Defoe contemptuously as a pretentious fraud: "The fellow that was pilloried (I have forgot his name) is indeed so grave, sententious, dogmatical a rogue that there is no enduring him." The claim to have forgotten Defoe's name is usually quoted as Swift's personal opinion, but actually he put it in the mouth of an imaginary member of the Irish House of Commons. It was quite true, though, that Defoe was sententious and humorless. Dickens remarked that *Robinson Crusoe* was "the only instance of an universally popular book that could make no one laugh and could make no one cry."[25]

Harley, as it would turn out, would soon offer Swift an avenue to the long-sought First Fruits prize, and to much else besides. At last, at the age of forty, Swift would be close to the center of power, and not relegated to the back stairs, either.

THE MANY BLANKS IN SWIFT'S STORY

It needs to be emphasized that during this time, as in the previous forty years of Swift's life, the documentary record is extremely spotty, and highlights his public life much more than his private. Thanks to a clever piece of modern detective work, an episode can be recovered that illustrates how much is missing. In October 1708, Swift sent a short letter to the poet Ambrose Philips, dating it from "Havisham" (or possibly "Harisham") and mentioning that he was staying with a Mr. Collier who had been at school with Philips.[26] There is no such place as Harisham, and nothing to associate Swift with the tiny hamlet of Haversham in Bedfordshire. As for Collier, until recently nothing was known about him either. But there are sufficient clues to establish that his name was actually spelled Coleire, and that he was the vicar of a town in Kent called Harrietsham. Swift probably met him when they were both at Oxford for their M.A. degrees, and evidently they remained friends, since they spent nearly a month together on this occasion.

During this visit Coleire undoubtedly regaled Swift with his remarkable story. Having gotten into financial straits, he signed on as a chaplain in the Royal Navy, and the records of the Navy Board describe what had happened to him two years before Swift's visit. Sent ashore in Portugal to bury a sailor who had been murdered, Coleire was left behind when his ship unexpectedly sailed off for the West Indies. Together with twenty-one companions who were stranded along with him, he chartered a Portuguese boat to get as far as Madeira, where they found another ship bound for England. This voyage too led to misadventure, since a storm forced a landing at the southern tip of Ireland. Still in charge of his band of tars, Coleire marched them to Kinsale, where he was able to turn them over to naval authorities. He then submitted a bill for £49 and 15 shillings as reimbursement for his expenses, which the navy duly paid.

Swift had a great appetite for picaresque travel stories, and it's easy to imagine that this one remained in his memory. Coleire was a young clergyman who was forced by bad financial management to leave his family and go to sea, was deserted on the shores of a strange land, and then had to make his way back to England. Change the profession from clergyman to physician, and this could be the germ of *Gulliver's Travels*. But if no one had taken the trouble to dig out the information that was misleadingly preserved in the letter to Ambrose Philips, we wouldn't have the slightest glimpse of an interesting episode.[27]

CHAPTER 12

Swift the Londoner

LONDON LIFESTYLE

As before, Swift found London alarmingly expensive, and he had to manage his finances with care. Whenever possible he walked rather than hiring a coach or sedan chair. Lodgings were relatively cheap, about £1 a month, and he moved often, though it's not clear why. His quarters were taken by the week or month, and it was easy to change them. At various times he lived in Pall Mall, Bury Street, St. Albans Street, Suffolk Street, St. Albans Street, St. Martin's Street in Leicester Fields, Little Panton Street, and Rider Street; he also lived in Chelsea and in an unidentified street in Kensington.[1]

The main meal was at midday. At no time did Swift have a cook or kitchen, so he would have a roast or fowl brought in from a "cook shop," or else go to a tavern. It would be a mistake to romanticize taverns. "We had a neck of mutton," he reported one evening, "that the dog could not eat." The next morning he added, "I was very uneasy last night with ugly, nasty, filthy wine that turned sour on my stomach."[2]

Swift was always on the lookout for invitations to dine with friends, but that could be expensive too, since servants in great houses expected generous tips, known as "vails." You could pay a footman a couple of shillings just for opening the door when you arrived, and be 10 shillings poorer by the time you went home. One footman whose annual salary was £4 collected £100 more per year in vails.[3]

A recent innovation that had caught on fast was the coffeehouse; by 1700 London had over two thousand of them. It was a place to have one's mail sent (there were no post offices), sit by a fire, gossip, make business appointments, catch up on the news, and argue about politics. Coffee was the social lubricant, as in Pope's description:

> Coffee, which makes the politician wise,
> And see through all things with his half-shut eyes.[4]

Some of these establishments developed impressively over the years. Maritime insurers did business at Edward Lloyd's coffeehouse, which became the ancestor of Lloyd's of London. "The spoken word," Trevelyan says, "did many things that print does today, and for merchants the word was spoken at Lloyd's." The stock exchange had its origin in a coffeehouse run by a man named John Castaing, who began to publish updated lists of stock prices in 1698.[5]

The coffeehouses are sometimes described as establishing a new kind of "public sphere" in which ideas could be freely exchanged. But whatever the buzz there was like, it didn't embody public opinion in the modern sense, since only a narrow slice of the public was represented. "It is the folly of too many," Swift commented, "to mistake the echo of a London coffee house for the voice of the kingdom." At another time he summed up the coffeehouse atmosphere as "tobacco, censure, coffee, pride, and port." And he once remarked, "The worst conversation I ever remember to have heard in my life was that at Will's coffee house, where the wits (as they were called) used formerly to assemble." Will's was where Dryden held forth.[6]

LONDON FRIENDS

During these years the cast of characters in Swift's life grew much larger. It can be hard to keep them straight, as T. H. White indicated in a whimsical sequel to *Gulliver's Travels*:

> He searched the Colonnade, where the great Pope himself had walked with William Broome, on the night when he was persuading the latter to persuade Tonson to publish a letter from Lintot, signed however by Cleland, and purporting to have been written by Bolingbroke, in which Lady Mary Wortley Montagu was accused of having suspected

a Mr. Green of persuading Broome to refuse permission to Tonson to publish a letter by Cleland, purporting to have been signed by Lintot, without the knowledge of Bolingbroke, about the personal habits of Dr. Arbuthnot, under the pseudonym of Swift.[7]

With the possible exception of Mr. Green, these were all real people, and many of them will appear in this volume.

Swift often stayed with the Berkeleys at one of their four homes, notably Berkeley Castle in Gloucestershire. Betty, now known by her married name as Lady Betty Germaine, remained a special favorite. A close friend of the Berkeleys was a celebrated beauty called Biddy Floyd, who was, Swift told Stella, "the handsomest woman that ever I saw" apart from herself. In a charming poem he wrote for Biddy, Venus and Cupid construct a brand-new type of beauty by discarding the defects normally found in society ladies, retaining only the good qualities. Since she came from far-off Chester, she is equipped from the outset with virtues seldom found in London, as Cupid discovers when Jove sends him on a quest:

> Jove sent and found, far in a country scene,
> Truth, innocence, good nature, look serene;
> From which ingredients, first the dext'rous boy
> Picked the demure, the awkward, and the coy.
> The Graces from the court did next provide
> Breeding, and wit, and air, and decent pride;
> These Venus cleansed from ev'ry spurious grain
> Of nice, coquette, affected, pert, and vain.
> Jove mixed up all, and his best clay employed;
> Then called the happy composition *Floyd*.

"Nice" in this context is defined by Johnson as "fastidious; squeamish." As Ehrenpreis observes, the poem says nothing about the lady's looks, only her mind and character.[8] Swift was a warm admirer of beautiful women, but he liked to compliment them by implying that their looks were the least of their charms.

For an extended period during 1707 and 1708, Stella was in England, apparently the only visit she made there after she moved to Ireland. Nothing is known about how often she and Swift saw each other. The sole trace is a casual remark he made in a letter to their Dublin friend John Stearne: "Pug is very well, and likes London wonderfully, but Greenwich better, where we could hardly keep him from hunting down the deer." Pug belonged to Stella's companion, Rebecca Dingley, who had a great fondness for dogs. Swift once composed a couplet for her pet's collar:

> Pray steal me not, I'm Mrs. Dingley's,
> Whose heart in this four-footed thing lies.

It seems unlikely, however, that Swift cared much for her dogs:

> May Bec have many an evening nap
> With Tyger slabbering in her lap.[9]

It may be that the ladies were not in England on Swift's account, but because Lady Giffard had requested their help. A niece of hers had just died, leaving a distraught husband with seven young children to care for. Lady Giffard suggested that they move from London to Moor Park, which belonged to her but was currently the residence of her nephew Jack Temple, and that she would find someone to look after the children. "If I were younger and had better health I would offer myself and Bridget," Lady Giffard said. Bridget was Stella's mother, still in Lady Giffard's employ; it would certainly have made sense to think of Stella and Rebecca for this task.[10]

One of Swift's longest-lasting friendships was formed in London at this time. This new friend was Charles Ford, a graduate of Trinity College fifteen years his junior, who had an estate near Dublin but mostly lived in London. Over the years he and Swift corresponded often, and his letters show him to have been intelligent, well read, and politically astute. He struck Laetitia Pilkington, though, as "one of the oddest little mortals I ever met with," and she was surprised that Swift let him dominate conversation and relate "a whole string of improbabilities."[11] As with many of Swift's friends, indeed, it's hard today to get Ford into clear focus; the very real attachment rested on qualities of personality that don't come through in documents.

In addition to friends like these, Swift was taken up by the leading writers of the day. William Congreve he already knew, of course, and they were rivals no longer, for Congreve had stopped writing. His last play was the sparkling *The Way of the World*, produced in 1700 when he was just thirty years old. His remaining twenty-nine years would be devoted to politics and pleasure, not in that order.

More important to Swift than Congreve was another Irishman, Richard Steele. Like Swift, Steele chose to think of himself as only accidentally Irish—"I am an Englishman born in the city of Dublin," he said.[12] Actually, his family had been in Ireland much longer than Swift's, settling near Kil-

39. William Congreve.

kenny in the 1630s and enjoying a close connection there with the great Duke of Ormonde. But whereas Swift was educated at Kilkenny and Trinity, Steele's mother took him to England (his father had died when he was five) and he went to the distinguished Charterhouse School and then to Oxford.

Steele's temperament was very different from Swift's. He was boisterous, impulsive, a heavy drinker, and addicted to living far beyond his means. "He knew the town," Macaulay said, "and paid dear for his knowledge. He was a rake among scholars and a scholar among rakes." A literary antagonist of Steele's thought he had a distinctively Irish temperament: "God has stamped his native country upon his face, his understanding, his writings, his actions, his passions, and above all his vanity. The Hibernian brogue is still upon all these, though long habitude and length of days have worn it from off his tongue."[13] Comments like this were by no means rare at the time, and they illustrate the ethnic prejudice that Swift and his countrymen had to contend with.

When Steele left Oxford, he became a cavalry officer in the Life Guards and fought in Flanders under the Duke of Marlborough, to whom he remained

40. Richard Steele.

deeply loyal. He nearly killed a man in a duel, and then became a spokesman for abolishing dueling. He was an occasional playwright, edited a political journal, and scored a big success with a new kind of periodical essay called the *Tatler*. He was also constantly on the lookout for employment. At various times he was gentleman-waiter to Prince George of Denmark (Queen Anne's consort), commissioner of the Stamp Office, surveyor of the royal stables at Hampton Court, governor of the Royal Company of Comedians, and commissioner of forfeited estates in Scotland.

Valued most of all by Swift was Joseph Addison, Steele's collaborator on the *Tatler* and afterward on the hugely popular *Spectator*. Five years younger than Swift, Addison was a clergyman's son who had seemed destined for an academic career until he decided to try his luck in London; he had spent twelve years at Oxford, where he excelled in writing Latin verse. It was he who celebrated rivers of blood in his poem on the Duke of Marlborough, but he was far from bloodthirsty in reality, and his view of humanity was far more benign than Swift's. As an example of malicious writers who "give mean

41. Joseph Addison.

interpretations and base motives to the worthiest actions," Addison instanced the duc de la Rochefoucauld, author of the celebrated *Maximes*. Swift, in contrast, called Rochefoucauld his favorite writer, "because I found my whole character in him." Years later he began a poem by invoking him:

> As Rochefoucauld his maxims drew
> From nature, I believe 'em true;
> They argue no corrupted mind
> In him; the fault is in mankind.

Steele was as sanguine as Addison. "The sense of shame and honour," he said, "is enough to keep the world itself in order." Swift did not agree. In his *Thoughts on Various Subjects* he observed, "I never wonder to see men wicked, but I often wonder to see them not ashamed."[14]

Close though Addison and Steele were, Swift seldom saw them together. As he told another friend, "The triumvirate of Mr. Addison, Steele and me come together as seldom as the sun, moon and earth. I often see each of them, and each of them me and each other." Perhaps Swift preferred it like that, for in later years he told his friends that he and Addison enjoyed their evenings together so much that "neither of them ever wished for a third person to support or enliven their conversation." Swift's relatives preserved a copy of Addison's *Travels in Italy* with this inscription: "To Doctor Jonathan Swift, the most agreeable companion, the truest friend, and the greatest genius of his age, this book is presented by his most humble servant, the author." "Genius" was a less exalted term then than now, but even so, it suggests that Addison knew that Swift was the author of *A Tale of a Tub*, in which Lord Somers is addressed as "the sublimest genius of the age."[15]

LONDON WRITER

Swift's writing was now branching out in many directions. In 1709 he wrote *A Description of the Morning*, and the next year *A Description of a City Shower*, both published for the first time in the *Tatler*. And he made a playful invention in *The Story of Baucis and Philemon*. Dryden had translated one of Ovid's *Metamorphoses*, in which Jupiter and Mercury, disguised as beggars, are turned away at house after house. Finally, an impoverished couple shows them hospitality, and the two are rewarded when their cottage turns into a magnificent shrine.

> The pavement polished marble they behold,
> The gates with sculptures graced, the spires and tiles of gold.[16]

Swift's version of the Ovid story is a sustained piece of deflation, but also an experiment in fantasy, stranger and more uncanny than the narrative in Dryden. The gear-driven chimney jack, used for turning meat on a spit, becomes a church clock. The bedstead is transformed into pews, still suitable for "folks disposed to sleep." And the walls and furniture come alive, with a hallucinatory vividness like that of *Alice in Wonderland*. Swift's pleasure is infectious as he creates detail after detail:

> Aloft rose every beam and rafter,
> The heavy wall went climbing after;
> The chimney widened and grew higher,
> Became a steeple with a spire.
> The kettle to the top was hoist,
> And there stood fastened to a joist,
> But with the upside down, to show

Its inclination for below;
In vain, for a superior force
Applied at bottom, stops its course,
Doomed ever in suspense to dwell,
'Tis now no kettle, but a bell.
The groaning chair began to crawl
Like a huge insect up the wall;
There stuck, and to a pulpit grew,
But kept its matter and its hue.[17]

The element of fantasy keeps surfacing throughout Swift's writing, and will do so unforgettably in *Gulliver's Travels*.

Swift was always willing to let friends advise him about revision. They might well be right, he thought, and it really didn't matter that much. He showed this poem to Addison and was advised to make some drastic changes. In later years Swift told friends cheerfully that "in a poem of not two hundred lines Mr. Addison made him blot out fourscore, add fourscore, and alter fourscore."[18]

It's worth noting that although he loved literature, Swift had surprisingly little interest in what would nowadays be called "the arts." He was bored by music, didn't care for paintings unless they were portraits of people he knew, and may have gone to a play only once in his life. He did read plays, but as literature, not as living drama. The sole occasion on which he is known to have seen a play was an act of friendship, since it was a tragedy by Addison— and even then Swift went to a rehearsal, not a public performance. As for the vogue of Italian opera that was then at its height, he told Archbishop King, "I design to set up a party among the wits, to run them down [that is, to ridicule them] by next winter." Eventually his friend John Gay would do exactly that in *The Beggar's Opera*. Meanwhile, Swift reported with amusement that an old lady "asked me t'other day what these *uproars* were that her daughter was always going to."[19]

SWIFT IN CONVERSATION

Swift never had a Boswell to transcribe his conversation, so we can only guess at what it was like, but there are plenty of tributes to his genial good humor. Steele called Swift "a friend of mine who has an inexhaustible fund of discourse, and never fails to entertain his company with a variety of thoughts and hints that are altogether new and uncommon." The elder Sheridan described him as an engaging storyteller "who speaks not a word too much or too little; who can, in a very careless manner, give a great deal of pleasure to others, and desires rather to divert than be applauded; who shows good understanding and a delicate turn of wit in everything that comes from him . . . and everything requisite not only to please the hearer, but to gain his favour and affection."[20]

Swift was fond of "raillery," which was, he explained, "to say something that at first appeared a reproach or reflection [criticism]; but by some turn of wit unexpected and surprising, ended always in a compliment, and to the advantage of the person it was addressed to." His sallies in this mode could seem aggressive, and sometimes they were, but in his mind raillery was the opposite of a sarcastic put-down. "It now passeth for raillery to run a man down in discourse, to put him out of countenance, and make him ridiculous, sometimes to expose the defects of his person or understanding; on all which occasions he is obliged not to be angry, to avoid the imputation of not being able to take a jest."[21]

Addison once wrote, "I have always preferred cheerfulness to mirth. The latter I consider as an act, the former as an habit of mind. Mirth is short and transient, cheerfulness fixed and permanent." Swift valued both. Mirth for him was an essential relief, and Charles Ford called him one of "those who are formed for mirth and society."[22] In a poem he distinguished between two styles of amusement:

> For wit and humor differ quite;
> That gives surprise, and this delight.

Even when deploying verbal wit, Swift rode the wave of conversation, contributing shared enjoyment rather than quotable bon mots. You had to be there, for as he said himself, "Some things are extremely witty today, or fasting, or in this place, or at eight o'clock, or over a bottle, or spoke by Mr. What d'y'call'm, or in a summer's morning: any of which, by the smallest transposal or misapplication, is utterly annihilate."[23]

Johnson missed the point when he complained that Swift's expression was "seldom softened by any appearance of gaiety; he stubbornly resisted any tendency to laughter." Johnson himself laughed like a booming ogre—Boswell remembered an occasion when "he burst into such a fit of laughter that he appeared to be almost in a convulsion; and, in order to support himself, laid hold of one of the posts at the side of the foot pavement, and sent forth peals so loud, that in the silence of the night his voice seemed to resound from

Temple Bar to Fleet Ditch." But Swift's style was deliberately deadpan, and that was a point of affinity with Addison. "True Humour," Addison said, "generally looks serious, whilst everybody laughs about him; False Humour is always laughing, whilst everybody about him looks serious."[24]

PRACTICAL JOKES

The younger Sheridan heard of an incident that occurred soon after Swift became friends with his father. An old classmate who hadn't seen Swift for a long time paid a visit to the school Sheridan ran, and Swift pretended to be a hopeless dullard named Jodrel, applying for a job there. "As he was an excellent mimic, he personated the character of an awkward country parson to the life." The former classmate was deputed to interview him, and got such inept responses that he exclaimed, "Was there ever such a blockhead? Who the devil put you in [holy] orders?"[25]

Swift also put on his awkward-parson act at a London coffeehouse where writers gathered, at a time when he was a new arrival and they had no idea who he was. He would lay his hat on a table and walk up and down in silence for half an hour, and then pay for his coffee and leave. "They concluded him to be out of his senses," Sheridan says, "and the name that he went by among them was that of the mad parson." On one occasion Swift unexpectedly accosted a gentleman who had just come to town from the country.

> They were all eager to hear what this dumb, mad parson had to say, and immediately quitted their seats to get near him. Swift went up to the country gentleman, and in a very abrupt manner, without any previous salute [salutation], asked him, "Pray, sir, do you remember any good weather in the world?" The country gentleman, after staring a little at the singularity of his manner and the oddity of the question, answered, "Yes, sir, I thank God, I remember a great deal of good weather in my time." "That is more," said Swift, "than I can say; I never remember any weather that was not too hot, or too cold, too wet, or too dry; but however God Almighty contrives it, at the end of the year 'tis all very well." Upon saying this, he took up his hat, and without uttering a syllable more, or taking the least notice of anyone, walked out of the coffee house, leaving all those who had been spectators of this odd scene staring after him, and still more confirmed in the opinion of his being mad.[26]

We know that Swift had a hobby of collecting trite conversational gambits. Commenting on the weather has to be the tritest of them all.

Another coffeehouse encounter was the start of a long and warm friendship. After hastily scribbling a letter, Dr. John Arbuthnot noticed that it was blotted and needed some sand to absorb the excess ink, a common practice at the time. "Pray, sir," he said to Swift, "have you any sand about you?" "No," Swift answered, "but I have the gravel, and if you will give me your letter I'll piss upon it." Johnson defines "gravel" as "sandy matter concreted in the kidneys; if the stone is brittle it will often crumble, and pass in the form of gravel." Arbuthnot was a humorist himself, and thought that this was funny.[27]

Swift had a special fondness for April Fool's jokes. Among the documents in his collected works is an advertisement that appeared in the *London Post-Boy* on March 31, 1709: "Tomorrow, being Friday, between the hours of 3 and 5, afternoon, will be sold by auction, at Mr. Doily's in the Strand, a small collection of about a hundred books of the choicest kinds and editions, . . . a porphyry urn, two bronze lamps, and a small parcel of medals, some very rare." The next day the paper grimly reported, "This is to give notice that there was no such auction designed, and that the said advertisement was taken in and inserted by the printer's boy's inadvertency."[28] No doubt Swift showed up in person to enjoy his victims' bafflement.

He may also have been exacting revenge against his own temptation to indulge in expensive books. "I itch to lay out nine or ten pounds for some fine editions of fine authors," he told Stella after viewing a library that was about to be sold. When the auction was held he couldn't afford to buy much, and "laid out one pound seven shillings, but very indifferently, and came away, and will go there no more." Two days later, though, he was back. "I went to the auction of Barnard's books, and laid out three pounds three shillings, but I'll go there no more; and so I said once before, but now I'll keep to it."[29]

It was at this time that Swift went public with his love of impersonation, concocting a hoax that had everyone laughing. He published a brief pamphlet entitled *Predictions for the Year 1708*, under the name of Isaac Bickerstaff, which he had noticed on the sign at a locksmith's shop. This was a sly, deadpan parody of popular almanacs based on astrology. The specific target was John Partridge, who had been turning out an almanac called *Merlinus Liberatus* for several decades, always with predictions too vague to be proved mistaken. Swift picked on him for two reasons: his attacks on the Church of England, and the radical politics that he covertly promoted in his almanacs.

"Bickerstaff" poses as a genuine astrologer who is disgusted by phonies like Partridge, and proceeds to mount an earnest defense of his art. Then comes a shocker: "My first prediction is but a trifle, yet I will mention it, to show how ignorant those sottish pretenders to astrology are in their own concerns. It relates to Partridge the almanac-maker. I have consulted the star of his nativity by my own rules, and find he will infallibly die upon the 29th of March next, about eleven at night, of a raging fever; therefore I advise him to consider of it, and settle his affairs in time."[30]

Swift's pamphlet was published early in the year, allowing lead time for this ominous claim to hang in the air. The rest of his predictions were highly specific, including the virtual extinction of the royal family of France. A follow-up pamphlet pulled the trigger. It was dated March 29 and published the next day, just in time to serve as an April Fool's joke.[31]

Readers were now informed that the fatal prediction had been fulfilled. A purported friend of Partridge's describes him on his deathbed, where he earnestly repudiated his life's work. "I then asked him why he had not calculated his own nativity, to see whether it agreed with Bickerstaff's predictions? at which he shook his head, and said, 'Oh! sir, this is no time for jesting, but for repenting those fooleries, as I do now from the very bottom of my heart.'" Partridge goes on to acknowledge his Dissenting leanings, and his end is related with novelistic realism:

> On his deathbed he declared himself a Nonconformist, and had a fanatic preacher to be his spiritual guide. After half an hour's conversation I took my leave, being almost stifled by the closeness of the room. I imagined he could not hold out long, and therefore withdrew to a little coffee house hard by, leaving a servant at the house with orders to come immediately and tell me, as near as he could, the minute when Partridge should expire, which was not above two hours after; when, looking upon my watch, I found it to be above five minutes after seven: by which it is clear that Mr. Bickerstaff was mistaken almost four hours in his calculation. In the other circumstances he was exact enough.[32]

Partridge, of course, proclaimed that he was very much alive, but Bickerstaff published an answer in which he refused to believe it. The most he would concede was that "if an uninformed carcass walks still about, and is pleased to call itself Partridge, Mr. Bickerstaff does not think himself any way answerable for that."[33] And if *Merlinus Liberatus* should continue to be published under Partridge's name, Swift could plausibly say that that proved nothing, since almanacs often kept the names of deceased founders. As it happens, Partridge's almanac did shut down for several years, and it used to be believed that the Stationers' Company that revoked his license had been taken in by Swift's hoax. In fact it had to do with an unconnected financial dispute.

Swift's deeper point was that whether Grub Street authors used their real names or not, they were nothing more than names to their readers. The blustering Partridge seemed hollow and insubstantial, even though he really existed, while the articulate Bickerstaff seemed convincingly real. And indeed, Bickerstaff got a new lease on life when Steele borrowed the name for the *Tatler*, deftly making the same point about virtual authors: "I have in another place, and in a paper by itself, sufficiently convinced this man that he is dead; and if he has any shame, I don't doubt but that by this time he owns it [that is, admits it] to all his acquaintance. For though the legs and arms and whole body of that man may still appear and perform their animal functions; yet since, as I have elsewhere observed, his art is gone, the man is gone."[34]

With brazen effrontery, Swift even drafted *An Answer to Bickerstaff*, in which he hinted that Bickerstaff was in reality the same man who wrote the *Tale of a Tub*. As Ehrenpreis says, "Here is Swift pretending to be a man who sees through a man whom Swift is pretending to be."[35] But he evidently realized that it would be most unwise to come out openly as author of the *Tale*, and the piece wasn't published until after his death.

Partridge never did figure out who his opponent was. "The principal author of it," he told a friend, "is one in Newgate, lately in the pillory for a libel against the state. There is no such man as Isaac Bickerstaff; it is a sham name, but his true name is Pettie." A pamphleteer named Pittis was indeed in Newgate Prison, but he had nothing to do with Bickerstaff. Partridge seems to have suspected him because he was a High Church pamphleteer whose politics resembled Swift's.[36]

Meanwhile, Swift's First Fruits negotiations continued to be stalled, but change was at last at hand, for Swift and for the nation. The next four years would find him welcomed unexpectedly at the very summit of power.

CHAPTER 13

At the Summit

THE DOWNFALL OF THE WHIGS

At the beginning of 1709 Swift was still calling himself a "moderate Whig," though Archbishop King teased him about it: "Pray, by what artifice did you contrive to pass for a Whig?"[1] But momentous changes were just beyond the horizon, and soon he would be a Whig no longer.

There was a personal loss just at this time. In April 1710, Abigail Swift died in Leicester, while Swift was still at Laracor. He wrote on a blank page in his account book, "I have now lost my barrier between me and death; God grant I may live to be as well prepared for it as I confidently believe her to have been! If the way to Heaven be through piety, truth, justice, and charity, she is there." The sentiments are appropriately pious, but very general, and Ehrenpreis is just guessing when he claims that Abigail's death "shook and depressed him profoundly." And as Nokes says, the conditional "if" is thought provoking. Could there be any doubt that a good life is the way to heaven?[2]

Despite the butchery of Malplaquet in September of 1709, the Whigs remained committed to continuing the war. Rumors spread that the Duke of Marlborough was getting rich from it and would never allow it to end. But Queen Anne's trust in the duke was waning, even as his duchess grew more and more imperious. Likewise Godolphin, the Marlboroughs' relative by marriage, was beginning to lose his grip on power. Once he had been the queen's intimate friend as "Mr. Montgomery"; he was her intimate no longer.

An unexpected crisis blew up in November of 1710. The spark that ignited it was a Guy Fawkes Day sermon, *In Perils among False Brethren*, preached at St. Paul's Cathedral by Henry Sacheverell. Invoking memories of the 1605 Gunpowder Plot that sought to blow up Parliament, Sacheverell called Dissenters a "brood of vipers" and a menace to church and state. He also invoked the old divine-right doctrine that forbade resistance to the Lord's anointed king, and the Whigs saw a chance to smear the Tories as closet Jacobites. So in February of the next year they launched a show trial of Sacheverell in the House of Lords.

The Tory defense was brilliantly managed by Francis Atterbury, dean of Carlisle Cathedral and soon to be bishop of Rochester. He argued that Sacheverell was entirely loyal to the Protestant succession and an innocent victim of Whig persecution. The Whigs did secure conviction by a narrow margin, but it was followed by a mere slap on the wrist. Sacheverell was suspended from preaching for three years, and the offending sermon was publicly burned.

Sacheverell was widely hailed as a martyr. There were violent riots in his support, and he received a hero's welcome when he went to Shropshire to take up a new parish. The excitement there was so contagious that the three-year-old Samuel Johnson insisted on mounting his father's shoulders to see him in Lichfield Cathedral.[3]

The Whigs had overreached, and Queen Anne decided that it was time for Godolphin to go. He possessed great abilities, but what had kept him at the top was his close relationship with her and the Marlboroughs. And at this point, the Marlboroughs too lost the queen's trust completely. The duke demanded to be appointed general-in-chief for life, which looked disturbingly like a bid for dictatorship. And the duchess finished things off by claiming that her successor as Queen Anne's confidante, Abigail Masham, was the queen's lesbian lover. Infuriated, the queen never spoke to the duchess again.

Godolphin's dismissal was carried out, as Swift later said, "in a manner not very gracious."[4] Godolphin had a right to be bitter. He had overseen the financing of a great war that established Britain as a world power. He had also managed a union with Scotland that created a genuinely united kingdom. And now the queen wouldn't even discharge him face-to-face, but sent the chief groom of her stables to tell him to break his white staff of office. As Swift heard the story, "Mr. Smith, Chancellor of the Exchequer, happening to come in a little after [the Queen's message was delivered], my Lord broke his staff and flung the pieces in the chimney, desiring Mr. Smith to be witness that he had obeyed the Queen's commands."[5]

Just a year previously, in a preface to the final volume of Sir William Temple's writings, Swift had praised Godolphin for serving as lord treasurer "with such universal applause, so much to the Queen's honour and his own, and to the advantage of his country." But times were changing fast. When Swift arrived from his stay in Ireland in September of 1710, he immediately found himself "equally caressed by both parties," as he told Archbishop King, since he could provide an able pen in this public relations emergency. "I was to visit my Lord Godolphin," he continued, "who gave me a reception very unexpected, and altogether different from what I ever received from any great man in my life, altogether dry, short, and morose."[6] It is not clear whether Swift knew yet that Godolphin was on the way out.

On the day of this meeting, Swift told Stella, "My Lord Treasurer received me with a great deal of coldness, which has enraged me so, I am almost vowing revenge."[7] The revenge was a clever poem, in a newly adopted style of brisk couplets just right for Swift's satiric voice. Its odd title was calculated to provoke interest: *The Virtues of Sid Hamet the Magician's Rod*. Godolphin's first name was Sidney, and the name Sid (or Cid) Hamet appears in *Don Quixote*, one of Swift's favorite books.

With inventive glee, Swift finds one analogy after another for the lord treasurer's staff. First it's Moses's rod, which turned into a serpent when he put it down. With Sid's rod it's just the opposite: the moment he lets go of it, its powers are gone.

> Our great magician, Hamet Sid,
> Reverses what the prophet did.
> His rod was honest English wood
> That senseless in a corner stood,
> Till metamorphosed by his grasp
> It grew an all-devouring asp:
> Would hiss, and sting, and roll, and twist,
> By the mere virtue of his fist;
> But when he laid it down, as quick
> Resumed the figure of a stick.[8]

In rapid succession the staff becomes a witch's broomstick, a divining rod useful for locating gold, the soporific rod of Hermes with which a passive House of Commons is drugged to sleep, a fishing rod for catching politicians with bribes, a magician's wand that draws a circle for "mischievous spirits" to congregate in, and a schoolmistress's rod with which the queen has meted out Godolphin's punishment. But after the playfulness, the poem turns harsh:

> For since old Sid has broken this,
> His next will be a rod in piss.[9]

Swift was playing on the expression "a rod in pickle," a term for a schoolmaster's cane, kept ready to administer beatings. Having had his fun with Godolphin, he dismisses him with a coarse sarcasm.

Swift had the poem published—anonymously, as he nearly always did—as a single-page broadsheet, and it was an immediate hit. As usual, he took pleasure in hearing people speculate as to who might have written it. "My lampoon is cried up to the skies, but nobody suspects me for it except Sir Andrew Fountaine; at least they say nothing of it to me."[10] Fountaine knew Swift so well that he could recognize his work.

HARLEY AND THE TORIES

Robert Harley, the former secretary of state, was now making his move. After being dropped from the cabinet in 1708, he had left the Whigs and joined the Tories. That was not really a drastic defection, since party lines were blurred and he was always committed to moderation. When he became chancellor of the exchequer in 1710, he knew that he needed an able writer and that Swift would be perfect for the role. Meanwhile, Swift was ready to change sides too. In 1709, in *A Letter concerning the Sacramental Test*, he had denounced the Whig policy of toleration for Dissenters. The "test" was the requirement that every officeholder take Communion at least once a year in an Anglican church, and the Whigs tried repeatedly to get it repealed.

Although this *Letter* was published anonymously, the Whig ministers strongly suspected that Swift had written it. They didn't forgive. "I have been assured," he said two years later, "that the suspicion which the supposed author lay under for writing this *Letter* absolutely ruined him with the late ministry."[11]

So it was time to listen to Harley. At the end of September Swift wrote to Stella, "The Tories dryly tell me I may make my fortune if I please, but I do not understand them; or rather, I do understand them." He was being coy because he needed more than hints before he would change sides openly. Soon, however, the courtship was irresistible. The Whig grandee Halifax invited

Swift to dine and he declined. Harley invited him and he accepted. "Today I was brought privately to Mr. Harley," he reported a week later, "who received me with the greatest respect and kindness imaginable." Four days later, Harley "knew my Christian name very well"—a great mark of familiarity—and when Swift proposed meeting at his public levee "he immediately refused, and said that was not a place for friends to come to."[12]

Next, Harley put Swift in touch with his chief colleague: "I dined today, by invitation, with the Secretary of State, Mr. St. John."[13] The youthful, dazzling Henry St. John was more of an ideologue than either Harley or Swift, and far less willing to work constructively with the Whigs. But for a time his partnership with Harley would flourish, and Swift would be deeply involved behind the scenes.

No sooner did Swift agree to come on board than Harley got him the prize he had sought in vain for so long. The queen, Harley reported, had promised to grant the remission of the First Fruits to the Church of Ireland. "I believe never anything was compassed so soon," Swift told Stella exultantly, "and purely done by my personal credit with Mr. Harley, who is so excessively obliging that I know not what to make of it, unless to show the rascals of the other party that they used a man unworthily who had deserved better." As for the Whigs, "I have done with them, and they have, I hope, done with this kingdom for our time." At court in November Swift saw the queen pass by "with all Tories about her—not one Whig."[14]

Swift had been told not to announce his First Fruits triumph until it became official, and at this very moment Archbishop King wrote to warn that he might not be the right man to keep up the negotiations, since he was "under the reputation of being a favourite of the late party in power." But before that discouraging message arrived, the queen's decision was made public. "A certain pride seizeth me," Swift told the archbishop, "from very different usage I meet with" in London as contrasted with Ireland, where the bishops refused to give him the least credit for his achievement. To this King replied generously, with an apt classical quotation: "I acknowledge you have not been treated with due regard in Ireland, for which there is a plain reason, *praegravat artes infra se positas*, etc." The allusion is to Horace's *Epistle to Augustus Caesar*: "A man scorches with his brilliance who outweighs merits lowlier than his own."[15]

It might seem that there was no longer any reason for Swift to stay in London, but he told the archbishop that the new administration had something important in mind for him. "I beg to tell your Grace in confidence that the ministry have desired me to continue here some time longer, for certain reasons that I may sometime have the honour to tell you."[16] It had been decided that he should promote Tory policies in a new periodical to be called the *Examiner*.

THE ODD COUPLE

The new Tory administration was headed by a pair of politicians who were unfortunately different in every way, from temperament to policies. There would be serious tensions between them from the start, and within a few years their partnership would collapse. Swift liked them both, however, and was trusted by both, which encouraged him to imagine that he had more influence than he actually did.

The more experienced of the two leaders was Robert Harley, six years older than Swift, who had been speaker of the House from 1701 to 1705, and secretary of state from 1704 to 1708. The queen trusted him, and at a time when personal connections mattered so much, his cousin Abigail Masham

42. Robert Harley, Lord Oxford. Harley carries the white staff, emblematic of the office of lord treasurer, and wears on his left shoulder the emblem of the Order of the Garter, which he received in 1712, together with the title of the Earl of Oxford.

was her faithful nurse, companion, and confidante. It was often through Mrs. Masham, rather than in direct conversations of his own, that Harley influenced the queen. Harley now held the office of lord treasurer, and his partner Henry St. John (pronounced "Sinjin") was secretary of state. Essentially, the lord treasurer was responsible for domestic affairs and the secretary of state for foreign.

Swift had much in common with Harley, who was a great reader and collector of manuscripts (eventually bequeathed to Oxford as the Harleian Miscellany), and also a firm supporter of the Anglican Church. Indeed, Harley never lost the rather puritanical values of his upbringing, trusting in divine providence in times of stress. At a critical juncture he wrote to his father, "I pray God direct and keep a poor worm sensible of his weakness."[17]

Harley appreciated Swift's charm and wit, and liked to call him Martin for the character in the *Tale of a Tub;* also, as Swift told Stella, "because martin is a sort of swallow, and so is a swift." In return Swift nicknamed Harley the Dragon—"so called by contraries," he explained, "for he was the mildest, wisest, and best minister that ever served a prince." They even shared a physical disability. Like Swift's, Harley's left ear was deaf: "He always turns to the right, and his servants whisper him at that only."[18]

Even after Harley was raised to the peerage as the Earl of Oxford, he treated Swift as an equal. Years later Swift recalled, "I often said, when we were two hours diverting ourselves with trifles, *vive la bagatelle.*" And after his friend had been dead for many years, Swift wrote to his son, "I knew your father better than you could at that time, and I do impartially think him the most virtuous minister, and the most able, that ever I remember to have read of. . . . I loved my Lord your father better than any other man in the world."[19]

Harley had defects, however. One that didn't bother Swift, but did get in the way of political leadership, was that he couldn't express himself clearly. "Lord Oxford," Pope said, "was huddled in his thoughts, and obscure in his manner of delivering them. He talked of business in so confused a manner that you did not know what he was about, and everything he went to tell you was in the epic way, for he always began in the middle." Pope thought that this awkwardness, rather than any intention to insult, explained a comment Harley once made. He advised a playwright named Nicholas Rowe that it would be a good idea to learn Spanish, which Rowe naturally took as a hint that he might receive a diplomatic appointment. When he came back later to report that he could speak Spanish, Harley said, "Then, sir, I envy you the pleasure of reading *Don Quixote* in the original."[20]

Harley was also a procrastinator, maddeningly so. Even when he was a boy, his mother complained, "He is sometimes extremely lazy so that I have been near whipping him," and in 1712 a colleague told him, "If I had that sloth in my temper that you have, I would on purpose keep a man to pull me by the sleeve to remember me of things that I was to do." Swift was once given, as a present, an elaborately decorated Venetian snuffbox. He showed it to Harley, who teased him by noting the image of a goose on the bottom and suggesting that it represented the clergy. Swift's riposte was that "the goose is there drawn pecking at a snail, just as I do at him, to make him mend his pace." As Deane Swift heard the story, Harley replied, "That is severe enough, Jonathan, but I deserve it."[21]

Harley was also exasperatingly secretive about his plans. In part this was because he preferred improvisation to long-range strategy. "He thinks it a more easy and safe rule in politics," Swift noted, "to watch incidents as they come, and then turn them to the advantage of what he pursues, than to pretend to foresee them at a great distance." But his detractors were convinced that the secrecy was a calculated policy. One of them said that Harley loved trickery "even where not necessary, but from an inward satisfaction he took in applauding his own cunning; if any man was ever born under necessity of being a knave, he was." A modern historian believes that "behind the obese, mumbling, lethargic bulk of the Earl of Oxford lurked cunning, weasel-toothed, sharp-sighted Robert Harley, watching patiently, taking his decisions suddenly and craftily."[22] Swift too, of course, was in his own way a secretive man of masks.

Policy or not, Harley certainly loved secrecy. His second marriage took place privately, after which he returned to his office without mentioning where he had been, and his own father learned of it only secondhand. In later years he took to keeping notes in a code of his own invention, and when Abigail Masham was giving him information about the court, they used a code in which entire messages purported to be about Harley's family in Herefordshire. Abigail was Cousin Kate Stephens, the queen was Aunt Stephens, and the Tories were Cousin Palmer. More peculiarly, "courage" was Ready Money, "victory" was Lawsuit, and "peace" was E. M. Barnett.[23]

Henry St. John (called Harry by his friends) was fifteen years younger than Harley, and in every way Harley's opposite. He was an eloquent writer and spellbinding orator, a political thinker with long-range views, and temperamentally rash and impulsive; he was widely known as "the man of mercury."[24] As for religion, he supported the Church of England because, like the Tories

43. Henry St. John, Lord Bolingbroke. These are the parliamentary robes he wore after being created Viscount Bolingbroke in 1712.

generally, he regarded it as essential for social order. But he was a freethinker, and it amused Johnson in his *Dictionary* (using St. John's later title of Lord Bolingbroke) to define "irony" as "a mode of speech in which the meaning is contrary to the words; as, 'Bolingbroke was a holy man.'"

From the moment Swift met St. John, who was thirty-two in 1710, he was bowled over. He told Stella, "I think Mr. St. John the greatest young man I ever knew; wit, capacity, beauty, quickness of apprehension, good learning, and an excellent taste; the best orator in the House of Commons, admirable conversation, good nature, and good manners; generous, and a despiser of money. His only fault is talking to his friends in way of complaint of too great a load of business, which looks a little like affectation; and he endeavours too much to mix the fine gentleman and man of pleasure with the man of business." The encomium is almost an echo of Hamlet's "in apprehension how like a god, the beauty of the world!" Swift did go on to say, "What truth and sincerity he may have I know not."[25] The caution was well advised. Beneath his air of frankness, St. John could be just as cunning as Harley. And although he had to defer to the older and more established Harley for the time being, he was watching for an opportunity to displace him.

Sir William Temple had been proud of declining the office of secretary of state, and as Swift continued to spend time with St. John, the analogy with Temple brought back disagreeable memories. "One thing I warned him of, never to appear cold to me, for I would not be treated like a schoolboy; that I had felt too much of that in my life already (meaning from Sir William Temple); that I expected every great minister, who honoured me with his acquaintance, if he heard or saw anything to my disadvantage, would let me know it in plain words, and not put me in pain to guess by the change or coldness of his countenance or behavior." St. John took the rebuke in good part, said Swift "had reason," and explained that he seemed distant only because he was worn down by "sitting up whole nights at business, and one night at drinking."[26]

Swift was surprisingly tolerant of St. John's well-known lifestyle as a rake. He mentioned casually to Stella that when he and Harley were strolling on the Mall, "Mr. Secretary met us and took a turn or two, and then stole away, and we both believed it was to pick up some wench; and tomorrow he will be at the cabinet with the Queen. So goes the world." With evident relish, Swift passed on to Stella some verses that a friend had given St. John at a time when he claimed to be finished with public life:

> From business and the noisy world retired,
> Nor vexed by love, nor by ambition fired;
> Gently I wait the call of Charon's boat,
> Still drinking like a fish, and —— like a stoat.

Swift added, "I think the three grave lines do introduce the last [line] well enough." Perhaps he secretly envied St. John's ability to gratify his appetites with impunity. Ehrenpreis splendidly calls him Swift's "super-id."[27]

What did greatly worry Swift, always a temperate drinker himself, was his colleagues' debauches. Harley was a borderline alcoholic and often neglected his responsibilities. St. John managed better, but not all that well, as Swift remarked with one of the pseudo-proverbs he liked to make up: "I dined with him, and we were to do more business after dinner. But after dinner is after dinner—an old saying and a true, Much drinking little thinking."[28]

In one way Swift identified deeply with St. John: they both paid a high price for being more intelligent than other people. Years later, when his friend was permanently out of politics, Swift told him that he had been too sharp for his own good: "Did you never observe one of your clerks cutting his paper with a blunt ivory knife? Did you ever know the knife to fail going the true way? Whereas if he had used a razor or a penknife, he had odds against him of spoiling a whole sheet." At another time Swift critiqued the middle-of-the-road discretion that allows mediocrities to weather any storm: "It will carry a man safe through all the malice and variety of parties, so far that whatever faction happens to be uppermost, his claim is usually allowed for a share of what is going."[29]

ASSASSINATION ATTEMPT

In March of 1711 an extraordinary incident occurred, frightening at the time and very helpful to Harley's prestige afterward. A Frenchman calling himself the marquis de Guiscard, which was probably not his real name, had worked his way into St. John's confidence; they both had illegitimate sons by the same mistress. Chronically short of money, Guiscard began spying for the French and smuggling information out in the diplomatic pouch of the British ambassador to France. After a while the ambassador grew suspicious and detected what was happening. Guiscard was accordingly called before the Cabinet Council for interrogation. Swift, who knew him, happened to pass him in the street on his way there, "and I wondered he did not speak to me."[30]

After trying at first to bluff it out, Guiscard rushed at Harley and stabbed him with a penknife that he had picked up from a table on his way in (in the days of quill pens, penknives were in use everywhere). Harley was wounded in the chest, but saved by luck. Because the anniversary of the queen's coronation had just been celebrated, he was wearing several layers of elegant formal clothing that partly cushioned the first blow. The tip of the blade broke off against his breastbone, and the second blow, which would otherwise have pierced his heart, caused only a nasty bruise.

Several of those present drew swords and rushed at Guiscard, wounding him severely. Harley, maintaining astonishing composure, called out that he should be allowed to live since it was important to put him on trial. It seemed to some people that St. John, who joined in the attack on Guiscard, was particularly eager to dispatch him then and there. Certainly St. John had reason to fear that under interrogation too much might be revealed about his own secret activities—he was never a wholehearted Jacobite, but he did have feelers out to the Pretender in case he should ever regain his throne.

In the event, Guiscard's condition deteriorated and he died before he could be tried. Meanwhile, St. John claimed that it was really he, and not Harley, who had been the intended target, but nobody believed that. Guiscard certainly knew that Harley was the biggest obstacle to the Pretender's return. It was also noted that Guiscard seemed to have free run of the court, had made odd inquiries in the royal kitchen, and was found to have a bottle of poison in his pocket. His ultimate intention may have been to kill the queen, in the hope that the country would turn to the exiled James III rather than accept the Hanoverian George I.

Swift wasn't present at the attack, but he described it to Stella immediately afterward and was deeply upset. "My heart is almost broken. . . . Pray pardon my distraction; I now think of all [Harley's] kindness to me. The poor creature now lies stabbed in his bed by a desperate French Popish villain. Good night, and God preserve you both, and pity me. I want it [that is, need it]." Ehrenpreis speculates, "I cannot help wondering whether Swift's identification of Harley with his own parent did not go so far that he felt the guilt of a resentful son over a father's near-death." It's not obvious that he felt guilty in that way, but he did acknowledge a kind of filial grief. He told Archbishop King that Harley "hath always treated me with the tenderness of a parent," and that his "violent pain of mind" was the greatest he had ever felt in his life.[31]

It turned out that Harley was never in real danger, once it was clear that gangrene wouldn't set in. He let it be thought, however, that he might be at death's door, and made the most of his slow recovery. Much to the disgust of Bolingbroke, who had been working covertly to supplant him, he was hailed everywhere as a martyr. Matthew Prior, a poet and diplomat with whom Swift was friendly, hastened into print with a poem that Swift charitably called "handsome":

> The sharp point of cruel Guiscard's knife
> In brass and marble carves thy deathless name.[32]

In the *Examiner* Swift himself saw an opportunity to boost Harley's reputation by describing his behavior as an extraordinary instance of magnanimity—the word still meant, as Johnson defines it, "greatness of mind; bravery; elevation of soul."

After the wound was given, he was observed neither to change his countenance, nor discover any concern or disorder in his speech. He rose up, and walked along the room while he was able, with the greatest tranquility, during the midst of the confusion. When the surgeon came he took him aside, and desired he would inform him freely whether

the wound were mortal; because in that case, he said, he had some affairs to settle relating to his family. The blade of the penknife, broken
by the violence of the blow against a rib, within a quarter of an inch
of the handle, was dropped out (I know not whether from the wound,
or his clothes) as the surgeon was going to dress him. He ordered it to
be taken up, and wiping it himself, gave it somebody to keep, saying,
he thought "it now properly belonged to him." He showed no sort of
resentment, or spoke one violent word against Guiscard, but appeared
all the while the least concerned of any in the company—a state of
mind which in such an exigency nothing but innocence can give, and
is truly worthy of a Christian philosopher.[33]

Ten days later Swift reported to Stella, "We have let Guiscard be buried at last,
after showing him pickled in a trough this fortnight for two pence apiece. . . .
'Tis hard our laws would not suffer us to hang his body in chains, because he
was not tried, and in the eye of our law every man is innocent till then."[34]

There was one thing in the *Examiner* version of the story that Swift soon
came to regret. He had been taken in by the claim that Guiscard, under interrogation, revealed that it was St. John whom he intended to stab, and that
"not being able to come at the Secretary as he intended, it was some satisfaction to murder the person whom he thought Mr. St. John loved best." This
turned out to be a shamelessly self-serving story invented by St. John himself,
who hoped that by getting it into print through Swift, he could make himself
the hero and Harley just an accidental victim. A Whig critic took pleasure
in highlighting Swift's embarrassment: "He has repented of that passage; he
cannot blot it out."[35]

At some later time Harley made Swift a present of the macabre relic,
which Deane Swift said he saw several times. "It was a common ordinary
penknife with a tortoise-shell handle, and when it was shut was just about the
length of a man's little finger. But as the blade was broken within half an inch
of the handle by the violence of the blow against one of the ribs of the Earl,
the Doctor had a hole drilled through that part of the blade which was broken off, and another hole through that piece which remained in the handle,
and by that contrivance they were both held together by a little silver chain."[36]

One would suppose that those details carry complete conviction, but
maybe they don't, which highlights the slipperiness of most evidence about
Swift. After Deane Swift published some remarks critical of Patrick Delany,
Delany responded indignantly, "I knew Dr. Swift fifty times better than you

did." Delany was certain not only that the knife was an ordinary one, not able to be closed up and never broken, but that Guiscard's weapon remained in Lord Oxford's family and was never given to Swift.[37]

Soon after Harley's recovery he received a double reward from Queen Anne. He had been serving until then as chancellor of the exchequer, and was now made lord treasurer in title as well as fact. In addition, he was raised to the peerage as the first Earl of Oxford, the name by which we will now refer to him.

St. John got no peerage at this point, since he was needed to manage debates in the House of Commons while Oxford went on to the Lords. And when he did get one a year later, he regarded it as an insult. His new title was Viscount Bolingbroke (pronounced "Bullenbrook"), and viscounts were outranked by earls. Swift heard that the lower rank was due to the widespread stories about his sexual escapades, which Her Majesty found offensive. "The Queen could not be prevailed with, because, to say the truth, he was not much at that time in her good graces, some women about the court having infused an opinion into her that he was not so regular in his life as he ought to be."[38]

HOW MUCH POWER DID SWIFT HAVE?

Swift was now at the center of political power, its valued spokesman, but that doesn't mean that he made policy or was privy to many secrets. After the first heady rush of excitement he admitted as much. Both Oxford and Bolingbroke permitted him to speak his mind freely, but as he later acknowledged, "I have known many great ministers ready enough to hear opinions, yet I have hardly seen one that would ever descend to take advice." On one occasion, when Bolingbroke asked to be left alone with Oxford, "I said it was as fit I should know their business as anybody, for I was to justify [that is, in print]; so the rest went and I stayed." As it turned out, the issue wasn't so mighty after all: "It was so important I was like to sleep over it."[39]

To outsiders it probably did appear that Swift had a great deal of influence, and no doubt he liked them to think so. An unsympathetic clergyman named White Kennett preached a sermon before the queen "against Popery and profaneness," and was gratified to notice that when he denounced "the prevailing foolishness of wit and humour so called," everyone looked at Swift. The hint referred to the *Tale of a Tub*. At a coffeehouse the next day, Kennett saw Swift receive respectful bows "from everybody but me, who I confess could not but despise him." According to Kennett, Swift put on something of a performance in the queen's antechamber, making sure he was being overheard as he went from one gentleman to another:

> Then he stopped Francis Gwynne, Esq., going in with his red bag to the Queen [the bag indicated a distinguished queen's counsel], and told him aloud that he had somewhat to say to him from my Lord Treasurer. He talked with the son of Dr. Davenant to be sent abroad, and took out his pocketbook and wrote down several things, as memoranda, to do for him. He turned to the fire and took his gold watch, and telling the time of the day, complained it was very late. A gentleman said "he was too fast." "How can I help it," says the doctor, "if the courtiers give me a watch that won't go right?" Then he instructed a young nobleman that the best poet in England was Mr. Pope (a Papist), who had begun a translation of Homer into English verse, for which he must have them all subscribe, "for," says he, "the author shall not begin to print till I have a thousand guineas for him." My Lord Treasurer (after leaving the Queen) went through the room, and beckoning Dr. Swift to follow him, they both went off just before prayers.

From Kennett's perspective, not only was Swift guilty of wit and humor, he was officious and self-important as well, parading his access to Lord Oxford and not even bothering to stay for prayers. But Ehrenpreis plausibly suggests a different angle: Swift knew that Kennett was hostile and "was deliberately overplaying the part of an insider."[40]

In a poem written after his London years were over, Swift had no illusions about the reality of his role.

> Now Finch alarms the Lords: he hears for certain
> This dangerous priest is got behind the curtain;
> Finch, famed for tedious elocution, proves
> That Swift oils many a spring which Harley moves. . . .
> Now Delaware again familiar grows,
> And in Swift's ear thrusts half his powdered nose.[41]

In another poem, Swift confessed that his conversations with the great man were all too mundane:

> Since Harley bid me first attend
> And chose me for an humble friend,

> Would take me in his coach to chat,
> And question me of this and that,
> As "What's o'clock?" and "How's the wind?
> Whose chariot's that we left behind?" . . .
> Where all that passes *inter nos*
> Might be proclaimed at Charing Cross.[42]

When Swift's friend Patrick Delany began to believe that a lord lieutenant was going to reward him in some way, Swift warned that people in power might enjoy the company of wits and scholars, but they reward only political favors.

> Suppose my Lord and you alone;
> Hint the least interest of your own—
> His visage drops, he knits his brow,
> He cannot talk of business now.[43]

Oxford once tried to pay Swift £50 for a pamphlet, and he turned down the money with indignation. He wanted it understood that he was expressing his own convictions freely, not serving as a paid drudge like Daniel Defoe. If he accepted no pay, they couldn't dictate what he wrote, and he could go back to Laracor at any time—as Sheridan said, "return to his willows at a day's notice, on any ill treatment, without the least reluctance."[44]

What Swift did want, as always, was a cushy appointment in the Church. That was still not forthcoming. The ministers, he told Stella, "call me nothing but Jonathan; and I said I believed they would leave me Jonathan as they found me; and that I never knew a ministry do anything for those whom they make companions of their pleasures." From their point of view, there was nothing wrong with that. Appointments in both church and state were bargaining chips in the world of power. They were useful to confer obligations or to block rivals, and Swift's colleagues had no reason to waste a bargaining chip on him. Besides, they needed his pen to defend their policies. Why would they give him an appointment that would mean losing him?[45]

Such power as Swift did exercise took the form of giving boosts to deserving people when he could. The boosting was even institutionalized in a club, known simply as the Club. "The end of our Club," he told Stella, "is to advance conversation and friendship, and to reward deserving persons with our interest and recommendation. We take in none but men of wit or men of interest [that is, people in power], and if we go on as we begin, no other club in this town will be worth talking of." In the beginning there were a dozen members, and eventually nearly twice as many, half of whom were peers.[46] They may all have been men of wit, but the reason they were there was that they were players on the political scene; the only writers were Swift, Matthew Prior, and John Arbuthnot. Although Prior was a poet, he was best known as a diplomat, and Arbuthnot published only occasionally. The Club valued him because he was the queen's physician, and an excellent source of information about her moods and intentions.

Swift liked to think of himself as disinterested, and he often put in a good word for writers on the other side of the political fence. "It was in those times," he said later, "a usual subject of raillery towards me among the ministers that I never came to them without a Whig in my sleeve." He recalled that he had been "officious to do good offices to many of that party, which was then out of power."[47]

It was not always possible to help writers if they refused to help themselves. Swift grew friendly at this time with an Irish clergyman, Thomas Parnell. He was a poet of some elegance, and a poem of his called *A Night-Piece on Death* remained popular for a long time, though as Johnson noted, "The general character of Parnell is not great extent of comprehension or fertility of mind." Unfortunately, Parnell was an alcoholic. Oxford had no prejudices in that direction, but there were limits to what he was prepared to tolerate. Johnson heard that Parnell "could not get through a sermon without turning his head, even in the pulpit, to drink a dram," and Swift related to Delany an example of Oxford's dry wit: "Parnell was miserably addicted to drinking. He could not refrain even in the morning that Swift introduced him to Lord Oxford. My Lord pressed through the crowd to get to Parnell, but he soon perceived his situation. He in a little said to Swift, 'Your friend, I fear, is not very well.' Swift answered, 'He is troubled with a great shaking.' 'I am sorry,' said the Earl, 'that he should have such a distemper, but especially that it should attack him in the morning.'"[48]

There were times when Swift would also use his influence to secure justice for someone at the bottom of society. Bolingbroke's undersecretary was urging him to pardon a rapist "upon the old notion that a woman cannot be ravished"—in other words, that she must have gone along with it instead of resisting. "'Tis true," Swift told Stella, "the fellow had lain with her a hundred times before, but what care I for that? What! must a woman be ravished because she is a whore?" At that time an accusation of rape was almost never believed in court if the victim had a reputation for promiscuity.[49]

POLITICAL PRINCIPLES AND POLEMICAL COMBAT

What the Tories wanted the *Examiner* to do was to articulate their fundamental ideology. In the Tory political creed, the nation rested on twin supports, the land and the Church. Landowners had the nation's interest at heart because it coincided with their own. And the established Church was the binding principle of shared community.

"Law in a free country," Swift wrote, "is, or ought to be, the determination of the majority of those who have property in land." That position was normal all over Europe. "Rule by a tiny group of privileged landowners," a historian says, "was the basis of the social structure right across the continent, and the assumption that landed property translated into political power was universal." Whigs differed from Tories only in wanting merchants and financiers to have a share in the spoils; there was no notion of extending the franchise to humble citizens. And in practice the merchants and financiers weren't really distinct from the landowners, since they constantly intermarried with them and acquired estates of their own.[50]

As for the Church, it is crucial to grasp that whatever Swift's private beliefs may have been, he saw its authority as essentially legal rather than spiritual. Having been officially "established," it exercised authority simply because it *was* established. A loyal member of his Church, Swift said, "would defend it by arms against all the powers on earth, except our own legislature." By this reasoning, in France and Italy the Catholic Church was likewise entitled to be obeyed. In Britain, Catholics and Dissenters were free to worship as they pleased, but not to enjoy the same civil rights as Anglicans. Bolingbroke the freethinker took exactly the same view: "There must be a religion; this religion must be national, and this national religion must be maintained in reputation and reverence; all other sects must be kept too low to become the rivals of it."[51]

In Swift's mind, therefore, it was entirely appropriate that he should go over to the Tories. He had worked with the Junto because, as he later said, he was "much inclined to be what they called a Whig in politics," accepting William III's right to the throne. "But as to religion, I confessed myself to be an high churchman, and that I did not conceive how anyone who wore the habit of a clergyman could be otherwise."[52] "High Churchmen" regarded Dissent as subversion and wanted the Test and Toleration acts rigidly enforced. "Low Churchmen," also known as "latitudinarians," wanted toleration of Dissenters to be extended. Whigs tended to be Low Churchmen and Tories High Churchmen.

Swift kept his authorship of the *Examiner* so secret that the Whigs were never sure whom they were arguing with. He was careful not to reveal that he was a clergyman, claiming at one point, "I understand not ecclesiastical affairs well enough" to comment on them. And he affected a pose of lofty objectivity that infuriated the Whigs. "An Examiner is a creature of power," one of them wrote, "a spaniel that fetches and carries at the command of his master."[53]

Swift often put a partisan spin on alleged facts, and he made it seem plausible because his writing was exceptionally clear and straightforward. As the editor of his prose observes, if an anonymous piece of writing is convoluted and wordy, you can be sure it's by someone else. He had a special technique for making sure his writing was intelligible. It was his practice, a friend said, to read aloud to two servants (he didn't say which ones). "When he had any doubt, he would ask them the meaning of what they heard; which, if they did not comprehend, he would alter and amend until they understood it perfectly well, and then would say, 'This will do; for I write to the vulgar, more than to the learned.'"[54]

Although Swift's style is deliberately "plain," it is also muscular and compelling. Commenting on a history of the Church, he once rewrote an overelaborate passage in order to bring it to life. Here is the original text, describing unworthy clergymen: "They are an insensible and degenerate race, who are thinking of nothing but their present advantages; and so that they may now support a luxurious and brutal course of irregular and voluptuous practices, they are easily hired to betray their religion, to sell their country, and to give up that liberty and those properties which are the present felicities and glories of this nation." That's barely readable. Swift's version gets rid of the big words and abstractions, and leaps from the page: "The bulk of the clergy, and one third of the bishops, are stupid sons of whores, who think of nothing but getting money as soon as they can. If they may but procure enough to supply them in gluttony, drunkenness, and whoring, they are ready to turn traitors to God and their country, and make their fellow subjects slaves."[55]

George Orwell once drew up a recipe for good prose:

(i) Never use a metaphor, simile, or other figure of speech which you are used to seeing in print.

(ii) Never use a long word where a short one will do.

(iii) If it is possible to cut a word out, always cut it out.

(iv) Never use the passive where you can use the active.

(v) Never use a foreign phrase, a scientific word, or a jargon word if you can think of an everyday English equivalent.

(vi) Break any of these rules sooner than say anything outright barbarous.[56]

Swift was consciously committed to every one of these principles, and his writing embodies them brilliantly.

In all, Swift turned out thirty-three *Examiner* papers, from November of 1710 to June of the following year (it was then carried on for a while, not very well, by others). It had been a major achievement, and it fills close to two hundred pages in a modern edition.

POLITICAL LYING

Swift still had old scores to settle with the Whig grandees who had failed to reward him. He didn't really hate Godolphin, though he pilloried him as Sid Hamet with his magician's rod. There was one man he did hate—"like a toad," he said—and that was Thomas, Earl of Wharton.[57] Wharton had served a term as lord lieutenant of Ireland as well as being a leading member of the Junto, and he infuriated Swift in every way. He actively promoted the Dissenting cause and wanted the Test Act abolished; he used his immense fortune to install his own creatures in Parliament; and he was a shameless libertine.

Swift launched his campaign against Wharton in the second of his *Examiner* papers, on "the art of political lying."

> [Wharton] never yet considered whether any proposition were true or false, but whether it were convenient for the present minute or company to affirm or deny it; so that if you think to refine upon him by interpreting everything he says, as we do dreams, by the contrary, you are still to seek, and will find yourself equally deceived whether you believe or no. The only remedy is to suppose that you have heard some inarticulate sounds without any meaning at all. . . . It often happens that if a lie be believed only for an hour, it hath done its work, and there is no farther occasion for it. Falsehood flies, and truth comes limping after it; so that when men come to be undeceived, it is too late.[58]

In later *Examiners* Swift kept up the attack, pretending to talk about a corrupt Roman governor called Verres but really referring to Wharton, and afterward retailing a scandalous anecdote about him:

That worthy patriot and true lover of the Church, whom a late *Examiner* is supposed to reflect on under the name of Verres, felt a pious impulse to be a benefactor to the Cathedral of Gloucester, but how to do it in the most decent, generous manner was the question. At last he thought of an expedient. One morning or night he stole into the church, mounted upon the altar, and there did that which in cleanly phrase is called *disburthening of nature*. He was discovered, prosecuted, and condemned to pay a thousand pounds, which sum was all employed to support the Church, as no doubt the benefactor meant it.

Apparently this actually happened, though the fine was reduced to £40.[59]

For a really thorough hatchet job, Swift needed more space than an *Examiner* paper, and after some months he brought out a pamphlet called *A Short Character of His Excellency Thomas Earl of Wharton*. The character assassination was masterful. "He is without the sense of shame or glory, as some men are without the sense of smelling. . . . He is a Presbyterian in politics and an atheist in religion, but he chooseth at present to whore with a Papist."[60]

Knowing that his letters to Ireland were likely to be opened by spies, Swift couldn't tell Stella he had written the *Short Character*, but he made sure she knew about it. "Here's a damned libelous pamphlet come out against Lord Wharton, giving the character first and then telling some of his actions. . . . I had one or two of them, but nobody knows the author or printer."[61] Two thousand copies were sold in two days.

Naturally, Wharton resented Swift's attacks, but when they ran into each other a year later he was as insouciant as ever. "I intended to dine with Mr. Masham today, and called at White's chocolate house to see if he was there. Lord Wharton saw me at the door, and I saw him, but took no notice, and was going away; but he came through the crowd, called after me, and asked me how I did, etc. This was pretty; and I believe he wished every word he spoke was a halter to hang me." Wharton never got back into power, and never had a chance to do further damage to Swift. For his part, Swift never forgave. Long afterward he encountered Wharton's name in a book and wrote in the margin, "The most universal villain I ever knew."[62]

TWO PECULIAR PUBLICATIONS

Producing political polemics was Swift's job, but that wasn't all he published. He brought out a volume called *Miscellanies in Prose and Verse*

anonymously, as usual, that included a number of his short pieces, including *An Argument against Abolishing Christianity* and *Sentiments of a Church
of England Man*. A prefatory note observes, "There are in every one of these
pieces some particular beauties that discover this author's vein, who excels too
much not to be distinguished, since in all his writings such a surprising mixture of wit and learning, true humour and good sense, does everywhere appear, as sets him almost as far out of the reach of imitation, as it does beyond
the power of censure." We can be sure that Swift agreed with this description.
He wrote it himself.[63]

It's not clear how much money Swift made from this book, and in any
case, publishers paid up front for a manuscript and that was all the author
would ever get, no matter what the sales turned out to be.

Swift also published two pamphlets that are extremely puzzling because
they make earnestly positive recommendations in a way that's uncharacteristic of him. One of these, *A Proposal for Correcting, Improving, and Ascertain-
ing the English Tongue*, calls upon Lord Oxford to sponsor a British academy
that will police changes in language usage. Most unusually, Swift signed his
real name.

Swift did believe that too much slang was getting into print. Since slang
changes constantly, he was afraid that future generations would be unable
to read the works of his own time. In a *Tatler* paper he acknowledged wryly,
"I have done my utmost for some years past to stop the progress of *mob* and
banter, but have been plainly borne down by numbers, and betrayed by those
who promised to assist me." "Mob" sounds like a fine old Anglo-Saxon word,
but it was a recent invention, a contraction of *mobile vulgus*, "the unstable
common people." Likewise "banter" originated in Swift's lifetime.[64]

Proposing an academy wasn't an idiosyncratic notion; there were many
similar suggestions. The Académie Française had been founded by Cardi-
nal Richelieu back in 1635, and there was a widespread feeling that England
should have an academy of its own. But Swift was normally contemptuous of
visionary proposals. What other agenda might he have had?

An obvious motive was to show how important he had become. He was
known only as a party journalist, good at his job but working at a subliterary
level, and of course he couldn't acknowledge his writings publicly. Now he
was making a bid to appear as a major player in culture. He was also making it
known that he was an intimate of the lord treasurer, mentioning chats about
language that the two of them had had. As Ehrenpreis says, "The style of the
essay is pushingly personal." Beyond that, the proposed academy would be a

Tory fiefdom, and Swift would in effect be the British Richelieu. No wonder he signed his name.[65]

The other piece is stranger by far. Called *A Project for the Advancement of Religion, and the Reformation of Manners*, it came out in 1709. This piece is interesting not for what it claims to say but for what it may imply. It may in fact be one of the booby traps that Swift was fond of setting, which explode beneath readers who take them at face value.

Writing anonymously again, Swift declares that although immorality and irreligion are widespread, Queen Anne has the power to stop them. She controls appointments in government and the military, and she should let it be known that anyone who behaves immorally will be dismissed. Graft and corruption would then be nonexistent in a ministry in which "every single person was of distinguished piety," and as their influence spread, "morality and religion would soon become fashionable court virtues." In society in general, all that is needed is ruthless enforcement of existing laws, which will be ensured by establishing "something parallel to the office of censors anciently in Rome." A team of commissioners should travel throughout the country to receive "complaints and informations" against offenders.[66]

Not everyone, of course, would experience a genuine change of heart, but at least people would have to pretend to. "Hypocrisy is much more eligible than open infidelity and vice. It wears the livery of religion, it acknowledgeth her authority, and is cautious of giving scandal. . . . And I believe it is with religion as it is with love, which by much dissembling at last grows real."[67]

Can Swift possibly have meant all this? Some distinguished Swiftians have thought he did. But it's hard to believe that the author of the *Argument to Abolish Christianity*, with its mordant critique of "nominal Christianity," could call for obligatory hypocrisy in a police state founded on censorship and spying. Throughout his life Swift regarded political informers with loathing. Years later he called them "the most accursed and prostitute and abandoned race that God ever permitted to plague mankind." We know too that he despised "projects" of every kind, especially ones that claimed to reshape human behavior. Can he really have believed, as the *Project* claims, that faith and morality would return to a high standard "in a short time, and with no very great trouble"?[68] And can he really have wanted ruthless censorship?

This may well be yet another instance of Swiftian impersonation, and one in which he has covered his tracks so well that even experts have been misled. Sheridan provided a clue long ago: this pamphlet is "a very strong though covert attack upon the power of the Whigs." By a brilliant stroke,

Swift appropriated what the queen herself had recently declared, in a proclamation to be read in churches: "For the greater encouragement of religion and morality, we will, upon all occasions, distinguish persons of piety and virtue by marks of our royal favour." A Society for the Reformation of Manners was digging up dirt on allegedly immoral persons and pressing to have them prosecuted. That was widely resented as a resurgence of Whiggish Puritanism, and it's inconceivable that Swift was in sympathy with it. But if the Whigs did suspect that the *Project* was aimed at them, they were helpless to do anything about it, since it mirrored so closely the views of the queen herself.[69]

CHAPTER 14

The Journal to Stella

AN INTIMATE VOICE

It is easy to forget that the documents that happen to survive record only a tiny fraction of people's lives. In 1708 Swift began saving his correspondence, including drafts of his letters to other people, and 97 percent of what we have comes after that. But by then he was forty-one years old and had lived more than half his life.[1]

For an extended period of nearly three years, from September 1710 to June 1713, we finally see Swift's life up close. During that time he kept a daily record, sent in sixty-five installments from London to Dublin and dubbed the *Journal to Stella* in 1779, six decades after it was written. Stella was twenty-nine when the journal began and had known Swift for twenty years.

Unfortunately, we have only Swift's side of the correspondence, though we know that Stella sent at least sixty replies (he kept a numbered list). Sometimes we can guess at their content from his replies, but we never hear Stella's own voice. Herbert Davis thinks he destroyed her letters at some time after her death, as he did all other correspondence between them. Altogether, in fact, we have just three letters written by Stella at any time in her life, and none of them is significant.[2]

The reason Swift sent the journal in installments was that postage was expensive—sixpence for a letter from London to Dublin, and a shocking

2 shillings per ounce for a package. When possible, a couple of weeks' entries would be sent off in a single parcel with someone who was traveling to Dublin. Packages always went that way. Swift sent Stella "palsy water" for some sort of numbing facial condition, and "the finest piece of Brazil tobacco for Dingley that ever was born."[3] Women didn't smoke, but they did use snuff, which was often prepared at home by grating dried tobacco.

Rebecca Dingley not only received occasional presents from Swift, she was the co-recipient of the *Journal to Stella*. Since there were no street addresses, Swift had to identify their house by location, which he did in various ways. One parcel was sent "to Mrs. Dingley, at her lodgings over against St. Mary's church near Capel Street, Dublin"; another was addressed "to Mrs. Dingley, at Mr. Curry's house over against the Ram in Capel Street, Ireland, Dublin."[4]

To save expensive paper, all of which had to be handmade, Swift wrote in a minuscule script. Stella had weak eyes, and Rebecca read the letters aloud. It has been suggested that by addressing both women, Swift was protecting himself from too much intimacy, but there are plenty of intimate moments in the *Journal*. The tiny script may itself have implied a private bond. "Methinks when I write plain," he commented, "I do not know how, but we are not alone—all the world can see us."[5]

The *Journal to Stella* has come down to us in two very different segments. Swift gave a bundle containing the first forty installments to his cousin, Martha Whiteway, who cared for him in his final years. From her they passed to Deane Swift, who made numerous minor alterations—impossible to identify today, since the originals have vanished—and in that form they found their way into print. The other twenty-five were discovered by Dr. John Lyon, one of Swift's executors, when he went through his papers after his death. These too were first published in edited form, but fortunately the originals survived, and are now in the British Library.

From the Lyon batch, it becomes apparent that there were curious short-hand nicknames for the three participants in the correspondence. Swift was "Pdfr," Stella (and perhaps Dingley as well) "Ppt." Both women together are "MD," and Rebecca is "DD" when the context requires mentioning her individually. These nicknames are usually interpreted as standing for "Poor Dear Foolish Rogue," "Poppet," "My Dears," and "Dear Dingley." The first seems rather far-fetched, and is based on nothing but guesswork, but no one has suggested anything better. We do know that it was pronounced "Podefar," because Rebecca wrote it out like that in a marginal note. As for "MD," a rhyme at one point shows that it was pronounced "Em Dee"—"Letters from MDs Must not be answered in ten days; 'tis but bad rhyme."[6]

Supposedly "MD" always means Dingley as well as Stella, but that's sometimes hard to believe. "Now I am in bed between eleven and twelve, just going to sleep, and dream of my own dear roguish impudent pretty MD."[7] Rebecca Dingley was not roguish, impudent, or pretty, but Stella was all of those things.

Deane Swift must have found the nicknames embarrassing, so he got rid of them. If his segment of the *Journal* was all that we had, we would imagine that Swift called himself "Presto" and that Hester Johnson was always "Stella." It's true that in later poems he made the name "Stella" familiar, but he never used it in the *Journal*. As for "Presto," Deane Swift picked that up from a single casual anecdote. Swift happened to repeat what St. John had laughingly told him: "The Duchess of Shrewsbury [who was Italian] asked him, was not that Doctor—Doctor—and she could not say my name in English, but said Dr. *Presto*, which is Italian for Swift."[8]

A motto Swift often invoked was *vive la bagatelle*. Years later, counseling Archbishop King on how to keep melancholy at bay, he said, "I have a receipt [recipe] to which you are a stranger; my Lord Oxford and Mr. Prior used to join with me in taking it, to whom I often said, when we were two hours diverting ourselves with trifles, *vive la bagatelle*."[9]

If we didn't have the *Journal to Stella*, we could only guess at what the informal, playful Swift was like, but now we hear him everywhere in the letters.

> I dined today with Patty Rolt at my cousin Leach's, with a pox, in the City. He is a printer, and prints the *Postman*, oh ho, and is my cousin, God knows how, and he married Mrs. Baby Aires of Leicester; and my cousin Thomson was with us; and my cousin Leach offers to bring me acquainted with the author of the *Postman*, and says he does not doubt but the gentleman will be glad of my acquaintance, and that he is a very ingenious man, and a great scholar, and has been beyond sea. But I was modest, and said maybe the gentleman was shy, and not fond of new acquaintance, and so put it off. And I wish you could hear me repeating all I have said of this in its proper tone, just as I am writing it. 'Tis all with the same cadence with "oh hoo," or as when little girls say, "I have got an apple, miss, and I won't give you some."

Patty Rolt was Swift's age, a distant relative. As for Mrs. Baby Aires, Sir Harold Williams explains in his edition of the *Journal* that she "may be fictitious."[10] One can imagine what Swift would have said about Sir Harold.

There are frequent glimpses of street life, from the night watchman's call— "Paaaast twelvvve o'clock"—to treats for sale on the twelfth day of Christmas. "Silly, silly, silly, you are silly, both are silly, every kind of thing is silly. As I walked into the city I was stopped with clusters of boys and wenches buzzing about the cake-shops like flies. There had the fools let out their shops two yards forward into the streets, all spread with great cakes frothed with sugar, and stuck with streamers of tinsel." The changing seasons are regularly noted. "The Canal and Rosamond's Pond [in St. James's Park] full of the rabble sliding, and with skates, if you know what those are." Ice skates were a novelty, brought over quite recently from Holland.[11]

Often Swift makes himself palpably present. He calls attention to the paper that his friends have in their hands, remarking on inkblots, tobacco smudges, and candle wax. And he dramatizes his moment-to-moment experience: "I have my mouth full of water, and was going to spit it out, because I reasoned with myself, how could I write when my mouth was full? Han't you done things like that, reasoned wrong at first thinking?" He also emphasizes the difference between the familiar self and the public one: "Pdfr is going to be very busy; not Pdfr, but t'other I." Or again, "Answer MD's letter, Pdfr, d'ye hear? No, says Pdfr, I won't yet, I'm busy: you're a saucy rogue. Who talks?" Michael DePorte comments, "Even Swift seems confused by the inner play of voices."[12]

There are thoughts of home in Ireland. "Oh, that we were at Laracor this fine day! The willows begin to peep, and the quicks [hawthorn hedges] to bud. My dream's out—I was a-dreamed last night that I ate ripe cherries. And now they begin to catch the pikes, and will shortly the trouts (pox on these ministers), and I would fain know whether the floods were ever so high as to get over the holly bank or the river walk. If so, then all my pikes are gone; but I hope not."[13] "Pox on these ministers" implies regret at being confined to London by politics. No doubt Swift wants the ladies to believe that he misses Laracor more than he actually does; yet he does miss it.

Swift never forgot that at any moment he might be staggered by an attack of nausea and vertigo. Recurring comments show what a handicap Ménière's syndrome was for him:

> *April 18.* I know not what's the matter. It has never been thus before: two days together giddy from morning till night, but not with any violence or pain; and I totter a little, but can make shift to walk.

Oct. 24. I had a little turn in my head this morning, which, though it did not last above a moment, yet being of the true sort [i.e., not an ordinary headache] has made me weak as a dog all this day.[14]

Swift's account books give a grimmer picture than he revealed to Stella and Rebecca. Thus, during a two-month period in 1708: ["Nov.] From 6 to 16 often giddy. God help me. So to 25th less. 16, brandy for giddiness, 2 shillings. [Dec.] 5, Horrible sick. 12th Much better, thank God and MD's prayers. 16, Bad fit at Mrs. Barton's. 24th. Better, but—dread a fit."[15]

As a sufferer from Ménière's, Swift was the victim of a condition that was always unpleasant and at times overwhelming. It would be difficult to exaggerate the lifelong burden this became. In the words of a modern medical expert, "The sufferer feels as though he is being violently seasick in the middle of an earthquake. . . . A disease in which one can fall out of a chair, which may make it necessary to lie prostrate to avoid injury through falling, while a world whirling in giddy circles mingles with a background of violent nausea, will leave its mark on any man."[16]

At one point Swift also had to endure an agonizing attack of shingles, which he described vividly in the *Journal*:

> I was not able to go to church or court to-day, for my shoulder. The pain has left my shoulder and crept to my neck and collarbone. It makes me think of pooppt's bladebone. Urge, urge, urge, dogs gnawing. . . . The pain increased with mighty violence in my left shoulder and collarbone and that side my neck. On Thursday morning appeared great red spots in all those places where my pain was, and the violence of the pain was confined to my neck behind, a little on the left side; which was so violent that I [had] not a minute's ease nor hardly a minute's sleep in three days and nights. The spots increased every day and had little pimples, which are now grown white and full of corruption, though small. The red still continues too, and most prodigious hot and inflamed. The disease is the shingles.

This description provoked Swift's Victorian biographer Craik to comment that "we are dealing with a man whose modes of thought were peculiar," living in an age "whose modes of expression differed from our own."[17]

When Swift's doctors decided it wasn't actually shingles, but something more obscure, he commented wryly, "I can never be sick like other people, but always something out of the common way." That was certainly true of the vertigo. He told Stella a bit later, "I think we both have that faculty never to part with a disorder forever; we are very constant. I have had my giddiness 23 years by fits."[18] It's impossible to be sure what Stella's chronic condition was, but she was never in very good health, and in her last years she was seriously ill.

Whenever Swift's health returned, he kept up his lifelong practice of walking. In the spring of 1711 he took lodging in Chelsea, which was then a rural village a couple of miles west of London, reached by a pleasant footpath through the fields. On a fine day in May he exclaimed, "About our town we are mowing already and making hay, and it smells so sweet as we walk through the flowery meads." He added, though, "The hay-making nymphs are perfect drabs, nothing so clean and pretty as further in the country."[19]

Increasingly portly in spite of regular exercise, Swift detested hot weather, and took the opportunity to swim in the Thames while his servant guarded his clothes on the bank. "I have been swimming this half-hour and more; and when I was coming out I dived, to make my head and all through wet, like a cold bath." The ability to swim, which he probably learned to do in the river at Kilkenny, was rare at the time. Several weeks later the heat wave broke, and Swift exclaimed with relief, "O this dear rain, I cannot forbear praising it; I never felt myself to be revived so in my life. It lasted from three till five, hard as a horn, and mixed with hail."[20]

Sometimes an element of strangeness enters the *Journal*, when Swift reports his dreams. Whenever he wrote about dreams in print, which wasn't often, he said that they had no special meaning and were just recycling images already present in a person's mind. That was the standard view of empiricist psychology at the time. Yet his dreams were clearly disturbing. "Lord, I dreamt of Ppt, etc., so confusedly last night, and that we saw Dean Bolton and Stearne go into a shop; and she bid me call them to her, and they proved to be two parsons I know not; and I walked without till she was shifting, and such stuff, mixed with much melancholy and uneasiness, and things not as they should be, and I know not how. And it is now an ugly gloomy morning."[21]

This is what Freud calls the uncanny, familiar things turning disconcertingly strange. "Things not as they should be" is a recurring theme, and as Michael DePorte observes, this dissolving world has much in common with the disorienting changes of perspective in *A Tale of a Tub* or *Gulliver's Travels*.[22] By "shifting" Swift means that Stella was changing her clothes, presumably in the shop. Why does he wait until then to go inside? Does he watch her?

Another dream is self-explanatory. "Morrow, little dears. O, faith, I have been dreaming; I was to be put in prison. I don't know why, and I was so afraid of a black dungeon; and then all I had been inquiring yesterday of Sir

Andrew Fountaine's sickness I thought was of poor Ppt. The worst of dreams is that one wakes just in the humour they leave one."[23] Entangled in risky political maneuvering, Swift might well dream about prison, and Stella's health was a constant concern.

Whatever was wrong with Sir Andrew, it was bad, because his doctors expected him to die and he sent for Swift to say prayers, "which you know is the last thing." Ten days later he was still "extremely ill" and paying his doctors £10 a day.[24] He got better, however, and lived another forty years.

One other dream got recorded during these years, not in the *Journal* but in a note that Swift jotted down. He woke at two in the morning with two lines of verse in his head, "which I had made in my sleep":

> I walk before no man, a hawk in his fist,
> Nor am I a brilliant, wherever I list.

He added that he wrote them down immediately so that "two such precious lines may not be lost to posterity," but admitted that he had no idea what they meant. Strange and even haunting, they would never have gone into a Swift poem during waking hours.[25]

FRIENDS AND ACQUAINTANCES

The *Journal to Stella* swarms with people, some of them close friends, others casual acquaintances. It occurred to Swift that he might be supplying more details than his Dublin correspondents wanted. "I fancy my talking of persons and things here must be very tedious to you, because you know nothing of them, and I talk as if you did."[26]

Closest at hand was Swift's servant Patrick, who made a fire in the morning, carried messages, and answered the door. That last duty was important, for a servant needed to know when to deny that his employer was at home. After Patrick was replaced by someone else, Swift complained, "My man is not such an artist as Patrick at denying me."[27]

In other respects, though, Patrick was exasperating. Londoners lived in fear of burglary, and they controlled access to a house by having a single key for each door. That meant that when Swift went out, Patrick was supposed to stay at home. One evening Swift was locked out until ten. When Patrick finally showed up, "I went up, shut the chamber door, and gave him two or three swingeing cuffs on the ear, and I have strained the thumb of my left hand with pulling him, which I did not feel until he was gone. He was plaguily afraid and humbled."[28] The strained thumb may have been some consolation for Patrick.

The biggest problem was that Patrick regularly got drunk, making implausible excuses afterward. In his ironic "directions to servants" Swift gave tongue-in-cheek suggestions for what a servant might say: "You were taking leave of a dear cousin who is to be hanged next Saturday. . . . Some nastiness was thrown on you out of a garret window, and you were ashamed to come home before you were cleaned and the smell went off. . . . You were told your master had gone to a tavern and come to some mischief, and your grief was so great that you inquired for his honour in a hundred taverns between Pall Mall and Temple Bar."[29]

Others who turn up in the *Journal* are Stella's mother and sister. "This morning Ppt's sister came to me with a letter from her mother, who is at Sheen, but will soon be in town and will call to see me. She gave me a bottle of palsy water, a small one, and desired I would send it you by the first convenience, as I will, and she promises a quart bottle of the same. Your sister looked very well, and seems a good modest sort of girl."[30] This was Anne Johnson, married at some point, but perhaps not yet, to a baker named Filby for whom Swift later tried to find a government position. She was a "girl" of twenty-seven in 1710.

Stella's mother was at Sheen because she was still in the employ of Lady Giffard, Temple's sister. Since Swift had quarreled with Lady Giffard over his publication of the Temple papers, he had no wish to go to Sheen; he had already written to Bridget Johnson to say that he wanted to see her "without hazarding seeing Lady Giffard, which I will not do until she begs my pardon."[31] That was never going to happen.

Bridget's employer limited her freedom severely. Swift wrote indignantly to Stella, "I will desire her to let Lady Giffard know that she hears I am in town, and she would go to see me to inquire after you. I wonder she will confine herself so much to that old beast's humour." Finally Bridget did come to see him, and they talked for an hour, mostly about Stella's finances. Swift was able to report, "She looks extremely well." They stayed in touch after that, as occasional mentions confirm: "Your mother's cakes are very good, and one of them serves me for a breakfast." There were further consignments of "palsy water" for Stella, too, brewed from cowslip, also known as palsy-wort. If she actually had palsy, that meant temporary paralysis of a facial nerve, but the concoction was used for other ailments as well.[32]

Someone else who appears is Swift's sister, Jane, about whom he was as unenthusiastic as ever. When the Moor Park household broke up she had married a tanner named Fenton, whom Swift detested. The marriage was not a success, and Jane was now working for Lady Giffard again. If Denis Johnston is right and Jane knew Temple family secrets, Lady Giffard may have thought it advisable to employ her.[33]

In the public world, Swift was constantly in contact with members of the nobility, and always on guard to make sure they didn't condescend to him. "The Duchess of Shrewsbury came up and reproached me for not dining with her. I said that was not so soon done, for I expected more advances from ladies, especially duchesses. She promised to comply with any demands I pleased." This might seem arrogant, but she got the point: he refused to be classed with the sycophants who swarmed around the court. And they knew he had power. As Virginia Woolf says, "Nobody could buy his services; everybody feared his pen."[34]

Often these people became good friends, the formidable Duke of Ormonde, for instance: "I have been five times with the Duke of Ormonde about a perfect trifle, and he forgets it; I used him like a dog this morning for it." In the same vein, "I lost my handkerchief in the Mall tonight with Lord Radnor, but I made him walk with me to find it, and find it I did not."[35]

Swift was especially pleased when friends would join in his favorite game of punning. Lord Carteret was in London, as happy to do it as he had been in Dublin, and others were too. As usual, the puns Swift reports make discouraging reading:

> We all pun here sometimes. Lord Carteret set down Prior t'other day in his chariot, and Prior thanked him for his *charity*. That was fit for Dilly [Dillon Ashe]. . . .
>
> Henley told me that the Tories were insupportable people, because they are for bringing in French claret, and will not *sup-port*. . . .
>
> I made a good pun on Saturday to my Lord Keeper. After dinner we had coarse doily napkins, fringed at each end, upon the table to drink with. My Lord Keeper spread one of them between him and Mr. Prior; I told him I was glad to see there was such a *fringeship* between Mr. Prior and his Lordship.

Perhaps the whole point was to think up groaners. Swift went on to say, "Prior swore it was the worst he ever heard; I said I thought so too." That was certainly the expectation for an especially labored attempt: "If there was a hackney coach at Mr. Pooley's door, what town in Egypt would it be? Why, it would be *Hecatompolis, Hack at Tom Poley's*. Silly, says Ppt."[36]

There were agreeable friendships with several noblewomen, who appreciated Swift's combination of witty banter and frank esteem. At Windsor, where the court migrated during the summer and Swift was working with Oxford and Bolingbroke, he got to know Lady Orkney, now in her midfifties, who had been one of William III's mistresses and lived at the Cliveden estate nearby. "She is the wisest woman I ever saw," Swift told Stella, "and the Lord Treasurer [Oxford] made great use of her advice in the late change of affairs." On another occasion, "I dined yesterday with Lady Orkney, and we sat alone from 2 till 11 at night." Soon he was able to report, "Lady Orkney is making me a writing table of her own contrivance, and a bed nightgown." (She didn't make the table with her own hands, of course, but gave instructions to a "joiner.") Swift especially relished an aphorism of hers: "In men, desire begets love, and in women, love begets desire."[37]

Great ladies were fond of giving Swift presents, and the Duchess of Hamilton seems to have personally constructed a belt with pockets, "for you know I wear no waistcoat in summer, and there are several divisions, and one on purpose for my box, oh ho." The box was for snuff, and the Duke of Hamilton, who had just been named ambassador to France, gave him a pound of snuff that was "admirable good." But just two weeks later Swift had a dreadful story to tell:

> This morning at 8 my man brought me word that Duke Hamilton had fought with Lord Mohun, and killed him, and was brought home wounded. I immediately sent him to the Duke's house in St. James's Square, but the porter could hardly answer for tears, and a great rabble was about the house. In short, they fought at 7 this morning. The dog Mohun was killed on the spot; and while the Duke was over him, Mohun, shortening his sword, stabbed him in at the shoulder to the heart. The Duke was helped towards the cake house by the Ring in Hyde Park (where they fought), and died on the grass before he could reach the house, and was brought home in his coach by 8, while the poor Duchess was asleep. Maccartney and one Hamilton were the seconds, who fought likewise, and are both fled. I am told that a footman of Lord Mohun's stabbed Duke Hamilton, and some say Maccartney did so too. Mohun gave the affront, and yet sent the challenge. I am infinitely concerned for the poor Duke, who was a frank, honest, good-natured man. I loved him very well, and I think he loved me better.

The incident has been called "the most celebrated duel of the age," all the more shocking because Mohun not only provoked the quarrel, but had been twice tried for murder by the House of Lords. Swift hurried to do what he could to comfort the duchess, who was in despair—"She has moved my very soul."[38]

Deaths provoked Swift's most emotional entries in the *Journal*, especially when those who died were young and he knew them well.

> I am just now told that poor dear Lady Ashburnham, the Duke of Ormonde's daughter, died yesterday at her country house. The poor creature was with child. She was my greatest favorite, and I am in excessive concern for her loss. I hardly knew a more valuable person on all accounts; you must have heard me tell of her. I am afraid to see the Duke and Duchess. She was naturally very healthy; I am afraid she has been thrown away for want of care. Pray condole with me; 'tis extremely moving. . . . I hate life, when I think it exposed to such accidents; and to see so many thousand wretches burthening the earth, while such as her die, makes me think God did never intend life for a blessing.

When Swift went to see the duke and duchess two days later, the duke "bore up as well as he could, but something accidentally falling in discourse, the tears were just falling out of his eyes, and I looked off to give him an opportunity (which he took) of wiping them with his handkerchief. I never saw anything so moving, nor such a mixture of greatness of mind and tenderness and discretion."[39]

THE LITTLE LANGUAGE

In addition to putting in the names "Presto" and "Stella," Deane Swift took out every instance of writing that sounds like this: "I go on with such courage to prate upon nothing to deerichar Md, oo would wonder"; "Meetinks I begin to want a rettle flom Md"; and "I assure oo it im vely rate now." This is a style of baby talk that Swift, Stella, and Rebecca called "ourrichar gangridge," which means "our little language." Over the years most of it has been deciphered on the basis of some fairly consistent rules: here, *r* takes the place of *l* and *ch* of *t* ("gangridge" seems to be a unique instance of *g* for *l*). "Deerichar" is therefore "dear little," "a rettle" is "a letter," and "vely rate" is "very late."[40]

Occasionally the gangridge is almost Joycean—"O Rold hot a cruttle" for "O Lord what a clutter"—but mostly it just seems like a private game.

Forster conjectured that it began when Stella was a child, and gloomily acknowledged, "It does not admit of doubt that Swift and Esther Johnson really talked, as well as wrote, such particular silliness." That is clearly true, because Swift says at one point, "Do you know what? when I am writing in our language I make up my mouth just as if I was speaking it. I caught myself at it just now."[41] This last comes from the transcription by Deane Swift, who must have replaced "ourrichar gangridge" with "our language."

What was it for? It can't have been for secrecy, since the prattle is never about anything scandalous (attempts to detect clues to passion have never gotten any traction). Woolf suggests that in a sophisticated society in which artificial politeness was obligatory, "to throw off the ceremonies and conventions and talk a 'little language' for one or two to understand is as much a necessity as a breath of air in a hot room."[42]

Swift liked to toss out teasing epithets, careful to call both ladies and not just Stella "naughty girls," "saucy rogues," "sauce boxes," "nauti nauti dear girls," and so on. Sometimes he addressed them as "sirrahs" ("sollahs" in the little language), not normally a female term, often as "young women" ("ung oomens"), and occasionally even as "boys." Rebecca was in her midforties and two years older than Swift. But he can be a boy too. Sometimes he sounds not like Joyce but like Leopold Bloom: "Now I am writing to saucy MD; no wonder, indeed, good boys must write to naughty girls." Occasionally he would forget to use the little language and have to correct himself: "Be good gals, dood dallars I mean."[43]

The *Journal* is written in a small, crabbed hand, hard to read and filling every inch of the paper. If an entry ended with blank space to spare it would often be filled it up with the little language: "Farewell deelest hearts & souls Md. Farewell Md Md Md FW FW FW FW Me Me Lele Lele Lele Sollahs lele." "FW" might stand for "farewell"; nobody knows what "lele" is supposed to mean. Sometimes it may be "there," but sometimes it clearly isn't. Anyway, that was the point. The private meanings were well known to the participants but not to anyone else.[44]

The conclusion to the entry for May 10, 1712 (in larger script than usual), begins with one of Swift's made-up rhyming proverbs and ends with the mysterious "lele."

This is a pitiful Letter for want of a better, but plagud with a Tetter, my Fancy does fetter—Ah my poor willows & Quicksets.—Well, but you must read John Bull. Do you understand it all? Did I tell you that

44. A page from the *Journal to Stella*.

young Parson Geree is going to be marryed, and asked my Advice—
when it was too late to break off. He tells me Elwick has purchased
40ll a year in Land adjoyning to his Living—Ppt does not say one
word of her own little Health. I'm angry almost; but I won't tause see
im a dood dallar in odle sings, iss ['cause she is a good girl in other
things, yes] and so im DD too. God bless Md & FW & Me, ay & Pdfr
too. farewell Md Md Md FW FW FW Me

Lele I can say lele it ung oomens

iss I tan, well as oo

[Lele, I can say lele yet, young women, yes I can, as well as you].[45]

The History of John Bull was a satire by Swift's friend Dr. Arbuthnot. John Geree
was the friend from Moor Park days who would describe, forty-five years after
this letter, his memories of Stella and suspicions about her parentage.

It appears that Stella did a good deal of teasing herself. "Faith, your letters
would make a dog silly, if I had a dog to be silly, but it must be a little dog."

And again, "I'll break your head in good earnest, young woman, for your nasty jest about Mrs. Barton. Unlucky sluttikin, what a word is there!" But we'll never know what word that was, and as Herbert Davis says, in passages like this one Stella is really a character in a play by Swift.[46]

Sometimes Swift imagines Stella interfering at the very moment he's writing. "Let me go, will you? and I'll come again tonight in a fine clean sheet of paper; but I can nor will stay longer now; no, I won't, for all your wheedling; no, no, look off, don't smile at me and say 'Pray, pray, Pdfr, write a little more.' Ah! you're a wheedling slut, you be so." Swift also enjoys pretending to overhear his friends. "Pray, love one another, and kiss one another just now, as DD is reading this; for you quarreled this morning just after Mrs. Marg'et [the maid] had poured water on Ppt's head. I heard the little bird say so." The bird was real enough. Patrick kept a pet linnet in a closet, which it disgustingly befouled.[47]

Often Swift imagines what Stella is doing. Usually it's playing cards, but sometimes it's taking walks or riding, as he constantly urges for the sake of her health.

> Ppt can't stay writing and writing; she must write and go a cock-horse, pray now. Well, but the horses are not come to the door; the fellow can't find the bridle; your stirrup is broken; where did you put the whips, DD? Marg'et, where have you laid Mrs. Johnson's ribband to tie about her? Reach me my mask: sup up this before you go. So, so, a gallop, a gallop: sit fast, sirrah, and don't ride hard upon the stones.— Well, now Ppt is gone, tell me, DD, is she a good girl?

At times Stella is permitted to mock Swift in reply: "So flap ee hand, and make wry mouth ee self sawci doxi."[48]

There is much talk about the physical reality of Stella's letters—anticipating them, receiving them, opening them, and reacting to them. Swift sometimes narrates the process moment by moment, in a sort of flirty foreplay. During the cold London winters he spent a lot of time reading and writing in bed, and Stella accompanies him there:

> I am now got into bed, and going to open your little letter; and God send I may find MD well, and happy, and merry, and that they love Pdfr as they do fires. Oh, I won't open it yet! yes I will! no I won't. I am going; I can't stay till I turn over [the page]. What shall I do? My fingers itch; and now I have it in my left hand; and now I'll open it

this very moment.—I have just got it, and am cracking the seal, and can't imagine what's in it."

At another time, "Now let us come and see what this saucy dear letter of MD says. Come out, letter, come out from between the sheets; here it is underneath, and it won't come out. Come out again, I say: so there. Here it is."[49]

There is a startling moment when Swift begins an entry right after waking up, and imagines Stella in Dublin getting up too: "Ppt is just now showing a white leg, and putting it into the slipper." Could this have some relation to an odd dream that he described earlier? In the dream he imagined that a mysterious saying was circulating about town: "I have desired Apronia to be always careful, especially about the legs." Stella had asked Swift to buy her an apron, and there was a good deal of discussion about it. Is Apronia, then, the apron with white legs underneath? Three days before this Swift had made an overt double entendre: "'Tis still terribly cold.—I wish my cold hand was in the warmest place about you, young women."[50]

In one respect Swift continues to be Stella's tutor: he reproves mistakes in spelling. "R*e*diculous, madam? I suppose you mean r*i*diculous; let me have no more of that." "Pray, Ppt, explain those two words of yours to me, what you mean by *villian*, and *dainger*." At one point Swift made a list of fourteen misspellings in a single letter, and Stella dutifully wrote in corrections beside each word:

Dineing—dining
Houeur—hour
Intellegence—intelligence
Phamphlets—pamphlets[51]

This wasn't pedantic bullying on Swift's part. He often pointed out that intelligent women weren't doing themselves justice if their spelling was terrible. He told a friend, "A woman of quality, who had excellent good sense, was formerly my correspondent, but she scrawled and spelt like a Wapping wench, having been brought up in a court at a time before reading was thought of any use to a female; and I knew several others of very high quality with the same defect." He may have been thinking of Lady Orkney, whom he described as "a person of as much good natural sense and judgment as I have ever known," but with "neither orthography, grammar, nor choice of words."[52]

Swift's own spelling was erratic at times, and he noted the experience of suddenly feeling unsure about a familiar word:

Pray let us have no more *bussiness*, but *busyness*—the deuce take me if I know how to spell it. Your wrong spelling, MD, has put me out: it does not look right. Let me see, *bussiness, busyness, business, bisyness, bisness, bysness;* faith, I know not which is right, I think the second. I believe I never writ the word in my life before; yes, sure I must, though; *business, busyness, bisyness.*—I have perplexed myself, and can't do it. Prithee ask Walls. *Business*, I fancy that's right. Yes it is; I looked in my own pamphlet, and found it twice in ten lines, to convince you that I never writ it before. Oh, now I see it as plain as can be; so yours is only an *s* too much.[53]

A note of affectionate intimacy pervades the *Journal to Stella*, especially at the ends of letters: "Farewell, my dearest lives and delights, I love you better than ever, if possible, as hope [to be] saved, I do, and ever will . . . and so farewell, dearest MD; Ppt, DD, Pdfr, all together, now and forever all together. Farewell again and again." But during the course of 1711 the endearments diminish, and so do the protestations that Swift misses Ireland. In November of that year we find the last emotional effusion: "Farewell, dearest MD, and love Ppt, who loves MD infinitely above all earthly things." A few days previously Swift had admitted that if Stella and Rebecca weren't in Ireland, "I believe seriously I should not think of the place twice a year."[54]

And how often, at this point, was he thinking even of them? Detailed and confiding as the *Journal to Stella* is, there is one very remarkable omission. Not once does he mention Esther Vanhomrigh, a young woman in whose company he had begun to spend a great deal of time.

CHAPTER 15

Enter Vanessa

A COVERT RELATIONSHIP

In 1707, during a previous stay in England, Swift spent the night at an inn in Dunstable in Bedfordshire, halfway between Leicester and London. It happened that a family just arrived from Dublin was there too, a widow named Mrs. Vanhomrigh, her sons Bartholomew and Ginkel, and her daughters Esther and Mary. Esther, the eldest, was nineteen and extremely good-looking. Swift found the whole group appealing, and when he returned to London in 1710 he began to see them regularly. We know Esther now by the name he gave her in a poem later on, Vanessa, combining the first syllable of her last name with her nickname, Hessy.

The late Bartholomew Vanhomrigh, pronounced "Vannummery," was a Dutch merchant who had come to Ireland after the arrival of William III. He was naturalized and became a prominent citizen of Dublin, serving in 1697 as its lord mayor. An acquaintance described him as "a small, funny, and quick-speaking man."[1] It's possible that Swift had known the family in Dublin, but the Dunstable encounter is the first that we know of. At Bartholomew's death in 1703, his widow had inherited £16,000, and was now on her way to settle in London.

Whenever Swift mentioned an attractive woman in the *Journal to Stella*, he was careful to forestall suspicions. After striking up a "mighty friendship"

with a Lady Kerry, he commented that "we are almost in love with one another," but hastened to add, "she is most egregiously ugly."[2] Vanessa was egregiously pretty.

Since Swift was also in the habit of reporting to Stella where he dined
every midday, he evidently thought it unwise to omit the Vanhomrighs completely. References to them were casual, however, and immediately followed
by something else:

> This has been an insipid day. I dined with Mrs. Vanhomrigh, and
> came gravely home, after just visiting the Coffee House. . . .
>
> I was mortified enough today, not knowing where in the world to
> dine, the town is so empty; I met H. Coote, and thought he would
> invite me, but he did not. Sir John Stanley did not come into my
> head, so I took up with Mrs. Van, and dined with her and her damned
> landlady, who, I believe, by her eyebrows, is a bawd. This evening I
> met Addison and Pastoral Philips in the Park, and supped with them
> at Addison's lodgings. We were very good company; and yet know no
> man half so agreeable to me as he is. I sat with them till twelve.

Stella knew about the pastoral poet Ambrose Philips, and when Addison
was working for the lord lieutenant in Dublin, she had met and liked him.
No doubt the mention of Addison would have mainly drawn her attention.
Swift's suspicion about the landlady, incidentally, was confirmed a few weeks
later, though it's not clear why her eyebrows were a tip-off.[3]

At least fifty-five meals at the Vanhomrighs' can be identified, and there
were doubtless more. And although Swift was apparently reluctant to lie
about where he dined, he felt no obligation to mention visits that didn't include
meals. He says, for example, "I dined with a friend in St. James's Street," but
fails to add, as his account book shows, that he then went on to play cards at
the Vanhomrighs'. A week later he says, "Mr. Lewis and I dined with a friend of
his," but not that there were once again cards at the Vanhomrighs'. The account
books also record occasions when he paid generously for Vanessa to travel by
coach in London, either riding with him or meeting him at some destination.[4]

But Stella did become suspicious. Just five weeks after Swift returned to
London in 1710, he wrote, "I was at a loss today for a dinner, unless I would
have gone a great way, so I dined with some friends that board hereabout, as
a sponger." We don't have the letter in which Stella called him on this, but
we have his indignant response to it: "What do you mean, 'that boards near
me, that I dine with now and then?' I know no such person; I don't dine with

boarders. What the pox! You know whom I have dined with every day since I left you, better than I do."[5] No, she didn't. Presumably the Vanhomrighs kept their own cook and were technically renters, not boarders, which makes his statement a white lie, but the smokescreen is obvious.

Mrs. Vanhomrigh had high social aspirations, and Swift often met interesting people at her house. One whom he did tell Stella about was a cousin of theirs named Anne Long, a noted beauty who was celebrated as a "toast" by the Kit-Cat Club to which Addison and other Whigs belonged. (The whimsical name came from the tavern where they met, run by a Christopher Catling.) In a facetious *Decree for Concluding the Treaty between Dr. Swift and Mrs. Long*, Swift declared his "sole and undoubted right" to require that a lady be the one to make the first advances, but that Anne has thus far held back, "to the great grievance and damage of Mrs. Vanhomrigh and her fair daughter Hessy." That was a name that Stella never once heard.

> We, out of our tender regard to truth and justice, having heard and duly considered the allegations of both parties, do declare, adjudge, decree, and determine that the said Mrs. Long, notwithstanding any privileges she may claim as aforesaid as a Lady of the Toast, shall, without essoin [excuse for not appearing in court] or demur, in two hours after the publishing of this our decree, make all advances to the said Doctor that he shall demand; and that the said advances shall not be made to the said Doctor as *un homme sans conséquence*, but purely on account of his great merit.[6]

Anne Long did become Swift's friend, but her story had an unhappy ending. In desperate money trouble, she fled her creditors by moving to King's Lynn in Norfolk and living there under an assumed name. She and Swift seem to have corresponded regularly, though few of their letters have survived. In November of 1711 she told him, "As to my health, that was much out of order last summer. My distemper was a dropsy or ahstma (you know what I mean, but I cannot spell it right) or both, lazy distempers, which I was too lazy to molest whilst they would let me sit in quiet." Her condition was now getting worse and she had seen a doctor, "by whose advice I am now well enough." Swift wrote back some weeks later with his customary advice: "Your illness is the effect of too little exercise." He added darkly, "Health is worth preserving, though life is not." It was too late. Three days later she was dead.[7]

Swift took it hard. He told Stella, "I never was more afflicted at any death," and he published a notice in the *Post Boy* saying that Anne was "celebrated for her beauty, virtue, and good sense." (The *Post Boy* was a pro-Tory paper run by a journalist named Abel Roper, whom Swift referred to as "my humble slave.") In his account book he noted Anne's death and called her "the most beautiful person of the age she lived in, of great honour and virtue, infinite sweetness and generosity of temper, and true good sense."[8]

Whatever Swift's feelings were toward Anne Long, it was Vanessa he was preoccupied with. His move to Chelsea afforded a reason to visit the Vanhomrighs more often than ever, for he would arrive hot and sweaty after his walk through the fields to London, and it was convenient to keep his best gown and wig at their house. He mentioned doing this to Stella in an offhand way that suggested boredom rather than interest: "I am so hot and lazy after my morning's walk that I loitered at Mrs. Vanhomrigh's, where my best gown and periwig are, and out of mere listlessness dine there very often, as I did today." Five days later it was the same story: "Heat and laziness, and Sir Andrew Fountaine, made me dine today again at Mrs. Van's."[9]

As for the return to Chelsea, Swift described it in detail, as if to deflect attention from the starting point. "My way is this: I leave my best gown and periwig at Mrs. Vanhomrigh's, then walk up the Pall Mall, through the Park, out at Buckingham House, and so to Chelsea a little beyond the church. I set out about sunset, and get here in something less than an hour; it is two good miles, and just five thousand seven hundred and forty-eight steps; so there is four miles a day walking, without reckoning what I walk while I stay in town." No doubt he didn't actually count every step, but was playfully naming an exact number. But was it a thought of Vanessa that then provoked an uncharacteristic innuendo? "When I pass the Mall in the evening it is prodigious to see the number of ladies walking there; and I always cry shame at the ladies of Ireland, who never walk at all, as if their legs were of no use but to be *laid aside*."[10] The emphasis is Swift's.

Only a few letters between Swift and Vanessa survive from this period, since they saw each other often and didn't need to write. But one evening Swift remarked in the *Journal*, "I have been writing letters all this evening till I am weary." Since the letters still exist, we know that one was to Anne Long and another to Vanessa, in which he signed off, "Adieu till we meet over a pot of coffee, or an orange and sugar, in the Sluttery, which I have so often found to be the most agreeable chamber in the world."[11] According to the *OED*, "sluttery" in this context means "an untidy room; a work-room." Perhaps it was a sewing room. At any rate, it wasn't the parlor in which guests would ordinarily be entertained. In the Sluttery, Vanessa and Swift could be alone.

What exactly was going on? Glendinning, though not prudish, believes it was just comfortable companionship: "I think they made coffee together in the Sluttery, bent over the fire or spirit lamp, making their private jokes, their heads close, their hands touching as they managed the kettle and coffeepot; and then sat back in their chairs, and talked, forgetting the coffee, reminding one another to drink it."[12] In this tenderly soft-core vision, their hands touched, but only their hands.

Ehrenpreis, who dismisses Vanessa as "a peripheral pastime," is sure it wasn't even that. Swift was inhibited, he says, by an "anxious asexualism," and explained to Vanessa that he lacked "the amative faculty" (Ehrenpreis's term, not Swift's). Confident that this most secretive of men has no secrets from his biographer, he concludes, "Judging from Swift's habits over many years, I believe he made no improper advances to Hessy."[13]

We know, however, that Vanessa contrived to be alone with Swift, for he told Anne Long, "She will bid her sister go downstairs before my face, for she has some private business with the Doctor." And mentions of "coffee" began to play a curiously prominent role. Writing from Windsor, Swift tells Vanessa that he's thinking of her in her bed. "I cannot imagine how you pass your time in our absence, unless by lying a-bed till twelve, and then having your followers about you till dinner. . . . What do you do all the afternoons? . . . I will steal to town one of these days and catch you napping. . . . I long to drink a dish of coffee in the Sluttery, and hear you dun me for secrets, and—drink your coffee—why don't you drink your coffee." Vanessa was in her midtwenties (seven years younger than Stella) and Swift in his midforties, "an age," as Johnson remarks, "when vanity is strongly excited by the amorous attention of a young woman."[14] And it is not usual for a person with high energy and strong appetites to be sexually apathetic.

Meanwhile, the tender passages in the *Journal to Stella* were drying up, and the apron that Swift sent can't have been much of a compensation. In Louise Bogan's crisp summary,

> Hypocrite Swift sent Stella a green apron
> And dead desire.[15]

One thing is certain, as Swift confirmed in a poem never meant for publication: Vanessa loved him passionately and longed to be loved in return. While he was at Windsor she alarmed him by threatening to bring their relationship into the open. In London it was Mrs. Van whom he ostensibly visited; for her young unmarried daughter to meet him elsewhere would be deeply imprudent. Vanessa's servant turned up at Windsor to give Swift a book and to say that Vanessa and her sister Mary (nicknamed Molkin or Molly) were on their way to Oxford, and were now spending the night at Beaconsfield, ten miles away. His hastily scribbled reply still exists, because Vanessa saved it, blotted because he sealed it before the ink had dried.

The note begins, "I did not forget the coffee," and then states decisively, "I would not see you for a thousand pounds if I could." He was afraid, too, that she might be recognized in Oxford. "I doubt [that is, suspect] you do wrong to go to Oxford, but now that is past, since you cannot be in London tonight; and if you do not inquire for acquaintance, but let somebody in the inn go about with you among the colleges, perhaps you will not be known, adieu."[16] Since Oxford is forty-five miles from Windsor, it's not clear what Swift was worried about. He may have been afraid she would encounter someone he knew and reveal too much about why she and Mary were traveling without their mother.

CADENUS AND VANESSA

In this increasingly precarious situation, Swift now wrote a very long poem, by turns playful and earnest, that would trace the course of their relationship and explain his reluctance to respond to Vanessa's desire. It is an enormous poem for a man who usually wrote short ones, nearly nine hundred lines long. Swift called it *Cadenus and Vanessa*, naming himself with an anagram of *decanus*, Latin for "dean," which indicates that the second half of the poem, which is where "Decanus" first appears, must have been written after he was appointed dean of St. Patrick's in 1713. He probably began it, however, at Windsor in 1712. It got into print after Vanessa's death only because she stipulated in her will that it should.[17]

In the story as Swift tells it, Vanessa is an exceptional being, created in an unprecedented partnership between Venus, goddess of love, and Athena, goddess of wisdom. The opening section of the poem is often described as absurdly artificial, since Venus holds a legal hearing to decide whether men or women are most responsible for the decline of true love, and then tricks Athena into helping to create Vanessa (Athena mistakes the infant for a boy). But it has been persuasively argued that Swift is using the pagan gods, as many writers did, to dramatize the complexities and contradictions of human nature. The God of the Bible is all-powerful and all-wise; the Greek gods are humanly fallible, and often in bitter conflict with each other.[18]

In a society in which women are conditioned to be shallow flirts, Vanessa embodies the virtues of both sexes—literally, in a lovely body. She has "a sweetness above all perfumes" and a "gentle, soft, engaging air," and also "knowledge, judgment, wit," and a soul endued with "justice, truth, and fortitude." Most of these were conventionally masculine qualities, though Swift always held that women ought to aspire to them just as much as men. Anne Long, who evidently saw an early draft, told Swift that "my poor cousin is taken for an hermaphrodite."[19]

Women, of course, despise Vanessa as a bookish prude, and in criticizing her unfashionable attire they provide a voyeuristic glimpse under her dress:

> A petticoat without a hoop!
> Sure, you are not ashamed to stoop,
> With handsome garters at your knees,
> No matter what a fellow sees.[20]

But men aren't attracted to her either, since she disdains conventional feminine wiles. Impatient at the lack of action, Cupid decides to forget about the young men and tries to plant his arrow in the middle-aged Jonathan Swift. Swift's books serve as a defensive shield, and Vanessa is hit instead. She too is holding a book by Swift, but the arrow goes straight through it and she falls desperately in love. He is flattered, but unable to respond in the way she wants. The rest of the poem is a fascinating debate in which they explain their conduct to each other and try to justify it.

Of course Cadenus and Vanessa is a poem, not a transcript, and we have no way of knowing how well it corresponds to what actually went on. Unquestionably, Swift wanted to put his own spin on how the relationship developed. All the same, he clearly expected Vanessa to appreciate the poem, and it's a unique window into his emotional life.

It seems likely that Swift, one of whose favorite authors was the unillusioned moralist Rochefoucauld, was strongly impressed by the French conception of romantic love. Venus may preside over love and sex, but individual choices are arbitrarily chosen by her son, whom Swift describes as "full of mischief." Falling in love is not much different from a serious illness; Rochefoucauld says, "The most accurate comparison one can make of love is with a fever—we have no more power over one than over the other, whether for its violence or its duration." A corollary in the French tradition is that the emotional storm provokes fantasizing, in which the victim projects impossibly ideal perfections onto the loved one.[21]

> Vanessa, not in years a score.
> Dreams of a gown of forty-four;
> Imaginary charms can find
> In eyes with reading almost blind;
> Cadenus now no more appears
> Declined in health, advanced in years.
> She fancies music in his tongue,
> Nor further looks, but thinks him young.[22]

If "not in years a score" is right, Vanessa fell in love as long ago as 1707, when she met Swift at the inn in Dunstable.

In some lines that were deleted by whoever eventually printed the poem, it's clear that Vanessa actively pursued Swift:

> Strange, that a nymph by Pallas nursed
> In love should make advances first.
> She wished her tutor were her lover,
> Resolved she would her flame discover;
> And when Cadenus would expound
> Some notion subtle or profound,
> The nymph would gently press his hand
> As if she seemed to understand,
> Or dext'rously dissembling chance
> Would sigh, and steal a secret glance.[23]

These lines were no doubt deleted because they made Vanessa seem too forward for a virtuous young woman of the time.

Vanessa's next move is to attack Swift at his weakest point. He prides himself on reason. Very well, it is his own ethical teaching that she has taken to heart:

> Two maxims she could still produce,
> And sad experience taught their use:
> That virtue, pleased by being shown,
> Knows nothing which it dare not own;
> Can make us without fear disclose
> Our inmost secrets to our foes;
> That common forms were not designed
> Directors to a noble mind. . . .
> Your lessons found the weakest part,
> Aimed at the head, but reached the heart.[24]

Swift always dreaded gossip, and as he indicated in his note at Windsor, this situation seemed sure to ignite it.

> Appearances were all so strong,
> The world must think him in the wrong;
> Would say, he made a treach'rous use
> Of wit, to flatter and seduce;
> The town would swear he had betrayed
> By magic spells the harmless maid,
> And every beau would have his jokes,
> That scholars were like other folks. . . .
> Five thousand guineas in her purse?
> The Doctor might have fancied worse.

Still, his vanity is tickled, and he lacks the resolution to dismiss Vanessa outright.

> Cadenus, to his grief and shame,
> Could scarce oppose Vanessa's flame,
> But though her arguments were strong,
> At least could hardly wish them wrong.
> Howe'er it came, he could not tell,
> But sure she never talked so well.
> His pride began to interpose,
> Preferred before a crowd of beaux.[25]

The poem ends with a meditation on the complexity of love, the milder pleasures of friendship, and a teasing hint that the story isn't over. First comes the meditation:

> Love, why do we one passion call,
> When 'tis a compound of them all?
> Where hot and cold, where sharp and sweet,
> In all their equipages meet;
> Where pleasures mixed with pains appear,
> Sorrow with joy, and hope with fear.

Swift offers instead "friendship, in its greatest height . . . which gently warms, but cannot burn." Vanessa prefers to burn.[26]

As for the teasing hint, it aroused intense curiosity from the moment the poem was published:

> But what success Vanessa met
> Is to the world a secret yet:
> Whether the nymph, to please her swain,
> Talks in a high romantic strain,
> Or whether he at last descends
> To act with less seraphic ends;
> Or to compound the business, whether
> They temper love and books together,
> Must never to mankind be told,
> Nor shall the conscious Muse unfold.

"Conscious" is used in the sense then current, defined by the *OED* as "having awareness of one's own wrongdoing; affected by a feeling of guilt." But what if sex and intellect can indeed be partners, tempering love and books together?[27]

It's hard to agree with Ehrenpreis that "by desexualizing both partners, the panicky poet removes the element that threatens him," or that he talks like "a fatherly admirer trying to cheer up a solitary spinster." Sheridan remarked long ago that if Swift was hoping to discourage Vanessa's passion, a poem that described her "in the most flattering colours was not likely to administer to her cure." And the modern critic is surely right who sums up *Cadenus and Vanessa* as "a darkly lustrous myth of dalliance."[28]

There is persuasive evidence that after 1714, when Swift went back to Ireland and Vanessa followed him there, they did descend to less seraphic ends. Even before then, the relationship seems to have been more intense than *Cadenus and Vanessa* might suggest. On an earlier trip to Ireland in 1713, Swift said this: "I promised to write to you, and I have let you know that it is impossible for anybody to have more acknowledgements at heart for all your kindness and generosity to me." He signed off, "Pray God preserve you, and make you happy and easy—and so adieu brat." Soon afterward there was another letter that has not survived, to which Vanessa replied joyously, "Now you are good beyond expression in sending me that dear voluntary from St. Albans; it gives me more happiness than you can imagine or I describe to find that your head is so much better already." The reference to Swift's head presumably means an attack of vertigo; a "voluntary" could be an extempore or spontaneous piece of writing. This time it's Vanessa who drops hints about coffee: "I am very impatient to hear from you at Chester. It is impossible to tell you how often I have wished you a cup of coffee and an orange at your inn."[29]

CHAPTER 16

Tory Triumph

A BROTHERHOOD OF WRITERS

Swift relished being called a brother by the members of the political Club, but even more enjoyable was the company of leading writers. At this time Addison and Steele were launching a sequel to the *Tatler*, called the *Spectator*, which came out every weekday from March 1711 to December 1712. There were 555 papers in all, on popular topics such as snuff taking, current fashions, courtship, the coffeehouses, and so on. There were also easy-to-understand discussions of intellectual topics, such as the excellence of *Paradise Lost* and the pleasures of imagination.

"Mr. Spectator" is presented as a coffeehouse regular, with a circle of friends who include a Whiggish merchant, the appropriately named Sir Andrew Freeport, and a lovable but hopelessly backward country squire, Sir Roger de Coverley. In politics Swift favored frontal attacks, but Addison's insidious portrait of Sir Roger is just as effective in its own way. C. S. Lewis comments, "The enemy, far from being vilified, is turned into a dear old man."[1]

From Swift's point of view, the *Spectator* was lightweight popularization. "I shall take it for the greatest glory of my work," Steele wrote, "if among reasonable women this paper may furnish tea-table talk." Addison declared, "Women were formed to temper mankind, and soothe them into tenderness and compassion." It's possible that Addison approached Swift for a contribution or two, but he told Stella, "I will not meddle with the Spectator, let him fair-sex it to the world's end."[2]

Besides, Swift was disgusted by the way his former friends were promoting the Whig agenda. One day in 1712 he ran into Addison and "Pastoral Philips" on the Mall and walked with them for a bit, "but they both looked terrible dry and cold—a curse of party."[3] Addison, at least, continued to be polite, but Steele did not. Like Swift, he was deeply involved in political polemics, and they ended up calling each other names in print.

After relations with Addison began to cool, Swift's closest friend was Dr. John Arbuthnot, an urbane Scotsman who was physician to the queen and a fellow "brother" in the Club. (His name was probably stressed on the second syllable, since Swift playfully rhymes "a good Arbuthnot" with "I know his worth not.") Swift gave his friend a deft inverted compliment: "All your honor, generosity, good nature, good sense, wit, and every other praiseworthy quality will never make me think one jot the better of you. That time is now some years past, and you will never mend in my opinion. But really,

45. Dr. John Arbuthnot.

brother, you have a sort of shuffle in your gait; and now I have said the worst that your most mortal enemy could say of you with truth." Apparently there was something peculiar about the way Arbuthnot moved. Pope recalled that when he was about to meet him for the first time, Swift commented, "He is a man that can do everything but walk."[4]

Arbuthnot was a writer, but only occasionally. His one extended work is *The History of John Bull*, in which he invented the bluff country squire as a symbol of Britain. It was in conversation that he shone, and he shared with Swift a fondness for deadpan irony. Late in life Swift acknowledged as much, managing to be ironic *about* irony:

> Arbuthnot is no more my friend,
> Who dares to irony pretend,
> Which I was born to introduce,
> Refined it first, and showed its use.[5]

One short piece gives a good sense of Arbuthnot's style, a mock epitaph on a scandalous aristocrat named Francis Charteris. As Pope said, Charteris was "a man infamous for all manner of vices," who got rich by unscrupulous means, was always in trouble with the law, and ended up imprisoned for alleged rape. This shameful career inspired Arbuthnot's little masterpiece:

> HERE continueth to rot
> the body of FRANCIS CHARTRES,
> who with an INFLEXIBLE CONSTANCY,
> and INIMITABLE UNIFORMITY of life,
> PERSISTED,
> in spite of AGE and INFIRMITIES,
> in the practice of EVERY HUMAN VICE,
> excepting PRODIGALITY and HYPOCRISY:
> his insatiable AVARICE exempted him from the first,
> his matchless IMPUDENCE from the second. . . .
> He was the only person of his time
> who could CHEAT without the mask of HONESTY,
> retain his primeval MEANNESS
> when possessed of TEN THOUSAND A YEAR,
> and, having daily deserved the gibbet for what he *did*,
> was at last condemned to it for what he could *not* do.
> Oh indignant reader!

think not his life useless to mankind!
PROVIDENCE connived at his execrable designs
to give to after-ages
a conspicuous PROOF and EXAMPLE
of how small estimation is EXORBITANT WEALTH
in the sight of GOD,
by his bestowing it on the most UNWORTHY of
ALL MORTALS.[6]

Pope himself, twenty-one years younger than Swift, came into the picture only at the end of Swift's time in London. At that point they saw each other a lot, but we know little about their meetings, since the *Journal to Stella* stops short in June of 1713.

Born into a loving Catholic family, Pope was astonishingly precocious, and his literary talent was warmly encouraged. His masterful *Rape of the Lock* was published in 1712, when he was twenty-four, and in a brilliantly enlarged version in 1714. Before he was thirty he brought out a volume of *Works* that

46. Alexander Pope.

contained a whole series of major poems. By then he was acknowledged to be the greatest poet of the time, at an age at which Swift had published nothing but the forgettable *Ode to the Athenian Society*.

Pope had painful handicaps as well as great abilities, and writing was essential compensation for him. In an era of anti-Catholic repression he was debarred from most careers and even from owning property. And in childhood he contracted Pott disease, in which a tubercular infection spreads to the spine. The usual consequences of this condition are progressive bone loss, nerve pain, and deformity, and he experienced all of them. He was hunchbacked and four and a half feet tall, condemned to continuous discomfort in what he wryly called, in his great *Epistle to Dr. Arbuthnot*, "this long disease, my life." "Let me tell you," he wrote to another friend, "my life in thought and imagination is as much superior to my life in action and reality as the best soul can be to the vilest body."[7]

Pope couldn't stand Addison, who seemed to him to be jealous of rising talent. The *Epistle to Arbuthnot* includes a devastating portrait of him, with phrases that have become proverbial:

> Damn with faint praise, assent with civil leer,
> And without sneering, teach the rest to sneer;
> Willing to wound, and yet afraid to strike,
> Just hint a fault, and hesitate dislike.[8]

Addison no doubt saw Pope as a pushy and presumptuous youth.

Another member of the circle of writers was John Gay, author of pleasantly chatty topical poems. At this time he was working on *Trivia; or, The Art of Walking the Streets of London*. Swift laughed at his claim to be a great walker, and told him that he always had "a rooted laziness, and an utter impatience of fatigue." Gay was impressively overweight, and getting fatter all the time; Congreve adapted Descartes' *Cogito ergo sum*—"I think, therefore I am"—and said that Gay's motto should be *Edit ergo est*—"He eats, therefore he is."[9]

For a brief period the wits banded together to collaborate on a satire called *The Memoirs of the Extraordinary Life, Works, and Discoveries of Martinus Scriblerus*. It is often claimed that the Scriblerus Club was a potent seedbed of later works. But all we really know is that the group met a few times in 1714, that Arbuthnot was the principal author of the *Memoirs*, and that he got bored with it almost immediately. It was not until 1741 that Pope finally put it into print, no doubt with revisions of his own. And the masterpieces that these writers went on to produce—Pope's *Dunciad*, Gay's *Beggar's Opera*, Swift's *Gulliver's Travels*—are so different from each other that it doesn't mean much to call them all "Scriblerian."[10]

WINNING THE PEACE

Meanwhile, in the public world, mighty events were taking place. After the British triumph at Oudenarde in 1708, France was eager for peace; its economy was bankrupt, and poor harvests threatened famine. And then, in 1709, the horrific bloodshed at Malplaquet made most people in England equally ready for peace. Negotiations began at The Hague in 1709, but the Whigs clung to their slogan "No Peace without Spain," which would take years to conquer if it could ever be achieved at all.

Many army officers were furious at the Tory determination to depose the Duke of Marlborough and shut down the war. Swift told Stella about a group of them who were discharged "for drinking destruction to the present ministry, and dressing up a hat on a stick and calling it Harley; then drinking a glass with one hand, and discharging a pistol with the other at the maukin [effigy]."[11] Death threats followed.

In November of 1712, Swift was personally present at a shocking near disaster. In a letter to the *Evening Post* he described what happened. A bandbox—a container for a lawyer's or clergyman's neck bands—was delivered to Harley. Something aroused his suspicions, and Swift asked to see the box. Referring to himself in the third person, he told what followed:

> He took it to the window, at some distance from my Lord, and opened it by cutting with a penknife the packthreads that fastened the lid. The first thing that appeared was the stock and lock of a pocket pistol, lying across the middle of the bandbox, and fastened at each end with two nails; on each side of the firelock were laid the middle pieces of two large inkhorns charged with powder and ball. . . . The small nails which fastened the stock at either end were so contrived that by taking it up at the first view, as it was natural to do with all the implements about it, the cock would have gone down and fired the whole train, which would immediately have discharged both barrels different ways."

It would thus fire at whoever opened the box, no matter which side of it he happened to be on. To Stella, Swift commented, "I wonder how I came to have so much presence of mind, which is usually not my talent; but so it pleased God, and I saved myself and him, for there was a bullet apiece."[12]

The campaign to bring down Marlborough was entrusted to Swift, and he prosecuted it enthusiastically. He detested war, and often described it with revulsion. Stranded in a land of rational horses, Gulliver describes his reaction when his host wonders how human beings, who lack claws and sharp teeth, could ever do each other much harm:

> I could not forbear shaking my head and smiling a little at his igno-
> rance. And being no stranger to the art of war, I gave him a descrip-
> tion of cannon, culverins, muskets, carbines, pistols, bullets, powder,
> swords, bayonets, sieges, retreats, attacks, undermines, countermines,
> bombardments, sea-fights; ships sunk with a thousand men; twenty
> thousand killed on each side; dying groans, limbs flying in the air;
> smoke, noise, confusion, trampling to death under horses' feet; flight,
> pursuit, victory; fields strewed with carcasses left for food to dogs and
> wolves and birds of prey; plundering, stripping, ravishing, burning,
> and destroying. And to set forth the valour of my own dear country-
> men, I assured him that I had seen them blow up a hundred enemies
> at once in a siege, and as many in a ship, and beheld the dead bodies
> drop down in pieces from the clouds, to the great diversion of all the
> spectators.

John Wesley quoted this passage and commented, "Is it not astonishing, beyond expression, that this is the naked truth?"[13]

Marlborough was a military genius, not vulnerable to criticism of his battlefield decisions. "Nobody that I know of," Swift acknowledged in the *Examiner*, "did ever dispute the Duke of Marlborough's courage, conduct, or success." What Swift did harp on was "the monstrous encroachments of exorbitant avarice and ambition," reaping personal profit from a war that wouldn't end. He also emphasized "the ungovernable rage, the haughty pride, and unsatiable covetousness of *a certain person*." That was the Duchess of Marlborough.[14]

At a time when the average income for a noble family was approximately £3,000 a year, the duke had an income of £55,000 and his wife another £9,000. Historians take seriously Marlborough's defense that much of his income was intended to pay military costs that were his personal responsibility. Still, an admiring biographer acknowledges that "his thirst for wealth was remarkable even by the standards of the age."[15]

Seizing on Whig claims that the nation hadn't shown the duke enough gratitude, Swift worked up a comparison of his gains by contrast with what ancient Rome gave victorious generals. The Roman would get a sacrificial bull worth £8, an embroidered garment worth £50, a laurel crown worth 2 pence, and so on, to a sum total of £994. Marlborough got Blenheim Palace, at £200,000 by this time and still unfinished, "employments" worth £100,000, and other plums in addition to these that added up to £540,000. "So that upon the whole," Swift concluded, "we are not yet quite so bad at *worst*, as the Romans were at *best*."[16]

Slyly, Swift added that he knew a highly favored servant who was expected to meet necessary expenses out of an allowance of £26, but managed to keep all but £4 of it for her own use. Multiplying these figures by a thousand, one gets the actual circumstances of the Duchess of Marlborough: as comptroller of the Privy Purse, she received £26,000 a year and held onto £22,000. Years later she handsomely acknowledged "the witty comparison that was made between me and the lady's woman, who out of her mistress's pin money of £26 put twenty-two into her own pocket." She also said, "I could not help wishing that we had had [Swift's] assistance in the opposition, for I could easily forgive him all the slaps he has given me and the Duke of Marlborough, and have thanked him heartily, whenever he would please to do good."[17]

On January 1, 1712, the House of Commons received an official report accusing Marlborough of misusing public funds, and the queen dismissed him from all his employments. She also sent the duke a letter so offensive that he flung it in the fire. No doubt he recalled that some months earlier, when Godolphin was commanded to break his white staff of office, he too threw the pieces in the fireplace. A few years later Swift commented with relish, "This Lord, who was beyond comparison the greatest subject [that is, nonruler] in Christendom, found his power, credit, and influence crumble away on a sudden."[18]

Swift took his final shot at Marlborough after the deposed general died in 1722. *A Satirical Elegy on the Death of a Late Famous General* is chilling in its contempt. It begins with casual chattiness, expressing surprise that the intrepid hero should have died peacefully:

> His Grace! impossible! what, dead!
> Of old age too, and in his bed!
> And could that mighty warrior fall?
> And so inglorious, after all!

When the Last Trump sounds it will bode ill for Marlborough, and meanwhile all that remains is a bad smell:

> This world he cumbered long enough;
> He burnt his candle to the snuff,
> And that's the reason, some folks think,
> He left behind so great a stink.

By the end of this angry poem, Marlborough is dismissed as one of the hollow bubbles that "float upon the tide of state," and his elevated rank furnishes a contemptuous rhyme:

> Let pride be taught by this rebuke
> How very mean a thing's a Duke;
> From all his ill-got honours flung,
> Turned to that dirt from whence he sprung.

The solemn language of the burial service—"Dust thou art, and unto dust shalt thou return"—collapses into the nastiness of dirt.[19]

Denigrating Marlborough was only part of the Tory strategy, though an essential part. The chief challenge was to justify the peace they were negotiating, whose anticipated terms were being denounced by the Whigs as a sellout. Behind the backs of Britain's Dutch and Austrian allies, the ministry secretly negotiated a peace treaty with France that would drop the whole issue of Spain. Matthew Prior, Swift's poet friend who was also a gifted diplomat, had carried out a covert mission to France, and Britain was about to renege on its commitment to the allies. What the Tories needed, therefore, was to argue that the allies themselves had done plenty of reneging already, while wasting British lives and money in a war that didn't serve Britain's interests at all. By implication, they had been so self-serving that they had lost the right to be consulted in negotiating peace.

For two months in the fall of 1711, Swift labored nonstop at this task. Oxford and Bolingbroke fed him information that wasn't yet public, reviewed his drafts, and went over everything in minute detail. By mid-November he was thoroughly fed up. "Something is to be published of great moment," he told Stella, "and three or four great people are to see there are no mistakes in point of fact; and 'tis so troublesome to send it among them and get their corrections that I am weary as a dog."[20] Perhaps what wearied him most was serving as a mouthpiece for other people.

47. Matthew Prior as a
plenipotentiary.

At the end of November the piece appeared at last, entitled *The Conduct of the Allies*. Sixty pages long in a modern edition, it made its case with what Trevelyan calls "cold, concentrated force." The first printing sold out within hours, and within a few days a fourth edition was for sale. The compositors were working around the clock; they had to start from scratch for each new edition, since it was impossibly expensive to keep whole pages of type intact. By the end of January Swift could boast that "eleven thousand of them have been sold, which is a most prodigious run."[21]

Seventy years later Johnson thought that what made *The Conduct of the Allies* so effective was its details, not its intrinsic interest. "Surely whoever surveys this wonder-working pamphlet with cool perusal will confess that its efficacy was supplied by the passions of its readers; that it operates by the mere weight of facts, with very little assistance from the hand that produced them." In conversation Johnson was still more dismissive: "Swift has told what he had to tell distinctly enough, but that is all. He had to count ten, and he has counted it right."[22] But by Johnson's time the once-urgent issues had faded, and he was taken in by Swift's cunning deployment of apparent common sense.

The Conduct of the Allies was designed not to convert Whigs, but to encourage the rural squires who formed the power base of the Tories. And although Swift's case was overstated, it was genuine. The war could have ended on advantageous terms two years previously, and the Whigs were insisting that it shouldn't end even now. "After ten years' war, with perpetual success," Swift exclaimed, "to tell us it is yet impossible to have a good peace is very surprising." So why did the war go on? Speaking for the Tories, Swift claimed it was to pay off "the moneyed men, such as had raised vast sums by trading with stocks and funds, and lending upon great interest and premiums, whose perpetual harvest is war."[23]

It was true that the national debt enriched investors who drew interest from it, but Swift deliberately exaggerated the gulf between peace-loving country gentlemen and warmongering financiers. In reality, many country gentlemen invested in stocks and bonds, and many financiers set up as country gentlemen. The Tory appeal was to a nostalgic picture of a simpler merry England that was allegedly being sold out. To some extent they actually believed in that picture, and were unable to conceive that a national debt could create wealth instead of draining it. Characteristically, Swift relied on homely domestic analogies: "It is obvious in a private fortune that whoever annually runs out, and continues the same expenses, must every year mortgage a greater quantity of land than he did before; and as the debt doubles and trebles upon him, so doth his inability to pay it."[24]

Tendentious or not, *The Conduct of the Allies* was indeed wonder-working, exploiting the psychological moment. And this Johnson did acknowledge: "The nation was then combustible, and a spark set it on fire." Swift was never a bureaucrat like Addison, or a diplomat like Prior, but as a political writer he was unrivaled. Trevelyan's verdict is impressive: "He had done more during three years' residence in London to settle the immediate fate of parties and nations than did ever any other literary man in the annals of England."[25]

Throughout 1711 the Whig peers steadfastly resisted the campaign for peace, and for a time it looked as if the Tory ministry would fall. But to Swift's bafflement, Oxford and Bolingbroke were perfectly calm. Their secret was that the queen had decided to break the impasse by creating twelve new members of the House of Lords. A Tory majority was thereby assured, and when Swift got the news he wrote exultantly from a coffeehouse, "I have broke open my letter, and tore it into the bargain, to let you know that we are all safe. . . . We are all extremely happy. Give me joy, sirrahs." Four of the twelve new peers were "brothers" in the Club.[26] The Whigs were furious, but they had to admit that the queen had the right to create as many peers as she wished.

The negotiations that followed were protracted and bewilderingly complex. One Austrian participant commented that Oxford's strategy was "to work up policy on two sides, so that he can choose the one which will involve him in least reproach from the nation, and to contrive matters so that he can always throw the blame on someone else." When the Treaty of Utrecht was finally concluded in 1713, it was actually a series of separate treaties and impenetrably complicated. The Earl of Peterborough said that it was like "the peace of God, beyond human understanding." Coincidentally, Archbishop King said the same thing.[27]

The nation as a whole was overjoyed, and the peace was welcomed, Swift said, "with louder acclamations, and more extraordinary rejoicings of the people, than had ever been remembered on like occasion."[28] The consequences of the Treaty of Utrecht were profound and enduring. The threat of a monstrous Bourbon superstate, joining France with Spain and uniting the overseas colonies of both, had been dispelled. Nor would the Habsburgs of the Holy Roman Empire achieve dominance. Instead a stable balance of power was in place, and would remain even after the British-French wars of midcentury and after. It was Britain, whose own empire would grow rapidly in the coming decades, that could now lay claim to being the leading power on the globe.

The Treaty of Utrecht did exact a dreadful human price for the future, though most people at the time would not have seen it that way. Until then the exclusive right to export slaves to South America had been held by France. It now went to Britain, and Oxford had a personal stake in securing it, since it would enrich the South Sea Company he had sponsored as a means of paying down the national debt. From now on the slave trade would play a central role in British imperial expansion. Under a treaty known as the Asiento (from *asentir*, to acquiesce or agree), British slave traders would eventually deliver a million and a half Africans to the Caribbean and American colonies.[29]

Swift was among the minority who disapproved of slavery, but most people took it for granted, and Whig spokesmen like Defoe positively celebrated it. Robinson Crusoe is shipwrecked after setting out to collect a cargo of slaves. On his desert island he has a religious conversion, and begins to understand the message God is sending him. The message is not that it was wrong to go and get slaves—it's that he should have *sent someone else* to get them.

CHAPTER 17

Tory Collapse

OFFENDING THE QUEEN

With the Peace of Utrecht concluded, the Tories were riding high, having ended what Bolingbroke called "such a war as I heartily wish our children's children may never see."[1] But trouble lay ahead. He and Oxford were increasingly at odds, and not just because of personality differences. Oxford, the former Whig, was always seeking compromise, while Bolingbroke wanted to break the Whigs' power forever.

Support for Bolingbroke within their own party came from a group called the October Club that sought to punish the Whigs for the war taxation, which had fallen heavily on landowners. Swift described the October Club to Stella as "a set of above a hundred Parliament men of the country, who drink October beer at home, and meet every evening at a tavern near the Parliament to consult affairs, and drive things on to extremes against the Whigs, to call the old ministry to account, and get off five or six heads." Bolingbroke wanted to use the club as leverage against Oxford, and they adopted a motto that alluded to Oxford's family name, Harley—"We will not be harled."[2] *Harl* looks like a made-up word, but according to the *OED* it was in frequent use in the north of England and in Scotland. Either of its two meanings would apply very aptly to Harley: "To drag, usually with the notion of friction or scraping the ground," and "to entangle, twist, or knot together; to ravel or confuse."

"The ministry is upon a very narrow bottom," Swift said anxiously, "and stands like an isthmus between the Whigs on the one side and violent Tories on the other. They are able seamen, but the tempest is too great, the ship too rotten, and the crew all against them."[3] For Swift personally, time was running short. He had always refused to be paid for his work, but it was understood that he would get an English bishopric in due course. That would bring not only prestige and income, but also a seat in the House of Lords, making him a political insider and not just a government spokesman.

But the queen's health was failing, and the elector of Hanover was bound to come to the throne before long. Since the future George I was sympathetic to the Whigs, Swift's hopes would then be at an end. It was now or never. He was close to Oxford, who saw the queen regularly, and to Abigail Masham, who spent most of every day with her. Surely they could get the thing done?

Although it was difficult for an Irishman to become a bishop in England, it was not impossible; two of Swift's Trinity classmates did. But the queen was determined not to make Swift a bishop in England—or in Ireland either. She was genuinely pious, and had never forgiven him for the *Tale of a Tub*. Swift probably had her hostility in mind, years later, when Gulliver quick-wittedly saves the Lilliputian palace from burning down, but outrages the tiny monarch because he does so by pissing on it. Unfortunately, a Lilliputian law forbids urinating within the royal precincts. Even though her palace has been saved, the empress is furious, "and in the presence of her chief confidants could not forbear vowing revenge."[4] The analogy is not altogether positive, of course. Urine is still urine.

Reluctantly, Swift began to grasp just how low an opinion the queen had of him. Oxford and Bolingbroke "thought to mortify me," he reported to Stella, "for they told me they had been talking a great deal of me today to the Queen, and she said she had never heard of me. I told them that was their fault and not hers, etc., and so we all laughed." It must have been hollow laughter—the whole point was that she knew very well who Swift was and detested him. A couple of days later he did finally get into Her Majesty's presence, joining twenty other people in her chamber, but it was an anticlimax. "She looked at us round with her fan in her mouth, and once a minute said about three words to some that were nearest her, and then she was told dinner was ready, and went out."[5]

Swift even turned down a chance to preach before the queen, which might have been a way to make a positive impression. "If it should happen," he explained unconvincingly, "all the puppies hereabouts will throng to hear me, and expect something wonderful, and be plaguily balked; for I shall preach plain honest stuff."[6] Perhaps he thought that plain honest stuff would offend Her Majesty, and felt unwilling or unable to fake the kind of emotional piety she liked.

As if the *Tale of a Tub* wasn't damaging enough, Swift chose this moment to self-destruct. When the scheme of creating new peers was still secret and the ministry seemed certain to be thrown out, he produced a staggeringly abusive satire aimed at a particular favorite of the queen. Called *The Windsor Prophecy* and full of quaint black-letter Gothic type, this short poem purported to be a medieval prediction of future disasters. It was packed with allusions to contemporary people and events, and any reader would have gotten the point.

> And dear *Englond*, if aught I understond,
> Beware of Carrots from Northumberland.
> Carrots sown Thyn a deep root may get,
> If so be they are in Sommer set;
> Their Conyngs mark thou, for I have been told
> They *Assassine* when young, and *Poison* when old.[7]

The target was the Duchess of Somerset, whom Swift had met at Moor Park when she was a friend of Lady Giffard's. This duchess was Abigail Masham's rival for the queen's favor, and Swift hated her. "Carrots from Northumberland" are mentioned because her father was the Earl of Northumberland and she had flaming red hair.

The Duchess of Somerset had a remarkable history. Her first husband, Lord Ogle, died shortly after she married him in 1679; she was only twelve at the time. Soon afterward her family forced her into a second marriage with a wealthy gentleman named Thomas Thynne, and a year later Thynne was murdered by thugs in the employ of still another suitor, the Count of Königsmark (spelled "Conigsmark" in England, as Swift's "Conyngs" hints).

The widow Thynne was suspected of having connived at her husband's death, but that was never proved. She went abroad for a while, returning to derision from anonymous satirists:

> Ogle's returned and will consider further
> Who next she'll show her arse to for a murder.[8]

At that point the widow Ogle-Thynne, still just fifteen, acquired a third husband, the Duke of Somerset.

Swift gave his poem to a printer and looked forward to scoring a big hit with it. "I like it mightily," he told Stella, adding that he was sure people would guess its author. When Mrs. Masham found out, however, she was horrified, and urged Swift to stop publication. It was too late. "I writ to the printer to stop them," he reported; "they have been printed and given about, but not sold."[9] That made no difference, since copies soon found their way to other printers who did publish. He himself had given copies to all the members of his Club. As Mrs. Masham anticipated, the queen was enraged.

Why ever did Swift permit himself this suicidal performance? No doubt he was sure that the Tories were about to lose office, and was taking a parting shot on his way out. But beyond that, he always had an impulsive, risk-taking streak. Given to strict self-control in his daily routine, he sometimes flaunted his indifference to consequences in larger matters. And perhaps by now he thought he could get away with anything. At any rate, the Duchess of Somerset became his implacable enemy, and if the *Tale of a Tub* hadn't sufficiently damaged his chances for promotion, he had now demolished them completely.

When he was supervising an edition of his works a quarter of a century later, Swift neglected to mention that *The Windsor Prophecy* had ever existed. But perhaps it, too, found an echo in *Gulliver's Travels*. This time Gulliver is in Brobdingnag, the land of the giants. "There was a cow-dung in the path, and I must need try my activity by attempting to leap over it. I took a run, but unfortunately jumped short, and found myself just in the middle up to my knees."[10]

AN IRISHMAN AFTER ALL

Only the queen could appoint bishops, but various other people had the right to appoint deans. A dean is the priest in charge of the daily affairs of a cathedral, while its bishop is responsible for the diocese as a whole. Giving up on becoming a bishop, Swift began working on his friends to get him a deanery.

For a while it looked as if that might be possible in England. After telling Stella that *The Conduct of the Allies* had helped to turn the tide in the House of Commons, Swift thought it was a good moment to drop Oxford a hint: "I most humbly take leave to inform your Lordship that the Dean of Wells died this morning at one o'clock. I entirely submit my poor fortunes to your Lordship; and remain, with greatest respect, my Lord, your Lordship's most obedient and most obliged humble servant J. Swift."[11]

That was in 1712. Nothing came of it, and by 1713 time was running out. In April three English deaneries were vacant, but none of them went to Swift. Oxford urged him to be patient, but he replied firmly, "I had nothing to do but go to Ireland immediately, for I could not with any reputation stay longer here, unless I had something honorable immediately given me."[12]

That same day Swift and Oxford dined with their mutual friend the Duke of Ormonde, a "brother" in their Club and currently lord lieutenant of Ireland. Ormonde was glad to help, and promised to make Swift dean of St. Patrick's Cathedral, the best appointment in Ireland at that rank. There was a problem, though: what to do with the present incumbent, Swift's friend John Stearne? The solution was to make Stearne a bishop, but for that the queen's approval would be needed.

There was another obstacle as well. Ormonde disliked Dean Stearne and was reluctant to get him a promotion. Swift wrote, "With great kindness he said he would consent, but would do it for no man alive but me." Swift was thus the cause of raising Stearne to the rank of bishop, a position he might never attain himself, as indeed he didn't. "They say here 'tis much to my reputation that I have made a bishop in spite of all the world, to get the best deanery in Ireland."[13]

As for Queen Anne, she was happy to make Stearne a bishop if that was the price of getting rid of Swift. "The Queen was willing enough," Sheridan says, "that Swift should have a moderate provision made for him in Ireland, in order to send him into banishment, in a decent though not very honourable manner."[14]

The whole business left a permanent sour taste. Swift never really blamed Oxford for not pushing harder, but perhaps he should have. Ten years later Bolingbroke told him that the reason he got no appointment in England was Oxford's failure to make it happen. "You are unjust when you say that it was either not in the power or will of a ministry to place you in England. Write 'minister,' friend Jonathan, and scrape out the words 'either power or,' after which the passage will run as well and be conformable to the truth of things. I know but one man who had power at that time, and that wretched man had neither the will nor the skill to make a good use of it."[15]

The person Swift did blame was Archbishop Sharp of York, second only to the archbishop of Canterbury in the Church hierarchy. Sharp was the queen's trusted adviser on religious matters, and Swift regarded him as "my mortal enemy." It may be that he was misled on this too. Bolingbroke later told the head of an Oxford college that "he had been assured by the Queen herself

that she never had received any unfavourable character of Dr. Swift, nor had
the archbishop or any other person endeavoured to lessen him in her esteem.
My Lord Bolingbroke added that this tale was invented by the Earl of Oxford to deceive Swift, and make him contented with his deanery in Ireland."
Bolingbroke's friend commented, sensibly enough, "If Lord Bolingbroke had
hated the Earl of Oxford less, I should have been readily inclined to believe
him."[16] It was true—Bolingbroke and Oxford did hate each other, and their
collaboration was on the verge of shipwreck.

After telling Stella that Stearne would become bishop of Dromore "to
make room for me," Swift added glumly, "Neither can I feel joy at passing my
days in Ireland, and I confess I thought the ministry would not let me go; but
perhaps they can't help it. Nite Md."[17]

The installation—literally, ceremonial occupation of the dean's stall in the
cathedral—happened in May. Dublin was depressing, and Swift preferred
to stay in Laracor instead, while Stella and Rebecca boarded with Anthony
Raymond and his wife in nearby Trim, where Raymond was the rector. The
account books show frequent charges for dinners, wine, "etc."

Swift's vertigo came on again, as it often did in times of stress. He wrote to
Vanessa about it, adding affectionately, "It is impossible for anybody to have
more acknowledgements at heart for all your kindness and generosity to me."
She responded with anxious concern, and then exclaimed,

> Oh what would I give to know how you do at this instant! My fortune
> is too hard, your absence was enough without this cruel addition. Sure
> the powers above are envious of your thinking so well, which makes
> them at some times strive to interrupt you. But I must confine my
> thoughts, or at least stop from telling them to you, or you'll chide,
> which will still add to my uneasiness. I have done all that was possible
> to hinder myself from writing to you till I heard you were better, for
> fear of breaking my promise, but 'twas all in vain. . . . I am impatient to
> the last degree to hear how you are. I hope I shall soon have you here.[18]

Deanship brought with it a major burden: it entailed taking on a massive debt. When Swift was still in London, Stearne had offered to sell him a
houseful of expensive furniture. "I shall buy Bishop Stearne's hair," Swift told
Stella, "as soon as his household goods." But he did have to pay £600 for the
deanery itself, because that was required by law. To encourage improvements
in church properties, a statute stipulated that when a clergyman spent his
own money on a residence, his successor had to pay him two-thirds of the

cost, receiving in turn one-third of the value from the next occupant. Stearne had recently spent £900 to have the deanery rebuilt.[19]

Foreseeing this hefty expense, Swift secured a promise from Lord Oxford to find £1,000 for him, and he looked forward confidently to receiving it. It never came, but his friendship with Oxford remained unshaken. Like his secrecy and procrastination, Oxford's inability to follow through on promises seems to have been accepted as a character trait that couldn't be altered. In later years Swift wrote repeatedly to implore him to fulfill one promise at least: to send a portrait of himself. Oxford never did that either.

"BROKE TO SHATTERS"

Swift was barely settled in Ireland when there was pressure to return to England. Erasmus Lewis, Oxford's chief aide, wrote urgently that only Swift could patch up the rift between Oxford and Bolingbroke. Since both of them liked and trusted him, they might listen to him. Swift ignored these pleas for a while, until Lewis made it clear that he was speaking for Oxford himself: "I have so often and in so pressing a manner desired you to come over [to England] that if what I have already said has no effect, I shall despair of better success by any further arguments. . . . You and I have already laid it down for a maxim that we must serve Lord Treasurer without receiving orders or particular instructions. . . . The *desires* of great men are *commands*, at least the only ones I hope they will ever be able to use."[20]

In September Swift was back in London, after just four months in Ireland. He had departed so abruptly for England that Archbishop King was offended, and the Irish lord chancellor wrote to tell Swift, "I cannot discharge the part of a friend if I omit to let you know that your great neighbor at St. Pulchers [the archbishop's palace] is very angry with you; he accuseth you for going away without taking your leave of him, and intends in a little time to compel you to reside at your Deanery."[21] It was a fair point.

Perhaps Swift was getting back at King, soon afterward, when he helped to block his promotion to an eminence he clearly deserved. When the archbishop of Armagh died, King was the obvious candidate to succeed him as Primate of all Ireland. But King had Whiggish sympathies, and Swift made that his reason for urging his colleagues to recommend someone else to the queen. He told Stearne, "I should be thought a very vile man if I presumed to recommend to a bishopric my own brother, if he were the least disinclined to the present measures of her Majesty and ministry here."[22]

Still, there is no reason to suspect that Swift was insincere when he assured King that despite their political differences, "I sincerely look upon your Grace to be master of as much wisdom and sagacity as any person I have known. . . . I conceive you to follow the dictates of your reason and conscience; and whoever does that will, in public management, often differ as well from one side as another." Nokes calls this a "poisonous compliment," but does not explain why. He also says mistakenly that Swift's letter to Stearne was addressed to King, which would indeed have been an insult.[23] The correction is important because Swift and King are often described as enemies when in fact they worked well together, and would become stalwart allies in the years to come.

Shortly after returning to England, Swift published a remarkable poem about his relationship with Lord Oxford. There was a fashion of adapting classical poems to modern circumstances, and he called this one *Part of the Seventh Epistle of the First Book of Horace Imitated*. Horace's poem describes a poor man who is given a farm, but gets so badly in debt that he asks his patron to put him back where he found him. In Swift's version, Oxford (still Harley at the time) encounters him browsing at a bookstall, invites him to dinner, and is offended when Swift assumes it's a joke and doesn't show up. After Oxford repeats the invitation, Swift arrives flustered and full of apologies:

> "My Lord—the honour you designed—
> Extremely proud—but I had dined—
> I am sure I never should neglect—
> No man alive has more respect"—[24]

They quickly become friends, and soon Swift is a regular guest at the family table.

Harley knows that Swift wants to be a bishop, but tells him to settle instead for St. Patrick's Cathedral, with assurances that it's a perfect choice:

> You need but cross the Irish Seas
> To live in plenty, power, and ease.

Far from living in ease and plenty, Swift as dean is harassed by debts and unable to collect his rightful income, which he describes in a torrent of detail:

> Suppose him gone through all vexations,
> Patents, installments, abjurations,
> First Fruits and tenths, and chapter-treats,
> Dues, payments, fees, demands, and cheats

(The wicked laity's contriving
To hinder clergymen from thriving).

When Swift can't stand any more of this, he returns to England, accuses Oxford of having managed the whole business as a practical joke, and ends with the same demand that Horace did:

> The Doctor in a passion cried,
> "Your raillery is misapplied:
> I have experience dearly bought;
> You know I am not worth a groat;
> But you resolved to have your jest,
> And 'twas a folly to contest.
> Then since you now have done your worst,
> Pray leave me where you found me first."[25]

This poem was something of a sensation, and quickly ran through eight editions in London, Dublin, and Edinburgh. Some critics believed it was a shameless attempt to get money from Oxford, and they had a point. Swift bitterly resented never getting the £1,000, and he may have thought that going public would embarrass Oxford into paying.

With no official duties in London any longer, Swift decided to write a major retrospective work in the ministry's defense, and he began a heavily slanted account of the peace negotiations, misleadingly titled *The History of the Four Last Years of the Queen*. For the rest of his life he would make efforts to get the thing published, but Erasmus Lewis, Bolingbroke, and (after Oxford's death) Oxford's son always dissuaded him. It was unacceptably biased, even though in their favor, and it distorted too many facts. *The History of the Four Last Years* does show how deeply Swift believed his own rhetoric. As a historian says, he and the Whigs bought into rival ideologies, each reflecting "a view of reality intensely perceived and experienced." Another historian says severely that Swift "displays a disquieting facility for tendentious argument, tunnel vision, and conspiracy theory."[26]

Also at this time, Swift effected a final breach with Steele. A year previously he had attacked Steele in *The Importance of the Guardian Considered*, pausing in his political argument to disparage Steele as a writer (and heavy drinker): "He hath no invention, nor is master of a tolerable style. His chief talent is humour, which he sometimes discovers [that is, reveals] both in writing and discourse, for after the first bottle he is no disagreeable companion." Now

Swift followed up with *The Public Spirit of the Whigs*. "He hath a confused remembrance of words since he left the university, but hath lost half their meaning, and puts them together with no regard except to their cadence; as I remember a fellow nailed up maps in a gentleman's closet, some sidelong, others upside down, the better to adjust them to the panels."[27]

That was just bad blood between former friends, but *The Public Spirit* was objectionable to the entire Whig party, since it claimed that the Whigs were smearing Oxford and Bolingbroke, charging the Tory ministers falsely with conspiring to bring back the Pretender. "They are most damnably wicked," Swift declared, "impatient for the death of the Queen [which would ensure the accession of George I]; ready to gratify their ambition and revenge by all desperate methods; wholly alienate from truth, law, religion, mercy, conscience, or honour."[28]

This accusation of disloyalty to the queen was offensive enough, and still worse, Swift gratuitously added some insulting comments about the Scots, suggesting that the Union had been a big mistake. There was a furious debate in Parliament, and *The Public Spirit of the Whigs* was formally censured by the House of Lords: "The said pamphlet is a false, malicious, and factious libel . . . tending to the destruction of the constitution, and most injurious to her Majesty."[29] A reward of £300 was offered for discovery of the writer, and when the publisher and printer refused to name him, they were imprisoned

Of course, everyone knew that the writer was Swift, but he had his protectors. This pamphlet was his culminating defense of the ministry, and it was unthinkable that Oxford and Bolingbroke would let him go to jail. Oxford sent him an urgent note promising to take care of the printer, John Barber; it still survives in the British Library, with Swift's annotation, "Lord Treasurer to me in a counterfeit hand, with the bill, when the printers were prosecuted by the House of Lords for a pamphlet." The "bill" was money for bail to get the bookseller and printer out of jail. "I have heard that some honest men who are very innocent," Oxford wrote circumspectly, "are under trouble touching a printed pamphlet. A friend of mine, an obscure person but charitable, puts the enclosed bill in your hands to answer such exigencies as their case may immediately require, and I find he will do more, this being only for the present. If this comes safe to your hands it is enough."[30]

There the controversy died. The ministry cleverly pretended to share in the Whigs' indignation, and stole the initiative by prosecuting Barber themselves. Not surprisingly, no informant appeared to make conviction possible, and that was the end of it.

Meanwhile, things were falling apart. Swift wrote to the Earl of Peterborough, who was abroad, "My head turns round, and after every conversation I come away just one degree worse informed than I went." He had believed he was a privileged insider, but he now admitted bafflement. "I thought myself twenty times in the right, by drawing conclusions very regularly from premises which have proved wholly wrong. I think this, however, to be a plain proof that we act altogether by chance; and that the game, such as it is, plays itself."[31]

The game wasn't playing itself, but Oxford and Bolingbroke had been poor teammates for a long time, and now they had lost control altogether. If compromise had ever been possible, it wasn't now. A couple of months previously Peterborough invoked a pithy proverb: "Betwixt two stools the arse goeth to the ground."[32]

Long afterward Swift recalled his hopelessness at this point, and his decision to get away before the crackup.

> He labored many a fruitless hour
> To reconcile his friends in power;
> Saw mischief by a faction brewing
> While they pursued each other's ruin.
> But finding vain was all his care,
> He left the court in mere despair.[33]

On the last day of May, Swift left London for the village of Letcombe Bassett in Berkshire, not far from Oxford. His host there was the Reverend John Geree, his friend from Moor Park days.

It was a relief to escape the political whirlpool, but Swift's claim to love rural obscurity rang hollow. Bolingbroke told him so. "I never laughed, my dear Dean, at your leaving the town. On the contrary, I thought the resolution of doing so, at the time when you took it, a very wise one. But I confess I laughed, and very heartily too, when I heard that you affected to find within the village of Letcombe all your heart desired."[34]

Swift had sent ahead a case of French wine that Bolingbroke had given him, which Geree called a "noble present," but he served it only sparingly, and life in the Letcombe rectory was a dismal contrast to London. After a week Swift wrote to Vanessa, "I am at a clergyman's house, an old friend and acquaintance whom I love very well, but he is such a melancholy thoughtful man, partly from nature and partly by a solitary life, that I shall soon catch the spleen from him. . . . We dine exactly between twelve and one, at eight we have some bread and butter and a glass of ale, and at ten he goes to bed. Wine is a stranger, except a little I sent him, of which one evening in two we have a pint between us. . . . I read all day, or walk, and do not speak as many words as I have now writ in three days."[35]

To cheer Swift up, Pope and Parnell came over for a visit, after which Pope reported to Arbuthnot that Swift "talked of politics over coffee with the air and style of an old statesman who had known something formerly, but was shamefully ignorant of the last three weeks." Pope added that Swift kept a magnifying glass by the window and amused himself by burning holes in paper with it. "We chanced to find some experiments of this nature upon the votes of the House of Commons. The name of Thomas Hanmer, Speaker, was much singed, and that of John Barber entirely burned out. There was a large gap at the edge of the Bill of Schism, and several specks upon the proclamation for the Pretender."[36]

These attentions by Swift do not suggest ignorance of affairs. An enormous reward of £5,000 had been proclaimed for anyone apprehending the Pretender in his expected invasion; Bolingbroke was about to force passage of a Bill of Schism making it illegal for Dissenters to be teachers (part of his effort to embarrass Oxford, who was relatively tolerant of Dissent). Why Swift deleted the name of his friend and printer Barber isn't clear—presumably to express resentment at the way Barber had been treated.

Meanwhile the queen dismissed Oxford at last. She had good reason. His right-hand man Lewis glumly told Swift that "he neglected all business; that he was seldom to be understood; that when he did explain himself she could not depend upon the truth of what he said; that he never came to her at the time she appointed; that he often came drunk; that lastly, to crown all, he behaved himself towards her with ill manner, indecency, and disrespect."[37] By now Oxford was a confirmed alcoholic, barely able to carry out his responsibilities.

Bolingbroke, of course, thought his lucky day had arrived when his rival fell, but his hopes were quickly dashed. Just four days after she discharged Oxford, Queen Anne departed this life at the age of forty-nine, probably from complications of gout. At the end she endured violent convulsions, and Dr. Arbuthnot, who was in attendance, told Swift, "I believe sleep was never more welcome to a weary traveler than death was to her." Psalms of rejoicing were sung in Dissenting chapels, and the Whig head of St. John's College, Oxford, ordered grateful prayers for King George. When he was told that the queen might not really be dead yet, he replied, "Dead! She's as dead as Julius Caesar."[38]

Bolingbroke wrote to Swift, "The Earl of Oxford was removed on Tuesday; the Queen died on Sunday. What a world is this, and how does Fortune banter us!" Swift himself said that her death left "all our schemes broke to shatters." For all his shrewdness and suspicion of motives, he was at bottom an idealist, and this catastrophe broke his heart. "His ideal order was the Roman Senate," a character in one of Yeats's plays says of Swift, "his ideal men Brutus and Cato. Such an order and such men had seemed possible once more, but the moment passed and he foresaw the ruin to come."[39]

While he was waiting for the end at Letcombe, Swift wrote (but didn't publish) a piece called *Some Free Thoughts upon the Present State of Affairs*, in which he lamented the ruin his friends were bringing down on themselves. Their disagreements, he said, "have been, for some time past, the public entertainment of every coffee house," and he compared their conduct to "a ship's crew quarreling in a storm, or while their enemies are within gunshot."[40]

Also at Letcombe, Swift composed an apologia called *The Author upon Himself*, which alternates between wry realism and furious resentment. The realism comes in acknowledging that he was never the sort of clergyman who gets promoted:

> Swift had the sin of wit, no venial crime:
> Nay, 'twas affirmed he sometimes dealt in rhyme;
> Humour and mirth had place in all he writ;
> He reconciled divinity and wit.
> He moved and bowed and talked with too much grace;
> Nor showed the parson in his gait or face.

That is genial enough, but the anger is just below the surface:

> By an old red-pate, murdering hag pursued,
> A crazy prelate, and a royal prude. . . .
> Now Madam Konigsmark her vengeance vows
> On Swift's reproaches for her murdered spouse;
> From her red locks her mouth with venom fills,
> And thence into the royal ear distills.[41]

Swift always personalized his troubles, and this was one more kick at Archbishop Sharp and the Duchess of Somerset. He blandly ignored the fact that

A Windsor Prophecy was outrageously libelous, since there was never any evidence that the duchess had conspired to murder her second husband. And she was never Madam Königsmark, either. Königsmark was the rejected suitor who organized the murder.

It was time to leave for Ireland. Swift had thirty-one years still to live, and during all that time he would be in England only twice, for six months each time. Long afterward he told Bolingbroke, "I was 47 years old when I began to think of death, and the reflections upon it now begin when I wake in the morning, and end when I am going to sleep." At another time he told Pope, "As to mortality, it hath never been out my head eighteen minutes these eighteen years." Both references are to 1714. Giving up England was a kind of death.[42]

Preparing to depart, Swift sent sad farewells, and Arbuthnot returned a moving reply. "Dear friend, the last sentence of your letter quite kills me. Never repeat that melancholy tender word, that you will endeavour to forget me. I am sure I never can forget you, till I meet with (what is impossible) another whose conversation I can delight so much in as Dr. Swift's; and yet that is the smallest thing I ought to value you for. That hearty sincere friendship, that plain and open ingenuity [that is, ingenuousness], in all your commerce, is what I am sure I never can find in another, alas. I shall want often a faithful monitor, one that would vindicate me behind my back and tell me my faults to my face. God knows I write this with tears in my eyes."[43]

CHAPTER 18

Reluctant Dubliner

THE DEAN

For the first thirty years of his life Swift had been an outlier. He never felt at home among the Swifts in Dublin, and at Moor Park he was treated as a mere employee. Then came the intoxicating years in London, with Laracor nothing more than a pleasant retreat whenever he was in Ireland. Still, the Church of Ireland was Swift's institutional home, and it was in that context that he saw himself as an Irishman at all. His long campaign to secure the First Fruits, as Trevelyan perceptively observes, was "a small act of justice to the island he hated and the Church he loved." The initial period as dean, in 1713, had been too brief to amount to anything, but now he buckled down to the job. He clearly liked the title, for in his poems he refers to himself as "the Dean" over 170 times.[1]

The two Dublin cathedrals, Christ's Church and St. Patrick's, looked much as they do today. Relics of medieval Catholicism, they were reminders of an ecclesiastical empire that now lay mostly in ruins, with roofless abbeys all over the country. St. Patrick's was located on marshy ground between two branches of the river Poddle, a site called by a later dean "extraordinarily unsuitable for a great building." It was apparently chosen because a well, known as St. Patrick's Well, was there and believed to have miraculous curative powers. The

48. St. Patrick's Cathedral. The cathedral as Swift knew it,
except that the pointed spire was added after his time.

Poddle itself, which flows beneath the streets today, is variously described by historians as "an unfortunate little river" and "a miserable trickle."[2]

Some brilliant clergymen in those days became famous preachers or theologians. Swift's interests and talents didn't run that way. His gift was as an administrator: running a big establishment efficiently, expanding its influence in the city and nation, and helping the needy poor who inhabited the immediate neighborhood. By his own estimate he had to manage a budget of £10,000 a year. It has been said of Samuel Pepys, the civil servant who played a major role in shaping the Royal Navy, "He had the mental powers, the physical vitality, and the love of order which go to the making of a great administrator." Exactly the same is true of Swift.[3]

Swift took his responsibilities very seriously. He attended services three times every Sunday, his own in the morning and evening, plus an afternoon service with a congregation of French Huguenot refugees. Holy Communion was celebrated every Sunday, as happened at no other church in Dublin. That was a sign of High Church allegiance; the usual frequency was once a month in city parishes, and less often than that in the country.[4]

Swift made sure that the cathedral choir was first rate. When the wife of a lord lieutenant recommended a singer, he replied that only the best could be considered. According to Dr. Delany, he told the lady, "I know nothing of music, madam; I would not give a farthing for all the music in the universe. For my own part, I would rather say my prayers without it. But as long as it is thought by the skilful to contribute to the dignity of the public worship, by the blessing of God it shall never be disgraced by me, nor, I hope, by any of my successors."[5]

It was well known that Swift would be in the pulpit every fifth Sunday, and according to Dr. Lyon, a large audience would show up. In an often-quoted comment, Ehrenpreis says that Swift's "entire career can be described as the partnership of a clown and a preacher."[6] But both terms are reductive. Although his writings usually have a message, they are never didactic and

49. St. Patrick's choir stalls and altar.

50. Swift's movable pulpit. Swift preferred this pulpit to the remote and massive one at the east end of the cathedral, no doubt because it brought him closer to his listeners.

preachy. And as for his wit, so varied and brilliant, to call it clowning suggests a determination to amuse that is very far from his style.

Unfortunately, Swift's delivery left something to be desired. Dr. Delany said that his voice was "sharp and high-toned rather than harmonious," and that he had an ear for rhythms of language "but not for harmony of sounds." But if his manner was a bit grating, he made sure that the language was easy to understand. "A divine hath nothing to say to the wisest congregation of any parish in this kingdom," he advised young clergymen, "which he may not express in a manner to be understood by the meanest among them."[7]

Visiting preachers at the cathedral found Swift intimidating, since he monitored their performance closely. "As soon as anyone got up into the pulpit," Delany recalled, "he pulled out his pencil and a piece of paper, and carefully noted every wrong pronunciation or expression that fell from him. Whether too hard, or scholastic (and, of consequence, not sufficiently intelligible to a vulgar hearer), or such as he deemed in any degree improper, indecent, slovenly, or mean; those he never failed to admonish the preacher of, as soon as he came into the chapter house."[8]

There was a large audience for published sermons, and some preachers made a lot of money from them. Swift not only didn't publish his sermons, he burned most of them, dismissing them as "rubbish."[9] The few that survived were rescued by Dr. Sheridan, who said he wanted to save labor by preaching them himself.

When Swift became dean, he inherited a large and fractious body of clergy who were attached to the cathedral in various ways. Many were prebendaries, as he himself had been at Laracor, with no real duties but a right to vote on cathedral business. It took Swift several years to force them all into line, but he did it. By 1721 he could say with satisfaction, "It is an infallible maxim that not one thing here is done without the Dean's consent."[10]

There were also two very able subordinates, who became close friends as well as colleagues. One was Archdeacon Thomas Walls, master of the cathedral school, and the other was John Worrall, director of music and a gifted financial manager as well. Whenever Swift was away from Dublin, he relied on the two of them to manage affairs in his stead.

Swift not only presided over the cathedral, he effectively ruled the surrounding neighborhood, known as the liberties. The term denoted a section of the city that had originally been exempted from municipal government and was subject only to the king. The Liberty of St. Patrick's occupied nine acres around the cathedral and was a haven in which debtors were safe from arrest.[11]

THE DEAN AT HOME

Swift's deanery (he spelled it "deanry") was close to the cathedral and adjacent to the grand archbishop's palace. He never cared for it much, and liked to describe himself as an exile in his own domain, "sitting like a toad in a corner of his great house." Shortly after settling in he told Pope, "I live in the corner of a vast unfurnished house," with a "family" (the term included everyone living there) of "a steward, a groom, a helper in the stable, a footman, and an old maid, who are all at board-wages." At about the same time Swift wrote gloomily in verse:

> On rainy days alone I dine
> Upon a chick and pint of wine.

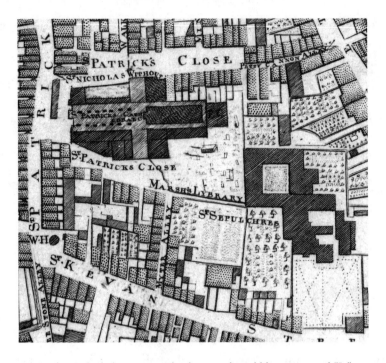

51. The Cathedral precincts. The deanery, shaped like an inverted "L,"
lies just below the center of the open space labeled "St. Sepulchres."
That was the name of the huge archbishop's palace to the right. Swift said,
"He lives within 20 yards of me, our gardens join."

> On rainy days I dine alone
> And pick my chicken to the bone.

It rains a lot in Ireland. An English visitor in 1728 commented that "the French have named it *le pot de chamber du Diable*, i.e. the Devil's piss pot, seldom dry, but often running over, the rains falling down so frequently as if the heavens were a wounded eye perpetually weeping over it, or the clouds dropping sponges."[12]

The deanery as Swift knew it no longer exists, having burned down in 1781, leaving only the stone-vaulted kitchen in the cellar.[13] It is remarkable how much of his world has vanished. One can still visit Samuel Johnson's birthplace in Lichfield, and the house in London where he worked on his *Dictionary*. In Dublin only the cathedral remains from Swift's many years there. His deanery is gone, and so are his house and church in Laracor.

Stella and Rebecca must have visited the deanery often, and according to their friends, whenever Swift was away they would move in and live there.

They had various different Dublin addresses over the years; at this time they lodged with their good friends Archdeacon Walls and his wife in Queen Street, just beyond the Liffey.

Swift believed that wine helped to relieve his vertigo, and although he drank it in moderation, it added up to a considerable expense. He ordered six hogsheads a year from France, each containing sixty-three gallons, and got a signed contract each time guaranteeing replacement if the wine should turn out sour.[14] It was decanted as needed into bottles, and of course often shared with friends.

When a bemused Houyhnhnm asks Gulliver why the British import expensive wine when they could drink water instead, he explains that "it was a sort of liquid which made us merry, by putting us out of our senses; diverted all melancholy thoughts, begat wild extravagant imaginations in the brain, raised our hopes, and banished our fears; suspended every office of reason for a time, and deprived us of the use of our limbs, until we fell into a profound sleep; although it must be confessed that we always awaked sick and dispirited, and that the use of this liquor filled us with diseases which made our lives uncomfortable and short." Swift had no desire to experience extravagant imaginations, impaired motor skills, and painful hangovers. But he very much desired to banish melancholy thoughts and fears. He drank, he said,

52. Swift's wine bottles. A nineteenth-century depiction of two of Swift's bottles, in dark green glass. Each held a pint and a quarter (the modern seventy-five-centiliter bottle holds a little more than a pint and a half).

"to encourage cheerfulness," and he would have appreciated Oscar Wilde's remark that he drank to keep body and soul apart.[15]

The vertigo was bad, and its attacks lasted longer than they used to. Unquestionably they contributed to the depression. In addition to nausea that often left Swift helpless in bed, the tinnitus got so bad that it was like "the noise of seven watermills in my ears," so that the only people he could stand to listen to were "trebles and countertenors." By now his left ear was effectively deaf, and he had to turn the right one toward people talking to him. These afflictions turn up in *Gulliver's Travels*, where the sound of a giant farmer's voice "pierced my ears like that of a watermill," and where sounds are frequently described as coming from the right.[16]

Medical intervention was useless. Swift submitted patiently to the whole range of treatments that were recommended: emetics to provoke vomiting, bloodletting, searing blisters on the back of the neck, and pills concocted from all sorts of revolting substances. In one letter he mentioned "blister upon blister and pills upon pills."[17]

Swift's close friend Arbuthnot was one of the most distinguished physicians of the day, but all he could suggest was "cinnabar of antimony and castor, made up into boluses with confect of alkermes." Alchermes was a liqueur colored red from the insect *kermes vermilio;* cinnabar of antimony was produced by combining antimony with mercury and sulfur. The castor oil promoted a purgative effect. At another time Arbuthnot recommended a bitter concoction of zedoary root, galangal, and wormwood, to be taken after first inducing vomiting with ipecacuana. Swift told Ford after one such treatment, "I have been twice severely vomited, to the utmost I could possibly bear, but without amendment." Ford replied sensibly, "Those sort of disorders puzzle the physicians everywhere, and they are merciless dogs in purging or vomiting to no purpose, when they don't know what to do." More harmless, but nonetheless weird, was a recommendation to wear a quilted cap stuffed with cloves, mace, and nutmegs.[18]

THE DEAN AND HIS SERVANTS

A sick man can be difficult to live with, as Sir William Temple was, and Swift's servants found him so. Though not a harsh employer, he was a demanding one. Leslie Stephen comments that Swift studied the behavior of servants with the same attention that Darwin gave to worms, with the difference that Darwin "had none but kindly feelings for worms."[19]

Orrery, though a nobleman and a snob, was startled by Swift's piercing scrutiny even of other people's servants:

> Dr. Swift dined with me one day in Dublin. . . . When the first dish was removed and the second was brought upon the table, the Dean became for some time pensive and very grave. I asked him the meaning. "I am thinking," says he, "how often, if your servant had been mine, I should have chid him for faults which I have seen him commit; and I find the number of times amount to twenty-two." These faults were: not giving a plate with the right hand; not taking off a dish with both hands; putting the plates too near or too far from the fire; and such kind of trifles, which gave him constant causes of fretfulness and passion, and made his servants, to whom he was in general a very kind and indulgent master, very fearful and uneasy."[20]

Laetitia Pilkington likewise noted Swift's surveillance techniques. When entertaining he would sit opposite a mirror in which he could watch his servants at the sideboard. On one occasion, "the Dean, turning his eye on the looking glass, espied the butler opening a bottle of ale, helping himself to the first glass, and very kindly jumbling the rest together, that his master and guests might all fare alike. 'Ha, friend!' says the Dean, 'sharp's the word. I find you drank my ale, for which I stop two shillings of your board wages this week, for I scorn to be outdone in anything, even in cheating.'"[21]

As usual, however, Swift was concealing an aspect of the situation that reflected well on himself. The point of board wages was that servants normally had to buy their own food. But Swift gave his servants three free meals a day as well as their regular wages, which meant that the board wages were a complete bonus. This butler, in particular, got 4 shillings a week in board wages, amounting to over £10 a year, which was as much as the total annual salary of most servants. And it has been suggested that the whole thing might have been a setup, prearranged between Swift and the butler to impress the guests. It seems improbable that a servant, knowing Swift well, would help himself to a drink right in front of a mirror.[22]

Perhaps with memories of the unreliable Patrick in London, Swift drew up "laws" for his household staff, with penalties strictly defined:

> Whatever servant shall be taken in a manifest lie shall forfeit one shilling out of his or her board wages.

The woman may go out when the Dean is abroad for one hour, but no longer, under the same penalty with the men, but provided the two men-servants keep the house until she returns. Otherwise, either of the servants who goes out before her return shall forfeit a crown out of his wages, as above.

Whatever other laws the Dean shall think fit to make, at any time to come, for the governance of his servants, and forfeitures for neglect or disobedience, all the servants shall be bound to submit to.[23]

Servants had to be especially careful not to offend against Swift's standards of cleanliness. He listed, with obvious irony, a variety of ways that they could extinguish candles, as alternatives to simply blowing them out: "You may run the candle end against the wainscot, which puts the snuff out immediately; you may lay it on the floor, and tread the snuff out with your foot; you may hold it upside down until it is choked with its own grease, or cram it into the socket of the candlestick; you may whirl it round in your hand till it goes out; when you go to bed, after you have made water, you may dip your candle end into the chamber pot." According to Dr. Lyon, "among all kinds of smells, none offended him so much as the snuff of a candle."[24]

In fact Swift rarely used candles, since they were very expensive. Instead he made do with rushlights, pincerlike holders for rushes that had been soaked in bacon grease or mutton fat. They gave a smoky flame and an unpleasant smell, which he evidently endured for the sake of economy. Dr. Delany remembered that he resolved to read by candlelight once he had increased the value of the deanery, but admitted ruefully that he never kept his resolution. Even in homes that did use candles, lighting was feeble by modern standards. "Much was invisible," a historian says, "in a world lit by candlelight, rushlight, and moonlight."[25]

At bottom the issue was not just "good" servants or "bad" ones but the vulnerability created by sharing one's life with poorly paid, often dishonest employees. Eighteenth-century novels are full of servants who conspire against each other, defame their masters, and steal whenever they can get away with it. In a sermon Swift reviewed their misdeeds:

If we consider the many misfortunes that befall private families, it will be found that servants are the causes and instruments of them all. Are our goods embezzled, wasted, and destroyed? Is our house burnt down to the ground? It is by the sloth, the drunkenness, or the villainy of servants. Are we robbed and murdered in our beds? It is by

53. Swift's rushlight, now in
St. Patrick's Cathedral.

confederacy with our servants. Are we engaged in quarrels and misun-
derstandings with our neighbours? These were all begun and inflamed
by the false, malicious tongues of our servants. Are the secrets of our
family betrayed, and evil repute spread of us? Our servants were the
authors. Do false accusers rise up against us (an evil too frequent in
this country)? They have been tampering with our servants.

Samuel Johnson, though notable for kindness to servants, said much the
same thing: "No condition is more hateful or despicable than his who has
put himself in the power of his servant. . . . He is condemned to purchase, by
continual bribes, that secrecy which bribes never secured, and which, after a
long course of submission, promises, and anxieties, he will find violated in a
fit of rage, or in a frolic of drunkenness."[26]

In his own way Swift tried to be tactful. Delany was present when a badly
overdone roast was served, whereupon Swift sent for the cook and said calmly,
"Sweetheart, take this down to the kitchen, and do it less." When she protested

that that was impossible, he pointed out that if it had been underdone, there would have been no difficulty. "Why then, sweetheart, let me advise you, if you must commit a fault, commit a fault that can be mended." Only when the cook had left the room did he permit his irascibility to emerge. "Turning to the company, he cried, 'You see, gentlemen, how I bear this; and yet I can assure you, this was the very thing that tried Job's patience and got the better of it, when none of his other calamities could: to wait for his victuals, as we have done, a great while, and then have them sent up to him roasted to rags.'"[27]

In truth, the roasts were never anything special. Dr. Delany teased Swift about the difference between Swift and his predecessor, John Stearne:

> In the days of good John, if you came here to dine,
> You had choice of good meat, but no choice of good wine.
> In Jonathan's reign, if you come here to eat,
> You have choice of good wine, but no choice of good meat.[28]

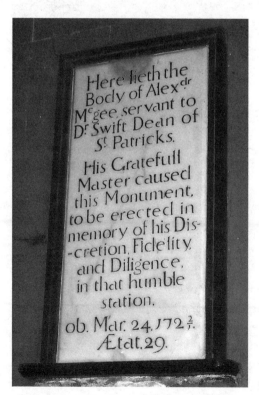

54. The Alexander McGee memorial.

Some servants became much more than employees. That was true of Swift's housekeeper, Anne Brent, who often dined with him when there were no guests. Swift also had the highest regard for his faithful manservant, Alexander ("Saunders") McGee. He was deeply distressed when McGee died in 1722 at the age of twenty-nine: "Poor Saunders died on Saturday last, and was buried on Easter Sunday, and in him I have lost one of my best friends as well as the best servant in the kingdom." He performed the funeral service himself "and was observed to shed tears." In his will McGee left Swift "a fusil, quail pipes and nets . . . as the last mark of duty and affection from a faithful servant." It's not clear whether Swift ever used the gun, let alone the "quail pipes," which were whistles to lure birds by imitating their call.[29]

In the southern side aisle in St. Patrick's Cathedral, a modest marble plaque stands out by its difference from the pompous memorials of the rich and famous: "Here lieth the body of Alexander McGee, servant to Dr. Swift, Dean of St. Patrick's. His grateful master caused this monument to be erected in memory of his discretion, fidelity, and diligence in that humble station." When Swift originally composed the epitaph, he called himself Saunders's "grateful friend and master." A snobbish friend persuaded him to omit the word "friend." And in a culture deeply imbued with class consciousness, even the revised version struck some people as outrageous. Swift's enemy Jonathan Smedley complained that it was "a kind of burlesque apotheosis that he celebrated in honour of his deceased servant, who used to squeeze his lemons, and for his faithful discharge of that important trust had an inscription engraved to his memory on his master's large punchbowl." Smedley thought the memorial must have been a joke.[30]

SOCIAL LIFE

Selective quotations from Swift's letters, especially in his later years, can give the impression that he was miserable in Ireland. He calls himself, in biblical language, "a stranger in a strange land." He says that Ireland is "the most disagreeable place in Europe," and that it is "a wretched, dirty dog-hole and prison, but it is a good enough place to die in." He even exclaims that he expects to "die here in a rage, like a poisoned rat in a hole."[31] But these are all deliberate exaggerations, usually to impress English friends with how unkind the world had been. Before long, Swift, who was always sociable, acquired a wide circle of friends. There were Worrall and Walls, and a pair of brothers named Dan and John Jackson, and no fewer than five Grattan brothers. All were intelligent and congenial, though we know them only indistinctly from casual references. Deane Swift the younger, who was still just a boy during these years, heard from members of Swift's circle that he spent most of the day with friends, from noon until bedtime at eleven.[32]

The most important friendship of all was with Stella, but it remains as hidden as ever, though occasional references confirm that she participated in the social evenings. A number of their closest friends were certain that in 1716 they were secretly married. Others were just as certain that they didn't. That strange mystery will be taken up later.

The closest male friends were two young clergymen, Thomas Sheridan and Patrick Delany, many of whose comments have already been quoted. Delany was the popular vicar of St. Werburgh's, the church in which Swift was supposedly baptized. He was unusually well off for a clergyman, having married a lady with money, and they regularly entertained at their impressive country house, which Swift dubbed Delville. "Of all the gentlemen I ever knew," Laetitia Pilkington recalled, "this I must say, that Dr. Delany excels in

55. Dr. Patrick Delany. Delany's comfortable, well-fed countenance reflects his excellence as a host.

one point particularly, which is in giving an elegant entertainment, with ease, cheerfulness, and an hospitality which makes the company happy."[33]

Delany was a man of wide interests, one of which was the native Gaelic language, and through him Swift became acquainted with the blind musician Turlough Carolan (more properly, Toirdhealbhach Ó Cearbhallain). Carolan, who went blind at eighteen and was then apprenticed to a harper, was a celebrity in Dublin and welcome at country estates, where he would sing verses in praise of his hosts.[34]

There is no evidence that Swift ever learned much Irish, but he picked up at least a smattering. Sheridan was amused by his chumminess with country people:

> Conforming to the tattered rabble,
> He learns their Irish tongue to gabble,
> And what our anger more provokes,
> He's pleased with their insipid jokes.[35]

Gaelic words do show up here and there in Swift's writings, and on one occasion, working from a literal translation, he produced a spirited version of a ballad that Carolan had set to music.

> O'Rourk's noble fare
>   Will ne'er be forgot
> By those who were there,
>   Or those who were not.
> His revels to keep,
>   We sup and we dine
> On seven score sheep,
>   Fat bullocks, and swine. . . .
> They dance in a round,
>   Cutting capers and ramping;
> A mercy the ground
>   Did not burst with their stamping.
> The floor is all wet
>   With leaps and with jumps,
> While the water and sweat
>   Splish, splash in their pumps.[36]

Swift liked to note down scraps of dialogue in which Gaelic words would mingle in with English ones.

A. He sometimes coshers with me, and once a month I
take a pipe with him, and we shoh it about for an hour
together.
B. Well, I'd give a cow in Connaugh to see you together. I
hear he keeps good horses.
A. None but garrawns, and I have seen him often riding
on a sougawn. In short, he is no better than a spawlpeen, a
perfect Monaghan.

This was the patois of the Anglo-Irish planters. "Shoh" comes from *seach*, to
take turns; a "spawlpeen" is a common laborer, from *spailpín*. To "cosher"
is to find lodging with friends or relatives, a "garrawn" is a gelding, and a
"sougawn" is a straw saddle. Connaught is the western province of Ireland,
named here for the alliteration with "cow"; a person from County Monaghan
is understood to be a rustic clod.[37] Indeed, there may be something especially
Irish in Swift's love of wordplay.

At bottom, however, Swift was no admirer of the native Irish tongue, because he thought it trapped its speakers in a cultural ghetto. He called it "barbarous," criticized its "abominable sounds," and said that it did more than
anything else "to prevent the Irish from being tamed." On another occasion
he talked about "civilizing" the Irish in much the same way that the English
would talk about people in India: "It would be a noble achievement to abolish the Irish language in this kingdom, so far at least as to oblige all the natives
to speak only English on every occasion of business in shops, markets, fairs,
and other places of dealing. . . . This would, in a great measure, civilize the
most barbarous among them, reconcile them to our customs and manner of
living, and reduce great numbers to the national religion, whatever kind may
then happen to be established."[38] That last comment might seem surprising,
coming from the dean of St. Patrick's, but it had always been Swift's principle
that the crucial thing was to enforce a single national religion, not to insist on
the Anglican Church as the sole repository of truth.

Most valued of all Swift's friends was Dr. Thomas Sheridan (not to be
confused with his son the actor and biographer, also named Thomas). Delany
said that the bond was obvious: Sheridan "had a faculty, and indeed a felicity,
of throwing out hints and materials of mirth and humor, beyond any man
I ever knew." The younger Sheridan concurred that his father "had a lively
fancy, and a surprising quickness of invention. He had such a perpetual flow
of spirits, such a ready wit and variety of humour, that I have often heard

56. Dr. Thomas Sheridan. The normally jocular Sheridan adopts an air of solemn dignity.

his acquaintance say it was impossible for the most splenetic man not to be cheerful in his company."[39] Wit is verbal, and often sarcastic and hostile; humor is situational, genial, and tolerant. It is rare for both to be highly developed in the same person. Voltaire had wit but not humor; Dickens had humor but not wit. Swift—like another great Irish writer, Oscar Wilde—had both, and in Sheridan he found a kindred spirit.

Physically, Sheridan was not prepossessing. In a playful Latin poem Swift said he had the voice of a cricket, the thighs of a fly, the hands of a mouse, and the shanks of a heron. In another poem a servant is made to call him "a spindle-shanked hoddy-doddy." Sheridan was incorrigibly impulsive. "His thoughts are sudden," Swift said in a character sketch of his friend, "and the most unreasonable always comes uppermost; and he constantly resolves and acts upon his first thoughts, and then asks advice, but never once before." Swift remarked to Charles Ford, his London friend who was now living at his estate near Dublin, "Sheridan is still the same—I mean in the sense that weathercocks are still the same."[40]

Sheridan was native Irish, not Anglo-Irish. His forebears were originally O'Sioradains in County Cavan, and had converted to the Church of Ireland a hundred years before. A graduate of Trinity College, Sheridan was deeply learned in Latin and Greek, and to supplement his clergyman's income he kept a school for boys. Dublin had no institution like Kilkenny College, and no public schools either. Schools run by private individuals had no fixed curricula, but in Sheridan's there was a steady diet of the classics, and the students even put on a Greek play once a year. Swift enjoyed visiting the school, where he often took part in the public examinations, and when Dr. Sheridan was sick or out of town he sometimes substituted for him in the classroom.[41]

Such schools for girls as existed had few academic pretensions. "At Mrs. Dawson's Boarding School the following work is to be taught, as embroidery, quilting, flourishing, cross stitch and tenth stitch, plain work and dressing of heads, with clearing and washing all manner of gauzes. . . . Likewise dancing, writing, and pastry is taught."[42]

If Sheridan had remained unmarried he would probably have had a distinguished career as a fellow of Trinity, but he became ineligible when he married Elizabeth McFadden, possibly before graduating. It was a horrendously unhappy marriage, as his friends all knew and as he freely acknowledged. He called her "a clog bound to me by an iron chain, as heavy as a millstone," and lamented that "a man should suffer all his life for the frenzy of youth. I was in the mad years of life when I married, and mad to marry, and almost mad after I had married." Swift said that Elizabeth Sheridan was "as cross as the Devil, and as lazy as any of her sister sows, and as nasty." But as Pat Rogers comments, this "wretched marriage" produced the actor and writer Thomas Sheridan the younger, and his son, the great playwright Richard Brinsley Sheridan.[43]

A favorite motto of Swift's was *vive la bagatelle*, keeping gloom at bay with playful trifles. In this, the younger Sheridan said, "no one was better qualified to keep up the ball" than his father. They regularly exchanged jocular verses, with the stipulation that they had to be composed in five minutes or less. Most of them were naturally thrown away.[44]

There were language games as well. Swift pretended to believe that words should be abbreviated whenever possible to letters of the alphabet—"The same thing men of business are not ignorant of, for thus three vowels shall stand for a promissory note, IOU £20." A letter to a lady would thus begin, "D R L n U r a Bu t. I s tm u a D t" ("Darling, you are a beauty. I esteem you a deity").[45]

And of course Sheridan was a willing participant in punning. He liked to refer to himself, in fact, as "Tom Punsibi," a name that was itself a pun since it means "a pun on himself." *Sibi* is Latin for "himself," and Sheridan's surname, sometimes spelled Siridan, was formed from the Irish *sír* (always) and *dán* (poetry).[46]

A poem by Sheridan on the origin of punning begins in mock homage to the androgynous primal human in Plato's *Symposium:*

> Once on a time, in merry mood,
> Jove made a pun of flesh and blood:
> A double, two-faced, living creature,
> *Androgynos*, of two-fold nature.

In Plato's myth, the subsequent division into sexes was the beginning of all our troubles. The *Symposium* ends with Socrates telling his drunken companions that tragedy and comedy are really the same thing. In Sheridan's irreverent version,

> Whatever words the male expressed,
> The female turned them to a jest;
> Whatever words the female spoke,
> The male converted to a joke.[47]

Swift's own puns tended to be desperately elaborate. Thus, "all eggs under the grate" becomes "Alexander the Great." He also came up with a nice imaginary derivation for the word "pun"—"from the French word *punaise*, which signifies a little stinking insect that gets into the skin, provokes continual itching, and is with great difficulty removed."[48] It may well be that punning, for Swift, was the reverse side of his obsession with stylistic correctness. Puns subvert propriety from within, a miniature expression of the anarchic inventiveness that created *A Tale of a Tub.*

CHAPTER 19

Political Peril

SWIFT UNDER SURVEILLANCE

Swift was now far from the world of London politics, but not from its influence, for the victorious Whigs were on the warpath. Back in 1712, when he prepared an index for his collected *Examiner* papers, he identified the Whigs complacently as "not properly a national party, but a little, inconsiderable, undone faction." Just two years after that they regained power, as he later said, "with wrath and vengeance in their hearts."[1] The Tory party, meanwhile, was in the process of committing political suicide. Swift's closest associates would be driven into exile or confined to prison, and for years to come he too would face the threat of arrest and imprisonment.

What wrecked the Tories was the well-grounded suspicion that they had been secretly colluding with the Pretender, promising that if he would convert to Protestantism, they would put him on the throne. Swift always denied that he had Jacobite sympathies, but of course he would need to deny it. Whatever his private feelings may have been, nothing in writing was ever found to incriminate him. The best guess is that he didn't actively support bringing back the Pretender, and might not have done so even if James turned Protestant—the danger of civil war would have been too great. On the other hand, he disliked William III and despised George I, and might have been glad to see the native Stuart dynasty restored.[2]

Early in 1715 Erasmus Lewis, Oxford's former right-hand man, wrote to warn, "If you have not already hid your papers in some private place in the hands of a trusty friend, I fear they will fall into the hands of your enemies." Swift's mail was definitely being opened, and he told a friend with amusement that the authorities thought they had found incriminating evidence, "but after opening several seals it proved only plum cake." Without Swift's knowledge, Archbishop King was shown some of the intercepted letters, but to King's relief they were entirely innocent. Still, Swift was alarmed, and he acquired a legal treatise entitled *A Collection of the Several Statutes, and Parts of Statutes, Now in Force, Relating to High Treason and Misprision of High Treason.* "This is not a time for any man to talk to the purpose," Pope wrote. "Truth is a kind of contraband commodity which I would not venture to export."[3]

In Ireland, Tories were systematically purged from office; eight of ten judges were removed, along with seventy-two justices of the peace. Bishops couldn't be deposed, but every vacancy henceforth was filled with a loyal Whig, guaranteeing that Swift would never be a bishop. And for several years, his Tory affiliation made many Dubliners distrust him. According to the younger Sheridan, "He was constantly insulted with opprobrious language as he walked the streets, and some of the more violent used to take up dirt from the kennel [gutter] to throw at him as he passed along; insomuch, that he was obliged never to go abroad without servants armed to protect his person."[4]

In the winter of 1715 a remarkable incident occurred when Swift was riding on the beach toward Howth, and he was so indignant that he made a formal petition to the Irish House of Lords. A Whig peer named Lord Blayney, riding in a fast chaise with another man, galloped after him with the clear intention of running him down. After taking evasive action Swift reached safety at a ditch that the chaise couldn't cross. In his account,

> The two gentlemen stopping their career, your petitioner mildly expostulated with them. Whereupon one of the gentlemen said, "Damn you, is not the road as free for us as for you?" and calling to his servant who rode behind said, "Tom (or some such name) is the pistol loaden with ball?" To which the servant answered, "Yes, my Lord," and gave him the pistol. Your petitioner then said to the gentleman, "Pray, sir, do not shoot, for my horse is apt to start, by which I shall endanger my life." The chaise went forward, and your petitioner took the opportunity to stay behind.[5]

The implication was that Lord Blayney was unlikely to hit anything he was aiming at, so that the only thing Swift had to fear was his horse's alarm when the gun went off. In the event, no action was taken against Blayney.

BOLINGBROKE DISGRACED

Meanwhile a government witch hunt was under way throughout Britain, searching for Jacobites. And Bolingbroke did something that was catastrophic for the future of the Tory party—he panicked and fled to France. One evening he appeared at a London playhouse, and the next day, disguised as a servant, he left the country.[6]

This was an obvious admission of guilt. Bolingbroke had indeed been negotiating with the Pretender. His gamble was that if James Stuart would agree to turn Protestant while Queen Anne was still alive, she might welcome a Stuart successor, replace Oxford with Bolingbroke, and smash the Whigs. J. H. Plumb believes the scheme could actually have worked, but it foundered on James's sincere devotion to his Catholic faith. "To a man of Bolingbroke's worldliness and agnosticism," Plumb comments, "a change of religion was a paltry matter."[7] But now the queen was dead, George I was on his way from Hanover, and the Tory party was in ruins.

From this perspective, Swift's abrupt retreat from London to Letcombe Bassett, in the months before the queen's death, was a prudent move to get out before it was too late. It's now certain that Oxford, as well as Bolingbroke, had been in touch with the Pretender, and although Ehrenpreis believes they successfully pulled the wool over Swift's eyes, it seems highly unlikely that Swift never suspected it. Even if they didn't confide in him explicitly, he had to guess what they were up to. And he was well aware that you could go to jail for not telling what you knew, even if you had done nothing wrong yourself.[8]

Two years later, in 1716, Archbishop King was afraid that Swift was still in danger, and pressed him to be frank about his situation. Swift answered, "Had there ever been the least overture or intent of bringing in the Pretender during my acquaintance with the ministry, I think I must have been very stupid not to have picked out some discoveries or suspicions; and though I am not sure I should have turned informer, yet I am sure I should have dropped some general cautions, and immediately have retired."[9]

What Swift had done was indeed to offer Oxford and Bolingbroke some "general cautions" and then leave town. King understood his meaning perfectly, and replied, "I never believed you [were] for the Pretender, but remember that when the surmises of that matter run high, you retired, which agrees with what you say you ought to have done in that case."[10] Staying in a country vicarage far from London, Swift avoided knowing too much.

In September of 1715, a rebellion broke out, known as the Jacobite Rising or "the Fifteen." Bolingbroke actively encouraged it, telling the Pretender, "Things are hastening to that point that either you, Sir, at the head of the Tories, must save the Church and Constitution of England, or both must be irretrievably lost forever."[11] Fighting began in Scotland, ancestral home of the Stuarts, and at first the Jacobite forces won some battles. The Pretender then joined them, but momentum flagged, and by early 1716 their campaign to recover his throne came to an ignominious end. The Pretender went back to France for good.

Swift's friend the Duke of Ormonde was charged with high treason for supporting the rebellion, and escaped to France. He never saw England or his wife again. Swift wrote that Ormonde's downfall was like an unreal dream "to those who will consider the nobleness of his birth, the great merits of his ancestors and his own, his long unspotted loyalty, his affability, generosity, and sweetness of nature. I knew him long and well." Swift added that Ormonde "no more conceived himself to be acting high treason than he did when he was wounded and a prisoner at Landen for his sovereign King William, or when he took and burned the enemy's fleet at Vigo."[12]

OXFORD IN THE TOWER

Bolingbroke panicked, but Oxford didn't. With characteristic caution, he had been careful to leave no paper trail, and he knew that the Whigs would never be able to convict him. He was given repeated opportunities to get away as Bolingbroke had, and he refused to do it. Lacking evidence for a trial, the government simply kept him in the Tower of London without charges for two whole years. He was the last high-ranking British statesman to be imprisoned there.

As soon as Swift heard of Oxford's arrest, he wrote to him to say that he was "the ablest and faithfullest minister and truest lover of your country that this age has produced. . . . Your heroic and Christian behavior under this prosecution astonisheth everyone but me, who know you so well, and know how little it is in the power of human actions or events to discompose you." Swift also assured Oxford in verse that even if other people were talking too much, he himself never would:

> Faithful silence hath a sure reward;
> Within our breast be every secret barred.
> He who betrays his friend shall never be
> Under one roof or in one ship with me.[13]

These lines strongly suggest that Swift did know what Oxford and Boling-broke had been up to. That he denied it in writing proves nothing; he would have been a fool not to deny it.

Finally, in June of 1717, Erasmus Lewis was able to assure Swift that Oxford's accusers "publicly own that they neither have, nor ever had any evidence." Two weeks after that Lewis reported, "My Lord Oxford's impeachment was discharged last night, by the unanimous consent of all the Lords present. . . . Our friend, who seems more formed for adversity than prosperity, has at present many more friends than ever he had before in any part of his life."[14] "All the Lords present" meant that a number of peers, bitterly opposed to setting Oxford free, absented themselves from the vote. The Duke of Marlborough, now in retirement but still eligible to sit in the House of Lords, was one of them.

Soon afterward Swift wrote to Oxford, offering to come and stay with him in Herefordshire and adding pointedly, "I have many things to say to you, and to inquire of you, as you may easily imagine." Oxford's reply was unenthusiastic. "Our impatience to see you should not draw you into uneasiness. We long to embrace you—if you find it may be no inconvenience to yourself." Oxford was probably hinting that he was still under suspicion, and it would be best for Swift to stay away. They went on exchanging occasional letters—Oxford was always a poor correspondent—but they never saw each other again. After Oxford's death seven years later, Swift wrote to ask his son whether he had any papers that could be used for a biography. "Such a work most properly belongs to me, who loved and respected him above all men, and had the honor to know him better than any other of my level did."[15] Oxford's son seems never to have sent the papers.

At about the time when Oxford was released from the Tower, Swift preached a sermon in St. Patrick's on the tenth commandment, "Thou shalt not bear false witness against thy neighbour." It was filled with biblical examples, but made obvious reference to current politics. In times of party rivalry, Swift said, "there is never wanting a set of evil instruments, who either out of mad zeal, private hatred, or filthy lucre, are always ready to offer their service to the prevailing side, and become accusers of their brethren without any regard to truth or charity." Writing to Pope (in a letter that may never have been sent), Swift called informers "the most accursed and prostitute and abandoned race that God ever permitted to plague mankind."[16]

As for Bolingbroke, he had to wait until 1723 for a pardon. He was permitted to return to England, but he didn't get his title back, and he was forbidden ever to engage in politics again.

THE FORMIDABLE SIR ROBERT

Rejoicing in their power in 1712, the Tories had pushed through a vote by which Robert Walpole, leader of the opposition in the House of Commons, was expelled for alleged corruption and imprisoned for five months in the Tower. He was charged with skimming money from military contracts, but that was never proved, though it's true that he got incredibly rich during this period. From the Tower, Walpole wrote to his sister, "You hear from me from this place, but I am sure it will be a satisfaction to you to know that this barbarous injustice being only the effect of party malice, does not concern me at all, and I heartily despise what I shall one day revenge."[17]

In 1713 Swift was still dismissing Walpole as a second-rater, adding that that readers "must excuse me for being so particular about one who is otherwise altogether obscure." He and his colleagues had no idea what they were up against. As Walpole's biographer, J. H. Plumb, summarizes his talents, "His powers of concentration were of the highest, and they were backed by an obstinate will, soaring ambition, and a greedy love of power, for he was a man utterly confident of his own capacity to rule." Plumb calls his ambition "aching," and says that he pursued power "with the greed and lust of a jealous lover."[18]

Oxford was never driven in that way. He enjoyed power, but not enough to master every detail or to manipulate allies and rivals with relentless skill. Bolingbroke was driven and self-confident, but it was fatal overconfidence. Brilliant though he was, he was erratic and untrustworthy, the type of person the English call too clever by half. He and Walpole had been rivals ever since they were schoolboys at Eton together, and at first it was Bolingbroke who shot to the top, but now the tables were turned. It was payback when he fled to France and Oxford went to the Tower.

Up until then it was taken for granted that the peers governed Britain, with the support, of course, of the House of Commons. That was why Harley and St. John expected to become peers as soon as they gained power. Walpole was the first to govern the nation from the House of Commons.[19] He didn't even become Sir Robert until 1725, and by then he was established as his country's first true prime minister.

Walpole liked to play the role of a bluff country squire, entertaining lavishly at his estate in Norfolk. One guest recalled, "We used to sit down to dinner a little snug party of about thirty odd, up to the chin in beef, venison, geese, turkeys, etc., and generally over the chin in claret, strong beer, and punch." Walpole had six different wine suppliers, and his bill with one of them for a single year was £1,118 (6,480 empty bottles were returned). He also laid on extravagant feasts for the money men of the City, as a newspaper ballad reported:

> For pipes by gross and wine by ton they called with might and main;
> They smoked and drank, and drank and spewed, and spewed and
>   drank again.[20]

Walpole's total mastery exasperated the Tories, and their apologists satirized him ceaselessly. Pope targeted him in poem after poem, Gay made him

57. Sir Robert Walpole. The artist has tactfully suggested Walpole's massive girth. Though not a tall man, he weighed 280 pounds.

an underworld chieftain in *The Beggar's Opera*, and Swift put him into *Gulliver's Travels* as Flimnap, the Lilliputian lord treasurer. Flimnap dominates the political competition of leaping and creeping, jumping over a horizontal pole and crawling under it. On one occasion he takes a tumble, and "would have infallibly broke his neck if one of the King's cushions, that accidentally lay on the ground, had not weakened the force of his fall." This is thought to refer to a mistress of George I.[21]

Walpole often turns up in Swift's poems, too, with a blank for his name that the rhyme makes obvious.

> How the helm is ruled by ——,
> At whose oars, like slaves, they all pull. . . .
> But why would he, except he slobbered,
> Offend our Patriot, great Sir R——?[22]

But unlike Bolingbroke and Pope, who dreamed of a virtuous Tory opposition that could restore integrity to politics, Swift now regarded politics as degrading if not corrupting. When he came to write *Gulliver's Travels* in the 1720s, he gave the nobly rational Houyhnhnms a republic, not a monarchy. The foul Yahoos, on the other hand, obey a vicious leader whom they turn against the moment they get a chance.

> This leader had usually a favourite as like himself as he could get, whose employment was to lick his master's feet and posteriors, and drive the female Yahoos to his kennel, for which he was now and then rewarded with a piece of ass's flesh. This favourite is hated by the whole herd, and therefore to protect himself keeps always near the person of his leader. He usually continues in office till a worse can be found; but the very moment he is discarded, his successor, at the head of all the Yahoos in that district, young and old, male and female, come in a body and discharge their excrements upon him from head to foot. But how far this might be applicable to our courts and favourites and ministers of state, my master said I could best determine.[23]

THE ATTERBURY DISASTER

The final chapter in the Tories' downfall came in 1722, when Oxford was back in the House of Lords and Bolingbroke about to return from exile. Francis Atterbury, bishop of Rochester, was the leader of the High Church wing that sought to establish the Church as separate from the monarchy, not subordinate to it. It now emerged that he was still negotiating with the Pretender.

Atterbury and his fellow conspirators exchanged heavily coded letters, which were intercepted by the government, and in which references to a dog named Harlequin supposedly furnished a damning clue. Swift wrote, but didn't publish, a mocking poem called *Upon the Horrid Plot Discovered by Harlequin, the Bishop of Rochester's French Dog:*

> I asked a Whig the other night
> How came this wicked plot to light;
> He answered that a dog of late
> Informed a minister of state.[24]

A dog from France did exist, though Atterbury never actually had it. It had arrived in England lame after an accident in transit, and was being cared for by the landlady of one of the minor conspirators, who said under interrogation that it was intended "for the Bishop of Rochester." That wouldn't have proved anything in itself, but in the letters the dog's owner was referred to as a certain T. Illington, who suffered from gout as Atterbury did, was away from London at just the times Atterbury was, and was distressed that a dog being sent from France had broken its leg.

The conspirators knew, of course, that their letters were likely to be opened, and they always took pains to deliver them by private means. So why were the three letters mentioning "Illington" and his dog sent by ordinary mail? Handwriting might have identified the writers decisively, but all the government presented was copies, claiming that the originals had been sent on to their addressees. Furthermore, there were blunders and errors of fact that the alleged senders would have been unlikely to make. The letters were probably forgeries, made necessary because without them there would have been no evidence at all.

For this reason, the government didn't dare to risk a judicial trial, fearing acquittal, and Atterbury was tried instead by the House of Lords. The Lords voted a special act—a most irregular law targeting a single individual—that imposed "pains and penalties" by which Atterbury was deposed from his bishopric and denied "any office, dignity, promotion, benefice, or employment in England." He went to France and died there nine years later.

A few years after his initial poetic reaction, Swift followed it up with a trenchant reprise in *Gulliver's Travels.*

It is first agreed and settled among them what suspected persons shall be accused of a plot; then, effectual care is taken to secure all their letters and papers, and put the owners in chains. These papers are delivered to a set of artists very dexterous in finding out the mysterious meanings of words, syllables, and letters. For instance, they can discover a close stool to signify a privy council; a flock of geese, a senate; a lame dog, an invader; the plague, a standing army; a buzzard, a minister; the gout, a high priest; a gibbet, a Secretary of State; a chamber pot, a committee of grandees; a sieve, a court lady; a broom, a revolution; a mouse trap, an employment; a bottomless pit, the treasury; a sink, a c——t; a cap and bells, a favourite; a broken reed, a court of justice; an empty tun, a general; a running sore, the administration.[25]

Even the lame dog is there, with the Pretender as the would-be invader. Atterbury is of course the "high priest" with the gout. The members of the House of Lords are the tame geese who went along with the administration's demands. The "close stool" and chamber pot evoke the Privy Council that advised the king and its special committee that conducted the investigation. By a sly allusion, its name becomes literal, since some of the government's documents had actually been retrieved from the bishop's privy. As for "c——t," no doubt it means "court," but since Swift had already used just that word without disguising it, other possibilities exist. It could suggest the undue influence of politicians' mistresses.

Atterbury's persecutors tried to put the best face on what they had done by claiming that a trial in a court of law would have imposed a more serious punishment than the Lords did, and they got King George to declare, "It is with pleasure I reflect that the justice of Parliament had been so tempered with mercy, that even those who are resolved to be dissatisfied must acknowledge the lenity of your proceedings."[26]

After Gulliver tries in vain to reconcile Lilliput with its rival island Blefuscu, a stand-in for France, he is convicted of treason. The Lilliputian ministry then demands that he be put to death as painfully as possible, possibly by sprinkling his clothes with a poisonous juice that will make him tear his own flesh and die "in the utmost torture." By the king's generosity, however, a milder punishment is decreed. "Your friend the Secretary will be directed to come to your house and read before you the articles of impeachment, and then to signify the great lenity and favour of his Majesty and Council, whereby you are only condemned to the loss of your eyes, which his Majesty does not question you will gratefully and humbly submit to; and twenty of his Majesty's surgeons will attend, in order to see the operation well performed, by discharging very sharp pointed arrows into the balls of your eyes as you lie on the ground."[27] The allusion to George I's speech about lenity and mercy is unmistakable, but the effect is chilling even for readers who have never heard of the bishop of Rochester.

CHAPTER 20

The Irish Countryside

SWIFT ON HORSEBACK

Swift enjoyed riding, chose his horses with care, and generally traveled on horseback, whereas his friends preferred carriages. He loved to be in motion, and in Ireland he could pass in a short time from one kind of world to another. "I have often reflected," he remarked, "in how few hours, with a swift horse or a strong gale, a man may come among a people as unknown to him as the Antipodes."[1]

When in Dublin, Swift took long rides on the broad sandy beaches, as he was doing when he had his confrontation with Lord Blayney. When he was away from town, visiting friends at their country houses or just commuting back and forth from Laracor, a servant with the luggage would follow on a second horse. On longer journeys there would be two servants.

On his return to Ireland in 1714, Swift brought over from England a horse he had named Bolingbroke. The name may have been facetious, implying that if he could never get the man Bolingbroke to listen to his advice, he could at least control the horse. But this Bolingbroke too proved a disappointment. First he had to get over an illness, and even afterward, "he is very fat and well, but I hate riding him."[2]

Shortly after Christmas 1714, a contretemps occurred. A footman named Tom showed up late and drunk at a ferry where he was supposed to retrieve

58. Swift on horseback. A satiric print from a 1714 parody of the *Tale of a Tub*, showing Swift outside the deanery in his customary clerical gown. It's not clear what is going on; a post boy is galloping off, blowing his horn, and a second clergyman is riding away.

Bolingbroke. It was like Patrick in London all over again, but this time there was a rearing, uncooperative horse to deal with. Tom mounted the horse, rode him wildly into the sea, fell off, and started fighting when Swift and a couple of passersby tried to wrestle the bridle out of his hands. Eventually they succeeded and Tom staggered away.[3]

Swift was well versed in the elaborate equipment that horses required, and he also understood that these encumbrances were aggravating and made long training necessary. Among the rational horses, Gulliver says, "I described, as well as I could, our way of riding; the shape and use of a bridle, a saddle, a spur, and a whip; of harness and wheels. I added that we fastened plates of a certain hard substance called 'iron' at the bottom of their feet, to preserve their hoofs from being broken by the stony ways on which we often travelled." His equine master reacts with "great indignation."[4]

To have a convenient place where his horses could graze, Swift leased a three-acre field and enclosed it with a brick wall nine feet high. Along the south-facing wall, which got the most sunlight, he planted fruit trees in imitation of Moor Park. The name he gave this plot was Naboth's Vineyard, and the allusion is disturbing. Close to King Ahab's palace, Naboth had a vineyard that he declined to sell because it had belonged to his forefathers. Ahab's queen, the infamous Jezebel, solved the problem by bribing two sons of Belial to testify falsely that Naboth was a blasphemer, after which he was stoned to death. The prophet Elijah was then sent by the Lord to warn the king: "In the place where dogs licked the blood of Naboth shall dogs lick thy blood, even thine."[5] In adopting this name, Swift was alluding once again to bearers of false witness.

Normally frugal, Swift could be extravagant once a project got going. He threw himself obsessively into this one, with much bullying of the workmen. "When the masons played the knaves, nothing delighted me so much as to stand by while my servants threw down what was amiss. I have likewise seen a monkey overthrow all the dishes and plates in a kitchen, merely for the pleasure of seeing them tumble and hearing the clatter they made in their fall." The eventual cost of the construction was a staggering £600, and Swift told his Laracor curate that he had "half ruined myself by building a wall, which is as bad as a lawsuit."[6]

COUNTRY HOUSE GUEST

Over the years, Swift grew accustomed to spending long visits, months on end at times, at the country houses of his friends. There were many of these, including the Grattans' Belcamp close to Dublin, Knightley Chetwode's Woodbrook in Queen's County (renamed County Laois after Irish independence), Charles Ford's Woodpark in County Meath, and Robert Rochfort's Gaulstown, also in County Meath.

At some point he wrote out detailed instructions for servants on the road. These were at least as detailed as his "laws" at the deanery. A servant should: ride no more than forty yards beyond the master; inquire along the way for the best inn at that day's destination; attend to stabling and feeding the horses (not removing saddles and bridles until they cool down); stand by while a smith repairs any loose horseshoes; keep an eye on the dinner while it is being

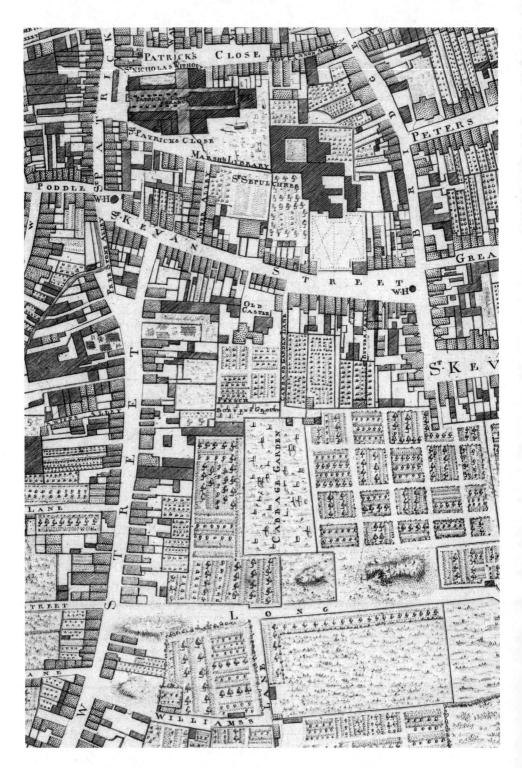

59. Naboth's Vineyard. St. Patrick's is at the top, and Naboth's Vineyard at
bottom right, showing Swift's fruit trees along two of the walls.

prepared; make sure the master's room is well aired; look under the bed "lest a cat or something else may be under it"; dry any damp bedclothes before a fire; lay out the master's belongings as they would be at home; sample the ale or wine to make sure it isn't sour; keep track of all expenses; "learn to have some skill in cookery, that at a pinch you may be able to make your master easy"; wake the master up an hour before departure time; and pack his belongings, taking care "that no two hard things be together, and that they be wrapped up in paper or towels."[7]

In a poem called *The Journal* Swift related the events of a single day (the root meaning of *journal*, as in "diurnal") when he was a guest at Gaulstown. It begins with his taking charge, as he could never resist doing:

> At seven, the Dean in nightgown dressed
> Goes round the house to wake the rest;
> At nine, grave Nim and George facetious
> Go to the Dean to read Lucretius.
> At ten, my Lady comes and hectors,
> And kisses George, and ends our lectures,
> And when she has him by the neck fast
> Hauls him, and scolds us down to breakfast.

George and John Rochfort were the sons of the baron and his lady; "Nim" was so called in allusion to Nimrod, the great hunter of the Bible, and indeed Swift says that he "brings us hares when he can catch them."[8]

The day unfolds in a series of minor mishaps. Dan Jackson, a mutual friend, liked to fish in the thousand-foot canal that the baron had constructed, and Swift remarks that a really full account would relate

> How Dan caught nothing in his net,
> And how his boat was overset;
> For brevity I have retrenched
> How in the lake the Dean was drenched.

There are too many guests for the modest size of the house, and some of them are extremely tedious. Years later, William Percival, dean of Emly, was offended when the poem was published and he came upon this account of himself:

> I might have told how oft Dean Percival
> Displays his pedantry unmerciful,

> How haughtily he lifts his nose
> To tell what every schoolboy knows.

The wounded Percival published verses of his own in reply, denouncing Swift as an ungrateful guest:

> Sometimes to Gaulstown he will go
> To spend a month or two or so,
> Admires the Baron, George and 's spouse,
> Lives well, and then lampoons the house.[9]

Swift seems to have left Gaulstown abruptly without saying why, and when he got back to Dublin he told Dan Jackson, "I had no mind to load you with the secret of my going, because you should bear none of the blame. I talk upon a supposition that Mr. Rochfort had a mind to keep me longer, which I will allow in him and you, but not one of the family besides, who I confess had reason enough to be weary of a man who entered into none of their tastes, nor pleasures, nor fancies, nor opinions, nor talk." Rather proudly, Swift added an account of his return journey that confirms his remarkable stamina: "I baited [spent the night] at Clancurry, and got to Leslip between three and four, saw the curiosities there, and the next morning came to Dublin by eight o'clock, and was at prayers in my Cathedral. There's a traveler."[10]

QUILCA

The place where Swift stayed oftenest and longest, though he also enjoyed lampooning it, was a little house in County Cavan that the Sheridans called by the Gaelic name of Quilca. Both spouses came from Cavan, and Elizabeth inherited the house from her family. It stood by a boggy lake in the middle of nowhere, fifty miles northwest of Dublin and eight miles from the town of Kells, which Swift mentioned as "the nearest habitable place." The surrounding area was known as the Great Bog, useless for farming.[11]

Thomas Sheridan the younger called the house "as inconvenient a cabin, and as dreary a country, as could anywhere be met with." In her illuminating book on Swift and landscape, Carole Fabricant says that he "seems to have had a love-hate relationship with Quilca; he was simultaneously attracted to and repelled by its unadulterated rusticity and primitive conditions, its severe climate, and its harsh, angular beauty." He wrote from there, "I live in a cabin, and in a very wild country, yet there are some agreeablenesses in

60. Mullagh Lake, Quilca, seen from the site of the Sheridans' house.

it, or at least I fancy so, and am leveling mountains and raising stones and fencing against inconveniencies of a scanty lodging, want of victuals, and a thievish race of people." As always, Swift liked to take charge. It should not be assumed that he was actually doing the work with his own hands. The weather being too wet to go out on horseback, "I have been forced for amusement to set Irish fellows to work, and to oversee them." It's unlikely that the Irish fellows enjoyed leveling mountains and raising stones in the rain, which fell virtually every day that year from May through August. "The harvest was spoiled," a Dublin official recorded, "and most of the fruit and vegetable productions of the earth."[12]

Sheridan, if not his wife, was tolerant of Swift's bossiness, and Swift was grateful for that. When his vertigo got bad, he needed to escape the social interchange of Dublin and live among understanding friends. He wrote to the second Earl of Oxford, who had recently succeeded to his father's title, "I have been four months in a little obscure Irish cabin about forty miles from Dublin [Irish miles were longer than English], whither I fled to avoid company in frequent returns of deafness. . . . While I am thus incommoded I must be content to live among those whom I can govern, and make them comply with my infirmities."[13]

Swift detailed the house's faults in a short poem with a long title, *To Quilca, A Country House in No Very Good Repair, Where the Supposed Author and Some of His Friends Spent a Summer in the Year 1725* (the friends were Stella and Rebecca):

> Let me my properties explain:
> A rotten cabin, dropping rain,
> Chimneys with scorn rejecting smoke,
> Stools, tables, chairs, and bedsteads broke. . . .
> Through all the valleys, hills, and plains,
> The goddess Want in triumph reigns,
> And her chief officers of state,
> Sloth, Dirt, and Theft around her wait.

Sheridan got back at Swift with a description of the furnishings at Laracor:

> An oaken, broken elbow chair;
> A caudle cup, without an ear;
> A battered, shattered ash bedstead;
> A box of deal, without a lid.[14]

During another visit Swift wrote up a catalogue of "the blunders, deficiencies, distresses, and misfortunes of Quilca." The few "vessels for drink" were leaky, bottles were uncleanable, only one chair was safe to sit on and even it was "in a very ill state of health," and peat was in such short supply that the guests had to go down to the bog to help gather it. Swift's room had a door full of chinks that the wind blew through, and a bed with "two damnable iron spikes" that threatened to break his shins. The room that Stella and Rebecca shared was no better, with a hole in the floor they had to avoid stumbling into, and two big gaps in the wall, "either of which would blow out a candle in the calmest day." The servants were shameless thieves, and even the cats gave offense, getting into the cellar to eat the food stored there, "for which one was tried, condemned, and executed by the sword."[15]

Sheridan was unrepentant. A couple of years later he wrote a poem cheerfully acknowledging similar defects of his Dublin house, starting with the parlor door:

How oft in turns have you and I
Said thus—"Let me"—"No, let me try."
"This turn will open it, I engage."
You push me from it in a rage!
Twisting, turning, trifling, rumbling,
Scolding, staring, fretting, grumbling;
At length it opens, in we go;
How glad are we to find it so!

Sheridan's joke is to find a solemn moral in every inconvenience, in the spirit of Swift's *Meditation on a Broomstick*.

If you're disposed to take a seat,
The moment that it feels your weight,
Out go its legs, and down you come
Upon your reverend Deanship's bum.
Hence learn, and see old age displayed,
When strength and vigor are decayed,
The joints relaxing with their years;
Then what are mortal men, but chairs?[16]

Once, when Swift was staying at Quilca, he heard that there was going to be a beggars' wedding nearby, and he proposed to show up at it dressed as a blind fiddler, with Sheridan leading him as his guide. They entered delightedly into the beggars' storytelling and joking, parted from them with hearty good wishes, and even accepted money from them. But there was a distressing sequel. When Swift and Sheridan went for a walk the next day and encountered the beggars, "they found some upon crutches, who had danced very nimbly at the wedding; others stone blind, who were perfectly clear-sighted at the feast. . . . The Dean, who mortally hated those sturdy vagrants, rated [that is, berated] them soundly, told them in what manner he had been present at the wedding and was let into their roguery; and assured them, if they did not immediately apply to honest labour, he would have them taken up and sent to jail.[17] It's far from clear how Swift, who knew nothing of music, managed to pass himself off as a fiddler.

All was not dreary at Quilca. Stella enjoyed working in the garden, and at one point Swift wrote to Sheridan, who was away in Dublin at the time, "She is so pleased with her pickaxe that she wears it fastened to her girdle [belt] on her left side, in balance with her watch." Someone who later owned the

MATTOCK PRESENTED TO STELLA BY SWIFT.

61. Stella's pickaxe.

pickaxe said it had a cherrywood handle sixteen inches long and a pointed head of nine inches.[18]

Since Quilca was the name of a house and not a town, it would be impossible to find the site today without local knowledge. It is as isolated as ever, buried among the woods a couple of miles from the village of Virginia (named by English settlers for the Virgin Queen). A Victorian visitor was shocked when the verdant landscape around Kells abruptly gave way to barren brown bogs, and the road grew rutted and bumpy. A "fine old peasant," whose name was coincidentally Sheridan, pointed the way to Quilca. Nothing remained there but some tumbledown walls, the beech trees that Swift had helped to plant, and his canal, "now filled up."[19] A house does stand today where Quilca used to be, but the one Swift knew is long gone.

CHAPTER 21

Stella

CAN WE KNOW HER?

Given that Stella was Swift's closest friend during her entire adult life, and also that mutual friends saw them both almost daily, it is extraordinarily difficult to get her into focus. What was she really like? Were they in love? Did she want to marry Swift, and did he refuse? Or did he indeed marry her but insist on keeping it secret?

We don't even know what Stella looked like, since no authentic portrait exists. The one certainty is that, as Swift said, "her hair was blacker than a raven." He confirms that she was beautiful but doesn't say in what way—"every feature of her face in perfection." Delany's wife told someone else, who subsequently told Sir Walter Scott, that Mrs. Delany "was struck with the beauty of her countenance, and particularly with her fine dark eyes. She was very pale, and looked pensive, but not melancholy, and had hair black as a raven." That's thirdhand testimony, and the raven comparison suggests that Scott, who edited Swift's works, may have been remembering his description. Black hair was definitely admired. Fielding's ravishing Sophia Western has black hair, and an English traveler describing an Irishwoman said, "Her hair is black, or near it (and then I need not tell ye it is charming)."[1]

Nor did the friends who knew Stella best—the elder Sheridan, Delany, Ford—record a distinct impression of what she and Swift were like together.

They all testified that to the best of their knowledge, the two of them were never alone without a third person present. That person was usually Rebecca Dingley, and about her, too, it's impossible to learn much. No one knows how close she and Stella had been at Moor Park, and whether their living together was evidence of an important friendship or just a way to preserve propriety and save money.

Swift's references to Rebecca after the *Journal to Stella* are few, unenthusiastic, and sometimes dismissive. A little song called *Dingley and Brent* describes her and the deanery housekeeper Anne Brent as empty-headed:

> Dingley and Brent,
> Wherever they went,
> Ne'er minded a word that was spoken;
> Whatever was said,
> They ne'er troubled their head,
> But laughed at their own silly joking.

When Swift himself is witty, however, Rebecca can't be bothered to pay attention:

> You tell a good jest
> And please all the rest;
> Comes Dingley, and asks you "What was it?"
> And curious to know,
> Away she will go
> To seek an old rag in the closet.[2]

Presumably Anne and Rebecca never saw this poem, which wasn't published until long after they and Swift were dead.

A little house near Laracor, in which Stella supposedly lived, is itself a symbol of uncertainty. It was first given the name "Stella's cottage" on an Ordinance Survey map of 1836, drawing on local tradition; but that tradition was more than a century old.

The cottage was located on the roadside halfway between Laracor and Trim, an easy mile's walk either way. But that's all we have to go on, and the latest writer on the question agrees with Sir William Wilde, who visited Laracor a few years after the Ordinance Survey map was made, that the association with Stella was "somewhat apocryphal."[3]

At any event, the uncertainty reflects the way in which most traces of Swift and his circle have vanished from the earth. The surviving foundation is a chal-

STELLA'S HOUSE.

62. Stella's cottage. The little house as it still appeared in the
mid-nineteenth century.

lenge even to find, hidden in an unmarked, overgrown patch behind a fence. Wildflowers and weeds fill the space in which Stella may possibly have lived.

Lacking clear evidence, interpreters project their own assumptions on the relationship between Stella and Swift. Victorian writers used to sentimentalize her as a sweet victim of fate. Thus Thackeray: "Gentle lady! so lovely, so loving, so unhappy! you have had countless champions, millions of manly hearts mourning for you. From generation to generation we take up the fond tradition of your beauty; we watch and follow your tragedy, your bright morning love and purity, your constancy, your grief, your sweet martyrdom. We know your legend by heart. You are one of the saints of English story."[4]

Stella was not so sweet as all that, and if she had been, it's hard to imagine that she and Swift would have gotten along. He made a list of her snappy replies: "A very dirty clergyman of her acquaintance, who affected smartness and repartee, was asked by some of the company how his nails came to be so dirty. He was at a loss; but she solved the difficulty, by saying, 'The doctor's nails grew dirty by scratching *himself*.'" The initial question was remarkably impolite; perhaps Swift himself gave Stella her setup. He also recorded a retort

63. The remains of Stella's cottage.

that was downright caustic: "A gentleman who had been very silly and pert in her company at last began to grieve at remembering the loss of a child lately dead. A bishop sitting by comforted him that he should be easy, because the child was gone to Heaven. 'No, my Lord,' said she, 'that is it which most grieves him, because he is sure never to see his child there.'"[5]

Swift claimed that Stella "excelled almost beyond belief" at bon mots. But as Johnson remarked, "Of her wit, so loudly vaunted, the smart sayings which Swift himself has collected afford no splendid specimen." This one is typical: "A Quaker apothecary sent her a phial corked; it had a broad brim, and a label of paper about its neck. 'What is that,' said she, 'my apothecary's son?' The ridiculous resemblance, and the suddenness of the question, set us all a-laughing."[6]

Victorian pieties are out of fashion nowadays, but it is still usual to imagine a docile Stella who willingly subordinated herself. When Swift was moody, Nokes says, she would play along, "and, if necessary, modify his ideas by soothing rather than ruffling him." There is no evidence for that. Swift did say, in a memorial description after her death, "Never was so happy a

64. Stella's ghost. Stella
imagined by a Victorian
artist: her spirit watches
tenderly over a grieving
Swift, while the sands of his
own mortality sift away in
the hourglass in front of him.

conjunction of civility, freedom, easiness, and sincerity." That's not docility,
however, and he also told her that she had a quick temper:

> Your spirits kindle to a flame,
> Moved with the lightest touch of blame,
> And when a friend in kindness tries
> To show you where your error lies,
> Conviction does but more incense;
> Perverseness is your whole defense.
> Truth, judgment, wit, give place to spite,
> Regardless both of wrong and right. . . .
> Stella, for once you reason wrong,

> For should this ferment last too long,
> By time subsiding, you may find
> Nothing but acid left behind.[7]

Ehrenpreis is certain that Swift was completely asexual, and also believes that since he never knew a father of his own, he had a powerful desire to play a father's role himself. Ehrenpreis invokes symbolic paternity in contexts of every kind, even in political ones—"With an instinctive pleasure in the duties of a father and a long training in the work of a priest, Swift naturally welcomed the *Examiner's* opportunities to form the opinions of Englishmen."[8]

Confident that he can always recognize unconscious motivations, Ehrenpreis offers a most peculiar interpretation of the relationship with Stella. The master key is the notion, based on a handful of instances, that Swift was profoundly drawn to women in poor health. "He worried incessantly about her health, her eyesight, her melancholy. . . . To all this solicitude there is a distasteful side. By attaching himself to an invalid, a man can relieve himself of angry impulses without openly admitting them, because the beloved is always suffering a punishment that he has not administered. Without feeling guilty, therefore, he can indulge a kind of sadism, even prolonging the existence of the woman in order to prolong his participation in her suffering."[9] There is not the slightest evidence for this quite offensive interpretation.

As for the asexuality, we have already noted hints to the contrary in Swift's correspondence with Vanessa. He was well known for his intensity, with a magnetic personality and a compelling gaze that people responded to instinctively. He had powerful, even volatile emotions. He had intense likes and dislikes. He flirted with attractive women all his life; when he visited his mother in Leicester she warned him to stop, and even in late middle age, so many women were drawn to him that a jealous friend, Lord Orrery, called them his "seraglio."[10] And the two women he deeply loved, both of whom were exceptionally good-looking, loved him in return and remained permanently bonded to him.

THE POEMS TO STELLA

From 1719 on, Swift wrote a birthday poem for Stella on March 13 nearly every year. In each of these poems, the depth and sincerity of affection are movingly apparent. The first one is short enough to quote in full.

> Stella this day is thirty-four
> (We won't dispute a year or more).

However, Stella, be not troubled,
Although thy size and years are doubled
Since first I saw thee at sixteen,
The brightest virgin of the green,
So little is thy form declined,
Made up so largely in thy mind.
Oh, would it please the gods to split
Thy beauty, size, and years, and wit,
No age could furnish out a pair
Of nymphs so graceful, wise, and fair,
With half the lustre of your eyes,
With half thy wit, thy years, and size.
And then, before it grew too late,
How should I beg of gentle Fate
(That either nymph might have her swain)
To split my Worship too in twain.[11]

Stella was thirty-eight, actually, as Swift well knew; he always liked to tease her by pretending to mistake her age. And there is a frank admission that they were both putting on weight, with the word "size" breaking in repeatedly until it finishes up a line. The age of sixteen is significant: not when Swift met Stella as a young girl, but when he returned from Ireland to Moor Park and realized she had grown into a woman. "My Worship" is a nice touch, a playful adaptation of the polite "Your Worship" with which people addressed the dean. Aging and fat though they are, outward changes only emphasize the changelessness of inner worth.

In the next year Swift sent a nonbirthday poem, *To Stella, Visiting Me in My Sickness*, expressing gratitude for her attention when he was laid up once again with vertigo.

When on my sickly couch I lay,
Impatient both of night and day,
Lamenting in unmanly strains,
Called every power to ease my pains,
Then Stella ran to my relief
With cheerful face, and inward grief. . . .
My sinking spirits now supplies
With cordials in her hands, and eyes;
Now with a soft and silent tread

Unheard she moves about my bed.
I see her taste each nauseous draught,
And so obligingly am caught:
I bless the hand from whence they came,
Nor dare distort my face for shame.[12]

The 1721 birthday poem is another compliment to Stella's excellence of mind. Just as people keep frequenting a favorite inn even after it begins to decay,

Now this is Stella's case in fact:
An angel's face, a little cracked
(Could poets or could painters fix
How angels look at thirty-six).
This drew us in at first to find
In such a form an angel's mind,
And every virtue now supplies
The fainting rays of Stella's eyes.[13]

In the same year, Stella reciprocated with a birthday poem of her own for Swift, written in his style:

St. Patrick's Dean, your country's pride,
My early and my only guide,
Let me among the rest attend,
Your pupil and your humble friend. . . .
When men began to call me fair
You interposed your timely care;
You early taught me to despise
The ogling of a coxcomb's eyes;
Showed where my judgment was misplaced,
Refined my fancy and my taste.[14]

Complimentary though the poem is to Swift, it seems a bit strange for a woman of forty to say that she is still his "pupil," and to describe herself as a "humble friend." But she knew that her poem would be seen by others in their circle, and perhaps this is how she wanted to appear.

By now Stella's health was starting to decline, though the cause is not known. She probably suffered from asthma, and may have contracted tuberculosis as well. As early as 1723 Swift told a neighboring vicar, "Mrs. Johnson eats an ounce a week."[15] By 1725, Swift's references to aging are more earnest than before:

> No poet ever sweetly sung
> Unless he were, like Phoebus, young,
> Nor ever nymph inspired to rhyme
> Unless, like Venus, in her prime.
> At fifty-six, if this be true,
> Am I a poet fit for you?
> Or at the age of forty-three
> Are you a subject fit for me?
> Adieu bright wit, and radiant eyes;
> You must be grave, and I be wise.
> Our fate in vain we would oppose,
> But I'll be still your friend in prose.

In a touching conclusion, Swift claims that it's just as well his eyesight is failing, but refers bleakly to his other affliction:

> No length of time can make you quit
> Honour and virtue, sense and wit;
> Thus you may still be young to me
> While I can better *hear* than *see*.
> Oh, ne'er may Fortune show her spite
> To make me *deaf*, and mend my *sight*.

Fifteen years later Swift wrote in the margin, "Now deaf 1740."[16]

Perhaps the best clue to the relationship is something Swift said after Stella was gone: "Violent friendship is much more lasting, and as much engaging, as violent love." As he made clear to Vanessa in London, he was skeptical of the swept-away kind of falling in love, and may well have feared it. He said the same thing in one of the first Stella poems:

> Thou, Stella, wert no longer young
> When first for thee my harp I strung,
> Without one word of Cupid's darts,
> Of killing eyes, or bleeding hearts;

> With friendship and esteem possessed
> I ne'er admitted love a guest.[17]

But if the friendship was truly violent, most people would call it love.

WERE THEY MARRIED OR NOT?

It is astonishing that on a question of such obvious importance, Swift's friends were about equally divided, and that no conclusive evidence was available then or later. Readers in those days were addicted to "secret histories" that purported to reveal the scandalous goings-on of the rich and powerful, and Swift admitted that when Stella moved to Ireland, people suspected that "there were a secret history in such a removal; which, however, soon blew off by her excellent conduct."[18] That implies that the gossip stopped; but it didn't, of course.

In 1713, after Stella had been living in Dublin for over a decade, Archbishop King sent Swift a friendly letter in which he expressed sympathy for renewed attacks of vertigo, and added, "An odd thought came into my mind on reading that you were among willows, imagining that perhaps your mistress had forsaken you and that was the cause of your malady. If that be the case, cheer up, the loss may be repaired, and I hope the remedy easy." King meant "mistress" in a blameless sense, and may have been hinting that Swift would soon marry her.[19]

Swift had a poor opinion of marriage as an institution. It wasn't only that a houseful of dependents was a burden for a clergyman to support, as Sheridan's experience showed. It was also that as an institution, marriage could damage love instead of sustaining it. In his *Thoughts on Various Subjects*, Swift invoked a pair of rival Olympians: "Venus, a beautiful good-natured lady, was the goddess of love; Juno, a terrible shrew, the goddess of marriage; and they were always mortal enemies." Swift added, "Matrimony hath many children: repentance, discord, poverty, jealousy, sickness, spleen, loathing, etc."[20]

In another aphorism Swift wrote grimly, "The reason why so few marriages are happy is because young ladies spend their time in making nets, and not in making cages." In other words, they work hard to catch a mate, but not to make him contented with his loss of freedom. Or perhaps love itself is a cage as well as net, as in Blake's haunting lyric:

> Underneath the net I stray,
> Now entreating burning fire,

> Now entreating iron wire,
> Now entreating tears and sighs—
> O! when will the morning rise?[21]

If Swift and Stella did get married, it probably happened in 1716, performed by St. George Ashe, who by then was bishop of Clogher in the north. That is what Sheridan told another clergyman, from whom Johnson in turn got the story. Delany and Deane Swift were likewise sure it took place then, as was the younger Sheridan, who presumably heard about it from his father. Supposedly the marriage took place in the garden of Ashe's house, and as bishop, he was well placed to keep it secret.[22]

On the other hand, Dr. Lyon said that despite what some friends believed about the marriage, "There is no authority for it but a hearsay story, and that very ill founded." Lyon added that Rebecca Dingley "laughed at it, as an idle tale founded on suspicion," and that Mrs. Brent, Swift's housekeeper, "thought it was all Platonic love."[23] But of course, if Stella as well as Swift was determined to keep the marriage secret, Rebecca would have participated in the cover-up. As for Anne Brent, she said that Stella never visited the deanery alone, but she couldn't have known what might have happened elsewhere.

John Hawkesworth, one of the first biographers of Swift, summed up the puzzle very well: "Why the Dean did not sooner marry this excellent person; why he married her at all; why his marriage was so cautiously concealed; and why he was never known to meet her but in the presence of a third person; are inquiries to which no man can answer, or has attempted to answer, without absurdity."[24]

One other anecdote survives from this time, and it is a most remarkable one, though again we have it thirdhand. It supposedly originates with Swift's close friend and fellow clergyman Patrick Delany. Delany was a man of the utmost probity, and if he was indeed the source, the report is most illuminating. Sir Walter Scott heard it from a friend of Delany's widow:

> Immediately subsequent to the ceremony, Swift's state of mind appears to have been dreadful. Delany (as I have learned from a friend of his relict) being pressed to give his opinion on this strange union, said that about the time it took place he observed Swift to be extremely gloomy and agitated, so much so that he went to Archbishop King to mention his apprehensions. On [Delany's] entering the library, Swift

rushed out with a countenance of distraction, and passed him without speaking. [Delany] found the Archbishop in tears, and upon asking the reason, [the archbishop] said, "You have just met the most unhappy man on earth; but on the subject of his wretchedness, you must never ask a question."[25]

This is a story told at two removes, by Delany's widow and her friend, and then retold with novelistic gusto by Sir Walter Scott. It is therefore impossible to know how much credence to give it. But it is not disproved by the mere fact that Delany himself didn't report it in his commentary on Orrery's memoir of Swift, nine years after Swift's death. At that time he could well have regarded the anecdote as too sensitive to make public.

If the encounter did actually happen, we will never know why Swift was so upset. But it has been conjectured that this was the moment when Swift learned, to his horror, that he and Stella were related by blood, with Sir John Temple as their common ancestor. If Swift and Sir William Temple were half brothers, then Swift was Stella's uncle. It was against canon law, and also against the law of the land, for an uncle and niece to marry. If they had already done so, the secret must never get out, and he may have hastened to tell the archbishop and implore his support.

The rumor of some sort of blood relationship was widespread, and it even reached Swift's English friends. Pope and Gay were said to believe that "Mrs. Johnson was Swift's sister, and that that was the reason of his not cohabiting with her."[26] Conceivably they picked up hints from Swift himself, or thought they did. And this was the reason why John Geree wrote his letter to the *Gentleman's Magazine* about the Moor Park ménage: he wanted to defend Swift from Orrery's claim that he broke Stella's heart by refusing to marry her. On the contrary, Geree said, it was impossible for such a marriage to take place, and he knew the reason why.

One other story, though a highly implausible one, should be mentioned. George Monck-Berkeley, a grandson of the philosopher Bishop Berkeley, heard from a St. Patrick's bell ringer named Richard Brennan "that when he was at school, there was a boy boarded with the master who was commonly reported to be the Dean's son by Mrs. Johnson." Brennan recalled "that the boy strongly resembled the Dean in his complexion, that he dined constantly at the deanery every Sunday, and that when other boys were driven out of the Deanery yard, he was suffered to remain there and divert himself." According to Brennan, the boy died shortly after Stella did. Monck-Berkeley himself was cautious in assessing this: "The story is, however, related merely as the report of the day, and no stress is meant to be laid upon it." More recent writers have called it "a fanciful yarn" and "a wild tale," which it almost certainly is.[27] Still, it's one more piece of evidence that questions about the Swift-Stella relationship refused to die.

CHAPTER 22

Vanessa in Ireland

A SECRET LIAISON

In January of 1714 Mrs. Vanhomrigh (named Hester, like her daughter) died, and her three surviving children were orphans. They stood to inherit ample wealth if complicated legal obstacles could be surmounted, and Swift gave Vanessa a good deal of advice about that. Meanwhile, they had to decide where to live. Bartholomew was on his own by then, and Ginkel had died, which left Vanessa and Molly by themselves.

Like Stella, Vanessa had inherited property in Ireland. Now that it was apparent that Swift would be returning there for good, Vanessa resolved to follow him, taking Molly with her. In August, when he was with Geree at Letcombe Bassett, she made a surprise trip to Wantage, just three miles away. As at Windsor two years before, Swift was alarmed, no doubt because he didn't want his host to find out. We have no way of knowing whether they met at Wantage, but a letter he sent after she returned to London made it clear that he would definitely see her again.

> You should not have come by Wantage for a thousand pound. You used to brag you were very discreet; where is it gone? It is probable I may not stay in Ireland long, but be back by the beginning of winter. . . . If you write to me, let some other direct it [that is, write the address], and I beg you will write nothing that is particular, but what may be

seen, for I apprehend letters will be opened and inconveniences will happen. If you are in Ireland while I am there, I shall see you very seldom. It is not a place for any freedom, but where everything is known in a week and magnified a hundred degrees. These are rigorous laws that must be passed through; but it is probable we may meet in London in winter. . . . God Almighty bless you. I shall, I hope, be on horseback a day after this comes to your hand. I would not answer your questions for a million, nor can I think of them with any ease of mind. Adieu.

Ehrenpreis sees this letter as reflecting "an amazing need to entice through discouragement," but it's hard to see why it's discouraging.[1] The message is simply that it's much harder to keep a secret in Dublin than in London. As for the questions Swift doesn't want to answer, they remain a mystery, though they keep coming up in later letters. They may have concerned the kind of commitment he would be willing to make, either now or later on.

It's not known exactly when Vanessa and Molly went to Ireland, but it was no later than the beginning of November, when Swift next wrote to her. They moved into a grand country house that had belonged to their father, in the town of Celbridge, ten miles west of Dublin. They also rented a town house in the city, and Vanessa stayed there often, not necessarily with Molly along.

And what were Stella's feelings? Since Vanessa was frequently in Dublin, surely mutual acquaintances would have mentioned her, whether or not they suspected her relationship with Swift. But we don't know what Stella herself knew or suspected. One clue, though, has been largely overlooked, even though it lies in plain sight. This is a poem Swift wrote in October, a month after his return to Dublin. One would suppose that his reunion with Stella, after nearly four years apart, must have been joyous. But the poem, *In Sickness*, suggests no such thing. Instead, Swift is strangely alone:

> 'Tis true—then why should I repine
> To see my life so fast decline?
> But why obscurely here alone,
> Where I am neither loved nor known?
> My state of health none care to learn;
> My life is here no soul's concern. . . .
> But no obliging, tender friend
> To help at my approaching end;
> My life is now a burthen grown
> To others, e'er it be my own.[2]

65. Celbridge. A nineteenth-century view of Marley Abbey, Vanessa's home,
later known as Selbridge Abbey. The Liffey flows in the foreground.

Does this imply that Stella, far from welcoming Swift after years of separation, was cold-shouldering him? Did she know that Vanessa was already in Ireland or about to arrive?

It appears that Vanessa, on the other hand, sought to be especially supportive at this time. She wrote a poem called *A Rebus*, with riddling clues that spell out Swift's name, followed by a generous compliment on his gifts and virtues. When the poem was later printed, it was attributed to "a Lady" without naming her, but people close to Swift knew that it was by Vanessa. The date is uncertain, too, but Swift's verse reply is suggestive of this period of anxiety and gloom. *A Rebus* is especially valuable because it's the only documented glimpse of Vanessa's relationship with Swift that's separate from the often fraught letters they exchanged.

A Rebus begins with some biblical clues that yield the names "Jo" (if you cut off the second half of "Joseph") and "Nathan," followed by a racehorse that's fast ("Swift") but that comes last in the name instead of first:

> Cut the name of the man who his mistress denied,
> And let the first of it be only applied
> To join with the prophet who David did chide.
> Then say what a horse is that runs very fast,
> And that which deserves to be first put the last;
> Spell all then, and put them together, to find
> The name and the virtues of him I designed.[3]

Is it just a coincidence that both biblical references have sexual implications? "The man who his mistress denied" sounds very much like Swift. Joseph resisted the advances of Potiphar's wife. As for Nathan, he reproved David for sending Bathsheba's husband to his death in battle so that he could marry her himself. David had been smitten with Bathsheba when he saw her bathing naked, he did marry her, and she gave birth to King Solomon, wisest of men. Don't both allusions speak directly to Jonathan Swift, who desires Vanessa but resists her?

However that may be, *A Rebus* continues by trying to cheer Swift up. He has political distinction, yet like a biblical prophet he speaks freely to men in power; and he is always ready to help friends or other deserving people when they need him. One of the deserving friends, of course, is Vanessa.

> Like the patriarch in Egypt, he's versed in the state;
> Like the prophet in Jewry, he's free with the great.
> Like a racer he flies to succor with speed
> When his friends want his aid, or desert is in need.

Swift sent back a reply in verse, in which he wrote glumly that he might have been like that when Vanessa first knew him in London, but that those days were gone forever.

> Her fine panegyrics are quite out of season,
> And what she describes to be merit is treason;
> The changes which faction has made in the state
> Have put the Dean's politics quite out of date.

Now no one regards what he utters with freedom,
And should he write pamphlets, no Great Man would read 'em;
And should want or desert stand in need of his aid,
This racer would prove but a dull foundered jade.[4]

"THOSE KILLING, KILLING WORDS"

As soon as Vanessa was settled in Celbridge, Swift wrote to warn that she must not expect to see him there. "I would not have gone to Kildrohood [a Gaelic spelling of the name] to see you for all the world. I ever told you, you wanted discretion." After that, letters passed frequently between them. Although Ehrenpreis says that "Vanessa saved some though not all of Swift's letters," in fact she did save them all; it was her executors, after her death, who destroyed many of them. It's a sobering thought, as Louise Barnett observes, that if all of the letters had been lost, we would have no idea how significant Vanessa was in Swift's life. What he himself once said about letters was borne out in his own case: "They are a standing witness against a man, which is confirmed by a Latin saying—for words pass, but letters remain."[5]

On Vanessa's side, what we have is drafts of her letters, not the versions that were sent. Because she didn't bother much with punctuation, they have a headlong quality that emphasizes their emotional urgency, though as quoted here they will be punctuated for clarity. Swift's letters are more measured and cautious—but not always.

If it was risky to meet in Celbridge, that was not so true of Dublin. In December, a month after refusing to go to Celbridge, Swift not only mentioned a recent encounter—presumably in Dublin—but promised another. "I will see you tomorrow if possible. You know it is not above five days since I saw you, and that I would ten times more if it were at all convenient." Soon after came another note: "I will see you in a day or two, and believe me, it goes to my soul not to see you oftener."[6] "It goes to my soul" is strong language indeed.

For Vanessa these encounters couldn't come often enough. At about this time (she numbered her letters but didn't always date them) she poured out her feelings of neglect, amounting really to betrayal. Her heartfelt plea needs to be heard in full:

> Once I had a friend that would see me sometimes, and either com-
> mend what I did or advise me what to do, which banished all my
> uneasiness. But now, when my misfortunes are increased by being in

a disagreeable place amongst strange prying deceitful people, whose company is so far from amusement that it is a very great punishment, you fly me, and give no reason but that we are amongst fools and must submit. I am very well satisfied that we are amongst such, but know no reason for having my happiness sacrificed to their caprice. You once had a maxim, which was to act what was right and not mind what the world said. I wish you would keep to it now. Pray what can be wrong in seeing and advising an unhappy young woman, I can't imagine. You can't but know that your frowns make my life insupportable. You have taught me to distinguish and then you leave me miserable. Now all I beg is that you will for once counterfeit (since you can't otherwise) that indulgent friend you once were.[7]

Swift had quoted the maxim about doing what was right in *Cadenus and Vanessa*, and clearly he didn't appreciate having it thrown back at him yet again. In reply, he reiterated his warning about the danger of gossip:

I received your letter when some company was with me on Saturday night, and it put me in such confusion that I could not tell what to do. I here send you the paper you left me. This morning a woman who does business for me told me she heard I was in —— with one ——, naming you, and twenty particulars, that little master and I visited you, and that the A-B did so; and that you had abundance of wit, etc. I ever feared the tattle of this nasty town, and I told you so, and that was the reason why I said to you long ago that I would see you seldom when you were in Ireland. And I must beg you to be easy if for some time I visit you seldomer, and not in so particular a manner.[8]

The "paper" may have been one of the financial documents Swift was helping with. The "A-B" was Archbishop King, who had known Vanessa's parents and was taking an interest in her welfare. The "woman who does business" was Swift's housekeeper, Mrs. Brent. Scott suggested that the blank should be filled in with "she heard I was in [love]," though of course it might just be a place-name. But who on earth was "little master"? Clearly it was a boy well known to Mrs. Brent, but why would he have accompanied Swift when he went to see Vanessa? Is it conceivable that this was the boy whom the aged bell ringer believed to be a child of Stella's?

Swift's warnings failed to persuade Vanessa to be "easy," and her next letter reflects a bitter encounter that must have taken place. "'Tis impossible to describe what I have suffered since I saw you last. I am sure I could have bore the rack much better than those killing, killing words of yours. Sometimes I have resolved to die without seeing you more, but those resolves, to your misfortune, did not last long. . . . The reason I write to you is because I cannot tell it you, should I see you, for when I begin to complain then you are angry, and there is something in your look so awful that it strikes me dumb."[9]

Awful in those days meant "that which strikes with awe, or fills with reverence," as Johnson defines it. Swift's flaring anger—not the sign of a passionless man—was well known to his friends. "Dr. Swift had a natural severity of face," Orrery recalled, "which even his smiles could scarce soften, or his utmost gaiety render placid and serene; but when that sternness of visage was increased by rage, it is scarce possible to imagine looks or features that carried in them more terror and austerity."[10]

Ehrenpreis, incidentally, quotes the phrase about "killing, killing words" and then puts Vanessa in her place: "Having concentrated her desires on the middle-aged priest, Vanessa could not bear the threat of his disengagement. Drawing on a well-stocked arsenal of emotional blackmail, she enjoyed the thrill of humiliating herself before the father-lover who remained deliciously out of reach." The index to Ehrenpreis's book cites this passage under two different headings, "emotional extortion" and "masochism." Nokes, quoting the same phrase, says contemptuously, "Her letters become morbid, whining, and accusatory."[11]

It is amazing how insensitive most biographers have been to Vanessa's predicament and pain, beginning with Orrery, who never knew her but saw in her story "a miserable example of an ill-spent life, fantastic wit, visionary schemes, and female weakness." Deane Swift's retort was more generous and also more accurate: she was "worthy of an happier fate, a martyr to love and constancy."[12]

At this point there is a gap of over four years in the letters, almost certainly destroyed by the executors. As a result, we know nothing about emotional ups and downs, or about how and where Swift and Vanessa met. It appears that his taboo against Celbridge was relaxed, for a gardener who had worked there as a boy remembered Vanessa's attractive bosom and her habit of planting a laurel or two whenever she expected a visit from Swift. They would sit together in an arbor overlooking the Liffey, with books and writing materials on a table in front of them.[13]

One brief note survives from the middle of the four-year gap. Swift must have sent it to Vanessa's Dublin house, warning her not to let one of his colleagues suspect a prearranged assignation—"He will think it was on purpose to meet me; and I hate anything that looks like a secret." It *was* a secret, of course, that Vanessa and Swift were arranging to meet, which is why it mustn't look like one.[14]

When the letters resume in 1719, there is a startling change in tone. Vanessa has evidently written to Swift in French, and he responds in the same language, though protesting that he's not really good at it. The protest turns into what, for him, is an extravagant series of compliments. Here is what he says, translated:

> As for me, I'm a fool to reply in the same language to you, who are incapable of any folly, unless it's the esteem that it pleases you to feel for me; for it is no merit or proof of my good taste to find in you everything that Nature has given to a mortal: I mean honor, virtue, good sense, wit, sweetness, agreeableness, and firmness of soul. But concealing yourself as you do, the world doesn't know you, and you lose the praise of millions of people. Since I've had the honor of knowing you, I have always observed that never, in private or in public conversation, has a single word come from your lips that could have been better expressed. And I swear to you that in often making the severest critique, I could never find any fault in your actions or your words. Coquetry, affectation, and prudishness are imperfections that you have never known. And with all of that, do you believe it's possible not to esteem you above the rest of humankind? What beasts in skirts [*bêtes en jupes*] are the most excellent of those whom I see dispersed through the world, in comparison with you.[15]

So was there a sexual relationship? A comment by the younger Sheridan is persuasive: "When it is known that he carried on a secret intercourse with the lady during the space of eight or nine years; that he passed many hours alone with a young and charming woman, who loved him to adoration, and for whom he himself was first inspired with the passion of love; it will be hardly credible that thus circumstanced they should not, in some unguarded moment, have given way to the frailty of human nature."[16] More probably, not unguarded at all.

At this point the coded references to "coffee," which had begun in London, reappear insistently. "Without health," Swift tells Vanessa, "you will lose all desire of drinking your coffee." And at another time, "I wish I were to walk with you fifty times about your garden, and then—drink your coffee." To this he adds, "The Governor was with me at six o'clock this morning, but did not stay two minutes, and deserves a chiding which you must give when you drink your coffee next."[17] Swift sometimes called Vanessa "Governor Huff," for her imperious manner, and surely he's hinting that he woke up in the midst of an erotic dream.

It may be relevant that coffee had a well-known association with sex at the time. A Swiss visitor reported that some London coffeehouses were frequented by wits and politicians, but others were "temples of Venus; you can easily recognize the latter, because they frequently have as sign a woman's arm or hand holding a coffee pot." An English writer said the same thing: "Where the sign is painted with a woman's hand in't, 'tis a bawdy house."[18]

One remarkable letter by Swift combines warm protestations in French with an even more suggestive allusion to coffee: "Soyez assurée que jamais personne du monde a été aimée honorée estimée adorée par votre ami que vous" (Be assured that no one on earth has ever been loved, honored, esteemed, adored by your friend but yourself). He then reverts to English: "I drank no coffee since I left you, nor intend till I see you again, there is none worth drinking but yours, if *my self* may be the judge—adieu."[19] The emphasis is Swift's.

Sheridan's suggestion is plausible: "This declaration seems to have been drawn from him by some desperate state of mind in which he had left her, probably occasioned by her jealousy of Stella." Woolley takes too many liberties when, in his edition of Swift's letters, he inserts an unnecessary word, "a été [plus] aimée." That would mean "No one on earth has ever been loved more than yourself," which it's hard to imagine Swift saying. Besides, it would obliterate the implication that he loves Vanessa in a different way from Stella—in short, romantically and erotically. The passage in French immediately follows this piece of advice: "Settle your affairs, and quit this scoundrel island, and things will be as you desire." Is Swift hinting that he has renewed hopes of an appointment in England, and that Vanessa might join him there?[20]

There are also repeated references to Vanessa's insistent "questions." On one occasion Swift says, "The questions which you were used to ask me, you may suppose to be all answered, just as they used to be after half an hour debate. . . . So drink your coffee, and remember you are a desperate chip; and that the lady who calls you bastard will be ready to answer all your questions." The "lady" is probably the Venus of *Cadenus and Vanessa*, who tells Athena that Vanessa is a daughter of Apollo; "chip" may be a teasing reference to diminutive size. At any rate, Vanessa replied tartly, "I have asked you all the questions I used ten thousand times, and don't find them answered at all to my satisfaction."[21]

Sometimes the coffee and the questions show up as a pair in Swift's letters.

It would have been infinitely better once a week to have met Kendall, and so forth, where one might pass three or four hours in drinking coffee in the morning, or dining tête à tête, and drinking coffee again until seven. I answer all the questions you can ask me in the affirmative. . . . Remember that riches are nine parts in ten of all that is good in life, and health is the tenth. Drinking coffee comes long after, and yet it is the eleventh, but without the two former you cannot drink it right. . . . I hope you will let me have some of your money when I see you, which I will pay you honestly again; répondez-moi si vous entendez bien tout cela, et croyez que je serai toujours tout ce que vous désirez [tell me whether you understand all of this well, and believe that I will always be all that which you desire].[22]

Kendall was a bookbinder in the neighborhood of Vanessa's Dublin house, and apparently he provided a hideaway where they could meet. Are riches really nine-tenths of what matters in life? Can money actually be meant in the talk about Swift repaying what he receives? And will he really be all that she desires? At any rate the allusions are deliberately veiled, as the comment in French confirms.

Finally, Swift offers a philosophical remark about trying to be satisfied with what one can get. "The best maxim I know in this life is to drink your coffee when you can, and when you cannot, to be easy without it. While you continue to be spleenatic, count upon it I will always preach. Thus much I sympathize with you, that I am not cheerful enough to write, for I believe coffee once a week is necessary to do that."[23]

In one letter, after reproving Vanessa for her eruptions of temper—"I am confident you came chiding into the world, and will continue so while you are in it"—Swift suggests using dashes to signify endearments that shouldn't be written down. "A stroke thus —— —— —— —— signifies everything that may be said to Cad—at beginning or conclusion. It is I who ought to be in a huff, that anything written by Cad—should be difficult to Skinage." "Cad" is "Cadenus," of course, and "Skinage" is a teasing allusion to Vanessa's skinny frame (he sometimes combined it with her first name as "Heskinage").[24]

Overjoyed, Vanessa replied, "——— ——— ——— ——— Cad—you are good beyond expression and I will never quarrel again if I can help it. . . . I am now as happy as I can be without seeing ——— ——— ——— Cad I beg you'll continue my happiness to your own Skinage."[25]

A further, and indeed surprising, sign of intimacy is that Swift shared the "little language" with Vanessa, and she used it when demanding that he treat her better. If all human arts should fail, she said, "I am resolved to have re-course to the black one . . . but there is one thing falls out very ruckily for you, which is that of all the passions, revenge hurries me least, so that you have it yet in your power to turn all this fury into good humor." Swift accepted this as playful "raillery" and replied, "You need make use of no other black art besides your ink. 'Tis a pity your eyes are not black, or I would have said the same of them; but you are a white witch, and can do no mischief."[26] Accord-ing to the *OED*, a white witch "uses witchcraft for beneficent purposes; one who practices 'white magic.'"

By now there was a long history of shared experiences, and Swift pours out an irresistible catalogue of them.

> What would you give to have the history of Cad—and—exactly writ-ten through all its steps from the beginning to this time? I believe it would do well in verse, and be as long as the other [*Cadenus and Va-nessa* is nearly nine hundred lines long]. I hope it will be done. It ought to be an exact chronicle of 12 years, from the time of spilling the coffee to drinking of coffee, from Dunstable to Dublin with every single passage since. There would be the chapter of the blister, the chapter of Madam going to Kensington, the chapter of the colonel's going to France, the chapter of the wedding with the adventure of the lost key. Of the strain, of the joyful return, two hundred chapters of madness. The chapter of long walks. The Berkshire surprise. Fifty chapters of little times; the chapter of Chelsea. The chapter of swallow, and clus-ter; a hundred books of my self and so low. The chapter of hide, and whisper. The chapter of who made it so.[27]

The blister must be the agonizing attack of shingles that Swift endured in London; the strain was caused by moving a heavy box of books, mentioned elsewhere. The wedding was probably that of a close friend of Vanessa's, though the story of the key is lost. What was the much-reiterated "mad-ness"? Was it amorous? We do know what the Berkshire surprise was: Vanessa's unannounced and potentially gossip-causing appearance at Wantage in 1712, which by now is an event to cherish in memory. As for the "hide, and whisper," and "who made it so," we have no way of knowing anything about that.[28] But it would be impossible to read all of this without feeling intense intimacy. How could this not have been love?

But the recriminations always return. A few months later Vanessa complains that she has heard almost nothing from Swift for "ten long weeks." Discreetly but unmistakably, she insists that her feelings are sexual as well as spiritual: "Nor is the love I bear you only seated in my soul, for there is not a single atom of my frame that is not blended with it." In another letter from this autumn or winter (they are undated) she tries even more eloquently to express her loneliness. Reproduced as she wrote it, without punctuation, her anguish is embodied in an unstoppable outpouring of words, with dashes in place of endearments as they had agreed:

> Tell me sincerely if you have once wished with earnestness to see me since I wrote to you No so far from that you have not once pitied me though I told you how I was distressed solitude is insupportable to a mind which is not easy I have worn out my days in sighing and my nights with watching and thinking of ——, ——, ——, —— who thinks not of me how many letters must I send you before I shall receive an answer can you deny me in my misery the only comfort which I can expect at present oh that I could hope to see you here or that I could go to you I was born with violent passions which terminate all in one that unexpressible passion I have for you consider the killing emotions which I feel from your neglect of me and show some tenderness for me or I shall lose my senses.[29]

It is hard to understand how Ehrenpreis and Nokes could interpret this kind of appeal as mere neurotic harassment. Nor is the claim plausible that Swift, in simple kindness, was remaining attentive in order to let Vanessa down gently. Ehrenpreis says, "I pass over the many piquant or touching sentences from Swift's letters to Vanessa because they would misrepresent the general effect of a man straining to transform a romantic obsession into a placid, playful intimacy."[30]

For anyone interested in this relationship, there is a special thrill in holding the actual sheets of paper with which they communicated. There is also a sense of illicit prying. How appalled Swift would have been to know that

Tell me sincerely if you have once a
wished with earnestness to see me since I wrote
to you No so far from that you have not
once pity'd me ~~though~~ though I told you how
I was distressed solitude is insupportable to
a mind which is not easie I have worn out
my days in sighing and my nights with
watching and thinking of —, —, —,
— — — who thinks not of me
how many letters must I send you before
I shall receive an answer con you
deny me in my misery the only comfort
which I can expect at present oh that I
could hope to see you here or that I could yet I was born
with violent passions which terminate
all in one that unexpressible passion I have
                                    killing
for you consider the violent emotions
which I feel from your neglect of me
and shew some tenderness for me
or I shall lose my senses sure you
con not possibly be so much taken
up but you might command a moment
to write to me and force your inclynations
to do so great a charrity

66. Vanessa to Swift.

these deeply private documents would be open to the world, in the reading room of the British Library! Vanessa, on the other hand, would probably have been delighted.

Here is the very last letter of Vanessa's that we have: "All other disappointments in life I can bear with ease, but that of being neglected by ——, ——, ——, Cad. He has often told me that the best maxim in life, and always held by the wisest in all ages, is to seize the moments as they fly. But those happy moments always fly out of the reach of the unfortunate."[31] One of Blake's lyrics reads, in its entirety:

> He who binds to himself a joy
> Does the wingèd life destroy,
> But he who kisses the joy as it flies
> Lives in eternity's sunrise.

Vanessa could never stop trying to bind the joy, even while her heart was breaking and her health was giving out.

THE END

The reason Vanessa was thin was that susceptibility to tuberculosis ran in her family. Ginkel, the youngest sibling, had died in 1710, and in 1721 it was Molly's turn. Swift was fond of Molly, and dashed off a note to Vanessa on a small scrap of paper: "I am surprised and grieved beyond what I can express. I read your letter twice before I knew what it meant, nor can I yet well believe my eyes. Is that poor good creature dead. . . . I was wholly unprepared against so sudden an event, and pity you most of all creatures at present."[32]

Two years later Vanessa herself was about to die of the same disease, and if the younger Sheridan is right, there was a bitter confrontation with Swift at that time. Sheridan had heard, presumably from his father, that Vanessa was tortured by suspicions that Swift had married Stella, and decided to put an end to the suspense by writing directly to Stella to ask if it was true. According to Sheridan, Stella replied that it was indeed true, and sent Vanessa's letter on to Swift, "after which [Stella] immediately went out of town without seeing him or coming to any explanation, and retired in great resentment to Mr. Ford's country seat at Wood Park." Infuriated, Swift rode straight to Celbridge. "He entered the apartment where the unhappy lady was, mute, but with a countenance that spoke the highest resentment. She trembling asked him, would he not sit down? No—he then flung a paper on the table, and immediately returned to his horse. When, on the abatement of her consternation, she had strength to open the paper, she found it contained nothing but her own note to Mrs. Johnson. Despair at once seized her, as if it she had seen her death warrant; and such indeed it proved to be."[33] On June 2, 1723, Vanessa was dead.

Sheridan was reporting all of this fully sixty years after the event, and without saying exactly when it supposedly occurred. As for Stella's side of the story, that could well have been passed on by Charles Ford. But if the confrontation at Celbridge did happen, presumably no one was present except Vanessa and Swift, and if either of them ever described it, we don't know how or to whom.

Swift left immediately—maybe even the very next day—on a four-month journey into the west of Ireland, while Stella did indeed make a stay of several months with Ford. Strikingly, Ford was the only member of their circle who was close to Vanessa as well as Stella, since he had been a frequent visitor to the Vanhomrighs in London. What he thought about the whole affair, nobody knows. As for Swift's departure, it's usual to say that he just wanted to escape gossip, but a stronger motive must have been reluctance to face Stella. And if Molly's death had grieved him more than he could express, what did he feel at Vanessa's?

As executors of her will, Vanessa chose George Berkeley, the philosopher and future bishop, and a young lawyer named Robert Marshall. Each of them got a generous bequest of £500, and Vanessa clearly expected them to publish her entire correspondence with Swift. As soon as his friends became aware of this possibility, however, they mobilized energetically to block it. The younger Sheridan heard that his father "applied so effectively to the executors that the printed copy was canceled, but the originals still remained in their hands."[34] As we have seen, many of the originals were almost certainly destroyed by them.

Rumors were nevertheless current. Six weeks after Vanessa's death, when Swift was far away, Bishop Evans of Meath, his superior at Laracor, wrote to the archbishop of Canterbury:

> I think it not improper for me to acquaint your Grace with a passage lately happened here wherein Jonathan Swift is concerned. A young woman, Mrs. Van Omrig (a pretended vain wit) and the Dean had great friendship, many letters and papers passed betwixt them (the subject I know nothing of); they give out there was a marriage prom-

ise between them, but this I can't affirm. . . . In April last, she discovered the Dean was married to Mrs. Johnson (a natural daughter of Sir W. Temple, a very good woman) upon which she expressed great indignation, making a new will and leaving all to Dr. Berkeley . . . and to one Mr. Marshall, who was charged by her (on her deathbed) to print all the letters and papers which had passed between the Dean and herself. . . . The Archbishop of Dublin and the whole Irish posse have (I fear) prevailed with Mr. Marshall (the lady's executor) not to print the papers, etc., as she desired, lest one of their own dear joys [an Irish term for "darlings"] should be trampled on by the Philistines.

The bishop also commented that Vanessa apparently died without religious belief, and that when the local minister offered to attend her at the end, she not only declined, but quoted "a scrap out of the *Tale of a Tub*."[35]

Evans hated Swift, who sent a rude reply when the bishop demanded that he be present at the annual "visitation" of his parish: "Your Lordship will please to remember in the midst of your resentments that you are to speak to a clergyman, and not to a footman." A couple of years later Swift was still firing off insults: "I am only sorry that you, who are of a country [Wales] famed for good nature, have found a way to unite the hasty passion of your own countrymen with the long, sedate resentment of a Spaniard." Soon after that, a slanderous fake obituary of Evans appeared in a London paper. It may well have been by Swift, and Evans was certain that it was.[36]

But however much Evans may have enjoyed Swift's predicament, his proper concern was to alert the head of the Church to an incipient scandal. In the process, interestingly, he confirmed Stella's blameless reputation in Ireland. It's remarkable how much Evans knew. Presumably the executors had been talking to him.

At this point Berkeley probably had no appetite for a confrontation with his Dublin colleagues, and as for young Marshall, he was in no position to jeopardize his career by alienating powerful enemies. The Swift-Vanessa letters remained unpublished for nearly half a century. In 1767, a selection was included in a multivolume edition of Swift's works, but they were not published in full until 1921. Meanwhile, many of them had vanished, as we know because Vanessa scrupulously numbered the whole sequence, which now has many gaps. Under pressure from Swift's friends, the executors clearly removed the letters they thought most damaging to him, though they left enough to confirm that Vanessa was an honorable and sincere person and that she spent an entire decade trapped in an agonizing situation. Berkeley did tell Delany that the letters contained "nothing which would either do honour to her character or bring the least reflection upon Cadenus," but he might well say that to divert suspicion. At that time he had no reason to believe that the letters would ever see the light of day.[37]

So despite Vanessa's wishes, the letters were not made public—but *Cadenus and Vanessa* was, in 1726. Marshall probably allowed people to read the manuscript, some of them made copies, and those were given to several printers. Soon after the poem appeared in Dublin there were London editions too, with variations that suggest that more than one transcript was being used. Naturally, the poem created a sensation, and fifteen separate editions came out within a year. Swift unquestionably didn't want the poem to be published, did his best to ignore it, and published it himself much later only when it was irretrievably in the public domain.[38]

By this time Stella seems to have been reconciled with Swift, and Delany heard her make a crisp retort when a tactless visitor said that Vanessa must have been "an extraordinary woman, that could inspire the Dean to write so finely upon her." Stella smiled and replied that she thought that wasn't quite clear, "for it was well known the Dean could write finely upon a broomstick."[39]

Even if we had all the missing letters between Vanessa and Swift, they would give only a limited perspective on a relationship that was conducted not just on paper but in person. And even so far as documents go, what others may have been lost or destroyed? Among the papers in Vanessa's desk was a poem entitled *To Love* that begins like this:

> In all I wish, how happy should I be,
> Thou grand deluder, were it not for thee.
> So weak thou art, that fools thy pow'r despise,
> And yet so strong, thou triumph'st o'er the wise.
> Thy traps are laid with such peculiar art
> They catch the cautious, let the rash depart.
> Most nets are filled by want of thought and care,
> But too much thinking brings us to thy snare;
> Where held by thee, in slavery we stay,
> And throw the pleasing part of life away.

The poem goes on to blame "discretion"—which Swift was constantly urging—as doing more damage than impulsiveness ever could.

But the poor nymph who feels her vitals burn,
And from her shepherd can find no return,
Laments and rages at the pow'rs divine,
When, curs'd Discretion, all the fault was thine.

Whether Vanessa or someone else wrote these lines, she certainly preserved them. And amazingly—unmentioned by all of Swift's biographers—the copy in her desk *was in Swift's handwriting.*[40] The poetic style is not his, but it could be Vanessa's, or this may have been a poem by someone else that struck her as expressing her own feelings. We will never know what she and Swift said to each other about it, but it does provide another glimpse into a woundingly troubled relationship.

CHAPTER 23

National Hero

SOUTH SEA BUBBLE

Swift and Vanessa both arrived in Dublin in 1714, and at that time he wrote to Charles Ford, "I hope I shall keep my resolution of never meddling with Irish politics." For six years he did keep clear of politics, motivated mainly by the surveillance he was under from the authorities. In 1719 he wrote bleakly to Bolingbroke,

> If you will recollect that I am towards six years older than when I saw you last, and twenty years duller, you will not wonder to find me abound in empty speculations; I can now express in a hundred words what would formerly have cost me ten. . . . I have gone the round of all my stories three or four times with the younger people, and begin them again. I give hints how significant a person I have been, and nobody believes me; I pretend to pity them, but am inwardly angry. . . . Nothing has convinced me so much that I am of a little subaltern spirit, *inopis atque pusilli animi* [of weak and insignificant spirit], as to reflect how I am forced into the most trifling amusements, to divert the vexation of former thoughts and present objects."[1]

The event that finally stimulated Swift to resume publication was a financial catastrophe in 1720, known as the South Sea Bubble. Nine years previously the Oxford-Bolingbroke ministry, with excellent intentions, had established the South Sea Company to attract investment in Latin American trade. The goal was to try to reduce the huge national debt caused by the war, by persuading investors who had purchased safe government annuities to exchange them for stock in the company.

In the beginning this seemed like a safe and potentially lucrative option, backed as it was by the sponsorship of the government. Swift promoted it wholeheartedly in the *Examiner*, praising Oxford as a "great person whose thoughts are perpetually employed, and ever with success, on the good of his country." He invested in South Sea stock himself, in partnership with Stella and Rebecca, putting in £400 of his own and borrowing another £100 to invest.[2]

For a number of years the value of South Sea shares appreciated respectably, though not at the spectacular rate that had been promised. In 1720, however, the company's directors made a fatal gamble. They bought outright half of the national debt, intending to remain profitable by encouraging increased speculation in their stock. For a few months the scheme worked. Between January and August the price of a share rocketed from £100 to nearly £1,000, and canny investors who got out at that point realized enormous gains. The chancellor of the exchequer doubled his investment in two months, and the Duchess of Marlborough sold out after making £100,000, with what her descendant Winston Churchill calls "her almost repellent common sense."[3]

The frenzy couldn't last, and in September the crash came. Within weeks the stock's value was back down to £100, and families all over Britain were ruined (Swift and Pope had both fortunately gotten out in time). There was a storm of outrage, and Edward Harley, the government auditor and brother of the Earl of Oxford, said that investors had been victimized by "a machine of paper credit supported by imagination." In Parliament it was suggested that the directors should be treated the way parricides were in ancient Rome— tied up in sacks and thrown into the Thames. To limit the damage, Walpole came up with a government bailout. The Bank of England bought part of the now-shattered South Sea Company, paying its investors interest that had to be funded by current taxation.[4]

This disaster, one of the first to reveal that paper wealth could simply vanish, inspired Swift to mordant verse. According to the book of Proverbs, reputedly written by King Solomon, "riches certainly make themselves wings; they fly away as an eagle to heaven," and Swift gleefully extended the metaphor:

> Riches, the wisest monarch sings,
> Make pinions for themselves to fly;
> They fly like bats on parchment wings,
> And geese their silver plumes supply.

Swift always enjoyed giving abstractions literal embodiment; the plumes were the quill pens used for contracts recorded on parchment. Similarly, he turned wax seals on documents into witches' effigies:

> Conceive the works of midnight hags,
> Tormenting fools behind their backs:
> Thus bankers o'er their bills and bags
> Sit squeezing images of wax.[5]

A couple of months later Swift followed up with a long poem called *The Bubble*, in which he derided the gullible investors as well as the cynical financiers who exploited them.

> As fishes on each other prey
> The great ones swallowing up the small,
> So fares it in the Southern Sea,
> But whale directors eat up all.[6]

Years later Swift would still be suggesting that the stockbrokers who promoted the South Sea Company were no better than thieves:

> A public, or a private robber;
> A statesman, or a South Sea jobber.

Even apologists for the stock market despised middlemen for preying on investors. Defoe was a warm admirer of the market, but he said that if stockjobbers ever told the truth, they would have to admit that "'tis a complete system of knavery; that 'tis a trade founded in fraud, born of deceit, and nourished by trick, cheat, wheedle, forgeries, falsehoods, and all sorts of delusions." He said that a year *before* the bubble. By 1755 Johnson was defining "stock-jobber" in his *Dictionary* as "a low wretch who gets money buying and selling shares in the funds."[7]

The Tory opposition saw the bubble not just as a passing episode, but as the inevitable consequence of financial speculation. Britain was becoming a world power, however, on the strength of its financial revolution—the wealth that provided "the sinews of power," in a historian's phrase—and there was no turning back. Some years later, Pope wrote bitterly,

> Alike in nothing but one lust of gold,
> Just half the land would buy, and half be sold. . . .
> While with the silent growth of ten per cent
> In dirt and darkness hundreds stink content.[8]

Neither Pope nor Swift thought that investment was immoral, but they did believe, with good reason, that a promised return of 10 percent was too good to be true.

"BURN EVERYTHING ENGLISH BUT THEIR COAL"

Swift took a keen interest in economics, and he was convinced that Ireland's position was almost uniquely vulnerable. According to the standard economic theory, known as mercantilism, nations got rich by importing cheap raw materials and selling expensive manufactured goods. The function of a colony, whether Jamaica or Massachusetts, was therefore to provide raw materials but not to compete in manufacturing. In fact if not in name, Ireland was just such a colony.

The British Parliament passed a protectionist Woolen Act in 1699, requiring Ireland to sell its wool exclusively to England, and forbidding the export of cloth to England or anywhere else. The resulting British monopoly of Irish wool brought down its price. Irish landowners, needing to rebuild their fallen income, then began to replace food crops with grass on which sheep could graze. "The politic gentlemen of Ireland," Swift lamented, "have depopulated vast tracts of the best land for the feeding of sheep." The domino effect continued to raise the cost of food in Ireland, leading to a "prodigious dearness of corn" (as all kinds of grain were called). Meanwhile, the Irish gentry spent freely on English manufactured goods, which caused a further wealth transfer from Ireland to England.[9]

In 1712 Archbishop King talked to a landlord who had trouble collecting rent from his hundred tenants, got rid of them all, and made more money from a single man who used the land for grazing. King told a colleague, Bishop William Nicolson, "I asked [the landlord] what came of the hundred families he turned off it. He answered that he did not know." That was damaging enough, but worse was to follow, for the entire decade of the 1720s brought a continuous economic depression. During 1720–21, seven thousand people were thrown out of work in Dublin, and in the countryside laborers were beginning to starve. Bishop Nicolson gave a striking example of rural desperation. While he was traveling in Ulster—a relatively prosperous region—one of his coach horses died in an accident. "My servants were surrounded with fifty or sixty of the neighbouring cottagers, who brought axes and cleavers and immediately divided the carcass, every man carrying home his proper dividend for food to their respective families."[10]

It was in this context that Swift broke his long silence as a writer, in a 1720 pamphlet entitled *A Proposal for the Universal Use of Irish Manufacture, in Clothes and Furniture of Houses, etc., Utterly Renouncing Everything Wearable That Comes from England.* The pamphlet was anonymous. The title page identifies it as "printed and sold by E. Waters, in Essex Street, at the corner of Sycamore Alley." Edward Waters, not one of Dublin's more distinguished printers, had to know he was sticking his neck out by taking responsibility for this piece, and events would show how true that was.

Swift's message was that since England was never going to treat the Irish fairly, their best hope of resisting exploitation was to boycott English goods. Even though they were prohibited from selling their cloth abroad, no one could stop them from wearing it at home. "Let a firm resolution be taken, by male and female, never to appear with one single shred that comes from England; *and let all the people say,* AMEN." The italicized phrase is the conclusion of Psalm 106, which says a few verses earlier, "Their enemies also oppressed them, and they were brought into subjection under their hand."[11]

This was a voice the Irish public had not heard before, straightforward and persuasive, but with an undercurrent of controlled anger—and sometimes more than an undercurrent. "I heard the late Archbishop of Tuam mention a pleasant observation of somebody's, 'that Ireland would never be happy till a law were made for burning everything that came from England, except their people and their coals.'" In a sentence that was softened in later editions, Swift added, "Nor am I *even yet* for lessening the number of those exceptions." The clear implication was that it might be a good idea to burn the English themselves. The anger was directed not against England only, but also against the Irish themselves for importing luxuries and contributing to their own exploitation. "I would now expostulate a little with our country landlords, who by unmeasurable *screwing* and *racking* their tenants all over the kingdom, have already reduced the miserable people to a worse condition than the peasants in France, or the vassals in Germany and Poland; so that the whole species of what we call substantial farmers will in a very few years be utterly at an end."[12]

The reference to "vassals in Germany" was a loaded one, since George I was a German and had vassals back in Hanover. And the publication of Swift's *Proposal* was timed to coincide with celebrations for the king's sixtieth birthday, when the privileged class would dress up in the imported finery that Swift was deploring. "I hope and believe," Swift said with deadpan irony, "[that] nothing could please his Majesty better than to hear that his loyal subjects, of both sexes, in this kingdom celebrated his birthday (now approaching) universally clad in their own manufacture."[13]

This was a subject that Swift would be speaking out about for years to come—the crushing rents charged by landlords, many of whom lived in England and allowed greedy middlemen to skim off their own share. But the ultimate implications were far broader. He was helping to create a new national self-awareness, from which the Republic of Ireland would eventually emerge. "The pamphlet is written," Orrery said thirty years later, "in the style of a man who had the good of his country nearest his heart; who saw her errors, and wished to correct them; who felt her oppressions, and wished to relieve her; and who had a desire to rouse and awaken an indolent nation from a lethargic disposition that might prove fatal to her constitution." In 1947, Ehrenpreis mentioned to an attendant in the National Library in Dublin that he was working on a biography of Jonathan Swift. "Oh, yes," was the reply, "burn everything English but their coal."[14]

The *Proposal for the Universal Use of Irish Manufacture* was about economics, but it was about politics too. A recent legal case had provoked stern reaction from England. By the terms of Poyning's Law, which went all the way back to 1495, the sole function of the Irish Parliament was to accept or reject bills that had already been approved by the English Privy Council. Now, in 1720, the Irish House of Lords had tried to reverse the judges' decision in a lawsuit and were overruled by the British Parliament, which proceeded to pass a Declaratory Act stating that the kingdom of Ireland was "subordinate and dependent upon the imperial crown of Great Britain."[15] In addition to reaffirming the right of the English Parliament to legislate for Ireland, this new act made it the court of final appeal in law as well. At this stage of history, Irish independence was never considered by either side. What Swift and other Irishmen wanted was that their own parliament be recognized as equal in authority to the one in London. That was what the Declaratory Act denied.

Irish resistance was based not on an appeal to fairness, which would have been ignored by England, but by a constitutional claim: ever since the Middle

Ages Ireland had been a distinct kingdom within Great Britain, not a dependent colony like the ones in North America and the Caribbean. This argument was energetically stated by William Molyneux in 1698, in *The Case of Ireland's Being Bound by Acts of Parliament in England Stated.* "Do not the kings of England," Molyneux asked, "bear the style of Ireland amongst the rest of their kingdoms? Is this agreeable to the nature of a colony? Do they use the title of kings of Virginia, New England or Maryland?"[16]

Was Ireland in fact a colony? The question is still debated, because it depends upon how one defines one's terms. So far as the constitutional argument went, Molyneux's case was pretty flimsy, which he no doubt knew. The historical claim was really just a rhetorical fiction, one argument among many that Molyneux deployed lawyer fashion in the hope that something might stick. In the past it might have made sense to see Ireland as an independent nation, though loyal to the British Crown. But with the emergence of modern politics, it was really the party in power that had to be obeyed, not the king in whose name it acted. The historian S. J. Connolly says that the argument Swift invoked was "a political blind alley, depending on a rigid distinction between crown and parliament that was already unrealistic in the 1720s." He adds, "Few Irish Protestants shared Swift's taste for pushing an argument to its confrontational limit."[17]

Still, the larger issue was that whatever the legal justification might be, England did indeed exploit Ireland. And whereas colonists in America were to a large extent self-governing, separated by months of sailing from the mother country, Ireland lay nearby and was easily micromanaged from London. In Connolly's summary, it was "too physically close and too similar to Great Britain to be treated as a colony, but too separate and too different to be a region of the metropolitan culture."[18] Much more was thus at stake than correct interpretation of constitutional issues. Ireland was awakening to a sense of its existence as a nation, and Swift's brilliant rhetoric was a major catalyst in bringing that about.

The implications of Swift's *Proposal* were not lost on the authorities, and a grand jury denounced the pamphlet as "false, scandalous, and seditious." It was widely suspected that he had written it, but no one would formally denounce him, and the printer Waters was arrested instead. Swift described with relish what happened next: "After his trial the jury brought him in not guilty, although they had been culled [that is, chosen for their docility] with the utmost industry. The Chief Justice sent them back nine times, and kept them eleven hours, until being perfectly tired out they were forced to leave the matter to the mercy of the judge, by what they call a special verdict. During the trial the Chief Justice, among other singularities, laid his hand on his breast and protested solemnly that the author's design was to bring in the Pretender; although there was not a single syllable of party in the whole treatise."[19]

The government soon realized that it was creating a martyr in Waters, and backed off. He was released from prison, and when a new lord lieutenant arrived he had the case dropped altogether. From this moment forward, the dean of St. Patrick's would be a hero in the land he still claimed to despise.

"HEWERS OF WOOD AND DRAWERS OF WATER"

Swift's four-month journey after Vanessa's death in 1723 took in much of Ireland. He got as far as Cork and Skibbereen in the south and southwest, and Ennis and Clonfert in the west. When he said that he traveled "without one companion," he must have meant "without one friend," for as usual he didn't travel alone. There were two servants with him, as we know from an alarming incident that he described to Delany. At Carberry Rocks on the south coast, he stretched out at full length to peer over a precipice, and suddenly began to slide forward, "which obliged him to call in great terror to his servants who attended him (for he never traveled, or even rode out, without two attendants) to drag him back by the heels; which they did, with sufficient difficulty and some hazard." The experience inspired an uncharacteristically romantic poem in Latin, *Carberiae Rupes*, on the steep cliffs and roaring waves.[20]

The trip gave Swift a visceral understanding of how dreadful the poverty was in regions far from Dublin. In part the cause was natural; large areas of Ireland are rocky or boggy, ill suited to agriculture. But much of the suffering was due to a combination of incompetent management and cynical exploitation.

Politically, the huge Catholic majority was victimized by the so-called Penal Code, which wasn't really a code, but instead a series of repressive laws that were enacted over the years after the revolution. Catholics were excluded from the university, had no vote, and were not permitted to be lawyers, judges, or military officers. It was even illegal for them to keep a school, act as private tutors, or send their children to be educated abroad. The intention was to force them into Protestant schools, and as Lecky says, "The alternative offered by law to the Catholics was that of absolute and compulsory ignorance or of an education directly subversive of their faith."[21]

As a result of the Penal Code, most land was owned by Protestants, and Catholics could only lease it from them. If a Catholic did still own property, the law required it to be divided equally among his heirs when he died. As a result, the size of individual Catholic holdings continually shrank. The ultimate motive of the laws was to coerce Catholics to convert to the Church of Ireland. If they did so, their estates could pass intact to their eldest sons. There were many such prudential conversions as time went on. Edmund Burke's father was a convert in 1722, while his mother continued to practice Catholicism discreetly. When Burke entered politics he became an eloquent advocate of Catholic emancipation, calling the penal laws a system "as well fitted for the oppression, impoverishment, and degradation of a people, and the debasement in them of human nature itself, as ever proceeded from the perverted ingenuity of man."[22]

The Catholic Church itself was driven underground. Bishops, monks, and friars were banished from Ireland. Parish priests were permitted to stay— there were nearly nine hundred at the start of the eighteenth century—so long as they did not worship openly. Some bishops did return, operating undercover. The laws were not always strictly enforced; their real purpose was intimidation, and they succeeded in that. If anything, however, these repressive measures strengthened allegiance to Catholicism. By providing a common bond for a population deprived of political rights, the Catholic Church filled the role that politics normally would. As a historian says, it became for the people "the one representative organization they had."[23]

Throughout his journey in the south and west, Swift saw the consequences of these policies in neglected farms and miserable hovels. The plain of Tipperary, so verdant and rich today, was "like the rest of the whole kingdom, a bare face of nature, without houses or plantations—filthy cabins, miserable, tattered, half-starved creatures, scarce in human shape. . . . There is not an acre of land in Ireland turned to half its advantage, yet it is better improved than the people, and all these evils are effects of English tyranny."[24]

The same diagnosis appears in *Gulliver's Travels*, where Lord Munodi invites Gulliver to visit his country estate. Along the way, Gulliver observes, "I never knew a soil so unhappily cultivated, houses so ill contrived and so ruinous, or a people whose countenances and habit expressed so much misery and want." Approaching Munodi's estate, however, "the scene was wholly altered. We came into a most beautiful country: farmers' houses at small distances, neatly built; the fields enclosed, containing vineyards, corn-grounds, and meadows. Neither do I remember to have seen a more delightful prospect."[25]

This sounds very much like Swift's perception of his friend Robert Cope's estate at Loughgall, County Armagh, in the north, where he stayed in the summer of 1722. He wrote to Charles Ford from Loughgall, "The people, the churches, and the plantations make me think I am in England. I mean only the scene of a few miles about me, for I have passed through miserable regions to get to it."[26] Cope was a Tory member of Parliament who had been arrested as a suspected Jacobite in 1715.

Even to call the peasant huts "cabins" makes them sound more substantial than they were. The walls were of sod or mud, and there were no windows, so that it was always dark inside. The roof would be thatched with bracken or heath, making the dwelling almost indistinguishable from the bog land around. There would be one single room, and a hole in the roof to serve as a chimney. It wasn't very efficient, and one writer says, "The smoke was often seen to rise up like a cloud from every inch of the roof, percolating through as the thatch grew old and thin."[27]

The native Irish were often described, for example by the lord chancellor in 1706, as "poor, insignificant slaves, fit for nothing but to hew wood and draw water." The allusion is to the Gibeonites, whom Joshua promised not to kill before he discovered that they were secret enemies. Obliged to honor his oath, he did the next best thing: he enslaved them. "Now therefore ye are cursed, and there shall none of you be freed from being bondmen, and hewers of wood and drawers of water for the house of my God." Swift picked up the allusion bitterly in a sermon on "causes of the wretched condition of Ireland": "The first cause of our misery is the intolerable hardships we lie under in every branch of our trade, by which we are become *as hewers of wood and drawers of water* to our rigorous neighbours."[28]

THE TRIUMPH OF THE DRAPIER

Swift's experience as a political pamphleteer in England had given him the rhetorical weapons that he was now ready to use. His six years of enforced silence, watching close friends persecuted or driven into exile, had embittered him against the land he once identified with so strongly. For years his mail had been opened by the authorities, and he knew that the Whig ministry in London sought evidence to prove he was a seditious Jacobite. He was spoiling for a fight, and what he needed was an issue.

Swift's call for a boycott of imports never got any traction among his countrymen, since it demanded an improbable commitment to self-denial for the common good. Similarly, the cruelty of rural poverty didn't interest members of the Anglo-Irish landlord class, because they were helping to create and profit from it. A more promising issue would concern the condition of Dublin artisans and the national economy as a whole. In 1724 an obscure English industrialist unexpectedly provided the subject.

The affair started with William Wood, an "ironmaster" in the English Midlands who produced and worked with metal. Wood paid the king's mistress, the Duchess of Kendal, £10,000 to obtain a royal patent that would allow him personally to furnish Ireland with halfpence. There was nothing unusual about empowering a private citizen in this way, since the government minted only gold and silver. But copper coins, which the new halfpence would be, were not legal tender, and therein lay the crux. The value of coins was based on the metal they were made of, so that if they were melted down they would still be worth just as much. For this reason, coins from countries all over Europe were widely used, regardless of the governments that issued them. But if Wood's halfpence were debased, he would get rich while bad money drove out good. As for paper money, governments didn't issue that at all. Banknotes came from private banks, and people who accepted them had to rely on the good faith of the bank in question. Even the great Bank of England, founded in 1694, was a private company, although the government granted it wide powers. It was not nationalized until 1946.

The crisis evolved with many twists and turns, too complicated to narrate here. Archbishop King and his associates realized that they needed a protest campaign, and they knew that Swift was highly skilled at publicity. Accordingly, Swift began to issue a series of pamphlets under the pseudonym of a cloth merchant who signed himself "M.B., Drapier" (Swift probably pronounced it "Draper"). The initials may have been an allusion to Marcus Brutus, the Roman patriot who brought down the tyrant Caesar, and whom Swift elsewhere praised for "the most consummate virtue, the greatest intrepidity and firmness of mind, the truest love of his country."[29]

Swift's cathedral was in the heart of the weavers' district in Dublin, already hit hard by the Woolen Act, and now experiencing the effects of a deep economic depression. Skilled workers in his neighborhood were begging for bread. "We have got a fund [for poor relief]," Archbishop King wrote, "which I hope will amount to near fifteen hundred, but what will this be amongst so many?" The allusion was to the miracle of the loaves and the fishes, when the disciple Andrew said to Jesus, "There is a lad here which hath five barley

loaves, and two small fishes, but what are they among so many?"[30] By implication, it would take another miracle to rescue Dublin's poor.

Although Swift and King had not been entirely comfortable with each
other until now, their common cause brought them to a complete rapproche-
ment. Seventeen years older than Swift and a fellow graduate of Trinity, King
was a man of high intelligence and absolute probity. The son of a tenant farmer,
he had risen to eminence by his own abilities, which was highly unusual, and
he was one of the few Irish bishops seriously committed to reforming the
Church. By 1720 a mutual acquaintance was able to report to the archbishop
of Canterbury, "The Archbishop and the Dean are now joined in great unity."
Swift especially admired King's optimism. He once told King that the world
was divided into "those that hope the best and those that fear the worst," and
that he himself was always in danger of falling into the second category.[31]

In due course there were five long *Drapier's Letters*, plus two others that
were not published until later, and they fill an entire volume in Swift's collected

67. Archbishop
William King.

works. The first was addressed "to the tradesmen, shopkeepers, farmers, and country people in general of the Kingdom of Ireland," and a sequel targeted "the nobility and gentry." By posing as a cloth merchant, Swift could use a pithy, commonsense style to reach a wide audience. Before long it was widely assumed that he was the real author, but as usual he left no paper trail that could provide evidence for prosecution.

Historians sometimes assert that there was nothing wrong with Wood's coins. It's true that Sir Isaac Newton, who was in charge of the London mint, supervised an assay that found they had full value. But since Wood was allowed to choose which coins to submit for the assay, he naturally sent ones that would pass inspection. In Ireland, however, when four different lots of Wood's coins arrived, they varied markedly in size and weight, and three were definitely debased.

Other things looked suspicious, too. When private citizens were authorized to issue money, they were normally required to replace it with legal currency on demand. This stipulation was omitted in the patent granted to Wood. Furthermore, he was licensed to produce the astounding sum of £100,000 in copper halfpence, four or five times as much as Ireland could conceivably need, and a sure pathway to inflation.[32]

Swift seized the opportunity to personalize the controversy by demonizing Wood. As Ehrenpreis says, "We are roused more quickly to hate a man than an idea." For the most part Swift stuck to sober arguments, but there were characteristic flights of fantasy as well, taking expressions literally so as to make them absurd. Picking up on a report that Walpole "hath sworn to make us swallow his coin in fireballs," Swift objected solemnly that unfortunately the project wasn't practical:

> Now, the metal he hath prepared, and already coined, will amount to at least fifty millions of halfpence to be swallowed by a million and a half of people; so that allowing two halfpence to each ball, there will be about seventeen balls of wildfire apiece to be swallowed by every person in the kingdom; and to administer this dose, there cannot be conveniently fewer than fifty thousand operators, allowing one operator to every thirty; which, considering the squeamishness of some stomachs, and the peevishness of young children, is but reasonable. Now, under correction of better judgments, I think the trouble and charge of such an experiment would exceed the profit.

In addition, if the halfpence ever got into circulation, they would depreciate so drastically that enormous quantities would be required: "They say Squire Conolly has sixteen thousand pounds a year. Now if he sends for his rent to town, as it is likely he does, he must have two hundred and fifty horses to bring up his half year's rent, and two or three great cellars in his house for stowage."[33]

But, as Swift explained, it was perfectly legal to refuse Wood's coins. The patent stated that his halfpence should "pass and be received as current money, by such as shall be willing to receive the same." But that meant that no one who was unwilling to receive them could be forced to do so. "Therefore, my friends, stand to it one and all, refuse this filthy trash. . . . The laws have not left it in the King's power to force us to take any coin but what is lawful, of right standard, gold and silver. Therefore you have nothing to fear."[34]

Swift's reference to "Squire Conolly" was a deliberate taunt. As speaker of the Irish House of Commons, he was Walpole's favored instrument in managing Irish affairs, and as chief revenue commissioner he had amassed an enormous fortune. Thought to be the richest man in Ireland, he was building a great mansion known as Castletown in Celbridge, very close to where Vanessa had lived. Since he came from a family in the west that had only recently converted to Protestantism, Swift regarded him as a parvenu and referred to him as a "shoeboy" who was "wholly illiterate and with hardly common sense." By "illiterate" he meant ignorant of Latin. The Swifts, of course, were parvenus themselves.[35]

Wood was stung into publishing a lengthy defense, which Swift contemptuously dismissed as "the last howls of a dog dissected alive." As for Walpole, who was the real target of the *Drapier's Letters*, he was slow to grasp what a mess had been created. Apparently he genuinely believed that the Irish were being obstreperous about nothing. At this point the English Privy Council escalated the crisis by bringing the underlying constitutional issue into the open. It ordered the Irish commissioners of revenue to accept Wood's coins as legal tender, and the commissioners refused. The struggle now wasn't just between Ireland and William Wood, it was between Ireland and England.[36]

To bolster the Irish cause, Swift and his allies appealed to Molyneux's *Case of Ireland*. The fourth of the *Drapier's Letters* was addressed not to a particular class but "to the whole people of Ireland." Invoking "the famous Mr. Molineaux, an English gentleman born here"—a description that Swift would have applied to himself—he declared, "In reason, all government without the consent of the governed is the very definition of slavery; but in fact, eleven men well armed will certainly subdue one single man in his shirt. But I have done. For those who have used power to cramp liberty have gone so far as to resent even the liberty of complaining; although a man upon the rack was never known to be refused the liberty of roaring as loud as he thought fit."[37]

The lord lieutenant at the time was the clueless Duke of Grafton, whom Swift once described as "almost a slobberer, without one good quality." Realizing belatedly that Grafton was no use, Walpole recalled him and sent over a much abler man, Lord Carteret, as his replacement. Swift greatly admired Carteret, who was an old friend, and Carteret in turn was anxious to defuse the crisis. He had to go through with a show of force, however. The Irish Privy Council declared the pamphlet treasonable and secured a vote to have the printer arrested, meanwhile announcing a reward of £300 for anyone who would establish the identity of the Drapier.[38]

This was the second time a price had been put on Swift's head, and as in London in 1713, no one betrayed him. A remarkable confrontation did occur, though. Robert Blakely, Swift's butler, had been employed to copy out the *Drapier's Letters* (so that Swift's handwriting would not appear) and to deliver them to the printer. When Blakely stayed out unusually late one night, Swift feared that he had turned informer, and ordered the deanery doors to be locked. As soon as Blakely showed up the next morning, Swift ordered him to strip off his livery. "What, you villain," he exclaimed, "is it because I am in your power you dare take these liberties? Get out of my house, you scoundrel, and receive the reward of your treachery!"[39]

Stella, who was present, was greatly alarmed, and sent for Sheridan to intervene. Sheridan found Blakely in tears. "What grieves me to the soul," he told Sheridan, "is that my master should have so bad an opinion of me as to suppose me capable of betraying him for any reward whatever." When Swift heard this he not only restored Robert to favor, but offered him a position as cathedral verger, the assistant responsible for making services go smoothly. Robert replied that the greatest favor he could receive was to be allowed to continue as Swift's butler.[40]

The printer of the *Drapier's Letters*, John Harding, courageously refused to provide evidence. A grand jury was impaneled to interrogate him, at which point Swift published an impudent pamphlet called *Seasonable Advice to the Grand Jury*, declaring again that Ireland was not a "depending kingdom." Since it was illegal to try to influence a jury, this pamphlet too became the target of the investigation, which may be what Swift intended, since it deflected attention from Harding. But when the chief justice instructed the jurymen to find *Seasonable Advice* seditious, they refused. He then dismissed them and called for a new grand jury, which was exceeding his proper authority, and as Ehrenpreis says, "the farce dragged on."[41]

Swift decided to renew the attack yet again, in a letter addressed to Lord Chancellor Middleton. This time he signed the letter not "M.B., Drapier" but "J.S., Deanery House." He held off on publication, however, until Archbishop King could show the manuscript to Carteret, who was working behind the scenes to make peace. They both warned Swift to drop the idea, and he agreed to keep the Middleton letter to himself. It didn't appear in print until 1735, when the affair had long blown over.[42]

In any event, there was no need for another volley. Walpole finally yielded to the inevitable and withdrew Wood's patent. For once in his life Swift had achieved total victory. He told his friend John Worrall with satisfaction, "The work is done, and there is no more need of the Drapier."[43]

In later life Swift always remembered the Drapier episode as his pinnacle of success.

> Fair LIBERTY was all his cry;
> For her he stood prepared to die;
> For her he boldly stood alone;
> For her he oft exposed his own.
> Two kingdoms, just as faction led,
> Had set a price upon his head,
> But not a traitor could be found
> To sell him for six hundred pound.[44]

The first £300 was the reward offered in 1713 for exposing the author of *The Public Spirit of the Whigs.*

When Parliament assembled in Dublin in 1782, the patriot Henry Grattan declared, "I found Ireland on her knees; I watched over her with an eternal solicitude; I have traced her progress from injuries to arms, and from arms to liberty. Spirit of Swift! spirit of Molyneux! your genius has prevailed! Ireland is now a nation!" On another occasion Grattan said, "Swift was on the wrong side in England, but in Ireland he was a giant."[45]

When he addressed "the whole people of Ireland," Swift may have been thinking primarily of his own Anglo-Irish caste, but he was honored by all as a hero fighting the common oppressor. A Bible quotation was widely repeated: "And the people said unto Saul, Shall Jonathan die, who hath wrought this great salvation in Israel? God forbid: as the Lord liveth, there shall not one hair of his head fall to the ground, for he hath wrought with God this day. So the people rescued Jonathan, that he died not." Carteret's secretary reported that this text "has been got by rote, by men, women, and children, and, I do assure you, takes wonderfully."[46]

Indeed, the Drapier's message cut right across class and religious boundaries. King commented, "I never saw the kingdom so universally averse to anything as they are to these halfpence, from the herb women to the nobles." And Archbishop Boulter of Armagh, Walpole's handpicked representative, lamented to a member of Walpole's cabinet, "People of every religion, country and party here are alike set against Wood's halfpence, and their agreement in this has had a very unhappy influence on the state of this nation, by bringing on intimacies between Papists and Jacobites and the Whigs, who before had no correspondence with them." Swift himself relished the irony by which "money, the great divider of the world, hath, by a strange revolution, been the great uniter of a most divided people." From this time forward there were annual celebrations, with bell ringing and bonfires, to commemorate Swift's birthday on November 30.[47]

National hero though he had become, Swift continued to occupy a deeply ambiguous position, just as he had when he wrote *The Story of the Injured Lady*. In that little allegory, Ireland had been jilted by her English lover, but Swift himself belonged to the Ascendancy that did the jilting. And now, although he spoke for "the whole people of Ireland," he had no interest whatever in emancipating the Catholic majority, who still spoke their own language and were loyal to their own religion. In much the same way, when Archbishop King referred to "the people of Ireland," he meant Protestants; when he had Catholics in mind he called them simply "the Irish." King wrote at this time to the archbishop of Canterbury, "The Protestants of Ireland are sensible that they have no other security for their estates, religion, liberty or lives but their union to England and their dependence on the crown thereof; and therefore, in all events that have happened since the Reformation, they have ever stuck close to it, and ever will and must, whilst there are six or seven Papists for one Protestant in it."[48]

William Wood landed on his feet, of course. In return for giving up his patent, he received a pension of £24,000. The Walpole administration was careful to manage this transaction in secrecy, and the funds—drawn from Irish taxes!—were issued to a nonexistent "Thomas Uvedale, Esq."[49]

68. Lord Carteret.

A final echo of the affair does Swift honor. He had mentioned in passing someone named John Browne as belonging to "the race of suborners, forgers, perjurers and ravishers." Browne later wrote to say that he was sure Swift's intentions were good, but that he had been misled by false reports and had ruined Browne's reputation. "The cause for which you undertook my ruin was the cause of my country. It was a good cause, and you shall ever find me of that side. You have carried it [that is, been victorious] and I know you will no longer be my enemy. But alas, sir, as long as your works subsist, wherever they be read even unto the end of time, must I be branded as a villain?" In the 1735 edition of Swift's works the unkind reference to Browne disappeared, and a grateful Browne later erected a monument to Swift.[50]

As for Carteret, Swift never blamed him for doing what he was required to do, especially since he did it diplomatically and was instrumental in resolving the crisis. Delany reports an occasion when Carteret was mounting a strongly reasoned argument and Swift exclaimed, "What the vengeance brought you amongst us? Get you gone, get you gone—pray God Almighty, send us our boobies back again." Five years after Carteret's term as lord lieutenant ended and he was back in England, he wrote prophetically to Swift, "As for futurity, I know your name will be remembered when the names of kings, lords lieutenant, archbishops, and parliament politicians will be forgotten." And long after that, when he hadn't seen Swift for many years, he asked a mutual friend to tell Swift "that he loved and honoured you, and so you should find on all occasions, and that he toasted your health."[51]

In his London days, Swift had looked down from above as a champion of those in power, the Tory ministry and the established Church. Now he was still defending the Church, but otherwise he was looking up from below. In the past, he could never have predicted that one day he would make himself the voice of Ireland. Yet he was discovering now that he identified strongly with his country. In the voice of the Drapier, he called Ireland his mother: "It is a known story of the dumb boy whose tongue forced a passage for speech by the horror of seeing a dagger at his father's throat. This may lessen the wonder that a tradesman, hid in privacy and silence, should cry out when the life and being of his political mother are attempted before his face, and by so infamous a hand." Yeats put it well: "Swift found his nationality through the *Drapier's Letters*."[52]

CHAPTER 24

The Astonishing Travels

"COUNTRIES HITHERTO UNKNOWN"

At the time he was writing the *Drapier's Letters*, Swift was nearing comple-
tion of *Gulliver's Travels*, his first full-length work since *A Tale of a Tub*. He
intended it to be a major achievement, and he took his time, beginning in
1721, five years before eventual publication. "I am now writing a history of
my Travels," he told Ford, "which will be a large volume, and gives account
of countries hitherto unknown; but they go on slowly for want of health and
humor."[1] The first two of the four books were finished by the end of 1723,
and the fourth early the next year. We know, incidentally, from an allusion
in one of her letters, that Vanessa read the first two. Book 3, which probably
incorporates some old material from Scriblerian days, was done in the fall
of 1725.

As the story evolves, Lemuel Gulliver sets forth on four sea voyages, first
as a ship's doctor and eventually as a captain. The voyages all end in disaster,
each worse than the one before. First a storm causes a shipwreck; next Gulliver is abandoned by shipmates when a terrifying giant appears; then pirates
board his ship and set him adrift in a small boat; and finally his own crew ma-
roons him on what they assume is a desert island. Each time he goes ashore,
Gulliver encounters remarkable inhabitants: miniature people in Lilliput; co-
lossal ones in Brobdingnag; people who rule the territory of Lagado from a

flying island above it; and intelligent horses called Houyhnhnms whose beasts of burden are apelike humanoids.

Swift loved books of travels and owned numerous volumes, including the huge Elizabethan anthologies of Hakluyt and Purchas. Some of his books still exist, for example, a 1634 volume by Sir Thomas Herbert called *A Relation of Some Years Travaille, through Divers Parts of Asia and Africke*. Its glossaries are very suggestive of the languages Swift invented for his own narrative: *Choggee shoechoro whoddaw* in Persian means "Well I pray God," and *bedil besar* in Javanese is "a great torment." But Swift was a critical reader. On the first page he wrote, "If this book were stripped of its impertinence, conceitedness, and tedious digressions, it would be almost worth reading, and would then be two-thirds smaller than it is. 1720. J. Swift."[2]

With *Gulliver's Travels* Swift reached a new pinnacle as a writer, and he knew it. What exactly that pinnacle *was* is another question. In an era that often used the word *invention* where we would say *originality*, a commentator said it was "founded in the utmost wantonness of invention." Pope did use "original," telling Orrery that Swift's writings were "absolutely original, unequaled, unexampled." The book is usually classified as a satire, but it's much more than that too—it's a novel, and an antinovel, and a fantasy, with parody and science fiction mixed in. As he developed it, Swift must have felt as Robert Louis Stevenson did when he wrote *Treasure Island*: "It seemed to me original as sin."[3]

Critics tell us that *Gulliver's Travels* can't be a novel because Gulliver is sometimes shrewd but sometimes naïve, and because he learns very little from his experiences until the end, when he learns too much. They also point out that he is often a mouthpiece for Swiftian irony, earnestly praising European warfare and legal systems that Swift despised. Obviously it's not like a novel by Jane Austen or Henry James, but that's irrelevant. Novels like theirs hadn't been dreamt of yet. When Steele mentioned "novelists" in 1710, he was referring to newspaper journalists, who report what is new and therefore novel.[4]

The appeal of travel writing during this period was that it seemed to show that truth was stranger than fiction. In an age that valued factuality, voyagers were encouraged to describe wonders in a matter-of-fact way. Swift alludes to this expectation when he makes Gulliver say, "I could perhaps, like others, have astonished thee [the reader] with strange improbable tales, but I rather chose to relate plain matter of fact in the simplest manner and style, because my principal design was to inform and not to amuse thee."[5]

Swift was the wittiest of men; Gulliver is humorless. Irony was a way of life for Swift; Gulliver is never ironic. And yet Gulliver seems *real*, in a way that suggests his creator identified with him and lived through the adventures with him. In George Faulkner's 1735 edition of Swift's collected works, the portraits of Swift and of Lemuel Gulliver are so similar as to make the connection obvious. The quote from Horace, *splendide mendax*, means "nobly mendacious," and implies telling an untruth in a good cause. *Gulliver's Travels* is a fantasy, but it is also true.

We are told that Gulliver had a good education at Cambridge and wanted to make a career there, "but the charge of maintaining me (although I had a very scanty allowance) being too great for a narrow fortune, I was bound apprentice to Mr. James Bates, an eminent surgeon in London."[6] There may well be a memory of Swift's scanty allowance at Trinity, and his subsequent

69. Dean Swift. D.S^t.P.D. means "Dean of St. Patrick's, Dublin."

70. Captain Gulliver, shown in the 1735 edition of Swift's *Works*.

employment by Sir William Temple. Gulliver's first voyage begins in 1699 and his last one ends in 1715; those dates correspond to the period in Swift's life between leaving Moor Park and leaving London for good. At the time of writing his travels, Gulliver is fifty-nine years old. Swift was about to turn fifty-nine when *Gulliver's Travels* was published.

At one point the tiny Lilliputians think that Gulliver's watch must be his god, because he never does anything without consulting it. According to Orrery, "Swift's hours of walking and reading never varied; his motions were guided by his watch, which was so constantly held in his hand, or placed before him upon his table, that he seldom deviated many minutes in the daily revolution of his exercises and employments." On this practice, Lady Orrery made an insightful comment: "The great regularity of his life, constantly measured by his watch, plainly showed his mind to be uneasy."[7]

Gulliver's Travels had something for everyone. "It offered personal and political satire to the readers in high life," Walter Scott said, "low and coarse incident to the vulgar, marvels to the romantic, wit to the young and lively, lessons of morality and policy to the grave, and maxims of deep and bitter misanthropy to neglected age and disappointed ambition." The reader is ingratiatingly addressed as "the gentle reader," and is called "indulgent," "courteous," "judicious," and a long list of other compliments. At times Swift teases or taunts, but he knows he also has to give pleasure. "Gulliver is a happy man," Arbuthnot told him, "that at his age can write such a merry book."[8]

"BIG MEN AND LITTLE MEN"

Always ready to disparage Swift, Johnson roared in conversation, "When once you have thought of big men and little men, it is very easy to do all the rest."[9] Nothing could be further from the truth. What makes *Gulliver's Travels* compelling is the miraculous balance between realism and fantasy. As in Tolkien's *Lord of the Rings*, the fantasy is grounded in a world of consistently believable details. The Lilliputians are exactly one-twelfth as tall as ourselves, and the Brobdingnagians twelve times taller. In early illustrations of Gulliver held down by tiny ropes, if you cover up his supine figure, everything else looks perfectly ordinary.

There's not much psychological characterization, but physical sensations are vividly recorded, and Swift constantly makes us feel what it would be like to *be* Gulliver. When he regains consciousness after the shipwreck, he discovers that he's unable to move:

71. Gulliver tied
down, shown in a
1727 French edition.

As I happened to lie on my back, I found my arms and legs were
strongly fastened on each side to the ground; and my hair, which was
long and thick, tied down in the same manner. I likewise felt several
slender ligatures across my body, from my armpits to my thighs. I
could only look upwards; the sun began to grow hot, and the light
offended mine eyes. I heard a confused noise about me, but in the posture I lay could see nothing except the sky. In a little time I felt something alive moving on my left leg, which advancing gently forward
over my breast, came almost up to my chin; when, bending my eyes
downwards as much as I could, I perceived it to be a human creature
not six inches high.[10]

In part, Swift was critiquing the naïve realism of writers like Defoe, whose
Robinson Crusoe, often described as the first modern English novel, came out
just seven years before *Gulliver's Travels*. Defoe could never decide whether
to admit that he had made up the story, or whether it required the pretense

of veracity. His full title appeals to the stranger-than-fiction fashion: *The Life and Strange Surprising Adventures of Robinson Crusoe of York, Mariner, Who Lived Eight and Twenty Years All Alone on an Uninhabited Island on the Coast of America, Near the Mouth of the Great River of Orinoco, Having Been Cast on Shore by Shipwreck Wherein All Men Perished but Himself.* In his preface Defoe said, with obvious equivocation, "The editor believes the thing to be a just history of fact; neither is there any appearance of fiction in it." But in a later defense he asserted defiantly, "It is most real that I had a parrot, and taught it to call me by my name; such a servant a savage, and afterwards a Christian, and that his name was called Friday."[11]

Swift had to be remembering these claims of Defoe's when he made "the publisher" declare at the start of *Gulliver's Travels*, "There is an air of truth apparent through the whole; and indeed the author was so distinguished for his veracity that it became a sort of proverb among his neighbours at Redriff, when any one affirmed a thing, to say it was as true as if Mr. Gulliver had spoke it." Arbuthnot was amused to hear of a sea captain who claimed he knew Gulliver personally, "but that the printer had mistaken, that he lived in Wapping and not at Rotherhithe." Even more delicious, as Swift reported, was an Irish bishop who said, "That book was full of improbable lies, and for his part he hardly believed a word of it." It isn't clear which parts the bishop did believe, if indeed Swift didn't make him up.[12]

Arbuthnot mentions also that a friend of his went straight to the atlas to locate Lilliput on the map. As a fan of voyages, Swift understood that maps contribute verisimilitude. He probably didn't see the ones that his London publisher commissioned until after the book came out, but since he let them stand in the 1735 edition, he must have approved of them. They look altogether plausible, with neighboring territories carefully traced from an atlas, but they make no sense if you compare them with a genuine map of the world.[13]

Proud of his circumstantial accuracy, Defoe was embarrassed when readers noticed that Crusoe stripped off his clothes before swimming out to the wrecked ship, but was still able to stuff his pockets with biscuits when he got there. More recently it has been observed that the contents of Gulliver's pockets, if you put them all together, would fill a suitcase. At the Lilliputians' orders he brings out, one by one, a handkerchief, a snuffbox, a diary, a comb, some coins, a razor, a clasp knife, a watch, a pair of pistols, spectacles, a telescope, and "several other little conveniences."[14] Conceivably this overload is Swift's joke for attentive readers to pick up. But it's also possible that he didn't care. He wanted the illusion of reality, but only an illusion, and at this point

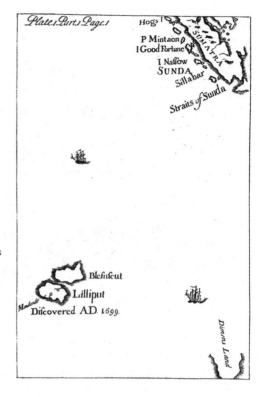

72. Lilliput on the map, from Motte's edition of 1726. The Sunda Straits, between Sumatra and Java, appear at the top. Van Diemen's Land, at the lower right, is the old name for Tasmania, but the location here is absurd, since Tasmania lies off the southeastern coast of Australia.

in the story he needed the comb and the watch and the rest, not to mention a sword with which Gulliver somehow swam to shore in the storm.[15]

Since the Lilliputians and Brobdingnagians are like us in every respect except size, the effect is to defamiliarize our everyday experience. Swift's genius lies in making us *see*. Nothing could be more ordinary than a pocket watch, but not in the eyes of the Lilliputians: "Out of the right fob hung a great silver chain, with a wonderful kind of engine at the bottom. We directed him to draw out whatever was at the end of that chain; which appeared to be a globe, half silver, and half of some transparent metal; for on the transparent side we saw certain strange figures circularly drawn, and thought we could touch them, until we found our fingers stopped with that lucid substance. He put this engine to our ears, which made an incessant noise, like that of a water-mill." Conversely, what is ordinary for the tiny people is strange for Gulliver, who watches a Lilliputian girl threading an invisible needle with invisible thread.[16]

73. Gulliver fighting the rat, by Willy Pogany.

A comparison with *Alice in Wonderland* helps to clarify Swift's use of scale. Size mutates constantly in *Alice*, with a sort of dream logic. There's nothing dreamy in *Gulliver*. Everything is completely normal, except that the relative proportions are disconcertingly altered. In Brobdingnag it's small things that become huge. Gulliver is cruelly bruised by hailstones, falls from a table and is luckily caught on a lady's pin, fights off a giant rat with his sword, struggles with an immense slimy frog that invades his little boat, and has a brush with death when a monkey as big as an elephant carries him up to a rooftop five hundred yards above the ground. As Claude Rawson says, these are Kafkaesque horrors.[17] The vividness of Swift's imagination is reflected in the wide range of superb illustrations, in many different styles, that artists have contributed to successive editions of his book.

On one occasion, when Gulliver witnesses a public execution, the difference in scale produces a nightmarish result. "The malefactor was fixed in a chair upon a scaffold erected for the purpose, and his head cut off at one blow with a sword of about forty foot long. The veins and arteries spouted up such a prodigious quantity of blood, and so high in the air, that the great *jet d'eau* at Versailles was not equal for the time it lasted; and the head, when it fell on the scaffold floor, gave such a bounce as made me start, although I were at least an English mile distant."[18]

We know that Swift was much concerned with the vulnerability of the body, and many incidents reflect that concern. Even ordinary functions become disturbing. When the Lilliputians chain Gulliver to a disused temple, he is deeply embarrassed by the need to defecate. Eventually it's arranged that servants should show up every morning and carry away the "offensive matter" in wheelbarrows. Gulliver says, "I would not have dwelt so long upon a circumstance that perhaps at first sight may appear not very momentous, if I had not thought it necessary to justify my character in point of cleanliness to the world; which, I am told, some of my maligners have been pleased, upon this and other occasions, to call in question."[19]

Perhaps this alludes to the scandal of the *Tale of a Tub*, as does the episode in which Gulliver puts out the palace fire by urinating on it. As usual, Swift is doing two things at once; Gulliver chained to the temple is evocative of Swift chained to St. Patrick's Cathedral. A further detail looks arbitrary but isn't, as Leslie Stephen noticed long ago. Gulliver is secured with "fourscore and eleven chains" that are fastened to his leg with "six-and-thirty padlocks." The ostensible author of the *Tale of a Tub* had boasted, "Fourscore and eleven pamphlets have I written under three reigns, and for the service of six-and-thirty factions."[20] By the time he wrote *Gulliver's Travels*, Swift had indeed worn himself out producing pamphlets, many of which were obstacles to career advancement.

When the subject of sex arises, it's not enticing. Gulliver is present while the Brobdingnagian maids of honor strip naked, and he finds it "very far from being a tempting sight, or from giving me any other motions [emotions] than those of horror and disgust." Seen close up, their skin is coarse and discolored, and when they toy with him he is revolted: "The handsomest among these maids of honour, a pleasant frolicsome girl of sixteen, would sometimes set me astride upon one of her nipples; with many other tricks, wherein the reader will excuse me for not being over-particular." Pope got the message, and sent Swift a poem in which Gulliver's wife exclaims after the returns to England,

> But on the maiden's nipple when you rid,
> Pray heaven 'twas all a wanton maiden did!

Nora Crow, who makes the plausible suggestion that Swift felt uneasy because he found women dangerously attractive, comments that "being employed as a dildo is the most literal form of female engulfment that a man could undergo."[21]

Even breastfeeding, a universal activity inseparable from maternal tenderness, excites revulsion when Gulliver watches a farm wife nursing her baby.

I must confess no object ever disgusted me so much as the sight of her monstrous breast, which I cannot tell what to compare with, so as to give the curious reader an idea of its bulk, shape and colour. It stood prominent six foot, and could not be less than sixteen in circumference. The nipple was about half the bigness of my head, and the hue both of that and the dug so varified with spots, pimples and freckles that nothing could appear more nauseous; for I had a near sight of her, she sitting down the more conveniently to give suck, and I standing on the table. This made me reflect upon the fair skins of our English ladies, who appear so beautiful to us only because they are of our own size, and their defects not to be seen but through a magnifying glass.[22]

People who believe that Swift loathed the body often quote this passage, but then they leave out that last sentence. A theme in *Gulliver's Travels* is that everything is relative. English ladies are lovely because we don't use magnifying glasses on them, and why would we want to? Gulliver recalls at this point that he himself seemed grotesque to the Lilliputians, who told him that they observed "great holes in my skin; that the stumps of my beard were ten times stronger than the bristles of a boar; and my complexion made up of several colours altogether disagreeable." Conversely, all Lilliputians looked equally attractive to him, though they themselves considered some people ugly and others beautiful. It follows that for the Brobdingnagians, it would be wrong to suppose that "those vast creatures were actually deformed; for I must do them justice to say they are a comely race of people."[23]

There was great interest in microscopes in Swift's day, and books were published with highly detailed illustrations. Swift was familiar with Robert Hooke's superbly illustrated *Micrographia*, from which the illustration of the louse (figure 74) is taken. Hooke was fascinated by a live louse under his microscope, noting that the blood it sucked from his hand "was of a very lovely ruby colour." Gulliver is revolted, however, by lice infesting the beggars of Brobdingnag: "The most hateful sight of all was the lice crawling on their clothes. I could see distinctly the limbs of these vermin with my naked eye, much better than those of an European louse through a microscope, and their snouts with which they rooted like swine."[24]

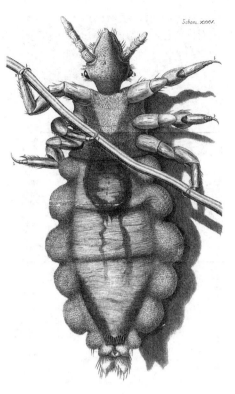

74. A louse as it appeared to Gulliver.

The closest bond Gulliver forms in Brobdingnag is with a daughter of the farmer who first discovers him, a nine-year-old girl who teaches him the language and becomes his faithful attendant.

> My mistress had a daughter of nine years old, a child of towardly parts for her age. . . . She was likewise my schoolmistress to teach me the language. When I pointed to anything, she told me the name of it in her own tongue, so that in a few days I was able to call for whatever I had a mind to. She was very good-natured, and not above forty foot high, being little for her age. She gave me the name of *Grildrig*, which the family took up, and afterwards the whole kingdom. The word imports what the Latins call *nanunculus*, the Italians *homunceletino*, and the English *mannikin*. To her I chiefly owe my preservation in that country. We never parted while I was there; I called her my *Glumdalclitch*, or little nurse.[25]

75. Glumdalclitch, by Arthur Rackham.

Stella was nine when Swift first knew her, and now the tutorial relationship is reversed. Arthur Rackham's Victorian illustration catches the affection well, though his Glumdalclitch looks more like an enchanting princess than a farm girl.

What really horrified Swift about the body was not physicality in itself, but decay. Most dreadful of all is the decay of the mind. Monitoring his occasional memory lapses with grim fascination, Swift dreaded the fate that finally did befall him, fifteen years after *Gulliver's Travels*. In Luggnugg, in the third book, there are rare individuals called Struldbruggs, identifiable at birth by a red spot on the forehead, who will never die. Gulliver is thrilled. "I cried out as in a rapture, 'Happy nation, where every child hath at least a chance for being immortal!'" But it turns out that when Struldbruggs get old they face eternal senility, unable to remember the beginning of a sentence when they get to the end. An eighteenth-century reader commented that the spectacle of the Struldbruggs can help "to reconcile old age to the thoughts of a dissolution."[26]

Gulliver's Travels immediately became a classic for children as well as adults, and for a century it never occurred to anyone to abridge it or clean it up. Starting in 1829, the nipples of the maids of honor had to go, and likewise the descriptions of urinating and defecating. It was then hard to understand why Gulliver gets into trouble for putting out the palace fire—in one version he grabs "a reservoir of water kept for the especial use of the empress," and in another there is vague mention of "a well meant but badly managed attempt to do her a service." Other passages were deleted if they seemed hard for young readers to understand, but in every version the story retained its power. Padraic Colum, Joyce's friend and a distinguished writer of children's stories, described it as an inverted fairy tale: "In the fairy tale the little beings have beauty and graciousness, the giants are dull-witted, the beasts are helpful, and

76. Struldbruggs, by
Arthur Rackham.

humanity is shown as triumphant. In *Gulliver* the little beings are hurtful, the giants have more insight than men, the beasts rule, and humanity is shown not as triumphant but as degraded and enslaved."[27]

Not just children have enjoyed the fantasy. Daniel Boone, of all people, used to read *Gulliver's Travels* aloud to his companions over the campfire. One of them came back one day boasting that he had just killed two Brobdernags near their capitol, Lulbegrud. He meant two buffalo, and the names were his version of Brobdingnag and Lorbrulgrud. Lulbegrud Creek still appears on maps of Kentucky.[28]

SATIRE

A Tale of a Tub is a satire from beginning to end; *Gulliver's Travels* is only intermittently satiric, and the satire seldom gets in the way of the story. Partly that's because Swift was highly skilled at making his allusions unspecific enough to escape prosecution. In his final revision he took care to anticipate potential problems, writing to Pope from Quilca, "I have employed my time (besides ditching) in finishing, correcting, amending, and transcribing my *Travels*, in four parts complete newly augmented, and intended for the press when the world shall deserve them, or rather when a printer shall be found brave enough to venture his ears." Prisoners at the pillory sometimes had their ears lopped off, as Pope pretended to believe had happened to Daniel Defoe: "Earless on high stood unabashed Defoe."[29]

The prizes for Lilliputian politicians who win the competition in leaping and creeping are silken threads, either blue, red, or green. These were the colors of the Orders of the Garter, the Bath, and the Thistle. Sir Robert Walpole was intensely proud of holding the Garter, but the allusion is too general to be actionable. Nevertheless, Swift's printer prudently changed the colors to purple, yellow, and white, and the correct ones weren't restored until later editions.[30]

Now and then a more elaborate narrative serves as an allegory of current events. Lord Munodi, the old-fashioned landlord whose estate was despised for prospering so well, is ordered to demolish an excellent watermill and replace it with a new one halfway up a hill. The rationale for this is that "wind and air" will add energy to the water, and so will gravity when it comes back down, making it twice as powerful as the river below. But of course an elaborate pumping system is now required, and the project is a complete failure.

As he loved to do, Swift has thus translated abstractions into concrete embodiment. A likely interpretation is that the old mill is the English economy, driven by the natural flow of trade and agriculture. The new mill is the South Sea Company, using the artificial pump of stockjobbing, which is as empty as wind and air, so inevitably the whole thing collapses.[31]

Closer to home for Irish readers is the story in book 3 of the flying island from which the rulers of Lagado govern their land. Managed by a huge movable lodestone, it can rise, descend, and travel from side to side. The nobles up there are totally out of touch with the real world, devoting themselves to abstract mathematics, and so absent-minded that servants called "flappers" have to touch their mouths with hollow bladders to remind them when it's time to speak. But there are totalitarian possibilities as well. If the populace rebels, the island hovers above them long enough to block both sun and rain, resulting in "dearth and diseases." The ultimate sanction would be to come all the way down and crush them, but this the king is reluctant to do, since the city's towers and an especially tall spire in the middle might shatter his island's base.

In an unpublished passage, Swift identified "the second city in the kingdom" as Lindalino, an obvious allusion to Dublin, second city after London. Its inhabitants build tall towers in which they secretly install lodestones of their own, and they also prepare "a vast quantity of the most combustible fuel, hoping to burst therewith the adamantine bottom of the island, if the lodestone project should miscarry." The island arrives and pelts the city with rocks, and when they refuse to plead for mercy, it does descend. But the descent begins to accelerate, and after lowering small bits of lodestone on strings and feeling them tugged from below, the government realizes the danger it's in. There is now no alternative but "to give the town their own conditions."[32]

The allegory is easy to decode. First, court patronage was withheld from Ireland; then, with the hail of rocks, moderate repression was tried; and finally, total retaliation was planned. But just as the island's base might be fatally shattered, so the hard-won equilibrium of the British political system is at risk. The combustible fuel is the stream of incendiary pamphlets, the *Drapier's Letters* above all, that stirred up popular resistance. And the high spire is St. Patrick's Cathedral.[33]

Once again, the narrative is effective even if one has never heard of William Wood and his halfpence. Swift was always skeptical of the claims of science, especially when it wastes its time on useless experimentation. Researchers at the Academy of Lagado kill a dog by pumping air into its anus, make pigs root around in fields to save the expense of plowing ("they had little or no crop"), and breed sheep that grow no wool (hoping "in a reasonable time to propagate the breed of naked sheep all over the kingdom").[34] But the flying island is different: it's prophetic of a threat to human existence. The mad scientist Frankenstein creates a monster that turns against him, and Winston Churchill, in his great "This was their finest hour" speech, warned against a new kind of tyranny "made more sinister, and perhaps more protracted, by the lights of perverted science."

Swift's care to avoid obvious attacks on individuals was rewarded. After *Gulliver's Travels* came out, Pope and Gay wrote to say that "the politicians to a man agree that it is free from particular reflections, but that the satire on general societies of men is too severe." Shortly afterward Pope added, "None that I hear of accuse it of particular reflections (I mean no persons of consequence or good judgment; the mob of critics, you know, are always desirous to apply satire to those that they envy for being above them)."[35] With great skill, Swift had achieved a trenchant critique of current affairs that applies equally well to other times and places. This universal relevance is what keeps *Gulliver's Travels* fresh and alive nearly three centuries after it was written.

"I HATE AND DETEST THAT ANIMAL CALLED MAN"

The extraordinary Fourth Voyage is the most disturbing thing Swift ever wrote. Set ashore by pirates, Gulliver encounters disgusting apelike creatures that "discharge their excrements" onto him from a tree, and then a pair of strangely thoughtful horses that display obvious intelligence. Soon, with his gift for languages, he is able to converse with them and their friends, and he learns that they call themselves Houyhnhnms. The name should be pronounced "whinnim," with a suggestion of whinnying, as T. H. White explains: "Swift used a 'hou' for the huffing part, and a Y for the squealy part, and the N's and M's are the part in the nose, Houyhnhnm. It is what a horse says."[36]

The Houyhnhnms are coolly rational, so much so that they can't understand the concept of lying and refer to it as "saying the thing which is not." They can make no sense at all of Gulliver's descriptions of money and lawsuits and warfare. For them, reason is a simple apprehension of reality, not the pretentious cleverness that humans call reason. They know nothing of metal or boats, don't practice agriculture, and haven't invented the wheel. Their oats grow naturally without needing to be cultivated, and they are pulled around on wheelless sledges by Yahoos—Swift invented the word—who serve them as beasts of burden. Illustrators always have trouble with the Houyhnhnms.

77. Yahoos pulling a Houyhnhnm, by Willy Pogany.

Drawn naturalistically, they just look like ordinary horses, but when shown behaving in a civilized manner they seem faintly absurd. Willy Pogany's Yahoos, however, are unusually well imagined.

The land of the Houyhnhnms—they don't even give it a name—is a utopia, which means "nowhere" in Greek. That term has gotten so debased that many people think it just means a really nice place. More properly, it means the opposite of everything we know, a standard to measure our inadequacies against. Thomas More was a hero of Swift's for standing up to Henry VIII and for his intelligence and wit, and More's *Utopia* (along with Plato's *Republic*) lies directly behind Swift's Houyhnhnms. A historian calls *Utopia* "the saddest of fairy tales—an indictment of humanity almost as terrible as *Gulliver's Travels*."[37]

One of Swift's brilliant catalogues, toward the end of the book, pours out a torrent of disgust at the way human beings behave. Long as the list is, one gets the impression it could have been much longer:

> I did not feel the treachery or inconstancy of a friend, nor the injuries of a secret or open enemy. I had no occasion of bribing, flattering, or pimping to procure the favour of any great man, or of his minion. I wanted no fence against fraud or oppression; here was neither physician to destroy my body, nor lawyer to ruin my fortune; no informer to watch my words and actions, or forge accusations against me for hire. Here were no gibers, censurers, backbiters, pickpockets,

highwaymen, housebreakers, attorneys, bawds, buffoons, gamesters, politicians, wits, splenetics, tedious talkers, controvertists, ravishers, murderers, robbers, virtuosos; no leaders or followers of party and faction; no encouragers to vice, by seducement or examples; no dungeon, axes, gibbets, whipping-posts, or pillories; no cheating shopkeepers or mechanics [workmen]; no pride, vanity, or affectation; no fops, bullies, drunkards, strolling whores, or poxes; no ranting, lewd, expensive wives; no stupid, proud pedants; no importunate, overbearing, quarrelsome, noisy, roaring, empty, conceited, swearing companions; no scoundrels raised from the dust upon the merit of their vices, or nobility thrown into it on account of their virtues; no lords, fiddlers, judges, or dancing masters.[38]

As Swift loved to do, he has made respectable professions alternate with the grossest crimes, as if there were no real difference.

The Houyhnhnms resemble the ancient Stoics, who sought to live according to nature, whatever that means, and according to reason. But if imaginary horses can live like that, real-life humans can't. Swift wrote, fifteen years earlier, "The Stoical scheme of supplying our wants by lopping off our desires is like cutting off our feet when we want shoes."[39]

From a human point of view, there's a lot that the Houyhnhnms lack. They have no sense of humor, which for Swift was a lifesaving gift. They have no religion, which might seem strange in a book by a clergyman, but the idea seems to be that with no experience of sin, they don't need it. It's not true, however, as is sometimes claimed, that they have no emotions. They just don't have destructive ones. When Gulliver is ordered to sail away, "I often heard the sorrel nag (who always loved me) crying out *Hnuy illa nyha, maiah Yahoo*, Take care of thyself, gentle Yahoo."[40]

The one thing the Houyhnhnms do hate is the Yahoos, their beasts of burden, who are incorrigibly vicious. For Gulliver it's a horrifying moment of truth when he realizes that under their hairy pelts the Yahoos are shockingly similar to himself. One day he wants to cool off in a river, so with his friend the sorrel nag on guard, he takes off his clothes.

> It happened that a young female Yahoo, standing behind a bank, saw the whole proceeding, and inflamed by desire, as the nag and I conjectured, came running with all speed and leaped into the water within five yards of the place where I bathed. I was never in my life so terribly frighted; the nag was grazing at some distance, not suspecting

any harm. She embraced me after a most fulsome manner; I roared as loud as I could, and the nag came galloping towards me, whereupon she quitted her grasp with the utmost reluctancy, and leaped upon the opposite bank, where she stood gazing and howling all the time I was putting on my clothes.

The conclusion seems inescapable. "I could no longer deny that I was a real Yahoo in every limb and feature, since the females had a natural propensity to me as one of their own species. Neither was the hair of this brute of a red colour (which might have been some excuse for an appetite a little irregular), but black as a sloe, and her countenance did not make an appearance altogether so hideous as the rest of the kind, for I think she could not be above eleven years old." Is it conceivable that this reflects Swift's anxiety about being sexually attracted to Stella as a girl? We know by his own report that her hair was "blacker than a raven." The point about red hair is that it was considered ugly and also associated with lecherousness. There's a curious "but" in a description of an acquaintance in the *Journal to Stella*: "The girl is handsome, and has good sense, but red hair."[41]

Even if physical resemblance were dismissed as irrelevant, the affinities go far deeper than that. We really are Yahoos, it turns out, because we share their strongest passions. They fight over possessions even when there's plenty to go around, they hoard "shining stones of several colours" and steal them from each other, they fawn on a leader who condescends to let his followers lick his rear end, and they "discharge their excrements" on anyone who loses favor with him. "But how far this might be applicable to our courts and favourites and ministers of state, my master said I could best determine." It would have amused Swift to learn the term *yahoo* is used frequently in Dublin today, "often without consciousness of its Swiftian source, to mean a graceless and ill-mannered fellow."[42] Not just in Dublin, either.

The Yahoos aren't fully human, of course, and none of them could ever be called "gentle" as Gulliver is, but that's the point. Just as we have degenerated from Adam and Eve, so they have degenerated even further, showing what our worst tendencies would be if nothing held them in check. They are brutes, but brutes that tell us something about ourselves, and Gulliver is jolted out of his complacency. It might seem shocking that the Houyhnhnms castrate Yahoos and that Gulliver fashions his boat out of Yahoo skins. But the Houyhnhnms are shocked that we castrate horses, and until we stop wearing leather jackets and shoes we are in no position to feel superior.

From the beginning, some readers complained that Swift's account of the Yahoos was a libel on human nature. "In painting Yahoos," Orrery said sententiously, "he becomes one himself." A century later Thackeray offered a wildly abusive impression of the author who could think them up: "a monster gibbering shrieks, and gnashing imprecations against mankind—tearing down all shreds of modesty, past all sense of manliness and shame; filthy in word, filthy in thought, furious, raging, obscene." That was in a book called *The English Humorists.*[43]

Other readers were less hostile, especially if they noticed that the Yahoos embody the traditional symbolism of original sin. Quoting Gulliver's description of the cruelty of European warfare, John Wesley commented, "Is it not astonishing beyond expression that this is the naked truth? that within a short term of years, this has been the real case in almost every part of even the Christian world? And meanwhile we gravely talk of the 'dignity of our nature' in its present state!"[44] Wesley was writing just as the Seven Years' War, soon to be the target of Voltaire's *Candide*, was getting under way.

For a long time after Swift's death, the dementia of his final years was misinterpreted as insanity. In Joyce's *Ulysses*, Stephen Dedalus has a lurid vision as he walks on the beach where Swift used to ride: "The hundredheaded rabble of the cathedral close. A hater of his kind ran from them to the wood of madness, his mane foaming in the moon, his eyeballs stars. Houyhnhnm, horsenostrilled."[45]

More recently, it has been suggested that if anyone goes crazy, it's Gulliver. He is so eager to emulate the Houyhnhnms that he starts trotting like them. When they tell him he has to leave, for fear that he may inspire the Yahoos to rebel, he does so with solemn respect:

> I took a second leave of my master; but as I was going to prostrate myself to kiss his hoof, he did me the honour to raise it gently to my mouth. I am not ignorant how much I have been censured for mentioning this last particular. Detractors are pleased to think it improbable that so illustrious a person should descend to give so great a mark of distinction to a creature so inferior as I. Neither have I forgot how apt some travelers are to boast of extraordinary favours they have received. But if these censurers were better acquainted with the noble and courteous disposition of the Houyhnhnms, they would soon change their opinion.[46]

This has been thought ridiculous, but is it any more so than kissing the hand of a king or the slipper of a pope? Swift has his joke about travelers' boastfulness, but the real target is our disposition to grovel before people in high places.

At the end of the story, Gulliver is revolted by human beings, even though a kindly Portuguese captain rescues him at sea. He can't endure the smell of his own family when he gets home, and spends his days communing with his horses in the stable. There is no doubt that the experience of Houyhnhnmland has gravely disenchanted Gulliver. It amused Pope to imagine his wife's distress:

> Where sleeps my Gulliver? O tell me where?
> The neighbours answer, "With the sorrel mare."[47]

Whether or not Gulliver is comically unhinged, the challenge to our complacency remains. As he was finishing the book, Swift wrote to Pope:

> I have ever hated all nations, professions, and communities, and all my love is towards individuals. For instance, I hate the tribe of lawyers, but I love Counselor such a one, and Judge such a one; for so with physicians (I will not speak of my own trade), soldiers, English, Scotch, French, and the rest. But principally I hate and detest that animal called man, although I heartily love John, Peter, Thomas, and so forth. This is the system upon which I have governed myself many years (but do not tell), and so I shall go on till I have done with them. I have got materials towards a treatise proving the falsity of that definition *animal rationale*, and to show it should be only *rationis capax*. Upon this great foundation of misanthropy (though not in Timon's manner), the whole building of my *Travels* is erected; and I never will have peace of mind till all honest men are of my opinion. By consequence you are to embrace it immediately, and procure that all who deserve my esteem may do so too. The matter is so clear that it will admit of little dispute; nay, I will hold a hundred pounds that you and I agree in the point.[48]

Rationis capax—"capable of reason," but rarely exercising it.

And why horses? Swift knew them well and liked them, of course, but it turns out that there was another reason too. The symbolism of the horse as irrational passion goes back to Plato's *Republic*, and when R. S. Crane looked at the logic textbooks that Swift studied at Trinity College, he discovered something even more specific. Not only is "man" defined as *animal rationale*, but the irrational opposite, the horse, is *animal hinnibile*. "The whinnying animal!" So that's where the Houyhnhnms got their name; and by putting them on top, Swift brought our own irrationality into sharp focus. Crane also found that while the textbooks distinguished between mankind in general and individuals, only one of them listed *Joannes, Petrus, Thomas, etc.*— the same names and sequence that Swift mentioned to Pope. That textbook was written by Narcissus Marsh, provost of Trinity College when Swift was there.[49]

Are we supposed to be like the Houyhnhnms, then? We're not, because we can't, and Gulliver's attempt to do so is hopeless. "The Houyhnhnms are not a statement of what man ought to be," Rawson says, "so much as a statement of what he is not."[50]

The Fourth Voyage will always be controversial, because it forces us to question our deep, self-flattering assumptions about that animal called man. "I am not in the least provoked," Gulliver says, "at the sight of a lawyer, a pickpocket, a colonel, a fool, a lord, a gamester, a politician, a whoremonger, a physician, an evidence, a suborner, an attorney, a traitor, or the like; this is all according to the due course of things. But when I behold a lump of deformity and diseases, both in body and mind, smitten with pride, it immediately breaks all the measures of my patience; neither shall I be ever able to comprehend how such an animal and such a vice could tally together." A central Christian tenet is that pride is the fundamental sin; a being consumed by pride has no right to flatter itself as the "rational animal." Wesley quoted this passage too with approval.[51]

Gulliver's Travels ends with these words: "I hereby entreat those who have any tincture of this absurd vice that they will not presume to appear in my sight." That's an extreme reaction, of course, and Gulliver isn't Swift. But in Swift's own opinion, even the best people fell far below the unattainable standard, and it's good to remember that. "I hate Yahoos of both sexes," he told Ford, adding that even the best, Stella included, were only tolerable "for want of Houyhnhnms."[52]

CHAPTER 25

Gulliver in England

GETTING GULLIVER *INTO PRINT*

In March of 1726, Swift set out for England, after an absence of twelve years. He had a triple motive for the trip. One was to arrange for the publication of *Gulliver's Travels,* which he wanted to come out in the center of the book trade, not in provincial Dublin. This would have to be accomplished in extreme secrecy in case of political reprisals. Another motive was the long-awaited reunion with English friends. And a third was an attempt, fruitless as it turned out, to angle yet again for a Church appointment in England. There would be, in fact, two successive stays in England, of six months apiece—March through August 1726, and April through September 1727.

The boat Swift took landed at Chester, and he left two inscriptions there, one on arrival and the other on his return journey. He scratched these verses on the window of an inn, presumably using a diamond, as it occasionally amused him to do. The first was satirical:

> The church and clergy here, no doubt,
> Are very near a-kin:
> Both weather-beaten are without,
> And empty both within.

The second inscription was bitter:

> J.S.D.S.P.D. hospes ignotus,
> Patriae (ut nunc est) plusquam vellet notus,
> Tempestate pulsus,
> His pernoctavit,
> A.D. 1726

"Jonathan Swift, Dean of St. Patrick's, Dublin, an unknown stranger, but in his own country (such as it now is) better known than he would wish, driven by a storm, spent the night here in the year 1726."[1] A stranger indeed, in the England where he always yearned to live. The initials "J.S.D.S.P.D."—Jonathan Swift, Dean of St. Patrick's, Dublin"—would have been understood in Ireland, but not here.

During his second visit the next summer, Swift stopped off at Goodrich in Herefordshire, where the Reverend Thomas Swift had suffered persecution from the Puritans. He ordered a plaque to be inscribed in his grandfather's memory, and presented the church of St. Giles with a pocket chalice that his grandfather had once used there. On the chalice he had a Latin text engraved: "Thomas Swift, vicar of this church, well known in history for what he did and suffered for King Charles I, administered out of this same chalice to the sick. Jonathan Swift, S.T.D., Dean of the Church of Saint Patrick, Dublin, grandson of the aforesaid Thomas, dedicates this cup to this church in perpetuity, 1726."[2] The chalice still exists, kept at Hereford Cathedral.

Swift was interested to discover that his grandfather's house was still standing, "which by the architecture," as he later described it, "denotes the builder to have been somewhat whimsical and singular." When Deane Swift printed Swift's account he added, "The whole seems to be three single houses all joining in one central point. Undoubtedly there never was, nor ever will be, such another building to the end of the world. However, it is a very good house, and perhaps calculated to stand as long as any house in England."[3]

Gulliver's Travels didn't yet have that title, and Gulliver's name never appears in the book itself. The title was *Travels into Several Remote Nations of the World,* and only on the first page is the author identified as Lemuel Gulliver, "first a surgeon, and then a captain of several ships." It may be that Swift picked up the name on his way from Chester, since he passed through a town whose innkeeper was Samuel Gulliver.[4]

In Dublin, meanwhile, there were rumors that some new satire by Swift was about to come out, and the authorities sent out feelers about it. Thomas

Tickell, an old acquaintance, wrote a friendly inquiry asking to see it. Tickell was secretary to Carteret, the lord lieutenant, and Swift replied pointedly, "As to what you mention of an imaginary treatise, I can only answer that I have a great quantity of papers somewhere or other, of which none would please you, partly because they are very uncorrect, but chiefly because they wholly disagree with your notions of persons and things. Neither do I believe it would be possible for you to find out my treasury of waste papers without searching nine houses and then sending to me for the key."[5]

Swift liked Tickell and admired Carteret, but he wasn't about to give them proof that he was the author of *Gulliver's Travels*. This letter warns Tickell that it would be a waste of time to have the deanery searched, and suggests that any incriminating papers were being moved from one hiding place to the next. It was like being in the underground in occupied territory, which Ireland in effect was. The next day Swift wrote to Sheridan and asked him and "the ladies" to spread the story about the nine houses, "and laugh at my humour in it, etc."[6]

Swift was in no hurry to get *Gulliver* into print, no doubt thinking that his wisest plan would be to leave England before it came out. In due course he made a secretive approach to a publisher named Benjamin Motte, with whose father he had had some dealings in the past, and who was about to publish a three-volume Pope-Swift *Miscellanies* that Pope had put together. Pope reported gleefully that the manuscript was delivered with an appropriate air of mystery. "Motte received the copy (he tells me) he knew not from whence, nor from whom, dropped at his house in the dark from a hackney coach."[7]

The package contained the first of the four voyages of *Gulliver's Travels*, with a promise to send the rest if Motte would give £200 to the anonymous messenger, "who will come in the same manner exactly at 9 o'clock at night on Thursday." In his cover letter Swift adopted the alias of a cousin of Gulliver's named Richard Sympson, promising solemnly that the money would be devoted to "the use of us poor seamen." Motte replied that he couldn't get his hands on that much cash at short notice, but that if Mr. Sympson would accept payment in six months, "I shall thankfully embrace the offer." It was the wisest decision Motte ever made.[8]

FRIENDSHIPS RENEWED

Swift made extended stays at various country estates, including grand ones belonging to Lord Cobham and Lord Bathurst, both of whom were correspondents of his and had poems by Pope dedicated to them. But the place Swift liked best was Pope's own villa at Twickenham on the Thames, ten miles west of London and three miles beyond Sheen. Pope had gotten rich from his translation of Homer, but as a Catholic he had to fear confiscation of his property, so he rented the estate rather than owning it. Swift, incidentally, had no quarrel with Pope's Catholicism, though he teasingly offered a bribe if he would convert to Anglicanism.[9]

Pope described his estate deprecatingly as "three inches of gardening," and added, "I have a theatre, an arcade, a bowling green, a grove, and what not, in a bit of ground that would have been but a plate of salad to Nebuchadnezzar, the first day he was turned to graze." Pope's biographer says sympathetically that he was "a species of country 'squire,' occupant and improver of a small 'estate,' living off annuities, investments, a small inheritance, and other revenues not gained by shopkeeping." Shopkeeping, presumably, was beneath him. But it's hard to see why "squire" and "estate" are put between ironic quotation marks. Nebuchadnezzar would have had to be a voracious feeder, since the theater, arcade, bowling green, and gardens occupied five acres.[10]

78. Pope's villa at Twickenham.

Pope liked to paint an idealized picture of his cozy retreat, secure in an artificial grotto that joined his house to the garden on the other side of the main road. During this period he was creating a personal mythology in which no virtuous person could possibly succeed in the corrupt public arena. To withdraw from the fray was therefore proof of virtue:

> Know, all the distant din that world can keep
> Rolls o'er my grotto, and but soothes my sleep.
> There my retreat the best companions grace,
> Chiefs out of war, and statesmen out of place;
> There St. John mingles with my friendly bowl
> The feast of reason and the flow of soul.[11]

They didn't drink from bowls, of course; Pope was being classical.

Swift never bought into this complacent pose, and when Pope wrote him a letter expressing similar thoughts, he replied, "I have no very strong faith in you pretenders to retirement. You are not of an age for it, nor have gone through either good or bad fortune enough."[12]

St. John was Bolingbroke, who was still addressed by that name although he had been deprived of his title (Oxford, who died in 1724, had been allowed to retain his). Bolingbroke's protestations of contented retirement were even less convincing than Pope's. He received a royal pardon in 1723, nine years after his flight to France, and in 1725 was granted the right to own property once again, at which point he purchased an estate at Dawley near Uxbridge, fifteen miles northwest of London. But far from retreating into obscurity, he immersed himself in anti-Walpole journalism and became the de facto leader of the opposition, which had almost no hope of regaining power.

Pope worshiped Bolingbroke, dedicating the *Essay on Man* to him and calling him "my guide, philosopher, and friend." Swift's feelings were more measured. The letters he and Bolingbroke exchanged show mutual respect, but nothing like the affection that fills Swift's correspondence with Pope or Arbuthnot. Bolingbroke's lament that he had been battered financially seemed especially hollow. "The fall from a million to an hundred thousand pounds," Swift remarked to Pope, "is not so great as from eight hundred pounds a year to one. . . . Such mortals have resources that others are not able to comprehend."[13]

Meanwhile, Bolingbroke went on taking crazy risks, as he always did. In 1733, needing funds to promote his political program, he would secretly

79. Bolingbroke in middle age. Bolingbroke as he would have appeared in 1727, considerably aged, with a receding hairline and no wig.

accept a pension of £3,000 a year from the French government, plus an initial payment of £11,000 up front. As his biographer says, "Such reckless conduct almost defies belief."[14] Rumors of what he was doing reached Walpole, of course, and in 1735 Bolingbroke would be forced to leave England |forever.

A frequent companion during Swift's English visits was John Gay, who hadn't done much since writing his poem on the London streets except to get extremely fat. Gay had made a lot of money with his writing, and then lost every bit of it in the South Sea Bubble. Johnson is probably right to say that Pope and Swift condescended to him: "Gay was the general favourite of the whole association of wits, but they regarded him as a play-fellow rather than a partner, and treated him with more fondness than respect."[15]

Gay's playfulness, though, was precisely what Swift appreciated. His *New Song of New Similes*, which Pope included in a volume of the *Miscellanies*, mingles clichés with preposterous analogies in a very Swiftian way.

As smooth as glass, as white as curds,
  Her pretty hand invites;
Sharp as a needle are her words;
  Her wit, like pepper, bites.

Brisk as a body-louse she trips,
  Clean as a penny dressed;
Sweet as a rose her breath and lips,
  Round as the globe her breast.[16]

Just at this time, Gay revived an idea that Swift had given him years before. Swift once suggested "a Newgate pastoral, among the whores and thieves there." Instead of a mock pastoral, Gay ended up creating a mock opera, and at Twickenham in 1726, with Pope and Swift offering suggestions, he wrote *The Beggar's Opera*. Pope said afterward that neither he nor Swift "did any more than alter an expression here and there." Gay's theme, a highly congenial one for Swift, was that there was no real difference between politicians

80. John Gay. The genial Gay affects an oddly skeptical expression, but has not required the artist to disguise his immense bulk.

and criminals. His Beggar says mordantly that he intended to show "that the lower sort of people have their vices in a degree as well as the rich, and that they are punished for them."[17] The difference is not in the vices, but in who gets punished.

Swift's most valued friend was Pope. It helped that they weren't really competing in the same arena, for as Scott says, Pope was obsessed with literary reputation and Swift with political—"His writings he only valued insofar as they accomplished the purpose for which they were written . . . and in almost every instance he sent them into the world without his name." Pope made this trenchant comment on his friend's anonymity: "Your method of concealing yourself puts me in mind of the bird I have read of in India, who hides his head in a hole while all his feathers and tail stick out."[18]

POETRY AND CULTURE

Though Swift was an accomplished poet, he never aspired to the polished grandeur of Pope's verse. He honored Pope's condensed eloquence:

> In Pope, I cannot read a line
> But with a sigh, I wish it mine:
> When he can in one couplet fix
> More sense than I can do in six,
> It gives me such a jealous fit
> I cry, "Pox take him, and his wit!"

Single lines from Pope have in fact acquired proverbial status. In *An Essay on Criticism*, published in 1711 when he was only twenty-three, familiar expressions repeatedly startle by turning up in their original contexts: "To err is human, to forgive, divine"; "Fools rush in where angels fear to tread"; "A little learning is a dang'rous thing"; "What oft was thought, but ne'er so well expressed."[19]

Swift's gift was for relaxed, colloquial freedom. It's especially interesting that he had a wonderful ear for rhyming, and made it seem natural rather than forced. Sir Walter Scott said of Swift, "Rhyme, which is a handcuff to an inferior poet, he who is master of his art wears as a bracelet." A greater poet than Scott, Lord Byron, told Percy Shelley, "If you are curious in these matters, look in Swift. I will send you a volume; he beats us all hollow, his rhymes are wonderful."[20]

At their best, Swift's poems seem effortless, but of course that's an illusion. He sometimes acknowledged as much:

> How oft am I for rhyme to seek?
> To dress a thought, may toil a week.

Or as he put it still more frankly, in another poem:

> Blot out, correct, insert, refine,
> Enlarge, diminish, interline;
> Be mindful, when invention fails,
> To scratch your head, and bite your nails.[21]

It was during Swift's stay at Twickenham that Pope began a major satire, the *Dunciad*. He later claimed that it seemed so trifling to him that he tried to burn it, but it was "snatched from the fire by Dr. Swift, who persuaded his friend to proceed in it."[22] It isn't likely that Pope needed any persuading, since he labored obsessively on this mock epic for fifteen years, publishing the first installment in 1728 and a final version in 1743. By then it had swollen to seventeen hundred lines denouncing modern culture. Pope named names in a relentless catalogue of Grub Street writers, and ended with a nightmarish vision of the death of civilization.

Swift, who often made use of Grub Street himself, was more sympathetic. He saw the so-called dunces not as villains, but as victims of the cynical consumerism of modern publishing.

> Poor starveling bard, how small thy gains!
> How unproportioned to thy pains!
> And here a simile comes pat in:
> Though chickens take a month to fatten,
> The guests in less than half an hour
> Will more than half a score devour.
> So, after toiling twenty days
> To earn a stock of pence and praise,
> Thy labours, grown the critic's prey,
> Are swallowed o'er a dish of tea;
> Gone to be never heard of more,
> Gone, where the chickens went before.

When Swift describes bad writing, it is with playful glee, not revulsion:

> Or oft, when epithets you link
> In gaping lines to fill a chink,
> Like stepping-stones to save a stride
> In streets where kennels are too wide;
> Or like a heel-piece to support
> A cripple with one foot too short;
> Or like a bridge that joins a marish
> To moorlands of a different parish.[23]

Feeble poets fill gaps with empty epithets; Swift fills them with exuberant analogies.

To some extent, however, Swift went along with the Pope circle's vision of impending doom. When their correspondence was published long afterward, Walpole's son Horace was outraged: "Last night I took up, to divert my thoughts, a volume of letters to Swift from Bolingbroke, Bathurst, and Gay; and what was there but lamentations on the ruin of England, in that era of prosperity and peace, from wretches who thought their own want of power a proof that their country was undone!" Johnson too was offended by their air of superiority. "In the letters both of Swift and Pope there appears such narrowness of mind as makes them insensible of any excellence that has not some affinity with their own, and confines their esteem and approbation to so small a number, that whoever should form his opinion of the age from their representation would suppose them to have lived amidst ignorance and barbarity, unable to find among their contemporaries either virtue or intelligence, and persecuted by those that could not understand them."[24]

There was certainly posturing on Pope's side, and no doubt some on Swift's too, but that's not surprising. In any case, Swift's attitude was more complicated and painful than Johnson's comment would suggest. When Pope plumed himself on constantly acquiring new friends, Swift asserted a deeper standard of friendship: "I believe every man is born with his quantum, and he cannot give to one without robbing another." For Swift the ideal was a close relationship among gifted and like-minded individuals. "I have often endeavoured to establish a friendship among all men of genius, and would fain have it done. They are seldom above three or four contemporaries, and if they could be united would drive the world before them. I think it was so among the poets in the time of Augustus, but envy and party and pride have hindered it among us." Stuck in Dublin, Swift knew he was settling for undemanding sociability rather than connection with kindred spirits: "I choose my companions among those of least consequence and most compliance."[25] Admittedly, "drive the world before them" is a highly aggressive way of describing a writer's stance toward his world.

IN ENGLAND AGAIN, FOR THE LAST TIME

In 1727 Swift was back at Twickenham again. *Gulliver* was in print by then, and the dream of an appointment in England was fading, but he wanted very much to stay close to his friends. During this visit, however, there were signs that he and Pope were beginning to wear on each other. In part they found each other's disabilities frustrating. The tubercular condition that was eroding Pope's bones made him alarmingly infirm. He needed help to get dressed and

81. Alexander Pope. The portrait was sketched by an artist named William Hoare while Pope was in conversation with a friend at the other end of a large gallery. Joseph Warton, who reproduced it in a 1797 edition of Pope's *Works*, said that Pope "would never have forgiven the painter had he known it—he was too sensible of the deformity of his person to allow the whole of it to be represented."

undressed, and was barely able to stand up until he had been laced into a stiff corset. Almost inevitably, he was a demanding companion.

Swift still had his remarkable energy. When he stopped off at Oxford, a clergyman who had known him years before commented, "He is as little altered, I think, of any man I ever saw, in so many years' time." But vertigo and deafness continued to plague him, as he acknowledged in *Dr. Swift to Mr. Pope, While He Was Writing the Dunciad*:

> Pope has the talent well to speak,
>> But not to reach the ear;
> His loudest voice is low and weak,
>> The Dean too deaf to hear.

So Pope would walk about, jotting down lines of verse, while Swift would wear out the day reading when he would rather have been conversing.

> A while they on each other look,
>> Then different studies choose:
> The Dean sits plodding on a book,
>> Pope walks, and courts the Muse.[26]

This little poem gives a vivid impression of the way Pope would play around with poetic fragments until they came together in a finished whole.

> Now backs of letters, though designed
>> For those who more will need 'em,
> Are filled with hints, and interlined,
>> Himself can hardly read 'em.

> Each atom by some other struck
>> All turns and motion tries,
> Till in a lump together stuck,
>> Behold a poem rise![27]

After some months, Swift could no longer stand trying to be sociable, and abruptly departed. Pope reported to the Earl of Oxford (the son of Swift's deceased friend), "The Dean is so much out of order, and withal so deaf, that he has conversed with nobody and fled all company." It was a sad parting, and they both felt it. Swift wrote to Pope from London, "I love and esteem you for reasons that most others have little to do with, and would be the same although you had never touched a pen, further than with writing to me."

Pope replied, "Besides my natural memory of you, you have made a local one, which presents you to me in every place I frequent . . . nor see one seat in my own garden, or one room in my own house, without a phantom of you sitting or walking before me."[28]

In the opinion of Lady Orrery, who knew them both well, "Swift certainly loved Pope from his soul; Pope rather feared than loved Swift." She also distinguished perceptively between Swift's brusqueness and Pope's sinuous politeness: "Pope's mind and conversation was like his gardens, full of windings neatly trimmed. . . . The nettles and thorns were all hid behind the hedges." Johnson said that Pope "hardly drank tea without a stratagem," whereas in Orrery's experience Swift, for all his ironical teasing, "was undisguised and perfectly sincere."[29]

Pope once told a story to illustrate Swift's "odd, blunt way that is mistaken by strangers for ill-nature." When he and Gay dropped in one evening—it's not clear when or where this took place—Swift demanded to know why they had left "all the great lords that you are so fond of to come hither to see a poor Dean." When they assured him that the only hospitality they wanted was his conversation, he proceeded to calculate what he would have had to spend if they had dined with him.

> "Let me see, what should I have had? A couple of lobsters? Aye, that would have done very well—two shillings. Tarts—a shilling. But you will drink a glass of wine with me, though you supped so much before your usual time, only to spare my pocket?"
>
> "No, we had rather talk with you than drink with you."
>
> "But if you had supped with me, as in all reason you ought to have done, you must then have drank with me: a bottle of wine—two shillings. Two and two is four, and one is five: just two and sixpence apiece. There, Pope, there's half a crown for you, and there's another for you, sir, for I won't save anything by you. I am determined."
>
> This was all said and done with his usual seriousness on such occasions, and in spite of everything we could say to the contrary, he actually obliged us to take the money.[30]

Very likely Pope was missing the point. Sheridan thought that Swift felt insulted by his friends' attempt not to put him to expense, with the implausible claim that they had already eaten and didn't even care for wine. "It was clear therefore to him that they had given credit to the common report of his covetousness; and in order to show that he was above such sordid thrift, and to punish them for supposing it, by this practical rebuke, he made them undergo the shame of putting into their pockets what would otherwise have been spent in good fellowship."[31]

There were odd irritations at Pope's table. After Swift was back in Ireland, Gay wrote to say teasingly that Gay's patron, the Duchess of Queensberry, had been shocked when she dined with Swift—"Never more despise a fork with three prongs. I wish too you would not eat from the point of your knife." Swift wrote back indignantly, "Pray tell her Grace that the fault was in Mr. Pope's poetical forks, and not in my want of manners." In a follow-up letter he elaborated: "A knife was absolutely necessary at Mr. Pope's, where it was morally impossible with a bidential fork to convey a morsel of beef with the encumbrance of mustard and turnips into your mouth at once." It seems that Pope liked to use old-fashioned utensils that he had inherited; by this time three-pronged forks had largely replaced two-pronged ones.[32]

When Pope brought out a fourth volume of Pope-Swift *Miscellanies* in 1728, there was further exasperation for Swift. Pope's goal was to get some of his odds and ends into print and to make a bit of money doing so. Swift assumed that each collaborator was going to offer his best work, as equal partners in a major achievement. He had been led to believe that the *Dunciad* would appear in the *Miscellanies*, and was shocked when it didn't. As it turned out, the volume was almost entirely filled by some of Swift's best poems, balanced inadequately by some very minor ones of Pope's.

Pope also left out, without warning that he would, *A Libel on Dr. Delany*, of which Swift was especially proud. The reason was that it praised Pope warmly for his independence:

> Hail! happy Pope, whose gen'rous mind
> Detesting all the statesmen kind. . . .
> His heart too great, though fortune little,
> To lick a rascal statesman's spittle.

Among friends Pope talked big about his independence from court and politics, but in reality he was angling for favor and had no intention of seeing this compliment in print.[33]

In the end, Swift's friendship with Pope was best conducted by mail, not in person, which doesn't make it any less real. Swift wrote from Dublin, "You are the best and kindest friend in the world, and I know nobody alive or dead to whom I am so much obliged; and if ever you made me angry, it was for your too much care about me." In his will he left a portrait of himself "to my dearest friend Alexander Pope of Twittenham, Esq."[34]

CHAPTER 26

Disillusionment and Loss

RENEWED HOPES FOR A LIFE IN ENGLAND

During his 1726 visit to England, Swift made an appointment to see Sir Robert Walpole, intending to make the Irish case for relief in a time of economic crisis. Before he left Dublin he and Archbishop King had worked up a full set of facts and figures. What they didn't know was that Hugh Boulter, the recently appointed archbishop of Armagh and head of the Church of Ireland, had already warned the prime minister to be on guard. Boulter wrote to Walpole: "The general report is that Dean Swift designs for England in a little time, and we do not question his endeavours to misrepresent his Majesty's friends here wherever he finds an opportunity; but he is so well known, as well as the disturbances he has been the fomenter of in this kingdom, that we are under no fear of his being able to disserve any of his Majesty's faithful servants by anything that is known to come from him. But we could wish some eye were had to what he shall be attempting on your side of the water."[1] It was not likely, anyway, that Walpole would have much patience with the Drapier.

When the meeting took place, Walpole did most of the talking, for over an hour. "I failed very much in my design," Swift admitted to the Earl of Peterborough, who had arranged the interview. "Sir Robert Walpole was pleased to enlarge very much upon the subject of Ireland, in a manner so alien from what I conceived to be rights and privileges of a subject of England, that I did not think proper to debate the matter with him as much as I otherwise might, because I found it would be in vain." There were rumors, then and later, that Swift offered concessions of some kind in return for appointment to a bishopric in England, but these were surely unfounded, since he declared that he had sought the meeting "without any view to myself," and asked Peterborough to show the letter to Walpole, who would obviously have known if Swift wasn't telling the truth.[2]

Still, Swift had never given up hope of an English bishopric. At this time he noted down the incomes of nearly fifty English bishops. The archbishop of Canterbury led the field with £6,000 per year. At the bottom were Hereford in England and St. Asaph's in Wales, both at a relatively modest £1,000, which was still £400 more than what Swift received at St. Patrick's.[3]

Giving up on Walpole, Swift pursued other contacts. Bishops were appointed by the Crown, and it was clear that the present king would never reward Swift. But what about the next one? The Prince of Wales, who would succeed his father as George II, was known to dislike the Whig ministry, and it was believed that when he came to the throne he might eject Walpole and bring back the Tories. That would be the chance Swift was waiting for.

Dr. Arbuthnot was a regular visitor to Caroline of Anspach, the prince's wife, and through Arbuthnot she invited Swift to visit at Richmond Lodge, her villa on the Thames near Twickenham. With his usual pride Swift neglected "at least nine times" to respond, or so he later claimed, but eventually he went and was graciously received. He took the occasion to make a joke: "I told her the first time that I was informed she loved to see odd persons, and that having sent for a wild boy from Germany, she had a curiosity to see a wild Dean from Ireland."[4] Princess Caroline promised to give Swift some valuable medals that were soon to be struck, which he took as a great compliment, and she gave the impression that he could expect a splendid promotion when she came to the throne.

In addition, Swift grew close to Henrietta Howard, Caroline's personal servant or "dresser" who was also—in a remarkable ménage à trois—the acknowledged mistress of the prince. She was separated from her disagreeable husband, whom the prince had bought out with a financial settlement. The prince also provided her with Marble Hill, a Thames-side villa not far from Richmond Lodge. Attractive and intelligent, Mrs. Howard was a valued member of the Pope-Arbuthnot-Bolingbroke circle, and Pope paid her a tribute in verse:

> I know the thing that's most uncommon,
> (Envy be silent and attend!)
> I know a reasonable woman,
> Handsome and witty, yet a friend.[5]

At this stage Swift's relationship with both ladies seemed highly promising. After he returned to Ireland in 1726, Arbuthnot wrote to say, "I had a great deal of discourse with your friend her Royal Highness. She insisted upon your wit and good conversation." Those were of course qualities that Arbuthnot himself appreciated, and he went on to say, "I told her Royal Highness, that was not what I valued you for, but for being a sincere honest man, and speaking truth where others were afraid to speak it."[6]

As Swift recalled the relationship later on, the princess enjoyed his teasing bluntness. As he described his own behavior,

> And to her Majesty, God bless her,
> Would speak as free as to her dresser.
> She thought it his peculiar whim,
> Nor took it ill, as come from him.[7]

The dresser was Mrs. Howard, and the expectation was that when her lover became king, she would enjoy the same kind of backstage influence that Abigail Masham once had. As an earnest of friendship, and as a hint to remember needy Ireland, Swift made Mrs. Howard a present of expensive Irish plaid. The princess admired it and had it made into dresses for herself and her children, exactly as Swift hoped would happen.

Delighted at the progress he was making, Swift sent Mrs. Howard a letter signed "Lemuel Gulliver," along with a toy crown. "I beg leave to lay the crown of Lilliput at your feet, as a small acknowledgement of your favours to my book and person. I found it in the corner of my waistcoat pocket, into which I thrust most of the valuable furniture of the royal apartment when the palace was on fire." Swift permitted himself a sly innuendo, recalling that the fire had started when a maid of honor fell asleep while reading a book of romances, and that Gulliver resourcefully put it out by urinating on it. "Did I make use of an improper engine to extinguish a fire that was kindled by a maid of honour?"[8]

In April of 1727 Swift was back in England, and by then it was obvious that the king didn't have long to live. The likelihood of imminent change at the top thwarted an opportunity that Swift would have loved to take advantage of, for Bolingbroke invited him to travel to France. He spoke French reasonably well and was thrilled at the possibility; it would have been the only trip outside the British Isles in his whole life. But just before it was time to depart, Bolingbroke sent an urgent warning: "Much less ought you to think of such an unmeaning journey, when the opportunity of quitting Ireland for England is, I believe, fairly before you." Mrs. Howard herself, in a letter that Swift described but that no longer exists, advised him "by all means not to go; it would look singular, and perhaps disaffected. And to my friends, she enlarged upon the good intentions of the Court towards me. I stayed."[9] There was a new attack of vertigo as well.

"PUT NO TRUST IN PRINCES"

A few days later George I did indeed die, and Swift soon had the opportunity to call upon the new king and queen and to kiss their hands. He also wrote a playful poem called *A Pastoral Dialogue between Richmond Lodge and Marble Hill*, reminding them of their friendship with him:

> Here wont the Dean, when he's to seek,
> To sponge a breakfast once a week;
> To cry the bread was stale, and mutter
> Complaints against the royal butter.[10]

That was Swift's favored posture of cocky independence, criticizing his hosts even while acknowledging that he was sponging off them. This probably felt pleasantly fresh to people who were accustomed to being flattered all the time.

Despite his hopes, Swift had too much experience of the great to be entirely confident, and he began to suspect that Caroline and Henrietta had been leading him on. In this poem, he makes Richmond Lodge quote King David to George II and Queen Caroline:

> The kingly Prophet well evinces
> That we should put no trust in princes.
> My royal master promised me
> To raise me to a high degree,
> But now he's grown a King, God wot,
> I fear I soon shall be forgot.[11]

To Henrietta, Swift was more blunt. Shortly before leaving Twickenham, he sent her a trenchant *Character of Mrs. Howard*. Pope commented, with something like awe, "You have a desperate hand at dashing out a character by great strokes, and at the same time a delicate one at fine touches." According to Swift, Mrs. Howard was exceptionally gifted at interpreting motives, and so subtle that "she can gather early intelligence without asking it, and often when even those from whom she hath it are not sensible that they are giving it to her." She knew how to make people believe that "all present proceedings" were exactly as they should be, "and the danger is that she may come in time to believe herself."[12]

Bitterly, Swift describes an otherwise worthy person who has sold out, in hopes of gaining power in the new court. "In all offices of life except those of a courtier she acts with justice, generosity, and truth. She is ready to do good as a private person, and I would almost think in charity that she will not do harm as a courtier, unless to please those in chief power. . . . If she had never seen a court, it is not impossible that she might have been a friend." With withering irony, Swift foretells what will happen to her good qualities now: "Her private virtues, for want of room and time to operate, will be laid up clean (like clothes in a chest) to be used and put on whenever satiety, or some reverse of fortune, or increase of ill health (to which last she is subject) shall dispose her to retire. In the meantime it will be her wisdom to take care that they may not be tarnished or moth-eaten, for want of airing and turning at least once a year."[13]

When this piece found its way into print after Swift's death, Mrs. Howard had become the Countess of Suffolk, her estranged husband having succeeded to the title. She protested to a friend, "It is very different from that which he sent me himself, and which I have in his own handwriting." No doubt she wanted to believe that, but the original letter has survived, and in fact the changes were trivial. As for Pope, he was more charitable than Swift, and was convinced that she simply didn't have much influence. "But after all, that lady means to do good, and does no harm, which is a vast deal for a courtier."[14]

Meanwhile, John Gay, who like Swift had been encouraged to have great expectations, was fobbed off with an appointment as gentleman usher to a two-year-old princess. Walpole regarded it as a huge joke, and Gay indignantly declined. From then on Swift complained to friends that Lady Suffolk had betrayed their trust, although Lady Betty Germaine told him repeatedly to stop imagining that she ever had that much power. Indeed, Caroline was now making a point of humiliating her rival. Lady Suffolk's biographer believes that this was the reason Gay was offered such an insulting position, and notes also that although Swift never forgave Henrietta for not getting him a position, Gay soon did, and remained on cordial terms with her. As for the downfall of the Whigs, that never happened. Walpole had shrewdly cultivated Caroline but not Henrietta all along, and he now boasted that he had the right sow by the ear.[15]

Lady Suffolk herself sent Swift a challenging rebuke. "You seem to think that you have a natural right to abuse me because I am a woman, and a courtier. I have taken it as a woman and as a courtier ought: with great resentment, and a determined resolution of revenge." She was speaking ironically: far from exacting revenge, she loyally defended Swift when he was falsely accused of writing a forged letter that offended the queen. Lady Suffolk ended her letter with one more attempt at reconciliation: "Am I to send back the crown and plaid, well packed up in *my own Character?* Or am I to follow my own inclination, and continue very truly and very much your humble servant?" Swift sent back a stiff reply, affirming that he knew she had good qualities, but that he could never again regard her as a friend. "If you are weary of your *Character*," he added, "it must lie upon my hands [that is, there was no one else to send it to], for I know no other whom it will fit."[16]

A couple of years later Swift got in a fresh dig at the queen in *Directions for a Birthday Song*, alluding to the odes that the poet laureate was expected to produce for royal birthdays. Unlike his father, George II could speak English when he came to throne, but Swift enjoyed sneering at German names, while urging poets to make the most of the mellifluous "Caroline."

> A skilful critic justly blames
> Hard, tough, cramp, guttural, harsh, stiff names. . . .
> In vain are all attempts from Germany
> To find out proper words for harmony;
> And yet I must except the Rhine,
> Because it clinks to Caroline. . . .
> Three syllables did never meet
> So soft, so sliding, and so sweet.
> Nine other tuneful words like that
> Would prove ev'n Homer's numbers flat.
> Behold three beauteous vowels stand
> With bridegroom liquids hand in hand,

In concord here forever fixed,
No jarring consonant betwixt.[17]

Swift's final salvo against Henrietta and Caroline was written in 1731 but not published until 1739. In *Verses on the Death of Dr. Swift*, he imagines what people will say about him when he's gone.

Kind Lady Suffolk, in the spleen,
Runs laughing up to tell the Queen.
The Queen, so gracious, mild, and good,
Cries "Is he gone? 'Tis time he should.
He's dead, you say? why let him rot;
I'm glad the medals were forgot.
I promised them, I own, but when?
I only was the Princess then;
But now, as consort of the King,
You know 'tis quite a different thing."[18]

An English friend named William King (coincidentally, the same name as the archbishop of Dublin), to whom Swift had entrusted the manuscript, wrote to say that he deleted these lines before publication "because I durst not insert them, I mean the story of the medals. However, that incident is pretty well known, and care has been taken that almost every reader may be able to supply the blanks."[19] Swift was indignant, and got George Faulkner to publish a corrected version in Dublin. Even then, however, it had to be riddled with blank spaces.

In the copy of the poem shown here, the gaps were filled in by someone who was clearly familiar with Swift's manuscript, which he was accustomed to show to his friends (figure 82). The long footnote was by Swift himself: "The medals were to be sent to the dean in four months, but she forgot them, or thought them too dear. The dean, being in Ireland, sent Mrs. Howard a piece of Indian plaid made in that kingdom; which the queen seeing, took from her, and wore it herself, and sent to the dean for as much as would clothe herself and children, desiring he would send the charge of it. He did the former. It cost thirty-five pounds, but he said he would have nothing except the medals. He was the summer following in England, was treated as usual, and she being then queen, the dean was promised a settlement in England, but returned as he went; and instead of favour or medals, hath been ever since under Her Majesty's displeasure."[20]

82. A page from *Verses on
the Death of Dr. Swift.*

THE GATHERING GLOOM

Beyond professional and political disappointment, Swift dreaded a terrible personal loss. Each of his two visits to England was cut short by messages from Sheridan warning that Stella seemed to be close to death. However, the thought of actually being with her when she expired was more than Swift could bear. "I would not for the universe be present at such a trial of seeing her depart. She will be among friends that upon her own account and great worth will tend her with all possible care, where I should be a trouble to her and the greatest torment to myself."[21]

Toward the end of 1726 Stella seemed on the mend, and Swift was able to report, "Mrs. Johnson is much recovered since I saw her first, but still very lean and low." The respite was temporary. In 1727, back in England, he wrote to Sheridan that he feared "the most fatal news that can ever come to me, unless I should be put to death for some ignominious crime."[22]

Four days later Swift wrote again to Sheridan to say that he had kept his latest letter (now lost) unopened for an hour, "with all the suspense of a man who expected to hear the worst news that Fortune could give him." With her usual callousness, Fortune was allowing the trivial Rebecca Dingley to live on. "I brought both those friends over [to Ireland] so that we might be happy together as long as God should please. The knot is broken, and the remaining person, you know, has ill answered the end, and the other who is now to be lost was all that is valuable."[23]

Swift was incapacitated just then by an onslaught of vertigo, which may well have been exacerbated by stress, but as soon as he was well enough to travel he set out for Chester. No ship there was ready to sail, so he pressed on and reached Holyhead three days later after an exhausting journey, up at four every morning and on horseback until nightfall. When he and his new servant, Watt, got close to Holyhead, both of their horses lost shoes and they had to proceed on foot with the horses limping along. As a result, they arrived just too late to catch a ship for Dublin.

The next day the wind had shifted and no ships could sail. The only option was to hang around waiting. To pass the time Swift began keeping a grumpy record now known as the *Holyhead Journal*, mentioning that when they arrived, "I walked on the rocks in the evening, and then went to bed, and dreamt I had got 20 falls from my horse."[24]

It was impossible to have laundry done, lest it be left behind in the hurry, which meant that "I am in danger of being lousy, which is a ticklish point." The inn had no wine, since a previous party had drunk it all. Worst of all, Swift was obliged to exchange grudging civilities with strangers, something he always hated. "In short, I come from being used like an emperor [that is, at court], to be used worse than a dog at Holyhead." Yet in a strange way this tiresome place was a refuge from the frustrations at home. "Here I could live with two or three friends in a warm house, and good wine—much better than being a slave in Ireland."[25]

Not knowing whether Stella was alive or dead, Swift vented his feelings in pungent verse:

> Lo here I sit at Holy Head
> With muddy ale and mouldy bread;

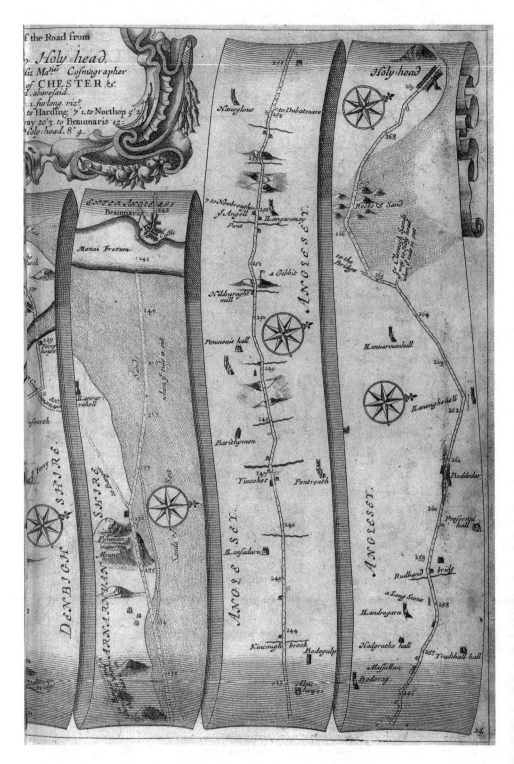

83. The road to Holyhead. In those days what travelers needed was reliable route maps to specific destinations. This one, published during Swift's time at Moor Park, shows the final thirty-six miles of the route from London to Holyhead; the full sequence fills twenty-two of these strips.

> All Christian vittles stink of fish,
> I'm where my enemies would wish. . . .
> But now, the danger of a friend
> On whom my fears and hopes depend,
> Absent from whom all climes are cursed,
> With whom I'm happy in the worst,
> With rage impatient makes me wait
> A passage to the land I hate.[26]

Swift recorded a memorable dream in the *Holyhead Journal*, one that was deeply suggestive, although he always denied that dreams have any meaning—"all are mere productions of the brain, / And fools consult interpreters in vain."

> Last night I dreamt that Lord Bolingbroke and Mr. Pope were at my Cathedral in the gallery, and that my Lord was to preach. I could not find my surplice, the church servants were all out of the way; the doors were shut. I sent to my Lord to come into my stall for more conveniency to get into the pulpit. The stall was all broken; they said the collegians had done it. I squeezed among the rabble, saw my Lord in the pulpit. I thought his prayer was good, but I forget it. In his sermon, I did not like his quoting Mr. Wycherley by name, and his plays. This is all, and so I waked.[27]

As Michael DePorte says, this is "a nightmare of impropriety, violation, and loss." The irreligious Bolingbroke has commandeered Swift's pulpit, and after somehow managing a suitable prayer, starts quoting from racy Restoration comedies instead of the Bible. Meanwhile Swift can't locate his clerical vestments or his church attendants, and he squeezes in among the "rabble" down below, noticing meanwhile that rowdy Trinity College undergraduates have been up to their usual tricks. In his own days at Trinity he was disciplined for causing "tumults" and insulting the authorities. Perhaps this dream is a message from Swift's anarchic hidden self, defying the proprieties he normally had to preach and observe. Bolingbroke, the unbeliever, impersonates Swift like an alter ego expressing his repressed thoughts, while Swift himself is displaced and merges into the crowd.[28]

Swift's concern for propriety is startlingly evident in a letter to John Worrall, his trusted subordinate at the cathedral. "By Dr. Sheridan's frequent letters I am every post expecting the death of a friend with whose loss I shall have very little regard for the few years that Nature may leave me. I desire to know where my two friends lodge." In other words, are Stella and Dingley still in the deanery, where they were accustomed to stay when he was away, or somewhere else? If it's the former—and then Swift switches to Latin for discretion: "I gave a caution to Mrs. Brent that it might not be in domo decanus, quoniam hoc minime decet, uti manifestum est, habeo enim malignos, qui sinistrè hoc interpretabuntur, si eveniet (quod Deus avertat) ut illic moriatur." What he warned his housekeeper was that Stella's death "might not be in the deanery, since that would be most improper, as is evident, for I have enemies who will give it an evil meaning if it happens (which God forbid) that she should die there."[29] It's unlikely that Mrs. Brent understood Latin, but Sheridan or Lyon would translate it for her. Swift was making sure that prying eyes wouldn't grasp his meaning.

Since Stella regularly stayed in the deanery when Swift was known to be away, it is far from clear why it would be scandalous for her to die there. As Sybil Le Brocquy says, "It is obviously impossible to reconcile the man, who so genuinely loved and valued a woman over many years, with the dean, whose chief concern was lest her death cause him embarrassment by taking place in his deanery."[30] If propriety was involved, perhaps it was Stella's reputation rather than his own that concerned Swift. And there may have been emotional anguish as well. If Stella should die in the deanery, he would have to live ever after in a house haunted by her ghost.

STELLA DIES

In 1721 Stella had written a poem for Swift's fifty-fourth birthday that ended,

> Long be the day that gave you birth
> Sacred to friendship, wit, and mirth;
> Late dying may you cast a shred
> Of your rich mantle o'er my head,
> To bear with dignity my sorrow,
> One day alone, then die tomorrow.[31]

Since she was fourteen years younger than Swift, Stella could imagine that she would outlive him. But it was not to be.

By 1725, Stella was wasting away, possibly from tuberculosis. No more jokes about fatness now, as a poem called *A Receipt to Restore Stella's Youth* acknowledges:

> Meager and lank with fasting grown,
> And nothing left but skin and bone.[32]

No annual birthday poem has survived for 1726, and 1727 saw the last, more somber than any before:

> This day, whate'er the fates decree,
> Shall still be kept with joy by me;
> This day, then, let us not be told
> That you are sick, and I grown old. . . .
> From not the gravest of divines
> Accept for once some serious lines.

The divine doesn't suggest that the prospect of eternal bliss will help Stella to face death. Instead, he encourages her to remember the past. She can have no regrets, at least, about how she has conducted her life.

> Say, Stella, feel you no content,
> Reflecting on a life well spent?

In the end the poem turns to Swift himself:

> Me, surely me, you ought to spare,
> Who gladly would your suffering share,
> Or give my scrap of life to you
> And think it far beneath your due;
> You, to whose care so oft I owe
> That I'm alive to tell you so.[33]

In October, Swift composed a prayer:

Restore her to us, O Lord, if it be thy gracious will, or inspire us with constancy and resignation to support ourselves under so heavy an affliction. Restore her, O Lord, for the sake of those poor, who by losing her will be desolate, and those sick, who will not only want [that is, lack] her bounty, but her care and tending; or else, in thy mercy, raise up some other in her place with equal disposition, and better abilities. Lessen, O Lord, we beseech thee, her bodily pains, or give her a double strength of mind to support them. And if thou wilt soon take her to thyself, turn our thoughts rather upon that felicity which we hope she shall enjoy, than upon that unspeakable loss we shall endure.

"Better abilities" must imply someone with as good a heart as Stella, but more money with which to do good. Ehrenpreis observes that he probably read this prayer in Stella's presence.[34]

By December it was obvious that the end was near. Writing to a Dublin clergyman's wife who had recently lost a child, Swift said bleakly, "Life is a tragedy, wherein we sit as spectators awhile, and then act our own part in it. . . . I fear my present ill disposition, both of health and mind, has made me but a sorry comforter."[35]

Stella died in her own lodgings, probably with Sheridan at her side, six weeks short of her fortieth birthday. The news was brought to Swift as he was entertaining friends in the deanery. Apparently he permitted them to stay on until the usual time, and then sat down to begin the memoir entitled *On the Death of Mrs. Johnson*: "This day, being Sunday, January 28th, 1728, about eight o'clock at night, a servant brought me a note with an account of the death of the truest, most virtuous and valuable friend that I, or perhaps any other person, ever was blessed with. She expired about six in the evening of this day, and as soon as I am left alone, which is about eleven at night, I resolve for my own satisfaction to say something of her life and character."[36]

The tone of this memoir is tender and generous, and it gives no hint of an extraordinary exchange that may have occurred shortly before Stella died. There are two versions of the story, both derived at secondhand from Dr. Sheridan. His son's version is the more sensational:

> As she found her final dissolution approach, a few days before it hap-
> pened, in the presence of Dr. Sheridan, she addressed Swift in the most
> earnest and pathetic terms to grant her dying request. That as the cer-
> emony of marriage had passed between them, though for sundry con-
> siderations they had not cohabited in that state, in order to put it out
> of the power of slander to be busy with her fame [that is, reputation]
> after death, she adjured him by their friendship to let her have the sat-
> isfaction of dying, at least, though she had not lived, his acknowledged
> wife. Swift made no reply, but turning on his heel walked silently out
> of the room, nor ever saw her afterwards during the few days she lived.
> This behavior threw Mrs. Johnson into unspeakable agonies, and for a
> time she sunk under the weight of so cruel a disappointment.[37]

Martha Whiteway, the cousin who cared for Swift in his last years, also got the story from Dr. Sheridan. As she recounted it, however, it was Swift who wanted to acknowledge the marriage and Stella who refused:

Before [Sheridan] gave her the sacrament for the last time, she talked largely to him on her intimacy with the Dean. She said she well knew how much her character had suffered: that what the world said had no effect on her because she knew herself his wife, but his being unable to acknowledge her as such had torn her mind until her body was unable to support life. That about three months before her death, he had offered and pressed her to let him acknowledge the marriage, which was all the satisfaction that was then in his power. She answered that it was then too late for her to enjoy the only honour she had ever wished; that her own conduct freed her from any fears of hereafter, and as she was now past the world's farther censures, it would do her no service. Thus died a woman whose merit deserved a better fate.

Is either version of this story true? And if so, how strange that it should echo an equally ambiguous final breach between Swift and Vanessa, five years previously! At any rate, the relationship between Swift and Stella ends as it began, in impenetrable privacy. Perhaps the last word should go to an old lady who lived, long afterward, in the cottage between Trim and Laracor that may have been Stella's. "Some says she was his wife, and some says she wasn't, but whatever she was, she was something to him."[38]

Two days after Stella died, Swift wrote, "This is the night of the funeral, which my sickness will not suffer me to attend. It is now nine at night, and I am removed into another apartment, that I may not see the light in the church, which is just over against the window of my bedchamber." The detail is woundingly revealing; he wouldn't look at the light, but he could well imagine the paving stones opened up and the coffin lowered beneath the cathedral floor. Lyon commented that as dean he would have been obliged to conduct the service himself.[39]

LIVING ON

In her will, signed and dated a month before her death, Stella identified herself as "Esther Johnson, of the city of Dublin, spinster." There were generous bequests to her mother and sister, and money to support a chaplain in Dr. Richard Steevens's hospital, with the thought-provoking proviso "that the said chaplain be an unmarried man at the time of his election, and so continue while he enjoys the office of chaplain to the said hospital; and if he shall happen to marry he shall be immediately removed from the said office, and another chosen in his stead."[40] Perhaps this stipulation reflects Swift's belief that unless a clergyman had independent wealth, he would be a fool to weigh himself down with dependents. He always urged young colleagues not to hurry into marriage, and Sheridan was a case in point of someone with too many mouths to feed.

One clause in particular has excited curiosity: "I bequeath to Bryan M'Loghlin (a child who now lives with me, and whom I keep on charity) twenty-five pounds, to bind him out apprentice as my executors or the survivors of them shall think fit." Nothing more is known about this boy, and there were apparently rumors that Swift might have been the father, though if that were true the bequest would surely have been more generous. Probably he was just what the will said he was.

More remarkably, "my friend, Mrs. Rebecca Dingley," got only "my little watch and chain, and twenty guineas"—a slender enough reward for thirty years of companionship. A servant named Robert Martain got £10 "in consideration of his long and faithful service," and Swift received "my strongbox, and all the papers I have in it or elsewhere." No one knows what those papers were, or whether he destroyed any of them.

One proviso in particular shows the enduring influence of Swift. The money intended for Dr. Steevens's projected hospital was to be carefully invested in land, and the value of the land judiciously improved—the language, indeed, may well have been drafted with Swift's help.

> It is likewise my will that the lands purchased by the said thousand pounds shall be let, without fine, to one or more able tenants for no longer term than forty-one years, at a full rent, with strict penal clauses for planting, enclosing, building, and other improvements; and that no new lease shall be granted till within two years after the expiration of the former lease; and then, if the tenant hath made good improvement and paid his rents duly, he shall have the preference before any other bidder by two shillings in the pound; provided that in every new lease there shall be some addition made to the former rent, as far as the land can bear, so as to make it a reasonable bargain to an improving tenant.

The executors of Stella's will were Sheridan and three other friends.

In the will Stella declared, "I desire that a decent monument of plain white marble may be fixed in the wall over the place of my burial, not exceeding the value of twenty pounds sterling." A white marble tablet did eventually

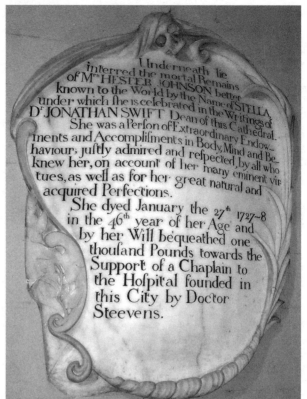

Underneath lie interred the mortal Remains of Mʳˢ HESTER JOHNSON better known to the World by the Name of STELLA under which she is celebrated in the Writings of Dʳ JONATHAN SWIFT Dean of this Cathedral. She was a Person of Extraordinary Endowments and Accomplishments in Body, Mind and Behaviour; justly admired and respected, by all who knew her, on account of her many eminent virtues, as well as for her great natural and acquired Perfections.

She dyed January the 27ᵗʰ 1727–8 in the 46ᵗʰ year of her Age and by her Will bequeathed one thousand Pounds towards the Support of a Chaplain to the Hospital founded in this City by Doctor Steevens.

84. Memorial to Stella, St. Patrick's Cathedral.

appear in St. Patrick's, identifying Hester Johnson as Stella, "justly admired and respected, by all who knew her, on account of her many eminent virtues, as well as for her great natural and acquired Perfections." No one knows who composed this, but it wasn't Swift. Lyon says, "The executors indeed waited for an inscription which he promised to write."[41] But he never did it.

Among Swift's effects, after his own death, was a lock of hair in an envelope on which he had written, "Only a woman's hair." Scott, who saw it, saw this as an instance of "striving to veil the most bitter feelings under the guise of cynical indifference"; Leslie Stephen thought it expressed "indignation at the cruel tragicomedy of life."[42] Nobody seems to have noticed that no name is given. For all we know, the hair could have been Vanessa's.

Stella died before Orrery entered the Swift circle, but when he was working on his biography he solicited recollections from Martha Whiteway, the cousin who cared for Swift in his final years. According to Mrs. Whiteway,

The Dean's grief was violent and lasting. He shut himself up for a week even from the sight of his servant, who was not permitted to make his bed, and took so little nourishment that his friends feared for his life. For many years after, he never named her, and to the last of his understanding [that is, until his final dementia], never without a sigh. He kept two public days [open house for guests] in every week from the time he was made Dean until her death, but then dropped it, and never cared after to see more in his house than a few select friends.[43]

Swift had known Stella for thirty-eight years, and for the past twenty-seven, apart from his stays in England, he had seen her almost every day of their lives.

CHAPTER 27

Frustrated Patriot

SWIFT THE CELEBRITY

In the years following his English trips and Stella's death, Swift's life settled into a general sameness, with few notable events. In his capacity as dean, he was deferred to throughout Dublin. "His reputation for wisdom and integrity was so great," Sheridan said, "that he was consulted by the several corporations [that is, incorporated guilds] in all matters relative to trade, and chosen umpire of any differences among them, nor was there ever any appeal from his sentence. . . . He assumed the office of Censor General, which he rendered as formidable as that of ancient Rome." Lord Carteret, who stayed on as lord lieutenant until 1730, remained on excellent terms with Swift, and afterward wrote to him, "I know by experience how much that city thinks itself under your protection, and how strictly they used to obey all orders fulminated from the sovereignty of St. Patrick's." At another time Carteret said, "When people ask me how I governed Ireland, I say that I pleased Dr. Swift."[1]

Swift once compiled a long list of noble actions recorded by historians, among which was occasion when a theater audience in Rome rose in homage when Virgil came in. It was especially flattering, therefore, when he arrived at Trinity College for a commencement ceremony and everyone spontaneously stood up.[2]

85. Dean Swift, by Francis Bindon.

The best portrait of Swift in his later years was by Francis Bindon. Swift wrote to Sheridan in 1735, "I have been fool enough to sit for my picture at full length by Mr. Bindon for My Lord Howth. I have just sat two hours and a half."[3] The scroll in the portrait reads "The Drapier's fourth letter to the whole people of Ireland." It would have delighted Swift to know that an adaptation of this likeness would one day appear on the Irish £10 note. He would probably have been less pleased to see the pound give way to the euro.

Swift's reputation for wit extended far beyond Dublin. He once had himself shaved by a village barber, who amused him with facetious chatter. When the man found out who his customer was he turned pale, fell on his knees, "and entreated the Dean not to put him into print; for that he was a poor barber, had a large family to maintain, and if his Reverence put him into black and white he should lose all his customers." Swift laughed delightedly, promised not to do it, and gave him a big tip.[4]

With the pronunciation of "dean" as "dane," Swift even became a character in folklore. In a series of tales about Jack (or Paddy) and "the Dane," a clever servant is rewarded for his wit by Swift. None of the tales had any basis in actual events, and Swift appears mainly as a straight man setting up Jack's (or Paddy's) punch lines.[5]

Though he had become Ireland's champion, Swift remained contemptuous of the Irish people for valuing personal comfort more than freedom from oppression. To the end of his days he regarded his confinement to Dublin as a cruel blow:

> With horror, grief, despair, the Dean
> Beheld the dire destructive scene:
> His friends in exile, or the Tower,
> Himself within the frown of power;
> Pursued by base, envenomed pens
> Far to the land of slaves and fens.

Lest any reader should miss the point, he added in a footnote, "The land of slaves and fens is Ireland."[6]

Just a year after the triumph of the Drapier, Swift dated a letter from "wretched Dublin in miserable Ireland," and described himself as "the Dean of St. Patrick's sitting like a toad in a corner of his great house, with a perfect hatred of all public actions and persons." In Yeats's deft aphorism, "Jonathan Swift made a soul for the gentlemen of this city by hating his neighbour as himself."[7]

It needs to be emphasized, however, that when Swift called the Irish slaves, he was referring to servile behavior, not to innate inferiority. Answering a letter from an Irish émigré in Spain, Swift expressed real sympathy for his countrymen. The exploits of the "Wild Geese," Catholic soldiers of fortune who emigrated after the defeat of James II, "ought to make the English ashamed of the reproaches they cast on the ignorance, the dullness, and the want of courage in the Irish natives—those defects, wherever they happen, arising only from the poverty and slavery they suffer from their inhuman neighbours, and the base corrupt spirit of too many of the chief gentry." Swift added that during his travels in Ireland, "I have found the poor cottagers here, who could speak our language, to have much better natural taste for good sense, humour, and raillery, than ever I observed among people of the like sort in England. But the millions of oppressions they lie under, the tyranny of their landlords, the ridiculous zeal of their priests, and the general misery of the whole nation, have been enough to damp the best spirits under the sun."[8]

In conversation with a friend—probably Delany, who told the story—Swift demanded to know "whether the corruptions and villainies of men in power did not eat his flesh, and exhaust his spirits." When the reply was negative, he asked in a fury, "Why—why—how can you help it, how can you avoid it?" His friend replied calmly, "Because I am commanded to the contrary: 'Fret not thyself because of the ungodly.' This raised a smile, and changed the conversation to something less severe and sour."[9]

Swift relished the esteem in which he was held. Celebrations, with bells ringing and bonfires, commemorated his birthday each November 30. Taverns sprang up called the Drapier's Head, with signs showing Swift in clerical garb, and ships were christened the *Drapier*. He was quick to take offense if he ever felt undervalued. In 1730 the Dublin Corporation voted to give him a gold box ("the value thereof not to exceed 25 pounds") as a freeman of the city, and Cork paid him the same compliment, offering a silver box rather than gold. But neither one was inscribed, and Swift was deeply offended. In his remarks to the lord mayor and aldermen of Dublin, he declared that he had done Ireland much service. He had obtained remission of First Fruits for the Church; he had lent his own money to tradesmen and thereby rescued "above two hundred families in this city from ruin"; and with the *Drapier's Letters* he had saved the nation from cynical exploitation by England. In short, it seemed only proper "that an inscription might have been graven on the box, showing some reason why the city thought fit to do him that honour."[10]

As for the silver box, Swift returned it to Cork, with the comment that the city should present it to "some more worthy person whom you may have an intention to honour, because it will equally fit everybody." After it was inscribed and re-sent, he accepted it, but it is mentioned sarcastically in his will: "I bequeath to Mr. John Grattan, Prebendary of Clonmethan, my silver box in which the freedom of the city of Cork was presented to me; in which I desire the said John to keep the tobacco he usually cheweth, called pigtail."[11]

THE DEAN IN HIS DOMINION

At the cathedral and in the surrounding Liberty of St. Patrick's, Swift ruled supreme. He told Pope in 1733, "I am Lord Mayor of 120 houses; I am absolute lord of the greatest cathedral in the kingdom; am at peace with the neighboring princes, the Lord Mayor of the city and the Archbishop of Dublin; only the latter, like the King of France, sometimes attempts encroachments on my dominions."[12] In 1729 death had come for Archbishop King; this reference is to his unworthy successor.

For most bishops Swift felt indifference or contempt; they were Whig mediocrities, notorious for neglecting their duties. One of the exceptions, Archbishop Bolton of Cashel, lamented that "a true Irish bishop has nothing more to do than to eat, drink, grow fat, rich, and die." The bishop of Elphin, who owed his appointment to impressing aristocrats with his skill in watercolors, hardly ever visited his diocese, and the bishop of Clonfert spent the last decades of his eighty-eight years in hopeless senility while his diocese was governed by his wife.[13]

An Irish peer remembered Swift's deadpan comment when someone complained about these appointments: "Ye are in the wrong to blame his Majesty before you know the truth. He sent us over very good and great men, but they were murdered by a parcel of highwaymen between Chester and London, who slipping on their gowns and cassocks here pretend to pass for those bishops."[14]

Swift took a strong interest in the financial plight of his Dublin neighbors, especially the weavers, whom repressive trade regulations condemned to poverty. Over the years he lent large sums of money, with the proviso that he be paid back in installments. As Craik observes, he believed that lack of self-reliance contributed to Ireland's suffering, and he wanted the people he helped to feel like independent businessmen, not recipients of charity. In a sermon on "doing good," he observed that "the very example of honesty and industry in a poor tradesman will sometimes spread through a neighbour-hood, when others see how successful he is." Fifty years later, the younger Sheridan said that many families "owed the foundation of their fortunes to the sums borrowed from this fund."[15]

Swift also made a constant practice of giving money to beggars. To avoid arrest for vagrancy, they usually had little odds and ends for sale, and he invariably overpaid, "for every halfpenny-worth, at least sixpence, and for every pennyworth, a shilling." He made a point of keeping coins in various denominations in different pockets, so that he would always have something to give.[16]

Perhaps it was in order to keep his distance from the beggars that Swift gave several old women satirical nicknames. "He called them his mistresses," Orrery said, "and carried his friends frequently to visit and relieve them in the streets. He named them Stumpanthe, Fritterilla, Ulcerissa, Cancerina and Fourleganda. Stumpanthe had lost one of her hands. Fritterilla was lame and made apple fritters for shoe boys. Ulcerissa was full of sores. Cancerina had a sore breast. Fourleganda went upon her arms and knees."[17]

Several hospitals were founded in Dublin during this period, and Swift decided to leave his own fortune to establish a hospital for the insane, who were wandering the streets with no support system at all. There was no thought of tactful euphemisms, and in his will Swift called them "idiots and lunatics." At the end of *Verses on the Death of Dr. Swift* he said sarcastically,

> He gave the little wealth he had
> To build a house for fools and mad,
> And showed by one satiric touch
> No nation wanted it so much.

The "satiric touch" was presumably Swift's last great satire, *A Modest Proposal*. But his bitterness in no way extended to the afflicted residents of St. Patrick's Hospital, as it came to be known. A history of the hospital emphasizes the sincerity of his concern for the mentally ill, and says that the foundation "was very far from being a satire in stone."[18]

"A PROJECT FOR EATING CHILDREN"

In 1728 Swift and Sheridan launched a weekly periodical called the *Intelligencer*, a popular name for newspapers since they gave "intelligence" of current affairs. Actually, it consisted of short essays, not news, in the manner of the *Examiner* years before. The authors were supposed to share the writing equally, but in the end Sheridan did most of it. It lasted barely a year, never made any money, and was discontinued after nineteen numbers.

Swift's gloom was deepening, and in 1729 he wrote to Bolingbroke and Pope: "I never wake without finding life a more insignificant thing than it was the day before, which is one great advantage I get by living in this country, where there is nothing I shall be sorry to lose; but my greatest misery is recollecting the scene of twenty years past, and then all on a sudden dropping into the present." Twenty years previously, the short-lived era of Tory rule was about to begin.[19]

Yet it was from this gloom that a masterpiece suddenly emerged, the short piece that Swift referred to as "a project for eating children." During the 1720s a series of terrible harvests had reduced the rural population to near starvation, and a brutally cold winter in 1728–29 made conditions intolerable. "The

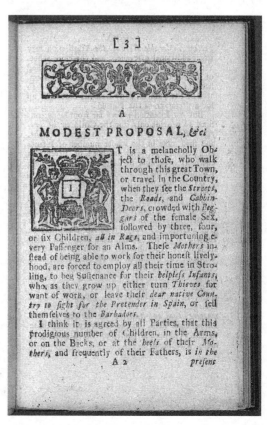

86. *A Modest Proposal.* The first page of the original 1729 edition (sixteen small pages in all, six and a half inches high). As is typical of Swift's pamphlets, it is quite crudely printed, in no way presented as a work of literature.

cry of the poor for bread," Archbishop King wrote movingly in the final year of his life, "is a stab to my heart, to find them dying every day for want, and being unable to relieve them."[20]

After publishing a long series of carefully thought-out commentaries, none of which had any effect, Swift brought out *A Modest Proposal for Preventing the Children of Poor People in Ireland from Being a Burden to Their Parents or Country, and for Making Them Beneficial to the Public.* It fills less than ten pages in a modern edition, and in its unimposing original form it looked like just another routine economic tract.

A number of writers had published "modest proposals" for addressing the crisis, and Swift begins by mimicking their earnest, objective tone. "It is a melancholy object to those who walk through this great town, or travel in the country, when they see the streets, the roads, and cabin doors crowded with beggars of the female sex, followed by three, four, or six children, all in rags, and importuning every passenger for an alms. These mothers, instead of being able to work for their honest livelihood, are forced to employ all their time in strolling to beg sustenance for their helpless infants." This was no exaggeration. During his tour of Ireland after the death of Vanessa, Swift had found the plain of Tipperary to be "like the rest of the whole kingdom, a bare face of nature, without houses or plantations—filthy cabins, miserable, tattered, half-starved creatures, scarce in human shape."[21] That was in 1723, and conditions were far worse now.

Economists at the time—like many later—took a detached view of experience, reducing lives to statistics and deploying coldly objective language. It was widely agreed that since labor creates value, people were the wealth of a nation. Swift had no quarrel with that principle, except that he believed England's abuse of Ireland made it the one country in which the truism wasn't true. "This is the only Christian country," he wrote, "where people, contrary to the old maxim, are the poverty and not the riches of the nation."[22]

Now, if people really are the wealth of a nation, it follows that small children must be a financial drain, since they're too young to contribute labor. But what if there were a way of cashing them in? A note of indignation begins to invade the reasonable tone: "A child just dropped from its dam may be supported by her milk for a solar year with little other nourishment, at most not above the value of two shillings, which the mother may certainly get, or the value in scraps, by her lawful occupation of begging." The term *dam* belongs to animal husbandry, while "the value in scraps" is a grim reminder of the depths of poverty.

Swift is entirely serious when he speaks of "that horrid practice of women murdering their bastard children, alas! too frequent among us; sacrificing the poor innocent babes, I doubt [that is, suspect], more to avoid the expense than the shame, which would move tears and pity in the most savage and inhuman breast." The lot of poor children was indeed dreadful, and infanticide was far from uncommon.[23]

So why not make infanticide commercially valuable? Colonial planters knew all about buying and selling human beings:

> I have been assured by a very knowing American of my acquaintance in London that a young healthy child, well nursed, is at a year old a most delicious, nourishing, and wholesome food, whether stewed, roasted, baked, or boiled; and I make no doubt that it will equally serve in a fricassee or a ragout. . . . A child will make two dishes at an entertainment for friends, and when the family dines alone, the fore or hind quarter will make a reasonable dish, and seasoned with a little pepper or salt, will be very good boiled on the fourth day, especially in winter. . . . I rather recommend buying the children alive, and dressing them hot from the knife, as we do roasting pigs.

Edmund Wilson once commented that Swift shared with Marx "a deadly sense of the infinite capacity of human nature for remaining oblivious or indifferent to the pains we inflict on others, when we have a chance to get something out of them for ourselves."[24]

A Modest Proposal continues in a strain that would be completely insane if it weren't so obviously ironic.

> I grant this food will be somewhat dear, and therefore very proper for landlords, who, as they have already devoured most of the parents, seem to have the best title to the children. . . . I have already computed the charge of nursing a beggar's child (in which list I reckon all cottagers, labourers, and four-fifths of the farmers) to be about two shillings per annum, rags included; and I believe no gentleman would repine to give ten shillings for the carcass of a good fat child, which, as I have said, will make four dishes of excellent nutritive meat, when he hath only some particular friend or his own family to dine with him. Thus the squire will learn to be a good landlord, and grow popular among his tenants; the mother will have eight shillings net profit, and be fit for work till she produceth another child. Those who are more thrifty

(as I must confess the times require) may flay the carcass; the skin of which, artificially dressed, will make admirable gloves for ladies, and summer boots for fine gentlemen.

And what about the elderly? "I am not in the least pain upon that matter, because it is very well known that they are every day dying, and rotting, by cold, and famine, and filth, and vermin, as fast as can be reasonably expected."

Swift's pamphlet is of course a protest against English exploitation of Ireland: "I could name a country, which would be glad to eat up our whole nation." But fundamentally it is a rebuke aimed at the Irish themselves, for complicity in their own exploitation. By their feckless inaction, Swift told Pope, they "are all inevitably undone; which I have been telling them in print these ten years, to as little purpose as if it came from the pulpit." In an earlier pamphlet he had quoted the book of Proverbs: "Wisdom crieth in the streets, because I have called and ye refused; I have stretched out my hand, and no man regarded. But ye have set at naught all my counsel, and would none of my reproof. I also will laugh at your calamity, and mock when your fear cometh."[25]

Terse and perfectly paced, *A Modest Proposal* is so skillfully constructed that it still has the power to startle, even if one has read it many times before. And for anyone who meets it for the first time, it explodes like a land mine. When the Gaiety Theatre reopened in Dublin in 1984, the actor Peter O'Toole gave a reading of *A Modest Proposal*, saying he had chosen a piece "with a little something to offend everybody." The result was a mass walkout. One headline reported, "O'Toole Defends 'Disgusting' Reading."[26]

Swift was rightly proud of his skill as an ironist, and what makes his irony distinctive is the passionate emotion that drives it. Simple irony merely says one thing but means the opposite. Swift's ironic mode is more profound. "Real irony," T. S. Eliot said, "is an expression of suffering, and the greatest ironist was the one who suffered the most—Swift."[27]

During the 1730s Swift published a few more pamphlets, cranky and eccentric for the most part, but his heart wasn't in them. *A Modest Proposal* is a cry of despair. When a stranger wrote to praise "your public spirit and great affection to your native country," Swift replied that he was "a Teague, or an Irishman, or what people please" only by accident of birth, and that "what I did for this country was from perfect hatred of tyranny and oppression." In another letter he said grimly, "Looking upon this kingdom's condition as absolutely desperate, I would not prescribe a dose to the dead."[28]

BADGING BEGGARS

One issue in particular did concern Swift during the 1730s, and one of the last things he wrote is also one of the most unsettling. Published in 1737 just before he turned seventy, it was entitled *A Proposal for Giving Badges to the Beggars in All the Parishes of Dublin, by the Dean of St. Patrick's*. Why badges?

A city workhouse had existed since 1704, but it never made much difference, and pedestrians like Swift found begging exasperating (people in coaches could ignore it). The situation was so bad, he claimed, that shopkeepers were letting crowds of beggars besiege their doors, "to the great disgust and vexation of many customers, whom I have frequently observed to go to other shops rather than suffer such a persecution." But there was a simple solution. "A 'prentice with a horsewhip is able to lash every beggar from the shop, who is not of the parish, and doth not wear the badge of that parish on his shoulder, well fastened and fairly visible."[29]

Ireland had no "poor law" like the one that had been passed in England in 1662, but Swift wished it did. Under the English law, a destitute person's parish was responsible for supporting him or her. The parish was defined as the place where one was born or married, rented a house, or had been employed for at least a year. The hordes of "vagrants" who congregated in towns and cities, seeking work that often didn't exist, were therefore supposed to be driven back to the villages they came from.

Swift's plan, first proposed back in 1726, was that every beggar should be required to display a badge, which would carry the initial letters of a parish and a number to identify the individual. Those who were physically unable to work needed help, but able-bodied people should be forced to do useful work instead of begging. Whether there were ever enough jobs was a serious question, and Swift did take it seriously—that was the burden of his many polemics against England's suppression of Irish industries. But if the immediate concern was to distinguish the truly needy from those who only pretended to be, then the best judges would be those who knew poor people in their local parishes.

Within the parish, though, Swift saw charity as a moral obligation. To illustrate the word "alms," Johnson quoted a sentence from one of Swift's sermons: "The poor beggar hath a just demand of an alms from the rich man, who is guilty of fraud, injustice, and oppression if he doth not afford relief according to his abilities." And Swift practiced what he preached, showing constant generosity to the poor in his own neighborhood. His account books are full of entries such as "charity 2s 8d," "poor woman 2s 8d," "gave old woman 6 1/2d," and "poor boy 6 1/2d." He was also a contributor to numerous hospitals and charity schools, and an active director of several.[30]

What makes Swift's pamphlet disturbing is not just the call for whipping, but the swelling contempt he shows for the poor. In his economic pamphlets he had described clearly how structural problems kept the nation in poverty: English policies drained wealth from Ireland, which was not allowed to make rational arrangements for itself, and agents working for absentee landlords ground down their tenants still further. But when it came to poor people themselves, Swift still thought in conventional moral terms and insisted that they were personally to blame for their plight. "I am confident that among the meaner people, nineteen in twenty of those who are reduced to a starving condition did not become so by what lawyers call the work of God, either upon their bodies or goods, but merely from their own idleness, attended with all manner of vices, particularly drunkenness, thievery, and cheating. . . . [They are] a profligate clan of thieves, drunkards, heathens, and whoremongers, fitter to be rooted out off the face of the earth than suffered to levy a vast annual tax upon the city."[31]

As Nokes says, this was "a chilly and unforgiving note" on which to end a publishing career, but it's also true that sensibilities were different then. The kindly Delany thought that the *Proposal for Giving Badges to Beggars* was "the wisest, the best judged, the most practicable, and the most Christian scheme for relieving all those who were proper objects of charity."[32]

It's true, too, as a historian comments, that Swift tended to see moral explanations for all kinds of social problems—"hence the recurrent denunciations of greedy landlords and graziers, vain women addicted to expensive imported fabrics, dishonest dealers and idle workmen, that supplement his complaints of English oppression." But if this moral emphasis neglected some deep structural causes of poverty, it gave Swift's writing its exceptional power. And as the same writer says, it enabled Swift "to point up contradictions and flaws in the fabric of early eighteenth-century Ireland which other members of that society ignored, glossed over, or concealed."[33]

Whatever people thought of Swift's views on beggars, his popularity was undiminished. In the year in which this pamphlet was published, his birthday was celebrated, according to the *Dublin Journal*, "with the utmost expressions of joy and gratitude by all the people in and about the Liberty of St. Patrick's, and in many parts of the city and suburbs. The bells rang as usual on the most solemn occasions, nineteen petararoes were fired several rounds, four large bonfires were upon the steeple, and the windows illuminated."[34] (A petararo was a small cannon.)

And Swift still had his remarkable energy, as attested in an anonymous poem, *A Pun on Dr. Swift, D.S.P.D., Proving Him Immortal:*

> If DEATH denotes to be at rest,
> Of SWIFT he'll never be possessed:
> As sure as water's in the ocean,
> While SWIFT is SWIFT, he is in motion;
> Then while in motion 'tis confessed
> That SWIFT will never be at rest.
> What's SWIFT is QUICK; then on this head,
> SWIFT can't at once be QUICK and DEAD.[35]

CHAPTER 28

Swift among the Women

LA BAGATELLE

When the 1730s arrived, Swift still had fifteen years to live, and his mood would darken throughout those years. He predicted to Bolingbroke that he would die in Ireland "in a rage, like a poisoned rat in a hole." Any writing he did now was only to while away the time, and he destroyed most of it. "I love *la bagatelle* better than ever; for finding it troublesome to read at night, and the company here growing tasteless, I am always writing bad prose or worse verses, either of rage or raillery, whereof some few escape to give offence or mirth, and the rest are burnt."[1] "Tasteless" probably means "insipid."

The bagatelles often took the form of language games with Sheridan, who addressed a letter "Tooth ay Revere End Dock tore Jo Nathan Dray Peer, Gull Liver, Inn They Dane a wry" (to the Reverend Doctor Jonathan Drapier, Gulliver, in the Deanery). The game was to find real English words and use them absurdly out of context. Another time Sheridan wrote, "Yew no eye promiss said too right yew a nun inn tell liege eye bell let her. He writ is. Eye main ass crop off it" (You know I promised to write you an unintelligible letter. Here it is. I mean, a scrap of it). Swift's riposte was a stream of gibberish that made sense if read as Latin—"eat red eye, add nose sight O." That translates as "et redi ad nos cito," which in English would mean "and return to us with haste."[2]

87. Swift in informal attire.

All of this may look like a waste of time, but verbal puzzles were at least evidence for Swift that his mind hadn't stopped working. Scott comments that Sheridan's playful humor coaxed him out of his dark moods, so that friends called Sheridan "the David who alone could play the evil spirit out of Saul."[3]

We don't hear much about other male friends during this period. Delany probably wearied Swift with his humorless earnestness, and when he made a list of "grateful" and "ungrateful" friends, Delany appeared in it as "indifferent partly grateful." "When [Swift] met with gratitude," Dr. Lyon said, "he got his reward, and expected no other."[4] He may not have expected favors to be reciprocated, but he did want them appreciated.

Other friends were leaving Ireland, as Ford did in 1732, or else departing from life altogether. Gay sent a chatty letter urging Swift to come over for a visit in the spring. Less than three weeks later Pope and Arbuthnot wrote to say that "an inflammatory fever hurried him out of this life in three days." Arbuthnot diagnosed it as "a mortification of the bowels; it was the most precipitate case I ever knew." Swift noted on this letter, "Received December 15, but not read till the 20th, by an impulse foreboding some misfortune."[5]

Pope composed a condescending epitaph for Gay:

> Of manners gentle, of affections mild;
> In wit a man; simplicity, a child. . . .
> A safe companion, and an easy friend,
> Unblamed through life, lamented in thy end.

These lines were inscribed on Gay's monument in Westminster Abbey, but so was a more memorable epitaph that he had composed for himself:

> Life is a jest, and all things show it;
> I thought so once, but now I know it.[6]

Swift's one new male friend of any consequence was John Boyle, fifth Earl of Orrery, who was twenty-five when he turned up in Dublin in 1732. Swift had known his father, the editor of the ill-fated *Epistles of Phalaris* that Sir William Temple championed, and he took to the young man immediately. He was "absolutely the most hopeful young gentleman I ever saw," he told Pope, and to Orrery himself he sent extravagant praise: "Your learning, your genius, your affability, generosity, the love you bear to your native country and your compassion for this [that is, Ireland]; the goodness of your nature, your humility, modesty, and condescension; your most agreeable conversation, suited to all tempers, conditions, and understandings."[7]

Swift's other friends were deeply resentful of Orrery's presumptuousness and aristocratic snobbery. They would doubtless have appreciated Johnson's devastating assessment: "Respect him you could not, for he had no mind of his own." Swift evidently came around to that view, and Orrery was shocked, going through some of Swift's papers after his death, to come upon an unopened letter from himself marked "This will keep cold." Lyon saw another letter that was dismissed even more decisively: "Sad this—very wretched!—Oh! sick—worse!—dead!—stone dead."[8] These discoveries no doubt help to explain why Orrery was often ungenerous in his memoir of Swift.

"A CONSTANT SERAGLIO"

The friends Swift enjoyed the most were all female. "A constant seraglio of very virtuous women," Orrery called them, adding that they "attended him from morning till night, with an obedience, an awe, and an assiduity that are seldom paid to the richest or the most powerful lovers; no, not even to the Grand Seignor [the Turkish sultan]." According to the younger Sheridan, Orrery himself "was during his lifetime Swift's greatest flatterer." To be sure, Swift didn't mind being flattered now and then. As he acknowledged in *Cadenus and Vanessa*,

> 'Tis an old maxim in the schools
> That flattery's the food of fools;
> Yet now and then your men of wit
> Will condescend to take a bit.[9]

These women clearly found it satisfying to have a brilliant friend who responded not only to their charm—which he did—but to their intelligence and wit as well. Besides, he loved to flirt, and they could flirt in return without compromising themselves; he was thirty or forty years older than most of them, and they saw him in company rather than alone. Lady Mary Wortley Montagu picked up on Orrery's analogy and called Swift "a master eunuch in a seraglio," but that was missing the point of these friendships.[10]

In *A Letter to a Young Lady on Her Marriage*, written in 1723 when tension in the Vanessa and Stella relationships was at its height, Swift's message was that a bride needs to develop qualities that will earn "true rational love and esteem" after her youthful attractions have faded. As for romantic love, it is dismissed: "I hope you do not still dream of charms and raptures, which marriage ever did and ever will put a sudden end to. Besides, yours was a match of prudence and common good liking, without any mixture of that ridiculous passion which hath no being but in play-books and romances."[11]

Samuel Richardson made his heroine Pamela say that "this piece looks more like the advice of an enemy to the *sex*, and a bitter one too, than a friend to the *particular lady*." But it helps to know who the particular lady was. She was a teenager named Deborah Staunton, recently married to John Rochfort, whom Swift knew by the nickname Nim (for Nimrod, because he loved to hunt). She was naïve, unworldly, poorly educated, and rather spoiled, and she was fourteen years younger than her headstrong and tight-fisted husband. The marriage was indeed arranged between the two families, and unlikely to have been a love match. So when Swift gave advice about books and behavior that can "in time make yourself worthy of him," he may well have believed that was Deborah's only hope for happiness.[12]

Far from being a misogynist, as is sometimes charged, Swift was ahead of his time in his attitude toward gender. In an unfinished essay, *Of the Education of Ladies*, he criticized "the modern way of training up both sexes in ignorance, idleness, and vice." He wanted to refute the assumption, then held by most women and nearly all men, that the last things to look for in a wife were "good natural sense, some taste of wit and humour, sufficiently versed in her own natural language, able to read and relish history, books of travels, moral or entertaining discourses, and be a tolerable judge of the beauties in poetry." The pioneer feminist Mary Wollstonecraft said similar things seventy years later: "Women are told from their infancy, and taught by the example of their mothers, that a little knowledge of human weakness, justly termed cunning, softness of temper, *outward* obedience, and a scrupulous attention to a puerile kind of propriety, will obtain for them the protection of man; and should they be beautiful, everything else is needless, for at least twenty years of their lives."[13]

Several members of the seraglio—Laetitia Pilkington, Constantia Grierson, Mary Barber—were aspiring writers, and Swift gave them generous encouragement. Writing to Pope, he referred to them affectionately as his "triumfeminate." Unfortunately, Mary Barber caused him serious embarrassment. He had enlisted Pope's help to get her poems published, and a forged letter reached Queen Caroline, ostensibly from Swift himself, that called her "the best female poet of this or perhaps of any age." Swift's own contribution to her book was a much more measured recommendation:

> She seemeth to have a true poetical genius, better cultivated than could well be expected, either from her sex or the scene she hath acted in, as the wife of a citizen [her husband was a woolen draper]. Yet I am assured that no woman was ever more useful to her husband in the way of his business. Poetry hath only been her favorite amusement; for which she hath one qualification that I wish all good poets possessed a share of, I mean that she is ready to take advice, and submit to have her verses corrected by those who are generally allowed to be the best judges.[14]

In truth Mary Barber's poems weren't much good, and Swift may have been making excuses for them. As for the forged letter, he was extremely upset about it, but for some reason he never suspected Barber herself of writing it.

In Dr. Delany's hospitable circle, Swift encountered Frances Kelly, a young admirer who knew how to respond to being teased. On one occasion he threatened to fine her a shilling for some transgression, and she responded with a saucy note (commenting, "I am half asleep, so don't be angry at these

88. Mary Pendarves.

blots"): "I acknowledge to be indebted to the Reverend Doctor Swift, Dean of St. Patrick's, the sum of o*l*. 1*s*. 1½ *d*. per value received, this 2nd day of Feb. 1733." The extra penny and a half was the difference between the Irish shilling and the English. Three months later, however, Frances's impertinence was less excusable, for she wrote abjectly, "I am sure if you knew what I have suffered for having offended you, your anger would be changed into pity; for indeed, Sir, my uneasiness cannot be expressed. . . . . I spent so bad a night from the thoughts of my misfortune that could you have had an idea of it, you would have been sorry for me."[15]

A friend whom Swift especially valued was the spirited and artistic Mary Pendarves, in her early thirties when she arrived in Dublin. She wrote to a relative, "Swift is a very *odd companion* (if that expression is not too familiar for so extraordinary a genius); he talks a great deal and does not require many answers; he has infinite spirits, and says abundance of good things in his common way of discourse." Frances Kelly was the favorite just then, and Mary Pendarves added with some asperity, "Miss Kelly's beauty and good humour have gained an entire conquest over him, and I come in only *a little by the by.*"[16] Soon afterward Frances fell seriously ill, and within a few months she was dead.

Mary Pendarves's story is a striking illustration of the predicament of women in eighteenth-century society. Born to a distinguished family as Mary Granville, she was forced at seventeen to marry a sixty-year-old family friend for financial reasons. "I thought him ugly and disagreeable; he was fat, much afflicted with gout, and often sat in a sullen mood, which I concluded was from the gloominess of his temper. . . . I was married with great pomp. Never was woe dressed out in gayer colours, and when I was led to the altar, I wished from my soul I had been led, as Iphigenia was, to be sacrificed. I *was* sacrificed. I lost, not life indeed, but I lost all that makes life desirable."[17] To her great relief, the unpleasant Mr. Pendarves died in 1724, after six years of marriage. But he had neglected to alter his will, and she inherited nothing.

Swift sent Mary some pleasantly witty compliments some years later, when she had moved back to England:

> A pernicious heresy prevails here among the men, that it is the duty of your sex to be fools in every article except what is merely domestic. . . . If you will come over [to Ireland] to my assistance, I will carry you about among our adversaries, and dare them to produce one instance where your want of ignorance makes you affected, pretending, conceited, disdainful, endeavouring to speak like a scholar, with twenty more faults objected by themselves, their lovers, or their husbands. But I fear your case is desperate, for I know you never laugh at a jest before you understand it, and I much question whether you understand a fan or have so good a fancy at silks as others.

"Want of ignorance" is a deft way of indicating the empty-headed state that most men wanted to find in women. As for not attempting to speak like a scholar, Swift despised pedantry and never talked that way himself. He added that the people he liked would eventually offend him with a *boutade*, "a sudden yerk from a horse's hinder feet which you did not expect," but that Mary had never once done so.[18]

In another letter Swift paid an even more striking compliment. "I believe, Madam . . . I think myself to be in your company, where I could never be weary; no, it is otherwise, for in such a case I would rather choose to be your silent hearer and looker-on." She was able to volley back witty compliments

89. Laetitia Pilkington.

in his own vein: "You call yourself by a great many ugly names, which I take ill, for I never could bear to hear a person I value abused."[19]

Mary Pendarves was good friends with the Delanys as well as with Swift, and when Delany's wife died she married him. But that happened not long before Swift's death, when he was no longer capable of grasping it. Edmund Burke knew her in later life, and told a friend, "I wish you had known Mrs. Delany! She was a perfect pattern of a *perfect* fine lady; a *real* fine lady of other days. Her manners were faultless; her deportment was of marked elegance; her speech was all sweetness; and her air and address were all dignity. I always looked up to Mrs. Delany as the model of an accomplished gentlewoman of former times."[20]

The friend about whom we know the most, because she left a sprightly memoir, was Laetitia Pilkington. She was married to a young clergyman named Matthew Pilkington whom Swift took up for a while, and she was unusually good at witty conversation in the style Swift enjoyed. Her account of her very first evening with him is brilliantly described. He immediately launched a disconcerting challenge:

> "Pray, madam," says he, "do you smoke?" "No indeed, Sir," says I. "Nor your husband?" "Neither, sir." "'Tis a sign," said he, "you were neither of you bred in the University of Oxford, for drinking and smoking are the first rudiments of learning taught there, and in those two arts no university in Europe can outdo them. Pray, Mrs. Pilkington, tell me your faults." "Indeed, Sir, I must beg to be excused, for if I can help it you shall never find them out." "No," says he, "then Mr. Pilkington shall tell me." "I will, Sir," says he, "when I have discovered them." "Pray, Mr. Dean," says Dr. Delany, "why will you be so unpolite as to suppose Mrs. Pilkington has any faults?" "Why, I'll tell you," replied the Dean; "whenever I see a number of agreeable qualities in any person, I am always sure they must have bad ones sufficient to poise the scale." I bowed, and told the Dean, "He did me great honour."[21]

As Swift knew perfectly well, no women smoked in those days, or were admitted to universities.

Next there was some impromptu acting. Scorched by the fire when he started to make coffee, Swift told Laetitia to put a glove on his free hand, and then pretended to be shocked. "Taking up part of his gown to fan himself with, and acting in character of a prudish lady, he said, 'Well, I don't know what to think! Women may be honest that do such things, but for my part, I never could bear to touch any man's flesh—except my husband's; whom perhaps,' says he, 'she wished at the Devil.'"

The performance concluded with another insulting compliment in "his peculiarly ironical strain."

> "Mr. Pilkington," says he, "you would not tell me your wife's faults, but I have found her out to be a damned insolent, proud, unmannerly slut." I looked confounded, not knowing what offense I had committed. Says Mr. Pilkington, "Aye, sir, I must confess she is a little saucy to me sometimes, but—what has she done now?" "Done! Why nothing, but sat there quietly, and never once offered to interrupt me in making the coffee; whereas had I had a lady of modern good breeding here, she would have struggled with me for the coffee pot till she had made me scald myself and her, and made me throw the coffee in the

fire, or perhaps at her head, rather than permit me to take so much trouble for her."

Johnson defines "slut" as "a word of slight contempt to a woman."

This aggressive style of Swift's was entirely in keeping with his ideal of "raillery," as he described it in the unpublished *Hints towards an Essay on Conversation*: "to say something that at first appeared a reproach, or reflection; but, by some turn of wit unexpected and surprising, ended always in a compliment, and to the advantage of the person it was addressed to."[22] It was a game, seeing how far he could go, and it was also a test. To become his friend, you had to understand the game and enjoy it.

Matthew Pilkington came in for his share. Finding some dregs in a glass when he was pouring out wine, Swift commanded Pilkington to drink it, "'for,' says he, 'I always keep some poor parson to drink the foul wine for me.'" Pilkington cheerfully agreed, which delighted Swift. "'Why then,' says the Dean, 'you shan't, for I'll drink it myself. Why pox take you, you are wiser than a paltry curate whom I asked to dine with me a few days ago; for upon my making the same speech to him, he told me he did not understand such usage, and so walked off without his dinner. By the same token, I told the gentleman who recommended him to me that the fellow was a blockhead, and I had done with him.'" As Louise Barnett says, the Pilkingtons were being auditioned. Unlike the paltry curate, they passed muster and were welcomed into the cast.[23]

Rather later than he might have, Swift finally saw through the ingratiating but self-serving Reverend Mr. Pilkington—"the rubberend Mr. Polkingtone," Joyce called him. By then the couple had left for England, where Matthew treated Laetitia badly and then left her. Eventually she became notorious for affairs with a series of men, and the chief reason she wrote her autobiography was to prove that she had been more sinned against than sinning. Swift didn't live to see her book, but long before then he had bitterly repudiated both Pilkingtons: "He proved the falsest rogue, and she the most profligate whore, in either kingdom."[24] Johnson defines "whore," in this sort of context, as "a fornicatress; an adultress." Like Johnson, Swift was unforgiving of female sexual transgression.

One friend Swift saw very little of was Rebecca Dingley, whom he had never much cared for, and whom he described in these years as "quite sunk with years and unwieldiness." She was apparently living alone, and a kindly note of his did survive: "If you are disposed to be easy and cheerful, I will send

something for dinner to your lodgings, and eat it with you and Mrs. Ridgeway, with a bottle of wine and bread. Speak freely and send me word. But
Mrs. Ridgeway shall take all the care upon her." Ann Ridgeway was the
daughter of Swift's housekeeper, Mrs. Brent, whose position she would eventually fill herself. Does "speak freely" suggest a sense that there was awkwardness about the suggestion? He also sent Rebecca an annual "Christmas box,"
along with a golden half guinea and a couple of bottles of wine.[25] There is no
evidence of real friendship.

In 1731 Swift wrote his finest poem, *Verses on the Death of Dr. Swift*. He
had no illusions about what his friends were saying behind his back:

> Yet thus, methinks, I hear 'em speak:
> "See, how the Dean begins to break!
> Poor gentleman, he droops apace,
> You plainly find it in his face;
> That old vertigo in his head
> Will never leave him till he's dead.
> Besides, his memory decays,
> He recollects not what he says;
> He cannot call his friends to mind;
> Forgets the place where last he dined;
> Plies you with stories o'er and o'er,
> He told them fifty times before.
> How does he fancy we can sit
> To hear his out-of-fashioned wit?
> But he takes up with younger folks,
> Who for his wine will bear his jokes."

As for the coterie of women, they may be better at lip service, but their
card-table chatter (the "vole" was winning all the tricks) belies their words:

> My female friends, whose tender hearts
> Have better learned to act their parts,
> Receive the news in doleful dumps:
> "The Dean is dead (and what is trumps?)"
> "Then Lord have mercy on his soul.
> (Ladies, I'll venture for the vole.)"
> "Six deans, they say, must bear the pall.
> (I wish I knew what king to call.)"

"Madam, your husband will attend
The funeral of so good a friend?"
"No, madam, 'tis a shocking sight,
And he's engaged tomorrow night;
My Lady Club would take it ill
If he should fail her at quadrille.
He loved the Dean (I lead a heart),
But dearest friends, they say, must part.
His time was come, he ran his race;
We hope he's in a better place."[26]

"I lead a heart"! They may hope that the dean has gone to "a better place,"
but they obviously have their doubts, and anyway they're content to bandy
tired clichés. But he has the last laugh, putting words in their mouths from
the grave.

LADY ACHESON OF MARKET HILL

One other relationship, which developed in the late 1720s, is a story in itself, because it inspired an outpouring of poems. Sir Arthur Acheson, of Scottish descent but an Anglican in the Armagh hotbed of Presbyterianism, had
recently been elected to the Irish Parliament, which no doubt explains how
Swift came to meet him in Dublin. An invitation soon followed to stay at his
country estate near the small town of Market Hill, seventy-five miles to the
north. Stella died in January of 1728, and in June of that year Swift began an
extraordinarily protracted visit to the Achesons. He was there for fully eight
months, followed by four more months in 1729 and another three in 1730. He
was thus at Market Hill for nearly two-thirds of the time during that period.
Evidently he had no qualms about letting the cathedral manage without him,
and staying away probably helped him to deal with the loss of Stella.

At Market Hill there was an attractive successor, if not an adequate substitute. Sir Arthur turned out to be a bore, but his sprightly wife, Anne, interested Swift greatly. Her father was Philip Savage, a distinguished lord chancellor of Ireland and a friend of Swift's in his London days. "I dined with Phil
Savage and his Irish club at their boarding place," he told Stella in 1710.[27]
Anne would have been a teenager then, and there's no evidence that Swift met
her. Now he found that she was attractive, willing to take advice about books,
and good at repartee.

Swift didn't produce much prose during this time but, perhaps to his own surprise, he became a prolific poet. As he had done long before in *The Humble Petition of Frances Harris*, he began impersonating other people's voices. In one of these poems, Lady Acheson's waiting woman, Hannah, imagines how exciting it would be if her employers were to rent out a building as an army barracks. A dashing captain might then say, after encountering Swift,

> Whenever you see a cassock and gown,
> A hundred to one but it covers a clown.
> Observe how a parson comes into a room:
> God damn me, he hobbles as bad as my groom;
> A scholard, when just from his college broke loose,
> Can hardly tell how to cry boo to a goose.
> Your Noveds, and Blutraks, and Omurs and stuff,
> By God, they don't signify this pinch of snuff. . . .
> Now, Madam, you'll think it a strange thing to say,
> But the sight of a book makes me sick to this day.

The names are distortions of Ovid, Plutarch, and Homer, and this speech strikes Hannah as supremely clever:

> Never since I was born did I hear so much wit,
> And, Madam, I laughed till I thought I should split.[28]

The most interesting impersonations are of Lady Acheson herself. She was exceptionally thin, as Stella had been toward the end, and Swift constantly urged her to take exercise. After she'd had enough of that, and also of his rather tyrannical reading program, she put up spirited resistance. The poems catch her irritation.

> Next, for his diversion,
> He rails at my person;
> What court breeding this is?
> He takes me to pieces
> From shoulder to flank;
> I'm lean and I'm lank.

"The short lines," Ehrenpreis comments, "are as thin as their subject." As for books, Swift was making Anne his student, as he had Stella.

> At breakfast he'll ask
> An account of my task.

Put a word out of joint,
Or miss but a point,
He rages and frets,
His manners forgets.[29]

A "point" is a punctuation mark—hardly a grave mistake to make.

In a poem with the telling title *Lady Acheson Weary of the Dean*, Swift gives a rare self-portrait, ruefully acknowledging his sallow complexion, "wainscot" hands (the color of oak paneling—tanned, perhaps, from being outdoors so much), heavy eyebrows, and protuberant eyes.

Oh! if I could, how I would maul
    His tallow face and wainscot paws,
His beetle brows and eyes of wall,
    And make him soon give up the cause.

Must I be every moment chid
    With skinny, bony, snip, and lean?
Oh! that I could but once be rid
    Of that insulting tyrant Dean.[30]

According to George Faulkner, "The neighbouring ladies were no great understanders of raillery." It was evidence of intelligence and wit that Lady Acheson did appreciate it, and Swift wrote complacently to Pope that he had been "writing family verses of mirth by way of libels on my Lady." To Sheridan he reported, "My Lady is perpetually quarreling with Sir Arthur and me, and shows every creature the libels I have writ against her."[31] If Swift had thought these poems insulting he would not have had them published, as he promptly did.

One poem, however, was not published, *An Excellent New Panegyric on Skinnibonia*. It has only recently come to light, in a notebook in which Swift and Lady Acheson copied out poems as he had formerly done with Stella. This poem is remarkable for the audacity with which it imagines what women conceal beneath their dresses. First described are country girls, too poor to wear underclothes that would defend their modesty when they relieve themselves:

When the smockless nymphs expose
Pairs of legs from knees to toes,
How you scold to see them naked,

> Grimed with dirt by Phoebus bakèd!
> In what fury when you spied
> Her that showed her brown backside?
> How your eyes were fixed upon her,
> Zealous for your sex's honor!
> Men might think that every dame,
> Were she stripped, would show the same.

Men can't be prevented from thinking, though Lady Acheson's backside would presumably be pale rather than brown. Immediately afterward, an impolite gust of wind threatens to expose all:

> Zephyr, when you chanced to stoop,
> Strove to get beneath your hoop,
> And to waft you Lord knows where,
> To his palace high in air;
> But the Dean with counter-charm
> Interposed his valiant arm,
> Lent a pin to make all tight;
> Zephyr fled with grief and spite.[32]

Rather than taking voyeuristic advantage, Swift chivalrously supplies the necessary pin to fasten her clothes together.

The strangest of the Market Hill poems is entitled *Death and Daphne*. The idea of Lady Acheson's thinness is pushed as far as it can go, with disturbing consequences. In a little myth that Swift conjures up, Pluto, god of the underworld, complains that he hasn't been getting enough dead souls since Marlborough's war ended. He orders Death to find a wife and produce some children. Death settles down in London (welcomed there by his friends, the physicians). After covering his skeletal frame with a lawyer's parchment as skin, he pays court to Daphne.

> She, as he came into the room,
> Thought him Adonis in his bloom. . . .
> For such a shape of skin and bone
> Was never seen, except her own.

They fall for each other because they look so much alike. But when Death reaches out to touch the lady, his ardor vanishes:

> For when by chance the meagre shade
> Upon thy hand his finger laid,
> Thy hand as dry and cold as lead,
> His matrimonial spirit fled;
> He felt about his heart a damp
> That quite extinguished Cupid's lamp.[33]

Nora Crow Jaffe proposes a persuasive interpretation: Death, paying court to a young woman, is a stand-in for Swift himself. As with the glimpse of Lady Acheson's backside in *Skinnibonia*, he clearly felt a strong attraction. And he had to be aware that even if he did acknowledge it, age and physical defects would make him an improbable lover. Death finds Daphne even colder than himself; Swift, Jaffe suggests, "probably feared to find her warm and moist."[34]

In any event, Lady Acheson took *Death and Daphne* as a great compliment. When Swift introduced Orrery to her she unlocked a cabinet, got out the poem, and read it aloud.

> While she was reading, the Dean was perpetually correcting her for bad pronunciation, and for placing a wrong emphasis on particular words. As soon as she had gone through the composition, she assured me smilingly that the portrait of Daphne was drawn for herself. I begged to be excused from believing it, and protested that I could not see one feature that had the least resemblance, but the Dean immediately burst into a fit of laughter. "You fancy," says he, "that you are very polite, but you are much mistaken. That lady had rather be a Daphne drawn by me than a Sacharissa by any other pencil." She confirmed what he had said with great earnestness, so that I had no other method of retrieving my error than by whispering in her ear, as I was conducting her downstairs to dinner, that indeed I found "her hand as dry and cold as lead."[35]

For a while Swift relished the life of a country gentleman, and during the second of his three stays he even bought some land from Sir Arthur, with the idea of calling it Drapier's Hill. But it was becoming increasingly obvious that he and his host had nothing in common.

> Where friendship is by fate designed,
> It forms an union of the mind;

> But here I differ from the Knight
> In every point, like black and white,
> For none can say that ever yet
> We both in one opinion met. . . .
> His guests are few, his visits rare,
> Nor uses time, nor time will spare;
> Nor rides, nor walks, nor hunts, nor fowls,
> Nor plays at cards, or dice, or bowls;
> But seated in an easy-chair
> Despises exercise and air.[36]

Besides, the charms of rural retreat were fading fast. For a while Swift had enjoyed joking with the farm workers:

> He's all the day sauntering,
> With labourers bantering. . . .
> Hail fellow, well met,
> All dirty and wet.
> Find out, if you can,
> Who's master, who's man;
> Who makes the best figure,
> The Dean or the digger,
> And which is the best
> At cracking a jest.

As for settling down at Drapier's Hill, that fantasy evaporated completely.

> How could I form so wild a vision,
> To seek, in deserts, fields Elysian?
> To live in fear, suspicion, variance
> With thieves, fanatics, and barbarians?[37]

The barbarians may be the Irish in general, though Swift was equally capable of using the term for booby squires. The fanatics, of course, are the Presbyterians who dominated Armagh.

Swift left Market Hill for the last time in 1730, and not long after that the Achesons separated, probably because it was obvious that they had very little in common. They can't have felt that the breakup (divorce wasn't possible) had anything to do with Swift, since both remained on friendly terms

90. Dean Swift's well.

with him. As he would no doubt have predicted, however, Lady Acheson got caught up in the frivolities of fashionable society. He wrote to Ford in 1732, "Lady Acheson presents her service to you, and chides you for neglecting your health, although her Ladyship be a greater criminal in that article (if possible) than yourself. She is an absolute Dublin rake, sits up late, loses her money, and goes to bed sick, and resolves like you never to mend. It is said that you will soon see Sir Arthur at London to lessen a pair of swelled legs."[38] That is the last we hear of the couple with whom Swift once spent so much time. Anne Acheson died in 1737, and Sir Arthur outlived Swift.

The Market Hill house is long gone, replaced by a faux-Gothic Victorian edifice known as Gosford Castle. The garden that Swift helped to lay out has gone to seed, and all that survives are stone walls that may possibly date from his time. There is also a well, known as "Dean Swift's Well," reputed to have curative powers, but there is no evidence that Swift knew or cared about it.

Markethill itself (as it is now spelled) would experience, much later, hatreds that were only latent in Swift's day. It remained a predominantly Protestant town, and in the 1990s there were three separate IRA bombings, including a thousand-pound blockbuster that detonated outside the police station and damaged hundreds of buildings. Fortunately, a warning had been received and the residents got to safety in time.

CHAPTER 29

The Disgusting Poems

Since Swift had warm friendships with women and respected their intelligence so highly, why should he have been regarded as a misogynist? The main reason is a group of half a dozen poems that he published in the early 1730s. They shocked many readers when they first appeared, and have gone on shocking ever since. Johnson's verdict is typical: "The greatest difficulty that occurs, in analyzing his character, is to discover by what depravity of intellect he took delight in revolving ideas from which almost every other mind shrinks in disgust. The ideas of pleasure, even when criminal, may solicit the imagination; but what has disease, deformity, and filth upon which the thoughts can be allured to dwell?"[1]

These are generally called the scatological poems, but that's too narrow. "Disgusting" is more accurate. Over the years apologists have advanced various rationalizations: this kind of thing was common at the time (it wasn't), or he was just making fun of idealizing love poetry (he was, but that's not the whole story), or he was a "conscientious priest" wanting to discourage fornication.[2] It seems obvious that these poems should tell us a good deal about Swift's psyche, but just what do they tell?

The first thing to say is that ordinary sex is largely invisible in Swift's works. He apparently disliked what he regarded as obscenity too deeply even to hint at it. Dr. Lyon, who knew him well, remembered that he hated lewd talk and always reproved it. But references to urination and excretion were another matter, and Lyon believed they were intended didactically. "He always distinguished between obscenity, in common discourse and writing, from what was only slovenly. The former was not to be endured, but he wrote and spoke of the latter merely in order to recommend cleanliness in dress and behaviour, by representing filthiness and sluttishness in the most contemptible light."[3]

Lyon was certainly right about the obsession with cleanliness. In *Cadenus and Vanessa* Venus sprinkles the infant Vanessa with nectar,

> From whence the tender skin assumes
> A sweetness above all perfumes;
> From whence a cleanliness remains,
> Incapable of outward stains.

Fortunately for her, Vanessa was up to Swift's high standards. People who knew her assured Deane Swift that "she was extremely nice [that is, fastidious] and delicate, as well in the cleanliness of her person as in everything she wore."[4]

But of course it's entirely possible to be obscene and still enjoy gratification, as the libertine Earl of Rochester did:

> Cupid and Bacchus my saints are;
> May drink and love still reign.
> With wine I wash away my cares,
> And then to cunt again.[5]

By Swift's time writers had to be more euphemistic than that, but there are numerous appreciations of sex in Fielding, and endless double entendres in Sterne (a clergyman) and Smollett. Smollett's Tabitha Bramble orders her housekeeper to "let Roger search into, and make a general clearance of the slit holes which the maids have in secret," and is confident that her pious servant Humphry "may have power given to penetrate and instill his goodness, even into your most inward parts."[6]

It may well be that Swift disapproved of obscene language but not of sex itself. At various times, after all, from the *Journal to Stella* down to the Market Hill poems, he did enjoy oblique innuendos. In defense of the offending poems, he translated Horace:

> Some actions must be always out of sight,
> Yet elegantly told, may give delight.[7]

D. H. Lawrence thought that Swift was "mad with sex and excrement revulsion," but that's far from clear. It's one thing to be reticent about sex, and another thing to be explicit about excrement. And the excremental references aren't all equally disgusting. There is justice in C. S. Lewis's comment on both Swift and Pope: "Their love of filth is, in my opinion, much better understood by schoolboys than by psychoanalysts: if there is something sinister in it, there is also an element of high-spirited rowdiness."[8]

In one of the Market Hill poems, *A Panegyric on the Dean*, Swift makes Lady Acheson thank him for supervising the construction of a pair of outhouses. These will provide a welcome refuge for the farm workers, as Swift observes in parodically religious language, with italics to highlight the double entendres (*cloaca* is Latin for "sewer"):

> Here gentle goddess Cloacine
> Receives all offerings at her shrine.
> In separate cells, the he's and she's
> Here pay their vows with *bended knees*.
> (For 'tis profane when sexes mingle,
> And every nymph must enter single;
> And when she feels an *inward motion*,
> Comes filled with *reverence* and devotion.)
> The bashful maid, to hide her blush,
> Shall creep no more behind a bush;
> Here unobserved, she boldly goes,
> As who should say, to *pluck a rose*.[9]

"Sirreverence" was a euphemism for excrement, and "plucking a rose" for urinating.

As the anti-pastoral goes on, it does seem that Swift is curiously fascinated:

> Yet some devotion still remains
> Among our harmless northern swains,
> Whose offerings, placed in golden ranks,
> Adorn our crystal river's banks;
> Nor seldom grace the flowery downs
> With spiral tops and copple crowns.[10]

"Copple" meant crested, like a cock's head. Since Swift put these words in Lady Acheson's mouth and shared the poem with her, he evidently thought they were droll rather than offensive.

At least one woman writer, Mary Jones of Oxford, enjoyed Swift's irreverence and imitated it. In a poem of hers, "two nymphs of chaste Diana's train," riding in a coach with a pair of beaus, feel the call of nature and hasten into an empty dairy house:

> The cream pot first she filled with liquor
> Fit for the thorax of the vicar. . . .
> A pan of milk, unskimmed its cream,
> Did next receive the bounteous stream.

When the farm wife returns, she rejoices to discover that her containers have been magically filled up, and she relishes the beer in particular, although it does taste a bit flat.

> Our beer is dead, but no great matter,
> 'Tis better still than common water.

Yet Swift's "spiral tops" are disconcertingly closely observed. As the poet Geoffrey Hill says, "It is the very coolness of the verbal draughtsmanship, the detailing of the fecal coils, that is so chilling."[11]

In Swift's Dublin neighborhood, the Liberty of St. Patrick, a visitor described "a degree of filth and stench inconceivable except by such as have visited these scenes of wretchedness. Into the back yard of each house, frequently not ten feet deep, is flung from the windows of each apartment the ordure and filth of its numerous inhabitants; from which it is so seldom removed that I have seen it nearly on a level with the windows of the first floor."[12] In American usage, that would be the second floor.

Swift commented on the same thing. Anyone walking the streets of Dublin "must needs observe the immense number of human excrements at the doors and steps of waste houses." Swift imagines that partisans of England have deposited these so as to make it appear that the Irish have enough to eat. Then fantasy takes over. "They would confirm this by pretending to observe that a British anus being more narrowly perforated than one of our own country, and many of these excrements, upon a strict view, appearing copple-crowned, with a point like a cone or pyramid, are easily distinguished from the Hibernian, which lie much flatter and with less continuity." But this claim is unfounded, for the writer has consulted a distinguished physician "who is well versed in such profound speculations, and at my request was pleased to make trial with each of his fingers, by thrusting them into the anus of several persons of both nations; and professed he could find no such difference between them as those ill-disposed people allege."[13]

References of this kind were not uncommon in Swift's time. A distant acquaintance, Lord Castle Durrow of Kilkenny, wrote to say that he was delighted to receive a letter from Swift, and then remarked that since he was fond of rural retirement, "once indeed in two years I appear in the anus of the world, our metropolis."[14]

Back in 1719, when Swift was nursing his grievances and seeing (but in what way, exactly?) the cleanly Vanessa, he wrote a poem called *The Progress of Beauty* that gives a highly unromantic glimpse of a lady's dressing room. In Pope's *Rape of the Lock*, when the lovely Belinda puts on makeup, she "sees by degrees a purer blush arise, / And keener lightnings quicken in her eyes." Swift's Celia likewise knows how to "teach her cheeks again to blush," but that's because she's a prostitute who has not only lost the ability to blush in earnest, but has all too many defects to cover up:

> To see her from her pillow rise,
>   All reeking in a cloudy steam,
> Cracked lips, foul teeth, and gummy eyes,
>   Poor Strephon! how would he blaspheme!
>
> The soot or powder which was wont
>   To make her hair look black as jet,
> Falls from her tresses on her front,
>   A mingled mass of dirt and sweat.

Nasty as this is, it's only partway along the road of Celia's fate as a victim of syphilis (for which mercury, though poisonous, was thought to be a remedy).

> When mercury her tresses mows,
>   To think of oil and soot is vain:
> No painting can restore a nose,
>   Nor will her teeth return again.
>
> Two balls of glass may serve for eyes,
>   White lead can plaster up a cleft;
> But these, alas, are poor supplies
>   If neither cheeks nor lips be left.[15]

Swift apparently had a horror of prostitutes. Twelve years after writing this, he returned to the theme in a poem with the innocuous title *A Beautiful Young Nymph Going to Bed.* It begins, as his satires often do, as a charming pastoral:

> Corinna, pride of Drury Lane,
> For whom no shepherd sighs in vain . . .

The name Corinna must have been chosen for its association with love poems, but the theater district around Drury Lane was a notorious hunting ground for streetwalkers. No one "sighs in vain" for Corinna because anyone who wants her can have her. They wouldn't want her, though, if they could see her undressing:

> Now, picking out a crystal eye,
> She wipes it clean, and lays it by. . . .
> Now dext'rously her plumpers draws,
> That serve to fill her hollow jaws;
> Untwists a wire, and from her gums
> A set of teeth completely comes.
> Pulls out the rags contrived to prop
> Her flabby dugs and down they drop. . . .
> With gentlest touch, she next explores
> Her shankers, issues, running sores.[16]

Plumpers were often used by respectable people, in an era of widespread tooth loss. Johnson defines them as "something worn in the mouth to swell out the cheeks."

Finally Corinna falls asleep, but there's no relief there. In a nightmare she experiences the punishments of the Bridewell house of correction, "and feels the lash, and faintly screams." Waking up, she finds the animal kingdom taking over:

> A wicked rat her plaster stole,
> Half ate, and dragged it to his hole.
> The crystal eye, alas, was missed,
> And Puss had on her plumpers pissed.

This poem has been well described as "aversion therapy."[17] It's not about sex, and in fact there isn't any. Corinna has returned to her garret at midnight because she found no "drunken rake" who was willing to touch her.

Satires on removing fake attractions go back to ancient times, as in an epigram by Martial that Swift certainly knew. When he printed three of his disgusting poems in a 1734 pamphlet, he introduced them with a line from Ovid, *Pars minima est ipsa puella sui*—"A woman is the least part of herself." But Ovid avoids describing images that, he says, are obscene, whereas Swift highlights them.[18]

This is not scatology, though. Its subject is the alarming vulnerability of the human body. Many diseases that could be cured today were chronic or fatal then, and Swift's own body was a torment to him, with the ever-recurring vertigo and nausea. He may not sympathize with Corinna, exactly, but his poem considers the anguish she must feel:

> But how shall I describe her arts
> To recollect the scattered parts?
> Or show the anguish, toil, and pain
> Of gathering up herself again?[19]

Three of Swift's poems, however, do invoke scatology. Instead of depicting diseased prostitutes, they are about naïve young gentlemen. In *The Lady's Dressing Room*, Strephon is alarmed when he takes a close view of Celia cleaning her face, much like Gulliver among the giantesses.

> The virtues we must not let pass
> Of Celia's magnifying glass.
> When frighted Strephon cast his eye on't
> It showed the visage of a giant,
> A glass that can to sight disclose
> The smallest worm in Celia's nose,
> And faithfully direct her nail
> To squeeze it out from head to tail;
> For catch it nicely by the head,
> It must come out alive or dead.

What really shatters Strephon is discovering the purpose of the mysterious chest beneath Celia's bed.

> So things which must not be expressed,
> When plumped into the reeking chest,
> Send up an excremental smell
> To taint the parts from whence they fell:

> The petticoats and gown perfume,
> Which waft a stink round every room.
> Thus finishing his grand survey,
> Disgusted Strephon stole away,
> Repeating in his amorous fits,
> "Oh! Celia, Celia, Celia shits!"[20]

Lawrence made an interesting suggestion: maybe it was Swift's sensitivity to language that was offended. "'Celia, Celia, Celia shits!' Now that, stated baldly, is so ridiculous it is almost funny. . . . The *fact* cannot have troubled him, since it applied to himself and to all of us." Lawrence also confessed a wish to go back across the years and say to the lady, "It's all right, don't you take any notice of that mental lunatic."[21] He doesn't indicate what other kinds of lunatic there are, or why we should assume that Swift is identical to foolish Strephon.

The most recent editor of Swift's poems tells us that this was one of the most popular in Swift's lifetime and was frequently reprinted.[22] He obviously felt no embarrassment about it, since he published it with two others in an elegant, large-type edition. And because the final word breaks off with a dash in the original editions, it's up to the reader to supply it. As with Swift's political poems, in which the rhyme makes clear what name to fill in, the rhyme on "fits" offers the reader a little puzzle-solving game.

Lady Mary Wortley Montagu saw an opportunity to get in a kick at Swift, and published a riposte in which he himself pays a lady £4 for sex but is humiliated by impotence. In his defense, he identifies the cause:

> Your damned close-stool so near my nose,
> Your dirty smock, and stinking toes.

At this the lady retorts, "The blame lies all in sixty-odd." When Swift then threatens to write a lampoon on the lady's dressing room,

> She answered short, "I'm glad you'll write,
> You'll furnish paper when I shite."

And she adds,

> Perhaps you have no better luck in
> The knack of rhyming than of ——.

Lady Mary's grudge was an enduring one, and a reminder that although official culture was decorous, obscenity was freely used in private. Twenty-five years later, she gleefully showed a visitor a commode lined with books by Pope, Bolingbroke, and Swift. This, she explained, "gave her the satisfaction of shitting on them every day."[23]

There may be an entirely different way, though, to hear Swift's message. The ending of *The Lady's Dressing Room* recalls the maneuver in *A Tale of a Tub* when Swift suggests that the only way to be really happy is to be "well deceived." So here he recommends that Strephon plug his nose—"smell no evil," as a commentator says—and learn to content himself with superficial appearances.

> I pity wretched Strephon blind
> To all the charms of female kind;
> Should I the Queen of Love refuse
> Because she rose from stinking ooze? . . .
> He soon would learn to think like me,
> And bless his ravished sight to see
> Such order from confusion sprung,
> Such gaudy tulips raised from dung.[24]

In a poem called *Strephon and Chloe*, the game again is to imitate the idealizing language of pastoral, and then to deflate it with frank colloquialisms.

> Strephon, who heard the fuming rill
> As from a mossy cliff distill,
> Cried out, "Ye gods, what sound is this?
> Can Chloe, heav'nly Chloe piss?"

Relieved to find that she's "as mortal as himself at least," he decides to borrow her utensil:

> But soon with like occasions pressed
> He boldly sent his hand in quest
> (Inspired with courage from his bride)
> To reach the pot on t'other side,
> And as he filled the reeking vase,
> Let fly a rouser in her face.

Geoffrey Hill remarks that "'he boldly sent his hand in quest' is the language of lyrical pornography applied to an unlyrical situation," and as for the surprising fart, "it would be difficult to find a word that blends the outrageous and the festive more effectively than this."[25]

This wasn't the first time Swift had associated farting with sex. Thirty years earlier, he wrote a furious lampoon on Lord Romney, who had promised to get him an appointment at Canterbury or Westminster and then did nothing about it. "The handsomest man of his time," a modern authority tells us, "he was a notorious profligate, and the terror of husbands." In Swift's poem the peer's mistresses, knowing the way his love expresses itself, position themselves at both ends.

> And now the ladies all are bent
> To try the great experiment:
> Ambitious of a Regent's heart,
> Spread all their charms to catch a fart.
> Watching the first unsav'ry wind,
> Some ply before, and some behind.
> My Lord, on fire amidst the dames,
> Farts like a laurel in the flames. . . .
> So from my Lord his passion broke;
> He farted first, and then he spoke.[26]

One last poem of this kind, a weaker effort called *Cassinus and Peter*, repeats the line "Oh! Celia, Celia, Celia shits!" but also has a strange classical allusion that may be revealing:

> I come, I come—Medusa, see,
> Her serpents hiss direct at me.

In the myth, anyone who looked at the serpent-haired Medusa would be turned to stone, but Athena provides Perseus with a shield in which he can safely watch her mirror image while he cuts off her head. As Freud interpreted it, the gorgon's head is a displaced symbol of the feared female genitals. Whether or not one finds that persuasive, Swift is certainly talking about forbidden sights that are psychologically fatal:

> Here Cassy lies, by Celia slain,
> And dying, never told his pain.

Perhaps what disturbs Swift most is the unsettling fact that Yeats described:

> Love has pitched his mansion in
> The place of excrement.

Freud, talking about children's jokes, observes that "in the imagination at this stage there exists a latrine, as it were, where what is sexual and what is excremental are distinguished badly or not at all."[27]

It's conceivable that Swift's imagination got stalled at a childish stage, or regressed there. In the days when psychoanalytic writers liked to deduce formative traumas without any evidence, the nurse who took him to England was identified as the culprit. "However devoted to her little charge," one analyst explained, "she was in some way overly conscientious and harsh in her early toilet training, and left this stamp of the nursery morals of the chamber pot forever on his character." Another writer was sure that she must have disturbed Swift with "caresses of a faintly lascivious character." A third interpreter scandalized Swift specialists with an essay called "The Excremental Vision," in which he claimed that Swift offered a valuable insight into "the universal neurosis of mankind" by restoring anality to its foundational role in personality development.[28]

It's apparent, at any rate, that some kind of obsession is involved, and that Swift felt compelled to share it with the world. Was he thinking of himself when he jotted a note, "A nice man is a man of nasty ideas"? And a couplet in *Strephon and Chloe* surely speaks from experience:

> For fine ideas vanish fast,
> While all the gross and filthy last.[29]

Ideas, in Locke's philosophy, were not abstract concepts but direct sense impressions—all too direct, for the hypersensitive Swift.

It's important to remember that these poems were written, as Lady Mary cruelly emphasized, by a man in his sixties who was haunted by mortality. As a recent critic suggests, the loss of Stella must have heightened Swift's horror of bodily decay: "Although the overt accusations in these poems are about whoredom, dirt and deceit, the underlying one seems to be that, like Stella, these women are physical beings in pawn to disease and death. Swift details their physicality with triumphant rage."[30]

At any rate, Swift had no inhibitions about sharing these poems with his women friends, as Martha Whiteway teasingly reminded him. "As you have been remarkable for never being severe on the ladies, I am surprised you should say that we forsake the men at forty. I deny the fact; while they sing our praises, we continue to hold them in admiration. For an example of this, I give the author of *The Lady's Dressing Room* and *Strephon and Chloe*, who, by writing these poems, gained the hearts of the whole sex."[31]

CHAPTER 30

Waiting for the End

The occasional writings that Swift produced in his final decade were mostly indignant, and sometimes furious. A couple of years after leaving Market Hill, he returned to a poem he had left unfinished there, *An Epistle to a Lady, Who Desired the Author to Make Verses on Her, in the Heroic Style*, and turned it into a fierce defense of satire. Although he invokes Democritus, the "laughing philosopher" of Greece, the laughter is bitter:

> Like the ever-laughing sage,
> In a jest I spend my rage
> (Though it must be understood
> I would hang them if I could). . . .
> Poultney deep, accomplished St. Johns,
> Scourge the villains with a vengeance.
> Let me, though the smell be noisome,
> Strip their bums; let Caleb hoyse 'em;
> Then apply Alecto's whip
> Till they wriggle, howl, and skip.[1]

"Hoyse" is "hoist"; Alecto, whose name means "unceasing anger," is one of the avenging Furies.

A disturbing poem from the same period is called *The Day of Judgment*. It begins by imitating pious poems about God's righteousness, and then springs its trap: human beings are so contemptible that it would be a waste of God's time to bother with a Last Judgment at all. The Almighty dismisses the human race with contempt:

> "So some folks told you, but they knew
> No more of Jove's designs than you;
> The world's mad business now is o'er,
> And I resent these pranks no more.
> I to such blockheads set my wit!
> I damn such fools! Go, go, you're bit."

This God is a bitter jester, in the spirit of the London "biters" whom Swift had described years before: "You must ask a bantering question, or tell some damned lie in a serious manner, and then she will answer or speak as if you were in earnest; then cry you, 'Madam, there's a bite.'"[2]

"Jove" was a common poetic equivalent for Jehovah, but the name perhaps reflects covert skepticism about Christian theology. Certainly Swift declined to publish this poem, and it didn't appear in print until thirty years after his death. At some level he may even have been haunted by the vision that Mark Twain's Satan reveals at the end of *The Mysterious Stranger*: "There is no God, no universe, no human race, no earthly life, no heaven, no hell. It is all a dream—a grotesque and foolish dream." In a letter to Pope, Swift said, "The common saying of life being a farce is true in every sense but the most important one, for it is a ridiculous tragedy, which is the worst kind of composition."[3]

Another poem, *The Place of the Damned*, is a relentless catalogue of human viciousness that pervades every known profession.

> Damned poets, damned critics, damned blockheads, damned knaves,
> Damned senators bribed, damned prostitute slaves;
> Damned lawyers and judges, damned lords and damned squires,
> Damned spies and informers, damned friends and damned liars,
> Damned villains, corrupted in every station,
> Damned time-serving priests all over the nation;
> And into the bargain I'll readily give you
> Damned ignorant prelates, and councilors privy.[4]

By this stage, frustrated by his inability to influence events, Swift was spoiling for a fight. When a bill was proposed in the Irish Parliament to extend toleration by abolishing the Test Act, Swift responded with *On the Words "Brother Protestants" and "Fellow Christians," So Familiarly Used by the Advocates for the Repeal of the Test Act.* In this poem he suggested sarcastically that Presbyterians were no more like Anglicans than horse turds in a flooded farmyard were like apples.

> A ball of new-dropped horse's dung,
> Mingling with apples in the throng,
> Said to the pippin, plump and prim,
> "See, brother, how we apples swim."

In passing, Swift threw in a jibe at Richard Bettesworth, a pompous serjeant-at-law (the title indicated a barrister) who had presumptuously referred to a distinguished friend of Swift's as "brother serjeant."

> Thus at the bar that booby Bettesworth,
> Though half a crown o'er-pays his sweat's worth,
> Who knows in law nor text nor margent,
> Calls Singleton his brother serjeant.[5]

The "margent" is the marginal commentary that interprets the meaning of a law.

As the younger Sheridan heard it, Bettesworth first encountered these lines when he was reading the poem to friends. "He read it aloud till he had finished the lines relative to himself. He then flung it down with great violence, he trembled and turned pale; and after some pause, his rage for a while depriving him of utterance, he took out his penknife, and opening it, vehemently swore, 'With this very penknife, by God, will I cut off his ears.'" According to Orrery, Bettesworth added that he intended to make Swift's head "as round as an apple," evidently alluding to the apples among the turds.[6]

Hastening to the deanery and then to another house where he was told Swift was visiting, Bettesworth, as Swift himself said, "repeated the lines that concerned him with great emphasis." Swift blandly denied having written them, at which Bettesworth, with surprising perceptiveness, declared that he was convinced of Swift's authorship because he knew that the words that rhymed with his name "could come from none but me."[7]

In Sheridan's account, Bettesworth then added: "Well, since you will give me no satisfaction in this affair, let me tell you, your gown is your protection;

under the sanction of which, like one of your own Yahoos who had climbed up to the top of a high tree, you sit secure, and squirt your filth round on all mankind." Swift was amused, saying afterward that "the fellow showed more wit in this than he thought him possessed of."[8]

Swift's neighbors rallied to his defense. Thirty-one of them signed a declaration promising to "defend the life and limbs of the said Dean." Ehrenpreis observes that the document is "suspiciously well-worded" and may have been drafted by Swift himself. He sent them a moving response: "I receive with great thankfulness these many kind expressions of your concern for my safety. . . . I am chiefly sorry that by two cruel disorders of deafness and giddiness, which have pursued me for four months, I am not in a condition either to hear or to receive you, much less to return my most sincere acknowledgments, which in justice and gratitude I ought to do. May God bless you and your families in this world, and make you forever happy in the next."[9]

The allusion to Yahoos clearly stung, but Swift had a countermove. In the next year he published a rollicking ballad called *The Yahoo's Overthrow*, in which it was Bettesworth who was the Yahoo.

> He kindled, as if the whole satire had been
> The oppression of virtue, not wages of sin;
> He began as he bragged, with a rant and a roar;
> He bragged how he bounced, and he swore how he swore.
>   Knock him down, down, down, knock him down.

After some horseplay the ballad ends by predicting that Bettesworth will make peace by kissing Swift's rear end.

> And when this is over, we'll make him amends;
> To the Dean he shall go, they shall kiss and be friends.
> But how? Why, the Dean shall to him disclose
> A face for to kiss, without eyes, ears, or nose.
>   Knock him down, down, down, knock him down.

That insult was a common one. Fielding's Squire Western frequently invites people to kiss his posterior, though as Fielding notes, "No one ever desires you to kick that which belongs to himself, nor offers to kiss this part in another."[10]

The clever rhyme of Bettesworth with "sweat's worth" was quoted everywhere, and Swift's antagonist must have rued the day he took him on. "By targeting Bettesworth's name," Stephen Karian comments, "Swift left him little defense, since one can deny various attacks on one's character and abilities, but one cannot escape one's name."[11] His feeble recourse was to complain that the rhyme was defective, since he preferred his name to be pronounced "Bett-es-worth."

One of the last poems Swift ever wrote was the most ferocious of all. It was provoked by an issue that had obsessed him all his life, attacks on the income of the Church. In 1736 the Irish Parliament took up a petition to excuse grazing land from the tithes that other farmland had to pay. There were far-reaching implications. If landowners could win this battle they would soon be launching new ones, and before long there might be no tithes at all.[12]

Swift rose to the challenge with an extended invective called *A Character, Panegyric, and Description of the Legion Club.* "The Club" was his contemptuous nickname for the Irish House of Commons; he told Sheridan that he was tired of hearing about "the follies, corruptions, and slavish practices of those misrepresentative brutes." In the poem he adapted the story of the Gadarene swine, in which Jesus rescues a man from demonic possession by causing "unclean spirits" to migrate into a herd of the animals. When he asks the spirits their name they reply, "My name is Legion: for we are many."[13]

The Legion Club begins casually enough, noticing the brand-new Parliament House (today it houses the Bank of Ireland) adjacent to Trinity College.

> As I stroll the city, oft I
> See a building large and lofty,
> Not a bow-shot from the College,
> Half the globe from sense and knowledge.

But that edifice turns out to be a madhouse, filled with the criminally insane:

> While they sit a-picking straws,
> Let them rave of making laws;
> While they never hold their tongue
> Let them dabble in their dung. . . .
> We may, while they strain their throats,
> Wipe our arses with their votes.[14]

More than a dozen members of Parliament are attacked by name. At times the tone is amused and witty:

Bless us, Morgan! Art thou there, man?
Bless mine eyes! Art thou the chairman?

But mostly the fury is overwhelming. Bettesworth predictably shows up, yoked to another fellow Swift despised:

Tie them, keeper, in a tether,
Let them stare and stink together;
Both are apt to be unruly,
Lash them daily, lash them duly;
Though 'tis hopeless to reclaim them,
Scorpion's rods perhaps may tame them.[15]

In *Verses on the Death of Dr. Swift*, Swift claimed that he avoided personal satire:

Yet malice never was his aim;
He lashed the vice, but spared the name.
No individual could resent
Where thousands equally were meant.

In fact he named a dozen people in that very poem. But he may not have thought there was a contradiction. As a writer commented soon after his death, his "general satire" exposed vice and folly without naming names, "but in his particular satire, when egregious monsters, traitors to the commonwealth and slaves to party, are the objects of his resentment, he cuts without mercy, in order that those who trespass in defiance of laws might live in fear of him."[16]

Swift took more than usual care to conceal his authorship of *The Legion Club*. He wrote to Sheridan, who was out of town at the time, "Here is a cursed long libel running about in manuscript, on the *Legion Club*. It is in verse, and the foolish town imputes it to me. There were not above thirteen abused (as it is said) in the original, but others have added more which I never saw, though I have once read the true one." A week later he wrote again, "I hear it is charged to me, with great personal threatenings from the puppies offended. . . . If I could get the true copy I would send it to you."[17]

Sheridan duly replied, "Surely no person can be so stupid as to imagine you wrote the panegyric on the *Legion Club*." Of course he knew perfectly well who wrote it. He and Swift expected their letters to be opened and were careful to leave a false trail. As for the actual manuscript, Swift undoubtedly gave it to someone else for safekeeping, possibly Sheridan himself.[18]

"THE SHADOW OF THE SHADOW OF THE SHADOW OF DR. SWIFT"

In *Verses on the Death*, Swift imagined himself as "cheerful to his dying day," but that was not to be. By 1732 he was noticing a serious deficit in short-term memory: "I often forget what I did yesterday, or what passed half an hour ago." It was a condition he had long foreseen. As early as 1720, when he was walking with Edward Young, secretary to the lord lieutenant at the time, he made a remark that Young put in print much later: "As I and others were taking with him an evening's walk, about a mile out of Dublin, he stopped short; we passed on; but perceiving that he did not follow us, I went back, and found him fixed as a statue, and earnestly gazing upward at a noble elm, which in its uppermost branches was much withered and decayed. Pointing at it, he said, 'I shall be like that tree, I shall die at the top.'"[19]

No reason has ever been given to doubt Young's anecdote; he was a highly principled clergyman as well as a moralizing poet. Ehrenpreis never mentions this story, however, since it apparently does not conform to his own conception of Swift. He may not have noticed that there is corroboration in an independent anecdote from Swift's friend Faulkner: "One time, in a journey from Drogheda to Navan, he rode before his company, made a sudden stop, dismounted his horse, fell on his knees, lifted up his hands, and prayed in the most devout manner. When his friends came up, he desired and insisted on their alighting, which they did, and asked him the meaning. 'Gentlemen,' said he, 'pray join your hearts in fervent prayers with mine, that I may never be like this oak tree, which is decayed and withered at the top, whilst all the other parts are sound.'"[20] It looks as if this was a comment Swift was in the habit of making.

Around 1734 there is a marked change in Swift's correspondence. Depressed, lonely, and sick, he was all too aware that his faculties were fading. The number of personal letters diminishes rapidly, partly because many friends were now dead, and partly because the strain of composing them was too great. Most of what remains is simple messages about practical matters.

Swift was finding it difficult even to write accurately, and when he read over his letters he was appalled at the number of blunders. "You see by my many blotting and interlinings," he wrote at the end of one of them, "what a condition my head is in." That particular letter contained the words "Give me leavelth," which were crossed out and replaced by "Give me leave to inquire after your health." There were bizarre spellings, too. The man who had once been so demanding about accurate spelling could now write "liquize" when he meant "likewise."[21] In Swift's time, the progressive symptoms of dementia were not adequately recognized; a general mental fuzziness was understood to reflect "senility," but confusion over words may have seemed puzzling.

Realizing that he was nearly finished as a writer, Swift allowed Faulkner to publish his collected writings in four handsome volumes, with an impressive list of subscribers who made payment in advance—over eight hundred of them, filling eleven pages, from the Earl of Abingdon to a Mr. Zouch. The Reverend Dr. Thomas Sheridan is there, of course, as are the Reverend Dr. Delany, who ordered no fewer than ten sets, and Mrs. Rebecca Dingley. It's not clear how direct a hand Swift had in the process of publication, but he definitely helped to locate copies of missing works, and took pains to restore passages in *Gulliver's Travels* that had been cut in earlier editions.[22]

When Motte, Swift's London publisher, complained that the Faulkner edition was competing with his own, Swift retorted that England had no right to enforce a publishing monopoly. To him this was just one abuse out of many. "I am so incensed against the oppressions from England, and have so little regard to the laws they make, that I do as a clergyman encourage the merchants both to export wool and woolen manufactures to any country in Europe, or anywhere else, and conceal it from the custom-house officers, as I would hide my purse from a highwayman if he came to rob me on the road, although England hath made a law to the contrary." Ehrenpreis exclaims, "The open appeal to lawlessness astonishes me."[23]

Swift's championing of Irish rights began to take on eccentric forms. One of his last public acts, in 1738, was to protest a new regulation of the coinage by raising a black flag and having the cathedral bells toll in mourning. A judge commented that with performances like that, "he makes it impossible for one in my station to converse with him."[24]

Swift tried to keep up his exercise program, hard though that was. "My giddiness is more or less constant," he told Pope in 1736; "I have not an ounce of flesh between the skin and bone, yet I walk often four or five miles, and ride ten or a dozen. But I sleep ill, and have a poor appetite. I can as easily write a poem in the Chinese language as my own."[25] Pope returned warmly affectionate letters, in which, however, Swift detected an element of self-interest. Pope was anxious to retrieve his own letters from Swift, with a view to revising and publishing them. Swift had alarmed him by declaring that he gave orders for all of his correspondence to be destroyed after his death, though that was most likely a teasing joke.

After a while Pope did get his letters back. And then, since it was considered pretentious for a living person to publish his correspondence, he tried to trick Faulkner into bringing out an allegedly unauthorized edition. His biographer calls the whole performance "a real-life comedy of intrigue, mystification, and deceit. . . . Pope's willingness throughout the affair to lay his own scheming on the backs of others is painful to behold."[26]

In the fall of 1735, Swift took his very last extended trip. It was to stay with Sheridan once again, who by now had moved to Cavan, ten miles from Quilca, and had opened a new school there. That meant closing down his successful school in Dublin, where Swift used to enjoy examining the students, and seeing much less of his friends. Swift dropped in at Sheridan's Dublin house just before the move and found workmen packing up furnishings in the parlor where he had often been entertained. As Sheridan's son remembered, "He burst into tears, and rushed into a dark closet [that is, a small room], where he continued a quarter of an hour before he could compose himself."[27]

In this decision, as in many others, Dr. Sheridan was his own worst enemy. Ten years previously, he had been offered a fine appointment in the diocese of Cork, but had ruined his chances at the last minute by preaching at random on the text "Sufficient unto the day is the evil thereof." The day happened to be August 1, the anniversary of George I's accession to the throne. Naturally enough, he was suspected of Tory sympathies, and the offer was withdrawn. It's probably true that he just preached, without thinking, a sermon that he happened to have with him. The archdeacon of Cork must have believed him, since he compensated for Sheridan's loss with a lease worth £250.[28]

The Cavan school was turning out to be a failure, and Swift was miserable during the visit. He told Martha Whiteway, in a letter written jointly with Sheridan, "I have been now the third day at Cavan, the Doctor's Canaan, the dirtiest place I ever saw, with the worst wife and daughter, and the most cursed sluts and servants, on this side Scotland."[29] "Canaan" was ironic, since Cavan was the opposite of a Promised Land. To make matters worse, Swift injured a shin and could neither ride nor walk.

The younger Sheridan got to know Swift well at this time. Swift was invariably kind to him, and since his eyesight was poor, he would have the boy read aloud for two or three hours every day. But the decline was obvious. No longer portly, "his person was quite emaciated, and bore the marks of many more years than had passed over his head. His memory greatly impaired, and his other faculties much on the decline." However genial he still was with people he trusted, outsiders found him short-tempered and difficult. "His temper [was] peevish, fretful, morose, and prone to sudden fits of passion."[30]

On one occasion Dr. Sheridan persuaded Swift to host a dinner at an inn for some town dignitaries, in return for the warm welcome they had given when Swift arrived in Cavan. In his own opinion the affair went well, as he told Mrs. Whiteway: "I invited the principal men in town to sup with me at the best inn here. There were sixteen of them, and I came off rarely for about thirty shillings. They were all very modest and obliging." He meant that he came off cheaply, which always gratified him. But the younger Sheridan remembered what happened very differently. Swift ordered "a very shabby dinner," began openly calculating the cost before his guests were finished, and yelled at the servants until they ran away. Dr. Sheridan was so disgusted that he left the inn without saying a word.[31]

Nevertheless, the next summer Sheridan tried to get Swift to visit again. "Well, when will you come down, or will you come at all? I think you may, can, could, might, would, or ought to come." But Swift was through with traveling, and he was beginning to part ways even from his closest friends. In 1737 he stopped seeing Delany altogether, though it's not known why.[32] It may well be that in his increasingly impaired state, he was finding it just too hard to keep his friendships up.

Sheridan turned fifty that year, suffering from severe asthma, which he treated by "whiskey with an agreeable mixture of garlic, bitter orange, gentian root, snakeroot, wormwood, etc." On a visit to Dublin he fell ill and was unable to leave the deanery for several weeks. After he recovered, he apologized for the trouble he must have caused, and added, "I fear, Mr. Dean, I have been an expensive lodger to you." Mrs. Whiteway spoke up and commented that Sheridan could easily resolve the situation by going to stay somewhere else. When Swift said nothing at all, Sheridan took it as his cue to leave, and they never saw each other again.[33]

This breach might have been healed eventually, like others before it, but Sheridan didn't have long to live. A year later, he drew up his will and then dined cheerfully with friends. When he dozed off at the table they went out for a walk, and when they returned an hour later they were shocked to find him dead. In after years, Swift had to acknowledge how much he missed his friend. One of his servants reported that he would repeatedly ask, "William,

91. Dean Swift, by Francis Bindon.

did you know Dr. Sheridan?" When William replied that he did, Swift would
sigh heavily and say, "Oh, I lost my right hand when I lost him."[34]

In 1738 Swift wrote to Orrery, "I have been many months the shadow of
the shadow of the shadow, of etc. etc. etc. of Dr. Swift—age, giddiness, deafness, loss of memory, rage and rancor against persons and proceedings (I have
not recovered a twentieth part)."[35] The decay is painfully apparent in a late
portrait by Bindon.

By now Swift was increasingly irascible, a symptom, perhaps, of advancing dementia. In one strange incident he got into a violent quarrel with a young cathedral prebendary named Francis Wilson. Wilson, who was secretly stealing money from Swift, took him for a carriage ride, got him drunk at a tavern, and then demanded to be made sub-dean. According to the man who was driving the carriage, when Swift refused, Wilson shouted, "You are a stupid old blockhead and an old rascal, and only you are too old, I would beat you, and God damn me but I will cut your throat!" If Wilson didn't strike him at that point, he must at least have twisted his arm painfully, for when Swift got home one of his arms was black and blue. But by then he had already forgotten the incident, and wondered why Wilson was not present as he would normally have been.[36]

Fearing total loss of his reason, Swift longed for death. Whenever he parted from a friend he would say, "Well, God bless you; good night to you, but I hope I shall never see you again." Once he and a guest happened to move away from a huge mirror just before it fell from the wall and shattered. "Was it not a mercy," said the clergyman, "that we moved from that spot the moment we did? For undoubtedly if we had stayed there any longer, we should both have been killed." "I am sorry for it," Swift replied. "I wish the glass had fallen upon me."[37]

As his condition deteriorated, Swift was well cared for by affectionate friends. Frequently on hand were his cousin Martha Whiteway and a surgeon named John Nichols, to whom her son was apprenticed. Her daughter, Anne Ridgeway, had been the deanery housekeeper ever since 1735, when Mrs. Brent died.

Swift had no use for the rest of his relatives, except for occasional visits from young Deane Swift, son of a cousin of the same name. During his last stay at Cavan, Swift wrote to Mrs. Whiteway, "Your letters have been so friendly, so frequent, and so entertaining, and oblige me so much, that I am afraid in a little time they will make me forget that you are a cousin, and treat you as a friend." She replied gratefully that she was "proud of being discarded from being a cousin." Not long afterward he wrote to a judge for advice on a family debt he had been saddled with: "There is a rascally cousin of mine called John Swift, his father is my cousin german, called Mead Swift, as great a rascal as his son. He was a son of my uncle Godwin, as arrant an old rascal as either. . . . I was desired to be a trustee of the marriage settlement, along with a rogue of an attorney, one Kit Swift, another son of old Godwin."[38]

Godwin Swift was the uncle who had grudgingly supported Swift in his youth—possibly with a secret bequest from someone else—and whose role biographers have sentimentalized in a way that Swift himself never did. Referring to the whole pack of Swifts, he was contemptuous: "Those are of all mortals what I most despise and hate, except one Mrs. Whiteway and her daughter."[39]

The very last of Swift's personal letters was sent to Mrs. Whiteway, and it is woundingly sad.

> I have been very miserable all night, and today extremely deaf and full of pain. I am so stupid and confounded that I cannot express the mortification I am under both in body and mind. All I can say is that I am not in torture, but I daily and hourly expect it. Pray let me know how your health is and your family. I hardly understand one word I write. I am sure my days will be very few; few and miserable they must be. I am, for those few days, yours entirely, J. Swift. If I do not blunder, it is Saturday, July 26th, 1740. If I live till Monday I shall hope to see you, perhaps for the last time.[40]

His remaining days were miserable indeed, but unfortunately not few. He still had five unhappy years to live.

DEMENTIA AND DEATH

By the fall of 1742 Swift's disability was so advanced that his food had to be cut up for him. He would ignore it for an hour or so, and then eat while walking restlessly about. At one stage an acute infection, orbital cellulitis, caused an eye to swell alarmingly, and the pain was so great that he had to be forcibly restrained from tearing at it. The episode did provoke a moment of lucidity, as Mrs. Whiteway reported: "What is more to be wondered at, the last day of his illness he knew me perfectly well, took me by the hand, called me by my name, and showed the same pleasure as usual in seeing me. I asked him if he would give me a dinner; he said 'To be sure, my old friend.' . . . But alas! this pleasure to me was but of short duration, for the next day or two it was all over, and proved to be only pain that had roused him."[41]

By now, according to Faulkner, Swift "forgot all his friends and domestics, could not call any of them by their names, nor for clothes, food, or any necessaries that he wanted." It was a second infancy. "He was treated like a newborn infant, being taken out of bed, dressed, led about the room by the servants and nurse-keepers, fed, undressed, and put into bed like the youngest child, and had the actions of one being fond of gold or silver toys, which he would play with or put into his mouth." Word of Swift's condition spread, and a bricklayer-poet from Drogheda came up with a memorable description: "Reason buried in the body's grave."[42]

In July of 1742 a writ of *De Lunatico Inquirendo* was entered, appointing a committee to confirm "that the Rev. Doctor Jonathan Swift, Dean of St. Patrick's, Dublin, hath for these nine months past been gradually failing in his memory and understanding, and of such unsound mind and memory that he is incapable of transacting any business or managing, conducting, or taking care either of his estate or person." The committee reported that Swift was indeed incompetent and should be placed under guardianship. Dr. Lyon, the young colleague who had been helping with cathedral business, then moved into a room in the deanery and was charged with responsibility for Swift.[43]

Swift's last recorded words are tragic. Anne Ridgeway said that when he hadn't spoken for an entire year, he was told that the usual bonfires were being lit to celebrate his birthday. He replied, "It is all folly, they had better let it alone." During this final period Delany, who was coming to see Swift now that he couldn't remember their quarrel, heard him "lamenting, in a manner that pierced me to the heart, that he was an idiot; that he was no more a human creature."[44]

Mrs. Ridgeway was with Swift on St. Patrick's Day, 1744, a year before he died. "As he sat in his chair, upon the housekeeper's moving a knife from him as he was going to catch at it, he shrugged his shoulders, and rocking himself, said, 'I am what I am, I am what I am.'" Is it possible that some memory of the First Epistle to the Corinthians surfaced in his distressed mind? Paul says, "Last of all he [Christ] was seen of me also, as one born out of due time. For I am the least of the apostles, that am not meet to be called an apostle, because I persecuted the Church of God. But by the grace of God I am what I am, and his grace which was bestowed upon me was not in vain; but I labored more abundantly than they all."[45]

Swift seems to have suffered a stroke not long before he died, and it was rumored that after he became completely helpless, the servants took bribes to let strangers come in and look at him. Picking up on this, and recalling that the Duke of Marlborough too had been incapacitated by a stroke, Johnson coupled Swift with the general he hated:

> From Marlborough's eyes the streams of dotage flow,
> And Swift expires a driveler and a show.[46]

The *Verses on the Death of Dr. Swift* had foretold the final moments, which arrived at last on October 19, 1745.

> Behold the fatal day arrive!
> "How is the Dean?" "He's just alive."
> Now the departing prayer is read.
> "He hardly breathes." "The Dean is dead."

For three days Swift lay in an open coffin in the deanery. Someone who saw him recalled that "he had on his head neither cap nor wig; there was not much hair on the front or very top, but it was long and thick behind, very white, and was like flax on the pillow." A few visitors managed to take away locks of hair, described charitably by Sheridan as "sacred relics."[47]

There was an autopsy, as Swift had also anticipated.

> The doctors, tender of their fame,
> Wisely on me lay all the blame:
> "We must confess his case was nice;
> But he would never take advice.
> Had he been ruled, for aught appears,

92. Memorial to Swift and Stella, St. Patrick's Cathedral.

He might have lived these twenty years,
For when we opened him we found
That all his vital parts were sound."

The doctors who performed the autopsy were looking mainly for defects of
the brain, and they didn't find any; they wouldn't have been able to diag-
nose Alzheimer's disease or vascular dementia. They did note a badly deviated
septum, which a modern specialist thinks could have caused a Eustachian
obstruction that triggered Ménière's disease.[48]

On October 22, Swift was laid to rest in St. Patrick's Cathedral, not far
from Stella. Their graves are marked today by a pair of handsome brass plaques
on the floor near the main entrance, but they weren't always there. Originally
Swift was buried ten feet away from Stella, and they only ended up in a single
coffin a hundred years later. As for the brass plaques, Swift's was installed soon
after his death, but Stella's wasn't added until the early twentieth century.
After that, in an ongoing tragicomedy, the plaques migrated from place to
place in the cathedral, according to whether each successive dean felt that
they belonged together or ought to be kept apart.[49]

Swift left directions in his will for an epitaph in Latin, and it was duly engraved on a large black wall plaque. It should be read as he intended it, not as
a prose statement but as a series of telling phrases. Here is the Latin original:

> Hic depositum est Corpus
> IONATHAN SWIFT S.T.D.
> Hujus Ecclesiæ Cathedralis
> Decani,
> Ubi sæva Indignatio
> Ulterius
> Cor lacerare nequit.
> Abi Viator
> Et imitare, si poteris,
> Strenuum pro virili
> Libertatis Vindicatorem.
> Obiit 19° Die Mensis Octobris
> A.D. 1745 Anno Aetatis 78°.

Literally translated it reads thus ("S.T.D." means Sacrae Theologiae Doctor):

> Here is deposited the body
> of Jonathan Swift S.T.D.

of this Cathedral church
the Dean
where savage indignation
can no longer
lacerate his heart.
Go, traveler,
and imitate, if you can,
a valiant champion
of manly freedom.

Translating loosely, Yeats wrote, "It is almost finer in English than in Latin: 'He has gone where fierce indignation can lacerate his heart no more.'"[50]

The Latin *indignatio* comes from the satirist Juvenal, and perhaps from the Bible as well: "Who can stand before his indignation? and who can abide in the fierceness of his anger?" In his will, Swift used the word *vindex*, translated here as "champion." It's not clear why the word on the plaque is *vindica-*

93. Bust of Swift in
St. Patrick's Cathedral.

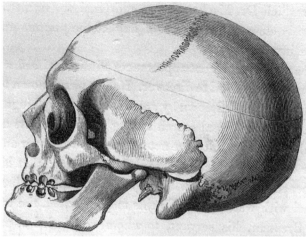

94. Swift's skull.

tor, whose meaning is closer to "avenger."[51] The challenge to the viewer is not in doubt: go and imitate if you can, but you probably can't.

Various proposals for a grand monument came to nothing, but twenty years later, when Swift's publisher Faulkner died, his son donated a bust by Patrick Cunningham that had occupied a place of honor in their bookstore window in Parliament Street. People who knew Swift regarded it as an excellent likeness, and the bust is now mounted high on the wall of the cathedral above the plaque. In 1749, a more accomplished bust by the celebrated sculptor Roubiliac was placed in the Long Room of Trinity College. But Roubiliac never saw Swift, and must have had to imagine a three-dimensional image by looking at portraits.[52]

There was a bizarre coda to come. In 1835, the river Poddle, which flows to this day in a tunnel beneath the streets of Dublin, overflowed into the cathedral. Repairs, which Swift himself had urged a century before, had to be made. His coffin was opened, and in accordance with the fad for phrenology, his skull and Stella's made the rounds of Dublin learned societies. The episode was described by a distinguished physician, Sir William Wilde: "The University where Swift had so often toiled again beheld him, but in another phase." The phrenologists concluded absurdly that the organs of wit, causality, and comparison were undeveloped, and also that "the portion of the occipital bone assigned to the animal propensities, philoprogenitiveness and amativeness, appeared excessive."[53] Perhaps Vanessa would have been able to confirm the truth of that.

In due course the remains were properly reburied, but in a macabre touch that might have amused Swift, "the only portion not returned was the larynx, the ossified fragments of which were abstracted by a bystander, a countryman of Swift's, and are now, we believe, in the city of New York."[54]

Stella's skull provoked Sir William Wilde to a romantic effusion. "It is no great stretch of the imagination to clothe and decorate this skull again with its alabaster skin, on which the rose had slightly bloomed; to adorn it with its original luxuriant dark hair, its white, expanded forehead; its level, penciled eyebrows, and deep, dark, lustrous eyes; its high prominent nose; its delicately chiseled mouth and pouting upper lip; its full, rounded chin, and long but gracefully swelling neck." Wilde confirmed what John Geree had remembered, sixty years after he knew Stella at Moor Park: "The teeth, which for their whiteness and regularity were in life the theme of admiration, were perhaps the most perfect ever witnessed in a skull."[55] Dr. Wilde was deservedly eminent in his profession, and could not have guessed that he would be later remembered, if at all, as the father of Oscar Wilde.

Even this was not quite the last of it. In 1882 the cathedral was flooded yet again, and the floor was opened up once more for repairs. The sexton then placed a memorandum with the remains: "The coffin was cleaned of the mud and water that was in it, and a box made by a carpenter who was working at the time in the Cathedral. And the two skulls and the remains of Swift put in the box. And from two to three feet of concrete put over it. I suppose never to be opened any more until the Great Day."[56]

A curious incident confirms how far from dated Swift still is. In 1969, a science writer read *Gulliver's Travels*, assumed it was a recent publication, and decided to request permission to quote from it. He addressed his letter to "Dr. Jonathan Swift, Dean, St. Patrick's Cathedral, Dublin, Ireland." The then dean, V. G. Griffin, sent this courteous reply: "Dr. Swift departed from here on 19th October, 1745. He left no forwarding address. Since that date, as far as I know, he has not communicated with friend or foe. Where he is at present, God only knows."[57]

Chronology

1699   Death of Sir William Temple; Swift goes to Ireland as chaplain to
        the Earl of Berkeley

1700   Appointed vicar of Laracor, County Meath, and prebendary of
        St. Patrick's Cathedral, Dublin

1701   Lord Berkeley returns to England; Swift accompanies him, and
        persuades Stella and Rebecca Dingley to move to Dublin; *Contests
        and Dissensions in Athens and Rome* (published 1709), *Humble
        Petition of Frances Harris, Meditation on a Broomstick* (published
        1710)

1702   Doctor of Divinity degree at Trinity College, Dublin; death of
        William III; War of the Spanish Succession begins

1703–4 In London seeking remission of the First Fruits in favor of the
        Church of Ireland

1704   Publication (in a single volume) of *A Tale of a Tub*, *The Battle of
        the Books*, and *The Mechanical Operation of the Spirit*; battle of
        Blenheim launches the Duke of Marlborough's fame; Robert Harley
        (later Lord Oxford) becomes secretary of state and Henry St. John
        (later Lord Bolingbroke) secretary at war

1704–7 In Ireland

1707   Union of England and Scotland

1708   *Bickerstaff Papers; Sentiments of a Church of England Man; Argument
        against Abolishing Christianity*

1708–13 In England most of the time; friendships with Joseph Addison,
        Richard Steele, and other writers, also with Esther Vanhomrigh
        (Vanessa) and Charles Ford

1709   *A Description of the Morning; Baucis and Philemon*

1710   Death of Abigail Swift; *The Virtues of Sid Hamet the Magician's Rod*;
        fifth edition of *Tale of a Tub* published, with added "Apology"; *A
        Description of a City Shower*; Harley and Bolingbroke persuade
        Swift to write the *Examiner* on behalf of their new Tory ministry

1710–11 Writes for the *Examiner*

1710–13 Writes *Journal to Stella*

1711   *Miscellanies in Prose and Verse; The Conduct of the Allies*; Harley
        becomes Earl of Oxford

1711–12 Addison and Steele's *Spectator*

1712   *Proposal for Correcting the English Tongue; Some Remarks on the Barrier Treaty;* St. John becomes Viscount Bolingbroke

1713   Installed as dean of St. Patrick's Cathedral, Dublin; *Cadenus and Vanessa* (published 1726); Scriblerus Club formed with Pope, Gay, Parnell, and Arbuthnot; Pope publishes *The Rape of the Lock* (enlarged version in 1714)

1714   Returns to England to try to repair a growing breach between Oxford and Bolingbroke; *Public Spirit of the Whigs;* Oxford dismissed by Queen Anne, who dies in August, succeeded by George I; Swift leaves London, stays with John Geree in the country, and then returns to Dublin; Vanessa follows, settling at nearby Celbridge

1715   Bolingbroke flees to France; Oxford impeached and committed to the Tower of London until 1717

1716   Rumored secret marriage with Stella

1718   Friendships with Thomas Sheridan senior and Patrick Delany

1719   First of the series of birthday poems for Stella; birth of Thomas Sheridan the younger; death of Addison; Defoe publishes *Robinson Crusoe*

1720   *A Proposal for the Universal Use of Irish Manufacture;* South Sea Bubble

1721   *Gulliver's Travels* begun; Sir Robert Walpole emerges as Whig leader, will retain power for twenty-one years

1722   *Satirical Elegy on the Death of a Late Famous General* (published 1764)

1723   Death of Vanessa; Swift makes four-month trip throughout Ireland; trial and exile of Bishop Francis Atterbury

1724   Book 4 of *Gulliver's Travels* finished, book 3 begun; *Drapier's Letters;* death of Lord Oxford

1725   Long stay with the Sheridans at Quilca, County Cavan, where *Gulliver's Travels* is completed; Bolingbroke returns to England from exile

1726   Swift visits England for the first time since 1714, arranges publication of *Gulliver's Travels; Cadenus and Vanessa* published without Swift's approval

1727   Final visit to England; *Holyhead Journal;* death of George I, succeeded by George II

1728   Death of Stella; *The Progress of Poetry; On the Death of Mrs. Johnson* (published 1765); collaboration with Sheridan on the *Intelligencer;* Gay publishes *The Beggar's Opera;* Pope publishes first installment of *The Dunciad*

1729   *A Modest Proposal;* deaths of Congreve and Steele

1730s   Friendships with Mary Pendarves, Mary Barber, and Laetitia Pilkington

1731   *Verses on the Death of Dr. Swift* (published 1739); *The Day of Judgment* (published 1762)

1732   *The Lady's Dressing Room;* friendship with Lord Orrery; death of Gay

1733   *On Poetry: A Rapsody*

1734   *A Beautiful Young Nymph Going to Bed; Strephon and Chloe; Cassinus and Peter*

1735   Dublin edition of Swift's *Works* published by George Faulkner; death of Arbuthnot; Bolingbroke returns to France

1736   *A Character of the Legion Club*

1737   *A Proposal for Giving Badges to Beggars*

1738   *Polite Conversation* (written over many years); death of Thomas Sheridan senior

1742   Swift declared "of unsound mind and memory"; Pope publishes new four-book *Dunciad*

1744   Death of Pope

1745   October 19, death of Swift, aged seventy-seven; buried near Stella in St. Patrick's Cathedral

Abbreviations

Account Books	*The Account Books of Jonathan Swift*, ed. Paul V. Thompson and Dorothy Jay Thompson (Newark: University of Delaware Press, 1984).
Boswell, *Life of Johnson*	James Boswell, *The Life of Samuel Johnson, LLD*, 6 vols., ed. G. B. Hill, rev. L. F. Powell (Oxford: Clarendon, 1934, 1950).
Cambridge *Works*	*The Cambridge Edition of the Works of Jonathan Swift* (Cambridge: Cambridge University Press, 2008–): vol. 1, *"A Tale of a Tub" and Other Works*, ed. Marcus Walsh; vol. 8, *English Political Writings, 1711–1714*, ed. Bertrand A. Goldgar and Ian Gadd. [These were the only volumes in print at the time this book went to press.]
Corr.	*The Correspondence of Jonathan Swift*, 4 vols., ed. David Woolley (Frankfurt: Peter Lang, 1999–2007).
Craik	Henry Craik, *The Life of Jonathan Swift*, 2 vols. (London: Macmillan, 1894).
Critical Heritage	*Swift: The Critical Heritage*, ed. Kathleen Williams (London: Routledge and Kegan Paul, 1970).
Deane Swift	Deane Swift, *An Essay upon the Life, Writings, and Character of Dr. Jonathan Swift* (London, 1755).
Delany	Patrick Delany, *Observations upon Lord Orrery's Remarks on the Life and Writings of Dr. Jonathan Swift* (Dublin, 1754).

Downie   J. A. Downie, *Jonathan Swift: Political Writer* (London: Routledge and Kegan Paul, 1984).

Ehrenpreis   Irvin Ehrenpreis, *Swift: The Man, His Works, and the Age*, 3 vols. (Cambridge: Harvard University Press, 1962–83): vol. 1, *Mr. Swift and His Contemporaries*; vol. 2, *Dr. Swift*; vol. 3, *Dean Swift*.

Elias   A. C. Elias Jr., *Swift at Moor Park: Problems in Biography and Criticism* (Philadelphia: University of Pennsylvania Press, 1982).

Ferguson   Oliver W. Ferguson, *Jonathan Swift and Ireland* (Urbana: University of Illinois Press, 1962).

Forster   John Forster, *The Life of Jonathan Swift*, vol. 1 [no second volume was ever published] (New York: Harper, 1876).

Glendinning   Victoria Glendinning, *Jonathan Swift* (London: Hutchinson, 1998).

Gulliver's Travels   Swift, *Gulliver's Travels*, vol. 11 of *PW*.

Johnson, *Life of*   Samuel Johnson, *Life of Swift*, in *Lives*, vol. 3.
Swift

Johnston   Denis Johnston, *In Search of Swift* (Dublin: Hodges Figgis, 1959).

Journal   Swift, *Journal to Stella*, 2 vols., ed. Harold Williams (Oxford: Blackwell, 1948); reprinted in *PW* as vols. 15 and 16.

Landa   Louis A. Landa, *Swift and the Church of Ireland* (Oxford: Clarendon, 1954).

Lives   Samuel Johnson, *Lives of the English Poets*, 3 vols., ed. G. B. Hill (Oxford: Clarendon, 1905).

Lyon   Dr. John Lyon's annotated copy of *The Life of Jonathan Swift*, by John Hawkesworth (1755), in the National Art Library, Victoria and Albert Museum, no. 579 in the Forster Collection (MS. 48. D. 39).

Macaulay   Thomas Babington Macaulay, *The History of England from the Accession of James the Second* (London: Longmans, Green, 1886).

Nokes   David Nokes, *Jonathan Swift, a Hypocrite Reversed: A Critical Biography* (Oxford: Oxford University Press, 1985).

Orrery   John Boyle, fifth Earl of Cork and Orrery, *Remarks on the Life and Writings of Dr. Jonathan Swift*, ed. João Fróes (Newark: University of Delaware Press, 2000).

Pilkington   *Memoirs of Laetitia Pilkington*, 2 vols., ed. A. C. Elias Jr. (Athens: University of Georgia Press, 1997).

Plumb   J. H. Plumb, *Sir Robert Walpole*, 2 vols. (London: Cresset, 1956–60).

Poems	*The Poems of Jonathan Swift*, 2nd ed., 3 vols., ed. Harold Williams (Oxford: Clarendon, 1958).
PW	*The Prose Works of Jonathan Swift*, 14 vols., ed. Herbert Davis (Oxford: Blackwell, 1939–68).
Reading Swift	Hermann J. Real and Heinz J. Vienken, eds., *Proceedings of the [First through Fifth] Münster Symposium on Jonathan Swift* (Munich: Wilhelm Fink Verlag, 1985–2008).
Rogers	Swift, *The Complete Poems*, ed. Pat Rogers (New Haven: Yale University Press, 1983).
Scott	Sir Walter Scott, *Memoirs of Jonathan Swift*, vol. 1 of *The Works of Jonathan Swift* (London: Bickers and Son, 1883).
Sheridan	Thomas Sheridan, *The Life of Jonathan Swift*, 2nd ed. (London, 1787).
Tale of a Tub	Swift, *A Tale of a Tub*, vol. 1 of *PW*.
Trevelyan	George Macaulay Trevelyan, *England under Queen Anne*, 3 vols. (London: Longmans, Green, 1930–34).

Notes

PROLOGUE

1. Vanessa to Swift, December 1714; Swift to Vanessa, July 5, 1721; Vanessa to Swift, August 1720, *Corr.*, 2:103, 386, 340. This letter of Swift's was written in French, perhaps for fear that a snooping servant might see it.
2. Swift to Vanessa, Aug. 4, 1720; Vanessa to Swift, November or December 1720, *Corr.*, 2:340, 352.
3. Swift to Vanessa, Oct. 15, 1720; July 5, 1721; July 13, 1722, *Corr.*, 2:348, 385–86, 425.
4. Deane Swift, 359; Orrery, 176.
5. Scott, 11n, repeating a story told to him by Theophilus Swift, the grandson of the uncle in question.
6. George Orwell, "Politics vs. Literature: An Examination of *Gulliver's Travels*," in *Inside the Whale and Other Essays* (London: Penguin, 1962), 138.
7. Ian Mortimer, *The Time Traveler's Guide to Medieval England: A Handbook for Visitors to the Fourteenth Century* (New York: Simon and Schuster, 2010), 1; William Butler Yeats, introduction to *Words upon the Window-pane* (1934), reprinted in *Fair Liberty Was All His Cry: A Tercentenary Tribute to Jonathan Swift*, ed. A. Norman Jeffares (London: Macmillan, 1967), 196.
8. Boswell, *Life of Johnson*, 2:100 (Oct. 26, 1769); Deane Swift, 367.
9. Swift to Bolingbroke, Mar. 21, 1730, *Corr.*, 3:295; *Journal*, 1:72–73 (Oct. 26, 1710).
10. E. D. Hirsch remarked in an obituary notice that little of Ehrenpreis's ironic wit carried over into his writing (*New York Review of Books*, Aug. 15, 1985). Ehrenpreis argued his case against literary ambiguity in *Literary Meaning and Augustan Values* (Charlottesville: University Press of Virginia, 1974) and again in *Acts of Implication:*

Suggestion and Covert Meaning in the Works of Dryden, Swift, Pope, and Austen (Berkeley: University of California Press, 1980).

11. Ehrenpreis, 1:41; 2:335, 331.

12. Ibid., 1:ix.

13. The Bolingbroke remark is quoted by Sheridan, introduction, unnumbered page.

14. Ashley Marshall, "The State of Swift Studies 2010," *Eighteenth-Century Life* 34 (2010): 87.

15. Glendinning, 10. Other recent biographies, each emphasizing a particular aspect of Swift's life, are J. A. Downie, *Jonathan Swift: Political Writer* (London: Routledge and Kegan Paul, 1984); Joseph McMinn, *Jonathan Swift: A Literary Life* (London: Macmillan, 1991); and Brean Hammond, *Jonathan Swift* (Dublin: Irish Academic Press, 2010).

16. Sheridan, introduction, unnumbered page.

17. Scott, 10.

18. William Godwin, "Of English Style" (1797), in *Critical Heritage*, 256.

CHAPTER 1. BEGINNINGS

1. Lyon, 11. Swift spelled the name of the church "Warbrow" in a letter to Knightley Chetwode, Dec. 3, 1714, *Corr.*, 2:98.

2. Orrery, 331.

3. Swift to Francis Grant, Mar. 23, 1734, *Corr.*, 3:730. Sheridan (214) reports the expression "dropped in Ireland."

4. The evidence for Abigail's origins will be taken up in chapter 2, when we return to some of the puzzles concerning her son's paternity.

5. The Earl of Essex, quoted by S. J. Connolly, *Religion, Law, and Power: The Making of Protestant Ireland, 1660–1760* (Oxford: Clarendon, 1992), 14; Patrick Reilly, "The Displaced Person: Swift and Ireland," *Swift Studies* 8 (1993): 69; Swift to Pope, June 1737, *Corr.*, 4:445.

6. Ehrenpreis, 1:3, 64.

7. Ibid., 1:30.

8. Quoted by Valerie Fildes, *Wet Nursing: A History from Antiquity to the Present* (Oxford: Blackwell, 1988), 100. Other details from Fildes, *Breasts, Bottles and Babies: A History of Infant Feeding* (Edinburgh: Edinburgh University Press, 1986), 158, 162–63, 173, 213, 245, 352, 364; and Fildes, "The English Wet-Nurse and Her Role in Infant Care, 1538–1800," *Medical History* 32 (1988): 142–73.

9. *Family of Swift, PW*, 5:192.

10. Pilkington, 1:31–32. Ehrenpreis (1:31n) calls this version "a garbled recollection," but it differs from the version in Swift's autobiographical sketch only in mentioning the nurse's husband and in suggesting that it was years before anyone knew where the child was.

11. Downie, 5; Deane Swift, 26.

12. Deane Swift, appendix, p. 42; *Gulliver's Travels*, book 4, ch. 5, p. 248.

13. Ehrenpreis, 1:32; Forster (40) conjectures that Abigail badly needed money.

14. *Gulliver's Travels*, book 1, ch. 6, p. 60.

15. *Journal*, 2:658 (Apr. 10, 1711). See Louise Barnett for a valuable chapter (5) on maternity, *Jonathan Swift in the Company of Women* (Oxford: Oxford University Press, 2007).

16. Franz Kafka, *Letter to His Father*, trans. Ernst Kaiser and Eithne Wilkins (New York: Schocken, 1966), 295. Jeffrey Meyers draws this comparison in "Swift and Kafka," *Papers on Language and Literature* 40 (2004): 334.

17. Amanda Vickery, *Behind Closed Doors: At Home in Georgian England* (New Haven: Yale University Press, 2009), 2.

18. *Family of Swift*, 5:187–89.

19. Ibid., 5:189; this piece was probably written between 1727 and 1729 (*PW*, 5:xxiii). Johnston (272–79) reviews the facts of Thomas Swift's career, and mentions the caltrop. The younger relative is Deane Swift, appendix, p. 24.

20. Swift to Pope, Apr. 28, 1739, *Corr.*, 4:575.

21. *Lines on Swift's Ancestors*, in *Minor Poems*, vol. 6 in the Twickenham edition of Pope's *Poems*, ed. Norman Ault and John Butt (London: Methuen, 1964), 251.

22. William Edward Hartpole Lecky, *A History of Ireland in the Eighteenth Century* (London: Longmans, Green, 1912), 1:166; the figures for population distribution are drawn from Edith Mary Johnston, *Ireland in the Eighteenth Century* (Dublin: Gill and Macmillan, 1974), 53.

23. *Family of Swift*, 5:192; Ehrenpreis, 1:35.

24. Details from Connolly, *Religion, Law, and Power*, 146; and W. G. Neely, *Kilkenny: An Urban History, 1391–1843* (Belfast: Institute of Irish Studies, 1989), 85–119.

25. Ormonde to Sir Robert Southwell, Mar. 20, 1679, quoted by Marilyn Frankus, *The Converting Imagination: Linguistic Theory and Swift's Satiric Prose* (Carbondale: Southern Illinois University Press, 1994), 194.

26. John Browne, "Kilkenny College," *Transactions of the Kilkenny Archaeological Society* 1, no. 2 (1850): 221–29.

27. Neely, *Kilkenny*, 108–9.

28. Samuel Pepys, *Diary*, ed. Robert Latham and William Matthews (Berkeley: University of California Press, 1979), 3:131 (July 4, 1662).

29. See Frankus, *Converting Imagination*, 11–18.

30. Swift to Charles Ford, Nov. 12, 1708, *Corr.*, 1:217.

31. Edward Gibbon, *Memoirs of My Life*, ed. Betty Radice (London: Penguin, 1984), 73; Boswell, *Life of Johnson*, 2:407 (end of 1775).

32. Swift to Pope, Feb. 13, 1729, *Corr.*, 3:209.

33. Lyon, 12.

34. Swift to Bolingbroke and Pope, Apr. 5, 1729, *Corr.*, 3:230.

35. George Faulkner to the Earl of Chesterfield, in John Nichols, *A Supplement to Dr. Swift's Works* (London: Nichols, 1779), 762. Sheridan (402–3) gives a somewhat abridged version of this anecdote, which he probably picked up from Faulkner.

36. Lyon, 12; John Timbs, *Lives of Wits and Humorists* (London: Bentley, 1862), 1:3.

37. T. C. Barnard, "'Grand Metropolis' or 'The Anus of the World'? The Cultural Life of Eighteenth-Century Dublin," in *Two Capitals: London and Dublin, 1500–1840*, ed. Peter Clark and Raymond Gillespie (Oxford: Oxford University Press, 2001), 203.

38. Sheridan, *An Oration, Pronounced before a Numerous Body of the Nobility and Gentry* (1757), quoted by Esther K. Sheldon, *Thomas Sheridan of Smock-Alley* (Princeton: Princeton University Press, 1967), 16.

39. Sheridan, 4.

40. *Tale of a Tub*, "A Digression in the Modern Kind," and section 8, pp. 80, 97; *Memoirs of Martinus Scriblerus*, ed. Charles Kerby-Miller (New York: Russell and Russell, 1966), 124.

41. Constantia Maxwell, *A History of Trinity College, Dublin* (Dublin: Dublin University Press, 1946), 74–75. Marsh died in 1701 and the library was founded in that year.

42. *A Character of Primate Marsh*, PW, 5:211–12.

43. *Gulliver's Travels*, book 3, ch. 5, pp. 180–82.

44. Forster, 53; Delany, 35.

45. Deane Swift, 42; T. G. Wilson, "Swift in Trinity," *Dublin Magazine* 5 (1966): 20.

46. Ehrenpreis, 69.

47. Deane Swift, 372; Edward Lloyd, in *A Description of the City of Dublin* (1732), quoted by Patrick Fagan, *The Second City: Portrait of Dublin, 1700–1760* (Dublin: Branar, 1986), 107.

48. George Faulkner, "Some Further Account," in Faulkner's 1763 Dublin edition of Swift's *Works*, 11:330; Joseph Spence, *Observations, Anecdotes, and Characters of Books and Men, Collected from Conversation*, ed. James M. Osborn (Oxford: Clarendon, 1966), 1:52.

49. Spence, *Observations*, 1:340–41.

50. Mentioned by Richard Holmes, *Marlborough: Britain's Greatest General* (London: Harper, 2008), 13, 221–22.

51. Imitation of Horace's *Epistle* 1.7.77–8; *Epilogue at the Theatre Royal*, lines 3–4; *A Serious Poem upon William Wood*, lines 27–28, *Poems*, 1:173, 275, 334. Swift's pronunciation is studied by Jonathan Pritchard in "Swift's Irish Rhymes," *Studies in Philology* 104 (2007): 123–58.

52. Baldwin is quoted by Wilson, "Swift in Trinity," 20; Lyon, 4; Delany, 175.

53. See Andrew Carpenter, "*A Tale of a Tub* as an Irish Text," *Swift Studies* 20 (2005): 30–40; and George Mayhew, "Swift and the Tripos Tradition," *Philological Quarterly* 45 (1966): 85–101.

54. Quoted in *A Tale of a Tub*, ed. A. C. Guthkelch and D. Nichol Smith (Oxford: Clarendon, 1958), 351. Recently discovered notes show that Dr. Lyon saw the original among Swift's papers after his death: see A. C. Elias, "Swift's *Don Quixote*, Dunkin's *Virgil Travesty*, and Other New Intelligence: John Lyon's 'Materials for a Life of Dr. Swift,' 1765," *Swift Studies* 13 (1998): 87.

55. Scott, 11, repeating a story told to him by Godwin Swift's grandson Theophilus Swift. Ehrenpreis (1:ix) dismisses the anecdote as an instance of "legendary Swiftiana."

56. For example, Wilson, "Swift in Trinity," 11.

57. Deane Swift, 54–55.

58. Swift to Deane Swift (senior), June 3, 1694, *Corr.*, 1:120.

59. Swift to Thomas Staunton, Dec. 15, 1726, *Corr.*, 3:65.

60. *Verses on the Death of Dr. Swift*, lines 107–8, *Poems*, 2:556.

61. John Dryden, *Absalom and Achitophel*, line 10; Macaulay, 1:214.

62. Lady Harvey, quoted by Tim Harris, *Revolution: The Great Crisis of the British Monarchy, 1685–1720* (London: Penguin, 2007), 239.

63. Macaulay, 1:584.

64. *Ireland's Lamentation* (1689), quoted by Toby Barnard, *Making the Grand Figure: Lives and Possessions in Ireland, 1641–1770* (New Haven: Yale University Press, 2004), 360. The first visit of a monarch in three hundred years is mentioned by Mark Kishlansky, *A Monarchy Transformed: Britain, 1603–1714* (London: Penguin, 1997), 287.

65. Harris, *Revolution*, 449. The Gaelic quotation is taken from Holmes, *Marlborough*, 168; other details are from S. J. Connolly, *Divided Kingdom: Ireland, 1630–1800* (Oxford: Oxford University Press, 2008), 188.

66. Quoted by W. MacNeile Dixon, *Trinity College, Dublin* (London: Robinson, 1902), 63, 65; the number of fellows who left is reported by Maxwell, *A History of Trinity College, Dublin*, 83.

67. Macaulay, 2:593.

68. Steve Pincus, *1688: The First Modern Revolution* (New Haven: Yale University Press, 2009).

69. Henry St. John, Viscount Bolingbroke, *Dissertation upon Parties* (1733–34), in *The Works of Lord Bolingbroke* (Philadelphia: Carey and Hart, 1841), 2:27.

70. Sheridan, 7–8.

CHAPTER 2. A PATRON AND TWO MYSTERIES

1. Laurence Eachard, *An Exact Description of Ireland* (London, 1691), 2.

2. www.irishferries.com.

3. Swift to Abigail Swift, Aug. 5, 1698, *Corr.*, 1:135. Ehrenpreis identifies half a dozen visits to Leicester: 1:44, 1:107, 2:44, 2:112, 2:195, 2:338.

4. Orrery, 331.

5. Jack Simmons, *Leicester Past and Present* (London: Eyre Methuen, 1974), 1:95; G. A. Chinnery, "Eighteenth-Century Leicester," in *The Growth of Leicester*, ed. A. E. Brown (Leicester: Leicester University Press, 1970), 48.

6. Swift to John Worrall, Jan. 18, 1729, *Corr.*, 3:207–8.

7. Swift to John Winder, Jan. 13, 1699, *Corr.*, 1:138.

8. Swift to Rev. John Kendall, Feb. 11, 1692, *Corr.*, 1:104.

9. *Family of Swift*, 5:193.

10. Trevelyan, 1:93; G. K. Chesterton, *The Rolling English Road*.

11. Deane Swift, 99–100.

12. Orrery, 96; Henri Misson, *M. Misson's Memoirs and Observations in His Travels over England, Written Originally in French and Translated by Mr. Ozell* (London, 1719), 332;

Johnson, *Life of Swift*, 6; George Faulkner to the Earl of Chesterfield, in Nichols, *A Supplement to Dr. Swift's Works*, 758–59.

13. See J. B. Owen, "Political Patronage in Eighteenth-Century England," in *The Triumph of Culture: Eighteenth-Century Perspectives*, ed. Paul Fritz and David Williams (Toronto: Hakkert, 1972). Swift's wages will be discussed below.

14. *Spectator* 469.

15. Quoted by Homer E. Woodbridge, *Sir William Temple: The Man and His Work* (New York: Modern Language Association, 1940), 106. The treaties were the short-lived Triple Alliance of 1668 between England, Holland, and Sweden, and the Treaty of Nijmegen in 1678–79 that concluded a naval conflict with Holland.

16. Sir William Temple, *Works* (1814), 2:569.

17. Jane Dunn calls the marriage "one of the great love stories of the century" in *Read My Heart: Dorothy Osborne and Sir William Temple, a Love Story in the Age of Revolution* (London: Harper, 2008), xvii. Woolf included an essay on the Osborne letters in *The Common Reader*.

18. Quoted by G. C. Moore Smith, *The Early Essays and Romances of Sir William Temple, Bt.* (Oxford: Clarendon, 1930), 194, 11.

19. Béat de Muralt, quoted by Woodbridge, *Sir William Temple*, 232.

20. Alexander Pope, *Windsor Forest*, line 344; Temple, *Upon the Gardens of Epicurus*, in *Five Miscellaneous Essays by Sir William Temple*, ed. Samuel Holt Monk (Ann Arbor: University of Michigan Press, 1963), 25.

21. Josua Poole, *The English Parnassus: A Help to English Poesie* (1657), quoted by Herman J. Real, "A Taste of Composition Rare: The *Tale*'s Matter and Void," in *Reading Swift*, 3:73 (I have abridged Poole's long catalogue a bit).

22. Temple's *Memoirs*, quoted by Samuel Holt Monk in his introduction to *Five Miscellaneous Essays*, xix; *An Essay upon the Ancient and Modern Learning*, in *Five Miscellaneous Essays*, 71.

23. Elias identifies several of them (124–25).

24. Ehrenpreis, 1:120, 3:1050; Carpenter, "*A Tale of a Tub* as an Irish Text," 39.

25. William Makepeace Thackeray, *The English Humourists of the Eighteenth Century*, in *Works* (London: Smith, Elder, 1879), 389; Thomas Babington Macaulay, "Sir William Temple," in *The Works of Lord Macaulay* (New York: Longmans, Green, 1897), 6:315.

26. Reported by Olivier de Corancez, *Mémoires de J.-J. Rousseau*, in *Mémoires biographiques et littéraires*, ed. Mathurin de Lescure (Paris: Firmin-Didot, 1881), 278.

27. Delany, 100; Temple to William Godolphin, Jan. 22, 1666, quoted by Elias, 125.

28. Lady Giffard, "The Character of Sir W. Temple," quoted by Thomas Peregrine Courtenay, *Memoirs of the Life, Works, and Correspondence of Sir William Temple* (London: Longman, 1836), 2:145; Temple, *An Essay upon the Cure of the Gout by Moxa*, in *Works* (1814), 3:270, 27; *An Essay upon the Cure of the Gout by Moxa*, in *Works* (1814), 3:270. Moxa, or mugwort, is a medicinal herb.

29. Elias (96) notes Swift's absence of comment on Gilbert Burnet's account of Temple's conceit.

30. The "swans" anecdote is quoted by Craik, 1:32; James Joyce, *Finnegans Wake* (London: Faber and Faber, 1950), 177. Joyce is quoted by Mackie L. Jarrell, "Swiftiana in

Finnegans Wake," *ELH* 26 (1959): 284; Jarrell shows that highly specific allusions to Swift and his circle are pervasive in *Finnegans Wake*.

31. Swift to Thomas Swift, May 3, 1692, *Corr.*, 1:110; Elias, 78.

32. Samuel Richardson to Lady Bradshaigh, Apr. 22, 1752, in *The Correspondence of Samuel Richardson*, ed. Anna Laetitia Barbauld (London: Phillips, 1804), 6:173–74. Ehrenpreis, as usual, ignores this anecdote.

33. *Journal*, 1:9, 113 (Sept. 9, Dec. 5, 1710); Courtenay, *Memoirs of the Life . . . of Sir William Temple*, 2:132; Elias, 143–46; Lyon, 27 (adding "it is certain" that Swift's relatives sent him money).

34. *Journal*, 1:230–31 (Apr. 3–4, 1711).

35. *Directions to Servants*, *PW*, 13:18. The relevance of this passage is noted by Sybil Le Brocquy, *Swift's Most Valuable Friend* (Dublin: Dolmen, 1968), 36.

36. Sir William Temple to Sir Robert Southwell, May 29, 1690, *Corr.*, 1:101. The letter was preserved in the Southwell papers.

37. Forster, 71.

38. *Family of Swift*, 5:193. Bruce Arnold reviews reasons why Swift might have been useful to Southwell in "Jonathan Swift: Some Current Biographical Problems," in *Reading Swift*, 4:39–43, but in the same volume James Woolley dismisses the connection as unlikely: "Swift's First Published Poem: *Ode to the King*," 277–78.

39. *PW*, 1:xxxvii.

40. Forster, 116.

41. *Gulliver's Travels*, book 1, ch. 6, p. 61. The Lilliputian system is drawn from Plato's *Republic* and More's *Utopia*.

42. Quoted by Courtenay, *Memoirs of the Life . . . of Sir William Temple*, 2:147–48.

43. Julia G. Longe, *Martha, Lady Giffard: Her Life and Correspondence* (London: George Allen, 1911), 197.

44. *Journal*, 1:183 (Feb. 8, 1711); see A. C. Elias Jr., "Stella's Writing-Master," *Scriblerian* 9, no. 2 (1977): 134–39; *To Dr. Swift on His Birthday, November 30, 1721*, line 2, *Poems*, 2:737.

45. *On the Death of Mrs. Johnson*, *PW*, 5:227. The evidence—or lack of it—for the alleged portraits is carefully reviewed by Henry Mangan in an appendix to the *Journal*, 2:687–703.

46. Swift to Stella, January 1698, *Corr.*, 1:129.

47. *On the Death of Mrs. Johnson*, 5:231; *Gulliver's Travels*, book 2, ch. 4, p. 114; see Margaret Anne Doody, "Swift and the Mess of Narrative," in *Locating Swift*, ed. Aileen Douglas et al. (Dublin: Four Courts, 1998), 115.

48. Details from Ehrenpreis, 1:260; and Elias, 148–50. Temple's will is printed by Courtenay, *Memoirs of the Life . . . of Sir William Temple*, 2:484–85.

49. Glendinning, 237; David P. French, "The Identity of C.M.P.G.N.S.T.N.S.," in *Jonathan Swift: Tercentenary Essays*, ed. French (Tulsa: University of Tulsa Press, 1967), 1–9; Swift to Vanessa, June 8, 1714, *Corr.*, 1:606. Since the *Gentleman's Magazine* letter contains facts that were not yet public knowledge, its author must have had a personal connection with Moor Park in the 1690s, and must have lived on until 1757. This drastically narrows the range of possible candidates.

50. All quotations are from "Anecdotes of Dean Swift and Miss Johnson," *Gentleman's Magazine and Historical Chronicle*, November 1757, 487–91; the letter is reprinted in full by Le Brocquy, *Swift's Most Valuable Friend*, 12–20.

51. Bruce Arnold saw a note by Denis Johnston explaining the *cum paganis satanas* identification: "Jonathan Swift," 4:44–47.

52. Ehrenpreis, 1:104.

53. Le Brocquy, *Swift's Most Valuable Friend*, 23–27. In this section I draw also on Johnston, 94–96. Geree thought that Stella was the youngest sibling rather than the oldest, which suggests that he never met the other two.

54. Frederick A. Pottle, *James Boswell: The Earlier Years, 1740–1769* (New York: McGraw-Hill, 1966), 98, 351–52; "a young diplomat's" comment is quoted by Ehrenpreis, 1:120.

55. Review of Orrery, *Monthly Review*, November 1751, 416; Ehrenpreis, 1:120.

56. Letter by a diplomat named de Cros, working for the Duke of Holstein, quoted by T. G. Wilson, "Swift's Personality," in Jeffares, *Fair Liberty Was All His Cry*, 34.

57. Johnston, 113; he gives sources (82) showing that Lady Temple stayed mainly in London.

58. Orrery, 83, 332 (the anecdote about Jane is a handwritten note in the margin of his own biography of Swift).

59. *Reminiscences Written by Mr. Horace Walpole in 1788*, ed. Paget Toynbee (Oxford: Clarendon, 1924), 144, reporting the opinion of Alexander Pope and John Gay.

60. *PW*, 5:227; Le Brocquy offers this interpretation in *Swift's Most Valuable Friend*, 25.

61. Orrery, 82. Temple's will is printed by Courtenay, *Memoirs of the Life . . . of Sir William Temple*, 2:484–85.

62. Shane Leslie, *The Script of Jonathan Swift* (Philadelphia: University of Pennsylvania Press, 1935), 12 (noting that Stella misspells the word *business* in exactly the way Swift had complained of in the *Journal to Stella*).

63. "Anecdotes of Dean Swift and Miss Johnson," 489. Elias (144) notes that Mose is mentioned in a 1697 Moor Park document.

64. Deane Swift, 35.

65. Downie, 342.

66. Johnston, ix, xi.

67. Lyon, 3.

68. *Monthly Review*, November 1751, 416.

69. The Black Book of King's Inns, quoted by Johnston, 33; on Swift's appointment as attorney, 50.

70. Ehrenpreis, 2:368n; Johnston, 45.

71. *Family of Swift*, 5:193; Temple to Sir Robert Southwell, May 29, 1690, *Corr.*, 1:101; Deane Swift, 34.

72. Robert Sidney, Earl of Leicester, served as lord lieutenant of Ireland, the representative there of the Crown (Johnston, 203–8).

73. Bruce Arnold, "Those Who Seek to Obtain My Estate: Swift on Love and Envy," *Swift Studies* 11 (1996), 42.

74. Johnston, 209–13.
75. This point is made by Le Brocquy, *Swift's Most Valuable Friend*, 32–33.

CHAPTER 3. "LONG CHOOSING, AND BEGINNING LATE"

1. Sydney Smith, quoted by Hesketh Pearson, *Lives of the Wits* (London: Heinemann, 1962), 125; John Milton, *Paradise Lost*, IX:26.
2. Macaulay, 2:419.
3. Deane Swift, 108.
4. Julian Hoppit, *A Land of Liberty? England, 1689–1727* (Oxford: Clarendon, 2000), 34; Macaulay, 1:406; quoted by Wilson (quoting the king's joke), "Swift in Trinity," 22.
5. Swift to William Swift, Nov. 29, 1692, *Corr.*, 1:116; Norman Sykes, *Church and State in England in the Eighteenth Century* (Cambridge: Cambridge University Press, 1934), 149. Swift specified Canterbury and Westminster in the autobiographical *Family of Swift*, 5:195.
6. On the king's offer to Swift: Deane Swift, 108, and Orrery, 81; Calhoun Winton, *Captain Steele: The Early Career of Richard Steele* (Baltimore: Johns Hopkins University Press, 1964), 39.
7. Johnson, *Life of Swift*, 4.
8. Macaulay, 2:499.
9. Elizabeth Hamilton, *The Backstairs Dragon: A Life of Robert Harley, Earl of Oxford* (London: Hamish Hamilton, 1969), 177.
10. Marginalia to Burnet's *History of His Own Times* and to Macky's *Characters of the Court of Britain*, *PW*, 5:285, 259.
11. Sermon, *On Mutual Subjection*, *PW*, 9:142–43; Orrery, 318, 424.
12. *Family of Swift*, 5:194; on the issues involved see Geoffrey Holmes, *The Making of a Great Power: Late Stuart and Early Georgian Britain, 1660–1722* (London: Longman, 1993), 222–23.
13. See John Brewer, *The Sinews of Power: War, Money and the English State, 1688–1783* (New York: Knopf, 1989), 159.
14. *Family of Swift*, 5:193; letter to Henrietta Howard, Aug. 19, 1727, *Corr.*, 3:120–21.
15. Locke, *Some Thoughts concerning Education*, in *The Educational Writings of John Locke*, ed. James L. Axtell (Cambridge: Cambridge University Press, 1968), section 20, p. 130; the relevance of this passage to Swift is noted by Carol Houlihan Flynn, *The Body in Swift and Defoe* (Cambridge: Cambridge University Press, 1990), 98. Scott, 1:23n; Johnson, *Life of Swift*, 4; Temple, *Upon the Gardens of Epicurus*, 35.
16. *Journal*, 1:338, 349 (Aug. 23, Sept. 1, 1711); Swift to Sheridan, July 1 and Aug. 12, 1727; *Corr.*, 3:103, 115.
17. Temple, *Of Health and Long Life*, in *Essays of Sir William Temple*, ed. J. A. Nicklin (London: Blackie, 1910), 142.
18. Swift to Ford, Nov. 20, 1733, *Corr.*, 3:707.
19. *Verses on the Death of Dr. Swift*, lines 83–84, 2:556. A full account of the disease's effects in Swift's life is given by Wanda J. Creaser, "'The Most Mortifying Malady':

Jonathan Swift's Dizzying World and Dublin's Mentally Ill," *Swift Studies* 19 (2004): 27–48. Even today, though its effects can be alleviated, it remains incurable: Alexander Thomas and Jeffrey Harris, "Current Epidemiology of Ménière's Syndrome," *Otolaryngologic Clinics of North America* 43, no. 5 (2010): 965–70.

20. Deane Swift, 272; Pilkington, 1:36. Deane Swift (100) mentions the medical advice against exercise.

21. *PW*, 1:xxxvii; Delany, 118–19; Johnson, *Life of Swift*, 55.

22. Glendinning, 226; Irvin Ehrenpreis, *The Personality of Jonathan Swift* (London: Methuen, 1958), 29.

23. Swift to Rev. John Kendall, Feb. 11, 1692, *Corr.*, 1:104 (annotating this letter, Woolley conjectures that the "person of great honour" may have been Henry Viscount Sydney); *Occasioned by Sir W—— T——'s Late Illness and Recovery*, lines 131–32, *Poems*, 1:55.

24. Swift to Thomas Swift, Dec. 6, 1693, *Corr.*, 1:118.

25. Roy Porter, *English Society in the Eighteenth Century*, rev. ed. (London: Penguin, 1982), 48.

26. Delany, 26.

27. Swift to Rev. Henry Clarke, Dec. 12, 1734, *Corr.*, 4:23; on the Oxford M.A., see Downie, 43.

28. Elias explains these arrangements in detail (50–54).

29. Swift to Deane Swift, June 3, 1694, *Corr.*, 1:120; on the requirement of the testimonial, see Landa, 6.

30. Swift to Temple, Oct. 6, 1694, *Corr.*, 1:122; Nokes, 29; Elias, 50.

31. See Landa, 5–8.

32. *Family of Swift, PW*, 5:194.

33. Sheridan, 16; Craik, 1:59; Ehrenpreis, 1:148; Elias, 229.

34. *Family of Swift*, 5:194.

35. Landa, 9–10, makes the case for Ashe's role.

36. Patrick Fitzgerald, "'Black 97': Reconsidering Scottish Migration to Ireland in the Seventeenth Century and the Scotch-Irish in America," in *Ulster and Scotland: History, Language, and Identity*, ed. William Kelly and John R. Young (Dublin: Four Courts, 2004), 79.

37. Details from Ehrenpreis, 1:157–67; and from Charles McConnell, *The History of the Parish of Kilroot* (St. Colman's Parish Church, 2003).

38. Landa, 12–14.

39. See Connolly, *Divided Kingdom*, 316.

40. Henry Fielding, *Tom Jones*, book 3, ch. 3; *Ode to the King*, lines 82–83, 88, 1:8–9; annotations to Burnet, *PW*, 5:276, 296, 302, 311; *A Letter concerning the Sacramental Test, PW*, 2:116.

41. Landa, 13.

42. Sheridan, 17; Desmond Clarke, *Arthur Dobbs, Esquire* (London: Bodley Head, 1958), 13–14, 17.

43. Toby Barnard, "What Became of Waring? The Making of an Ulster Squire," in Barnard, *Irish Protestant Ascents and Descents, 1641–1770* (Dublin: Four Courts, 2004), 235–65; Deane Swift, 93; Sheridan, 255; Ehrenpreis, 1:164–66.

44. Swift to Rev. John Kendall, Feb. 11, 1692, *Corr.*, 1:105; 1 Corinthians 7:9.

45. Nokes, 15.
46. Swift to Jane Waring, Apr. 29, 1696, *Corr.*, 1:126–27, with minor emendations from the recently discovered original manuscript, printed by Herman Real in *Securing Swift: Selected Essays* (Dublin: Maunsel, 2001), 100–104.
47. Swift to Jane Waring, May 4, 1700, *Corr.*, 1:142.
48. Ehrenpreis, 2:22; Johnston, 124.
49. George Rutherford, *Gravestone Inscriptions: County Antrim* (Belfast: Ulster Historical Foundation, 1981), 1:47, 60.

CHAPTER 4. MOOR PARK ONCE MORE

1. Swift to Rev. John Winder, Apr. 1, 1698, *Corr.*, 1:131; Craik, 1:76n.
2. Landa, 26.
3. William Flower to Swift, Mar. 18, 1729, *Corr.*, 3:217; Swift to Lord Castle-Durrow, Mar. 22, 1734, *Corr.*, 3:729. Flower turned ten in 1696, which confirms that the incident happened during this period in Swift's life.
4. For example, he can be shown to have read Thucydides in Hobbes's English translation and Theophrastus in the French translation of Jean de la Bruyère: see Heinz J. Vienken and Hermann J. Real, "'Ex Libris' J.S.: Annotating Swift," in *Reading Swift*, 1:310. Lyon (19) mentions the dual texts in Latin and Greek. Swift's list was reproduced by Lyon; also Craik, 72–73.
5. Voltaire, *Essai sur les moeurs et l'esprit des nations*, ed. René Pomeau (Paris: Garnier, 1990), 2:810; this work was published ten years after Swift's death. *Gulliver's Travels*, book 2, ch. 7, p. 132.
6. Delany, 34–35.
7. *Thoughts on Various Subjects*, PW, 4:253; *Tale of a Tub*, "An Apology," 1.
8. Temple, *An Essay upon the Ancient and Modern Learning*, 61.
9. David Hume, *The History of England*, final 1778 version (Indianapolis: Liberty Classics, 1983), 6:544; Boswell, *Life of Johnson*, 3:257 (Apr. 9, 1778) and 1:218–19.
10. Sheridan, 25.
11. Johnson, *Lives* 1:48; Dryden, preface to *Ovid's Epistles*, in *The Works of John Dryden*, ed. E. N. Hooker and H. T. Swedenberg (Berkeley: University of California Press, 1956), 1:117; Cowley, *The Praise of Pindar*, lines 12–15, in *Works* (London, 1674), 18; Swift to Thomas Swift, May 3, 1692, *Corr.*, 1:110.
12. Elias, 83; *Ode to Sir William Temple*, lines 135, 138, 157, *Poems*, 1:30–31.
13. *Ode to Temple*, lines 59–61, 178–79, 1:28, 32; Swift to Bolingbroke, Oct. 13, 1729, *Corr.*, 3:261.
14. Ehrenpreis, 1:112.
15. The first quotation is from Ann Cline Kelly, *Jonathan Swift and Popular Culture* (New York: Palgrave Macmillan, 2002), 14; the final three questions and answers are taken from *Athenian Mercury* 1, no. 21 (question 13); 1, no. 18 (question 6); and 7, no. 30 (question 7) (1691–95).
16. Line 62, *Poems*, 1:18.
17. *Ode to Temple*, line 191, 1:32; *To Mr. Congreve*, lines 39–40, *Poems*, 1:44.

18. John Dryden, *To My Dear Friend Mr. Congreve, on His Comedy, Called The Double Dealer*, lines 1–2, 66–67, 76–77.

19. Johnson, *Life of Swift*, 7; Joseph Warton, *An Essay on the Genius and Writings of Pope* (London, 1782), 2:250 (the source was a friend of Warton's father, the minor poet Elijah Fenton).

20. *On Poetry: A Rapsody*, lines 265–66, *Poems*, 2:649; *Tale of a Tub*, section 5, pp. 81–82. The "Nature has never formed you" version comes from Theophilus Cibber, relating a story told him by Laetitia Pilkington (see Robert M. Philmus, "Dryden's 'Cousin Swift' Re-examined," *Swift Studies* 18 [2003]: 99–103).

21. *Thoughts on Various Subjects*, 4:243; *To Mr. Congreve*, lines 133–34, 1:47; *Ode to Dr. William Sancroft*, line 91, *Poems*, 1:37.

22. *Ode to Temple*, line 205; *Occasioned by Sir William Temple's Late Illness and Recovery*, lines 151–55, *Poems*, 1:33, 55.

23. Charles Perrault, *Parallel between the Ancients and the Moderns*. The other important voice was Bernard le Bovier de Fontenelle's in *A Digression on the Ancients and Moderns*.

24. Temple, *An Essay upon the Ancient and Modern Learning*, 56–57.

25. Ibid., 64.

26. This point is made by James Henry Monk, *The Life of Richard Bentley, D.D.* (London: Rivington, 1830), 70.

27. Thomas Babington Macaulay, "Francis Atterbury," in *Miscellaneous Writings* (London: Longman, Green, and Roberts, 1860), 2:211; Joseph M. Levine, *The Battle of the Books: History and Literature in the Augustan Age* (Ithaca: Cornell University Press, 1991), 61.

28. *The Battle of the Books, PW*, 1:163, 157.

29. Ibid., 1:140, 150–51. The contrast between Bentley's and Temple's values is explored by John F. Tinkler in "The Splitting of Humanism: Bentley, Swift, and the English Battle of the Books," *Journal of the History of Ideas* 49 (1988): 453–72.

30. *Index Expurgatorius*, in *The Miscellaneous Works of Edward Gibbon*, ed. John Sheffield (London: John Murray, 1814), 5:564.

31. "These were Swift's own words in a conversation with the author about three or four and twenty years ago, upon the merits of Homer" (Deane Swift, 237; the date would have been around 1730). Temple's attitude toward burlesque is mentioned by Courtenay, *Memoirs of the Life . . . of Sir William Temple*, 2:191.

32. Lyon, preliminary page in his copy of Hawkesworth's *Life*; Elias, 97–98.

33. Scott, 38. What little is known about this text is reconstructed by George Mayhew, "Jonathan Swift's 'On the Burning of Whitehall in 1697' Re-examined," *Harvard Library Bulletin* 19 (1971): 404. Ehrenpreis, 1:257, 259; Elias, 100–101.

34. Details from Elias, 149–50.

35. Courtenay, *Memoirs of the Life . . . of Sir William Temple*, 2:485, 229.

36. Elias, 262.

37. Swift to Lady Giffard, Nov. 10, 1709, *Corr.*, 1:270.

38. *Journal*, 1:9, 113 (Sept. 9, Dec. 5, 1711).

39. Swift to Viscount Palmerston, Jan. 1 and Jan. 29, 1726; Palmerston to Swift, Jan. 15, 1726, *Corr.*, 2:629–32.

40. Jane Swift to Deane Swift (senior), May 26, 1699, *Corr.*, 1:139.

41. Swift to Sir John Temple, February 1737, *Corr.*, 4:388.

42. *The Poems and Fables of John Dryden*, ed. James Kinsley (Oxford: Oxford University Press, 1962), 838–39.

CHAPTER 5. THE VILLAGE AND THE CASTLE

1. Quoted in *Atlas of the Irish Rural Landscape*, ed. F. H. A. Aalen, Kevin Whelan, and Matthew Stout (Toronto: University of Toronto Press, 1997), 19.

2. Eachard, *An Exact Description of Ireland*, 79; J. G. Simms, "The Establishment of Protestant Ascendancy, 1691–1714," in *A New History of Ireland*, vol. 4, *Eighteenth-Century Ireland*, ed. T. W. Moody and W. E. Vaughan (Oxford: Clarendon, 1986), 22; J. L. McCracken, "The Social Structure and Social Life, 1714–60," in Moody and Vaughan, *Eighteenth-Century Ireland*, 44.

3. Details from Simms, "The Establishment of Protestant Ascendancy, 1691–1714," 22; McCracken, "The Social Structure and Social Life, 1714–60," 44; Barnard, *Making the Grand Figure*, 22.

4. Landa, 37; Joseph McMinn, *Jonathan's Travels: Swift and Ireland* (Belfast: Appletree, 1994), 39; Forster, 135, 197; Swift to Vanessa, July 8, 1713, *Corr.*, 1:513.

5. Swift to Dean Stearne, Apr. 17, 1710, *Corr.*, 1:279; Orrery, 95; Sheridan, 390.

6. Swift to Pope, Feb. 26, 1729, *Corr.*, 3:285.

7. *Considerations upon Two Bills*, PW, 12:200; Archbishop Hugh Boulter, quoted by J. L. McCracken, "The Ecclesiastical Structure, 1714–60," in Moody and Vaughan, *Eighteenth-Century Ireland*, 88.

8. Richard Haworth, "Jonathan Swift and the Geography of Laracor," *Swift Studies* 24 (2009): 25; Landa, 43; Connolly, *Religion, Law, and Power*, 180, 183.

9. Porter, *English Society in the Eighteenth Century*, 62; Macaulay, 1:161.

10. *Some Arguments against Enlarging the Power of Bishops*, PW, 9:58.

11. To John Winder, Apr. 1, 1698, *Corr.*, 1:132; Landa, 36; Ehrenpreis, 2:97–98.

12. Haworth, "Jonathan Swift and the Geography of Laracor," 9. My account of Laracor is greatly indebted to this article. "Bumford" (Lawrence Bomford) is mentioned in a letter from Swift to Vanessa, July 8, 1713, *Corr.*, 1:514.

13. *A Character of Primate Marsh*, PW, 5:211.

14. Laurence Sterne, *A Sentimental Journey through France and Italy*, ed. Graham Petrie (London: Penguin, 1967), 46 ("The Remise Door, Calais").

15. Edward Lloyd, *A Description of the City of Dublin* (1732), quoted by Fagan, *The Second City*, 37. On the powers of the office, see Ian McBride, *Eighteenth-Century Ireland: The Isle of Slaves* (Dublin: Gill and Macmillan, 2009), 283.

16. Swift's note in his copy of Macky's *Characters*, PW, 5:249.

17. *Journal*, 1:280 (May 25, 1711).

18. Deane Swift, 112.

19. *Family of Swift*, PW, 5:195.

20. Ibid.

21. Landa, 29–34.

22. *Verses Wrote in a Lady's Ivory Table Book*, lines 7–16, *Poems*, 1:60. This poem may have been first drafted in 1698, but it seems to have been revised later, and it reflects a milieu much more like that of the castle than of Moor Park.

23. *A Complete Collection of Genteel and Ingenious Conservation* (usually referred to as *Polite Conversation*), *PW*, 4:102, 139, 145; see Ann Cline Kelly, "*Polite Conversation*: An Eschatological Vision," *Studies in Philology* 73 (1976): 204–24.

24. *The Humble Petition*, lines 24–33, *Poems*, 1:70–71.

25. Ibid., lines 64–65, 1:73; *Directions to Servants*, *PW*, 13:57.

26. *The Works of Jonathan Swift*, ed. Walter Scott (1814), in *Critical Heritage*, 300.

27. Craik, 1:173; Robert Boyle, *Occasional Reflections upon Several Subjects* (Oxford: Masson, 1848), 66, 88, 304.

28. Sheridan, 38–39.

29. *A Meditation upon a Broomstick*, *PW*, 1:239–40.

30. Ehrenpreis (2:66) says Sheen, Craik (139) says Farnham. Both seem to be guesses, with no evidence one way or the other.

31. *On the Death of Mrs. Johnson*, 5:227–28.

32. Ibid, 5:228.

33. Swift to Martha Blount, Feb. 29, 1728, *Corr.*, 3:164; Swift to Gay and Pope, Nov. 23, 1727, *Corr.*, 3:142.

34. Swift to Martha Blount, Feb. 29, 1728, *Corr.*, 3:164; Swift to Gay and Pope, Nov. 23, 1727, *Corr.*, 3:142; Real, *Securing Swift*, 109.

35. Thomas Swift to Deane Swift, senior, *Corr.*, 1:163.

36. Deane Swift, 90; Ehrenpreis (2:69) gives reasons for placing Rebecca's age between thirty-five and forty.

37. On the annual allowance, see *Journal*, 1:137n, and Rebecca's receipt to Swift for a quarterly payment of £13, in *The Correspondence of Jonathan Swift*, 6 vols., ed. F. Elrington Ball (London: G. Bell, 1910–14), 6:40; Vickery, *Behind Closed Doors*, 24.

38. Swift to Rev. William Tisdall, Dec. 16, 1703, *Corr.*, 1:148.

39. Swift to Tisdall, Feb. 3, 1704, *Corr.*, 1:150–51.

40. Swift to Tisdall, Apr. 20, 1704, *Corr.*, 1:153–54.

41. Ehrenpreis, 2:138; *Journal*, 2:671 (June 6, 1713).

42. *On the Death of Mrs. Johnson*, 5:229–30.

43. John Geree's 1757 *Gentleman's Magazine* letter, reprinted by Le Brocquy, *Swift's Most Valuable Friend*, 16–17.

44. *A Letter to a Young Lady, on Her Marriage*, *PW*, 9:93; *To Stella, Visiting Me in My Sickness*, lines 71–74, *Poems*, 2:725.

45. Richard Burn, *The Justice of the Peace*, quoted by Vickery, *Behind Closed Doors*, 30–31.

CHAPTER 6. LONDON

1. Jeremy Boulton, "London 1540–1700," in *The Cambridge Urban History of Britain*, ed. Peter Clark (Cambridge: Cambridge University Press, 2000), 2:316; *The Diary of John Evelyn*, ed. E. S. de Beer (Oxford: Clarendon), 1955), 3:454.

2. Simon Ford, *The Conflagration of London Poetically Delineated* (1667), quoted by Cynthia Wall, *The Literary and Cultural Spaces of Restoration London* (Cambridge: Cambridge University Press, 1998), 24. Wall gives a richly detailed account of the rebuilding and reimagining of London.

3. See Lawrence E. Klein, "The Polite Town: Shifting Possibilities of Urbanness, 1660–1715," in *The Streets of London: From the Great Fire to the Great Stink*, ed. Tim Hitchcock and Heather Shore (London: Rivers Oram, 2003), 27–39.

4. Daniel Defoe, *A Tour through the Whole Island of Great Britain* (London, 1724–26), 1:317; Macaulay, 1:175.

5. Cynthia Wall, "'At Shakespeare's-Head, Over-Against Catharine Street in the Strand," in Hitchcock and Shore, *The Streets of London*, 10.

6. Maureen Waller, *1700: Scenes from London Life* (London: Hodder and Stoughton, 2000), 3–4.

7. Boswell, *Life of Johnson*, 2:337, 3:178 (Apr. 2, 1775, and Sept. 20, 1777); *Hell upon Earth* (1729), quoted by Roy Porter, introduction to Hitchcock and Shore, *The Streets of London*, xv.

8. J. H. Plumb, *England in the Eighteenth Century* (London: Penguin, 1950), 95; Emily Cockayne, *Hubbub: Filth, Noise and Stench in England, 1600–1770* (New Haven: Yale University Press, 2007).

9. Boswell, *Life of Johnson*, 1:110 (1737).

10. *A Character . . . of the Legion Club*, lines 219–20, *Poems*, 3:839.

11. Henry Fielding, *An Inquiry into the Late Encrease of Robbers* (1751), 142–43; Kirstin Olsen, *Daily Life in 18th-Century England* (Westport, Conn.: Greenwood, 1999), 203.

12. *Part of the Seventh Epistle of the First Book of Horace Imitated*, lines 58–60, *Poems*, 1:172; *Tale of a Tub*, "Preface," 28. The *OED* doesn't define "fit" as used here, but Johnson gives "any short return after intermission; interval" (as in the expression "fits and starts").

13. *Journal*, 2:647 (Mar. 27, 1713); *Account Books*, 77; *Gulliver's Travels*, book 2, ch. 3, p. 103. See Dennis Todd, "The Hairy Maid at the Harpsichord: Some Speculations on the Meaning of *Gulliver's Travels*," *Texas Studies in Literature and Language* 34 (1992): 239–83.

14. John Gay, *Trivia* (1716), 2:247–53.

15. Ibid.; Pepys, *Diary*, 1:269 (Oct. 19, 1660); Daniel Defoe, *Due Preparations for the Plague* (1722), in *Writings on Travel, Discovery and History by Daniel Defoe*, ed. W. R. Owens and P. N. Furbank (London: Pickering and Chatto, 2002), 5:48.

16. Richard Steele, *Tatler* 9; *A Description of the Morning*, lines 1–8, *Poems*, 1:124–25; John Dryden, translation of *Aeneid* IX, lines 459–60.

17. *London in 1710: From the Travels of Zacharias Conrad von Uffenbach*, trans. W. H. Quarrell and Margaret Mare (London: Faber and Faber, 1934), 16; Pepys, *Diary*, 3:301 (Dec. 31, 1662); on hackneys: Susan E. Whyman, "Sharing Public Spaces," in *Walking the Streets of Eighteenth-Century London*, ed. Clare Brant and Susan E. Whyman (Oxford: Oxford University Press, 2007), 45.

18. *A Description of the Morning*, lines 11–14, 1:124; Cockayne, *Hubbub*, 107.

19. Von Uffenbach in 1709, quoted by Real, *Securing Swift*, 200–201. Addison, *Spectator* 251.

20. *Verses Made for Women Who Cry Apples, etc., Poems,* 3:952–53.
21. Von Uffenbach, *London in 1710,* 35; John Evelyn, *Fumifigium; or, The Inconvenience of the Air and Smoke of London Dissipated* (1661), 6.
22. *A Description of the Morning,* lines 15–18, 1:125.
23. Ned Ward, *The London Spy* (1709), ed. Paul Hyland (East Lansing, Mich.: Colleagues, 1993), 39–40, 336–58 (dictionary of street lingo).
24. *A Description of a City Shower,* lines 1–6, *Poems,* 1:136; *Journal,* 1:87 (Nov. 8, 1710).
25. *A Description of a City Shower,* lines 55–56, 61–63, 1:139; Cockayne, *Hubbub,* 189.
26. There are various estimates of the number of voyages, and a 1704 notation in one of Swift's account books refers surprisingly to "my 16th voyage." See Irvin Ehrenpreis, "Swift's Voyages," *Modern Language Notes* 65 (1950): 256–57; and *Account Books,* 41.

CHAPTER 7. "A VERY POSITIVE YOUNG MAN"

1. Holmes, *The Making of a Great Power,* 339.
2. Kishlansky, *A Monarchy Transformed,* 315.
3. As Frank H. Ellis observes in his edition of the *Contests and Dissensions* (Oxford: Clarendon, 1967), 156–57. The political context is very fully explained by Ellis (1–79), and by Mark Goldie, "Situating Swift's Politics in 1701," in *Politics and Literature in the Age of Swift: English and Irish Perspectives,* ed. Claude Rawson (Cambridge: Cambridge University Press, 2010), 31–51.
4. *A Letter concerning the Sacramental Test,* 2:283 (in Herbert Davis's endnotes, from a variant edition of this work).
5. *Contests and Dissensions, PW,* 1:232–33, 227.
6. *Memoirs Relating to That Change Which Happened in the Queen's Ministry in the Year 1710, PW,* 8:119; Johnson, *Life of Swift,* 10.
7. Deane Swift, 122–23 (with some repetitions silently deleted).
8. *Memoirs Relating to That Change Which Happened in the Queen's Ministry in the Year 1710,* 8:119.

CHAPTER 8. THE SCANDALOUS TUB

1. *Tale of a Tub,* "Preface," 24–25.
2. Boswell, *Life of Johnson,* 2:319 (Mar. 24, 1775); William Cobbett, *Autobiography,* ed. William Reitzel (London: Faber and Faber, 1947), 13–14; Harold Bloom, ed., *Modern Critical Views: Jonathan Swift* (Philadelphia: Chelsea House, 1986), 1.
3. Orrery, 34: handwritten note in a copy of Orrery's book, quoting a letter to Orrery from Deane Swift. The relative was Martha Whiteway.
4. *Tale of a Tub,* 4.
5. Jean le Clerc (1721), in *Critical Heritage,* 59; note by Lyon in the University of Pennsylvania version of his annotations to Hawkesworth's biography: Elias, "Swift's *Don Quixote,* Dunkin's *Virgil Travesty,* and Other New Intelligence," 72.

6. *Tale of a Tub*, "A Digression concerning Madness," 113; Claude Rawson, *Gulliver and the Gentle Reader: Studies in Swift and Our Time* (London: Routledge and Kegan Paul, 1973), 12.

7. Swift complained to Pope about bad writing full of "abominable curtailings and quaint modernisms" (June 23, 1737, *Corr.*, 4:446; the *OED* follows a 1741 edition of the letters that mistakenly gave the date July 23); *Tale of a Tub*, "A Digression in the Modern Kind," 80–81.

8. Henry Fielding, *Covent-Garden Journal*, ed. Gerard Edward Jensen (New York: Russell and Russell, 1964), 2:48 (no. 52, June 30, 1752); Pope is quoted by Spence, *Observations*, 1:55; *The Dunciad*, ed. James Sutherland (London: Methuen, 1963), 1:19–20; Coleridge, *Table Talk*, quoted in *Critical Heritage*, 333. Coleridge was remembering the actual words of Rabelais: "The soul, says St. Augustine, cannot dwell in a dry place" (Rabelais, *Gargantua and Pantagruel*, trans. Jacques Le Clerq [New York: Modern Library, 1944], book 1, ch. 5, p. 17).

9. As Melinda Alliker Rabb suggests in "Postmodernizing Swift," in *Reading Swift*, 5:29–43.

10. James Ralph, *The Case of Authors by Profession or Trade* (London, 1758), 22.

11. *Tale of a Tub*, "Conclusion," 133.

12. Ibid., "Preface," 27.

13. Ibid., section 2, p. 44.

14. Ibid., section 6, p. 87.

15. William Empson, *Some Versions of Pastoral* (New York: New Directions, 1974), 60.

16. *Tale of a Tub*, section 2, p. 45.

17. Ibid., section 8, pp. 96, 99; the biblical quotation is 2 Timothy 2:21.

18. *The Mechanical Operation of the Spirit*, PW, 1:189. See Philip Harth, *Swift and Anglican Rationalism: The Religious Background of "A Tale of a Tub"* (Chicago: University of Chicago Press, 1961), 66. There were precedents for the sexual innuendo in seventeenth-century writers and in the early church fathers; see the notes in Cambridge *Works*, 1:417, 424.

19. *Tale of a Tub*, section 11, pp. 123–24 (the original version is recorded in the textual notes, 298).

20. Ibid., section 2, pp. 46–47.

21. *Critical Heritage*, 74 (I have altered the translation of the French *pretend* from "pretends" to the more accurate "claims").

22. *Tale of a Tub*, section 4, p. 73.

23. This point is made by William J. Roscelli, "*A Tale of a Tub* and the 'Cavils of the Sour,'" *Journal of English and Germanic Philology* 64 (1965): 47.

24. *Tale of a Tub*, "A Digression concerning Madness," 104; Horace *Satire* 1.3.107–8.

25. *Tale of a Tub*, "A Digression concerning Madness," 110.

26. Orrery, 125–26.

27. Erasmus, *Praise of Folly*, trans. Betty Radice (London: Penguin, 1971), 135; Rochester, "A Letter from Artemisia in the Town to Chloe in the Country" (1679), lines 114–15, in *The Complete Poems of John Wilmot, Earl of Rochester*, ed. David M. Vieth (New Haven: Yale University Press, 1968), 107.

28. *Tale of a Tub*, "A Digression concerning Madness," 109.

29. John Dunton, *Some Account of My Conversation in Ireland* (1699), in *The Dublin Scuffle*, ed. Andrew Carpenter (Dublin: Four Courts, 2000), 242–43. On public flogging, see Olsen, *Daily Life in 18th-Century England*, 219.

30. Denis Donoghue, *Jonathan Swift: A Critical Introduction* (Cambridge: Cambridge University Press, 1971), 7. Robert Mahony has an acute discussion of "I saw a woman flayed" in "Certainty and Irony in Swift: Faith and the Indeterminate," in *Swift as Priest and Satirist*, ed. Todd C. Parker (Newark: University of Delaware Press, 2009), 46–47.

31. *Tale of a Tub*, "Introduction," 40.

32. Ibid., "A Digression concerning Madness," 108.

33. Claude Rawson, "The Character of Swift's Satire: Reflections on Swift, Johnson, and Human Restlessness," in *The Character of Swift's Satire: A Revised Focus*, ed. Rawson (London: Associated University Presses, 1983), 71.

34. *Tale of a Tub*, section 6, p. 87; I borrow the term *psychopathology* from John Traugott, "A Tale of a Tub," in Rawson, *The Character of Swift's Satire*, 100.

35. *Tale of a Tub*, "A Digression concerning Madness," 111. See Michael DePorte, *Nightmares and Hobbyhorses: Swift, Sterne, and Augustan Ideas of Madness* (San Marino: Huntington Library, 1974), ch. 1.

36. *Journal*, 1:122 (Dec. 13, 1710).

37. *Tale of a Tub*, section 10, p. 118.

38. *Examiner* 29, *PW*, 3:92; see Phillip Harth, "Recent Religious History and *A Tale of a Tub*," *Swift Studies* 14 (1999): 34–36.

39. Defoe, *The Consolidator; or, Memoirs of Sundry Transactions from the World in the Moon* (London, 1705), p. 62. On the ministry, Defoe said, "It was my disaster first to be set apart for, and then to be set apart from, the honour of that sacred employ" (*Review*, Oct. 22, 1709).

40. 2 Corinthians 12:7; *Tale of a Tub*, "A Digression concerning Madness," 102; William Wotton, *A Defense of the Reflections . . . with Observations upon "The Tale of a Tub"* (1705), *Critical Heritage*, 45.

41. Francis Atterbury to John Trelawney, bishop of Exeter, July 1, 1704, *Critical Heritage*, 36.

42. *An Apology*, *PW*, 1:2; *The Author upon Himself*, lines 11–12, *Poems*, 1:194. The attacks on the *Tale* are surveyed by Roger D. Lund, "*A Tale of a Tub*, Swift's Apology, and the Trammels of Christian Wit," in *Augustan Studies: Essays in Honor of Martin C. Battestin*, ed. Albert J. Rivero (Newark: University of Delaware Press, 1997), 87–109.

43. Swift to Benjamin Tooke, June 29, 1710, *Corr.*, 1:282; the question is thoroughly surveyed by Marcus Walsh in Cambridge *Works* 1:xli–xlvi, concluding that it's unlikely that much by Thomas Swift survived in the final version.

44. *Thoughts on Various Subjects*, 4:249.

CHAPTER 9. SWIFT AND GOD

1. [Jonathan Smedley], *An Hue and Cry after the Examiner. Dr. S——t* (1727), 15; anonymous, *A Letter to Dean Swift* (1719), quoted in *PW*, 9:xiii.

2. Delany, 30–31.

3. George Monck-Berkeley, *Literary Relics* (London, 1789), xxvii; Lyon, 31.

4. Boswell, *Life of Johnson*, 1:444 (July 21, 1763); *Further Thoughts on Religion*, *PW*, 9:264; C. S. Lewis, "Addison," in *Eighteenth-Century English Literature: Modern Essays in Criticism*, ed. James L. Clifford (New York: Oxford Galaxy Books, 1959), 148.

5. *Thoughts on Religion*, *PW*, 9:261–62. Rawson has some penetrating comments on this question in *Order from Confusion Sprung: Studies in Eighteenth-Century Literature from Swift to Cowper* (London: George Allen and Unwin, 1985), 5–10.

6. Thomas Szasz, *The Second Sin* (New York: Anchor, 1973), 101; Dirk F. Passmann and Heinz J. Vienken, *The Library and Reading of Jonathan Swift: A Bio-Bibliographical Handbook*, 4 vols. (Frankfurt: Peter Lang, 2003), 2:1382; Blaise Pascal, *Pensées*, no. 197 (Brunschvicg numeration). Émile Pons was unable to find definite echoes of Pascal in Swift's writings, and thought that occasional similarities of thinking were due to both of them having read the same authors: "Swift et Pascal," *Les langues modernes* 45 (1951): 135–52.

7. W. E. H. Lecky, *The Leaders of Public Opinion in Ireland* (London: Longmans Green, 1871), 21; *The Mechanical Operation of the Spirit*, 1:180; Voltaire, *Candide*, trans. John Butt (London: Penguin, 1947), ch. 30, p. 141.

8. *A Letter to a Young Gentleman, Lately Entered into Holy Orders*, *PW*, 9:70, 66.

9. Ibid., 9:77; Boswell, *Life of Johnson*, 5:88 (the Hebrides tour).

10. *Gulliver's Travels*, book 4, ch. 5, p. 246.

11. Quoted in T. W. Moody and F. X. Martin, eds., *The Course of Irish History* (Lanham, Md.: Roberts Rinehart, 2001), 177.

12. *Concerning That Universal Hatred Which Prevails against the Clergy*, *PW*, 13:123; marginalia to Lord Herbert of Cherbury, *Life and Reign of Henry VIII* (1649), *PW*, 5:248–51.

13. *Thoughts on Various Subjects*, 1:241; *Some Arguments against Enlarging the Power of Bishops*, 9:56; *Thoughts on Religion*, 9:263.

14. *Gulliver's Travels*, book 2, ch. 6, p. 131; book 1, ch. 4, pp. 49–50. Swift's practice with eggs is mentioned by Arnold in "Those Who Seek to Obtain My Estate," 26.

15. *Verses on the Death of Dr. Swift*, lines 293–96 (targeting Thomas Woolston), 2:564; Pat Rogers explains "God's in Gloucester" in "Swift and the Reanimation of Cliché," in Rawson, *The Character of Swift's Satire*, 220.

16. The context is fully explained by Frank Ellis, "*An Argument against Abolishing Christianity* as an Argument against Abolishing the Test Act," in *Reading Swift*, 2:127–39; and by Ian Higgins, "*An Argument against Abolishing Christianity* and Its Contexts," in *Reading Swift*, 5:203–23.

17. *An Argument against Abolishing Christianity*, 2:35, 27, 37–38.

18. Orrery, 146; Sir Walter Scott, ed., *The Works of Jonathan Swift* (Edinburgh, 1814), 8:183.

CHAPTER 10. FIRST FRUITS

1. Proverbs 3:9.

2. See Trevelyan, 1:47–48; Landa, 53.

3. Quoted by Landa, 58; on the negotiations, too complicated to describe here, see Landa, 58–66; and Ehrenpreis, 2:323–26.

4. J. H. Plumb, in *The Growth of Political Stability in England, 1675–1725* (London: Penguin, 1967), 112, says that Queen Anne attended cabinet meetings more frequently than any other British monarch.

5. Quoted by Holmes, *Marlborough*, 7.

6. Sir John Clerk of Penicuick, quoted by ibid., 353.

7. Porter, *English Society in the Eighteenth Century*, 55.

8. *Gulliver's Travels*, book 4, ch. 6, p. 257.

9. Orwell, "Politics vs. Literature," 131; Plumb, 1:55–56, 59; Trevelyan, 3:71.

10. *History of the Last Four Years of Queen Anne's Reign, PW*, 7:5–6.

11. Macaulay, 1:197; Johnson, *Life of Dryden*, in *Lives*, 1:359, 399.

12. *Tale of a Tub*, Dedication, 15.

13. Ibid., "An Apology," 1; see Robert Phiddian, *Swift's Parody* (Cambridge: Cambridge University Press, 1995), 168–70, 199–200.

14. *Intelligencer* 5, *PW*, 12:40; on the incompatibility of Somers's principles with Swift's, see Ian Higgins, *Swift's Politics: A Study in Disaffection* (Cambridge: Cambridge University Press, 1994), 122–28.

15. On Swift's financial straits, see Ehrenpreis, 2:142.

16. On ecclesiastical jockeying during this period, see ibid., 2:152–65.

17. Quoted by ibid., 2:178.

18. Delany, 144; Virgil *Eclogue* 9.28.

19. Lyon, 10.

20. *Thoughts on Various Subjects*, quoting Ovid *Metamorphoses* 6.136, 1:244.

21. *Verses Said to be Written on the Union*, lines 1–4, *Poems*, 1:96; Trevelyan, 1:175.

22. *The Story of the Injured Lady, PW*, 9:3–4.

23. See Rick G. Canning, "'Ignorant, Illiterate Creatures': Gender and Colonial Justification in Swift's *Injured Lady* and *The Answer to the Injured Lady*," *ELH* 64 (1997): 77–97.

24. *A Letter Concerning the Sacramental Test*, 2:116.

CHAPTER 11. THE WAR AND THE WHIGS

1. J. P. Kenyon, *The Stuarts* (London: Fontana/Collins, 1970), 146.

2. Edward Gregg, *Queen Anne* (New Haven: Yale University Press, 2001), 29.

3. Macaulay, 1:453.

4. *History of the Last Four Years of Queen Anne's Reign*, 7:8.

5. Correlli Barnett, *The First Churchill: Marlborough, Soldier and Statesman* (New York: Putnam, 1974), 168; Holmes, *Marlborough*, 343.

6. Trevelyan, 1:363–64.

7. Ibid., 1:391.

8. Ibiid., 1:395–96.

9. Winton, *Captain Steele*, 73.

10. *The Campaign*, in *The Works of Joseph Addison*, ed. Richard Hurd (London: Bohn, 1854), 1:42, 48, 49–50 (this edition gives no line numbers); casualty figures from Holmes, *Marlborough*, 296–97.

11. Holmes, *Marlborough*, 433–34.

12. John A. Lynn, *The Wars of Louis XIV, 1667–1714* (London: Longman, 1999), 334.

13. Brewer, *The Sinews of Power*, xi; and Holmes, *Marlborough*, 441. See also P. G. M. Dickson, *The Financial Revolution in England: A Study in the Development of Public Credit, 1688–1756* (London: Macmillan, 1967).

14. *Spectator* 69.

15. *The Conduct of the Allies*, PW, 6:5, 61; and *The Public Spirit of the Whigs*, PW, 8:47. My attempts to find another origin for "blood and treasure" have consistently turned up sources later than these. On Tory opposition, see Trevelyan, 1:292–93.

16. *Examiner* 13, *PW*, 3:5.

17. Swift to Pope, Jan. 10, 1721, *Corr.*, 2:360; *A Short View of the State of Ireland*, PW, 12:11.

18. Winston S. Churchill, *Marlborough: His Life and Times* (New York: Scribner, 1938), 6:652.

19. King to Swift, Nov. 20, 1708; Swift to King, Apr. 15, 1708; King to Swift, Sept. 7, 1708; *Corr.*, 1:221, 187, 205.

20. *Journal*, 1:85 (Nov. 8, 1710); *A Description of a City Shower*, lines 39–42, 1:138.

21. Trevelyan, 1:184.

22. Swift to Halifax, June 13, 1709, *Corr.*, 1:256; Halifax to Swift, Oct. 6, 1709, *Corr.*, 1:265; Scott, 112; Swift's marginalia to John Macky, *Characters of the Court of Britain* (1733), *PW*, 5:258. Craik (1:235n) traced the identity of the "sinecure" of Islip.

23. Quoted by Paula R. Backscheider, *Daniel Defoe: His Life* (Baltimore: Johns Hopkins University Press, 1989), 156.

24. Details from Backscheider's *Daniel Defoe*.

25. *A Letter concerning the Sacramental Test*, 2:113; John Forster, *The Life of Charles Dickens* (Philadelphia: Lippincott, 1874), 3:135n.

26. Swift to Ambrose Philips, Oct. 20, 1708, *Corr.*, 1:210.

27. See Michael Treadwell, "Swift, Richard Coleire, and the Origins of *Gulliver's Travels*," *Review of English Studies* 34, no. 135 (1983): 304–11.

CHAPTER 12. SWIFT THE LONDONER

1. *Journal*, 1:142–43n; and Downie, 166.

2. *Journal*, 1:48–49 (Oct. 8–9, 1710).

3. Olsen, *Daily Life in 18th-Century England*, 126–27. Ehrenpreis, 2:300–301, gives examples of outlays from Swift's account books.

4. Pope, *The Rape of the Lock*, 3.117–18.

5. Waller, *1700*, 196, 201; Trevelyan, 1:84.

6. *The Conduct of the Allies*, 6:53; *The Author upon Himself*, line 22, 1:194; *Hints towards an Essay on Conversation*, PW, 4:90. See J. A. Downie, *Robert Harley and the Press:*

Propaganda and Public Opinion in the Age of Swift and Defoe (Cambridge: Cambridge University Press, 1979), 92, 151–52, and Downie's critique of the "public sphere" thesis of Jürgen Habermas in "Public and Private: The Myth of the Bourgeois Public Sphere," in *A Concise Companion to the Restoration and Eighteenth Century*, ed. Cynthia Wall (London: Blackwell, 2005), 58–79.

7. T. H. White, *Mistress Masham's Repose* (New York: G. P. Putnam's Sons, 1946), 169. White's book imagines the Lilliputians whom Gulliver brought to England living secretly in the grounds of a great estate.

8. *Journal*, 2:382 (Oct. 12, 1711); *To Mrs. Biddy Floyd*, lines 3–12, *Poems*, 1:118; Ehrenpreis, 2:309.

9. Swift to Dean Stearne, Apr. 15, 1708, *Corr.*, 1:184; *On the Collar of Mrs. Dingley's Lapdog* and *Bec's Birthday, 1726*, lines 39–40, *Poems*, 2:763, 761.

10. See Le Brocquy, *Swift's Most Valuable Friend*, 64–65.

11. Pilkington, 1:31.

12. *Englishman*, no. 46, Jan. 19, 1714, quoted by Winton, *Captain Steele*, 2. My account of Steele is largely based on Winton's two volumes; the sequel is *Sir Richard Steele, M.P.* (Baltimore: Johns Hopkins University Press, 1970).

13. Thomas Babington Macaulay, *The History of England in the Eighteenth Century*, ed. Peter Rowland (London: Folio Society, 1980), 37 (Macaulay did not live to write his projected history of this period, but touched on it in many of his essays, from which Rowland assembled this volume); John Dennis, *The Characters and Conduct of Sir John Edgar* (1720), in *The Critical Works of John Dennis*, ed. E. N. Hooker (Baltimore: Johns Hopkins University Press, 1939–43), 2:213.

14. Addison, *Tatler* 108; Swift to Pope, Nov. 26, 1725, *Corr.*, 2:623; *Verses on the Death of Dr. Swift*, lines 1–4, 2:553; Steele, *Spectator* 157; Swift, *Thoughts on Various Subjects*, 4:251.

15. Swift to Ambrose Philips, July 10, 1708, *Corr.*, 1:198; Delany, 23; Scott, 83, citing a communication from Theophilus Swift; *Tale of a Tub*, Dedication, 14. Ehrenpreis (2:320) notes the echo of the *Tale of a Tub* dedication.

16. Dryden, *Baucis and Philemon, Out of the Eighth Book of Ovid's* Metamorphoses, in *Fables Ancient and Modern* (1700), lines 161–62.

17. *The Story of Baucis and Philemon* (manuscript version), lines 152, 93–108, *Poems*, 1:92–94.

18. Delany, 13–14. In the passage from the poem quoted here, however, the revisions from Swift's draft are minimal.

19. Swift to King, Mar. 12, 1708; to Ambrose Philips, Mar. 8, 1709, *Corr.*, 1:245, 239. On Swift's indifference to the arts, see Ehrenpreis, 2:301; and Joseph McMinn, "Swift and Theatre," *Eighteenth-Century Ireland* 16 (2001): 35–46; McMinn offers a more comprehensive view in *Jonathan Swift and the Arts* (Newark: University of Delaware Press, 2010). Swift owned plays by Plautus, Terence, Corneille, Racine, Molière, and Jonson, and probably Shakespeare as well.

20. Steele, *Tatler* 249; Sheridan, *Intelligencer* 13, p. 161.

21. *Hints towards an Essay on Conversation*, 4:91.

22. Addison, *Spectator* 381; Ford to Swift, July 8, 1736, *Corr.*, 4:329.

23. Swift, *To Mr. Delany*, lines 23–24, *Poems*, 1:215; *Tale of a Tub*, "Preface," 26. Arno Löffler discusses the concept of humor in "The Dean and Lady Anne: Humour in Swift's Market-Hill Poems," in *Reading Swift*, 2:113–24; more largely, see Stuart M. Tave, *The Amiable Humorist* (Chicago: University of Chicago Press, 1960).

24. Johnson, *Life of Swift*, 55–56; Boswell, *Life of Johnson*, 2:262 (May 1773); Addison, *Spectator* 35.

25. Sheridan, 341.

26. Ibid., 40–41. Sheridan believed that this happened at Button's coffeehouse, but Craik (1:172) notes that Button's wasn't yet established at that time.

27. Sheridan, 41.

28. *PW*, 4:267.

29. *Journal*, 1:219, 240, 242 (Mar. 19, Apr. 11, Apr. 13, 1711).

30. *Predictions for the Year 1708*, *PW*, 2:145.

31. See George Mayhew, "Swift's Bickerstaff Hoax as an April Fool's Joke, *Modern Philology* 61 (1964): 270–80. On political and religious contexts, see Valerie Rumbold, "Burying the Fanatic Partridge: Swift's Holy Week Hoax," in Rawson, *Politics and Literature in the Age of Swift*, 81–115; also John McTague, "'There Is No Such Man as Isaack Bickerstaff': Partridge, Pittis, and Jonathan Swift," *Eighteenth-Century Life* 35 (2011): 83–101.

32. *The Accomplishment of the First of Mr. Bickerstaff's Predictions, Being an Account of the Death of Mr. Partridge, the Almanac Maker, upon the 29th Inst.*, *PW*, 2:154–55.

33. *A Vindication of Isaac Bickerstaff*, *PW*, 2:162.

34. *Tatler* 1 (Swift himself may possibly have written this passage). On implications of Bickerstaff and Partridge as authors, see Phiddian, *Swift's Parody*, ch. 5.

35. Ehrenpreis, 2:202. The *Answer to Bickerstaff* is included without explanation by Davis among "Bickerstaff papers not written by Swift" (*PW*, 2:195–99). I agree with Ehrenpreis that Swift did indeed write it.

36. John Partridge to Isaac Manley, Apr. 24, 1708, *Corr.*, 1:189–90; see Rumbold, "Burying the Fanatic Partridge," 91.

CHAPTER 13. AT THE SUMMIT

1. Swift to Robert Hunter, Jan. 12, 1709; King to Swift, Feb. 10, 1709; *Corr.*, 1:229, 233.

2. *PW*, 5:196; Ehrenpreis, 1:29; and also Ehrenpreis's *The Personality of Jonathan Swift*, 12; Nokes, 114.

3. See Kenyon, *The Stuarts*, 198–204; and Holmes, *The Making of a Great Power*, 364; Boswell, *Life of Johnson*, 1:38–39.

4. *Memoirs Relating to That Change Which Happened in the Queen's Ministry in the Year 1710*, 8:118.

5. Swift to Archbishop King, Sept. 9, 1710, *Corr.*, 1:291.

6. Preface to part 3 of Temple's *Memoirs*, *PW*, 1:268; Swift to Archbishop King, Sept. 9, 1710, *Corr.*, 1:291.

7. *Journal*, 1:6 (Sept. 9, 1710).

8. *The Virtues of Sid Hamet the Magician's Rod*, lines 5–14, *Poems*, 1:132.

9. Ibid., lines 85–86, 1:135.

10. *Journal*, 1:59 (Oct. 14, 1710).

11. Preface to *Miscellanies* (1711), quoted in *PW*, 2:xxxix.

12. *Journal*, 1:36, 41, 46–47 (Sept. 30, Oct. 4, Oct. 7, 1710).

13. *Journal*, 1:91 (Nov. 11, 1710).

14. *Journal*, 1:66, 55, 84 (Oct. 21, Oct. 13, Nov. 7, 1710).

15. King to Swift, Nov. 2, 1710; Swift to King, Dec. 30, 1710; King to Swift, Jan. 9, 1711, *Corr.*, 1:310, 324, 329. King quotes Horace's *Epistle* 2.1.13–14 (translation by H. Rushton Fairclough, *Satires, Epistles and Ars Poetica*, Loeb Classical Library [Cambridge: Harvard University Press, 1929], 397).

16. Swift to King, Dec. 30, 1710, *Corr.*, 1:324.

17. See Keith Feiling, *A History of the Tory Party, 1640–1714* (Oxford: Clarendon, 1924), 314; and Christopher Fox, "Swift and the Rabble Reformation: *A Tale of a Tub* and State of the Church in the 1690s," in *Swift as Priest and Satirist*, ed. Todd C. Parker (Newark: University of Delaware Press, 2009), 103. Swift probably never realized that the elder Harley had headed the committee that imprisoned his grandfather, Thomas Swift of Goodrich.

18. *Journal*, 2:381 (Oct. 11, 1711); Swift's annotation to Erasmus Lewis's letter of July 17, 1714, *Corr.*, 2:9; *Journal*, 1:353 (Sept. 7, 1711).

19. Swift to Archbishop King, Sept. 28, 1721, *Corr.*, 2:399; Swift to the Earl of Oxford, June 14, 1737, *Corr.*, 4:440.

20. Pope, as quoted by Spence, *Observations*, 1:96.

21. Hamilton, *The Backstairs Dragon*, 3, 222; Swift to John Hill, Aug. 12, 1712, *Corr.*, 1:434; Deane Swift, 164.

22. *A History of the Four Last Years of Queen Anne's Reign*, 7:73; William Cowper (later Earl Cowper), quoted by Plumb, 1:170; Kenyon, *The Stuarts*, 203.

23. Hamilton, *The Backstairs Dragon*, 17, 128.

24. H. T. Dickinson, *Bolingbroke* (London: Constable, 1970), 59.

25. *Journal*, 2:401 (Nov. 3, 1711); Shakespeare, *Hamlet*. 2.2.

26. *Journal*, 1:230 (Mar. 3, 1711); the editor, Harold Williams (230n), notes that the parenthetical "meaning from Sir William Temple" may have been added to Swift's manuscript, as a clarification, by Deane Swift.

27. *Journal*, 1:339, 164 (Aug. 23, Jan. 13, 1711); Ehrenpreis, 2:457.

28. *Journal*, 2:499 (Feb. 26, 1712).

29. Swift to Bolingbroke, Dec. 19, 1719, *Corr.*, 2:316; *Intelligencer* 5 and 7, *PW*, 12:41. The comment to Bolingbroke about the paper knife was repeated in *Thoughts of Various Subjects*, 4:251.

30. Swift to Archbishop King, Mar. 8, 1711, *Corr.*, 1:337.

31. *Journal*, 1:210–12 (Mar. 8, 1711); Ehrenpreis, 2:468; Swift to King, Mar. 8, 1711, *Corr.*, 1:338.

32. Prior, *To Mr. Harley, Wounded by Guiscard, 1711*, lines 15–16, in *The Literary Works of Matthew Prior*, ed. H. Bunker Wright and Monroe K. Spears (Oxford: Clarendon, 1959), 1:398; *Journal*, 1:228 (Mar. 30, 1711).

33. *Examiner* 32, *PW*, 3:109.

34. *Journal*, 1:224 (Mar. 25, 1711).

35. *Examiner* 32, *PW*, 3:109; John Oldmixon, *A Letter to the Seven Lords of the Committee, Appointed to Examine Gregg* (1711), quoted by Frank Ellis in *Swift vs. Mainwaring: The Examiner and The Medley* (Oxford: Clarendon, 1985), 303n.

36. Deane Swift, 163.

37. Delany, *A Letter to Deane Swift* (London, 1755), 16, 20–21.

38. *An Enquiry into the Behaviour of the Queen's Last Ministry*, *PW*, 8:151.

39. *A Letter from Dr. Swift to Mr. Pope* (1721), *PW*, 9:28; *Journal*, 2:589 (Dec. 26, 1712).

40. Kennett's diary is quoted in an appendix to Williams's edition of the letters, *The Correspondence of Jonathan Swift*, 4 vols., ed. Harold Williams (Oxford: Clarendon, 1963–65), 5:228–29; Ehrenpreis, 2:608.

41. *The Author upon Himself*, lines 37–40, 67–68, 1:194–96.

42. *Horace, Lib. 2. Sat. 6: Part of It Imitated*, lines 65–70, 79–80, *Poems*, 1:201.

43. *A Libel on Doctor Delany and a Certain Great Lord*, lines 13–16; *Poems*, 2:480.

44. Sheridan, 121.

45. *Journal*, 1:193–94 (Feb. 17, 1711). Ehrenpreis (2:210) makes the point about the ministers wanting to hold on to Swift.

46. *Journal*, 1:294 (June 21, 1711). The membership of the Club is listed at 2:505n.

47. Swift to Pope, Jan. 10, 1721, *Corr.*, 2:358; Swift to Lady Betty Germaine, Jan. 8, 1733, *Corr.*, 3:575.

48. Johnson, *Life of Parnell*, in *Lives*, 2:54; the anecdotes about Parnell's drinking (from Hester Piozzi's memoir of Johnson and from a friend of Delany's) are quoted by G. B. Hill in an appendix to that *Life*, 55.

49. *Journal*, 1:320 (July 25, 1711); Gregory Durston, "Rape in the Eighteenth-Century Metropolis," *British Journal for Eighteenth-Century Studies* 28 (2005): 15–16.

50. *Thoughts on Various Subjects*, 4:245; McBride, *Eighteenth-Century Ireland*, 113. See also G. E. Mingay, *English Landed Society in the Eighteenth Century* (London: Routledge and Kegan Paul, 1963).

51. *The Sentiments of a Church of England Man*, *PW*, 2:5; Bolingbroke, quoted by Dickinson, *Bolingbroke*, 164.

52. *Memoirs Relating to That Change Which Happened in the Queen's Ministry in the Year 1710* (written 1714, published 1765), 8:120.

53. *Examiner* 21, *PW*. 3:50; Thomas Burnet, *Essays Divine, Moral, and Political* (1714), v.

54. George Faulkner, preface to his 1763 edition of Swift's *Works*, *PW*, 13:202–3; Herbert Davis makes the point about Swift's style in *Jonathan Swift: Essays on His Satire and Other Studies* (New York: Oxford University Press, 1964), 217, 229–30.

55. *A Preface to the Right Reverend Dr. Burnet, Bishop of Sarum's Introduction to . . . the History of the Reformation of the Church of England* (1712), *PW*, 4:69.

56. George Orwell, "Politics and the English Language," in *A Collection of Essays by George Orwell* (New York: Doubleday Anchor Books, 1954), 176.

57. *Part of the Seventh Epistle of the First Book of Horace Imitated*, line 36, 1:171.

58. *Examiner* 14, *PW*, 3:11. Wharton's career is surveyed by Christopher Robbins in "'The Most Universal Villain I Ever Knew': Jonathan Swift and the Earl of Wharton," *Eighteenth-Century Ireland* 18 (2003): 24–38.

59. *Examiner* 22, *PW*, 3:57; see Ellis's note in *Swift vs. Mainwaring*, 152. The original "Verres" attack is in no. 17.

60. *A Short Character of His Excellency Thomas Earl of Wharton*, *PW*, 3:178–79.

61. *Journal*. 1:115 (Dec. 8, 1710).

62. *Journal*, 2:427 (Dec. 1, 1711); marginalia to John Macky, *PW*, 5:259.

63. *PW*, 4:270; on the *Miscellanies*, see Ehrenpreis, 2:422–24.

64. *Tatler* 230, *PW*, 2:176; on "banter," see the "Apology" to *A Tale of a Tub*, 10.

65. Ehrenpreis, 2:547; and see Ann Cline Kelly, *Swift and the English Language* (Philadelphia: University of Pennsylvania Press, 1988), ch. 6.

66. *A Project for the Advancement of Religion*, *PW*, 2:48–50.

67. Ibid., 2:57.

68. Swift to Pope (letter perhaps never sent), Jan. 10, 1721, *Corr.*, 2:361; *Project for the Advancement of Religion*, 2:44. For interpretations that accept Swift's serious intentions, see Ehrenpreis, 2:289–97; and Rawson, *Order from Confusion Sprung*, 28–35. Rawson advances a subtle argument according to which Swift's anarchic impulses and his commitment to order meet in "the kind of intimate mirror-opposition where self and anti-self complete one another."

69. I follow the argument of Leland D. Peterson, "Swift's *Project*: A Religious and Political Satire," *PMLA* 82 (1967): 54–63. This article is sometimes referred to as mistaken, but I have not seen it convincingly refuted.

CHAPTER 14. THE JOURNAL TO STELLA

1. See *Corr.*, 1:182n.

2. Herbert Davis, *Stella: A Gentlewoman of the Eighteenth Century* (New York: Macmillan, 1942), 52. Davis reproduces Swift's record of letters sent and received in an appendix to the *Journal*, 2:685–86. Woolley (*Corr.*, 2:377n) confirms that there are only three surviving letters by Stella.

3. *Journal*, 1:39, 31 (Oct. 3, Sept. 28, 1700). On postage costs, see *Corr.*, 1:177n.

4. *Journal*, 2:547 (July 1, 1712); letter 3, Sept. 9, 1710 (not noted in the printed *Journal*; British Library Add. ms. 72710).

5. *Journal*, 1:79 (Nov. 3, 1710). Abigail Williams suggests that "the tiny knotted scrawl becomes an embodiment of the ties between the three adults it joins." "The Difficulties of Swift's *Journal to Stella*," *Review of English Studies* 62 (2011): 761. Williams considers possible explanations for Swift's occasional covering over of endearments with looping cancellations, but concludes that "we will never know the real answer" (775); she offers a related analysis in "'I Hope to Write as Bad as Ever': Swift's *Journal to Stella* and the Intimacy of Correspondence," *Eighteenth-Century Life* 35 (2011): 102–18.

6. *Journal*, 1:142 (Dec. 27, 1710). These interpretations go back to Forster, 308, and have been repeated with occasional variations by numerous later writers. On "MD" and "Podefar," see *Journal*, 1:142 and 2:552n.

7. *Journal*, 1:131 (Dec. 17, 1710).

8. *Journal*, 1:325 (July 2, 1711).

9. Swift to King, Sept. 28, 1721, *Corr.*, 2:399.

10. *Journal*, 1:72–73 (Oct. 26, 1710) and 73n; on Patty Rolt, see *Corr.*, 1:640n.

11. *Journal*, 1:95, 157, 178 (Nov. 13, 1710, Jan. 6, Jan. 31, 1711).

12. *Journal*, 1:89, 344, 380 (Nov. 9, 1710, Aug. 25 [substituting "Pdfr" for Deane Swift's "Presto"], Oct. 9, 1711); Michael DePorte, "Swift's Horses of Instruction," in *Reading Swift*, 2:209. Robert C. Elliott discusses these passages in "The Self and t'Other I," in *The Literary Persona* (Chicago: University of Chicago Press, 1982), 89–106.

13. *Journal*, 1:220 (Mar. 19, 1711).

14. *Journal*, 1:245, 2:394 (Apr. 18, Oct. 24, 1711).

15. *Account Books*, 62–63.

16. T. G. Wilson, "The Mental and Physical Health of Dean Swift," *Medical History* 2, no. 3 (1958): 187; Wilson, "Swift's Deafness, and His Last Illness," *Irish Journal of Medical Science* 162 (1939): 249–50.

17. *Journal*, 2:528 (Mar. 30–31, 1712); Craik, 1:320.

18. *Journal*, 2:531–32, 564 (May 10, Oct. 9, 1712).

19. *Journal*, 1:272 (May 19, 1711).

20. *Journal*, 1:286, 293 (May 5, June 7, 1711).

21. *Journal*, 1:56 (Oct. 14, 1710), substituting "Ppt" for Deane Swift's "Stella."

22. Michael DePorte, "Night Thoughts in Swift," *Sewanee Review* 98 (1990): 646–63.

23. *Journal*, 1:152 (Jan. 4, 1711), substituting "Ppt" for Deane Swift's "Stella."

24. *Journal*, 1:143, 164 (Dec. 29, 1710, Jan. 14, 1711).

25. Lyon, loose notes in his copy of Hawkesworth.

26. *Journal*, 2:476 (Jan. 30, 1712)

27. *Journal*, 2:565 (Oct. 11, 1712).

28. *Journal*, 2:376 (Sept. 3, 1711). On house keys, see Vickery, *Behind Closed Doors*, 26, 43.

29. *Directions to Servants*, 13:8.

30. *Journal*, 1:39 (Oct. 3, 1710, substituting "Ppt" for "Stella"); her husband Filby is mentioned at 2:576 (Nov. 18, 1712).

31. *Journal*, 1:26 (Sept. 21, 1710).

32. *Journal*, 1:93, 99, 105 (Nov. 11, 21, 25, 1710).

33. Johnston, 215.

34. *Journal*, 2:378 (Oct. 7, 1711); Virginia Woolf, *The Common Reader, Second Series* (New York: Harcourt, Brace, 1932), 70.

35. *Journal*, 2:468, 1:342 (Jan. 21, 1712, and Aug. 24, 1711).

36. *Journal*, 1:153, 236, 249–50, 2:641 (Jan. 4, Apr. 6, Apr. 23, 1711, Mar. 19, 1713).

37. *Journal*, 2:558, 565, 569–70 (Sept. 18, Oct. 11, Oct. 30, 1712). In a letter to Lady Orkney Swift mentions "the workman you employed and directed" (Nov. 21, 1712, *Corr.*, 1:452).

38. *Journal*, 2:559, 569, 570–72 (Sept. 15. Oct. 30, Nov. 15, 1712); Holmes, *Marlborough*, 19.

39. *Journal*, 2:594–97 (Jan. 3, Jan. 5, 1713).

40. *Journal*, 2:484, 491, 494, 518 (Feb. 9, Feb. 18, Feb. 22, 1712). The "little language" got its first systematic analysis in 1948 in a valuable essay by Irvin Ehrenpreis, later collected in his *Personality of Jonathan Swift*, 50–58.

41. *Journal*, 2:518, 1:210 (Mar. 21, 1712, Mar. 7, 1711); Forster, 124, 307.

42. Woolf, *The Common Reader*, 68.

43. *Journal*, 1:30; 2:541 (Sept. 26, 1710, June 17, 1712).

44. *Journal*, 2:507 (Mar. 7, 1712). Deborah Baker Wyrick makes the point about private understanding in *Jonathan Swift and the Vested Word* (Chapel Hill: University of
North Carolina Press, 1988), 86.

45. *Journal*, 2:531–32 (May 10, 1712).

46. *Journal*, 1:205, 109 (Mar. 3, 1711, Nov. 30, 1710); Herbert Davis, *Jonathan Swift*, 63.

47. *Journal*, 1:154, 276–77, 154 (Jan. 4, May 23, 1711), replacing "Presto" with "Pdfr," etc.

48. *Journal*, 1:301, 2:539 (June 30, 1711, June 17, 1712), substituting "Ppt" for "Stella," etc.

49. *Journal*, 1:56–57, 146 (Oct. 14 [substituting "Pdfr" for "Presto"], Jan. 1, 1710).

50. *Journal*, 2:410, 1:182, 181 (Nov. 12, 1711, Feb. 8, 1711, Feb. 5, 1711).

51. *Journal*, 1:123, 234, 2:392 (Dec. 14, 1710, Apr. 5, Oct. 23, 1711).

52. Swift to Mary Pendarves, Jan. 29, 1736, *Corr.*, 4:257; the comment about the person
with "natural good sense and judgment" is quoted by Woolley from the Portland
papers: *Corr.*, 4:258n.

53. *Journal*, 2:426 (Dec. 1, 1711), conjecturing that Deane Swift substituted "Madam
Stella" for "MD."

54. *Journal*, 1:302–3, 2:414, 405 (June 30, Nov. 17, Nov. 6, 1711), altering "Presto," etc.

CHAPTER 15. ENTER VANESSA

1. Journal of C. Huygens (1690), quoted by Bruce Arnold, "'A Protestant Purchaser':
Bartholomew Van Homrigh, Merchant Adventurer," *Swift Studies* 15 (2000): 42. Orrery (154) mentions the pronunciation of Vanhomrigh.

2. *Journal*, 1:260 (May 4, 1711).

3. *Journal*, 1:95, 360, 2:382 (Nov. 14, 1710, Sept. 14, Oct. 12, 1711).

4. *Journal*, 2:417, 421 (Nov. 19, Nov. 26, 1711); Ehrenpreis, 2:641, 644. Harold Williams's
index identifies fifty-five meals (*Journal*, 2:794).

5. *Journal*, 1:48, 86–87 (Oct. 8, Nov. 8, 1710).

6. *PW*, 5:197–98.

7. Anne Long to Swift, Nov. 18, 1711; Swift to Anne Long, Dec. 18, 1711, *Corr.*, 1:397,
401.

8. *Journal*, 2:445, 446n, 519 (Dec. 25, 1711, Mar. 21, 1712); *Death of Mrs. Long, PW*,
5:198.

9. *Journal*, 1:283, 285 (May 30, June 4, 1711).

10. *Journal*, 1:270 (May 15, 1711).

11. *Journal*, 2:441 (Dec. 18, 1711); Swift to Vanessa, Dec. 18, 1711, *Corr.*, 1:399. The coincidence of dates is remarked by Williams in his footnote in the *Journal*.

12. Glendinning, 132–33.

13. Ehrenpreis, 2:661, 3:396, 2:647, 642.

14. Swift to Anne Long, Dec. 18, 1711, *Corr.*, 1:402; Swift to Vanessa, Aug. 15, 1712, *Corr.*,
1:436–37; Johnson, *Life of Swift*, 31.

15. Louise Bogan, *Hypocrite Swift*, in *The Blue Estuaries: Poems, 1923–1968* (New York: Farrar, Straus and Giroux, 1968), 68–69.

16. Swift to Vanessa, Sept. 28, 1712, *Corr.*, 1:443.

17. A full account of the poem's development and eventual publication is given by Peter J. Schakel, "'What Success It Met': The Reception of *Cadenus and Vanessa*," in *Reading Swift*, 3:215–24. "Cadenus" is first named at line 462.

18. Ellen Pollak makes this point in *The Poetics of Sexual Myth: Gender and Ideology in the Verse of Swift and Pope* (Chicago: University of Chicago Press, 1985), 133.

19. *Cadenus and Vanessa*, lines 161, 178, 205–7, 13–14, *Poems*, 2:691–93, 697; Anne Long to Swift, Nov. 18, 1711, *Corr.*, 1:398.

20. *Cadenus and Vanessa*, lines 400–403, 2:699.

21. Ibid., line 466, 2:701; François, duc de la Rochefoucauld, *Maximes*, ed. Jacques Truchet (Paris: Flammarion, 1977), 98.

22. *Cadenus and Vanessa*, lines 524–31, 2:703.

23. *Poems*, 2:703–4, deleted lines given in the textual notes.

24. *Cadenus and Vanessa*, lines 608–13, 622–23, 2:705–6.

25. Ibid., lines 642–55, 744–751, 2:707, 710. In line 746 I follow "but though her arguments," as in Faulkner's edition, which makes more sense than Williams's "and" (2:710, textual note).

26. Ibid., lines 772–77, 780, 785, 2:711.

27. Ibid., lines 818–27, 2:712 (I follow the alternative reading of "act" instead of "like" in line 823). This is the conclusion that John Irwin Fischer reaches in a thoughtful article, "'Love and Books': Some Early Texts of Swift's *Cadenus and Vanessa*," in *Reading Swift*, 4:309–10.

28. Ehrenpreis, 2:650–51; Sheridan, 273; William K. Wimsatt, "Rhetoric and Poems: The Example of Swift," in *Essential Articles for the Study of Swift's Poetry*, ed. David M. Vieth (Hamden, Conn.: Archon Books, 1984), 88.

29. Swift to Vanessa, May 31, 1713; Vanessa to Swift, June 6, 1713, *Corr.*, 1:498, 502.

CHAPTER 16. TORY TRIUMPH

1. Lewis, "Addison," 146.

2. *Spectator* 4, 57; *Journal*, 2:482 (Feb. 8, 1712).

3. *Journal*, 2:589 (Dec. 27, 1712).

4. *To Charles Ford*, lines 75–76, *Poems*, 1:314; Swift to Arbuthnot, July 25, 1714, *Corr.*, 2:26; Pope to Robert Digby, Sept. 1, 1724, *The Correspondence of Alexander Pope*, ed. George Sherburn (Oxford: Clarendon, 1965), 2:253.

5. *Verses on the Death of Dr. Swift*, lines 55–58, 2:555.

6. Pope's comment and Arbuthnot's epitaph in *Epistles to Several Persons*, vol. III-ii of the Twickenham edition of *The Poems of Alexander Pope*, ed. F. W. Bateson (London: Methuen, 1961), 85–86n.

7. Pope, *An Epistle to Dr Arbuthnot*, line 132; Pope to Lord Bathurst, Dec. 18, 1730, *Correspondence of Alexander Pope*, 3:156.

8. Pope, *An Epistle to Dr. Arbuthnot*, lines 201–4.

9. Swift to Gay, May 4, 1732, *Corr.*, 3:469; Congreve, quoted by Craik, 2:204.

10. Ashley Marshall subjects the alleged "Scriblerian" tradition to trenchant criticism in "The Myth of Scriblerus," *Journal for Eighteenth-Century Studies* 31 (2008): 77–99.

11. *Journal*, 1:120 (Dec. 13, 1710).

12. Swift's letter to the *Evening Post*, Nov. 12, 1712, *PW*, 6:196–97; *Journal*, 2:572–73 (Nov. 15, 1712).

13. *Gulliver's Travels*, book 4, ch. 5, p. 247; John Wesley, *The Doctrine of Original Sin* (1756), in *Works* (New York: Waugh and Mason, 1835), 5:512.

14. *Examiners* 28 and 37, *PW*, 3:87, 133–34.

15. Holmes, *Marlborough*, xix–xx, 438.

16. *Examiner* 16, *PW*. 3:22–23.

17. *An Account of the Conduct of the Dowager Duchess of Marlborough* (London: George Hawkins, 1742), 153; *Memoirs of Sarah, Duchess of Marlborough* (1736), in *Critical Heritage*, 101.

18. HMC 8th Report, Marlborough Papers, quoted by Barnett, *The First Churchill*, 262; Swift, *History of the Last Four Years of Queen Anne's Reign*, 7:30.

19. *A Satirical Elegy on the Death of a Late Famous General*, lines 1–4, 13–16, 29–32, *Poems*, 1:297; the "dust thou art" text quotes Genesis 3:19.

20. *Journal*, 2:408 (Nov. 10, 1711).

21. *Trevelyan*, 3:192; *Journal*, 2:474 (Jan. 28, 1712).

22. Johnson, *Life of Swift*, 3:19; Boswell, *Life of Johnson*, 2:65 (summer 1768).

23. *The Conduct of the Allies*, 6:6, 41.

24. Ibid., 6:19.

25. Johnson, *Life of Swift*, 19; Trevelyan, 3:254.

26. *Journal*, 2:449–50 (Dec. 29, 1711).

27. A. D. MacLachlan, "The Road to Peace, 1710–13," in "The Revolution and the People," in *Britain After the Glorious Revolution*, ed. Geoffrey Holmes (London: Macmillan, 1969), 213, 197; King to Swift, May 29, 1712, *Corr.*, 1:425.

28. *History of the Last Four Years of Queen Anne's Reign*, 7:167.

29. Porter, *English Society in the Eighteenth Century*, 37.

CHAPTER 17. TORY COLLAPSE

1. Quoted by Holmes, *The Making of a Great Power*, 254.

2. *Journal*, 1:195 (Feb. 18, 1711); "we will not be harled" quoted by Downie, 149.

3. *Journal*, 1:206 (Mar. 4, 1711).

4. *Gulliver's Travels*, book 1, ch. 5, p. 56.

5. *Journal*, 1:327–28 (Aug. 6, Aug. 8, 1711).

6. *Journal*, 1:126 (Dec. 14, 1710).

7. *The Windsor Prophecy*, lines 15–20, *Poems*, 1:148.

8. Quoted by Real, *Securing Swift*, 232.

9. *Journal*, 2:444–46 (Dec. 24, Dec. 16, 1711).

10. *Gulliver's Travels*, book 2, ch. 5, p. 124; Carole Fabricant suggests the application to Swift's experience at court, *Swift's Landscape* (Baltimore: Johns Hopkins University Press, 1982), 227–28. On Swift suppressing any mention of *The Windsor Prophecy*, see Hermann J. Real, "The Most Fateful Piece Swift Ever Wrote," *Swift Studies* (1994): 79n.

11. *Journal*, 2:480; Swift to Oxford, Feb. 5, 1712, *Corr.*, 1:414.

12. *Journal*, 16:660 (Apr. 13, 1713).

13. *Journal*, 2:663, 666 (Apr. 20, Apr. 23, 1713).

14. Sheridan, 138.

15. Bolingbroke to Swift, Dec. 25, 1723, *Corr.*, 2:479.

16. *Journal*, 2:665 (Apr. 23, 1713); Dr. William King's *Anecdotes*, quoted by Forster, 169n.

17. *Journal*, 2:662 (Apr. 18, 1713).

18. Swift to Vanessa, May 31, 1713; Vanessa to Swift, June 1713, *Corr.*, 1:498, 510.

19. *Journal*, 2:669 (May 16, 1713); see Louis A. Landa, "Swift's Deanery Income," in *Essays in Eighteenth-Century Literature* (Princeton: Princeton University Press, 1980), 115–16.

20. Erasmus Lewis to Swift, Aug. 6, 1713, *Corr.*, 1:525.

21. Sir Constantine Phipps to Swift, Oct. 24, 1713, *Corr.*, 1:542.

22. Swift to Bishop Stearne, Dec. 19, 1713, *Corr.*, 1:566.

23. Swift to King, Dec. 31, 1713, *Corr.*, 1:574; Nokes, 201–2.

24. *Part of the Seventh Epistle of the First Book of Horace Imitated*, lines 67–70, 1:173.

25. Ibid., lines 91–92, 101–6, 131–38, 1:173–75.

26. On specific points that the second Lord Oxford objected to, see *PW*, 7:xv. The historians quoted are W. A. Speck, "Swift and the Historian," in *Reading Swift*, 1:257–68; and S. J. Connolly, "Swift and Protestant Ireland: Images and Reality," in Douglas et al., *Locating Swift*, 35.

27. *The Importance of the Guardian Considered*, *PW*, 8:5–6; *The Public Spirit of the Whigs*, *PW*, 8:36.

28. *The Public Spirit*, 8:53.

29. *PW*, 8:xxi.

30. Oxford to Swift, Mar. 3, 1714, *Corr.*, 1:589.

31. Swift to Peterborough, May 18, 1714, *Corr.*, 1:600–601.

32. Peterborough to Swift, Mar. 5, 1714, *Corr.*, 1:591.

33. *Verses on the Death of Dr. Swift*, lines 365–70, 2:567.

34. Bolingbroke to Swift, July 13, 1714, *Corr.*, 2:1–2.

35. John Geree to Swift, Apr. 24, 1714; Swift to Vanessa, June 8, 1714, *Corr.*, 1:598, 606.

36. Pope to Arbuthnot, July 11, 1714, *The Correspondence of Alexander Pope*, 1:234–35.

37. Erasmus Lewis to Swift, July 27, 1714, *Corr.*, 2:31.

38. Arbuthnot to Swift, Aug. 12, 1714, *Corr.*, 2:70; Oxford college head, quoted by Gregg, *Queen Anne*, 395.

39. Bolingbroke to Swift, Aug. 3, 1714, *Corr.*, 2:47; Swift to Archdeacon Walls, Aug. 8, 1714, *Corr.*, 2:63; *The Words upon the Window-Pane*, in *The Collected Works of W. B. Yeats*, vol. 2, *The Plays*, ed. David R. Clark and Rosalind E. Clark (New York: Scribner, 2001), 468.

40. *Some Thoughts upon the Present State of Affairs*, PW, 8:86–87.

41. *The Author upon Himself*, lines 9–14, 1–2, 53–56, 1:193–95. Several blanks in the poem have been filled in with names supplied by Orrery (Rogers, 670).

42. Swift to Bolingbroke, Oct. 31, 1729; Swift to Pope, Mar. 23, 1733, *Corr.*, 3:261, 615.

43. Arbuthnot to Swift, Aug. 12, 1714, *Corr.*, 2:70–71.

CHAPTER 18. RELUCTANT DUBLINER

1. Trevelyan, 3:97; *A Concordance to the Poems of Jonathan Swift*, ed. Michael Shinagel (Ithaca: Cornell University Press, 1972).

2. J. H. Bernard, *The Cathedral Church of Saint Patrick*, rev. J. E. L. Oulton (Dublin: Talbot, 1940), 7–8; Fagan, *The Second City*, 23; Maurice Craig, *Dublin, 1660–1860: The Shaping of a City* (Dublin: Liberties, 2006), 31.

3. Swift to Gay, Nov. 20, 1729, *Corr.*, 3:268; introduction to Pepys, *Diary*, 1:xxxi.

4. Trevelyan, 1:52.

5. Delany, 131.

6. Lyon, 75; Ehrenpreis, 2:277. Peter Steele borrows Ehrenpreis's words for the title of *Jonathan Swift: Preacher and Jester* (Oxford: Clarendon, 1978).

7. Delany, 29; *A Letter to a Young Gentleman, Lately Entered into Holy Orders*, 9:66.

8. Delany, 140.

9. "Some Further Account," in Faulkner's 1763 edition of *Works*, 11:324.

10. Swift to Dean Mossom, Feb. 14, 1721, *Corr.*, 2:366. On the various ecclesiastical confrontations, see Downie, 211–12.

11. Elgy Gillespie, ed., *The Liberties of Dublin* (Dublin: O'Brien, 1973), 28–38.

12. Swift to Rev. James Stopford, Nov. 26, 1725, *Corr.*, 2:619–20; Swift to Pope, June 28, 1715, *Corr.*, 2:133; *The Author's Manner of Living*, *Poems*, 3:954; Erasmus Jones, "A Brief and Merry Character of Ireland," in *A Trip through London* (1728), 53–54.

13. Bernard, *The Cathedral Church of Saint Patrick*, 21.

14. See *Corr.*, 3:502n, 505n; Woolley prints one of Swift's wine contracts, *Corr.*, 4:117–18.

15. *Gulliver's Travels*, book 4, ch. 6, p. 252; Swift to Charles Ford, Dec. 20, 1718, *Corr.*, 2:286. Swift's many references to wine are surveyed by Michael DePorte, "*Vinum Daemonum*: Swift and the Grape," *Swift Studies* 12 (1997): 56–68.

16. Swift to Knightley Chetwode, October 1724, *Corr.*, 2:524; *Gulliver's Travels*, book 2, ch. 1, p. 89.

17. Swift to Charles Ford, Feb. 16, 1719, *Corr.*, 2:290.

18. Arbuthnot to Swift, Dec. 11, 1718, and Nov. 5, 1730; Swift to Ford, Oct. 9, 1733; Ford to Swift, Nov. 6, 1733, *Corr.*, 2:282, 3:331, 692, 698; on the quilted cap, *Corr.*, 3:714n.

19. Leslie Stephen, *Swift* (New York: Harper, 1887), 197.

20. Handwritten note by Orrery in a copy of his book, Orrery, 432.

21. Pilkington, 1:28.

22. See Ehrenpreis, 3:833; Pilkington, 2:239 (Elias's note on wages); and Barnett, *Jonathan Swift in the Company of Women*, 84.

23. *Laws for the Dean's Servants*, PW, 13:161–62.

24. PW, 13:14–15; Lyon, 751.

25. Delany, 6; Porter, *English Society in the Eighteenth Century*, 19.

26. *Causes of the Wretched Condition of Ireland*, PW, 9:204; Samuel Johnson, *Rambler* 68.

27. Delany, 127–28.

28. Patrick Delany, *Verses on the Deanery Window*, *Poems*, 1:261.

29. Swift to the Daniel Jackson, Mar. 26, 1722, *Corr.*, 2:418; see 417n; Lyon, 35.

30. Delany, 133; Ehrenpreis, 3:323 (suggesting that the snobbish friend was Sheridan); Jonathan Smedley, *Gulliveriana* (London, 1728), 10, 3, xi; and see Ann Cline Kelly, "Written in Stone: Swift's Use of St. Patrick's Cathedral as a Text," *Swift Studies* 21 (2006): 109–10.

31. Swift to Pope, Aug. 11, 1729, (quoting Exodus 2:22); Swift to Knightley Chetwode, Nov. 23, 1727; Swift to Sheridan, July 8, 1726; Swift to Bolingbroke, Mar. 21, 1730, *Corr.*, 3:245, 3:139, 2:651–52, 3:295.

32. Deane Swift, 181.

33. Pilkington, 1:283.

34. See Brian Boydell, "Music Before 1700," in Moody and Vaughan, *Eighteenth-Century Ireland*, 562–63. The Gaelic form of the name is given by Carole Fabricant, "Speaking for the Irish Nation: The Drapier, the Bishop, and the Problems of Colonial Representation," *ELH* 66 (1999): 342.

35. *A New Year's Gift for the Dean of St. Patrick's Given Him at Quilca, 1724*, in *The Poems of Thomas Sheridan*, ed. Robert Hogan (Newark: University of Delaware Press, 1994), 133.

36. *The Description of an Irish Feast*, lines 1–8, 37–44, *Poems*, 1:244–45. Fabricant, *Swift's Landscape*, 245–48, gives examples of Gaelic words in Swift, but she accepts as his a ballad that Williams was dubious about (*Poems*, 3:840) and that Rogers (595) rejects altogether.

37. *A Dialogue in Hibernian Style*, in *Swift's Irish Writings*, ed. Carole Fabricant and Robert Mahony (New York: Palgrave Macmillan, 2010), 184 (a more accurate transcription than the version in PW, 4:278). My identification of the Gaelic words relies on the notes in this edition.

38. *On Barbarous Denominations in Ireland*, PW, 4:280; *Answer to Several Letters from Unknown Persons*, PW, 12:89. See Robert Mahony, "Jonathan Swift and the Irish Colonial Project," in Rawson, *Politics and Literature in the Age of Swift*, 270–89.

39. Delany, 73; Sheridan, 321.

40. *Ad Amicum Eruditum Thomam Sheridan*, *Poems*, 1:213; see James Woolley's introduction to the *Intelligencer* 18; *Mary the Cook-Maid's Letter to Dr. Sheridan*, line 10, *Poems*, 3:985; *The History of the Second Solomon*, PW, 5:223; Swift to Ford, Jan. 19, 1724, *Corr.*, 2:487.

41. The Sheridan family name is mentioned by Fintan O'Toole, *A Traitor's Kiss: The Life of Richard Brinsley Sheridan* (New York: Farrar, Straus and Giroux, 1998), 3–10; Sheridan, 322.

42. Fagan, *The Second City*, 28, 30.

43. Sheridan, quoted in Woolley's edition of the *Intelligencer* 8; Swift to Mrs. Whiteway, Nov. 28, 1735, *Corr.*, 4:238–39; Sheridan to Swift, Apr. 5, 1735, *Corr.*, 4:81–82; Rogers,

735. See James Woolley, "Thomas Sheridan and Swift," *Studies in Eighteenth-Century Culture* 9 (1979): 93–114.
44. Sheridan, 321.
45. Undated letter (first printed by Faulkner), Ball, *The Correspondence of Jonathan Swift*, 5:436.
46. Woolley, "Thomas Sheridan and Swift," 101–2; and Woolley's introduction to the *Intelligencer* 17.
47. "The Original of Punning, from Plato's *Symposiacs*," in *The Poems of Thomas Sheridan*, 95.
48. *Discourse to Prove the Antiquity of the English Tongue*, PW, 4:236; *A Modest Defense of Punning*, PW, 4:206.

CHAPTER 19. POLITICAL PERIL

1. Index to the *Examiner*, PW, 14:12; *Verses on the Death of Dr. Swift*, line 380, 2:568.
2. Swift's relations with known Jacobites, and the similarity of some of his opinions to theirs, are surveyed by Higgins in *Swift's Politics*. Higgins is sometimes criticized for claiming that Swift actually was a Jacobite, but he doesn't make that claim, confirming that he kept clear of actual involvement.
3. Erasmus Lewis to Swift, Feb. 1715; Swift to Chetwode, June 21, 1715, *Corr.*, 2:112, 129; King to Christopher Delafaye, June 4, 1715, in Williams, *The Correspondence of Jonathan Swift*, 5:233; Passmann and Vienken, *The Library and Reading of Jonathan Swift*, 1:437; Pope to Swift, June 30, 1716, *Corr.*, 2:174.
4. Sheridan, 183.
5. *PW*, 5:199–200; see Ehrenpreis, 3:22.
6. Dickinson, *Bolingbroke*, 135.
7. Plumb, 1:189.
8. Ehrenpreis, 2:585. These issues are explored by Jeanne Clegg, "Swift on False Witness," *Studies in English Literature* 44 (2004): 461–85.
9. Swift to King, Dec. 22, 1716, *Corr.*, 2:205.
10. King to Swift, Jan. 12, 1717, *Corr.*, 2:215.
11. Quoted by Wolfgang Michael, *England under George I: The Beginnings of the Hanoverian Dynasty* (New York: AMS, 1970), 152.
12. *An Enquiry into the Behaviour of the Queen's Last Ministry*, 8:133.
13. Swift to Oxford, July 19, 1715, *Corr.*, 2:139; *To the Earl of Oxford . . . in the Tower*, lines 15–18, *Poems*, 1:210.
14. Lewis to Swift, June 15, July 2, 1717, *Corr.*, 2:244, 246.
15. Swift to Oxford, July 9, 1717; Oxford to Swift, Aug. 6, 1717; Swift to the second Earl of Oxford, July 9, 1724, *Corr.*, 2:249, 256, 504.
16. *On False Witness*, PW, 9:180; Landa's introduction (117–18) discusses Swift's sense of vulnerability in these years. Swift to Pope, Jan. 10, 1721, *Corr.*, 2:361.
17. Quoted by Plumb, 1:180–81.
18. *History of the Last Four Years of Queen Anne's Reign*, 7:65; Plumb, 1:xi, 92, 2:91.
19. As Trevelyan notes (1:276).

20. Plumb, 2:88, 90, 111.

21. *Gulliver's Travels*, book 1, ch. 3, p. 39; but the usual identification with the Duchess of Kendal is probably wrong. See Harold Williams's introduction in *PW*, 11:xix; and Higgins, *Swift's Politics*, 173–74.

22. *Epistle to a Lady*, lines 159–60, *Poems*, 2:635; *The Life and Genuine Character of Doctor Swift*, lines 107–8; *Poems*, 2:548.

23. *Gulliver's Travels*, book 4, ch. 3, pp. 262–63.

24. *Upon the Horrid Plot*, lines 1–4, *Poems*, 1:298. The poem was first published in 1735, in Faulkner's edition of Swift's *Works*. My account of the Atterbury affair is drawn from Edward Rosenheim Jr., "Swift and the Atterbury Case," in *The Augustan Milieu: Essays Presented to Louis A. Landa*, ed. Henry Knight Miller et al. (Oxford: Clarendon, 1970), 174–204; G. V. Bennett, *The Tory Crisis in Church and State* (Oxford: Clarendon, 1975); and Eveline Cruickshanks and Howard Erskine-Hill, *The Atterbury Plot* (New York: Palgrave Macmillan, 2004).

25. *Gulliver's Travels*, book 3, ch. 6, p. 191.

26. Quoted by Rosenheim, "Swift and the Atterbury Case," 202.

27. *Gulliver's Travels*, book 1, ch. 7, pp. 69, 72.

CHAPTER 20. THE IRISH COUNTRYSIDE

1. Swift to Pope, Aug. 25, 1726, *Corr.*, 3:19.

2. Swift to Archdeacon Walls, May 22, 1715, *Corr.*, 2:127; the suggestion about the name Bolingbroke comes from DePorte, "Swift's Horses of Instruction," 2:206.

3. Swift describes the incident in a letter to Walls, Dec. 27, 1714, *Corr.*, 2:105–6.

4. *Gulliver's Travels*, book 4, ch. 4, p. 241.

5. 1 Kings 21:1–29.

6. Swift to Bolingbroke, Mar. 21, 1730, *Corr.*, 3:295; Swift to Rev. Stafford Lightburne, Apr. 22, 1725, *Corr.*, 2:553.

7. *The Duty of Servants at Inns*, *PW*, 13:163–65.

8. *Journal*, lines 9–16, 74, *Poems*, 1:278, 281. In line 14 I follow Rogers in giving "ends our lectures"; *Poems* has "ends or lectures," which makes no sense.

9. Ibid, lines 65–68, 77–82. The poem was written in 1721 and published as a broadside in 1722. Percival, *A Description in Answer to the Journal* (published in 1722 as an anonymous broadside), quoted by Ann Cline Kelly, *Jonathan Swift and Popular Culture*, 71.

10. Swift to Daniel Jackson, Oct. 6, 1721, *Corr.*, 2:401.

11. Swift to Knightley Chetwode, May 27, 1725, *Corr.*, 2:555; see Joseph McMinn, "The Humours of Quilca: Swift, Sheridan, and County Cavan," in *Walking Naboth's Vineyard: New Studies of Swift*, ed. Christopher Fox and Brenda Tooley (Notre Dame, Ind: University of Notre Dame Press, 1995), 143–53.

12. Sheridan, 308; Fabricant, *Swift's Landscape*, 160; Swift to Chetwode, May 27, 1725, *Corr.*, 2:554; "the harvest was spoiled" quoted by James Kelly, "Harvests and Hardship: Famine and Scarcity in Ireland in the Late 1720s," *Studia Hibernica* 26 (1992): 72.

13. Swift to the 2nd Earl of Oxford, Aug. 14, 1725, *Corr.*, 2:583.

14. *To Quilca*, lines 1–4, 9–12, *Poems*, 3:1035; Sheridan, *A True and Faithful Inventory of the Goods Belonging to Dr. Swift, Vicar of Laracor*, lines 1–4, *Poems*, 3:1044.

15. *The Blunders, Deficiencies, Distresses, and Misfortunes of Quilca*, PW, 5:219–21.

16. Sheridan, *Tom Punsibi's Letter to Dean Swift*, lines 20–26, 29–36, *Poems*, 3:1046. I follow a different reading for lines 31–32, as given in Hogan, *The Poems of Thomas Sheridan*, 113.

17. Sheridan, 344.

18. Swift to Dr. Sheridan, June 25, 1725, *Corr.*, 2:559, 561n.

19. "A Pilgrimage to Quilca in the Year 1852," signed "B" [R. S. Brooke], *Dublin University Magazine*, November 1852, 509–25.

CHAPTER 21. STELLA

1. *On the Death of Mrs. Johnson*, 5:227; Scott, 223 (adding that his unnamed informant was a lady "equally distinguished for high rank, eminent talents, and the soundest judgment"); Dunton, *Some Account of My Conversation in Ireland*, 200.

2. *Dingley and Brent: A Song* (probably written around 1724), *Poems*, 2:755–56.

3. Haworth, "Jonathan Swift and the Geography of Laracor," 23, quoting William R. Wilde, *The Closing Years of Dean Swift's Life* (Dublin: Hodges and Smith, 1849), 97.

4. Thackeray, *The English Humourists of the Eighteenth Century*, 408.

5. *Bon Mots de Stella*, PW, 5:238.

6. *On the Death of Mrs. Johnson*, 5:229; Johnson, *Life of Swift*, 42; *Bon Mots de Stella*, 5:238.

7. Nokes, 165; *On the Death of Mrs. Johnson*, 5:228–29; *To Stella, Who Collected and Transcribed His Poems*, lines 87–94, 131–34, *Poems*, 2:730–31.

8. Ehrenpreis, 2:419.

9. Ibid., 2:661

10. Orrery, 168.

11. *On Stella's Birthday, Written A.D. 1719*, *Poems*, 2:721–22.

12. *To Stella, Visiting Me in My Sickness*, lines 97–102, 109–16, 2:726–27.

13. *Stella's Birthday, Written A.D. 1721*, lines 15–22, *Poems*, 2:734–35.

14. *To Dr. Swift on His Birthday, November 30, 1721*, lines 1–4, 9–14, *Poems*, 2:737. Deane Swift (81) said that Swift gave the original to "a lady of his acquaintance," presumably his cousin Martha Whiteway, with an assurance that it was "entirely genuine from the hands of Stella, without any sort of correction whatsoever."

15. Swift to Rev. Thomas Wallis, Feb. 12, 1723, *Corr.*, 2:450. Wallis was vicar of Athboy, seven miles from Laracor.

16. *Stella's Birthday* (1725), lines 19–30, 53–54, *Poems*, 2:757–58 and footnote.

17. Swift to James Stopford, July 20, 1726, *Corr.*, 2:660; *To Stella, Who Collected and Transcribed His Poems*, lines 9–14, 2:728.

18. *On the Death of Mrs. Johnson*, 5:228.

19. King to Swift, Aug. 5, 1713, *Corr.*, 1:524; Harold Williams makes the suggestion about the hint, Williams, *The Correspondence of Jonathan Swift*, 5:238.

20. *Thoughts on Various Subjects*, PW, 4:247, 252.

21. *Thoughts on Various Subjects* [a different collection], *PW*, 1:245; William Blake, *The Golden Net*.

22. Johnson, *Life of Swift*, 30, quoting Dr. Samuel Madden; Delany, 36; Deane Swift, 92; Sheridan, 279.

23. Lyon, 19.

24. John Hawkesworth, *The Works of Dr. Jonathan Swift* (London, 1766), 1:46.

25. Scott, 219–22. Names in brackets clarify Scott's meaning in a long sequence of "he" and "him."

26. As told by Lady Suffolk to Horace Walpole: *Reminiscences Written by Mr. Horace Walpole*, 144.

27. Monck-Berkeley, *Literary Relics*, xxxvi; Johnston, 80; Mackie L. Jarrell, "'Jack and the Dane': Swift Traditions in Ireland," in Jeffares, *Fair Liberty Was All His Cry*, 318.

CHAPTER 22. VANESSA IN IRELAND

1. Swift to Vanessa, Aug. 12, 1714, *Corr.*, 2:71–72; Ehrenpreis, 3:92.

2. *In Sickness*, lines 1–6, 19–22, *Poems*, 1:203–4.

3. Vanessa, *A Rebus, Written by a Lady*, lines 1–7, *Poems*, 2:715–16.

4. Ibid., lines 8–11, and (by Swift) *The Answer*, lines 21–228, *Poems*, 2:716–17; Faulkner and others identified the lady as Vanessa. Rogers (706–7) thinks that some allusions at the end of Swift's poem place it around 1721 or later, but I believe—as does Williams in his edition of the *Poems*—that the discouraged tone puts it closer to 1714.

5. Swift to Vanessa, Nov. 5, 1714, *Corr.*, 2:93; Ehrenpreis, 3:96; Barnett, *Jonathan Swift in the Company of Women*, 67; Swift to Knightley Chetwode, May 8, 1731, *Corr.*, 3:391.

6. Both letters, Swift to Vanessa, December 1714, *Corr.*, 2:99–100 (correcting "possibly" to "possible").

7. Vanessa to Swift, December 1714, *Corr.*, 2:101.

8. Swift to Vanessa, December 1714, *Corr.*, 2:102.

9. Vanessa to Swift, December 1714, *Corr.*, 2:103.

10. Orrery, 158.

11. Ehrenpreis, 3:94, 1056–57; Nokes, 215.

12. Orrery, 159; Deane Swift, 264.

13. Scott, 230–31 (citing "a most obliging correspondent" who knew the gardener when he was an old man).

14. Swift to Vanessa, Dec. 2, 1716, *Corr.*, 2:194; Michael DePorte makes this point in "Riddles, Mysteries, and Lies: Swift and Secrecy," in *Reading Swift*, 4:130.

15. Swift to Vanessa, May 12, 1719, *Corr.*, 2:304–5.

16. Sheridan, 291–92.

17. Swift to Vanessa, July 5, 1721, Oct. 15, 1720, *Corr.*, 2:385, 348.

18. *A Foreign View of England in the Reigns of George I and George II: The Letters of Monsieur César de Saussure to His Family*, trans. Madame Van Muyden (London: John Murray, 1902), 164; Thomas Brown, *Amusements Serious and Comical, Calculated for the Meridian of London* (London, 1700), 115.

19. Swift to Vanessa, July 5, 1721, *Corr.*, 2:386 (with minor errors in French corrected).

20. Sheridan, 283–84. The suggestion that Swift may be hoping to return to England is made by Sybil Le Brocquy, *Cadenus* (Dublin: Dolmen, 1962), 86.

21. Swift to Vanessa, July 13, 1720, *Corr.*, 2:337–38; Vanessa to Swift, July 28, 1720, *Corr.*, 2:339.

22. Swift to Vanessa, June 1, 1722, *Corr.*, 2:421. Swift was at Clogher for the installation of his friend Stearne as bishop.

23. Swift to Vanessa, July 13, 1722, *Corr.*, 2:425.

24. Swift to Vanessa, Aug. 4, 1720, *Corr.*, 2:340; Woolley notes that in common speech, "skinage" could mean "skinny," with examples going back to 1605.

25. Vanessa to Swift, Aug. 1720, *Corr.*, 2:341–42.

26. Vanessa to Swift and Swift to Vanessa, January 1720 [date not certain], *Corr.*, 2:319–20.

27. Swift to Vanessa, Aug. 12, 1720, *Corr.*, 2:343.

28. In identifying these references I have been helped by Le Brocquy, *Cadenus*, 74–75, as well as by Woolley's notes. "The strain by the box of books at London" is mentioned in a letter of June 1, 1722, *Corr.*, 2:421.

29. Vanessa to Swift, both letters November or December 1720, *Corr.*, 2:351–52.

30. Ehrenpreis, 3:395.

31. Vanessa to Swift, July 1722, *Corr.*, 2:426.

32. Swift to Vanessa, Feb. 27, 1721, *Corr.*, 2:367; the original little note is in the British Library, Add. 39839.

33. Sheridan, 285.

34. Ibid., 286.

35. Bishop Evans to the archbishop of Canterbury, July 27, 1723. Evans's phrase about the *Tale of a Tub* is quoted by Ehrenpreis, 3:390; the rest of the long quotation (not mentioned by Ehrenpreis) comes from Le Brocquy, *Cadenus*, 43–44. The elisions are Le Brocquy's.

36. Swift to Bishop Evans, May 22, 1719, June 5, 1721, *Corr.*, 2:306, 381. On the fake obituary, see Ehrenpreis, 3:57.

37. Delany, 84.

38. The complicated evidence is carefully analyzed by Fischer, who emphasizes that no certainties are possible, in "'Love and Books.'"

39. Delany, 40.

40. *To Love*, lines 1–10, 21–24, *Poems*, 2:717–18; Williams quotes Sheridan as confirming that the handwriting was Swift's.

CHAPTER 23. NATIONAL HERO

1. Swift to Ford, Aug. 29, 1714, *Corr.*, 2:76; Swift to Bolingbroke, Dec. 19, 1719, *Corr.*, 2:316–17 (adapting a phrase from Horace's *Satire* 1.4.17–18).

2. *Examiner* 44, June 7, 1711, *PW*, 3:170; Ehrenpreis, 2:556–57.

3. These events are lucidly summarized by Holmes in *The Making of a Great Power*, 274–76; see also Helen J. Paul, *The South Sea Bubble: An Economic History of Its Origins and Consequences* (London: Routledge, 2011).

4. Plumb, 1:301, 335.

5. Proverbs 23:5; *The Run upon the Bankers*, lines 21–24, 29–33, *Poems*, 1:239–40.

6. *The Bubble* (titled *Upon the South Sea Project* in Rogers), lines 65–68, *Poems*, 1:253.

7. *On Poetry: A Rapsody*, lines 161–62, *Poems*, 2:645; Defoe, *The Anatomy of Exchange Alley* (1719), in *Political and Economic Writings of Daniel Defoe*, ed. W. R. Owens and P. N. Furbank (London: Pickering and Chatto, 2000), 4:130.

8. Brewer, *The Sinews of Power*; Pope, imitation of Horace *Epistle* 1.1.124–25, 132–33.

9. *A Proposal for the Universal Use of Irish Manufacture*, *PW*, 9:15; see Louis A. Landa, "Swift's Economic Views and Mercantilism," in *Essays in Eighteenth-Century Literature*, 13–38.

10. King to Nicolson, Dec. 20, 1712; Nicolson to Archbishop Wake, June 2, 1721; both quoted by Ehrenpreis, 3:115–18; unemployment figure from Toby Barnard, *A New Anatomy of Ireland* (New Haven: Yale University Press, 2003), 284.

11. *A Proposal for the Universal Use of Irish Manufacture*, 9:16; Psalm 106:48, 42.

12. *A Proposal for the Universal Use of Irish Manufacture*, 9:17, 21; Swift's original language quoted from the textual notes, *PW*, 9:369.

13. Ibid., 16; see Downie, 229-30.

14. Orrery, 221; Ehrenpreis, 3:126n.

15. Connolly, *Divided Kingdom*, 220.

16. Quoted by Connolly, *Religion, Law, and Power*, 105.

17. Connolly, *Divided Kingdom*, 210, 224–25.

18. S. J. Connolly, "Eighteenth-Century Ireland: Colony or *Ancient Régime?*" in *The Making of Modern Irish History: Revisionism and the Revisionist Controversy*, ed. D. George Boyce and Alan O'Day (London: Routledge, 1996), 26.

19. *A Letter from Dr. Swift to Mr. Pope*, 9:27. (This long manifesto was probably not actually sent to Pope.)

20. Swift to Robert Cope, June 1, 1723, *Corr.*, 2:459; Delany, 94; *Poems*, 1:315–19. The details of the journey are traced by McMinn, *Jonathan's Travels*, 76–84.

21. Lecky, *History of Ireland*, 1:149.

22. McBride, *Eighteenth-Century Ireland*, 236; Burke, *Letter to Sir Hercules Langrishe*, in *The Works of Edmund Burke* (London: Bohn, 1896), 3:343.

23. See Toby Barnard, *The Kingdom of Ireland, 1641–1760* (London: Palgrave Macmillan, 2004), 51–52; Lecky, *History of Ireland*, 1:160–69; and Robert Kee, *Ireland: A History* (London: Abacus, 2003), 54–55.

24. Swift to Dean Brandreth, June 30, 1732, *Corr.*, 3:493–94 (recalling the 1723 trip).

25. *Gulliver's Travels*, book 3, ch. 4, pp. 175–76.

26. Swift to Ford, July 22, 1722, *Corr.*, 2:427.

27. Daniel Corkery, *The Hidden Ireland: A Study of Gaelic Munster in the Eighteenth Century* (Dublin: M. H. Gill, 1941), 14.

28. Sir Richard Cox, quoted by McBride, *Eighteenth-Century Ireland*, 167; Joshua 9:23; *Causes of the Wretched Condition of Ireland*, 9:200.

29. *Gulliver's Travels*, book 3, ch. 7, p. 196; see Ehrenpreis, 3:207–8. Swift sometimes wrote "draper" rather than "drapier," for instance, in a letter to Ford, Apr. 2, 1724, *Corr.*, 2:494.

30. King to Col. Flower, Apr. 8, 1721, quoted by Ferguson, 64; John 6:9.

31. Bishop Goodwin to Archbishop Wake, quoted by Landa, 172; Swift to King, Jan. 6, 1709, *Corr.*, 1:226.

32. See A. Goodwin, "Wood's Halfpence," *English Historical Review* 51 (1936): 653.

33. Ehrenpreis, 3:214; *To the Whole People of Ireland*, PW, 10:67–68; *To the Shop-keepers*, 7.

34. *To the Shopkeepers*, 11; Wood's patent is quoted by Ferguson, 99.

35. Swift to Gay and the Duchess of Queensberry, Aug. 28, 1731, *Corr.*, 3:428; see McBride, *Eighteenth-Century Ireland*, 114.

36. *To the Whole People of Ireland*, 10:54; see Ferguson, 107.

37. *To the Whole People of Ireland*, 10:62–63.

38. Swift, marginalia to *Characters of the Court of Britain* (1733), PW, 5:258 (he wrote "slobber," but undoubtedly meant "slobberer"); Ferguson, 115.

39. Sheridan, 211–13.

40. Ibid. Deane Swift (190–91) has a somewhat different version of the story, which according to Sheridan is full of errors.

41. Ehrenpreis, 3:280.

42. See Ferguson, 124; and Ehrenpreis, 3:275–76.

43. Swift to Worrall, Aug. 31, 1725, *Corr.*, 2:593.

44. *Verses on the Death of Dr. Swift*, lines 347–54, 2:566–67.

45. It is possible that Grattan didn't actually speak those words in 1782, but added them later in an edition of his speeches that was published after his death: Gerard O'Brien, "The Grattan Mystique," *Eighteenth-Century Ireland* 1 (1986): 191–94. "Swift was on the wrong side": Samuel Rogers, *Recollections*, 2nd ed. (London: Longmans, Green, 1859), 95.

46. Thomas Tickell, quoted in PW, 10:xx; the text is 1 Samuel 14:45.

47. King to Edward Southwell, June 9, 1724, quoted by Goodwin, "Wood's Halfpence," 674; Boulter to the Duke of Newcastle, Jan. 19, 1925, quoted by Ehrenpreis, 3:259; *To the Whole People of Ireland*, 10:61; on the birthday celebrations, see Clive T. Probyn, "Jonathan Swift at the Sign of the Drapier," in *Reading Swift*, 3:226.

48. Connolly, *Religion, Law, and Power*, 119; McBride, *Eighteenth-Century Ireland*, 38.

49. Ferguson, 138.

50. John Browne to Swift, Apr. 4, 1728, *Corr.*, 3:175–76; see PW, 10:210; and Probyn, "Jonathan Swift at the Sign of the Drapier," 236.

51. Delany, 17; Carteret to Swift, Mar. 6, 1735; John Barber to Swift, Aug. 6, 1733, *Corr.*, 4:64, 3:686.

52. *To Viscount Molesworth*, PW, 10:89; William Butler Yeats, *Explorations* (London: Macmillan, 1962), 348.

CHAPTER 24. THE ASTONISHING TRAVELS

1. Swift to Ford, Apr. 15, 1721, *Corr.*, 2:372.

2. Sir Thomas Herbert, *A Relation of Some Years Travaille, through Divers Parts of Asia and Africke* (London, 1634), 181, 204. Swift's inscription is in the Harvard University copy, f HEW 6.11.2. On Hakluyt and Purchas, see Real, *Securing Swift*, 114–15.

3. "Character of Jonathan Swift," *European Magazine* (1790), in *Critical Heritage*, 253; Mar. 4, 1737, *The Correspondence of Alexander Pope*, 4:59; Robert Louis Stevenson, *Treasure Island* (New York: Heritage, 1941), "How This Book Came to Be," xiii.

4. *Tatler* 178.

5. *Gulliver's Travels*, book 4, ch. 12, p. 291; see Neil Rennie, *Far-Fetched Facts: The Literature of Travel and the Idea of the South Seas* (Oxford: Clarendon, 1995).

6. *Gulliver's Travels*, book 1, ch. 1, p. 19.

7. Orrery, 127, and letter to Orrery from his wife, 391. Brean Hammond assembles these biographical clues in *Jonathan Swift*, 155.

8. Scott, 306; *Gulliver's Travels*, book 2, ch. 1, pp. 94, 90; book 2, ch. 6, p. 127; book 3, ch. 2, p. 162; Arbuthnot to Swift, Nov. 5, 1726, *Corr.*, 3:44.

9. Boswell, *Life of Johnson*, 2:319 (Mar. 24, 1775).

10. *Gulliver's Travels*, book 1, ch. 1, p. 21.

11. Daniel Defoe, *The Life and Strange Surprising Adventures of Robinson Crusoe*, ed. J. Donald Crowley (London: Oxford University Press, 1972), 1; "Robinson Crusoe's Preface," in *Serious Reflections during the Life and Surprising Adventures of Robinson Crusoe*, in *Romances and Narratives of Daniel Defoe*, ed. George A. Aitken (London: Dent, 1895), 3:xi.

12. "The Publisher to the Reader," *PW*, 11:9; Arbuthnot to Swift, Nov. 15, 1726; Swift to Pope, Nov. 17, 1726, *Corr.*, 3:45, 56.

13. See John Robert Moore, "The Geography of *Gulliver's Travels*," *Journal of English and Germanic Philology* 40 (1941): 214–28; and Frederick Bracher, "The Maps in *Gulliver's Travels*," *Huntington Library Quarterly* 8 (1944): 59–74.

14. *Gulliver's Travels*, book 1, ch. 2, pp. 34–35.

15. See J. Paul Hunter, *Gulliver's Travels* and the Novel," in *The Genres of Gulliver's Travels*, ed. Frederik N. Smith (Newark: University of Delaware Press, 1990), 67–68.

16. *Gulliver's Travels*, book 1, ch. 2, 6, pp. 35, 57.

17. Rawson, *Order from Confusion Sprung*, 170.

18. *Gulliver's Travels*, book 2, ch. 5, p. 120.

19. Ibid., book 1, ch. 2, p. 29.

20. Ibid., book 1, ch. 1, pp. 27–28; *Tale of a Tub*, "Introduction," 42; Stephen, *Swift*, 38.

21. *Gulliver's Travels*, book 2, ch. 5, p. 119; *Mary Gulliver to Captain Lemuel Gulliver*, lines 87–88, *Minor Poems*, vol. 6 in the Twickenham edition of Pope's *Poems*, 278–79; Nora F. Crow, "Swift in Love," in *Reading Swift*, 4:62.

22. *Gulliver's Travels*, book 2, ch. 1, pp. 91–92.

23. Ibid., book 2, ch. 1, p. 92.

24. Robert Hooke, *Micrographia* (London, 1665), 213; *Gulliver's Travels*, book 2, ch. 4, p. 113.

25. *Gulliver's Travels*, book 2, ch. 2, p. 95.

26. Ibid., book 3, ch. 10, p. 208; John Hawkesworth, *Notes on Gulliver's Travels* (1755), in *Critical Heritage*, 153.

27. M. Sarah Smedman describes expurgated editions in "Like Me, Like Me Not: *Gulliver's Travels* as Children's Book," in Smith, *The Genres of Gulliver's Travels*, 83–89; *Gulliver's Travels*, ed. Padraic Colum, illus. Willy Pogany (London: Harrap, 1919), unpaginated introduction.

28. John Mack Faragher, *Daniel Boone: The Life and Legend of an American Pioneer* (New York: Holt, 1992), 83.

29. Swift to Pope, Sept. 29, 1725, *Corr.*, 2:606; Pope, *Dunciad*, 2.147.

30. *Gulliver's Travels*, book 1, ch. 3, p. 39, and textual note, p. 303.

31. The analogy with the South Sea Bubble has been largely accepted ever since Arthur E. Case proposed it in *Four Essays on Gulliver's Travels* (Princeton: Princeton University Press, 1945), 88–89. There is a possible association as well with Wood's halfpence: J. A. Downie, "Political Characterization in *Gulliver's Travels*," *Yearbook of English Studies* 7 (1977): 116–17.

32. *Gulliver's Travels*, book 3, ch. 3, p. 172, and textual notes, pp. 309–10.

33. This interpretation, which has won general acceptance, was likewise proposed by Case, *Four Essays*, 83–84.

34. *Gulliver's Travels*, book 3, ch. 5, pp. 180, 182.

35. Gay and Pope to Swift, Nov. 7, 1726; Pope to Swift, Nov. 16, 1726, *Corr.*, 3:47, 52.

36. White, *Mistress Masham's Repose*, 209.

37. J. W. Allen, *A History of Political Thought in the Sixteenth Century* (New York: Barnes and Noble, 1928), 154.

38. *Gulliver's Travels*, book 4, ch. 10, pp. 276–77.

39. *Thoughts on Various Subjects*, 1:244 (published 1711, written 1706). A. D. Nuttall has valuable remarks on Stoicism in "Gulliver among the Horses," *Yearbook of English Studies* 18 (1988): 51–67.

40. *Gulliver's Travels*, book 4, ch. 11, p. 283.

41. Ibid., book 4, ch. 8, pp. 266–67; *On the Death of Mrs. Johnson*, 5:227; *Journal*, 2:407 (Nov. 8, 1711).

42. *Gulliver's Travels*, book 4, ch. 7, pp. 260–62; Terence Brown, notes to James Joyce, *Dubliners*, ed. Brown (London: Penguin, 1967), 298n.

43. Orrery, 216; Thackeray, *The English Humourists of the Eighteenth Century*, 406.

44. Wesley, *The Doctrine of Original Sin*, 5:512; see Roland M. Frye, "Swift's Yahoo and the Christian Symbols for Sin," *Journal of the History of Ideas* 15 (1954): 201–17.

45. James Joyce, *Ulysses*, ed. Hans Walter Gabler (New York: Random House, 1986), ch. 2, p. 33.

46. *Gulliver's Travels*, book 4, ch. 10, p. 282. Interpretations in which Gulliver is mad go back to Samuel H. Monk's article "The Pride of Lemuel Gulliver," *Sewanee Review* (1955): 48–71, dubbed the "soft school" by James L. Clifford in "Gulliver's Fourth Voyage: 'Hard' and 'Soft' Schools of Interpretation," in *Swift Springs of Sense: Studies in the Eighteenth Century*, ed. Larry S. Champion (Athens: University of Georgia Press, 1974), 33–49. Later variations run to the dozens if not hundreds.

47. Pope, *Mary Gulliver to Captain Lemuel Gulliver*, lines 105–6, p. 279.

48. Swift to Pope, Sept. 29, 1725, *Corr.*, 2:606–7.

49. R. S. Crane, "The Houyhnhnms, the Yahoos, and the History of Ideas," first published in 1962, reprinted in Crane's *The Idea of the Humanities* (Chicago: University of Chicago Press, 1967), 2:261–82.

50. Rawson, *Gulliver and the Gentle Reader*, 31.

51. *Gulliver's Travels*, book 4, ch. 12, p. 296; Wesley, *The Doctrine of Original Sin*, 512.
52. *Gulliver's Travels*, book 4, ch. 12, p. 296; Swift to Ford, Jan. 19, 1724, *Corr.*, 2:487.

CHAPTER 25. GULLIVER IN ENGLAND

1. *Poems*, 2:401, 405. Sheridan said the first was written at Chester; Scott printed the second, reproducing the report of Rev. Richard Graves. (Without explanation, Davis gives the date as "17—.")
2. Real, *Securing Swift*, 92–94.
3. *Family of Swift*, 5:188; Deane Swift, appendix, p. 9.
4. See *Corr.*, 3:11n.
5. Swift to Tickell, July 7, 1726, *Corr.*, 2:649.
6. Swift to Sheridan, July 8, 1726, *Corr.*, 2:651.
7. Pope to Swift, Nov. 16, 1726, *Corr.*, 3:52.
8. Swift to Benjamin Motte, Aug. 8, 1726; Motte to Swift, Aug. 11, 1726, *Corr.*, 3:9–10, 12. Ehrenpreis (3:493–508) gives a full account of the publication of *Gulliver's Travels*.
9. Swift to Pope, Feb. 7, 1736, *Corr.*, 4:259.
10. Pope to the Earl of Stratford, Oct. 5, 1725, in *The Correspondence of Alexander Pope*, 2:328; Maynard Mack, *The Garden and the City: Retirement and Politics in the Later Poetry of Pope* (Toronto: University of Toronto Press, 1969), 233.
11. Pope, imitation of Horace *Satire* 2.1.123–28.
12. Swift to Pope, Sept. 20, 1723, *Corr.*, 2:469.
13. Pope, *Essay on Man*, 4.390; Swift to Pope, July 16, 1728, *Corr.*, 3:190.
14. Dickinson, *Bolingbroke*, 241.
15. Johnson, *Life of Gay*, in *Lives* 2:268.
16. John Gay, *Poetry and Prose*, ed. Vinton A. Dearing (Oxford: Clarendon, 1974), 2:377–78.
17. Swift to Pope, Aug. 30, 1716, *Corr.*, 2:178; Spence, *Observations*, 1:57, 107; John Gay, *The Beggar's Opera*, 3.16.
18. Scott, 295; Pope to Swift, Jan. 6, 1734, *Corr.*, 3:716–17.
19. *Verses on the Death of Dr Swift*, lines 47–52, 2:555; Pope, *An Essay on Criticism*, lines 525, 625, 215, 297.
20. Scott, 453; E. J. Trelawney, *Recollections of the Last Days of Shelley and Byron* (Boston, Ticknor and Fields, 1858), 37.
21. Swift, *To Doctor Delany*, lines 65–66, 2:502; *On Poetry: A Rapsody*, lines 87–90; *Poems*, 2:643.
22. *The Dunciad*, appendix to the 1729 edition, 201n.
23. *On Poetry: A Rapsody*, lines 61–70, 167–74, 2:642, 645–46.
24. Horace Walpole to Horace Mann, Jan. 13, 1780, in *The Letters of Horace Walpole*, ed. Mrs. Paget Toynbee (Oxford: Clarendon, 1904), 11:102; Johnson, *Life of Pope*, in *Lives*, 3:212.
25. Swift to Pope, Sept. 20, 1723, *Corr.*, 2:469–70.

26. Canon Francis Stratford, quoted by Ehrenpreis, 3:518; *Dr. Swift to Mr. Pope, While He Was Writing the Dunciad*, lines 1–8, *Poems*, 2:405.

27. *Dr. Swift to Mr. Pope, While He Was Writing the Dunciad*, lines 9–16, 2:406.

28. Pope to the Earl of Oxford, Aug. 15, 1727, *The Correspondence of Alexander Pope*, 2:443; Swift to Pope, Aug. 4, 1726; Pope to Swift, Aug. 17, 1726, *Corr.*, 3:5, 16.

29. Letter from Lady Orrery to her husband, in Orrery, 404, 67; Johnson, *Life of Pope*, 200 (quoting a famous line by Edward Young).

30. Spence, *Observations*, 1:54–55.

31. Sheridan, 451.

32. Gay to Swift, Nov. 9, 1728; Swift to Gay, Nov. 20, 1729, Nov. 10, 1730, *Corr.*, 3:264–65, 269, 334; Mack, *The Garden and the City*, 256.

33. *A Libel on Doctor Delany and a Certain Great Lord*, lines 71–72, 81–82), 2:482. The whole story, too complicated to trace here, is surveyed by James McLaverty, "The Failure of the Swift-Pope *Miscellanies* (1727–32) and *The Life and Genuine Character of Doctor Swift*," in *Reading Swift*, 5:131–48.

34. Swift to Pope, Oct. 12, 1727, *Corr.*, 3:131; Swift's will, *PW*, 13:154.

CHAPTER 26. DISILLUSIONMENT AND LOSS

1. Quoted by Scott, 297.

2. Swift to the Earl of Peterborough, Apr. 28, 1726, *Corr.*, 2:642; see Ferguson, 140–41, and Ehrenpreis, 3:484–85.

3. *Corr.*, 3:29–30 (written on a blank sheet of a letter from Arbuthnot); see Louis A. Landa, "Swift's Deanery Income," in *Essays in Eighteenth-Century Literature*, 109. He had an additional £200 a year from Laracor.

4. Swift to Lady Betty Germaine, Jan. 8, 1733, *Corr.*, 3:574. My account of this period is much indebted to James Woolley, "Friends and Enemies in *Verses on the Death of Dr. Swift*," *Studies in Eighteenth-Century Culture* 8 (1979): 205–32.

5. Pope, *On a Certain Lady at Court*, lines 1–4.

6. Arbuthnot to Swift, Sept. 20, 1726, *Corr.*, 3:28.

7. A pair of supplementary couplets to *Verses on the Death of Dr. Swift*, written in the margin of some copies of Faulkner's Dublin edition (*Poems*, 2:566n.).

8. "Lemuel Gulliver" to Mrs. Howard, Nov. 28, 1726, *Corr.*, 3:59.

9. Bolingbroke to Swift, June 17, 1727, *Corr.*, 3:96. James Woolley says, "It is likely that Bolingbroke was relaying a message from Mrs. Howard" ("Friends and Enemies," 229n); Swift to Lady Betty Germaine, Jan. 8, 1733, *Corr.*, 3:576.

10. *A Pastoral Dialogue between Richmond Lodge and Marble Hill, Poems*, 2:409–10.

11. Ibid., lines 13–18; Psalm 146:3.

12. Pope to Swift, Oct. 9, 1729, *Corr.*, 3:258; *Character of Mrs. Howard, PW*, 5:213–14.

13. *Character of Mrs. Howard*, 5:214–15.

14. Lady Suffolk is quoted by John Wilson Croker in *Letters to and from Henrietta, Countess of Suffolk, and Her Second Husband, the Hon. George Berkeley, from 1712 to 1767* (London: J. Murray, 1824), 1:xliii; the full text is printed on xxxviii–xliv. (A comment

by David Woolley (*Corr.*, 3:99n) implies that the two versions differ substantially, but that is not the case.) Pope to Swift, Oct. 9, 1729, *Corr.*, 3:258.

15. Tracy Borman, *Henrietta Howard: King's Mistress, Queen's Servant* (London: Jonathan Cape, 2007), 152–65; Plumb, 2:163, 175.

16. The Countess of Suffolk to Swift, Sept. 25, 1731; Swift to the Countess of Suffolk, Oct. 26, 1731, *Corr.*, 3:434, 438.

17. *Directions for a Birthday Song*, lines 209–10, 217–20, 225–36, *Poems*, 2:467.

18. *Verses on the Death of Dr. Swift*, lines 170–88, 2:559–60.

19. William King to Swift, Jan. 23, 1739, *Corr.*, 4:557.

20. *Poems*, 2:557n.

21. Swift to Worrall, July 15, 1726, *Corr.*, 2:656.

22. Swift to James Stopford, Oct. 15, 1726; Swift to Sheridan, Aug. 29, 1727, *Corr.*, 3:33, 122.

23. Swift to Sheridan, Sept. 2, 1727, *Corr.*, 3:123–24.

24. *Holyhead Journal*, PW, 5:203.

25. Ibid., 5:204–7.

26. *Holyhead, Sept. 25, 1727, Poems*, 2:420.

27. *On Dreams*, lines 5–6, *Poems*, 2:363; *Holyhead Journal*, 5:205–6.

28. My interpretation is indebted to DePorte, "Night Thoughts in Swift," 658–59. See also DePorte's "Swift, God, and Power," in Fox and Tooley, *Walking Naboth's Vineyard*, 92.

29. Swift to Worrall, Sept. 12, 1717, *Corr.*, 3:126.

30. Le Brocquy, *Swift's Most Valuable Friend*, 10.

31. *To Dr. Swift on His Birthday, November 30, 1721*, lines 53–58, 2:738.

32. *A Receipt to Restore Stella's Youth*, lines 7–8, *Poems*, 2:759.

33. *Stella's Birthday, March 13, 1727*, lines 1–4, 13–14, 35–36, 83–88, *Poems*, 2:763–66.

34. *Prayers for a Person during Her Sickness*, PW, 9:254; Ehrenpreis, 3:546.

35. Swift to Mrs. Moore, Dec. 7, 1727, *Corr.*, 3:145–46.

36. *On the Death of Mrs. Johnson*, 5:227.

37. Sheridan, 311–12.

38. Orrery, 332–33; the Laracor lady quoted by R. Wyse Jackson, *Swift and His Circle* (Dublin: Talbot, 1945), 32.

39. *On the Death of Mrs. Johnson*, 5:229; Lyon, 19.

40. Stella's will is reprinted in full by Wilde, *The Closing Years of Dean Swift's Life*, 97–100.

41. Lyon, 48.

42. Scott, 223n (he says the envelope was in the possession of "Dr. Tuke of St. Stephen's Green"); Stephen, *Swift*, 139.

43. Orrery, 333.

CHAPTER 27. FRUSTRATED PATRIOT

1. Sheridan, 235; Carteret to Swift, Mar. 24, 1733, Mar. 24, 1737, *Corr.*, 3:608, 4:406.

2. Letter from George Faulkner to the Earl of Chesterfield, in Nichols, *A Supplement to Dr. Swift's Works*, 763.

3. Swift to Sheridan, June 15, 1735, *Corr.*, 4:123.

4. Sheridan, 368–69.

5. These tales are surveyed by Jarrell, "'Jack and the Dane.'"

6. *Verses on the Death of Dr. Swift*, lines 391–98, 2:568.

7. Swift to Rev. James Stopford, Nov. 26, 1725, *Corr.*, 2:619–20; William Butler Yeats, "The Tables of the Law," in *Mythologies* (New York: Collier, 1959), 301 (the speaker is a recurrent character in Yeats's writings, Owen Aherne).

8. Swift to Charles Wogan, Aug. 2, 1732, *Corr.*, 3:514–15.

9. Delany, 102; Psalm 37:1 (also Proverbs 34:19).

10. *The Substance of What Was Said by the Dean of St. Patrick's*, *PW*, 12:147–48. On bonfires and tavern signs, see Probyn, "Jonathan Swift at the Sign of the Drapier," 3:226; and Jarrell, "'Jack and the Dane,'" 314.

11. Swift to the Corporation of Cork, Aug. 15, 1737, *Corr.*, 4:468; *The Last Will and Testament of Jonathan Swift*, *PW*, 13:155.

12. Swift to Pope, July 8, 1733, *Corr.*, 3:663.

13. Lecky, *A History of Ireland in the Eighteenth Century*, 1:205–7.

14. Lord Egmont, quoted by Ehrenpreis, 2:771.

15. Craik, 2:177; *Doing Good*, *PW*, 9:234; Sheridan, 234.

16. Delany, 7, 133.

17. Orrery, 425; Lyon (146) remembered the name as Stumpa-Nympha.

18. *The Last Will and Testament of Jonathan Swift*, 13:150; *Verses on the Death of Dr. Swift*, lines 479–82, 2:572; *The Legacy of Swift: A Bi-Centenary Record of St. Patrick's Hospital, Dublin* (Dublin: Colm O Lochlainn, 1948), xii. See also Creaser, "'The Most Mortifying Malady.'"

19. Swift to Bolingbroke and Pope, Apr. 5, 1729, *Corr.*, 3:230.

20. Swift to Pope, June 12, 1732, *Corr.*, 3:489; King to Edward Southwell, Apr. 23, 1728, quoted by Ehrenpreis, 3:571. The historical context is reviewed in two articles by James Kelly: "Jonathan Swift and the Irish Economy in the 1720s," *Eighteenth-Century Ireland* 6 (1991): 7–36, and "Harvests and Hardships," 65–105.

21. *A Modest Proposal*, *PW*, 12:109; subsequent quotations are from 110–18; Swift to Dean Brandreth, June 30, 1732, *Corr.*, 3:493. George Wittkowsky describes several *Modest Proposals* by earlier writers: "Swift's *Modest Proposal*: The Biography of an Early Georgian Pamphlet," *Journal of the History of Ideas* 4 (1943): 88.

22. *A Proposal for Giving Badges to Beggars*, *PW*, 13:135.

23. See James Kelly, "Infanticide in Eighteenth-Century Ireland," *Irish Economic and Social History* 19 (1992): 5–25.

24. Edmund Wilson, "Karl Marx: Poet of Commodities," *New Republic*, Jan. 8, 1940, 46.

25. Swift to Pope, Oct. 31, 1729, *Corr.*, 3:263; *An Answer to a Paper Called a Memorial*, *PW*, 12:23, quoting Proverbs 1:20–26 (condensed by Swift).

26. Ann Cline Kelly, *Jonathan Swift and Popular Culture*, 185.

27. T. S. Eliot, *The Varieties of Metaphysical Poetry*, ed. Ronald Schuchard (London: Faber and Faber, 1993), 219.

28. Francis Grant to Swift, Mar. 14, 1734; Swift to Grant, Mar. 23, 1734; Swift to the Countess of Suffolk, Oct. 26, 1731, *Corr.*, 3:727, 730, 437.

29. *A Proposal for Giving Badges to Beggars*, 13:138.
30. *The Duty of Mutual Subjection*, *PW*, 9:144; *Account Books*, 3, 13, 104, 156. See Louis A. Landa, "Jonathan Swift and Charity," in *Essays in Eighteenth-Century Literature*, 49–62.
31. *A Proposal for Giving Badges to Beggars*, 13:135, 139.
32. Nokes, 400; Delany, 6.
33. Connolly, "Swift and Protestant Ireland," 43, 46.
34. *Dublin Journal*, Nov. 26, 1737, quoted in *PW*, 13:xl. The *Dublin Journal* was edited by Swift's publisher, George Faulkner.
35. Quoted in *PW*, 13:xl.

CHAPTER 28. SWIFT AMONG THE WOMEN

1. Swift to Bolingbroke, Mar. 21, 1730, *Corr.*, 3:294–95.
2. Sheridan to Swift, May 26, 1735; Sheridan to Swift, Dec. 25, 1734; Swift to Sheridan, Jan. 3, 1735, *Corr.*, 4:115, 31, 33. I have been gratefully reliant on David Woolley's unraveling of the verbal conundrums.
3. Scott, 288.
4. Note on a blank page bound at the beginning of Lyon's annotated copy of Hawkesworth's *Life*.
5. Gay to Swift, Nov. 16, 1732; Pope and Arbuthnot to Swift, Dec. 5, 1732, *Corr.*, 3:560–62, 563n.
6. Pope, *Epitaph on Mr. Gay*; Gay, *My Own Epitaph*.
7. Swift to Pope, Mar. 23, 1733; Swift to Orrery, Aug. 12, 1733, *Corr.*, 3:617, 680–81.
8. Boswell, *Life of Johnson*, 4:29, under 1780 (diplomatically, Boswell didn't give Orrery's name, but other sources confirm it); Monck-Berkeley, *Literary Relics*, xvi; note by Lyon in the University of Pennsylvania version of his annotated copy of Hawkesworth: Elias, "Swift's *Don Quixote*, Dunkin's *Virgil Travesty*, and Other New Intelligence," 75.
9. Orrery, 168; Sheridan, introduction, unnumbered page; *Cadenus and Vanessa*, lines 758–61, 2:710 and textual note (which I follow in giving "flattery" rather than "vanity").
10. Lady Mary Wortley Montagu, *Commonplace Book*, quoted in Montagu's *Complete Letters*, ed. Robert Halsband (Oxford: Clarendon, 1967), 3:56n.
11. *Letter to a Young Lady on Her Marriage*, 9:90, 89.
12. Samuel Richardson, *Pamela; or, Virtue Rewarded* (London: Chapman and Hall, 1902), 4:294. Details of the Staunton-Rochfort marriage, and information about the two families, are given by George P. Mayhew in *Rage or Raillery: The Swift Manuscripts at the Huntington Library* (San Marino, Calif.: Huntington Library, 1967), 37–57.
13. *Of the Education of Ladies*, *PW*, 4:225–28; Mary Wollstonecraft, *A Vindication of the Rights of Woman*, ed. Carol H. Poston (New York: Norton, 1975), ch. 2, p. 19.
14. Swift to Pope, Feb. 6, 1730, *Corr.*, 3:279; preface by Swift to *The Poetry of Mary Barber*, ed. Bernard Tucker (Lewiston, Maine: Edwin Mellen, 1992), 40. The Barber affair is explored by Barnett, *Jonathan Swift in the Company of Women*, 87–92; see also Mar-

garet Anne Doody, "Swift among the Women," *Yearbook of English Studies* 18 (1988): 68–92.

15. Frances Arabella Kelly to Swift, Feb. 2, May 4, 1733, *Corr.*, 3:586, 643.

16. *The Autobiography and Correspondence of Mary Granville, Mrs. Delany*, 1st ser. (London: Richard Bentley, 1861), 1:396.

17. Ibid., 1:24, 29.

18. Swift to Mary Pendarves, Oct. 7, 1734, *Corr.*, 4:3–4.

19. Swift to Mary Pendarves, Jan. 29, 1736; Mary Pendarves to Swift, May 16, 1735, *Corr.*, 4:258, 109.

20. Frances Burney, *Memoirs of Dr. Burney* (London, 1832), 3:169.

21. The full conversation is in Pilkington, 1:28–31.

22. *Hints towards an Essay on Conversation*, 4:91.

23. Barnett, *Jonathan Swift in the Company of Women*, 85.

24. Joyce, *Finnegans Wake*, 144; see Jarrell, "Swiftiana in *Finnegans Wake*," 283; Swift to John Barber, Mar. 9, 1738, *Corr.*, 4:501–2.

25. Swift to Rebecca Dingley, Aug. 29, 1733, *Corr.*, 3:688. The Christmas gifts are mentioned in a note from Swift on Dec. 28, 1734, *Corr.*, 4:33.

26. *Verses on the Death of Dr. Swift*, lines 79–94, 225–42, 2:556, 562.

27. *Journal*, 1:119 (Dec. 12, 1710).

28. *The Grand Question Debated*, lines 153–60, 171–74, *Poems*, 3:872–73. Peter J. Schakel brings out the significance of all of the poems written at Market Hill—not just the ones collected in *Poems* under that title—in "Swift's Voices: Innovation and Complication in the Poems Written at Market Hill," in *Reading Swift*, 4:310–25.

29. *My Lady's Lamentation and Complaint against the Dean*, lines 67–72, 137–42, *Poems*, 3:853, 855; Ehrenpreis, 3:604.

30. *Lady Acheson Weary of the Dean*, lines 37–44, *Poems*, 3:861.

31. Faulkner, quoted in *Poems*, 3:890n; Swift to Pope, Feb. 13, 1729; Swift to Sheridan, Sept. 18, 1728, *Corr.*, 3:209, 3:194.

32. *An Excellent New Panegyric on Skinnibonia*, lines 31–40, 43–50. The poem is printed in full, with interesting commentary by James Woolley, in "Swift's 'Skinnibonia': A New Poem from Lady Acheson's Manuscript," in *Reading Swift*, 5:309–42. The poem was transcribed by Lady Acheson, with a few corrections in Swift's handwriting.

33. *Death and Daphne*, lines 57–58, 61–62, 93–96, *Poems*, 3:904–5.

34. Nora Crow Jaffe, "Swift and the 'Agreeable Young Lady, but Extremely Lean,'" in *Contemporary Studies of Swift's Poetry*, ed. John Irwin Fischer and Donald C. Mell (Newark: University of Delaware Press, 1981), 149–57. (More recently, Nora Crow Jaffe has published under the name Nora Crow, as cited earlier.)

35. Orrery, 168.

36. *The Dean's Reasons for Not Building at Drapier's Hill*, lines 69–72, 85–94, *Poems*, 3:901.

37. *My Lady's Lamentation*, lines 159–60, 165–72, *Poems*, 3:856; *The Dean's Reasons for Not Building at Drapier's Hill*, lines 15–18, 3:856, 899.

38. Swift to Charles Ford, Dec. 9, 1732, *Corr.*, 3:566.

CHAPTER 29. THE DISGUSTING POEMS

1. Johnson, *Life of Swift*, 62–63.
2. Ehrenpreis, *The Personality of Jonathan Swift*. 39. An often-cited defense of Swift as moralist is Donald Greene, "On Swift's 'Scatological' Poems," in Vieth, *Essential Articles for the Study of Swift's Poetry*, 223.
3. Lyon, 33.
4. *Cadenus and Vanessa*, lines 160–63, 2:691; Deane Swift, 264.
5. "Upon His Drinking a Bowl," in *The Complete Poems of John Wilmot, Earl of Rochester*, 53.
6. Tobias Smollett, *Humphry Clinker*, ed. Angus Ross (London: Penguin, 1967), 313.
7. *A Modest Defence of a Late Poem by an Unknown Author, Called "The Lady's Dressing Room"* (translating Horace, *Epistola ad Pisones*, lines 179–88), *PW*, 5:339, appendix C. Herbert Davis relegates this essay to an appendix because of uncertainty that Swift wrote it. Faulkner, however, who enjoyed Swift's full confidence, identified it as "by D——n S——t."
8. Lawrence's introduction to an undated *Paintings of D. H. Lawrence*, quoted by Maurice Johnson, "Dryden's 'Cousin Swift,'" *PMLA* 68 (1953): 1234; Lewis, "Addison," 144.
9. *A Panegyric on the Dean*, lines 205–16, *Poems*, 3:893.
10. Ibid., lines 299–304, 3:896.
11. Mary Jones, *Holt Waters: A Tale*, quoted by Doody, "Swift among the Women," 85; Geoffrey Hill, "Jonathan Swift: The Poetry of Reaction," in *The World of Jonathan Swift*, ed. Brian Vickers (Oxford: Basil Blackwell, 1968), 209.
12. Rev. James Whitelaw in 1798, quoted by Fabricant, *Swift's Landscape*, 26–28.
13. *An Examination of Certain Abuses, Corruptions, and Enormities in the City of Dublin*, *PW*, 12:220.
14. Lord Castle Durrow to Swift, Dec. 4, 1736, *Corr.*, 4:368.
15. Pope, *The Rape of the Lock*, 1.143–44; *The Progress of Beauty*, lines 13–20, 109–16, *Poems*, 1:227–29.
16. *A Beautiful Young Nymph Going to Bed*, lines 1–2, 11–12, 17–22, 29–30, *Poems*, 2:580, 583.
17. Ibid., lines 42, 59–62, 2:582–83 ; Brean S. Hammond, "Corinna's Dream," *Eighteenth Century: Dream and Interpretation* 36 (1995): 106. I have drawn on this article at several points.
18. Martial 9.37, discussed with other analogous works by N. W. Bawcutt, "'News from Hide-Park' and 'A Beautiful Young Nymph Going to Bed,'" *British Journal for Eighteenth-Century Studies* 23 (2000): 125–34; *Remedia Amoris*, line 344, in *Ovid*, trans. J. H. Mozley, Loeb Classical Library (Cambridge: Harvard University Press, 1929), 2:200.
19. *A Beautiful Young Nymph Going to Bed*, lines 67–70, 2:583. My reading of the poem is indebted to Louise Barnett, *Swift's Poetic Worlds* (Newark: University of Delaware Press, 1981), 175–76; and to Hammond, *Jonathan Swift*, 149–51.
20. *The Lady's Dressing Room*, lines 59–68, 109–18, *Poems*, 2:527, 529.

21. D. H. Lawrence, introduction to *Pansies*, in *Phoenix: The Posthumous Papers of D. H. Lawrence*, ed. Edward D. McDonald (London: Heinemann, 1936), 281–82.

22. Rogers, 827.

23. "The Reasons That Induced Dr. S. to Write a Poem Called 'The Lady's Dressing Room,'" in Lady Mary Wortley Montagu, Essays and Poems, ed. Robert Halsband (Oxford: Clarendon, 1977), 273–74. Swift's poem was published in June 1732, and Lady Mary's in February 1734. The two lines beginning "She answered short" appear in a manuscript draft but not in the published version. On the book-lined commode, see Isobel Grundy, *Lady Mary Wortley Montagu* (Oxford: Oxford University Press, 1999), 566; and Robert Halsband, "New Anecdotes of Lady M.W. Montagu," in *Evidence in Literary Scholarship*, ed. René Wellek and Alvaro Ribeiro (Oxford: Clarendon, 1979), 245.

24. *The Lady's Dressing Room*, lines 129–32, 141–44, 2:530. The connection with the *Tale of a Tub* is brought out by Nora Crow Jaffe, *The Poet Swift* (Hanover, N.H.: University Press of New England, 1977), 112–13; the phrase "smell no evil" comes from Christine Rees, "Gay, Swift, and the Nymphs of Drury-Lane," *Essays in Criticism* 23 (1973): 15.

25. *Strephon and Chloe*, lines 175–78, 186–92, *Poems*, 2:589–90; Hill, "Jonathan Swift: The Poetry of Reaction," 206.

26. *The Problem*, lines 33–40, 47–48, *Poems*, 1:66. The description of the "handsomest man" is in Williams's headnote to the poem, 65.

27. *Cassinus and Peter*, lines 85–86, 77–78, *Poems*, 2:596; William Butler Yeats, *Crazy Jane Talks with the Bishop*, lines 15–16; Sigmund Freud, *The Joke and Its Relation to the Unconscious*, trans. Joyce Crick (London: Penguin, 2002), section 3 (b), p. 93. Pollak notes the possible relevance of Freud in *The Poetics of Sexual Myth*, 162–63, 167.

28. Phyllis Greenacre, *Swift and Carroll: A Psychoanalytic Study of Two Lives* (New York: International Universities Press, 1955), 108; Donald R. Roberts, "A Freudian View of Jonathan Swift," *Literature and Psychology* 4 (1956): 10; Norman O. Brown, "The Excremental Vision," in *Life against Death: The Psychoanalytical Meaning of History* (New York: Vintage Books, 1959), 179–201.

29. *Thoughts on Various Subjects*, 4:247; *Strephon and Chloe*, lines 233–34, 2:591.

30. Felicity Rosslyn, "Deliberate Disenchantment: Swift and Pope on the Subject of Women," *Cambridge Quarterly* 23 (1994): 296.

31. Martha Whiteway to Swift, Dec. 2, 1735, *Corr.*, 4:243.

CHAPTER 30. WAITING FOR THE END

1. *An Epistle to a Lady*, lines 175–80, *Poems*, 2:635. William Pulteney was a Tory collaborator of Bolingbroke's, and "Caleb D'Anvers" was the pseudonym they used in their periodical, the *Craftsman*.

2. *The Day of Judgment*, lines 17–22, *Poems*, 2:579; Swift to William Tisdall, Dec. 16, 1703, *Corr.*, 1:148. Contemporary poems on the Last Judgment are surveyed by Real, *Securing Swift*, 239–79; see also Richard H. Rodino, "Varieties of Vexatious Experience in Swift and Others," *Papers on Language and Literature* 18 (1982): 331–35.

3. Swift to William Tisdall, Dec. 16, 1703, *Corr.*, 1:148. *The Mysterious Stranger*, in *Selected Shorter Writings of Mark Twain*, ed. Walter Blair (Boston: Houghton Mifflin, 1962), 388; Swift to Pope, Apr. 20, 1731, *Corr.*, 3:382.

4. *The Place of the Damned*, lines 7–14, *Poems*, 2:576.

5. *On the Words "Brother Protestants" and "Fellow Christians," So Familiarly Used by the Advocates for the Repeal of the Test Act*, lines 11–14, 25–28, *Poems*, 3:811–12. It is sometimes claimed that Swift resented Bettesworth's support for a bill that would deprive the clergy of tithes on flax, but there is really no evidence for this; see Stephen Karian, *Jonathan Swift in Print and Manuscript* (Cambridge: Cambridge University Press, 2010), 226, n29.

6. Sheridan, 377; Orrery, 424. Ehrenpreis is skeptical about the accuracy of some of Sheridan's anecdotes, but Luis Gamez offers persuasive reasons for accepting this one, in "Richard Bettesworth's Insult and 'The Yahoo's Overthrow,'" *Swift Studies* 12 (1997): 80–84.

7. Swift to the Duke of Dorset, January 1734, *Corr.*, 3:719.

8. Sheridan, 378–79.

9. Ehrenpreis, 3:771; the document and reply are in *PW*, 5:341–43.

10. *The Yahoo's Overthrow; or, The Kevin Bail's New Ballad* [St. Patrick's was in the parish of Kevin Bail], lines 41–45, 61–65, *Poems*, 3:816–17; Henry Fielding, *Tom Jones*, ed. Thomas Keymer (London: Penguin, 2005), book 6, ch. 9, p. 270.

11. Karian, *Jonathan Swift in Print and Manuscript*, 89.

12. The controversy is fully described by Landa, 135–50.

13. Swift to Sheridan, June 15, 1735, *Corr.*, 4:122; Mark 5:9.

14. *The Legion Club*, lines 1–4, 49–52, 61–62, *Poems*, 3:829, 831.

15. Ibid., lines 189–90, 153–58, 3:835–37.

16. *Verses on the Death of Dr. Swift*, lines 459–52, 2:571; W. H. Dilworth, *The Life of Dr. Jonathan Swift* (1758), in *Critical Heritage*, 171.

17. Swift to Sheridan, May 15, May 22, 1736, *Corr.*, 4:296, 302.

18. Sheridan to Swift, June 2, 1736, *Corr.*, 4:306; see Karian, *Jonathan Swift in Print and Manuscript*, 150–51.

19. *Verses on the Death of Dr. Swift*, line 477, 2:572; Swift to Lady Worsley, Nov. 4, 1732, *Corr.*, 3:551; Edward Young, *Conjectures on Original Composition* (1759), in *Eighteenth-Century English Literature*, ed. Geoffrey Tillotson et al. (New York: Harcourt, Brace, 1969), 881. The lord lieutenant at the time was the second Duke of Wharton, son of Swift's old adversary; on the 1720 date, see *Corr.*, 2:336n.

20. Letter from Faulkner to the Earl of Chesterfield, in John Nichols, *A Supplement to Dr. Swift's Works*, 765.

21. Swift to John Barber, Mar. 21, 1735; Swift to Thomas Beach, Apr. 12, 1735, *Corr* 4:62, 63n, 88.

22. See Swift's letter to William Pulteney, May 12, 1735, *Corr.*, 4:108; and Karian, *Jonathan Swift in Print and Manuscript*, 30–43.

23. Swift to Benjamin Motte, May 25, 1736, *Corr.*, 4:304; Ehrenpreis, 3:790.

24. John Wainwright to the second Earl of Oxford, June 24, 1738, quoted in Ehrenpreis, 3:866.

25. Swift to Pope, Feb. 7, 1736, *Corr.*, 4:259–60.

26. Maynard Mack, *Alexander Pope: A Life* (New Haven: Yale University Press, 1985), 666, 671, 652ff. See also Ehrenpreis, 3:884–87, 898.

27. Sheridan, 332.

28. *The History of the Second Solomon*, 5:222; see Woolley, "Thomas Sheridan and Swift," 97–98.

29. Swift and Sheridan to Mrs. Whiteway, Nov. 8, 1735, *Corr.*, 4:213.

30. Sheridan, 332–33.

31. Swift to Mrs. Whiteway, Nov. 18, 1735, *Corr.*, 4:227–28; Sheridan, 333.

32. Sheridan to Swift, June 23, 1736, *Corr.*, 4:320; Ehrenpreis (3:870) mentions the break with Delany.

33. Sheridan, 338; on Sheridan's illness and medication, see Woolley, "Thomas Sheridan and Swift," 99–100.

34. Sheridan, 340.

35. Swift to Orrery, Feb. 2, 1738; *Corr.*, 4:494.

36. See Maxwell B. Gold, "The Brennan Affidavit," *TLS*, May 17, 1934, 360; and Deane Swift to Orrery, Nov. 19, 1742, *Corr.*, 4:660–63.

37. Deane Swift, 189 (page misnumbered by the printer; it ought to be 217). Sheridan (337) also tells this story, in somewhat different words, perhaps adapting it from Deane Swift's account.

38. Swift to Mrs. Whiteway, Nov. 28, 1735; Mrs. Whiteway to Swift, Dec. 2, 1735; Swift to Robert Lindsay, Jan. 22, 1736, *Corr.*, 4:239, 243, 254–55.

39. Swift to John Barber, Feb. 16, 1739, *Corr.*, 4:560–61.

40. Swift to Martha Whiteway, July 26, 1740, *Corr.*, 4:627–28.

41. Mrs. Whiteway to Orrery, Nov. 22, 1742, *Corr.*, 4:664.

42. Letter from Faulkner to the Earl of Chesterfield, in Nichols, *A Supplement to Dr. Swift's Works*, 765; Henry Jones, *The Bricklayer's Poem* (1745), quoted by Robert Mahony, *Jonathan Swift: The Irish Identity* (New Haven: Yale University Press, 1995), 7.

43. The document is preserved among the Lyon papers, and reprinted in Ball, *The Correspondence of Jonathan Swift*, 6:181–85.

44. Delany, 103.

45. Deane Swift to Orrery, Apr. 4, 1744, *Corr.*, 4:670; 1 Corinthians 15:8–11. My comments are indebted to DePorte, "Swift, God and Power," 94.

46. Samuel Johnson, *The Vanity of Human Wishes*, lines 315–16.

47. *Verses on the Death of Dr. Swift*, lines 147–50, 2:558; William Monck Mason, *The History and Antiquities of the Collegiate and Cathedral Church of St. Patrick* (Dublin: W. Folds, 1820), 412; Sheridan, 244.

48. *Verses on the Death of Dr. Swift*, lines 169–76, 2:558–59. On the septum, see Wilson, "Swift's Deafness, and His Last Illness," 250.

49. The story of the plaques is told by Johnston, 192, 200.

50. Yeats, *The Words upon the Window-Pane*, 469.

51. Juvenal *Satire* 1.79; Nahum 1:6; on *vindicator*, see Frank Boyle, *Swift as Nemesis: Modernity and Its Satirist* (Stanford: Stanford University Press, 2000), 5. See also Maurice

Johnson, "Swift and 'The Greatest Epitaph in History,'" *PMLA* 68 (1953): 814–27. The version of the epitaph in Swift's will is in *PW*, 13:149.

52. Mahony, *Jonathan Swift: The Irish Identity*, 12–13, 23. Roubiliac moved from Paris to London in 1730, after Swift's last visit to England.

53. Wilde, *The Closing Years of Dean Swift's Life*, 53.

54. Ibid., 56.

55. Ibid., 121.

56. Johnston, 199.

57. *Publishers Weekly*, Aug. 25, 1969, as quoted in *Swift Studies* 3 (1988): 125.

Illustration Credits

1. Gulliver on Dollymount Strand: photograph by Jack MacManus, courtesy of *The Irish Times*.
2. Godwin Swift's house, Hoey's Court: W. R. Wilde, *The Closing Years of Dean Swift's Life* (Dublin: Hodges and Smith, 1849).
3. Map of Swift's first neighborhood: John Rocque, *Exact Survey of the City and Suburbs of Dublin* (1756), courtesy of Harvard University Map Collection.
4. Kilkenny Castle: photograph by Leo Damrosch.
5. The Dublin Custom House (now demolished) and Essex Bridge (now rebuilt as Grattan Bridge), Dublin: no. 4 of 6 views of Dublin, courtesy of National Gallery of Ireland.
6. Map of Dublin showing Trinity College: John Rocque, *Exact Survey of the City and Suburbs of Dublin* (1756), courtesy of Harvard University Map Collection.
7. Jonathan Swift, by Charles Jervas: courtesy of the Bodleian Library, Oxford.
8. Holyhead in 1742: Holyhead Collegiate Church, by Samuel and Nathaniel Buck (1742), by permission of Llyfrgell Genedlaethol Cymru / The National Library of Wales.
9. Map of Leicester in 1741: by Thomas Roberts, by permission of the Record Office for Leicestershire, Leicester and Rutland.
10. Sir William Temple in his youth: Thomas Peregrine Courtenay, *Memoirs of the Life, Works, and Correspondence of Sir William Temple* (London: Longman, Rees, 1836).
11. Moor Park in Temple's time: by Johannes Kip, reproduced by permission of Surrey History Centre.
12. Moor Park today: photograph by Leo Damrosch.

13. A page of Swift's work as secretary to Sir William Temple: courtesy of Trinity College, Cambridge, Rothschild Collection 2258.

14. "When I come to be old": John Forster, *The Life of Jonathan Swift* (New York: Harper, 1876).

15. King William III: engraving by Bernard Picart, after Adriaen van der Werff, from an extra-illustrated copy of James Boswell, *Life of Johnson*, ed. G. B. Hill, MS Hyde 76, courtesy of Houghton Library, Harvard University.

16. Queen Mary II: engraving by William Henry Worthington, after Sir Godfrey Kneller, from an extra-illustrated copy of James Boswell, *Life of Johnson*, ed. G. B. Hill, MS Hyde 76, courtesy of Houghton Library, Harvard University.

17. Map of the Irish Sea (detail): William Camden, *Britannia* (London, 1695), f Br 3615.90.10, courtesy of Houghton Library, Harvard University.

18. John Dryden: engraving after Sir Godfrey Kneller, from an extra-illustrated copy of *The Letters of Samuel Johnson*, MS Hyde 77, courtesy of Houghton Library, Harvard University.

19. Trim Castle: photograph by Leo Damrosch.

20. Laracor Church: John Savage, *Picturesque Ireland* (New York: Thomas Kelly, 1884).

21. Laracor Communion table, now in St. Patrick's Cathedral: photograph by Leo Damrosch.

22. Swift's account book: courtesy of Trinity College, Cambridge, Rothschild Collection 2253.

23. Lord Berkeley: Mrs. M. O. W. Oliphant, *Historical Characters of the Reign of Queen Anne* (New York: Century, 1894).

24. St. Paul's Cathedral in 1695: Thomas Babington Macaulay, *The History of England from the Accession of James the Second*, ed. Charles Harding Firth (London: Macmillan, 1914), vol. 6.

25. Map of part of Middlesex County, 1695 (detail): William Camden, *Britannia* (London, 1695), f Br 3615.90.10, courtesy of Houghton Library, Harvard University.

26. Map of part of central London, 1720 (detail): John Stow, *A Survey of the Cities of London and Westminster*, augmented by John Strype (London, 1720), 2:66, f Typ 705.20.810, courtesy of Houghton Library, Harvard University.

27. William Hogarth, *The Second Stage of Cruelty*: *The Works of William Hogarth* (London: E. T. Brain, 1841), *44W-1879, courtesy of Houghton Library, Harvard University.

28. Mackerel seller: Marcellus Laroon, *The Cries of London Drawn after the Life* (London, 1711), f HEW 13.9.9, courtesy of Harry Elkins Widener Collection, Harvard University.

29. Frontispiece of *A Tale of a Tub*: *A Tale of a Tub*, 5th ed. (1710), *EC7 Sw55iT 1710, courtesy of Houghton Library, Harvard University.

30. The preacher in his tub: *A Tale of a Tub*, 5th ed. (1710), *EC7 Sw55iT 1710, courtesy of Houghton Library, Harvard University.

31. Bedlam: *A Tale of a Tub*, 5th ed. (1710), *EC7 Sw55iT 1710, courtesy of Houghton Library, Harvard University.

32. Queen Anne: Mrs. M. O. W. Oliphant, *Historical Characters of the Reign of Queen Anne* (New York: Century, 1894).

33. Lord Somers: Thomas Babington Macaulay, *The History of England from the Accession of James the Second*, ed. Charles Harding Firth (London: Macmillan, 1914), vol. 5.

34. The Duke of Marlborough: Mrs. M. O. W. Oliphant, *Historical Characters of the Reign of Queen Anne* (New York: Century, 1894).

35. The Duchess of Marlborough: Mrs. M .O. W. Oliphant, *Historical Characters of the Reign of Queen Anne* (New York: Century, 1894).

36. Lord Godolphin: Mrs. M. O. W. Oliphant, *Historical Characters of the Reign of Queen Anne* (New York: Century, 1894).

37. Lord Halifax: Mrs. M. O. W. Oliphant, *Historical Characters of the Reign of Queen Anne* (New York: Century, 1894).

38. Daniel Defoe: Walter Wilson, *Memoirs of the Life and Times of Daniel Defoe* (London: Hurst, Chance, 1830).

39. William Congreve: from an extra-illustrated copy of James Boswell, *Life of Johnson*, ed. G. B. Hill, MS Hyde 76, courtesy of Houghton Library, Harvard University.

40. Richard Steele: engraving by George Vertue, George A. Aitken, *The Life of Richard Steele* (London: Isbister, 1889).

41. Joseph Addison: after a portrait by Godfrey Kneller, Mrs. M. O. W. Oliphant, *Historical Characters of the Reign of Queen Anne* (New York: Century, 1894).

42. Robert Harley, Lord Oxford: after a portrait by Godfrey Kneller, Mrs. M. O. W. Oliphant, *Historical Characters of the Reign of Queen Anne* (New York: Century, 1894).

43. Henry St. John, Lord Bolingbroke: *The Works of Lord Bolingbroke* (Philadelphia: Carey and Hart, 1841).

44. A page from the *Journal to Stella:* ©The British Library Board, MS. Add 4804, f65.

45. Dr. John Arbuthnot: George A. Aitken, *The Life and Works of John Arbuthnot* (Oxford: Clarendon, 1892).

46. Alexander Pope: *The Works of Alexander Pope*, ed. John Wilson Croker (London: John Murray, 1871), vol. 6.

47. Matthew Prior as a plenipotentiary: Thomas Babington Macaulay, *The History of England from the Accession of James the Second*, ed. Charles Harding Firth (London: Macmillan, 1914), vol. 6.

48. St. Patrick's Cathedral: William Monck Mason, *The History and Antiquities of the Collegiate and Cathedral Church of St. Patrick* (Dublin: W. Folds, 1820).

49. St. Patrick's choir stalls and altar: photograph by Leo Damrosch.

50. Swift's movable pulpit: photograph by Leo Damrosch.

51. Map of the cathedral precincts (detail): John Rocque, *Exact Survey of the City and Suburbs of Dublin* (1756), courtesy of Harvard University Map Collection.

52. Swift's wine bottles: *The Correspondence of Jonathan Swift*, ed. F. Elrington Ball (London: Bell, 1910), vol. 6.

53. Swift's rushlight: photograph by Leo Damrosch.

54. The Alexander McGee memorial: photograph by Leo Damrosch.

55. Dr. Patrick Delany: *Dr. Patrick Delany, Dean of Down*, enamel on copper by Rupert Barber, c. 1740, courtesy of National Gallery of Ireland.

56. Dr. Thomas Sheridan: MS Hyde 76 2.4.258.1, courtesy of Houghton Library, Harvard University.

57. Sir Robert Walpole: engraving after Jonathan Richardson, from an extra-illustrated copy of James Boswell, *Life of Johnson*, ed. G. B. Hill, MS Hyde 76, courtesy of Houghton Library, Harvard University.

58. Swift on horseback: [Thomas Burnet?], *Essays Divine, Moral, and Political* (1714), *EC7 Sw551 H714b, courtesy of Houghton Library, Harvard University.

59. Map showing Naboth's Vineyard (detail): John Rocque, *Exact Survey of the City and Suburbs of Dublin* (1756), courtesy of Harvard University Map Collection.

60. Mullagh Lake, Quilca: photograph by Leo Damrosch.

61. Stella's pickaxe: illustration by Thomas Morten in *Gulliver's Travels*, ed. John Francis Waller (London: Cassell, Petter and Galpin, 1865), Depository Lowell 1816.7.3, courtesy of Houghton Library, Harvard University.

62. Stella's cottage: William Howitt, *Homes and Haunts of the Most Eminent British Poets* (London: Routledge, 1894).

63. The remains of Stella's cottage: photograph by Leo Damrosch.

64. Stella's ghost imagined by a Victorian artist: illustration by Thomas Morten in *Gulliver's Travels*, ed. John Francis Waller (London: Cassell, Petter and Galpin, 1865).

65. Celbridge: Mrs. M. O. W. Oliphant, *Historical Characters of the Reign of Queen Anne* (New York: Century, 1894).

66. Letter from Vanessa to Swift: ©The British Library Board, MS. Add 39839, f. 42–73, P. 60/341.

67. Archbishop William King: mezzotint by Charles Jervas, courtesy of National Gallery of Ireland.

68. Lord Carteret: engraving by Thomas Major, after Dominicus van der Smissen, from an extra-illustrated copy of *The Letters of Samuel Johnson*, MS Hyde 77, courtesy of Houghton Library, Harvard University.

69. Dean Swift: Swift's *Works* (Dublin: Faulkner, 1735), vol. 1, frontispiece, *EC7 Sw551 B735w, courtesy of Houghton Library, Harvard University.

70. Captain Gulliver: Swift's *Works* (Dublin: Faulkner, 1735), vol. 3, frontispiece, *EC7 Sw551 B735w, courtesy of Houghton Library, Harvard University.

71. Gulliver tied down: *Voyages du Capitaine Lemuel Gulliver* (La Haye: P. Gosse and J. Neaulme, 1727), vol. I, facing p. 8, *EC7 Sw551G Eh727vb v.1/2, courtesy of Houghton Library, Harvard University.

72. Lilliput on the map: *Gulliver's Travels* (London: Motte, 1726), *EC7.Sw551G.1726b, courtesy of Houghton Library, Harvard University.

73. Gulliver fighting the rat: *Gulliver's Travels*, ed. Padraic Colum, illus. Willy Pogany (London: Harrap, 1919).

74. A louse as it appeared to Gulliver: Robert Hooke, *Micrographia* (1665), *90W–122F, courtesy of Houghton Library, Harvard University.

75. Glumdalclitch: *Gulliver's Travels*, illus. Arthur Rackham (London: Dent, 1906).

76. Struldbruggs: *Gulliver's Travels*, illus. Arthur Rackham (London: Dent, 1906).

77. Yahoos pulling a Houyhnhnm: *Gulliver's Travels*, ed. Padraic Colum, illus. Willy Pogany (London: Harrap, 1919).

78. Pope's villa at Twickenham: anonymous ink wash drawing, from an extra-illustrated copy of *The Letters of Samuel Johnson*, MS Hyde 77, courtesy of Houghton Library, Harvard University.

79. Bolingbroke in middle age: from an extra-illustrated copy of James Boswell, *Life of Johnson*, ed. G. B. Hill, MS Hyde 76, courtesy of Houghton Library, Harvard University.

80. John Gay: engraving by John Romney after Michael Dahl, from an extra-illustrated copy of James Boswell, *Life of Johnson*, ed. G. B. Hill, MS Hyde 76, courtesy of Houghton Library, Harvard University.

81. Alexander Pope: *The Works of Alexander Pope*, ed. Joseph Warton (London, 1797), vol. 1, Houghton Depository 15443.1797, courtesy of Houghton Library, Harvard University.

82. A page from *Verses on the Death of Dr. Swift*: courtesy of Monash University Library, Rare Books Collection.

83. Map of the road to Holyhead: John Ogilby, *Britannia; or, The Kingdom of England and Dominion of Wales, Actually Survey'd* (London, 1698), f EC65 Og454 675bb, courtesy of Houghton Library, Harvard University.

84. Memorial to Stella, St. Patrick's Cathedral: photograph by Leo Damrosch.

85. Dean Swift: portrait by Francis Bindon, oil on canvas, courtesy of National Gallery of Ireland.

86. *A Modest Proposal*, original 1729 edition: *EC7 Sw551 729m, courtesy of Houghton Library, Harvard University.

87. Swift in informal attire: *Jonathan Swift, Dean of St. Patrick's Cathedral*, graphite on paper, by Isaac Whood (1730), courtesy of National Gallery of Ireland.

88. Mary Pendarves: *The Autobiography and Correspondence of Mary Granville, Mrs. Delany*, ed. Lady Llanover (London: Richard Bentley, 1861), vol. 2.

89. Laetitia Pilkington: John C. Pilkington, *The Real Story of John Carteret Pilkington* (1760), courtesy of Beinecke Rare Book and Manuscript Library, Yale University.

90. Dean Swift's well: photograph by Leo Damrosch.

91. Dean Swift: portrait by Francis Bindon, oil on canvas, courtesy of National Gallery of Ireland.

92. Memorial to Swift and Stella, St. Patrick's Cathedral: photograph by Leo Damrosch.

93. Bust of Swift in St. Patrick's Cathedral: photograph by Leo Damrosch.

94. Swift's skull: W. R. Wilde, *The Closing Years of Dean Swift's Life* (Dublin: Hodges and Smith, 1849).

Index

Page numbers in *italic* type indicate illustrations.